A HISTORY

OF THE

Old Town

OF

STRATFORD

AND THE CITY OF

BRIDGEPORT

CONNECTICUT.

BY

Rev. SAMUEL ORCUTT,

AUTHOR OF THE HISTORIES OF WOLCOTT, TORRINGTON, NEW MILFORD,
DERBY AND INDIANS OF THE HOUSATONIC VALLEY.

PART I.

PUBLISHED UNDER THE AUSPICES OF THE
FAIRFIELD COUNTY HISTORICAL SOCIETY.

PRESS OF TUTTLE, MOREHOUSE & TAYLOR,

NEW HAVEN, CONN.

PREFACE.

HE task of making this book, such as it is, is
ended. The work upon it as the history of
one of the oldest towns in the State, including one of the youngest and most prosperous cities, has been very attractive and
entertaining, and the only regret the author
has concerning it is that the income from the
sale of the work would not pay for another year's labor, by
which a degree of completeness, somewhat satisfactory,
might have been attained. This is especially applicable to
the genealogies, which in their present state are only the
beginning of what might have been secured; which is true,
after all the gratuitious labor, put upon them for several
years, contributed by the Rev. B. L. Swan, formerly pastor
in Stratford, Bridgeport and Monroe, in which he collected
a large amount of historical facts which have made the work
much more complete than it otherwise would have been.

The author has also profited very much from the research and historical collections made, during many years
of thoughtful gathering by R. B. Lacey, Esq., Major W.
B. Hincks and George C. Waldo, Esq. Many items which
they had gathered were as seed producing a hundred fold,
when improved. This is particularly true of Mr. Lacey as to
his collections and memory concerning old Stratfield Society and the city of Bridgeport, and the public are to be con-
gratulated upon the fact that this part of the book was written
largely under his eye, while yet his memory was in its sun-

niest noontide and his physical strength nothing abated. It is also probable that but for his interest in the matter of local history, this work would not have been commenced, and certainly without his counsel and aid at various points in its progress it would have been very difficult to have gone on with the work to its completion.

The aid received by the most cordial and continuous commendatory support of the Fairfield County Historical Society, and the financial support rendered by several of its members, have been, not only greatly helpful to the work, but without these the enterprise would have gone no further than the publication of the first one hundred and eighty pages. Much cordial friendly aid has been rendered by the town clerks, Mr. Henry P. Stagg of Stratford, and Mr. Daniel Maloney of Fairfield, they having spared no effort for the success of the work.

The author has great pleasure in acknowledging the honor and value bestowed upon the work by those persons who have contributed illustrations to it, especially the steel plate prints, which are first-class in respect to the art of engraving and of very great satisfaction in such a historical book.

It is due also to say that, with a few exceptions of no particular importance, whatever errors may be found in the book the fault lies with the author and not with the proof-readers at the office of publication.

It is a matter of some considerable satisfaction that such a memorial work, although costing the untiring effort of three years of most diligent labor, however imperfect it may be, is a realized fact.

THE AUTHOR.

ERRATA.

Page 20 and 157—C. " H." Hoadley should be C. J. Hoadley.

Page 152—Bottom of the page the date " 1662," should be 1692.

Page 157—" Winfield " Benham should be Winifred and her daughter Winifred.

Page 135—" Robert," should be Thomas Tomlinson.

Page 223—Rev. " Jackson," should be Rev. Joshua and Sarah Leavitt.

Page 226—The name " Patterson" should be Batterson.

Page 390—Mrs. Benjamin Fairchild died 1874, aged 88.

Page 454—The Lasper K. " Whitney" should be Whiting.

Page 454—J. W. " Dufow," should be Dufour.

Page 454—The name " Hendric" should be Hendee.

Page 454—Lasper K. " Whitman," should be Whiting.

Page 455—" A. W." Lewis, should be W. A. Lewis.

Page 505—Under the title Benjamin Hubbell should read, Polly, who m. Gale Ensign and had Howell.

Page 535—The record should be Abigail Hurd, not " Rebecca."

Page 550—" Charles H." should be Charles R. Brothwell.

Page 601—12th line from bottom " 1692 " should be 1792.

Page 627—Thaddeus " Barr" should be Burr.

Page 642—" Billings," should be Phillips Academy.

Page 675—" Harwinton" should be Rev. Daniel Harrington.

Page 704—The title should be Parallel Railroad Company, and H. R. Parrott, president of the company as well as of the directors.

Page 754—" Griffin " should be Grippin.

Page 721—" Northnagle " should be Nothnagle.

Page 791—" Both sides of Wall and State " should be both sides of Bank and State streets.

Page 1166—Brown, Dea. " Isaiah," should be Josiah.

Page 1247—L. N. Middlebrook was graduated in 1848, not " 1828."

Page 1251—The name Nicoll, should be Nicolls, making it Sir Richard Nicolls ; but on page 1258, the name is correct as Nicoll.

CONTENTS.

STEEL PLATES.

ENGRAVINGS ON WOOD.

HISTORY OF STRATFORD.

CHAPTER I.

STRATFORD INDIANS.

NDIAN history, under whatever circumstances found, excites a melancholy sympathy, which partakes of extreme loneliness as if one were lost in an interminable wilderness from which there could be no escape by the ingenuity or power of man. As we pass over the site of their ancient wigwams, although not a stick or stone is left to mark the place, we seem to be traveling amid the ruins of some ancient Persian or Egyptian city, long celebrated for its beauty and magnificence and from which, although the glory has all faded or crumbled to dust, we hesitate to depart, as though expecting still to see the forms of the long-departed coming forth to newness of life, to exhibit the wonders of ancient days. Occasionally we discover about traditional localities, some stone implement, arrow-head, pestle or axe, that seems as a spirit resurrected by enchantment to portray the marvelous, wild life that wrought it, for the severest needs of earth, which is like the recovery of some long-lost painting of kingly banquet or national pride and glory. The hatchet, although of stone, was the Indian's ensign of renown; the bow and arrow, his national flag of wild but unconquerable liberty, and his tent, because it was not immovable, declared

an inheritance in a vast continent rather than a few circum-
scribed acres of walled distributions.

Sometimes the rolling waters of a mighty river, or the
heights of immense mountain ranges barred his progress for
a time, but no mountain was too high and no valley too low
for the unwearied feet of the Red man in the greatness of
his freedom and the inexhaustible resources of his physical
strength.   Nothing but the mighty ocean ever stayed his
wandering footsteps, until the white man took possession of
the rocky and sandy shores of the Algonkin country, afterwards called New England; when "the poor Indian" fled to
the inland wilderness as if pursued by a devastating pesti-
lence; nor has he yet, after nearly three hundred years, found
a sure resting place.   To him the shores of Long Island
Sound were an enchanted country, in the abundance it gave
to supply his wants, and the beauty of its climate and scenery
reminding him of the native tropical clime of his ancestors.

Here on these shores he had dwelt many ages, when the
glittering sails of the white man came bearing the pilgrim
planters to their new life of freedom.   In the winter many of
them had retired to the sheltered valleys of the inland wilderness, where they secured their daily food by the hunter's
sport, and then in the spring they returned to their old sea-
side haunts, just as their white successors now, in the same
season of the year, flee from the hot breath of the inland valleys to the cool breezes of the New England coast.   These
"children of the wilderness" have been called "Red men,"
"wild Indians," "savage beasts," but with all, they have
exhibited a manliness of character and rectitude of life, according to the instructions received, that leaves no room for
boasting by those who now inhabit the same beautiful country.   To these untutored inhabitants the pilgrim immigrants
were rather unceremoniously introduced, and to them in
turn they gave a cordial welcome, not knowing what the final
result would be.   And now, after the lapse of ages, the pen
of the historian is importuned for some memorial record,
which, although inadequate to the object sought, shall be as
a brief epitaph to commemorate the greatness of those, of
whom there is now nothing but ashes and fragments left.

On the shores of Long Island Sound various clans or settlements of these Indians were found by the incoming English, which belonged to the same general class,—the Mohicans, the name having been localized or modified to Mohegans in the south-eastern part of the state. Those on the Housatonic river appear to have retained a system of general government, with head-quarters at New Milford, and when their lands further south had been sold they gradually returned thither, and thence to Scatacook and to Pennsylvania. Tradition and implements found, indicate that at first the Indians came from the Hudson river—the Mohicans—to the valley of the Housatonic in the vicinity of the town of Kent, and finding several falls in the river, to them of unusual grandeur, they named it Pootatuck, meaning 'falls river.' This was the only name to the river when the first white settlers came, and those natives inhabiting its valley, were the Pootatuck Indians,[1] but being settled at that time in quite large numbers at various places, were spoken of by their local names. There are also evidences that these local clans retained the general name of Mohegan Indians, specially as this is the tradition now among the intelligent survivors of all these clans.

The first Indian settlement on this river, south of the Massachusetts line, seems to have been in the southern part of Kent, near what is now called Bull's Bridge, and afterwards, two or three miles north where a few families still reside. This locality they named Scatacook, or Schaghticoke, signifying the confluence of two streams,[2] which is true where what is now called Ten Mile River comes into the Housatonic a little below Bull's Bridge.

The second settlement was made, probably, at New Milford, called Weantinock, which remained the capital, or place of the great council-fire for the whole tribe (or all the clans) on the river, until that territory was sold to the New Milford company in 1703. Thus gradually the Indians made their

---

[1] Indians of the Housatonic Valley, 6 to 12.

[2] See Indian Names of Conn., by J. H. Trumbull, and Indians of the Housatonic.

settlements down the river until they reached Long Island
Sound; and afterwards they dwelt on the Sound more largely
in the summer than in the winter on account of fish, oysters
and clams, and of the hunting inland in the winter.

The Cupheags and Pequannocks.

When the English first came to Stratford they found
there a settlement of Indians, their local name being Cuph-
eags, the name denoting 'a harbor' or 'a place of shelter,'
literally, 'a place shut in.'' The clan was small, and was
governed by Okenuck, who soon after, if not at that time,
resided at Pootatuck—now Shelton—whither his people removed soon after Stratford village was settled. Okenuck
was the son of Ansantaway of Milford, and his brother
Towtanimow, son of Ansantaway, was sachem or chief at
Paugasitt.

The name Pequannock⁴ means 'cleared field,' land
'opened' or 'broken open,' and was applied by the Indians
to the tract of land on the east side of Uncaway river (which
river is now called Ash creek) extending northward to the
old King's Highway and southward to the Sound, including
two or three hundred acres of land, on which were probably
several pieces of a kind of open woods, as well as the Indians'
planting ground. This name was not applied to the water
now called Pequannock river, but to the beautiful plain as
above described and now constituting the western portion of
the city of Bridgeport. On this plain "at the north end of
the cove in the Black Rock harbor" was the old Indian
planting field, limited to about one hundred acres, and on this
field was the old Indian Fort, standing near the end of the
cove where now is the flower garden of Mr. James Horan.
In 1752, the General Assembly in describing the boundaries
of the Stratfield Society gives the precise location of this
fort.⁵

---

³ Indian Names, J. H. Trumbull.

⁴ Indian Names, J. H. Trumbull.

⁵ "General Court, October, 1752. Whereas, in the setting off the parish of
Stratfield, it so happened that the act of this Assembly setting off said parish did

The Pequannock Indians were more numerous than any other clan from New London west, on the shore of the Sound. They had three encampments or villages of wigwams; one on the west bank of the Uncoway river, as we may hereafter see in the testimony of Thomas Wheeler, one at the Old Fort, and one at the foot of Golden Hill on the south side; the last, some years later, is said to have contained about one hundred wigwams. The one on the west side of Uncoway river was at the head of a cove near a fresh water pond, just south of the old King's Highway, and a few rods west of the mile-stone which is standing one mile east from Fairfield village, on that old highway, south of which the Indians had a planting field which afterwards constituted a part of the territory called by the first settlers the Concord field. This place we are told in a future chapter by Thomas Wheeler, was the old established place of residence for the Sachem of the Pequannock tribe many generations.

There seems to have been, at first, no reservations of land for the Indians at Cupheag, or Stratford village, and none elsewhere in the town except at Golden Hill, and this was not measured to them until twenty years after the first settlers came, or until 1659. The planting ground at the Old Fort, in the edge of Fairfield, was retained by the Indians as their planting ground until 1681, when it was sold, and after that the field at the Old Fort was called the Old Indian field, and is so referred to frequently on the Fairfield records.

Stratford and Fairfield Conquered and Ceded Territory.

It appears by various authorized records, that the territory of Stratford and Fairfield was not at first purchased of

---

not settle and fix the line dividing between the said first society and said parish any nearer the south-westerly extent of both said societies than where said line intersects the country road [the King's highway] near Jackson's mill, so-called [now, 1884, Moody's mill] . . . which line runs from said country road southerly as the river or creek runs on which Jackson's mill stood, commonly known by the name of Uncoway River or creek, till it comes due west from the north end of the cove in the Black Rock harbor, which said cove heads or terminates at, or near the place called the Old Fort, and then to run straight from said creek to the head of said cove, and so straight to the sea or Sound." Col. Rec., x. 147.

the Indians, as has been asserted by all historians, but was
held nearly twenty years as conquered and ceded territory,
and so declared by the General Court, but afterwards, as a
matter of friendliness to the Indians, was purchased by various agreements and deeds.

At the time the whites came, Queriheag was Sachem of
the Pequannocks, with his dwelling-place on the west side of
Uncoway river, but a large part of his people were dwelling
on the east side of that river—at the "old field" and at the
foot of Golden Hill.

The settlements of Stratford and Fairfield were commenced under the supervision of the Connecticut, in distinction from the New Haven Colony, and the territory was
granted to them by the General Court to which the Indians
had previously given it in regular form in 1638. On neither
of the town records are there any Indian deeds recorded
earlier than 1656, and in 1681 when all former deeds are mentioned in the final sale, no reference is made to any as having
been given earlier than 1656. Nothing is said in the records
in regard to the purchase of this territory, until 1656, when
we find the following statement made by the court at Hartford :

"This Court, at the request of Stratford, do grant that
theire bounds shall be 12 myle northward, by Paugusitt
River, if it be att the dispose, by right, of this Jurisdiction."[§]

This action of the Court was soon proclaimed, and the
Pequannock Indians denied the right of Stratford to the territory as thus described, as the Court intimated would probably be the case. The immediate cause for the desire that
the Court should fix the boundary of the Stratford plantation,
was the fact that a tract of land had just been sold by the
Indians in the western part of Fairfield, and considerable
trouble had arisen between the settlers and the Indians, in
consequence of the cattle and swine of the whites trespassing
on the Indians' corn at Pequannock. One item is thus recorded :

"General Court, October, 1651. Upon the complaint of
the Deputies of Stratford to this Court, in behalf of Richard

§ Col. Rec., i. 281.

Buttler, against an Indian named Nimrod, that wilfully killed some swine of said Buttler's, this Court consenteth that Mr. Ludlow may prosecute the said Indian according to order made by the commissioners in that respect.'"

Another reason for this desire by the Stratford planters was that the Indians being quite numerous at Fairfield, the settlers there were pushing them over on the Stratford territory as much as possible to make room for themselves, as was acknowledged afterwards. There had been several efforts made by the General Court to settle the boundaries between Stratford and Fairfield and the Indians at Pequannock commencing soon after these places began to be settled; and also it is shown that these Indians having agreed to pay tribute to the Connecticut Court, as conquered and protected subjects, as appears from the records, neglected to fulfill their agreement.

"General Court, February, 1640. It is ordered that Mr. Haynes, Mr. Wells, and Capt. Mason shall go down to Paquanucke to settle the bounds betwixt them and the plantations on both sides of them, according as they judge equal, as also to hear and determin the difference betwixt the inhabitants of Cupheag amongst themselves. They also with Mr. Ludlow, are to require the tribute of the Indians about those parts that is behind unpaid, due by articles formerly agreed upon, as also to inquire out the particular Indians that are under engagement, within the limit of the ground belonging to them, and upon refusal, to proceed with them as they shall see cause."[8] The next June the Court ordered that "the magistrates shall send for the tribute of the Indians about Cupheag, Uncoway and there about," and that another committee should survey between the two plantations. Again in General Court, 1648: "It is ordered, that Capt. Mason shall go to Long Island and to such Indians upon the mayne as are tributaries to the English, and require the tribute of them, long behind and yet unpaid, and to take some strict and righteous course for the speedy recovering thereof, and it is

---

[7] Col. Rec., i. 226.　　　　　　　[8] Col. Rec., i. 62.

judged equall and allowed that he shall have the one-half for
his paynes."

Not only did the Indians neglect to pay their tribute, but
they committed depredations in many ways and manifested
so much hostility, from 1643 to 1655, that the plantations on
different occasions kept soldiers on watch nights and Sundays, and at several times called out the militia. Also, the
Indians made continued trouble by their demands for pay for
their lands, for after the Court had given its decision, in 1656,
the Milford Indians made a claim to some of the land within
the Stratford territory. Ansantaway was chief then at Milford, and he gave a deed* for all the land his people claimed
on the west side of the Housatonic river, and leaves the English to give him whatever they should see fit, thus indicating
that his claim had but little real merit.

In order to secure satisfaction among the Indians, and
quiet to their English neighbors, the Connecticut Colony
made another effort to settle the matter among all parties, by
the following order:

"Hartford, March 7, 1658–59. By the Court of Magistrates. This Court having taken into consideration the business respecting the Indians pertayning to the plantations of
Stratford and Fayrefeyld and finding in the last agreement
made with the Indians while Mr. Willis and Mr. Allin were

---

* *Ansantaway's Deed to Stratford.*

"This present writing declareth, we Ansantaway and my wife do make over
and alienate unto the Inhabitants of Stratford all our right in a tract of land being
as far as the River called the further milne river by Woronoke and westward as
far as the bounds of us our Paugusit Indians lies, with the English of the aforesayd Town and mark the trees as our bounds did goe before it was alienated to
the English as abovesayd. We also do engadge that no other Indians shall lay
any charge unto any of the aforesayd lands, and we doe leave it to the town aforesayd to give us for this land as they shall see good and meet. And we doe give
free liberty for the aforesayd Town their cattle to go beyond that further milne
River northward and north-west as they did, peaceably and quietly; we and Paugusit Indians doe thus agree as witness our hands in the name of the rest. This
Febu. 22, 1658."

The recorder of this deed says: "This is a true copy of a bill of sale signed
by Ansantaway, his wife and Towtanamy the chief Sagamore," but he was mistaken, for he did not transcribe the Indian names, for the deed is without any sig-
natures.

down there, that those two plantations aforementioned are ingaged to asure and alow unto those respective Indians pertayning to each town sufitient land to plant on for their subsistance and so to their heayres and sucsessors:

"It is therefore ordered by this Court, and required that each plantation forementioned exercise due care that the agreement made by the magistrates be fully attended without unnecessary delay, that so the lndians may have no just cause to complayne agaynst the English, but rather may be incouragéd to attend and observe the agreement on their parts, that peace may be continued on both sides; and further it is desired that the Indians may be allowed to improve theire antient fishing place which they desire.

"To the Constables of Stratford to be forthwith published and sent to Fayrfiyld to be published and recorded by the Register."[10]

Three days after the above record the Court took further action:

"March 10, 1658–59. This Court having considered the agreement with the Indians as also for other reasons as particularly that which the town of Fayrfeyld pleaded why their bounds should be enlarged was because they might provide for theire Indians which were many, do therefore order that the towne of Fayrfeyld shall forthwith attend the order as above sent from the magistrates and alow and lay out unto theire Indians that formerly did and now do belong unto that plantation, sufitient planting land for the present and future, that so there may be no disturbance twixt the Indians and the town of Stratford about any former improprieties which we find are renownced for the future by the last agreement. And the Court judges that the Indians that have for so many and several years been inhabitants of Fayrfeyld bounds shall now and for future be acounted as those that do properly belong to that plantation.

"Mr. Camfield and the deputies of Norwoke are apointed to see this efected by Fayrfeyld men or do it themselves.

DANIEL CLARKE, Secretary."

---

[10] Stratford Records.

About a month later a paper was recorded giving the agreement made between the two towns as above referred to.

The great hindrance in settling the boundaries between these two plantations and the Indians was the open or cleared land on the east side of what is now called Ash Creek, formerly Uncoway River. It was good soil, and probably much of it cleared besides the portion which the Indians had planted for many years, called afterwards the Indian field. This is revealed in part by a paper from John Strickland,[11] giving the reason that Fairfield wanted more room, and so desired the Indians pushed over east on Stratford territory, but the old line was retained while a tract of land was set off for the Indians on Golden Hill, and they retained their old field at the head of Black Rock Cove until 1681, when they sold it to Fairfield. There were, probably, several hundred acres of partially cleared land, now constituting the western part of the city of Bridgeport and Sea-Side Park, of which the Indian field containing about one hundred acres, with their fort, formed a central part.

In the spring of 1659, the question of title or right to the land in the plantations of Stratford and Fairfield was brought before the General Court at Hartford and settled. The Indians agreed that if the English could prove that they had received the land by purchase, gift or conquest, it should be theirs; whereupon a number of men gave their testimony in writing under oath on the subject, and the Court decided in favor of the plantations, and the affidavits were recorded in the town book, and they are here produced in foot-notes because of various items of historical interest. These papers are prefaced on the records with the statement: "A Rec-

---

[11] *The Testimony of John Strickland.* "I John Strickland, of Huntington Long Island having formerly lived at Uncoway now called Fayrfeyld do remember that I was deputed with some others to treat with Stratford men about the bounds of those towns and accordingly we mett, we of Uncoway desired some inlargement of our bounds towards Stratford because we were burdened with many Indians, and to my best remembrance it was by Stratford men granted and by us all concluded that we of Uncoway should keep our Indians upon our own bounds.   John Strickling,   his mark.

April 23, 1659.
Taken upon oath before me.   Thomas Benedict."

ord of several letters presented to the Court of Hartford, whereby together with other evidences the town of Stratford proved, and the Court granted a clear right to their land in reference to Paquannock Indians with whom they had to do."

The first paper is by the Rev. John Higginson,[11] of Guil-

---

[11] "*A Testimony of Mr. Higison late pastor of the church at Guilford.*

"Being desired to expose wt I remember concerning the transaction between the English at Conneckticott and the Indians along the Coast from Quilipioke to the Manhatoes about the land, the substance of it I can say is briefly this:

"That in the beginning of the year 1638, the last week in March Mr. Hopkins and Mr. Goodwin,* being employed to treat with the Indians and to make sure of that whole tract of land in order to prevent the dutch and to accommodate the English who might after come to inhabit there, I was sent with them as an interpreter (for want of a better) we having an Indian with us for a guide, acquainted the Indians as we passed with our purpose and went as far as about Narwoke before we stayed. Coming thither on the first day we gave notice to the Sachem and the Indians to meet there on the second day that we might treat with them all together about the business. Accordingly on the second day there was a full meeting (as themselves sayd) of all the Sachems, old men and Captaynes from about Milford to Hudson's River. After they had understood the cause of our coming and had consulted with us and amongst themselves, and in as solemn a maner as Indians used to do in such cases they did with an unanimous consent approve their desire of the English friendship, their willingness the English should come to dwell amongst them and professed that they did give and surrender up all their land to the English Sachems at Coneckticott and hereupon presented us with two parcells of wampem the lesser they would give us for our mesage, the greater they would send as a present to the Sachims at Coneckticott, it being not long after the English conquest and the fame of the English being then upon them.

"It being moved among them which of them would go up with us to signifie this agreement and to present their wampem to the Sachem at Coneckticott, at last Waunetan and Wouwequock Paranoket, offered themselves, and were much applauded by the rest for it. Accordingly those two Indians went up with us to Harford. Not long after there was a comitee in Mr. Hooker's barne, the meeting house then not buylded, where they two did appeare and presented their wampum, (but ould Mr. Pinchin one of ye magistrates there then) taking him to be the interpreter, then I remember I went out and attended the business no farther, so that what was further done or what writings there were about the buysness I cannot now say, but I supose if search be made something of the business may be found in the records of the Court, and I supose if Mr. Goodwin be inquired of he can

* Mr. Edward Hopkins and Mr. William Goodwin were among the principal planters at Hartford.

ford, Conn., in which he states that the land was given to the Connecticut Colony in 1638, and gives the reasons why the Indians did it, namely, for the security thereby obtained. These are corroborated by the fact that Towtanemow, Sagamore at Paugassett, gave to Lieut. Thomas Wheeler of Fairfield, about forty acres of land, what is now the southern part of Birmingham village, in Derby, if he would come and reside upon it, which he did some five or six years; then sold the land and improvements for two hundred pounds money.

This paper of Mr. Higginson informs that a convention was held with the Indians from New Haven to the Hudson river, at Norwalk in the last week in March (as we now reckon time), 1638, he himself being interpreter, when the Indians gave this territory to Connecticut, reserving only room to plant, and the treaty was ratified with due solemnity at Norwalk and at Hartford, the council being held in Mr. Hooker's barn at Hartford because the meeting-house was not then completed.

The date of this Norwalk Indian council shows it to have been held about fifteen days before the New Haven company landed at Quinnipiac.

The next testimony is that of Thomas Stanton," who was

---

say the same for substance as I doe and William Cornwell at Sebrook who was there."

Mr. Nicholas Knell [one of the first settlers at Stratford] testifies to ye same with Mr. Higgison as respecting ye Indians giving ye land to ye English, and recommended payment of money to ye Indians as gratuity for ye gifts.

Taken this 3d Aprill   Nicholas Knell

Guilford May 5, 1659   John Higgison."

" *Testimony of Thomas Stanton.*

"Loving friends I received your's dated may the 4th 1659, by John Minor wherein I understand of the insolent and unreasonable behavior and demands of the natives in your parts as chalenging all or the greatest part of your land so long since by you possest. Their chalenge is that if the English can prove the lands they possess were ever sould them or given them or conquered by them.

I much wonder at these times; this lesson they have leayrned but of late years certainly. They well know the English did possess all these parts as Conquered lands for from Newhaven to Sashquaket we did pursue the Pequets, killed divers at Newhaven and at Cupheag, only one house, or the karkise of one, we found at Milford without inhabitants. At the cuting [off] of the Pequets all

for many years the Indian interpreter at Hartford, which informs us that Connecticut Colony conquered the Pequots and Pequannocks at the same time—1637—took hostages of the Pequannock Indians and sold some of their women into servitude into Massachusetts. He also says the Pequots had conquered the tribes along the Sound west of Quinnipiac, and made them tributary before the English came, and states that the Pequannocks engaged with the Pequots, as their allies, in the fight at Cupheag, and also at the swamp on the western boundary of Fairfield. The fight said to be at Cupheag was probably at Pequannock river where afterwards a gun was found as shown by the following record.

"General Court, April, 1639. Thomas Bull informed the

---

their friends and confederates fled also being under the same condemnation with them. Tis true some at Paquannocke did formerly stand out but the Pequets did kill severell of them [i. e. in previous wars,] and conquered the country, [and] so brought all the Indians at [on] Long Island and the mayne [land] their tributaries from Pequet to Accomket beyond Hudson River. The English conquering the Pequets conquered them also and took Captains from Sashquaket [and] Poquan-ocke, for they several of them lived with the Pequets in time of their prosperitie and fought against the English also at Sashquaket, Poquanocke Indians fought against us, likewise some of those women are at ⟨ ⟩ and the Bay [Massachusetts] as captives to this day. I have informed some of the most Rational Pequets of this and they say that if the English do grant that the western Indians may sell their land, they [the Pequots] may do the like, for they say their land [the Pequannocks] is conquered as well as ours. Severall of themselves debate the poynt with them and prove it to the English before their faces. Also since the wars I can testify that the Indians at Paquanock did intreat Mr. Haynes and Mr. Hopkins [then Magistrates] that some (?) of the English would dwell by them that so they might not be in fear of their enemies, the uplanders, and that the English should have all their land only providing them some place for plant-ing; which I think is but a reasonable request, and I hope you will atend rules of mercie in that case; not that they shall be their own carvers what they will and where for exhorbitant humor will cary them to disposes you of your houses. Experience proves it; give an Indian an inch and he will take an ell. I will Ingage myself to prove the land as before sayd conquered, and if I mistake not very much the English by gift firstlie from themselves desiring as above sayd the English to come and sit down upon it. I could wish this matter had been in question in Mr. Haynes days and Mr. Hopkins, but the commanders of the Bay [Massachusetts] soldiers, and commanders of Coneckticott, the antient Pequets, will prove it Conquered land, and I never heard of other ground by which the English did posses it but by Conquest and gift . . . Not else at present to trouble you I comit you to God and rest your's, to love and serve as God shall enable.

Thomas Stanton. Stratford Records."

Court that a musket with two letters, J. W., was taken up at Pequannocke in pursuit of the Pequatts, which was conceived to be John Woods who was killed at the River's mouth. It was ordered for the present [that] the musket should be delivered to John Woods friends until other appear."[14]

It has been generally maintained that at the time the English came here these Indians were tributary to the Mohawks, which has been an error according to this paper.

Mr. Stanton also says "only one house or the karkise of one we found at Milford without inhabitants." This was the last week in March, 1637, two weeks before the New Haven and the Milford companies arrived on what is now Connecticut territory. The question arises, who built this frame of a house at Milford in, or before 1638, before any of the Milford people came there?

Another paper was given by Lieut. Thomas Wheeler,[15] one of the first settlers at Fairfield, with his father as he himself informs, and as the records show, from which place he

---

[14] Col. Rec. i. 29.

[15] *Lieutenant Thomas Wheeler's Testimony.*

"That in the time of his being an inhabitant of the town of Fayrefeyld and having several times in discourse ocation to speake with some of the cheife of that company which are now caled Uncaway Indians as Matawmuck, Nimrod and Anthony the Sagamore's brother of Uncoway, men well known to themselves, did relate to him concerning the land now in controversie as followeth:

"That they could lay no clayme or chalenge to any of the land on the east side [of] Hawkins' Brooke only they had liberty to hunt and fish.

"The ground of this discourse partly came from this the Lieutenant having a farm on the east side of this Hawkins Brooke and fearing least the Indians should lay clayme to it as well as to the land on the west side of the aforesayd named Broke did inquire of aforesayd named Indians concerning it. This the Lieutenant will take his oath to, it being legaly demanded.

"This Deponent further sayth, that Paquanock Sachem, the chief of the Paquanock Indians had his place of residence on the west side of the River comonly called Unkcaway River and that it was the proper wright of their predisesours from generation to generation. This was afirmed to this deponent by Queriheag the cheefe Sagamore of the Indians at the English first coming here. To this the deponent Lieutenant Wheeler offers to take his oath legally caled thereto.

                              Thomas Wheeler. Stratford Rec."

No date, but it was probably given in 1659, it following directly Mr. Higginson's letter.

removed about 1657 to Derby, where the Indians gave him
land, as heretofore stated. Mr. Wheeler says, the Pequannock sachem, whose name was Queriheag, being chief sagamore, when the English first came, had his residence on the
west side of Uncaway river, and that it was the home and
inheritance of his predecessors from generation to generation,
giving us some idea of the importance and antiquity of this
tribe. Hence it appears that the Pequannock Indians possessed the territory from what is now the Pequannock river
to Sasqua swamp."

These Indians were numerous as appears from the many
names attached to deeds, and as we are informed by Squire
Isaac Sherman, that twenty years later, when some of them
had removed farther north, there were one hundred wigwams
occupied by them at Golden Hill. This on a medium estimate would give from five to eight hundred persons when
the English first came here, and they were all Pequannock
Indians, as shown by the names attached to Fairfield Indian
deeds.

Another testimony is that of John Minor," one of the

---

[14] See Fairfield Indian Deed dated Mar. 20, 1656, hereafter. —

[11] " *The Testimony of John Minor taken upon oath.*

"Being desired to speake to what I remember in order to what was spoken
and acted by the Indians or English about Captain Beebee's action commenced
against the town of Stratford at Fayrfeyld about Lands. The substance of what
I can say is briefly thus without any correction or bias of affection contrary to
truth and equity.

" Being desired by the Court then at Fayrfeyld with James Beers to treat with
the Indians of Pequanocke who in regard of the present contagion* were not
admitted into the meeting house when the Court sate about the land then in
debate. At our first coming to them the Indians there present did all agree in
one that they had never given any land particularly to Captain Beebee but that
they gave it to Mr. Hopkins and Mr. Haynes and the other comtee of Conecticoate
Generally. Having received this answer we went a little remote from the
Indians.

"The better to certifie each other how we understood them, several words
passed between us but at last I related to the aforesayd Beers what I understood
as above sayd. James Beers contradicted me saying he understood it otherways,
whereupon we went to the Indians a second time before we went into the Court
and they confirmed the same and sayed Captain Beebee had no particular interest

* The contagion was a severe sickness in the winter or spring of 1663.

early settlers and prominent men of Stratford, for many years an interpreter between the English and Indians and he was also town clerk of Stratford. His statement was taken for the particular purpose of disproving the claims of one Captain Beebe, in 1662, but it also shows that the Indians declared, at that time, that the land was given to Mr. Hopkins and Mr. Haynes twenty-four years previous, as stated by Rev. John Higginson. In this paper, also, Mr. Minor states incidentally, that there was then a "contagion" among the Indians, in consequence of which they were not permitted to go into the church at Fairfield, where the Court held its proceedings, and he also reveals the efforts made by unprincipled men to turn the Indians from truth and right, for selfish purposes.

The decision of the Court was rendered in 1659, and Golden Hill reservation was then laid out.

Golden Hill Reservation.[18]

"General Court, May, 1659. This Court having considered the business respecting the Indians at Paquanack, and the difference twixt Stratford and Fairfield about the said

---

in any land from them but they gave it as above sayd. Several questions I propounded to the Indians at this time so that now James Beers sayd I understood them well enough and as we were going from the Indians, as before Captain Beebee being a little ways from us James Beers caled to him, Captayne said he the land is gone, the Indians now uterly disown any perticular gift to you. Then gone it is says he.

"We now both agreeing that we understood the Indians aright went into the Court house to return our answer to the Court. Whilst we were abroad before we went into Court Captayne Beebee went to the Indians and the Captayne's Sonn. What they sayd to the Indians I know not but presently before we had delivered to the Court what the Indians had sayd there was a caling out that the Indians had something more to say. Upon which the Court desired us to go forth agayne and be fuly resolved what their minds were. At which then coming to them we found them of another turn, as may apear by our testimony upon oath.

This shall legally if called thereto to take my oath of 8th, 3d, 1663.

John Minor.

This action was tried about Michelmas, Anno, 1662.
Taken upon oath this 11th, 3d, 1663.

Samuel Sherman.   Stratford Records."

[18] Col. Rec., i. 335.

Indians; do see cause to order that according unto the desire of the Indians they may quickly possess and enjoy from henceforth and for the future, that parcel of land called Gold Hill; and there shall be forthwith so much land laid out within the liberties of Fairfield as the Committee appointed by the Court shall judge fit, and in as convenient a place as may best answer the desire and benefit of the Indians forementioned, for the future. And the said committee is to see so much land laid out within the bounds of Fairfield, for the use and accommodation of Stratford as that Golden Hill forementioned is, for quantity and quality, and as may be most convenient for the neighbors of Stratford. And in case Stratford men are unwilling to accept of land, then the committee shall appoint how much and in what kind the inhabitants of Fairfield shall pay unto Stratford, in way of satisfaction. And it is ordered that this parcel of land called Gold Hill, surrendered by Stratford unto Paquanack Indians, according to the premises, shall be full satisfaction from them unto the Indians forenamed, and that neither they nor their successors shall make any further claims or demands of land from Stratford, but shall henceforth be accounted as Fairfield Indians, .or belonging to Fairfield, to be provided for by them for future as is forementioned in the order. And it is ordered that in case these Indians shall wholly at any time relinquish and desert Gold Hill, that then it shall remain to Stratford plantation, they repaying to Fairfield the one half of that which they received in consideration of the said land.

" The committee appointed by the Court to see this order put into execution are, of Norwalk, Mr. Camfield, Mr. Fitch, Richard Olmstead, Nathaniel Elye, who are to bound out the lands at Gold Hill, about 80 acres, beginning at the foot of the hill where the wigwams stood, and to run upwards on the hill and within Fairfield bounds, as is above mentioned. And the said committee is to make return to the Court in October, what they do in reference to this order."

The Report of the Committee.

" Loving neighbors of Stratford we whose names are underwritten have according to the order we had from Gen-

2

eral Court, without any respect to persons considered of the
value that Fairfield men shall pay to Stratford for the 80 acres
of land that the Indians do possess at Paquanocke with a due
consideration of the land and the place where it lies, wherein
we are agreed and do appoint that the Fairfield men shall pay
to the Stratford men for the 80 acres of land that the Indians
do possess at Paquanocke, twenty pound ; this to be paid in
beefe, porke, wheat and pease. Of beefe 2 barrels, [and] of
porke, good and merchantable, which we value at twelve
pound, and 8 pounds to be payd in wheat and pease ;—wheat
at 4 shillings 6 pense the bushill, pease 3 shillings 6 pense the
bushell, good and merchantable, and this to be payed of Fairfield to Stratford men betwixt this and the first day of March
next ensuing. This being our agreement we have set to our
hands

Narwoke May 2, 1660.

> Matthew Camfeyld
> Thomas Fitch."

When this settlement was effected in obedience to the
directions of the Court, an arrangement was made directly
with the Indians.

Agreement between the Indians of Pequannock and the inhabitants of Stratford.

"Whereas there hath been a difference between the
Indians of Pequanack and the inhabitants of Stratford, for the
issuing of which it is agreed the Indians aforesayd acknowledging their former irregular carriage and misdemeanor and
promising reformation in the particulars hereafter mentioned,
it is then agreed that the aforesaid Indians shall have liberty
to plant and improve the land between the fence that the
Indians made and the bounds which the committee laid for
the aforesaid Indians, till they shall forfeit the same in the
apprehension of the inhabitants of Stratford by breaking
their engagement in the particulars following :

"The Indians do hereby ingage not to kill or any way
molest our cattle and swine.

" They ingadge to medle with none of our corn or pease to steale from us.

" They do ingadge so to mayntayne their fence which joynes to the fence of the Inhabitants of Stratford that the corn may be secured, and if any damage comes through any defect in their fence they are to make satisfaction.

" They are further, to keep up their fence winter and summer to prevent damaging either them or us.

" They do further engadge to suffer none of the in-habitants of Fayrefeyld and those of the farmers to get in or drive any cattle through the aforesaid ground which the Indians improve, that is to say the whole bounds layed out by the committee upon and about Golden Hill.

" The Indians aforesaid are well satisfied with what the committee had done, every particular, and concerning the two highways likewise.

" These Indians have subscribed in the name of all the rest, this 24th Aprill 1660.

Musquattat's	mark	Nimrod's	mark
Nesuposu's	mark	Nomledge's	mark
Pechekin's	mark."		

Thus rested the question of the ownership of the Soil of the Stratford township at the end of twenty years of occu-pancy by the English. It had not been purchased by the whites, not a rod square of it so far as has been ascertained unless it had been one piece bought by Moses Wheeler—deed dated April 12, 1659—as he alleged in 1684, but which was never recorded on Stratford records, although he said he made the purchase at the request of the principal men of the town ; and therefore all the statements by historians that Stratford territory was purchased in 1639, by Mr. Thomas Fairchild or any others were made for want of information, which might easily have been obtained from the Stratford first book of Town Records.

CHAPTER II.

INDIAN DEEDS AND RESERVATIONS.

SCARCELY had the proceedings instituted before the General Court come to a close declaring that Stratford, in 1659, already owned the land it claimed, before the Indians began to clamor for pay for their long possessed inheritance, and the people of the town began to yield in hope of obtaining a peaceful end, and to buy the land at the most favorable terms possible.

The first deed of purchase which has come to light was recorded in the first book of land records for the Colony at Hartford and was received by Moses Wheeler and dated April 12, 1659, and seems to have been executed while the question of title was before the Court at Hartford. It was a deed of "a parcel of ground lying along the side of Potatuck river, the east end of it being on a small river, which they say is Nayump, the west end bounding to a great rock [from which the name—*nai-ompsk* ' point of rock ' was derived] which reacheth the full length of all that plain piece of ground, and also to have two miles and a half of ground on the upland and all the meadow within that bounds.'" " Moses Wheeler alleged that the purchase was made at the solicitation of the principal inhabitants of Stratford, to prevent it from falling into other hands and that it cost him upwards of forty pounds.'" After the Court in 1659 decided that the territory belonged to Stratford with-

¹ Col. Land Rec., i. 213, 214.
² Mr. C. H. Hoadly in Col. Rec., iii. 164.

out paying for it, the town allowed Moses Wheeler to keep his land twenty-five years and then began to lay it into division lots among its own members without regard to Moses Wheeler, although he was one of their own citizens. But they were brought to time by the General Court in October, 1684, by a profitable suggestion, thus: " This Court do recommend it to the town of Stratford to come to an agreement with Moses Wheeler, sen. about the purchase he made of the Indians of a tract of land within their bounds," and some of the townsmen were required to appear at the next court and report the proposition of settlement to be ratified by the Court, which they did by giving Mr. Wheeler half of the land. Charity suggests that possibly these brethren of Moses Wheeler had forgotten, or were taking a little nap on, the subject of the golden rule as the reason why they left him with the expense of the land for twenty-five years, without fulfilling their agreement.

On June 5, 1660, a little over one year after the Court rendered its decision in favor of Stratford, a deed from the Indians for Stratford land was received by Bray Rossiter of Guilford,[1] and this act by one outside of the town, set the ball

---

[1] " June 5, 1660. An agreement betwixt Wampeagy, Ansutu, Wampeug, Aquiump and Onepenny, Indians of ye one party and Bray Rosseter of Guilford ye other party as followeth : All the afores'd Indians do passover, assign and sell (for a debt due) unto ye sd. Bray Rosseter one hundred acres of land on ye west side of ye river yt passeth up by Stratford ferry, (a little below ye land of Milford men at Paugesutt) the said hundred acres to begin at ye River and to take all ye breadth betwixt two small brooks and soe backward until ye said sume be made upp, with all ye privileges of ye River for fishing lying before ye said land, and ye sd Indians doe further promise and ingage to sell what other lands ye sd Bray Rosseter shall desire to buy behind ye same father in ye woods uppon like indifferent terms, in witness our hands.

A marke of Wampeagy.
A marke of Aquiump.
The marke of Wompeug.
The marke of Nansuty.
The marke of Onepenny.

Wampeagy, Nansutu and Onepenny desired to set down ye names of Wumpeug and Aquiump, Sagemes, affirming yt they consented unto ye same in presence of, etc.

Wampeagy approved the above before Andrew Leete, Assistant at Guilford Feb. 28, 1684."

moving, or rather set the Indians crazy to sell the land they had just been told they did not own. This piece of land seems to have been on the west side of the Housatonic about one mile above the two mile Island in that river, but whether Mr. Rossiter held it or not after 1684 has not been ascertained.

Another deed[4] was given by the Indians of land called by the English at the time Mohegan Hills, bounded on the west with the "near sprayne" (or stream, or branch) of the Farmill river, the date being 1661, but the name of the month being obliterated. The peculiar item in this deed is the information that there was then "a hop garden hard by ye River though on ye other side." In 1654 Edward Wooster was the first settler in Derby for the special purpose of raising hops

---

[4] This writing made ye —— 1661.

" For and upon good consideration moving me thereunto I make over alienate and freely give to my loving friend Joseph Judson of Stratford in ye jurisdiction of Connecticot, to him, his heirs and assigns (to have and to hold without molestation or trouble from any Indian or Indians whatsoever laying clayme or challenge) forever a parcell of land bounded on the northwest by ye lower part of Moose hill, on ye west with ye nere sprayne of ye far Mill River, on ye south at ye parting of ye spraynes of ye far Mill River called by ye English ye Trapfalls, and on ye east by ye northwest spraine of ye far Mill River, soe running to ye pine swamp at ye head of ye River. This parcell of land called by ye English ye Mohegan Hills and by ye Indians Ackquunokquahou I Amantaneag doe give as aforesd with all ye privileges and appertenances, the meadow or what else belongs thereto as witness my hand and seale ye day and date above written.

There is also a hop garden hard by ye River, though on ye other side, which I doe also freely give to aforesaid Joseph Judson and his forever.

	The mark of	Amantaneag.
	The mark of	Akenotch,
		Sagamore of Pagasett.
	The mark of	Ansantaway.
	Acquiumps	his mark.

Acquiumps doth hereby confirm this act of Amantaneag's witness his hand the 4th of 10th, 1663.

Per me John Minor.	
Poidge,	his mark.
Patequeno,	his mark.
Chepon,	his mark."

Witnesses :
The mark of Suchsquoke.
The mark of Wunnubber.

on the bottom land now a little way below Ansonia, and here in what is now Huntington was another hop garden only seven years later, and may have been there several years earlier than 1661.

There are also in this deed as well as others that follow several local names of interest.

A second deed* was given the same year, probably a

* " This present writing witnesseth yt I Wampegan who am ye lawful heir to all ye Indian Rights and privileges yt did aforetime belong to ye Sachems and my grandfather and since to other Sachems my uncles who were ye legall proprietors of a great tract of land lying west from ye farr mill River at Woronoke bounded on ye east with a pine swamp at ye east spraine of ye far mill River bounded on ye west with ye west spraine of Paquannuck River, on ye South with ye lower part of Moose hill and bounded on ye north with ye Assuntokereag a place soe named about a mile and a half north from ye upper part of Moose hill, and norwest with a place called Manantock running as far as Pootatuck path ; I say I Wampegan doe not only hereby confirm what hath been formerly granted and freely bequeathed to Joseph Judson of Stratford in ye Jurisdiction of Connecticut by Weenepes my uncle, I being a witness to what he did and it being for substance ye same which I do at present, but also I doe hereby give and freely bequeath to ye aforesaid Joseph Judson ye aforementioned tract of land, to him his heires and assignes forever to have and to hould without molestation or trouble from any person or persons Indian or Indians whatsoever yt shall lay clayme or challenge to any part of ye sd land by virtue of any title or interest whatsoever therein ; I say I give and freely bequeath the aforesaid land with all ye appurtenances and privileges belonging, as hunting, &c., with all dues to said land as if I were personally to enjoy the customs thereto belonging myself. The aforesaid Joseph Judson promising yt upon this consideration Wompegan his first cousins named Poidge, Heenummojeck, Momowetah shall have free liberty to hunt for deare, &c., uppon ye aforesd tract of land. For ye assurance hereof yt this is my act and deed is written freely and subscribed, this ninth of September one thousand six hundred and sixty-one, 9th Sept., 1661.

Wampegan,   his mark.
The mark of Akenotch the
    Sagamore of Pagusett.
The mark of Ansantaway.

"This writing made ye 14th May, 1662, witnesseth yt I Acquiumph upon good consideration doe confirm ye abovesd gift by Wompegan or any before, to Joseph Judson of Stratford. I Acquiumph Sachem of Pootatuck doe confirm ye same in every particular by subscribing ye day and date above written.

The mark of Quiump, Sachem of
  Pootatuck being related to Wampegan.
   Poidge,   his mark.
   Chepenett,   his mark."

month or two later, of land lying west from the Far-mill
river, extending west to the west branch of the Pequannock
river. "There was a Pootatuck path" bounding the land on
the northwest. Pootatuck was at that time the name of the
Indian settlement occupying land now covered by the southern part of the village of Shelton in Huntington, the place
of the same name in Newtown not being then established.
This deed was given by another party than the latter previous one, and was confirmatory of the other, yet the same
Sachem signed both. This strikingly illustrates the separate
interests in the lands by the Indians and also the relation
between the Pequannocks or Stratford Indians and the Pau-
gasetts, the Paugasett chief signed both deeds.

A third deed' was given in the year 1661, which was by
Towtanimow and his mother the wife of Ansantaway, the
old chief of Milford, who also signed the deed. Towtanimow
was the chief Sachem at Paugassett at that time, but died
that same winter, for in the spring—April, 1662—Okenuck

---

⁴ "This indenture made the 4th day of December, in the year of our Lord
Christ one thousand six hundred and sixtie one between Towtanamy and his
mother the wife of Ansantaway being the Chief Sagamore of Pagusit on the one
parte and Samuel Sherman and John Hurd and Caleb Nichols, Townsmen in the
name of the inhabitants of the town of Stratford in the colony of connecticoute
on the other part: Whereas the said Towtanimy is now lawfully seized to him
and his heayers and asigns forever of and in all that plat of land lying and being
between the nerer Milne River and the father Milne River comonly so caled by
the English and being the bounds south and northeast upon Stratford River and
west with the bare swamp caled by the Indians Makoron, northwest on black
brook's mouth : now this indenture witnesseth that the sayd tantanimy and in the
name of all the rest of the Indians of pawgasit for and in consideration of twelve
pound [worth] of trading cloath and one blankit to him in hand payd before the
writing hereof by the say'd Samuel Sherman, John Hurd and Caleb Nichcols
and for other considerations him the sayd towtanamy thereunto moving hath
given, granted, bargained, sould enfeoffed and confirmed by these presents do
give . . . . to Samuel Sherman, John Hurd and Caleb Nichcols and the inhabitants of Stratford aforesayd for ever all and every part of the sayd parcell of land
above written being between the Mill Rivers ; and all the sayd Towtanamy's right
and interest thereunto.

Towtanomow, Sagamore, his mark.	
Ansantaway,	his mark.
Uncktine,	his mark.
Chipes,	his mark."

Dec. 4, 1661.

signs a deed in which he states that he is the only Sachem of Paugassett.

In April, 1662, a deed[1] was given by Okenonge (more commonly called Okenuck, on Derby deeds) of land at the western boundary of Paugassett lands, which is a matter of interest although not quite explainable. West and northwest of this land is met the territory controlled and deeded by Pocono, then the Sachem at Weantinock (New Milford), for he gave a deed in 1671 to Henry Tomlinson for more than twenty thousand acres apparently extending to or into Newtown. This deed to[1] Henry Tomlinson was secured upon a permit by the General Court for establishing a plantation, and was recorded in Stratford, where Mr. Tomlinson resided, claiming seven miles in length, three miles wide from the river on each side, or six miles in breadth, which was to be three miles up, and three down the river from Goodyear's Island in the Housatonic just below Falls Mountain in New Milford. This locality, if not the most, is one of the most sublime, on the Housatonic river, but the lower half of the territory covered by the deed was of small value in consequence of the steep rocky hills along the river.

The accompanying cut is a good representation of Falls

---

[1] " Know all men by these presents yt I Okenonge ye only Sachem of Pagasitt doe freely give and bequeath unto my loving friends Ensign Joseph Judson and Joseph Hawley and John Minor of Stratford in ye Colony of Connecticott a parcell of Land bee it more or less lying on ye west of ye land wch ye aforesd Town of Stratford hath purchased of mee and it being all yt lyes on ye west of w^t is already purchased yt belongs to me and Pagassett Indians. That I give the above sd tract of land to ye aforenamed persons to have and to hold wthout molestation or trouble by any Indian or Indians w'soever: I say to them and theire Heires forever as witness my hand this 22d April 1662.

Witnessed by us		Okenonge	his marke."
Nansantaway's	marke		
Chipps	his marke "		

[8] Deed to Henry Tomlinson for 26,880 acres signed by the following Indians:

Pocono,	his mark.	Mataret, the Sachem's	Toto,	his mark.
Ocomunhed,	his mark.	eldest son.	Mohemat,	his mark.
Wesonco,	his mark.	Tomo, his mark, the second Son of Mataret.	Chetemhehu,	his mark.
Pomuntock,	his mark.		Othoron,	his mark.
Ringo,	his mark.	Quocanoco, his mark.	Papisconas,	his mark.
Coshushamock,	his mark.	Weekpenos, his mark.		

FALLS MOUNTAIN ON THE HOUSATONIC RIVER.

Mountain at the gorge looking up stream from the northern extremity of Goodyear's Island. The river just below the gorge has been called the Cove and Fishing Place since the first settlement of New Milford, because here the shad and herring were stopped in their progress up the river, and hence afforded a great supply of fish for the whole region of country—shad having been sold there many times at one penny each; and the most advantageous part of the west shore having been rented in the early settlement of the town, for 999 years, for one shad of every thirteen that should be caught there. The gorge is over half a mile long, at the upper end of which are the Great Falls where now is located the large Wood-finishing Mill built by Bridgeport men, and where in olden times were caught by Indians and whites immense numbers of lamprey-eels. These falls are not very high but are called the great falls in comparison with smaller ones two miles further up the river. The Island was named Goodyear's Island from the fact that Mr. Stephen Goodyear of New Haven about the year 1642 built a trading house upon it or near it, for purposes of commerce with the Indians.

The point of rocks on the right hand in the picture is called Lover's Leap from a legend said to have been historic of an ancient chief's daughter, but the legend being about the same in all its parts as is told of several other localities in Connecticut, receives but little credence.

The Indian name of the Great Falls was Metichawan, denoting an " obstruction " or " turning back," and hence since the fish stopped at the cove except the eels, the name may have been applied more immediately to the cove by the Indians.

The falls are celebrated as having been the locality— adjacent on the west bank—where was built the wonderfully ornamented bark tent of the renowned chief Warhaumaug, the last but one of all the chiefs of the Indians of Western Connecticut, or of the original Pootatuck tribe.[9]

The old chief Warhaumaug's monument stands on the

[9] See Trumbull's Indian Names.

[10] See " Indians of the Housatonic Valley."

hill a little to the east of Lover's Leap. Sometime within later years the white people have piled the stones, which lay scattered about for one hundred years at the old chief's grave, into a monumental pile, as represented in the accompanying cut. From it there is a beautiful outlook over the surrounding country, for which reason the old chief requested to be buried there.

WARHAUMAUG'S MONUMENT.

The gathering of the Indian tribes from the south and east with the old chief Warhaumaug at the falls was the last of any considerable number until they concentrated at Scata-cook, where now only a few families are left.

Warhaumaug seems to have been the chief " Tom King " of Turkey Hills in Milford and of Coram in Stratford, in 1714, who coming to this locality took his name, which means "good fishing place," from the place. He died about 1735, being attended in his last sickness by the Rev. Daniel Boardman of New Milford.

Henry Tomlinson's deed was reaffirmed[11] with an additional grant in 1702 extending it northward " five miles and a half in length from the Still River, to run southwest to a small brook called Susumene Brook and so in breadth three miles on both sides the great river." This was given to Richard Blackleach and Daniel Shelton, who had probably inherited or purchased it from Henry Tomlinson or his heirs. This was the land that John Read was heir to from his father who resided in Stratford as one of its first settlers. Mr. Read, who afterwards settled at Reading, Conn., and from whose family that town took its name, and who became very celebrated in the profession of law in Boston, sued the New Milford company for trespass when they settled there ; gained his suit before the Hartford Court fifteen times but lost it on the sixteenth, and then surrendered his claim.[12]

In the year 1671, the inhabitants of Stratford having become tired of purchasing the soil by piecemeal which they already owned, entered into an agreement to purchase all the claims of the Indians, within the town, except the reservations sanctioned by the Court, and in order to make a full end of the matter brought it before the General Court, by their deputies, and the Court ordered a full settlement,

---

[11] Henry Tomlinson's deed confirmed with addition to Richard Blackleach and Daniel Shelton, August 9, 1702, and signed by the following :

		Poconos,	his mark.
Indian witnesses.		Werneitt,	his mark.
Papepetito,	his mark,	Cush,	his mark.
Sachem of Oantenocke.		Paquahim,	his mark.
Siccus,	his mark.	Nunhotuho,	his mark, the
Metach,	his mark.		Indian interpreter.
Mattecus, his mark,			
Poconos' son.			

[12] See History of New Milford, Conn.

appointing the deputies to attend the execution of the matter and make report. The agreement with the Indians, and the deed are both recorded. In this deed[18] they acknowledge all previous agreements and confirm all sales. They restate the boundaries as follows:

"The line running from ye southward to ye northward twelve miles as it is now settled by ye court and from that north line, ye north end of it to runn away easterly to a pine swamp and so to a little River commonly called ye halfway River and soe to ye g[t] River called Stratford River—the north bounds being ye half-way River, ye east bounds Stratford River and ye South bounds ye Sound on ye Sea, ye west bounds Fayrefeyld as aforesd."

It was agreed that the Town of Stratford shall pay or cause to be paid for and in consideration of the premises of Musquatt or his assigns, ten coats and five pounds of powder and twenty pound of lead. By this purchase was secured, or rather the Indians released from any claims, a large proportion of what is now the northern half of the township of Huntington in which there were some sandy hills of light color, and hence the name "White Hills Purchase," by which the territory was designated on the town records, and the name is still retained in the White Hills school districts.

This purchase, which cost the town of Stratford according to the tax list made specially for this purpose, over £40, quieted the Indians just thirteen years, when another squad of claimants had grown up, or at least made their appearance, and doubtless for a consideration—as whenever did they without—confirmed the previous sale, thus: "We whose names are hereunto subscribed have had a full understanding of the contents of the above written bill of sales,—we do fully concur with those that formerly signed the same, and do approve

---

[18] This deed which secured particularly the White Hills was dated May 25, 1671, and signed by the following Indians:

Indian witnesses.		Musquatt,	his mark.
Sucksquo,	his mark.	Nesumpaw,	his mark.
Susqua James,	his mark.	Sasapaqun,	his mark.
Peonseck,	his mark.	Shoron,	his mark.
Totoquan,	his mark.	Tackymo,	his mark.

thereof and do oblige ourselves and our heirs to stand thereto, Golden Hill as stated by the Court excepted."[14]

Thus ended apparently all Indian claims to Stratford lands, except in the reservations at Golden Hill and Coram. Of those who signed this last release two deserve a passing notice. Siacus, who signed a deed in Fairfield, retired to Gaylordsville in New Milford where he resided some years after the Gaylord family settled there about 1724, and where the site of his hut is still pointed out, as having stood in the midst of an orchard of apple-trees. He was a kindly remembered old Indian.

Chickens was also of the Pequannock tribe, and removed, probably, first to the Newtown or southern part of New Milford, thence to Reading, where he claimed and held a reservation, and after some years traded his reservation there for land at Ten Mile River near Kent, with John Read, and became one of the Kent tribe. His grandson, Tom Warrups, figured somewhat amusingly as well as patriotically during the Revolution at Reading,[15] and after some years he removed and settled on the east side of Mount Tom in New Milford, where he enjoyed much liberty, lived cheerfully, loved strong water, had a wife who was a complete slave in waiting on him, but quite content in her home. Nothing is known of his death and hence probably he removed to Kent about 1810.

The local name Pootatuck, where the southern part of the village of Shelton now stands in the town of Huntington,

---

[14] Confirmation of the White Hills sale, April 28, 1684.

		Papuree,	his mark.
	Indian witness.	Ponamscut,	his mark.
Nasumpawes,	his mark.	Acunhe,	his mark.
		Robin,	his mark.
		Matach,	his mark.
		Siacus,	his mark.
		Chickens,	his mark.
		Sashwake James,	his mark.
		Crehero,	his mark.
		Nasqurro,	his mark.
		Cheroromogg,	his mark.

[15] Hist. of Redding, 65. Indians of Housatonic, Hist. New Milford.

was within the original limits of the town of Stratford, and was occupied by Indians, apparently, until 1684, some forty years after the town began to be settled, although it was not a reservation. It was probably the most ancient settlement on that river below Weantinock and retained the original name of the river, which was Pootatuck, meaning "falls river" or the river with many falls. From the distribution of relics as well as the name of the river it is suggested that the Mohican, or Hudson river Indians, came through the opening of the mountains a little below the present town of Kent, Conn., and finding the magnificent cascade or falls at the place now called Bull's Bridge, and on ascertaining the falls at New Milford and at Canaan, they named the river Pootatuck, 'falls river.' So far as ascertained, this was the only name applied by the Indians to this river when the whites first came here," and from it came the general classification of Pootatuck Indians to all who resided upon it; except that they always retained—even to this day—the ancestral origin of Mohegans (usually pronounced by the Indians, Mohegans.) The first settlement they made on the river of any considerable account was at New Milford which was retained as the Council-fireplace, or the capital, until the locality was sold in 1705. A small settlement was perhaps first made at Kent called Scata-cook (Pish-gach-tigok) signifying 'the confluence of two streams,' for here were found by the first settlers such implements as were not made in this part of the country, as described by Dr. Trumbull and as have been ascertained at more recent dates, but the favoring circumstances at that locality for a large and permanent settlement were almost nothing compared to New Milford, where were the richest bottom lands and greatest in extent of any place on the river, besides the great abundance of fish and eels two miles below, at Falls Mountain. Then, also, it has been handed down from the Rev. Daniel Boardman the first minister at New Milford, by his

---

[16] On Stratford and Derby records the only Indian name for this river at first was Pootatuck, with various spellings, and as late as 1723 in Newtown in a public vote they say, "the Great or Potatuck River," in a proposition to purchase the Indian claims of Quiomph and his tribe then residing there, thus showing that the Indians still retained their old name for the river.

son Sherman Boardman in writing that New Milford was the chief seat of government for all the tribes or clans on the Housatonic river. The only locality that retained the original name was at Shelton, and the extensiveness of the burials made there indicates greater antiquity than elsewhere except at New Milford. There was here also at the old Pootatuck village, an old fort when the English first came, and a new one had been built, just before, or was built soon after, at what is still called Fort Hill on the west side a little further up the river.

CONFLUENCE OF THE HOUSATONIC WITH THE NAUGATUCK.

The accompanying illustration represents the Naugatuck river coming from the north, at the right hand, into the Housatonic. The cove at the north end of the fields opposite the old Leman Stone store and shipping house, was known many years as Huntington Landing (belonging to Stratford 150 years); and about half a mile up the river on the west side was the old Pootatuck settlement and fort; and a mile

3

above it on the same side of the river was the new fort on
what is still Fort Hill, while about a mile further up is the
Indian Well. This Huntington and Derby Landing was a
great shipping port for about one hundred years.

It was at this place, being within the bounds of Stratford,
that the Indians in 1663 agreed to abandon their old planting
field for the sake of peace, and probably for the purpose of
being allowed to occupy the locality longer as a settlement
or residence, after the land had been turned over to the English more than twenty years, in the following language :

" Upon consideration of friendly and loving correspondence between us and the town of Stratford, we will no more
plant on the south side of the Great River at Paugusitt to
prevent a ground of future variance between us, in order to
avoid any damage that might be done to corn."[11] The cattle
and swine of the English were pastured in the wilderness,
and if the Indians planted corn without making substantial
fences about it, damage would be the inevitable result ; therefore rather than build a fence around land they could not
legally hold, they concluded not to plant at that place. A
large proportion of the Paugasitt tribe were residing then on
Derby Neck, a mile north of the present village of Birmingham, where they had a large planting field.

The relics found at Pootatuck have been numerous and
some of them very fine in workmanship. Two pestles dug
up in excavating for a cellar in 1879, near the river, in the
lower part of Shelton, were the most perfect of any seen in
this part of the country.

The Indian Well is the only remaining monument or
visible reminder of the old Pootatuck tribe. This was located
on the west side of the river about a mile above the dam
across the Housatonic. A stream of water pours through
the opening of the rocks and descends about twenty feet into
a deep pool or well, said to have been measured to the depth

---

[11] The agreement between Okenunge and Stratford, May 28, 1663, was signed
by the following names:

Okenunge,	his mark.	Ansantaway,	his mark.
Amantaneage,	his mark.	Mansuck,	his mark.
Asquetmougu,	his mark.	Nomponucke,	his mark.

of one hundred feet without finding the bottom. It is said that the Indians held some superstition of awe or veneration for the place, but the appearance would indicate the awe to have partaken more of the nature of thankfulness for the coolness and agreeableness of the place and the abundance of good water. It is a pleasing resort for visitors in the summer, and many improve its inviting shades and romantic scenery. Whether the Indians had as much or more pleasure in the locality than the whites have since may be a question of doubt, but certain it is that the name is the Indian Well.

Pootatuck in Newtown.

About 1680 the Indians on the lower part of the Housatonic made a considerable migration with their wigwams up the Housatonic river, those on the south side to Pootatuck in Newtown and those on the east side to the mouth of the Shepaug on the north side. In 1681, the Pequannock Indians sold their old planting field in Fairfield, and in 1685, 1686 and 1687 they completed the sale of all their claims in that town. Golden Hill and Coram in Stratford were left, but Coram they never liked as a place for wigwams and but few dwelt there, and the whites had already settled to the north of that place, so that game was scarce, the forests were disappearing, and they felt compelled to move West, as many of their successors have done since.

Newtown and New Milford became the points of rendezvous from 1680 until about 1705, when they sold again and moved on west.

Newtown from 1680 until 1705 must have been the home of several hundred natives. In the latter year they sold the territory for that township,[19] making some reservation and in

---

[19] The deed for the purchase of Newtown is dated July 25, 1705, and was for a " tract of land bounded south on a Pine Swamp and land of Mr. Sherman and Mr. Rossiter, Southwest upon Fairfield bounds, Northwest upon the bounds of Danbury, Northeast on land purchased by Milford men at or near Caentonoack, and Southeast on land of Nannawaug, an Indian, the line running two miles from the river right against Potatuck, the said tract of land containing in length, eight miles and in breadth six miles . . . . . in consideration of four guns, four Broadcloth coats, four Blanketts, four Buffalo Coats, four Kettles, ten shirts, ten pair of

1723, they by their chief, Quiumph, sold all their claims in
that town "except a corner of intervale lying by ye River
where Cocksures fence" is." The Newtown deed of 1705,
contains the names of several Indians who signed deeds in
Fairfield and Stratford, showing that they retired from their
old wigwams along the coast to Pootatuck in Newtown. New
Milford and Newtown were purchased at nearly the same
time. At New Milford they sold their last land, which was
their old planting field, in 1705, and with those from Newtown
and Shepaug in Woodbury began to center in considerable
numbers at Kent. There is a sense of sadness connected
with their leaving Weantinock, their old council-fire place,
where their warriors had gathered during many generations
to decide the great questions of peace or war, and where
their wigwams and fort had stood, perhaps hundreds of
years, and where also they had buried a large number of
their kindred ancestors. It was a beautiful locality, with

Stockings, fortie pound of Lead, ten Hatchetts, ten pound of powder and fortie
knives."

Macroremee,	his mark.	Siams,	his mark.
Wachunaman,	his mark.	Sudragumqua,	his mark.
Walwatup,	his mark.	Wompenoch,	his mark.
Martenech,	his mark.	Wachunanee,	his mark.
Awashkeran,	his mark.	Saununtawan,	his mark.
Ammeruetas,	his mark.	Manapok,	his mark.
Mattouchsqua,	his mark.	Magusquo,	his mark.
Gonnehampishe,	his mark,	Tarrosque,	his mark.
Wompeowash,	his mark.	Meramoe,	his mark.
Murapash,	his mark.	Sosauso,	his mark.
Punnauta,	his mark.	Wamatup,	his mark.
Wannome,	his mark.	Materook,	his mark.
Mesaukseo,	his mark.	Awashkeram,	his mark.
Taroosh,	his mark.	Mattoacksqua,	his mark.
Merammoe,	his mark.	Mauquash,	his mark.
Sachamoque,	his mark.	Massumpo,	his mark.
Sassousoon,	his mark.	Nannawaug,	his mark.

[19] *Newtown deed, called Second Purchase, dated Aug. 7, 1723.*

Indian Witnesses.   Quiumph, his mark.

Manchero,	his mark.
Nalumkeotunk,	his mark.
Machekomp,	his mark.
Mansumpus,	his mark.

INDIAN FIELD AND BURYING GROUND, NEW MILFORD, 1884.

most charming surroundings. Their wigwams stood on the high bluff, seen in the accompanying picture, with the mountain in the rear stretching to the north, and their rich planting field at the foot of the bluff stretching eastward to the river and along its shore for a mile or more. On the edge of the bluff, now covered with a beautiful chestnut and oak grove, was their burying place, where now after one hundred and eighty years, fifty mounds may be counted; it being, probably, the most perfect native memorial place that can be seen in all New England. The accompanying cut shows first, beyond the bridge, the old field, then the bluff where a dwelling stands; a little to the left of which are the mounds, in the grove, and beyond these the mountains. In front of all these, flowing beneath the bridge is the Indians' grand old Pootatuck river. All these are but memorial of these native children of America.

Notwithstanding there were only eighty acres of land reserved for the Indians on Golden Hill, the white settlers were unwilling to allow them even these acres, but the General Court faithfully tried to protect them, as seen in the following record:

" May, 1678. Whereas this Court have been informed that some of Stratford have been claiming and laying out land upon Golden Hill to themselves, which hath been settled upon the Indians by agreement in this Court about nineteen years since, the Indians having not relinquished their right in the said Golden Hill, the Court confirms the same to the said Indians, according to former grant, without molestation; and this Court orders that the said Indians shall not be molested or interrupted in their right there until they do wholly relinquish their right publicly, and come and record the same before this Court. This Court allows the Indians two coats to be delivered them by Stratford for their trouble." [20]

In May, 1680, Ackenach, Sachem of Milford and Paugassett Indians asked for more land for the support of his people; in reply to which the Court appointed two commit-

[20] Col. Rec., iii.

tees, one to lay out one hundred acres at Turkey Hill, for Milford Indians,—which accomplished its work—and the other to lay out one hundred acres at Corum hill. The latter say in their report: "We have been at Corum hill and have laid out one hundred acres of land, be it more or less, for the use of those Indians that properly belong to Stratford to provide land for, by the law of this Colony, bounded with marked trees and Stratford River and Samuel Judson's ground; sufficient highways and conveniences for fishing on that side the river to be allowed in that said land when and where occasion shall require from time to time.

Oct. 3, 6, 1680.

William Fowler.
Jehu Burr."

This Coram land the Indians did not like, reporting it as very stoney and poor, but they occupied it many years, although not in large numbers. In 1714, they sold about twenty acres of it,[1] for the sum of nine pounds and other land. This other land is described as "in Stratford township near a place called Quorum, bounded on the east partly on the river and on the north with a brook called Quorum brook."

In the deed to Harger is the name Tom, whom Harger in his deed to the Indians says was son of Cockapotane, who was the last chief at Paugassett, about 1730, and Tom in signing the deed made the same mark Antsantaway had used a number of times, namely, the bow and arrow.

Tom was somewhat accustomed to high times when young, as appears from the sale of a piece of the Coram reservation in 1724. The following is the record:

"Know all men by these presents, that whereas certain

---

[1] The deed to Abraham Harger, dated May 31, 1714, was signed by ten Indians as follows:

Windham,	his mark.	Mishallin,	his mark.
Ackomie,	his mark.	Robin,	his mark.
Tom,	his mark.	Curan,	his mark.
Tackamore,	his mark.	Rauneton,	his mark.
Pequet,	his mark.	Chips,	his mark.

Turkey Hill Indians upon Stratford River did about May
last and before, steal sundry sheep from Stratford side out of
Quorum plain and being convicted of the same before
Authority—the Indians were these: Montigue, Tom Will,
Ponocurate, Chashamon, Mojono, Chipunch, Nenoco, Peico-
curet,—their Sachem Tomtonee or Munshanges, engaging to
pay eleven pounds ten shillings in money which the said
Indians promised to pay for the damage in stealing of sheep,
and not having money to pay, the aforesaid Tomtonee, Sagamore, in the behalf of all the other Indians doth make over
two parcels of land; the one being about two acres called by
the name of lower Quorum upon the great River, that they
had of Abraham Harger, the other ten acres of land near the
Narrows, bounded with the land of Daniel Shelton, north,
south and easterly by the Indians' land in ye bounds of Stratford for the aforesaid sum of eleven pound ten shillings, and
forty shillings more in money which we do own to have
received already, in all being thirteen pounds ten shillings:
all the aforesaid land with all the privileges, etc., hath made
over unto Daniel Shelton of Stratford in the Colony of Connecticut, to quitclaim unto the said Daniel Shelton and his
heirs forever, or so long as he the said Shelton or his heirs
shall own that they are paid by the improvement of said
land. The said Shelton of his own accord doth say that if
the General Court or the town of Stratford saith he hath
done amiss, he will relinquish the land. The aforesaid Tomtonee paying the sum of thirteen pounds ten shillings to
aforesaid Shelton. . . . . and the said Tomtonee, Sagamore,
does promise for himself and the rest of said Indians that if
ever the land is taken out of the hand of Daniel Shelton or
his heirs, that the said Tomtonee will pay back the aforesaid
thirteen pounds ten shillings to the aforesaid Shelton or his
heirs."[21]   •

The special reason why Mr. Shelton so freely offered to

---

[21] Derby, Jan. 7, 1723-4, Tomtonee's deed for stealing sheep.

Mashages,	his mark.	Tomtonee,	his mark.
Tom Will,	his mark.	Cheponan,	his mark.
Punto,	his mark.		

restore the land if called upon was that it was unlawful for any person or company to purchase land of the Indians without a permit from the Court.

It has been reported that the Indians had a reservation at Oronoque, or Woronoque, as the early Stratford town clerks wrote it, but no record of such reservation has been seen by the author of these pages. They may have resided there, or occupied a particular locality for many years by sufferance from the town, as they did at Pootatuck, but there was no reservation in the town but at Golden Hill, at first, and then at Coram afterwards, and the wood lot at Rocky Hill.

Golden Hill Reservation Sold.

The settlement made with the Pequannock Indians in 1659, in the appropriation of eighty acres of land on Golden Hill, by the General Court through the towns of Stratford and Fairfield, remained in force nearly one hundred years, or until October, 1763, when three Indians—Tom Sherman, Eunice Shoran his wife, and Sarah Shoran, petitioned the General Court for redress, claiming that they and their ancestors " had quietly enjoyed said lands till within a few years last past, Gamaliel French, widow Sarah Booth, Elihu Burret, Joseph Booth, Mary Burret, the Rev. Robert Ross, Ezra Kirtland, Aaron Hawley and Samuel Porter, all of said Stratford, and Daniel Morriss, John Burr, Jr., and Richard Hall, all of Fairfield, have entirely ejected and put the memorialists out of the whole of said lands and pulled down their wigwam without right." Upon this complaint, Jabez Hamlin, Benjamin Hall and Robert Treat, Esqrs., were appointed a committee to inquire into the matter and report, which report was made the next May, but the Court was wholly dissatisfied with it and appointed Jabez Hamlin, Elisha Sheldon and Robert Treat, Esqrs., a second committee " with full power and authority to examine into and discover said matters of grievance." This committee reported the next October, 1765, an agreement with the Indians to sell all the eighty acres except "a certain piece or parcel of land called .

Nimrod lot, containing about twelve acres, with the spring at
the point of Golden Hill aforesaid, bounded westerly by an
highway, eastwardly by Poquonnuck River, northerly by
Jabez Summer's land, and southerly by the Cove and common land, also about eight acres of wood-land at Rocky Hill,
to be purchased for them by the petitioners, they also paying
to them the said Indians, thirty bushels of Indian corn and
three pounds worth of blankets.'" This report and agreement was accepted and ordered by the Court to be executed,
and to be in full for all demands by the Indians.

Besides the thirty bushels of Indian corn and three
pounds worth of blankets, those who had trespassed on the
rights of the Indians were ordered by the Court to pay to
Thomas Hill, the Indian agent, £52 11ˢ 2ᵈ, to defray the
expenses of the Indians in the suit.

In the agreement with Fairfield in 1659, this land upon
the Indians leaving it, was to revert to the town of Stratford,
upon their returning half the amount of money that Fairfield
paid for it. If this was carried out, then these trespassers
must have paid this item also to the town of Stratford, if no
more, provided they retained the land. It is probable, however, that they paid a still further charge to Stratford for the
land.

It will be seen by the above quotation that the wood
land was not an original reservation but a purchase at this
time.

The Last Families.

Tom Sherman, the last owner of the Golden Hill reservation, married, in the Indian way, Eunice Shoran, and had
children: I, Tom; II, Eunice; III, Sarah.

I. *Tom* 2ᵈ, m. Sarah (?) and had IV Ruby.

II. *Eunice*, m. Mack or Mansfield, formerly of Kent, and
had V, Jim, Garry and Eunice.

III. *Sarah*, m. Ben Roberts, a negro, and lived at the
Eagles' Nest at Stratford Tide Mill. Some of their descend-

" Conn. Col. Records, xii.

William Sherman

ants still reside in Orange, Conn., but are not claimants on the Indian funds of Stratford.

V. *Jim Mansfield*, son of Eunice Shoran, m. his cousin Ruby, dau. of Tom 2^d, and had Nancy, who had VI, William Sherman; after which she m. John Sharpe, and had Beecher, Nancy and Charles, and Sharpe being sent to State's Prison, she lived with a man Rensler, and had Olive.

VI. *William Sherman*, son of Nancy and grand-son of Tom 2^d and Ruby, was born in 1825 in Poughkeepsie, N. Y., and is still living at Nichols Farms in Trumbull, Conn., being the sole claimant on the Indian money from the sale of Golden Hill. He m. Nancy Hopkins of New London, and was a sailor in a whaling ship seventeen years; has been 'round the world nine times; was first mate of the ship five years and earned an honorable standing and reputation, which he has retained to the present time. He educated himself, and could perform the full services of a first mate on a vessel correctly as well as intelligently. He has long been a respected farm laborer at Nichols Farms, and long trusted with considerable responsibility in the management of the farm and properties of Mr. F. P. Ambler and Sons, while they were engaged in the business of Saddletree manufacturing at that place. He has been the Sexton of the Cemetery at Nichols Farms about thirty years and performed the work of his position with much satisfaction to the community. He and his wife have acted in the capacity of nurses in severe sicknesses in the community for many years, and as such won many expressions of thankfulness and confidence. The tradition is that he is a descendant of Molly Hatchet of Derby; and in the healthy locality where he resides has attained to the standard weight of about three hundred and sixty pounds.

His children are: I, William; II, Henry, died aged 17 years; III, George, who m. Mary A. Hamilton; IV, Mary Olive, who died young; V, Caroline; VI, Huldah; VII, Mary Olive; VIII, Charles; IX, child that died.

CHAPTER III.

AIRFIELD and Stratford were both held by the Connecticut Colony as conquered and ceded territory when these settlements were first commenced, and for ten years they were treated in several respects as one plantation. They were taxed as one; they were served with magistrates as one, and jointly they provided for the Pequannock Indians after 1659 until 1680; Stratford furnishing the land for the Golden Hill reservation in part and Fairfield contributing something towards the supply of the land, and also the agents to oversee the Indians were appointed from Fairfield.

In order, therefore, to understand the whole history of this tribe of Indians it is important to refer to the deeds they gave of land in Fairfield, and to preserve their names the same as the signers of Stratford deeds.

The division line between Stratford and Fairfield passed through, north and south, the territory which these Indians had long cultivated, which constituted the open plains that the new settlers so much desired, that they could not settle the boundary line themselves and hence called on the General Court to do it. This they did by retaining the old line, nearly through the centre of the plain, allowing the Indians to still cultivate about eighty acres, called the old Indian field, near Uncoway River, in Fairfield, and appropriating eighty more on Golden Hill in Stratford, but making Golden Hill the place of residence for all of them.

The first deed[1] is a quitclaim of a large part of the original town of Fairfield, and is given by Pequannock Indians in 1656, nearly seventeen years after Mr. Ludlowe took possession of the territory. In this deed they reserve the " propriety " or ownership of the Indian field, which they, being at Fairfield say, " is a small neck of land on y⁰ other side of ye creeke ;" meaning Uncoway creek as elsewhere explained. That was the neck where the Gentlemen's Trotting Park is now located, the original field extending northward some distance from the present park. At the time the deed was given they were about to build a fort, and the only consideration that they received at the time, apparently, was an agree-

---

[1] *Fairfield Indian Deed, dated March 20, 1656.*

" Whereas several Indians have made claim to much of y⁰ land y¹ ye Town of Fairfield have and do possess, ye Town of Fairfield having taken ye matter into consideration, ordered and appointed Alexander Knowles, Henry Jackson, Francis Purdy with several others to treat with Poquanuck Indians concerning and upon y⁰ treaty with those Indians whose names are under written in y⁰ behalf of all y⁰ Pequannock Indians they have agreed as followeth :

" First they owne y¹ ye land y¹ ye Town is built upon from ye Creeke y¹ ye tide mill of Fairfield southwestward is called Sasqua which they owne has been purchased* from ye Indians and is now y⁰ English land.

" 2. Secondly y⁰ sd. Indians have acknowledged, consented to and granted y¹ all that tract of land which they call Uncoway and which is from y⁰ above sd Creek eastward unto ye bounds between Fairfield and Stratford, from y⁰ See to run into y⁰ country seven or eight miles, for y⁰ future it shall be y⁰ land and propriety of y⁰ inhabitants of y⁰ Town of Fairfield, giving and granting to ye sd Town all ye above sd tract of land called Uncoway with all creeks rivers etc. . . . . only it is to be noticed that the field which y⁰ Indians now possess called y⁰ Indian field, which is a small neck of land on y⁰ other side of y⁰ creeke is excepted, y⁰ Indians still keeping their propriety in that small neck or field. Ye Indians are to have y⁰ privilege of killing deer within y⁰ aboves[d] tract of land, only they are not to set any traps within y⁰ sd tract of land.

In witness, 20th March, 1656.

" Whereas ye above said land is granted to ye Town of Fairfield by ye sd Indians : We also manifest our respect unto them y¹ wee doe engage upon sufficient warning to cart their stuff for them to erect and build a fort yr. Upon this consideration y⁰ sd Indians have acknowledged y⁰ abovesd grant.

Umpeter Noset,	marke.	Nimrod or Pocunnoc,	marke.
Matamuck,	marke.	Anthonyes, alias Lotashun,	marke.
Weshun,	marke."		

* " Purchased," means obtained, for in a later deed where all previous deeds are referred to, this one is the first mentioned.

ment on the part of the English to "draw the stuffe," with which to build this fort, but this may have taken time sufficient to balance quite a sum of money. Whether there had been a fort there or anywhere within Fairfield bounds is not stated, but a fort was at some time here, for in 1752, in giving the bounds of the Stratfield Society at this place, they say, "which said cove heads or terminates at or near the place called the Old·Fort."[1]

Another deed[2] of the same date—March 20, 1656—was given for "land commonly called Sasqua, lying west of Sasqua swamp, or on the west side of the present Mill River; Musquat, the first name on this deed, is the same as that on a deed in Stratford in 1671.

The third deed[4] was given to cover this same territory or a part of it because the Indians at Norwalk claimed an interest in it.

---

[1] Col. Rec., x. 147.

[2] *Second Indian Deed in Fairfield, date March 20, 1656.*

" This was a deed of "land commonly called Susqua, . . . bounded on yᵉ northeast with yᵉ land called Uncaway, on yᵉ southwest with ye land at Maximus, yᵉ line on· ye southwest runs close to ye English farms at Maximus, ... from the sea Straight up into ye country six miles at yᵉ least."

Musquatt,	his mark.	Santamartous poppoos,	his mark.
Taspee,	his mark.	Willecon,	his mark.
Ponuncamo,	his mark.	James, alias Watusewa-	
Cramkeago's Squaw,		satum,	his mark.
Selamartous' Sister		Wompegan,	his mark.
Wissashoes,	her mark.		

The following signed October 16, 1679.

| Creconoe's | mark. | Chickens' | mark." |

Indian Witnesses.

| Nimrod's | mark. | Antony's | mark." |

[4] Fairfield Indian Deed of Land claimed by Indians of Norwalk, in which it is said " Susqua did run west as far as Muddy Creek."

Dated April 11, 1661.

Momechemen,	mark.	Wenam,	mark.
Tolpee,	mark.	Quanumsooe,	mark.
Aucan,	mark.	Panoucamus,	mark.
Maskot,	mark.	James,	marke."

Indian Witnesses.

| Mamachim's | mark. | Weenam's | mark." |

The next deed* here noticed—for the deed given in 1670 has not been seen—was given for claims, again, on the whole township, and a large part of it is given in the note to show the inside track of the business of buying lands of the Indians, and also because it was the final one, except for reservations, for the southern part of the township.

The interpreter in these sales was John Minor of Stratford, and several of these deeds are recorded on Fairfield

---

* *Fairfield Indian Deed, quitclaim, date October 6, 1680.*

" Know all men by these presents yᵗ whereas yᵉ towne of Fairfield hath formerly bought of yᵉ true Indian proprietors all ye lands contained within their township bounds which is seven miles broad upon ye sea coast and from ye sea at least twelve miles into ye country to yᵉ northward of their bounds, bounded on yᵉ east with yᵉ sd. Town bounds as yᵉ Court hath settled, on ye west with ye town bounds of Norwake, also Compaw Neck from ye old road to Norwake to Sagatuck River on ye west, and to ye sea on ye south, for which lands ye Indian proprietors have given ye sd Towne severall bills of sale—one bill bearing date 20th March, 1656, another bill dated 21 March, 16⁴⁷, ye 3d bill bearing date ye 19th Jan., 1670, by all which bills of sale ye above lands are made over to ye Towne, Yet for ye maintenance of love and peace between ye sd Towne and us ye Indians yᵗ wee may prevent trouble, yᵗ neither we nor our heirs nor successors shall make any further claims . . . . . . We the surviving Indians, inhabitants of Poquanock, Uncoway, Susqua and Aspetuck do covenant, etc. . . . . for a valuable consideration do alienate, etc. . . . . [In this deed the old Indian field was still reserved.] Witness this 6th day of October, 1680.

John Minor, } Witnesses and Interpreter.
John Sherwood, }

Old Anthony,	his mark.	Panumset,	his mark.
Nimrod,	his mark.	Pupurah,	his mark.
Woywegun Nasque,	his mark.	Mamarashock,	his mark.
Yeerusqua,	her mark.	Nausouate,	his mark.
Washannaesuck,	his mark.	Sasqua James,	his mark.
Koewop,	his mark.	Nusenpawes,	his mark.
Cooreco,	his mark.	Creconoc,	his mark.
Weequombe,	his mark.	Norwake James,	his mark.
Poueri,	his mark.	Capt. Witree,	his mark.
Youyowwhy,	his mark.	Iletorow,	his mark.
Patchcock,	his mark.	Nasacoe,	his mark.
Sasapequun,	his mark.	Quatiart,	his mark.
Aquonke,	his marke.	Siacus,	his mark."

October 13, 1680, the following names were added.

" Hassahan,	marke.	Wampum,	marke.
Mittacke,	marke.	Warenet,	marke.
Womsoncowe,	marke.	Choromoke,	marke.
Chickins,	marke."		

book in John Minor's handwriting, but testified to by Fairfield town clerk.

On this last deed are many names, some of which we find on Stratford deeds, and also on deeds given some years later further up the Housatonic river. Old Anthony, whose Indian name was Lotashun, was, we imagine, a noble old Indian, and really very old. Nimrod, whose Indian name was Pocunnoe, had been prosecuted thirty years before for killing a Mr. Buttler's hogs, being then a prominent man, and must have been quite old, and he it was who had his wigwam on the eastern part of the Golden Hill reservation, and after whom the lot was named, and known many years, near where the Bridgeport Gas Works now stand, and in his honor also was named a steamboat sailing from Bridgeport nearly two hundred years after Pocunnoe was named Nimrod. Quite a number of these names with variations of spelling are to be seen several times in other deeds hereafter noticed..

Only one year after the date of the last deed the Pequannock Indians prevailed with Fairfield men to buy their old field near Uncoway creek, although the Fairfield people urged them to keep it, as the bill of sale says, and on the 18th of May, 1681, the deed was signed; the deed saying, " the Old Indian field on ye east side of Uncoway River."[*]

It is conclusive from the few names attached to this deed

---

[*] *Fairfield Indian Deed for the Indian field, dated May 18, 1681.*

" This sale we have made for a valuable consideration."

Mamerushee Umperenoset's		Cape,	his mark.
son,	mark.	Sowwahose squaw,	her mark.
Ponees,	his mark.	Naushuta's squaw,	her mark.
Old Anthony,	his mark.	Nassansumk Young,	
Washaganoset,	his mark.	Anthony's son,	his mark.
Wissawahem squaw,	her mark.	Choraromokes,	his mark."

" Indian Witnesses.

Sasqua James,	his mark.	Runsh squa,	her mark.
Crovecoe,	his mark.	Pascoe,	his mark.
Rorocway,	his mark.		

" Trushee an Indian who speaks very good English " was employed by both parties and signed this deed.

Trushee's   mark."

that quite many of the natives had removed, and we find also that during the previous year the Paugassett chief petitioned the General Court for more land to plant, and in October the Court ordered, and the reservation called Coram was devoted to their use, so that probably about this time a considerable emigration occurred to Pootatuck in Huntington, Pompe-raug on the Housatonic and to Pootatuck in Newtown.

Several other Indian deeds are recorded on Fairfield books; one of a piece of land called Wolf Pit Neck, in the southeast part of the town joining Stratford line, dated February 12, 1685, and sold to Fairfield town.[1]

This deed and several others are signed by John Burr as Commissioner, and since it was unlawful for any persons or towns to purchase lands of the Indians without an order from the General Court, probably he was appointed to act in that capacity, and hence may have effected the purchase under the great oak tree, as tradition has reported, on the plain about a mile west of the wigwams at the foot of Golden Hill and in the northern part of the old open field.

This was a grand ancient tree, celebrated as such for the last two hundred years, but like all the lords of this earth, it had its day when it flourished and extended its branches to a great distance, and then came the processes of decay which were in operation probably more than one hundred years before the great monarch bowed his proud head and yielded to inevitable fate. It had attained to about six feet in diameter two feet above ground, and by actual count of the layers of wood so far as decay would permit, it must have attained to about four hundred years of age; when in a strong east-

---

[1] *Fairfield Indian Deed dated Feb. 12, 1685.*

" We Indians sell . . . for a valuable consideration . . . a neck of land called Wolf Pitt Neck . . . on Stratford bounding line on ye northeast, on ye other sides with ye land of ye inhabitants of Fairfield. . . . .

The mark of Penomscot.	The mark of Matamhe.
Cheroramag, his mark.	The mark of Kahaco.
The mark of A soraimpom.	The mark of Shaganoset.
The mark of Machoka, acunk's Daughter.	The mark of Old Anthony.
The mark of Pony.	The mark of Matamhe.
The mark of Pascog, Interpreter."	

4

erly storm in the spring of 1884, it was blown down, and
"great was the fall of it," and then by the fiat of the world-
renowned showman' whose tender mercies and great respect
for old age allowed it standing room in a most beautiful field
for a number of years, although unfruitful, it was hewn in
pieces and disappeared forever.

It is probable, that this celebrated ceremony took place
under the branches of this great spreading oak, when the
old Indian field was sold, which occurred in the balmy
weather of spring on the 18th of May, 1681, just two hundred and three years before it fell by the strong winds from
the great sea. Col. John Burr who held the council with the
Indians and his descendants, owned the land on which this
tree stood nearly two hundred years, their dwelling standing
but a little distance from it. Miss Polly Burr, the last owner
in the family name died in 1874, but had sold it to Hon. P. T.
Barnum previous to her decease.

Another deed' was signed by the Indians for a highway
through their reservation on Golden Hill in June, 1686, which
was very nearly what is now Washington avenue, and this
highway was for the convenience of the English and Indians.
There were residing here then several English families, John
Beardsley, Samuel Gregory, Henry Summers and others, on
and near the old division line between Fairfield and Stratford, which was afterwards called Division street, and now
Park avenue.

The next spring (in 1687) the General Court ordered the
old King's highway laid out from Stratford to Fairfield, which
highway, after nearly two hundred years, was so unfortunate
as to have its name changed to the insignificant name of

---

8 The Hon. P. T. Barnum.

9 *Fairfield Indian Deed for highway, dated June 8, 1686.*

"A highway from the highway between Fairfield and Stratford [now Park
avenue] into the Indian field called Golden Hill, ... near where the path
lieth from Samuel Gregory's across the Indian field that goeth toward Stratford."

John Beardsley.

Wowompon,	his mark.	Pascob,	his mark.
Panomscot,	his mark.	Pany,	his mark.
Siacus,	his mark.	Robin,	his mark.

North avenue, thereby losing all its ancient renown and honor.

Two other deeds are recorded on the Fairfield book; one of land " called Umpawage lying westward from Fairfield in the wilderness ;"[10] the other[11] " a piece of land about eighteen or twenty miles from the town of Fairfield . . . to the westward of north Fairfield in the woods, called Ompaquag, a mile square." All the Indians signing these deeds were probably of the Pequannock tribe, and the last witness to this last deed—Cashesamay—was the Sachem at Pootatuck (Shelton) and afterwards at Newtown.

Trouble with the Indians.

The Indians made much trouble and brought many difficulties to the English settlers of Connecticut. The expenditures by the latter to defend themselves from the hostilities and trespasses of the former were more than a fair or proper value of the land as it was purchased from time to time until it was all secured by honorable deeds. There were two wars between the English and Indians in Connecticut ; the one in 1637, and the other in 1675 and 1676, and both, under the circumstances then existing, were great wars with heavy expend-

---

[10] *Fairfield Indian Deed dated Dec. 29, 1686.*

[11] " This land is by estimation about two miles square, northwest bounds is by Sagatuck River . . . . . . which runeth by the path that goeth from Paquiag the English plantateon."

Nanascrow,	his mark.	Mattake,	his mark.
Crekano,	his mark.	Mamorussuck,	his mark.
Tontasonahas,	his mark.	Washogenoset,	his mark.
Womumkaway,	his mark.	Aquetwake,	his mark.
Taquoshe,	his mark.		

" Indian Witnesses.

Sasco James,	his mark.	Panomscot,	his mark.
Roben,	his mark.	Messhawmish,	his mark."

[11] *Fairfield Indian Deed dated Sept. 12, 1687.*

" A parcel of land in Connecticut called Ompaquag, it being a mile square."

Monaquitarah, Sen.,	his mark.	Wamouncaway,	his mark.
Nathascon,	his mark.	Wukerowam,	his mark.

" Indian Witnesses.

Mamoroset, Sagawin,	his mark.	Robben,	his mark.
Wanachecompum,	his mark.	Cashesamay, Sachem,	his mark."

itures and terrible consequences. The first of these was the
Pequot war which began in May, 1637, and closed in June the
same year in a swamp near what is now the village of Southport, in the town of Fairfield. The attack on the fort of the
Pequots was made by Capt. John Mason and his ninety men
about day-break in the morning of June 5th, and a great victory was gained, resulting in the killing of many of the Indians, and the remainder fleeing westward in great haste.
These were pursued by the soldiers, crossing the Connecticut
river and continuing along the shore of the Sound. At New
Haven a number of Indians were killed in a skirmish or battle, and the same in Stratford where the fugitives were joined
by the Pequannock Indians; and finally the flying Indians
took refuge in a swamp, now located a little north of the village of Southport, where they were surrounded, and after
hard fighting some escaped with their lives.

At this time some hostages were taken of the Pequannock Indians and some of their women were sold to servitude
in Connecticut and Massachusetts. The Pequot and Pequannock women and children taken in this war numbering two
hundred[12] were all devoted to slavery for life, being distributed, probably, sold by the governments of Connecticut and
Massachusetts to pay expenses of the war, to the inhabitants
of these commonwealths, and many of them, especially the
male children, according to Governor Winthrop,[13] were sold
as slaves at the Bermuda Islands. This Pequot war was a
savage war on the part of the English and produced terrible
results. The historians have apparently nearly always
avoided the full particulars and the disgrace of its barbarity.
Even Dr. Trumbull either was ignorant of the aggravating
facts or passed over them too lightly for a historian of high
integrity. The slaughter of so many Indians—six or seven
hundred—besides those assigned to slavery, produced on the
minds of those who remained in the tribes, savages though
they were, a terrible fear, a shudder of horror, but the reac-
tion in their minds was an almost insatiable thirst for revenge,
and this the colonists understood, and so dreaded that it is

---

[12] Morton, 114.

[13] Ibid, 113.

apparent on almost every movement they made for self-protection, for fifty years, and the Narraganset, or King Phillip's War, was planned and carried on by the Indians with double secrecy and energy by the remembrance of this Pequot slaughter, for without it King Phillip could never have formed the combination of tribes which he did. Also from the day the Pequots were slain the western Connecticut Indians had no faith in the white man's religion. Think of it! There were at the time in the Housatonic valley, from Long Island Sound northward, between two and three thousand docile, friendly Indians, but a dozen reported conversions to Christianity were not made until the Moravian Missionaries came to Scatacook in 1743, and yet these natives mingled freely and in scores of cases, familiarly with the white settlers during all these one hundred years.

As has been stated, the colonists dreaded and expected retaliation. Several times during the next seventy-five years it was rumored, with no foundation for the rumor but the fears of the whites or the threats of a few irritated natives, that the Indians of Fairfield county had joined with the Mohawks in a war of extermination ; and the General Court sent out companies of soldiers, into Fairfield and Litchfield counties, to detect, and resist such a combination, even as late as 1724. As late as during the French and Indian wars in 1758, this dread and expectation were still cherished and acted upon all along the western boundaries of Connecticut.

The destruction of the Pequots was ended in the town of Fairfield, and the Pequannocks were allies and joined in the fight against the whites, thus connecting Stratford and Fairfield with that war.

The causes which have been set forth by Dr. Trumbull for this war were entirely inadequate to the terrible massacre of seven or eight hundred men, women and children, even in an Indian fort, and the enslaving of two hundred other women and children, and the only excuse for the persons who did it lies in the fact that they had just emigrated from England where such barbarity was the sentiment of the people, as was clearly exhibited by that people in the American Revolutionary War.

Until the year 1643, following the Pequot war, the
Indians were comparatively quiet and friendly, and the General Court saw the need of making but few restrictions and
regulations in regard to them, and what they did enact had
as much, or more reference to the conduct of the English than
to the Indians, but in this year and several following, the
doings of the Indians in what is now Fairfield County were
such as to awaken great apprehension for the safety of the
people.

Five plantations were seriously in danger; Stratford,
Fairfield, Norwalk, Stamford and Greenwich, but the last of
these was at the time under the jurisdiction of the New York
Governor. The settlers in each of these localities were not
numerous, and they had had but little time or means to make
preparations against any Indian hostilities. The settlement
at Stratford had been in progress four years, that of Fairfield,
four years, that of Norwalk, three, that of Stamford, two, and
that of Greenwich, three. The number of the Indians then
within the five plantations and their vicinities were, probably, four or five to every white person, and they had all
advantageous facilities for a complete massacre, or destruction of the white people. The immediate cause for this disturbance was the war between the Hudson River Indians
and the Dutch at New York. Dr. Trumbull[14] gives the following account of the origin of this Indian and Dutch War:

" The war between the Dutch and Indians began in this
manner. A drunken Indian, in his intoxication, killed a
Dutchman. The Dutch demanded the murderer, but he was
not to be found. They then made application to their governor to avenge the murderer. He, judging it would be
unjust or unsafe, considering the numbers of the Indians, and
the weak and scattered state of the Dutch settlements, neglected to comply with their repeated solicitations. In the
mean time the Mohawks, as the report was, excited by the
Dutch, fell suddenly on the Indians, in the vicinity of the
Dutch settlements and killed nearly thirty of them. Others
fled to the Dutch for protection. One Marine, a Dutch cap-

---

[14] Vol. i. 138.

tain, getting intelligence of their state, made application to the Dutch Governor, and obtained a commission to kill as many of them as it should be in his power. Collecting a company of armed men, he fell suddenly upon the Indians, while they were unapprehensive of danger, and made a promiscuous slaughter of men, women and children, to the number of seventy or eighty. This instantly roused the Indians, in that part of the country, to a furious, obstinate and bloody war.

" In the spring, and beginning of the summer, they burnt the Dutch out-houses; and driving their cattle into their barns, they burned the barns and cattle together. They killed twenty or more of the Dutch people, and pressed so hard upon them that they were obliged to take refuge in their fort, and to seek help of the English. The Indians upon Long Island united in the war with those on the main, and burned the Dutch houses and barns. The Dutch governor, in this situation, invited captain Underhill from Stamford to assist him in the war. Marine, the Dutch captain, was so exasperated with this proceeding that he presented his pistol at the governor, and would have shot him, but was prevented by one who stood by him. Upon this one of Marine's tenants discharged his musket at the governor, and the ball but just missed him. The governor's sentinel shot the tenant and killed him on the spot. The Dutch, who at first were so forward for a war with the Indians, were now, when they experienced the loss and dangers of it, so irritated at the governor, for the orders which he had given, that he could not trust himself among them. He was obliged to keep a constant guard of fifty Englishmen about his person. In the summer and fall the Indians killed fifteen more of the Dutch people, and drove in all the inhabitants of the English and Dutch settlements west of Stamford.

" In the prosecution of their works of destruction, they made a visit to the neighborhood where Mrs. Hutchinson, who had been so famous, at Boston, for her Antinomian and familistical tenets, had made a settlement. The Indians, at first, appeared with the same friendship with which they used to frequent her house; but they murdered her and all her family, Mr. Collins her son-in-law, and several other persons belonging to other families in the neighborhood. Eighteen persons were killed in the whole. The Indians, with an implacable fury, prosecuted the destruction of the Dutch, and of their property, in all that part of the country. They killed and burned their cattle, horses and barns without resistance. Their case was truly distressing."

Notwithstanding these calamitous circumstances the governor and Court at New Haven felt that they were not at liberty to go to the relief of the Dutch with an armed force until consultation could be had with the Commissioners of the other colonies.

"The war was continued several years, and was bloody and destructive both to the Dutch and Indians. Captain Underhill had the principal management of it, and was of great service to the Dutch. He collected a flying army of a hundred and fifty men, English and Dutch, by which he preserved the Dutch settlements from total destruction. It was supposed, that, upon Long Island and on the main, he killed between four and five hundred Indians.

"The Indians at Stamford too much caught the spirit of the western Indians in their vicinity, who were at war with the Dutch. They appeared so tumultuous and hostile, that the people of Stamford were in great fear, that they should soon share the fate of the settlements at the westward of them. They wrote to the general court at New Haven, that in their apprehensions there were just grounds of a war with those Indians, and that if their houses should be burned, because the other plantations would not consent to war, they ought to bear the damage.

"At the same time the Narraganset Indians were enraged at the death of their sachem. The English were universally armed. The strictest watch and guard was kept in all the plantations. In Connecticut, every family, in which there was a man capable of bearing arms, was obliged to send one complete in arms, every Lord's day, to defend the places of public worship. Indeed all places wore the aspect of a general war.

"In the year of 1644 the Indians were no more peaceable than they were the year before. Those in the western part of Connecticut still conducted themselves in a hostile manner. In the spring they murdered a man, belonging to Massachusetts, between Fairfield and Stamford. About six or eight weeks after the murder was discovered, the Indians promised to deliver the murderer, at Uncoway [Fairfield], if Mr. Ludlow would appoint men to receive him. Mr. Ludlow sent ten men for that purpose; but as soon as the Indians came within sight of the town, they, by general consent, unbound the prisoner and suffered him to escape. The English were so exasperated at this insult that they immediately seized on eight or ten of the Indians, and committed them to prison. There was among them not less than one or two Sachems. Upon this, the Indians arose in great numbers about the town, and exceedingly alarmed the people, both at Fairfield and Stamford. Mr. Ludlow wrote to New Haven for advice. The court desired him to keep the Indians in durance, and assured him of immediate assistance, should it be necessary and desired; and a party of twenty men were draughted forthwith, and prepared to march to Stamford at the shortest notice. The Indians were held in custody until four Sachems, in those parts, appeared and interceded for them, promising that if the English would release them, they would, within a month, deliver the murderer to justice."

"Not more than a month after their release, an Indian went boldly into the town of Stamford, and made a murderous assault upon a woman, in her house. Finding no man at home, he took a lathing hammer, and approached her as though he were about to put it into her hand; but, as she was stooping down to take her child from the cradle, he struck her upon her head. She fell instantly with the blow; he then struck her twice, with the sharp part of the hammer, which penetrated her skull. Supposing her to be dead, he plundered the house, and made his escape; but soon after, the woman so far recovered, as to be able to describe the Indian, and his manner of dress. Her wounds, which at first appeared

[15] N. H. Col. Rec., i. 134.

to be mortal, were finally healed; but her brain was so affected that she lost her reason.

"At the same time, the Indians rose in those parts, with the most tumultuous and hostile appearances. They refused to come to the English, or to have any treaty with them, and appeared in a very alarming manner about several of the plantations, firing their pieces, and exceedingly terrifying the inhabitants. They deserted their wigwams, and neglected to weed their corn. The English had intelligence that the Indians designed to cut them off, and therefore many judged it unsafe to travel by land, and some of the plantations were obliged to keep a strong guard and watch, night and day. And as they had not numbers sufficient to defend themselves, they made application to Hartford and New Haven for assistance, and they both sent aid to the weaker parts of their respective colonies. New Haven sent help to Fairfield and Stamford, as they were much nearer to them than to Connecticut.

"After a great deal of alarm and trouble, the Indian who had attempted the murder of the woman, was delivered up and condemned to death, and was executed at New Haven. The executioner cut off his head with a falchion, but it was cruelly done. He gave the Indian eight blows before he effected the execution; yet the Indian sat erect and motionless, until his head was severed from his body."[14]

"The Indians this year were almost everywhere troublesome, and in some places in a state of high hostility. In Virginia they rose and made a most horrible massacre of the English. The Narragansets, regardless of all their convenants with the English and with Uncas, continued in such hostilities that a party of soldiers were sent to preserve the peace and security of the people."

Under such circumstances these small plantations on the shore of the Sound, now within Fairfield county, made but slow progress. Greenwich was nearly, if not entirely, deserted, and but for Captain Underhill, Stamford, Norwalk,

---

[14] See Records of the Colonies, and Winthrop's Journal, p. 352.

Fairfield and Stratford must have been given up for a time.
And as it was, what a living death it must have been to
remain steadfast and not desert the localities. Every family
that could raise a soldier as a watchman, must bring him
forth, if it was the last and only man in the family. What
sleepless nights in those homes; what anxiety if a member
of a family, being out at work, did not return home at the
expected or appointed time. What a war-like appearance
was witnessed every "Lord's day" at the meeting-house,
with one soldier from every family, armed and equipped with
a gun and sword, and all possible war implements.

The cost of this Indian war to the seven plantations
along the Sound was sufficient to have purchased, established,
and perpetuated a separate plantation, if there had been no
Indians. The court at New Haven assessed fines almost
weekly, on persons who were found delinquent in watching
at their posts, or insufficiently provided with arms or ammunition, as the following items from the New Haven records
most fully show. At a Court holden March 7, 1643:

Matthew Hitchcock, for a willful neglect to walk the
round when the officers called him, was fined 5ˢ.

James Haward, Joseph Thompson, William Bassett,
Anthony Thompson, David Evance, Samuel Wilson and Samuel Haskins, [were] fined, each man, 6ᵈ "for foole guns."

"Thomas Yale and Jonathan Marsh for the same, 6ᵈ a
piece.

"Richard Perry and his 2 men, William Gibbard and
James Stewart and William Ball, for late coming fined each.
man 1ˢ.

"Roger Knapp, defective, all except gun, fined 5ˢ.

"Brother Lamson, defective gun, fined 4ˢ.

"Thomas Higginson, James Stewart and James Haward,
defective belt, fined 6ᵈ.

"Mr. Eaton's 3 men, Thomas Higinson and his man, for
coming without arms on the Lord's day, fined each man 2ˢ.

"Matthew Crowder, Thomas Caffins, Theodore Higginson, James Stewart, Thomas Meaks, Isaac Whitehead, Matthew Row, Richard Mansfield, Thomas Iles, Lawrence Wade,
John Hill, John Cooper, Jarvice Boykin, and Mr. Eaton's

3 men, fined each man 6ᵈ, for late coming to the meeting with their arms, Feb. 18, 1643.

"It was ordered that the 2ᵈ drum shall be the period of the soldiers coming on the Lord's day.

"Court holden, May 1, 1644.

Brother Perry, being master of a watch and willfully neglecting it, was fined 40ˢ.

"Matthew Row, for sitting down to sleep when he should have stood sentinel, was fined 5ˢ. Brother Nichols, brother Gibbert, Richard Webb, Thomas Wheeler, Henry Lendell and William Bassett, fined each man 1ˢ for late coming on the Lord's day with their arms."

Court held June 5, 1644.

"John Chapman being master of a watch and neglecting it, was fined 10ˢ.

"Mr. Gilbert's man, being absent at his watch, was fined 5ˢ.

"George Larrymore for neglecting his watch, fined 2ˢ6ᵈ."

Court held at New Haven June 23, 1644.

"It was ordered that the night watches be carefully attended, and the ward of the Sabbath days be dilligently observed, and that every one of the trainband bring their arms to the meeting every Lord's day; also that the great guns be put in readiness for service; also that the drum be beaten every morning by break of day, and at the setting of the sun.

"It was ordered that every Lord's day 2 men shall go with every heard of cattle, with their arms fitted for service until these dangers be over.

"It was ordered that the farmers shall be freed from watching at the town while there is need of watch at the farms, provided they keep a dilligent watch there."

New Haven and Milford were much less exposed to the hostilities of the Indians than the plantations west of them, and if they needed so great diligence and strictness, how much more must have been needed by the others?

The troubles resulting from the Dutch and Indian war quieted down to a considerable extent, after three or four years, but the Indians of Fairfield County continued to indicate hostile feelings, and committed various depredations, and some acts of personal violence. In 1649, this spirit became so threatening, in connection with a murder committed by an Indian, that the General Court felt compelled to take definite action,[12] and did in effect declare war against them, but by a committee consisting of Mr. Ludlow and Mr. Talcott, the matter was quieted and a siege of war avoided.

During all these efforts for peace and safety, great pains were taken to keep the Indians from obtaining guns and ammunition, or means for making war upon the English. In securing obedience to these regulations they had occasion to pass a somewhat unusual sentence in 1648, upon David Provost, a Dutchman, that if he repeated the offence he should be "shipped for Ireland and sent to the Parliament."[13]

Again in 1652, fears concerning the Indians were aroused anew, in consequence of the declaration of war between England and Holland, and it was expected that the war would be extended to America and assume serious proportions between New England and the Dutch at New Amsterdam, but after great preparations by the colonies, the war closed without any serious collisions here, between the whites, or damages done by the Indians.

---

[12] "This Courte taking into serious consideration what may be done according to God in way of revenge of the bloude of John Whittmore, late of Stanford, and well weighing all circumstances, together with the carriages of the Indians (bordering thereupon) in and about the premises, do declare themselves that they do judge it lawful and according to God to make war upon them.

"This Courte desires Mr. Deputy, Mr. Ludlow and Mr. Taylecoate [Talcott] to ride to-morrow to New Haven, and confer with Mr. Eaton and the rest of the magistrates there about sending out against the Indians, and to make return of their apprehensions with what convenient speed they may."

General Court, May, 1648.

[13] "Whereas, David Provost and other Dutchmen (as the Court is informed) have sould powder and shotte to Several Indeans, against the express Lawes both of the Inglishe and Dutch, It is now Ordered, that if upon examination of witnesses the said defaulte shall fully appeare, the penalty of the lawes of this Commonwealth shallbe laid upon such as shallbe found guilty of such transgression, the which if such delinquents shall not subject unto them shall be shipped for Ingland and sent to the Parliament." Col. Rec., i. 163.

"May 1707 This' Assembly judgeth it expedient that the Indian murderer in durance at Fairfield shall and may be returned to the Indians, that so the Indians may have the opportunity to execute on him as they shall determine.'"[11]

It is a matter of conjecture that this Indian was hung at a place called Gallows Hill, in the southwestern part of the present town of New Milford, for such an occurrence took place there, probably, by which the name is found there when that town was first settled about 1710.

The Golden Hill Indian Fund.

In 1802 on the petition of Tom Sherman, Eunice Sherman and others of the Golden Hill Indians, the State appointed an agent or overseer to administer their affairs. Abraham Y. De Witt held this office first, and after him were Josiah Lacey, Elijah Burritt, Smith Tweedy, Daniel O. Wheeler, Dwight Morris and Russell Tomlinson, the present incumbent.

Besides the dwelling and land at Nichols Farms now occupied by William Sherman, the Golden Hill fund amounts to about three hundred dollars.

The Samp Mortar Rock is a peculiarity and mystery. It is located about three miles north of Fairfield village, in the town of Fairfield, and is so called, or was so named because it was supposed that the Indians ground their corn in it. It is on the very verge of overhanging rocks of about fifty or sixty feet in height, and consists of a cavity in the top of the rock about thirteen inches in diameter and ten in depth, and has been pronounced by the younger Professor Dana, of Yale College, who has seen it, a "Pot-hole" or cavity worn there by the action of water and small cobble stones at some period far back in the ages. The rocky ridge on which it is located is of several miles in extent, and has been a place of frequent resort for pic-nics and visiting parties for many years. The locality forbids the idea of its being constructed there by the Indians and it is seemingly equally unreasonable that it should have been made where it is by the action of water, even were

---

[11] Col. Rec., v. 28.

the valleys around it filled. It is a curiosity. There is no evidence that the Indians had any encampment of consequence, nearer than three miles from it.

A Powwow or Medicine Camp.

A few years after the New York and New Haven railroad was completed, or about twenty-five years ago, Mr. Thomas B. Fairchild of Stratford saw a number of stone posts standing like hitching posts on a line with the sidewalk in front of the premises of Mr. William Tuttle, near the lower wharf in Stratford village, and the novelty and peculiar appearance of them attracted his attention. Mr. Tuttle had set them, a few years previous, and left the place, and all that could be learned as to them by careful inquiry was that they were dug up in making the railroad between Stratford and Bridgeport, and Mr. Tuttle had brought them to his home and placed them along the sidewalk as hitching posts and novel ornaments. Thus the matter passed some years, but Mr. Fairchild, whose business was in Bridgeport, while in a state of mysterious inquiry as to these stones, frequently looked along the road, to ascertain, if possible, where they were found, and to learn who made them and for what purpose. About two years since, with increasing inquiry as to these posts, while passing along the road near Pembroke Pond where some men were excavating by the railroad bank to lay some pipe to secure fresh water for the Holmes and Edward's Silver Works, in West Stratford, he saw one of these posts, but wondered why it should be at that place as constituting a part of the railroad embankment. On meeting a cartman employed at the Cartridge Works, he pointed out the post and requested him to bring it in the cart to the office, for it was a peculiar stone and he wanted to preserve it. Upon which Mr. Bernard Judge said, " Don't I know all about the posts, and how this post got where it is? Didn't I do the first work that ever I did in America on the railroad at this very place a few rods east of the iron bridge here in West Stratford? We dug out loads and loads of these posts, and threw them into the mill pond on the brush and limbs and then heaped the dirt upon them. These posts lay in heaps, partly covered, or under the ground, when we found them, and we talked about them a good deal, some saying they were put there by the Indians."

The larger number of these posts are nearly round, six and seven feet long, from seven to eight inches in diameter; one that is nearly square, only the corners rounded, being now in the possession of Mr. Thomas B. Fairchild, at Stratford, has a slot from the top downwards about eight inches deep and half an inch wide, on the side, as if to let in a wide band surrounding a sacred inclosure to keep out intruders. One of these posts is much larger than any of the others, and is of oval shape, from ten to twelve inches wide and about seven thick. Some are broken in pieces, but probably the larger number of them are still under the railroad bed. They were found on ground nearly level, at the foot of the hill, near a large, fine spring of water, and were thrown together, or near each other as if taken from their original positions and placed aside, to be out of the way; and are supposed to have been used to protect a powwow ground or a medicine camp.

The following is a description of a powwow place found among the Mandan Indians in Dakota Territory, published recently in London, in the " North American Indians :"

" In the centre of the village is an open space or public square, 150 feet in diameter and circular in form, which is used for all public games and festivals, shows and exhibitions. The lodges around this open space fronts in, with their doors toward the centre ; and in the middle of this stands an object of great religious veneration, on account of the importance it has in connection with the annual religious ceremonies. This object is in the form of a large hogshead, some eight or ten feet high, made of planks and hoops, containing within it some of their choicest mysteries or medicines. They call it the Big Canoe."—*Atlantis*, by Ignatius Donnelly, 111.

In the present town of Stratford there are but few relics of the natives to be seen, except quantities of oyster and clam shells in three localities. At the edge of the marsh west of the Lordship farm and a hundred rods north of the dwelling on that farm, is still a quantity of clam shells probably left there by the Indians, but it is not extensive. At a small fresh water pond on the northern part of the Lordship farm on the north side of the pound the oyster shells, many of large size, are in considerable quantities. They are largely covered by the soil but are in some places nearly two feet deep. On the east side of the great neck in several places are beds of oyster shells left by the Indians, which indicate a long occupation of the region in order to make the accumulations.

In some historical notes by Major W. B. Hinks, published in 1871, the following note is found: "Several interesting relics of the Indians were discovered in Stratford a few years since by the Rev. B. L. Swan. They consisted of a fire-place, and mortar for grinding corn, excavated in a ledge of rock near the house recently occupied by Mr. William Strong, which was built on the site of an ancient inn, kept during and before the Revolutionary War by George Benjamin. The fire-place was a semi-cylindrical upright hollow in the rock, several feet in height, from the top of which a pot could be suspended by a cross bar. Below it was the mortar with a rounded stone pestle, as large as a man's head, still lying in it. Unfortunately these relics were destroyed before measures could be taken for their preservation.

"Arrow heads in considerable numbers have also been found at the foot of another ledge a little west of the town on the lower road to Bridgeport, and it is believed that this was the place of their manufacture."

Indian Burying Places.

In three places have Indian skeletons been exhumed in considerable numbers within the territory now covered by the city of Bridgeport; one in or near what was the old Nimrod field near the present Gas Works, one where the Prospect Street School building now stands and the other on the bluff or hill as it was, South of State street and east of Main. The one at the Gas Works was greatly disturbed when the railroad was constructed, and quite a number of skeletons were taken out, but no implements of any considerable amount were found, at least none are reported, but this seems to have been the burial place for the Indians more largely after the whites came here.

As to the place where the Prospect Street School building now stands a paragraph from the Bridgeport *Standard*

5

for October 28, 1870, is given: "The frequent finding of Indian bones and skulls in different places about the city suggests the question whether Bridgeport may not have been at some remote period in the past, one immense Indian hunting and burying ground. Every few days these bones are being brought to light by excavation, and now we find by digging for the new wing of the Prospect Street school house that the ground there was once quite a large burying place. Some fifty graves have been exposed and a large number of human bones and skulls are found buried a few feet below the surface. In some instances these skull bones are perfect, the jaws with full sets of teeth, being also found in sound condition. Tobacco pipes have been discovered buried in the same graves, also a genuine Indian dinner pot, and other signs and evidences that the bones of many aborigines have been for many long years quietly resting there, are found. In each case the body was probably buried in a sitting posture."

Sacrificed Indian Implements.

In the autumn of 1883, Mr. L. B. Beers and Mr. Robert W. Curtis, of Stratford, were hunting for Indian relics on the bank, near the mouth of the Housatonic river, when coming to a place of clean loam ground Mr. Beers picked up a small piece of soapstone pot or dish, and Mr. Curtis soon found another stone that had the appearance of being worked out, but on examination it was thrown away as of no value. The hunt being continued Mr. Curtis found a broken piece of spear head, and directly Mr. Beers picked up a poll or head of a stone axe and called for the piece that had been thrown away, which being secured fitted to the head of the axe perfectly. The idea then came to Mr. Curtis that Indians would be likely to bury in light loamy earth, and that this place would be favorable in that respect, and proposed to his fellow laborer to dig up the ground, and thereupon went to work with his cane. Soon he struck something hard and dug it out with his hands and found it to be a large spear head. After working a little time longer Mr. Beers proposed to look elsewhere, but Mr. Curtis continued the work and soon found a small nest of implements, all broken, apparently, by fire heat. On further digging the articles found at this time were pieces of two axes, two chisels and a few pieces of other implements.

The search has been continued with intervals to the present time, and the result is the following, all the articles being in small pieces in consequence of fire heat:

One axe 10½ inches long, 6 wide, nicely worked; one axe 7½ inches long and 4½ wide, approaching round in form; one axe 8 inches long and 5 wide, nearly entire and nicely worked; one tomahawk 4½ inches by 2½; one pestle 13½ inches long, nicely worked; one pestle 12 inches long, rough; one 9 inches long, rough; eighteen pieces of other pestles; nineteen chisels from 3½ inches to 9 in length, some of them very fine grain stones, some of them coarse; one soapstone food dish 11 inches long, 8 inches wide, 4 in depth, nearly complete and ornamented with notches on the edge, the shape is triangular, oval; one soapstone food dish 12 inches long, 7 inches in width and 3 in depth; five rubbing stones; one drill 2½ inches in length, very delicate; one coarse triangular, cone shaped stone about 4 pounds in weight, use not known; 75 pieces of different sizes, comprising knives, spear and arrow heads; 1,000 pieces of small implements broken beyond designation.

The supposition is that these implements were from time to time thrown into sacrificial fires as offerings in worship, and afterwards buried with quantities of hickory nuts which were found as charred ashes in great numbers. This subject may be further treated in a following part of this book in regard to Indian worship.

CHAPTER IV.

THE CUPHEAG PLANTATION.

1639-1645.

BEAUTIFUL township, inhabited by a noble people, is the theme of discourse in the following pages. Antiquity has a charm for many thousands of persons whose lives never reach the half of three-score years and ten, while equally as many, as the allotted years are added, grow pathetic by the increasing remembrance of the halcyon days which will never more return; and yet we love to linger in our thoughts amidst the realities of early years and the recollection of those, the number of whose years were long since inscribed on marble tablets in the cemetery. Almost two hundred and fifty years—or from the year 1639 to that of 1884 —is the measure of the period which is to pass in review, as compassing the history of this locality, to the present time.

Stratford was, and is, a beautiful spot of earth, and they who have wandered from it have looked back with pride as well as with longing hearts, and have almost wished that the destinies of men would have allowed them to tarry by the old hearthstones of their ancestors until the work of life should have been accomplished; and many more will look back from far distant countries and proclaim with joy that they descended from the early planters of this good old town. "Beautiful for situation" was written thousands of years ago, and yet it is equally applicable to this distinguished locality. "Old Stratford" was a name fondly cherished, while yet it was young in years, by those who had gone forth to establish new plantations, and "Old Stratford" is still a sound of joy

and pride to a great circle of its acquaintances as well as its
descendants. Its situation, being bounded toward the sun-
rising by the placid Housatonic, and on the south by the
ever charming Long Island Sound, was, and is, one of remarkable attractiveness, and such as never to be forgotten by any
of its wandering sons and daughters. By the side of the
great sea where the tide of the mighty ocean, ever obedient
to the nod of the queen of night, ceases not its life-giving
toil, Stratford sat down as a child in 1639, and thereafter
grew towards maturer years. In historic time, it is still
young, but compared with many of its inland neighbors it is
truly old ; and, as the tale of its legends pass in review, the
ages will seem to have greatly multiplied, and its multitude
of descendants indefinitely extended from ocean to ocean.

Stratford village is located on the Housatonic river
about one and a half miles from Long Island Sound, in Fairfield county, Connecticut, fourteen miles from New Haven
and fifty-eight miles from New York City. The original
township, being twelve miles in length north and south, and
about seven miles wide east and west, comprised most of the
territory now included in the five townships of Stratford,
Bridgeport, Huntington, Trumbull and Monroe ; and in this
history it is proposed to complete the record of the whole
of this territory, in uniform style, from the commencement
down to the present time, and as each town is organized out
of the old territory, to lay its history aside until the original
township by name shall have been completed, and then to
take up again each of the new towns in the order of the date
of their organization, and thus complete the work.

The picturesqueness of the locality is remarkable. The
general slope of the land is towards the Housatonic on the
east and the Sound on the south, and the face of the country
is divided with small elevations of land, called hills, but
scarcely equal to the name, such as Old Mill Hill, Toilsome
Hill, Chestnut Hill, Long Hill, Coram Hill, and the White
Hills ; rising only to such a height as to afford numerous
sites for dwellings, in full view of many miles of water
scenery of the Sound and landscape on Long Island beyond,
and such as to guarantee a high degree of health from the

balmy breezes of the Atlantic and the bracing, if not sometimes the biting winds from the hills at the west and north.
Great vigor of health, longevity of life, and beauty of locality,
have been characteristic of the region, until the fame thereof
has reached from ocean to ocean, and is likely never to grow
less.

Stratford was the seventh plantation settled within the
present territory of Connecticut. Windsor, Hartford and
Wethersfield, the three first, were commenced in the years
1635 and 6; Saybrook was commenced under John Winthrop,
the younger, in 1635, although but few families had arrived
there in 1636. Mr. Davenport's company from London, with
Mr. Pruden's, arrived at New Haven the middle of April,
1638, and the next spring Mr. Pruden and his people who
had remained all winter at New Haven, settled at Milford ;
and in the spring of 1639, a number of families settled at
Stratford, then known by the Indian name of *Cupheag*.

The right of soil and manner of settlement.

The *Patent*[1] for the territory of Connecticut, given by
the Earl of Warwick in 1631, under King Charles I., included

---

[1] *The first Patent of Connecticut, given under King Charles I.*

"To all people, unto whom this present writing Shall come, Robert, Earl of
Warwick, sendeth greeting, in our Lord God everlasting.

Know ye, that the said Robert, Earl of Warwick, for divers good causes and
considerations him thereunto moving, hath given, granted, bargained, sold,
enfeoffed, aliebated, and confirmed, and by these presents doth give, grant, bargain, sell, enfeoff, aliene, and confirm, unto the right honorable William, Viscount
Say and Seal, the right honorable Robert, Lord Brook, the right honorable Lord
Rich, and the honorable Charles Fiennes, Esq., Sir Nathaniel Rich, Knt., Sir
Richard Saltonstall, Knt., Richard Knightly, Esq., John Pym, Esq., John Hampden, John Humphrey, Esq., and Herbert Pelham, Esq., their heirs and assigns,
and their associates forever, all that part of New England, in America, which lies
and extends itself from a river there called Narraganset river, the space of forty
leagues upon a straight line near the sea shore towards the southwest, west and
by south, or west as the coast lieth towards Virginia, accounting three English
miles to the league ; and also all and singular the lands and hereditaments whatsoever, lying and being within the lands aforesaid, north and south in latitude
and breadth, and length and longitude of and within, all the breadth aforesaid,
throughout the main lands there, from the western ocean to the south sea, and all
lands and grounds, place and places, soil, wood, and woods, grounds, havens,

"all that part of New England, in America, which lies and extends itself from a river there called Narraganset river, the space of forty leagues upon a straight line near the sea shore towards the southwest, west and south, or west as the coast lieth towards Virginia," and therefore covered more area than the present State of Connecticut. President Clap of Yale College described it thus: "All that part of New England which lies west from Narraganset river, a hundred and twenty miles on the sea coast; and from thence in latitude and breadth aforesaid to the sea, which grant extended

---

ports, creeks and rivers, waters, fishings, and hereditaments whatsoever, lying within the said space, and every part and parcel thereof. And also all islands lying in America aforesaid, in the said seas, or either of them, on the western coasts, or parts of the said tracts of lands, by these presents mentioned to be given, granted, bargained, sold, enfeoffed, aliened, and confirmed, and also all mines and minerals, as well, royall mines of gold and silver, as other mines and minerals, whatsoever, in the said land and premises, or any part thereof, and also the several rivers within the said limits, by what name or names soever called or known, and all jurisdictions, rights, and royalties, liberties, freedoms, immunities, powers, privileges, franches, preeminences, and commodities whatsoever, which the said Robert, Earl of Warwick, now hath or had, or might use, exercise, or enjoy, in or within any part or parcel thereof, excepting and reserving to his majesty, his heirs, and successors the fifth part of all gold and silver ore, that shall be found within the said premises, or any part or parcel thereof: To have and to hold the said part of New-England in America, which lies and extends and is abutted as aforesaid. And the said several rivers and every parcel thereof, and all the said islands, rivers, ports, havens, waters, fishings, mines, minerals, jurisdictions, powers, franchises, royalties, liberties, privileges, commodities, hereditaments and premises, whatsoever with the appurtenances, unto the said William, Viscount Say and Seal, Robert, Lord Brook, Robert, Lord Rich, Charles Fiennes, Sir Nathaniel Rich, Sir Richard Saltonstall, Richard Knightly, John Pym, John Hampden, John Humphrey and Herbert Pelham, their heirs and assigns and their associates, to the only proper and absolute use and behoof of them the said William, Viscount Say and Seal, Robert, Lord Brook, Robert, Lord Rich, Charles Fiennes, Sir Nathaniel Rich, Sir Richard Saltonstall, Richard Knightly, John Pym, John Hampden, John Humphrey and Herbert Pelham, their heirs and assignes, and their associates for ever more. In witness whereof the said Robert Earl of Warwick, hath hereunto set his hand and seal, the ninteenth day of March, in the seventh year of the reign of our sovereign Lord Charles, by the Grace of God, King of England, Scotland, France and Ireland, defender of the faith, &c. Annoq. Domini, 1631.

Signed, sealed, and delivered,   Robert Warwick."
    in the presence of
Walter Williams
Thomas Howson

from Point Judith to New York; and from thence in a west line to the South Sea: and if we take Narraganset river in its whole length, this tract will extend as far as Worcester, and comprehends the whole of the colony of Connecticut and much more."[1]

The title to this land was given to the Earl of Warwick by the Plymouth Company of England. On "the 3d of November, 1620, just before the arrival of Mr. Robbinson's people in New England, King James 1., by letters patent, under the great seal of England, incorporated the Duke of Lenox, the Marquis of Buckingham and Hamilton, the Earls of Arundel and Warwick, and others, to the number of forty noblemen, knights and gentlemen, by the name 'of the Council established at Plymouth in the county of Devon, for the planting, ruling and governing of New England in America,'—'and granted unto them and their successors and assigns, all that part of America, lying and being in breadth from forty degrees of north latitude from the equinoctial line, to the forty-eighth degree of said northerly latitude inclusively, and in length of and within all the breadth aforesaid, throughout the main lands from sea to sea.' The patent ordained that this tract of country should be called New England in America, and by that name have continuance forever."[2] In 1630, this Plymouth Company conveyed to the Earl of Warwick the territory named in the Connecticut Patent, and which he sold, as above, to the parties named in that Patent to the number of eleven persons.

When the companies settled at Windsor and Hartford, they supposed they were within the jurisdiction of the Massachusetts Bay company, but soon became aware of their mistake, and on the arrival of the younger Governor Winthrop soon after to make a settlement at Saybrook and to be governor of Connecticut one year, there was talk of removing from Hartford, Windsor and Wethersfield, but finally the two governments were united at Hartford.

It was in the latter part of the year 1636 that trouble

---

[1] Manuscripts of President Clap. Trumbull, p. 28.

[2] Trumbull, p. 20.

began between the Pequots and the Connecticut settlements, which resulted in the annihilation of that tribe in June of the next year, and by which the English took the Pequot country as conquered territory; and by which also they took possession in March, 1638, of the country west of the Quinnipiac to the Hudson river, as conquered country, in consequence of the Indians of this territory being allies of the Pequots, and joining with them in the fight.

Before giving proof of the above statements some notice must be taken of the declarations of historians, that the first planters at Stratford and Fairfield bought these townships of the Indians, in favor of which there is scarcely a scrap of record to be found, except in the publications hereafter mentioned.

Dr. Trumbull, who was a very careful collector of history—although he made a decided mistake this once, at least —says:

"The whole township [Stratford] was purchased of the natives; but first Cupheag and Pughquonnuck only, where the settlements began."[4] The settlement did not begin at Pequannock, within Stratford bounds, until twenty years after that at Cupheag; besides, in the Colonial records the Indian name Pequannuck was sometimes applied in a general way to the settlement at Cupheag, or Stratford village, but generally to the open country in Fairfield adjoining Stratford line and including a part of Stratford territory at that place. Of Fairfield he says: "The first adventures purchased a large tract of land of the natives,"—which was, as will be seen, wholly erroneous, so far as any records show.

Noah Webster, LL.D., in his *History of the United States*, printed in 1842, says:

"Mr. Ludlow, of Windsor, who had traversed the lands west of Quinnipiac, in pursuit of the Pequots in 1637, was so well pleased with their fertility, that he and a few friends purchased a large tract at Unquoway, and began a settlement in 1639, called Fairfield. In the same year a company of

---

[4] Dr. Trumbull, i. 110, Ibid., 109.

men from England and Massachusetts purchased Cupheag
and Poquonnoc, and began the town of Stratford."[1]

Mr. J. W. Barber and others have followed this same
erroneous supposition concerning the purchase of these
plantations of the Indians before 1659, for which there was
never a scrap of record or an authenticated tradition until
these historians made them, as far as can be ascertained.
Every Indian deed of lands in Stratford bears a date of more
than twenty years later than the first settlement of the town
and the deeds were then made more as a mutual friendship
act than for any other reason. The truth is—and it only
illustrates, that historians have too little time to bestow on
their work—that Dr. Trumbull and all the other writers
wholly overlooked certain papers recorded in the first volume of Stratford records, which give a clear elucidation of
this subject. Indeed, the Indian deeds of later years prove,
in their statements, that there were no purchases of these
lands before 1656.

The plantations of Stratford and Fairfield were always
under the government of the Connecticut Colony and never
under or connected with the New Haven Colony. The
cause securing this relation was the possession of this territory by Connecticut and the direction given by that Colony
in the settlement of these localities. The claim to this territory was based on the acquisition of it as conquered country,
and, in addition, a treaty was made with the Indians for the
specific purpose of settlement. The evidence of these facts
is contained in several papers, made under oath, and recorded
at Stratford in 1659, twenty years after the whites first came,
by which the Court at Hartford decided that the lands then
occupied by Stratford and Fairfield rightly belonged to those
towns.

These papers may be seen in full on pages 10 to 15 of this
book, as a part of the Indian history; and as authority they
are important documents. These persons were: the Rev.
John Higginson, a prominent minister living at Guilford at
the time, Thomas Stanton, of Hartford, Indian interpreter,

---

[1] Webster's Hist. U. S., 97.

Lieut. Thomas Wheeler, at first of Fairfield but afterwards
of Milford, and John Minor, interpreter to the Indians
and for some years town clerk at Stratford before his removal
to Woodbury. The items given by these persons are the following. Mr. Edward Hopkins and Mr. William Goodwin,
then prominent men, were employed by the Court at Hartford to "treat with the Indians in regard to the land from
Quinnipiac to the Manhattoes" (New York), and that Mr.
Higginson accompanied them, as interpreter : that after giving notice to, and inviting the sachems and principal men of
the tribes from Quinnipiac to the Hudson river, they met at
Norwalk in the last week in March in 1638 (really the beginning of the year 1638), not quite a year after the conquest of
the Pequots, and after a day's consultation in full council, all
the tribes being well represented, the Indians gave the land
to the English, without consideration except the protection
they should thereby secure against other Indians. In this
surrender they reserved only their planting grounds, which
were located at that time on the Pequannock plain.

In these papers it is also claimed that the territory,
specially of Stratford and Fairfield, was conquered country,
for the reason that the tribes inhabiting it were tributary to
the Pequots at the time, and that they being led specially by
the Pequannock tribe, which was the most numerous, joined
with the Pequots as they fled, the year previous, and aided
them in the battles or skirmishes at Quinnipiac, Cupheag,
Pequannock and Sashquaket swamp. It was claimed, and it
is said that the Indians acknowledged, that if the Pequot
country was conquered territory and not to be paid for, so
also was that owned by those who joined them in the fight.
Mr. Higginson states that the object of this treaty was particularly to secure the land for future settlements, and keep
it from the possession of the Dutch ; and that a deputation
of Indians returned with the commissioners to Hartford and
did ratify the agreement with a meeting of the Court, held
in Mr. Hooker's barn.

Mr. Nicholas Knell, a prominent planter at Stratford,
confirmed the testimony of Mr. Higginson, and it is said that
numbers of persons would do the same, and that it was upon

the right to the soil thus obtained that the Connecticut Colony proceeded to induce settlers to locate upon these lands, beginning in 1638, probably within two months after the council held with the Indians at Norwalk.

The New Haven and Milford companies, not being aware of this acquisition by the cost of many lives, and the treaty, took possession of the Quinnipiac lands about fifteen days after the treaty was ratified, and afterwards purchased the same of the natives; but they were, as appears from these papers, as to the right of the soil obtained from the Indians, squatters on Connecticut territory. Also the planters at Norwalk, Stamford and Greenwich, not being aware of the acquisition and treaty, and the General Court not urging its claims, purchased their lands of the tribes living at those places.

The Connecticut Court, however, proceeded at once to induce settlers to establish themselves at Stratford and Fairfield, and probably succeeded in directing a few families to locate in each place in the year 1638, and several more in 1639.

On the 10th of October, 1639, Mr. Ludlow then residing at Windsor, and being Deputy Governor, made a journey to New Haven and thence to Pequànnock and Uncoway, where he located some cattle for the winter, and laid out lots of land "for himself and others." Upon his return to Hartford, there arose some misunderstanding as to what he had done, and the Governor—Mr. Haynes—and Mr. Wells were appointed a commission to visit these places, already inhabited by a number of settlers, under the following directions:[*]

"They are desired to confer with the planters at Pequannocke [Fairfield and Stratford], to give them the oath of fidelity, make such free as they see fit, order them to send one or two deputies to the two General Courts in September and April, and for deciding of differences and controversies under 40^s among them, to propound to them and give them power to choose seven men from among themselves, with

---

[*] Conn. Col. Records, 36.

liberty of appeal to the Court here; and also to assign Sergeant Nichols for the present to train the men and exercise them in military discipline; and they are farther desired to speak with Mr. Pruden and that Plantation, that the difference between them and Pequannocke plantation [Stratford] may be peaceably decided, and to this end that indifferent men may be chosen to judge who have most right to the places in controversy and most need of them, and accordingly determined as shall be most agreeable to equity and reason."[1]

This act of the Court in October, 1639, to make freemen in addition to some who already resided here, who should vote in the election of representatives, was the legal recognition of these plantations as a part of the Government of Connecticut; and the fulfillment of these orders constituted the organization of the towns, but this was done only in part according to the acceptance of the report of the Governor and Mr. Wells the following 16th of January, 1639;[8] and the commission was renewed the next April (9, 1640), as follows:

"It is ordered that Mr. Haynes, Mr. Ludlow and Mr. Welles shall settle the division of the bounds betwixt Pequannocke and Uncowaye, by the 24th day of June next, according to their former Commission: And also that they tender the Oath of Fidelity to the Inhabitants of the said Townes, and make such free as they shall approve of."[9]

But before the date specified had arrived, namely, the 15th of June, 1640, other persons were appointed to attend this work, as follows:

"It is Ordered, that Mr. Ludlow, Mr. Hopkins and Mr. Blakeman shall survey and divide and set out the bounds betwixt the Plantations of Cupheag and Uncoway, provided if they cannot accord, Mr. Welles at his next coming to those parts shall issue it."[10]

---

[1] Col. Rec. i. 36.

[8] The year ending the 25th of March, 1639; but 1640 as we now begin the year.

[9] Conn. Col. Rec., 47.

[10] Conn. Col. Records, 53.

In the order for April 9, 1640, these plantations are called *towns*, indicating their standing as incorporated parts of the government; and the same, with other items may be seen in another order of the Court in June 15, 1640,[11] when Mr. William Hopkins of Cupheag is appointed and sworn as the first Magistrate of that town. On the 13th of April, 1643, it was "Ordered, that one or two of the Magistrates shall be sent to Stratford and Uncoway, to join with Mr. Ludlow for the execution of justice, twice this year, namely, the last Thursday in April and the last in September. Captain Mason and Mr. Wells are appointed for the last in April."[12]

Stratford does not appear to have sent representatives to the General Court until 1642, when Philip Groves filled that position. The taxes for Stratford and Fairfield were collected together as one plantation until 1647, when they were ordered by the Court to be divided. Also their courts were held jointly some years by magistrates appointed for the purpose.

The difficulty of ascertaining the date when Stratford was made a town, with many other items as to its organization and first settlement, is in consequence of the town records for ten of the first years having disappeared. These records probably consisted of a volume or small book, foolscap size, about half an inch thick, which was called "folio."

Not only were the plantations of Stratford and Fairfield called towns in April, 1640, but they had freemen who no doubt voted in the adoption of the first constitution, in January, 1638 (O. S.), they being a part of the government at the time, and hence in no great hurry to effect an organization of the town which would be burdensome to maintain; for dur-

---

[11] " Whereas by an Order the 14th of January 1638, none is to be chosen a Magistrate but such as are propounded in some General Court before, yet not-withstanding, as Cupheag and Uncoway are somewhat far distant from this Court, and there is a necessity for the dispensation of justice in those Towns, therefore in the mean and until the next General Court of Election, that it is thought meet and so ordered, that Mr. William Hopkins of Cupheag be a Commissioner to join with Mr. Ludlow in all Executions in their particular Court or otherwise, and is now sworn to that purpose." Col. Rec., 53.

[12] Col. Rec., 86.
6

ing several years after the commencement of the settlement
they seem to have been released from taxes, and perhaps this
is the reason why representatives were not sent earlier than
they were.

This first Constitution of Connecticut was a remarkable
paper, and ever will be a great honor to Roger Ludlow, then of
Fairfield, who drew it, as well as to the men who adopted it.
The basis of this paper was an independent republic, there
being in it no reference to king or queen or monarchy or any
other government except itself, which is very remarkable
when remembering that all those who were then to act as
freemen under it were just come from a kingdom of remarkable dignity and renown.

Dr. Trumbull, in his History of Connecticut, remarks
upon this instrument as follows:

"This probably is one of the most free and happy con-
stitutions of civil government which has ever been formed.
The formation of it, at so early a period, when the light of
liberty was wholly darkened in most parts of the earth, and
the rights of men were so little understood in others, does
great honor to their ability, integrity and love to mankind.
To posterity indeed, it exhibited a most benevolent regard.
It has been continued, with little alteration, to the present
time [1818]. The happy consequences of it, which, for more
than a century and a half, the people of Connecticut have
experienced, are without description."[13]

A recent writer[14] has the following passage in regard to
this constitution as formulated by Mr. Ludlowe:

"The salient feature of Ludlowe's career, the grand
achievement of his life, was his large share in originating and
putting into practical operation the original laws of Connecticut. When, after the Pequot war, the General Court
met to decide upon a frame of government, he was unanimously appointed to make the draft. Of this great paper it
is not too much to say, briefly, that in its immediate applica-

---

[13] Trumbull, 103.

[14] Mr. Wm. A. Beers, in Magazine of American History, April, 1882.

tion and far-reaching results it ranks with the best that have been formulated by the profoundest statesmen. It was not perfect: Ludlowe was not a perfect legislator; but it approached so near completeness that Dr. Leonard Bacon said of it: ' It is the first example in history of a written Constitution—a distinct organic law, and defining its powers.' "

CHAPTER V.

THE FIRST PLANTERS.

1639–1651.

EGINNING in a wilderness, bordering on the great sea, a settlement of English inhabitants, for the perpetuation of posterity under the broad principles of religious freedom and uprightness, as well as an enlarged perception of civil rights, was the honored privilege of the first planters of Stratford. Admitting that their opinions of religious and civil liberty were not equal to those entertained two hundred years later, yet, the advanced position which they took upon emigrating from the terrible restrictions placed by their native country, upon the ideas which they did entertain, was and is still, a marvel in itself; and it has proved already to be the germinating seed which has been scattered to a joyful extent to nearly every nation under the sun. Notwithstanding some odium of *Blue Laws*, the originating point of liberty in its best applications, for two hundred and fifty years, has been the State of Connecticut; and, among the very earliest protéstants against restrictions upon such freedom were found prominent planters at Stratford. Darkness in the thought-world as well as in the physical, is only dispelled by the incoming of light; and as light penetrates, the mental soil becomes prolific, the same as the physical, and hence America has grown from its small beginnings at the germ principles of mighty freedom, to its present marvelously grand proportions of *national liberty and government*. In the history of the world, nothing has ever half equaled

this growth, nor the completeness, and marvelous develop-
ments of *national* government and freedom.

Stratford began with a few families ; grew and prospered
until it surpassed many of its neighbors and thereafter sent
forth an innumerable number of families to establish and
replenish other plantations in the exercise of the same energy
and expanding thought that marked its own early history,
and which have secured for it a fame highly honorable to any
people. It was recognized first as an established plantation,
in 1639, although tradition reports that one family—William
Judson—if not more, settled here in the year 1638.

That it was settled by a number of inhabitants in 1639, is
evident not only from tradition, but from the following
extracts from the records of the General Court, October 10,
1639:[1] "And Mr. Governor [John Haynes] and Mr. Wells
[Thomas Wells, afterwards Governor] were intreated to
attend this service, [to view the plantation laid out by Mr.
Ludlow], and they are desired to confer with the planters at
Pequannocke, to give them the oath of fidelity, make such
free as they see fit, order them to send one or two deputies
to the General Courts of September and April, and for
deciding of differences and controversies under 40ˢ, among
them, to propound to them and give them power to choose
7 men from among themselves, with liberty of appeal to
the Court here; as also to assign Sergent Nichols for the ·
present to train the men and exercise them in military discipline: and they are further desired to speak with Mr.
Prudden, and that plantation that the difference between
them and Pequannocke plantation may be peaceably decided,
and to this end that different men may be chosen to judge
who have most right to the places in controversy and most
need of them, and accordingly determine as shall be most
agreeable to equity and reason."

According to this the plantation was settled so far as to
have men enough to be exercised in training, and so as to
choose seven men as a court for matters under 40ˢ of value;
and also there was a difference as to boundaries between the

---

[1] Col. Rec., i. 36.

two plantations, Stratford being called Pequannock; and the Court sought to have them send deputies, as a township.

This indicates that Mr. Blakeman and his company had arrived from Wethersfield, for without them there would have been too few to meet the supposition of the Court.

At this time the plantation is called Pequonnocke, by the Court, and in June 1640, it is called Cupheag, and the same the next September, and in April, 1643, it is called Stratford. The name therefore, must have been changed between September, 1640, and April, 1643.

As to the name, Stratford, and how it became the name of this locality, there are some interesting items. Hon. James Savage, author of a Genealogical Dictionary, speaking of Thomas Alsop and his brother Joseph Alsop at New Haven, says: "It may be that the father of these youth was that of John Alsop, rated for a subsidy in 1598, to the same parish and at the same time with William Shakespear, nor would it be very extravagant to suppose, that he too went up to London from Stratford on Avon," and thence came to America, and also to Stratford among the first settlers, perhaps in 1639, and that through him the name was thought of and used. It has been suggested that since Samuel Sherman, an early settler at Stratford, came from near Stratford, Essex county, England, quite another place from that where Shakespear was born, the place may have been named after this town in Essex by the suggestion of Mr. Sherman; but it should be remembered that the Connecticut Stratford was so named ten years or more before Samuel Sherman settled in it, and therefore he had nothing to do with naming it.*

A company, it is said, was organized at Wethersfield with Mr. Adam Blakeman as minister, for the purpose of settlement at Cupheag. Some of this company were persons who had been connected in church relations with Mr. Blakeman in England and had accompained him thither, and others joined him at Wethersfield. Tradition says there were fourteen or fifteen in this company, and it has appeared in print that there were seventeen, but it is impossible, now,

---

* See Biographical Sketch of Wm. Beardsley.

to fix the number. Several of the first planters had grown-up sons, over twenty-one years of age, and if these were counted, the number, apparently, must have been over seventeen.

The location at first of quite a number of families in the southern part of the present village of Stratford, near the site of the first meeting house, may indicate that they came to the place at the same time and made their homes near each other for better protection against the Indians.

It is also improbable that a company of families with Mr. Blakeman as their minister, should come from Wethersfield to settle at Stratford without some agreement or specific understanding about the ownership of the land, as it was then not only under the supervision of the Court, but claimed by it as conquered and ceded territory. Hence we find in 1656 the General Court confirms the boundaries and consequently the right of the soil to the inhabitants then residing here, in these words: "This Court, at the request of Stratford, doe graunt that their bounds shall be 12 myle northward, by Paugasitt River, if it be att the dispose by right of this Jurisdiction;" and therefore the inhabitants then in the town, some of them or all, were the owners of this territory, by agreement with the Court.

All the proceedings of the town, from the first record now remaining, are founded upon the implied ownership by a company of first settlers. It appears by the records, and tradition confirms the same, that about the year 1650 the records, then kept in a private house, were accidentally burned, destroying every entry made from 1639 to that time, and then the claims of the settlers, most of them, were reëntered by the town clerk, as the parties described them and as was generally known to be the facts. After this, when new parties came into the town, they were granted a home lot of about two acres free, upon condition that they would build upon and improve it for three years, after which they could sell it to their own profit if they desired so to do. Hence most of the entries are dated in 1651 or later; one land record bears the date of 1648, and one town meeting act bears that of 1650.

If a definite authoritative account or biographical sketch
of each of these original first settlers could be given, including the place of birth, social and civil relations and a
statement of the leading occurrences which drove them to
emigrate to this country, it would be a portion of history of
much value as well as of decided interest. We know in a
general way the causes of this emigration, but as to individuals we have no particulars except those of Mrs. Mirable, the
wife of John Thompson. In the absence of such information
as we would be delighted to obtain, we must be content with
the few items which can now be gleaned from the desolated
and long neglected field.

The settlement of Stratford was not made by a company
organized for the purpose in England as was the case with
several other towns, but by individuals, in a kind of independent or isolated way, except those who came in company
with Mr. Blakeman. These seem to have been more numerous than has been generally conceded. Of some of the
families settled here it is stated that they came direct from
England, but as no vessels landed at Stratford these must
have come through Massachusetts, and hence may have
joined Mr. Blakeman's company at Wethersfield, or, under
a concert of arrangement, joined him at Stratford in the
Spring of 1639. The fact that there were a certain number
of proprietors, or patentees, or owners of the whole territory,
necessarily requires concert of action under some specific
agreement with the General Court, and that, too, for some
consideration of value, else they could have had no right to
the exclusion of others. These were 15, perhaps 17, and if
any others came they were required to buy land of these 17,
individually or collectively, or receive it by gift from the
town. Dr. Trumbull's statements, for want of thoroughness
of research as to the purchase of the township of the natives,
are so erroneous that his other statements may be taken with
some doubt, yet in regard to the coming of the first principal
settlers he may be nearly correct, for he probably obtained
his information in this particular from aged living persons
who at that date would be likely to retain the facts. He
says:

"Mr. Fairchild, who was a principal planter, and the first gentleman in the town vested with civil authority,[2] came directly from England. Mr. John and Mr. William Curtiss and Mr. Samuel [should be Joseph] Hawley were from Roxbury, and Mr. Joseph [should be William] Judson and Mr. Timothy [should be William] Willcoxson from Concord in Massachusetts. These were the first principal gentlemen in the town and church of Stratford. A few years after the settlement commenced, Mr. John Birdseye removed from Milford and became a man of eminence both in the town and church. There were also several of the chief planters from Boston, and Mr. Samuel Wells, with his three sons, John, Thomas and Samuel, from Wethersfield, Mr. Adam Blakeman, who had been episcopally ordained in England, and a preacher of some note, first at Leicester and afterwards in Derbyshire, was their minister, and one of the first planters. It is said that he was followed by a number of the faithful into this country, to whom he was so dear, that they said, in the language of Ruth, 'Intreat us not to leave thee, for whither thou goest we will go; thy people shall be our people, and thy God our God!' These, doubtless, collected about him in this infant settlement."

Mr. John W. Barber, writing in 1836, says:

"The first settlers appear to have located themselves about one hundred and fifty rods south of the Episcopal Church, the first chimney being erected near that spot; it was taken down about two years since. The first burying ground was near that spot. Mr. William Judson, one of the first settlers, came into Stratford in 1638. He lived at the southwest corner of Meetinghouse hill or green, in a house constructed of stone. Mr. Abner Judson, his descendant, lives on the same spot, in a house which has stood one hundred and thirteen years, and is still in good repair."

The fact, repeatedly recorded, of the divisions of the common land proves that the town was owned by a certain number of persons, who, as proprietors of the whole (and if so then these persons obtained these shares or rights of the General Court which claimed the ownership at the time), secured the same for some consideration or stipulation, which was, probably, the simple fact of taking possession by actual settlement by a certain number of inhabitants within a specified time; for this was a method pursued in other towns at the time and soon after.

Common land, or "the commons," was land not divided or disposed of; "sequestered" was that given away, either

---

[2] This is an error according to the Conn. Col. Records, i. 53, "Genl. Court, June 15, 1640, . . . It is so ordered that Mr. William Hopkins of Cupheage be a commissioner to join with Mr. Ludlowe in all Executions in their particular court or otherwise and is now sworn to that purpose." This was for Cupheag and Uncoway, before Mr. Fairchild was elected magistrate.

for public or private use, but generally for public; "divisions" were a certain number of acres surveyed to each and every proprietor, which sometimes were measured into lots which were numbered and the numbers being put on paper and into a hat or box were drawn out, one to each proprietor; this was called drawing lots.

The "Common Field" was land for cultivation, owned by several or all of the proprietors, and a fence made around the whole instead of each making a fence around his own, for which latter work too much time would be required. There were two of these common fields. The first was constructed by making a fence from the brook on the west side of Little Neck to the swamp west and then down to the marsh, and thus shutting all the cattle and swine out into the forests northward. When the present records begin this first common field is frequently called the Old Field, and this name is still applied to a considerable part of the territory immediately south of Stratford village.

The second common field was made before the year 1648, since that is the date when Robert Rice has land recorded as being in that field. This was called the New Field, and was made by a fence running west across Claboard hill to what is now Buce's brook or still further to Mill creek. This is indicated by a record made March 5, 1665–6, locating a part of the fence at the northeast corner of the field and southward.' This field was then reserved for a "winter field;" that is, the fence was kept up and gates closed in order to leave the corn and stacks of hay and grain in that field secure from the cattle during the winter. Some years the Old Field was kept for the same purpose—a "winter field."*

A few years later, that is before 1652, another field was constructed by a fence across the neck about where Old Mill Green now is, from Mill Creek to Pequannock River, which

---

.   * "It was agreed at a lawful [town] meeting that the New field shall be kept for a winter field the two following years and liberty for a fence to be drawn along the swamp on the east side of Claboard Hill and so down to the old swamp land to the creek."

    * " Oct. 10, 1664. It was agreed that the Great Neck shall be kept this year for a winter field."

was called the "New Pasture," and afterwards the southern part of this field was called "New Pasture Point." About the same time, perhaps a little earlier, another field was made up the Housatonic river, called the "Oxe Pasture," which is frequently mentioned on the records.

It should be remembered that these fields were largely without forests when the white settlers first came. Probably the Old Field, and perhaps some part of the land where Stratford village was located had been somewhat cultivated by the Indians before the settlers came, at least it was largely cleared from forests, for if it had not been, so few inhabitants could not have cleared it and laid out a village with such regularity, to such an extent, as was done within four or five years. For in 1639 or 1640 the principal company of settlers came from Wethersfield, and in 1648 the village plot was all laid out, and, apparently, had been for several years. The tradition is that they came on foot and horseback, and forded the river to reach the west side, which seems almost if not quite incredible since the depth of the river at present precludes a supposition of fording it. The strong indications are that they came by boat, and if they did not their household goods did, and were landed at the mouth of Mack's creek, where they made their first tents or huts, houses, and meeting house, and afterwards laid out their village upon a very appropriate and beautiful plan, and thus it remains to-day with but few changes as to its principal streets. When they had laid the highways they proceeded to make the first division, which was a home lot, a piece of meadow, and a piece of upland for planting; the home lot containing usually two and a half acres, and the other pieces varying according to quality; all distribution of lands being passed by vote at the town meetings. When after planters came a grant of two and a half acres was made to them free of cost upon condition that they should build a dwelling upon it and improve it during three years, after which they could keep it or sell it at their own pleasure. These grants were called "home lots," but when a dwelling had been erected upon them they were called "house lots." *

The oldest date of such a lot or of anything, now upon

record, is that of Robert Rice's lands, Sept. 16, 1648; all previous to this having been lost or destroyed ;—said to have been burned, probably by accident, they having been kept in a private house.

It is quite certain that dwellings were not builded upon every home lot granted, but in some cases they were sold and united to other lots, as in the case of John Birdseye at the south end of the village, who purchased several.

Running through the New Field was a stream called Nesumpaw's Creek, and a portion of the territory in the New Field was called Nesumpaws' ; which title was first the name of an Indian and applied to a tract of land on which his wigwam stood. The name is spelled at first on the town records Nesingpaws or Neesingpaws, and later Nesumpaws.

"Claboard Hill" lay at the north of the New Field, a part of the hill being included in that field. Stony Brook Hill was afterwards called Old Mill Hill.

The Pequannock field was constructed, probably, about 1655, for it had been sometime established according to a town vote in January, 1661. It was on the Pequannock plain south of Golden Hill, east of Fairfield bounds.

The Calf-pen plain or Upper plain was north of, and, probably, included a part of, the Golden Hill Reservation, as the Reservation was laid out in 1659.' This plain was established for young cattle very early, probably before 1650. This locality was afterwards and even yet is known as Bull's head. It was here probably where Richard Butler's swine were pastured when Nimrod " willfully killed some of them," and a law suit followed, or at least was granted to follow, by the Court.

The following is the list of the owners of fence about the first common field, the fence being a little over 353 rods in length, which if it surrounded the entire field inclosed nearly fifty acres, but if it was a fence direct across the neck to Fresh Pond it would have inclosed several hundred acres, or all of Great Neck as well as Little Neck.

This list is without date but must have been recorded before 1651, since William Burritt's name is on it and he died that year.

"A note of every man's fence in the old field with what numbers and the several rods.

	rods.	feet.	inch.			rods.	feet.	inch.
1 Thomas Skidmore,....12	3	0		22 William Crooker,.... 2	10	2
2 John Wells, ...6	0	0		23 John Hurd,..........43	8	0
3 John Reader, ...10	9	0		24 Arthur Bosticke,..... 6	9	0
4 Adam Blakeman, ...11	14	0		25 John Tomson,.......10	9	0
5 Richard Harvey, ... 9	1	6		26 Robert Cooe,........ 0	10	2
6 John Peacock,........ 5	4	6		27 Thomas Ufford,.....12	6	3
7 William Quenby, ... 4	0	0		28 Joseph Hawley,...... 6.	9	0
8 Robert Rice, ...13	8	0		29 Jeremiah Judson,....11	14	0
9 William Burritt, ... 5	4	6		30 Joshua Judson,.....		
10 Mr. Knell, ... 5	4	6		31 Mr. Seabrook, ... 4	00	0
11 John Peatite, ...10	9	0		32 Henry Gregory,...... 8	00	0
12 John Brownsmayd,... 9	1	6		33 Richard Booth, ... 8	00	0
13 William Wilcoxson,..12	3	0		34 Mr. Waklin,........ 2	10	0
14 Richard Butler, ... 6	9	0		35 Widow Curtis,....... 2	10	2
15 John Peake,..........10	9	0		36 Thomas Sherwood,.. 5	4	6
16 Thomas Fayrchild,... 6	9	0		37 Francis Hall,........18	3	0
17 Joseph Judson, ... 4	0	0		38 William Beardsley,..24	6	0
18 Adam Hurd, ... 4	0	0		39 John Curtis,......... 4	10	0
19 Daniell Titterton,.....11	14	0		40 John Birdzie,........10	9	0
20 Philip Groves,........ 9	1	6		41 Isack Nickoles,..... 2	10	0"
21 Francis Peacocke, .. .5	4	6				

It is probable that this is not a complete list of the original company. Robert Cooe—number 26—was Robert, Junior, and just twenty-three years of age, and hence was not an original proprietor, yet his father, who was at Wethersfield at the time, may have been. Thomas Alsop appears to have been one of the original company, but his name is not on this list.

The following sketches of the first settlers at Stratford are much less complete than they would be if written at the end of the work. It is probable that these men had not the least surmise or apprehension of the relation they were to occupy in regard to a free people for many centuries to come. Each supposed himself to be simply an individual, seeking the prosperity of himself and family, but time has revealed that each was a pillar in a great temple of human government, for freedom and marvelous success. They sought, modestly and mainly, a simple home of personal possession and comforts, and in securing these, laid, in connection with other like plantations which were as independent republics, the foundations for a government which, after a little less than two centuries and a half, is, for the elevation of mankind, the most sublime the sun ever shone upon. It is often the case that the most perfectly carved marble statue occupies but an unobtrusive corner in a great temple, so the work and life of each family in such a plantation may seem at the time but an insignificant space partially filled, yet in the ages to follow, that which was the obscure germ will bloom into the crowning national glory; even as accomplished Presidents of the United States from the back-woods log cabins. Under such possibilities no family is too obscure to be noticed in a work like the present; and even if it were, the fact of a faithful mention of all, may prove a stimulant to high ambition and success in a most obscure corner; and therefore, so far as time and cost will allow, it is the purpose to mention in a historical manner as far as possible, every person that has had a residence in the good old town of Stratford. But few books if any in the English language have had greater influence to incite noble ambition and historical culture than *Plutarch's Lives*, and following in this same line America has already an unprecedented number of large volumes of Biographical Dictionaries and Cyclopedias. It is not then unseemly or aside from good historic order to allow local history to partake largely of the biographical style.

When the years are counted over, and the generations numbered who have already passed away since Stratford was first settled, the time seems long, and the various paths through which its citizens have journeyed seem wearisome to think of, but when we bring to mind the courage, endurance, toil and enjoyments which were the portion of these citizens we are both sad and delighted. Two hundred and thirty-four years have passed since the date of the paper which contains the forty-one names of whom we give, first, a brief outline of their remarkable lives—remarkable, if for nothing else, yet for the circumstances which surrounded them, and for the nation planted by them, and for that which has grown from their intellectual and religious planting. And what changes have taken place since those forty-one built their rude log houses at or near Sandy Hollow Banks, where they erected their first meeting-house! Some years since while digging near the site of the old meeting-house a party exhumed a skull-bone : that was a representative of one of these early settlers, which one it matters not ; it was one of them ; —all gone to dust but one bone—and so are they all.

> " Two hundred years ago ! how strange
> To look back o'er the way
> And think of the great, amazing change
> From that until th' present time.
>
> Slow rising in the eastern sky,
> Our fathers hailed the rising sun ;
> But saw not in the western skies
> What wonders should be done."

The old meeting-house, after about forty years' service, disappeared in 1683, but some of the timbers were used as sills and sleepers in a house now standing a little way west from the site of the old meeting-house, on the north side of the street, which is now occupied by Mr. Joseph Savage. These timbers having been in use about two hundred and forty years, are interesting as showing the work of human hands which have slept in the dust two centuries.

A barn now stands on the site of the old meeting-house, with a stone cellar which was long used as a kind of store or storage house, and is rather an unseemly sentinel to tell where the first bell that called worshipers together in the state of Connecticut was suspended to perform its weekly musical task. There Goodman Peat stood for ten or fifteen years pulling the rope that caused the sound of the bell to echo across the placid waters of the old Pootatuck, but now Housatonic river ; and after him Goodman Pickett performed the same duties to save Stratford from being in fashion in coming to the meeting at the beat of the drum.

1—Thomas Skidmore was of Cambridge, Mass., in 1642; in 1636 he had been engaged for John Winthrop in his preparation for planting Saybrook, Conn. He was early in Stratford, with his son-in-law Edward Higby, probably before 1649, when they had a suit in law tried before the Court at Hartford. He was in Stratford in 1659, but appears to have removed not long after to Fairfield, where his descendants continued many years. His will was dated April 20, 1684, and proved soon after. Judge Savage says he had a wife Ellen, but in his will he speaks of his wife Sarah, which may have been a second. He had two sons and several daughters.

2—John Wells, son of Gov. Thomas Wells of Wethersfield, was probably one of the original proprietors of Stratford, or sent there by his father to occupy the lands which he, the father, owned as one of the proprietors of the plantation, and he afterwards received considerable land in Stratford from his father. John Wells was made a freeman in 1645, perhaps in Stratford, but was here in 1650; was made an Assistant in 1656 and again in 1658 and 1659. He was a prominent man while he lived, but died in 1660, or in 1661, about the same time his father did, a comparatively young man, not far from thirty-five years of age.

Governor Thomas Wells, the father of John Wells, above, was an original proprietor at Hartford and Wethersfield; appears there on the records first as the Secretary Magistrate at the General Court, May 1, 1637, when war was declared against the Pequots. It is uncertain when he came from England and whether he brought a wife or not, but he brought three sons and three daughters. He married a second wife Elizabeth, widow of Nathaniel Foot of Wethersfield. In 1654, he was chosen Deputy Governor, and Governor Hopkins being in England, he acted as Governor all the year, and in 1655 he was elected Governor of Connecticut, and then re-elected again in 1658. Governor Wells died in Wethersfield Jan. 14, 1660.

3—John Reader, of New Haven, 1643, came to Stratford among the first settlers. His home lot, No. 10, he sold with several pieces of land in 1659, to David Mitchell, and appears to have removed from the town.

4—*Rev. Adam Blakeman,*' was the son of a private citizen of Staffordshire, Eng.; born in 1598, and entered Christ College, Oxford, May 23, 1617, when nineteen years of age,' where he wrote his own name, Blakeman.' Mather says of him: " He was a useful preacher of the gospel, first in Leicestershire, then in Derbyshire, England." Mather also gives the impression that he was attended to this country by several families of his parish, but in what year he came over or by whom accompanied he does not say. Allen, Hinman and other writers have asserted that he first preached a while in Scituate, Mass., but they were led into this error by Deane's History of Scituate, the author of which afterward acknowledged that he had mistaken the name of " Mr. Blackman" for that of Rev. Christopher " Blackwell." Cotton Mather also represents him as having preached in Guilford before Stratford, but of this no evidence appears, nor could it have been, since Guilford was settled not a year before Stratford, and its people had with them their minister, Mr. Henry Whitfield. In June, 1640, the General Court appointed him with Mr. Ludlow of Uncoway and William Hopkins of Cupheag to run the line between these two plantations, and from this it is concluded he was already settled at Cupheag.

On May 17, 1649, the Court directed: " Concerning Mr. Blakeman's maintenance, Mr. Ludlowe is directed, both for what is behind as also for the future, to take care that it be levied according to the several seasons as is provided by the order of the country." This indicates that his salary was so long in arrears as to make it important for the Court to take action in regard to it. In 1651, " by the town in public meeting it was agreed that Mr. Blakeman shall have 63 pounds and pay part of his own rate." His name occurs only a few times on the existing town records. In 1660, he is named

---

¹ Taken largely from MS. of Rev. B. L. Swan.

² Mass. Hist. Coll., vol. viii. 249.

³ His sons James and Benjamin wrote their names Blakeman and Blackeman.

7

as executor of William Beardsley's will, and on April 20, 1665,. he is named in a vote inviting Mr. Chauncey to help him in the ministry for one year. Mr. Blakeman died Monday, Sept. 1665, æ. 67 years.' His home lot was number 20 on the plan of the village of Stratford.

From Mather's brief notice of him Mr. Blakeman appears to have been a man of learning, prudence and fervent piety. The famous Rev. Thomas Hooker said of him : " for the sake of the sacred and solemn simplicity of the discourse of this worthy man, if I might have my choice, I would choose to live and die under Mr. Blakeman's ministry."

Nothing remains of .Mr. Blakeman's writings except his will on the Fairfield probate records and his autograph in the Connecticut Historical Society's Collections, at the bottom of a document in Mr. Chauncey's handwriting, and dated in the spring of 1665. It is the answer of the Church of Stratford to questions by the General Court of the preceding year, relating to the matters transacted in the Synod at Boston in 1662 : chiefly respecting the membership and rights of baptized persons.

A paragraph in Mr. Blakeman's will indicates that he was a member of the Synod from 1646 to 1648 which drew up the Cambridge platform.

Extracts from Rev. Adam Blakeman's Will.

The will was dated March 16, 1665–66.

" Item. Concerning my books which I intended for my son Benjamin, seeing his thoughts are after another course of life—that his thoughts be not to attend the work of Christ in the ministry, my wish is that my son Atwater [son-in-law] make his son Joshua a scholar and fit him for that work. I give unto him all my Latin books ; but if not they shall be put into my estate and disposed of as my wife any my overseers shall think fit.

" Item. Because many of God's servants have been falsely accused concerning the judgment of the kingly power of Christ, though I have cause to bewail my great ignorance and weakness in acting, yet I do hope I shall, through the strength of Christ to my dying day, adhere to that form of Church discipline agreed upon by the honored Elders and Brethren, now in print, and to the truth of God concerning that point left on record by that famous and Reverend Servant of God, of blessed Memory, Mr. Thomas Hooker, in his elaborate work called

---

' Savage, vol. ii. 472.

The Survey of Church Discipline, to which most in all the churches of Christ then gathered in this Colony gave their consent as appears in the Rev. Author's Epistle—so at Milford, New Haven, Guilford, and those in the Bay who could be come at in that stress of time. And being one who in the name of our church subscribed that copy, could never (through the Grace of Christ) see cause to receive any other in judgment, nor fall from those principles so solemnly backed with Scripture, and arguments which none yet could overturn."

Mr. Blakeman is described by Mr. Mather as having been attended on his departure for New England with a considerable and "desirable company of the faithful" who would not be separated from him. He also describes him as a very "holy man" and as greatly beloved by his people.

Mr. Blakeman's death should have been on Stratford town records, but is found only on his tombstone, which was removed to the second grave yard. There is a pretence (in accordance with repeated orders of the Court) of keeping a burial record, which begins (p. 49) with John, son of Nicholas Knell, January, 1651, and ends with Elizabeth Porter in 1683, but in these thirty-two years only twenty-four names— and one or two infants without names—are recorded. Mr. Blakeman had five sons and one daughter, all except perhaps, Benjamin, were born in England.

Mrs. Jane Blakeman, widow of the Rev. Adam, appears to have been sister to Moses Wheeler of Stratford, for her son John in his will dated in 1662, mentions his "Uncle Wheeler." Moses Wheeler was born in 1598, and if she was next younger, and born in 1600, she was two years younger than her husband, and at her death in 1674, was 74 years of age. Her name appears several times on the Colonial and Town records, in consequence of the misconduct of her son Deliverance, in whose behalf she was obliged to intercede more than once with the Colonial authorities, but who afterwards retrieved himself from his former life, married and settled in Stonington about 1685, where he died in April, 1702. Her will is on the Fairfield Probate records.

John Blakeman, son of the Rev. Adam Blakeman, married Dorothy, daughter of the Rev. Henry Smith of Wethersfield about 1653, removed to Fairfield where he died

in 1662, leaving a widow and three sons, Joseph, John and
Ebenezer; from the last of these, who married a Willcoxson,
descended the Blakeman families of Newtown and Monroe.

The widow Dorothy (Smith) Blakeman appears to have
possessed remarkable charms, either of person, intellect or
heart, for besides passing through a case of litigation in
Court for her hand, she was married four times, twice after
she was over fifty years of age. Rev. Adam Blakeman, who
survived his son John, in his will—1665—says: " I give to my
daughter [Dorothy] Blakeman, if she marry not John Thomas,
and shall take her friends' consent in the matter, or continue
a widow, five pounds," and the General Court, Oct. 10, 1665,
recorded: " The magistrates do order that in case John
Thomas and the widow Blakeman do not issue their difference by reference now concluded on, that the said Thomas
shall make good his claim to that woman at the next Court
at Fairfield, otherwise the widow shall have liberty to marry."
Upon this John Thomas seems to have abandoned his claims
instanter, for Francis Hall of Stratford, who had been the
attorney for the widow of Rev. Mr. Blakeman in this case
before the Court, became charmed with his opponent and
married her that same month, October 31, 1665, his former wife having died on July 6th previous. Twenty-two
years afterwards, before the decease of Francis Hall, his son
Isaac Hall entered a claim in Fairfield to recover certain
amount of money which was his own mother's estate at marriage, and guaranteed to her in writing by her husband
Francis Hall, when he sold the estate in England, in 1664, the
apparent object being to keep it from the possession of this
brilliant step-mother. Francis Hall died, apparently, in
Stratford, but this is not certain, in 1690, and his widow
Dorothy still possessing charms too attractive to be confined
to widowhood, married Mark Sension (St. John) of Norwalk,
who died in 1693, after which she married Dea. Isaac Moore
of Farmington.

Samuel Blakeman, son of Rev. Adam Blakeman, married Elizabeth, daughter of Moses Wheeler in 1660, and died in
1668, leaving several children. His widow married Jacob

Walker, a lawyer, in 1670. He was the son of Robert Walker of Boston and brother of the Rev. Zachariah Walker, pastor of the Second Congregational Church in Stratford, and which removed to Woodbury. Samuel Blakeman was only forty-eight years of age.

Mary Blakeman, the daughter of the Rev. Adam Blakeman, was born in 1636, and when fifteen years of age—in 1651—married Joshua Atwater of New Haven, who seems to have resided for a time in Stratford, purchasing a considerable estate here, and then removed to Boston where he died in 1676, leaving several children. After his death she married the Rev. John Higginson, then of Salem, Mass., but formerly assistant minister to Rev. Henry Whitfield of England and Guilford, Conn., whose daughter was his first wife. Mr. Higginson was an interpreter of the Indian language while in Connecticut, and gave a valuable paper in the settlement of the claims of Stratford territory in 1659, in which year he removed to Salem. He died in 1708, and his widow Mrs. Mary Higginson died March 9, 1709. Her character is finely set forth by Cotton Mather as illustrative of the noble women of that age.[*]

5—Richard Harvey, a tailor by trade, came from Great St. Albans, Hertfordshire, England, in the ship Planter, in which also came Rev. Mr. Blakeman and William Willcoxson, in 1635; was probably among the first settlers in Stratford in 1639. He appears to have had no sons but three daughters. His home lot was number 43. If this was his first lot, then either he did not come as early as is supposed above, or did not obtain one until some years after he came.

6—John Peacocke, was of New Haven in 1638, Milford, 1642, and came to Stratford before 1651. He had a home lot in the southern part of the village on Main street, and died in 1670. He had four children born before he came to Stratford, and his only son died while a child and hence his descendants of the name soon became extinct in the town.

---

[*] Thoughts on the Sleep of Death, by Cotton Mather, D.D. 1712. Pp. 4, 5, 6, 7, 8, MS. Rev. B. L. Swan.

7—William Quenby was one of the first proprietors
in Stratford territory, his lands being re-entered on the town
books in 1652; a house lot, two pieces of land in the New
field, and three acres on the Neck. These possessions he
sold April 1, 1657, to Henry Tomlinson. William Quenby,
probably, was a resident of Stratford only about four years.

8—Robert Rice was not of the original proprietors,
but came soon after them and was granted land from the
town which was recorded Sept. 16, 1648, which is the earliest
record now on the town books. Hence the plan or plot for
the village was laid before this date, else the lot could not
have been bounded on the highway. The record says: "One
house lot, two acres, more or less, butting south upon the
highway, north upon William Beardsley, west upon Mr.
Knell and east upon John Brownsmayd." He had also
"meadow and upland in the Old Field, 8 acres in the New-
feyld upon Mr. Waklin's Neck," and other pieces elsewhere.
On February 6, 1660, Mr. Rice sold these parcels of land,
including "one house lot, one dwelling house upon it and
barn" to "Thomas Wheeler now of Paugusit," and removed
to New London. A family of the same name have been resident on the south side of Long Island for many years to the
present time, in the vicinity of Bellville. This dwelling and
lot was afterwards owned by Richard Beach, and then Rev.
Israel Chauncey.

9—William Burritt came from England with wife
Elizabeth and settled in Stratford among the first planters
and died in 1651, the inventory of his estate is dated May 28,
1651. His home lot was at the south end of the village, west
side of Main street. He left two sons and one daughter, and
the name has been perpetuated with honor in the line of
blacksmiths as well as in other pursuits, in various interior
towns of Connecticut, as well as in the person of the "learned
blacksmith," the late Elihu Burritt of New Britain, Conn.

10—Nicholas Knell, married in 1650, Elizabeth, widow
of Thomas Knowles and daughter of Francis Newman of
New Haven. He was in Stratford probably before his
marriage and appears to have been an original proprietor·

The record of his land that is preserved is without date, but was made soon after 1650. Besides his house lot and other pieces of meadow and upland there was given to him by the town as a part of his first division "One Island of meadow lying in the midst of our harbor, lying for five acres and a half;" and hence the island has always borne his name—Knell's Island—and should never be spelled without the K. Mr. Knell seems to have been an influential man as to character and public efficiency and work. He died April 2, 1675, and the town clerk added to the record: "that aged benefactor in ye county." He had four children—one died an infant, and the family name continued in the town quite a number of years, but has long since disappeared.

Eleazer Knowles was the son of Mrs. Elizabeth Knell. His father, Thomas Knowles, was in New Haven in 1645, and died before 1648, leaving widow Elizabeth and sons Thomas and Eleazer. The widow married Mr. Knell as above, but what became of Thomas Knowles, Jr., does not appear; probably he died young. Eleazer Knowles settled in Stratford, married Jane Porter and had two sons, Eleazer and Thomas, and Eleazer removed to Woodbury, Conn., where his descendants still continue. Thomas Knowles, the first in New Haven, was one of a company of seventy who sailed in a new ship from New Haven for Liverpool in January, 1646, of whom nothing was ever heard.

11—John Pettit was in Roxbury in 1639, and was at Stratford in 1651, removed soon, probably to Stamford and thence to Newtown, Long Island.

12—John Brinsmade united with the church at Charlestown, Mass., in March, 1638, and in October, 1639, his wife Mary joined also; but he seems to have removed that year to Dorchester, Mass., where in 1640 his son John was born. He settled in Stratford before 1650, and became prominent in the town. He has been reported as a Ruling Elder in Stratford church, which is an error arising from the fact of his name being on the town records as John Brinsmade the elder, that is, not the younger, who was his son. The only Ruling Elder this church had was Philip Groves.

First Inhabitants and their Home Lots.[1]

Home Lots.		Home Lots.	
1-2	John Birdsey,	41	William Judson, then / Joseph Judson,
3	Thomas Sherwood,		
4	Wid. Elizabeth Beardsley,	42	First Parsonage Lot
5-8	Jeremiah Judson.	43	taken from Public Green.
6	John Minor, 1667.	44	Hugh Griffin, then / John Wheeler,
7	William Burritt,		
9	Nathaniel Porter,	45	Richard Harvey,
10	John Reader, then / David Mitchell,	46	Francis Hall,
		47	John Blakeman,
11	John Hurd,	47a	
12-13	Robert Seabrook,	48	Wid. A. Kimberly, 1680,
14	John Peacock,	49	David Sherman, 1686,
15	Henry Wakelyn,	50	Common,
16	Thomas Uffoot,	51	Land of I. Nichols,
17	Robert Coe,	52	Samuel Sherman, Jr., 1665,
18	Samuel Sherman, 1652,	53	Street.
19	Philip Groves,	54	John Beers,
20	Rev. Adam Blakeman,	55	Nathaniel Foot,
21	John Barlow, then / John Hurd,	56	Burial Place, 1678,
		57	Daniel Titterton, Jr.,
22	James Harwood,	58	Timothy Willcoxson,
23	Edward Higby,	59	Jabez Harger,
24	John Jenner,	60	John Hull,
25	Arthur Bostwick,	61	John Pickett,
26	Jeremiah Judson,	62	Robert Lane,
27	Joshua Judson,	63	John Young,
28	Thomas Fairchild, Sen.,	64	Thomas Wells,
29	Richard Booth,	65	John Thompson's 2d lot,
30	Isaac Nichols, Sen.,	66	John Wells,
31	Adam Hurd,	66a	Daniel Titterton, Sen.,
32	Francis Nichols, then / Caleb Nichols,	66b	John Wilcoxson, Sen.,
		67	John Peake, [Peat],
33	Thomas Quenby, then / Joshua Atwater, then / Henry Tomlinson,	68	Moses Wheeler,
		69	Thomas Curtis,
		70	William Wilcoxson,
34	William Curtis,	71	William Beardsley, 1st,
35	Adam Hurd,	72	John Brinsmade,
36	John Beach, 1660, / bought of A. Bryan,	73	Nicholas Knell,
		74	Robert Rice,
37	Richard Miles, then / Joseph Hawley,	75	First Meetinghouse,
		76	Thomas Uffoot,
38	John Thompson,	77	
38a	Francis Jecockes,	78	Jehiel Preston, 1662,
39	William Read,	79	Second Meetinghouse, 1678,
40	William Crooker,	80	Third Meetinghouse, 1743, / Burned by lightning, 1785.

---

[1] This Map was first constructed by the Rev. B. L. Swan, and has been carefully revised by the deeds of the first settlers. It is intended to have a map double this size in a future part of the book. The numbers have no significance, except for convenience in referring to the Map. For want of room lots 57, 58, 59, 60, 61, 62 and 63 are not designated on the map.

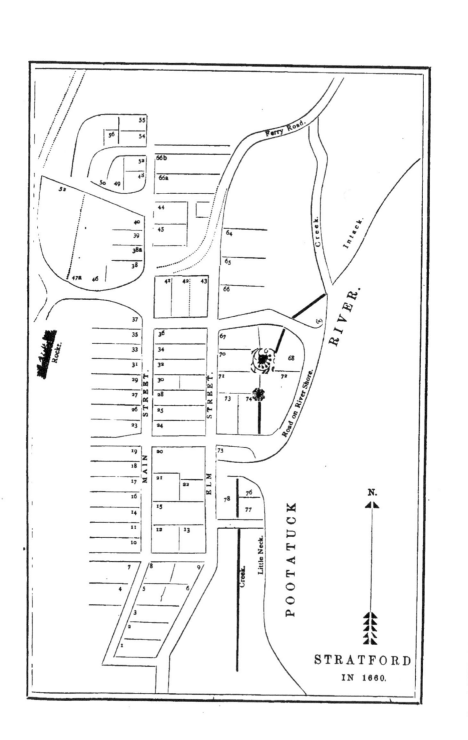

STRATFORD
IN 1660.

Hence, with the fiction of Mr. Brinsmade's office as Elder goes also the silly story of the leather mitten ordination.

John Brinsmade died in 1673 leaving an estate valued at £519. He had a brother William who entered Harvard College in 1644, and was settled minister in Marlborough from 1660 to 1701.[1]

By a town vote in 1664, it is ascertained that the Indian wigwams, some of them at least, were located in the southwest part of what is now Stratford village, west of Main street, along the path that went to the first mill at the "Eagle's Nest."[2] A tract of land there was called Wigwam Meadow, in consequence of the wigwams having stood there. It may not have been the only place where wigwams were located.

13—*William Willcoxson* came from England in April, 1635, in the ship Planter, in company with Richard Harvey and William Beardsley who settled in Stratford. He was made freeman in Massachusetts in 1636, and came from Concord, Mass., to Stratford, probably, in 1639, and hence was one of the first proprietors and a prominent man of the township. In his will, dated May, 1651, he gave £40 to the church in Concord. He left a widow and five sons, through whom the descendants of his name are widely scattered in the nation. The name has become contracted in some localities to that of Willcox.

---

[1] See Allen's Biog. Dictionary.

[2] "Oct. 10, 1664. In consideration of some meadow being not answerable to the grant given to Goodman Brinsmade the town at a lawful meeting gave him a little island below the ferry being south of the ferry, and one acre of land in the swamp on the right hand of the path as they go from Beardsley Gate to the meadow called by the place where the wigwams used to be and three, more or less, on the other side of the path by the swamp side, John Hurd's ground on the west side of it."

CHAPTER VI.

THE FIRST PLANTERS.

(Continued.)

1639–1651.

OMMONS or "commoning" was land not deeded from the town to any purposes. Hence in their deeds parties frequently sold their "commoning" or interest in the undivided lands. Rights of this kind are said to exist still in the town.

Sequestered land was that given away or devoted to some specific public purpose, but when given to settlers, as many of the home lots were, it was not called sequestered land. When the first parsonage lot was given by the town, which comprised the two lots 42 and 43 in the map on page 105, it was taken out of sequestered land, that is out of the public highway or green, and probably the highway now called Elm street was proportionally wide as these lots would make it at that place. Many changes have occurred in regard to the topography of the place since the first settlement. A brook once crossing where the railroad and the Old Mill road intersect and known as Gallows brook, has disappeared. Tanner's brook, so called from the earliest settlement, was then a larger stream than now, having one tannery, probably the oldest, standing on it where Dorman's blacksmith shop now stands.

The salt meadow and sedge on the west and south of the creek below New Lane were largely covered with water, and the point where the shipyard is, being then described as bounded east, south and west by the river, cove and beach.

Knell's island contained five or six acres. An island just below the old Washington bridge, once known as Brinsmade's island, has, the last of it, disappeared within the memory of persons now living.

The creek setting back from the river into Sandy Hollow and now almost choked up was two hundred years ago open and navigable. At the elbow of that creek where the barn now stands was the center of the first settlement, and the meeting-house and the burying ground.

14—Richard Butler was a proprietor in Stratford and received his divisions of lands as others, but may not have resided here until after 1660. He was a juryman in Hartford in 1643, and in 1648 was made executor of his brother William's estate at Hartford, who seems to have had no heirs but this brother Richard and two sisters in England. In 1651 the General Court granted him liberty to prosecute the Indian Nimrod at Pequannock who had "willfully killed some of his swyne." In 1659 he is appointed Custom officer at Stratford and allowed for his duty as collector 2s. for every butt of wine entered, and 12d. for every anker of liquor, and in proportion for other casks ; and the Colonial Records make him one of the grand jury for Hartford in 1660. He died in Stratford in 1676, having an estate of £350. His home lot was the southern part of lot number 68 on the diagram of home lots in this book. He was prominent in the organization of the Second Church from 1666 to 1670.

15—John Peake, afterward written Peat and then Peet, is said to have come from Duffield Parish, county of Derby, England, in the Hopewell, Capt. Bundock, master, in 1635. He had a wife, Sarah, but whose daughter she was is not certain, although the Fairfield Brand book[1] in 1669, styles Richard Osborn, John Peat's father, which in modern terms would be father-in-law. He may have been one of the original proprietors in Stratford ; had his house lot, No. 67, on Front street, now Elm, bordering on Salt Pond, and died in 1678, aged 81 years. His descendants have been and are still quite numerous, and scattered in the States. He was sexton,

---

[1] Manuscript of the Rev. B. L. Swan.

and rang the bell of the first meeting-house some years, giving up his position in 1660, in consequence of age.

Thomas Fairchild, Sen., was among the first settlers of Stratford, but whether he came here in 1638 or 1639 is not known. He was a merchant and may have come with his brother-in-law Thomas Sherwood, and with William Judson in 1638, for the purpose, principally, of trading with the Indians, or he may have joined Mr. Blakeman's company at Wethersfield and come in 1639. Mr. Fairchild's wife was the daughter of Robert Seabrook, and therefore sister to the wives of Thomas Sherwood, William Preston, of New Haven, and Lieut. Thomas Wheeler, of Milford. Mrs. Sherwood was much older than her sisters, she having been married twenty-one or twenty-two years when she came here, and probably two of her sisters were married after they came, about 1640. In what year Mrs. Fairchild died is not known, but her last child was born in 1653, and Mr. Fairchild married, 2d, Catharine Craigg, of London, a relative of Mrs. Elizabeth Whiting, of Hartford, to whom he secured in writing[*] £200 out of his estate, but he died without fulfilling the agreement, and the matter being brought before the General Court with the contract in writing, that body ordered it paid, but that she must support her three children by Mr. Fairchild. He died, Dec. 14, 1670, and the selectmen reported his inventory at £350. He had four sons by his first wife and two by his second, and the descendants are numerous.

The family name is of long standing in England, the coat-of-arms indicating that members of it were in the Crusades from (A. D. 1096 to 1400). The name is said to have been Fairbairn in Scotland, whence the family passed into England.

---

[*] A foot note in the Col. Rec. ii. 199, gives the following facts: "A copy of the marriage contract between Thomas Fairchild of Stratford, merchant, and Katharine Craigg, a sister of Elizabeth Whiting, widow, of London (executed in England, Dec. 22, 1662, is in Priv. Controv., Vol. I, Doc. 20), in which Mr. Fairchild binds himself to convey to the said Katharine a life estate in his lands at Stratford, or, in case of his death before his arrival in New England, to cause to be paid to the said Katharine the sum of £200.

Mr. Fairchild was one of the most prominent and respected men of Stratford. He was appointed by the General Court, with Thomas Sherwood and the Constables of Stratford, to draft men in 1654 for the then proclaimed Narraganset war; and again on a committee with Philip Groves, as leather sealer of Fairfield county. In 1654 he was elected Deputy, and a number of times after that, and in 1663 he was nominated for an Assistant, and the same for three successive years, but was not elected. As these nominations were made at or by the General Court, this shows the estimation of him by that body.. In 1664 he was appointed a Commissioner, which was a Justice of the Peace, for Stratford and was reappointed afterwards.

Dr. Trumbull's statement, repeated by Mr. J. W. Barber, that "Mr. Fairchild was the first gentleman vested with civil authority,"[1] appears to be erroneous, since the Colonial Records state that William Hopkins was appointed in 1640 Assistant, which must have been the first; and that Philip Groves was appointed several successive years from 1654.

17—*Lieut. Joseph Judson,* son of William, was born in 1619 in England, and died in 1690, aged 71 years. He became so prominent in the town, and his name so frequent in the records, that he was supposed by Dr. Trumbull and others to have been the first of the name in Stratford, but he came with his father, probably among the first settlers, and married Sarah, daughter of John Porter of Windsor, about 1644. He was made a freeman in 1658, elected a Deputy the next year, and was one of the foremost men in the work and offices of the town about thirty years. He died in 1690, aged 71 years, having been for quite a number of years the highest military officer in the town.

William Judson, born in Yorkshire, England, emigrated to Concord, Mass., in 1634, and settled in Stratford in 1638, the first inhabitant in the place, if here in that year; and the only one unless Thomas Fairchild or Thomas Sherwood, one or both of them, were with him.

---

[1] Trumbull, i. 109.

After residing in Stratford some years he became an owner in the iron works in East Haven and made his residence in New Haven, where he died July 29, 1662.

His will, recorded in New Haven, was dated 20th of ninth month, 1661, in which he gives to his son Joseph twenty pounds, and to his sons Joseph and Jeremiah Judson " all my part in the iron works (and the privilege I have in it) which are near Stony river, belonging to New Haven." He says also: " I give to my wife's daughter, Hannah Willmott, five pounds; to my wife's daughter, Mercy Willmott, five pounds; and to my wife's daughter, Elizabeth Willmott, five pounds; and the remaining time of service of my servant Peter Simson I give to my wife, and for his encouragement therein, he being a diligent servant to his dame, I give unto him five pounds, to be paid him when he hath served out his time according to his indenture; and the residue I give unto my loving and beloved wife Elizabeth Judson."

The inventory of his estate was taken Dec. 15, 1662, and amounted to £369, 16s. 6d.

Widow Elizabeth's will was made in January or February, 1685, and the inventory of her estate was taken Nov. 10, 1685, amounting to £63, 8s. 1d.

18—Adam Hurd, son of John Hurd, Sen., came with his father from Windsor, Conn., where they had been among the first settlers, to Stratford, before or not later than the spring of 1644. Instead of there being two brothers, it is quite evident that there were the father and two sons, and yet it is not certain. A clause in the will of John Thompson, who was brother to Sarah, the wife of John Hurd (1681), represents said John Hurd as having become senior by the death of his father, and if so, his father came to Stratford and was one of the first settlers there. The town records style this John brother of Adam, uncle to Adam's son John, and yet Adam's son John styles him cousin.

Adam Hurd had two house lots, Nos. 31 and 35, and other lands, but his name, while prominent on the records, is not as much so as his supposed brother John's.

19—Daniel Titterton (also spelled Titharton) appears to have been in Boston in 1643, removed to Stratford before

1647, for he was Representative from Stratford in 1647 and also in 1649, 1652 and 1654. He died in 1661, his will being proved July 6, 1661, in which he mentions three sons, Daniel, Samuel and Timothy, the last being the only one whose birth is recorded in Stratford, which was March 25, 1651. To these he gave his estate and lands in England, besides some in New England. He mentions three daughters; one, name not given, had married John Wilcoxson, and Mary and Elizabeth, to whom he gave £30 each, and besides £10 for marriage dresses. His wife Jane outlived him, and two sons may have returned to England to enjoy the estate there, yet Timothy and Samuel are here in the year 1700.

20—Philip Groves was among the first settlers at Stratford and was early appointed the Ruling Elder, and the only one, of the Stratford church. He seems to have married Ann, the daughter of the Rev. Henry Smith of Wethersfield, for John Blakeman, Jr., who married another daughter calls Philip Groves "brother." Mr. Groves was prominent in the town. He was, in 1642, the first Deputy of this town, and in 1647 a juryman at Hartford, but living at Stratford; in 1653 he was appointed with William Beardsley by the General Court to settle a question of boundaries between Fairfield and Norwalk; and the same year was directed as "Goodman Groves with Goodman Thornton," both of Stratford, to assist the Constables in making the draft of soldiers and provisions for the supposed impending war against the Dutch at New York; in 1654 he was appointed by the Court, with others, an Assistant to the Magistrates,[4]

---

[4] General Court, May 1654.

"It is ordered by this Court, that Mr. George Hull and Alexander Knowles of Fairfield, Philip Groves of Stratford, and Matthew Camfield of Norwalk, shall be Assistant to such Magistrates as the Court shall at any time send among them, in the execution of justice, and they hereby empower them to examine misdemeanors, to grant out summons, or bind over delinquents to Court, in this Jurisdiction, for either of them to marry persons, to press horses by warrant from them as the public welfare of this Comonwealth and their particular Towns may or shall at any time require; they giving an account to this Court of the same when required thereunto." In 1658 this office was further defined and restricted in the following language: "to assist Mr. John Wells and Assistant Camfield in procuring wills and taking inventories, and distributing estates of

which might be sent to execute justice in the town, and reappointed in 1655 and '56, thus showing that at this date this town had no regularly elected Magistrate. In 1655 he was elected Deputy; in 1656 he was again appointed Assistant; in October, 1656, he, with Robert Rice, was appointed leather sealer for Stratford, perhaps the first in that office; and in May, 1660, he was appointed one of the grand jury for the Colony. He died in 1675, having been a useful, prominent man in the church, town and state.

21—Francis Peacock, supposed brother of John Peacock, was a land owner in Stratford, but no further account of him has been seen.

22—William Crooker was a land owner in Stratford, but probably did not reside here, or if he did it was but a short time. His wife was the daughter of Henry Gregory. William Crooker, an original proprietor, deeded his land in Stratford to Henry Wakeley, and probably went to Norwalk, 1654, and thence to Newtown, L. I.

23—John Hurd, Sen., the emigrant, among the first settlers in Windsor, Conn., was in Stratford in October, 1644, when he and William Judson were appointed by the General Court to solicit subscriptions in the town of Stratford for the maintenance of scholars at Cambridge, and this collection was "to continue yearly," such being the enterprise of that day in behalf of education. In May, 1649, he was a chosen deputy to the General Court, and was appointed by that Court on a committee with Daniel Titterton to view land desired by the town of Fairfield for an enlargement of their territory, and in May, 1650, the report being favorable, the request of Fairfield was allowed, which extended their bounds to the Saugatuck river. He was deputy also at other times. Hence it seems that this John must have been an older man than the John who was married in 1662, and is credited with being the first of the name at Stratford.

---

persons that died intestate, and to appoint administrators. . . . This order respects Stratford, Fairfield and Norwalk." Hence the origin of the Probate Court. Col. Rec. i. 257, 323.

8

A grave-stone of " John Hurd, 1681, aged 68," taken from
the old burying-ground, is probably his, and hence he was
born in 1613, seven years before the landing at what we now
know as the old Plymouth Rock. Stratford should be proud
of such a monument as this stone, for, although naught but a
rude field stone, yet what visions of long years gone by are
brought to our minds by it. Two hundred and three years
this plain and often unnoticed stone has borne its unpreten-
tious title—*John Hurd, 1681, aged 68*—a fitting monument for
the plain, earnest life he and his associated brethren lived, as
emigrants to the then New World, for the sake of the truth
as they viewed it, in obedience to the Gospel of the Son of
God. Standing by such a stone in the light of two hundred
years is sufficient inspiration to cause every man to defy
religious proscription, bigotry or oppression.

John Hurd was a miller, and in connection with Thomas
Sherwood built the first mill at Old Mill Green, in 1653,
where he himself probably was the first or among the first
residents in that part of the town. He and Thomas Sherwood, or one of Sherwood's sons, may have located there
together.

24—*Arthur Bostwick,* came from Cheshire, county
of Chester, England, with son John, and probably a wife, and
was an early settler in Stratford, before 1650, and probably in
1639. In 1659 he had a second wife, a widow Ellen Johnson,
who petitioned the General Court in regard to her husband's
lands, and by the order of the Court their united property
was divided equally between them, and in the same year
Arthur gave the most, if not all of his estate, to his son John,
by contract, in which John agrees to maintain his father with
whatever he shall need for his comfort, and among other
things " to find him wines and spirituous liquors, and a horse
when he shall wish to ride forth." The widow, Ellen, in
after years gave a portion of her property to her son Johnson
by a former husband. The reason for dividing the property
appears from the use they made of it, in each bestowing it on
children by their former marriage ; a matter of no surprise.
Arthur was in the list of freemen in 1669, and probably died
within four years thereafter.

His home lot, 25, indicates him to have been among the first settlers. His descendants have been numerous in New Milford as well as in Fairfield county.

25—John Thompson,' being a little over twenty-one years of age, came.to New England on a visit of inspection, and being satisfied with its appearance returned home to dispose of his property and come here for life. From the seaport where he landed in England to his home in the interior was a distance of many miles, which he journeyed on foot. While passing at early morn a farm-house where the daughters were bringing the milk, he stopped for some refreshments, and disclosing the fact that he was from New England, he found himself among ardent friends of the Puritan Colonies. Conversation grew earnest and he was urged to stay. Many questions were asked in regard to the land of the exiles. "It is a goodly land," said he, "but as yet full of wild beasts and savage men, but a place where we may worship God with a true conscience."· "Would God I were there," said Mirable, a younger daughter of the farmer, protesting that for love of Christ and to be free from the severe restrictions then laid upon Puritan worship, she would gladly endure the hardships and peril in order to attain that end. Not long before this she had been imprisoned for attending a conventicle. Thompson's stay was prolonged; the interest between him and Mirable increased and they were engaged to be married. He went home, closed his business affairs, returned, married her, and they came to New England. · It is thought that his first coming was in the Elizabeth and Ann in 1635, he being then twenty-two years of age, yet this is not certain, nor is it certain in what year he came the second time, nor what year he arrived at Stratford, although he was there before 1646.

This sketch is taken from the narrative of these events by the Rev. Nathan Birdseye who died in 1818, aged 103 years, who relates among other things that Mr. Thompson brought to Stratford some of the first fruit trees introduced there, and also that he harvested the first wheat raised there.

---

* From the manuscript of Mr. Curtis Thompson.

The family tradition was that he and his wife, walking in the field by the Fresh Pond, found that numerous heads of wheat had already become yellow, whereupon he gathered hand-fulls of these heads and she rubbed out the wheat until nearly a peck was secured, which they dried, and probably pounded in a mortar, and made bread from it, the first made from wheat grown in the town.

Mr. Thompson died in July or August, 1678; his will being drawn in July and the inventory was made in August, and he is supposed to have been 65 years of age. His widow, Mirable, died April 13, 1690. The story is related that on a certain day soon after their settlement in Stratford, while engaged in her house with her face from the door two Indians rushed in, the one giving a fearful yell, and the other just then buried his tomahawk in the head of the first, who fell dead across the table. Mr. and Mrs. Thompson had two sons and four daughters, whose descendants still abide within the limits of the old town.

26—Robert Coe, Jr., settled in Stratford before 1651, where he purchased of widow Ramble (?) a house lot recorded in 1652, bounded "east upon the highway, west upon the swamp, Samuel Sherman on the north and Thomas Uffoot on the south; with land in the New Field, at Carman's Neck, at Nesumpaws and in the great meadows." Previous to this purchase he held land in the Old Field, and hence was one of those who kept up the fence around it, and therefore it is probable that his father was one of the original owners of Stratford and afterwards gave his share to this son Robert, else why should he have left Hempstead to settle at Stratford? He died in 1659, at the age of 32, leaving a widow, three daughters and one son, among whom his estate, amounting to £179, 18s. was divided, the daughters receiving £35 each. The widow, Susannah Coe, married, 2d, Nicholas Elsey of New Haven, and upon her son John, becoming of age she, with her husband, made over to him the homestead of his father, December, 1682.

The following verses were made by the Rev. Abraham Pierson, pastor at Branford, on the death of Robert Coe:

" Rest blessed Coe, upon thy bed of ease ;
I'the quiat grave with the is no desease.
all, all our anguish hath its perod fixt,
Err hens we goe : not any joy but mixt.
Raer grace which maks the life of man the best.
this young man lived to God and now is blest.
Come parallel this saint : now far exceed :
Omit no means that may true goodness breed.
are tryals come, bestowed for days of need ?
the Lord his widow bless, and take his seed."

Cooe or **Coe.** It is an interesting fact that during Queen Mary's reign, in the year 1555, Roger Cooe, of Suffolk county, England, the section of the country whence the family came to America, was burned at the stake, in his extreme old age, a martyr to the truths of the gospel. His trial is related by Fox in the Book of Martyrs, where it is represented that he most decidedly and faithfully testified to the truth and suffered patiently but firmly for Christ and his teachings.

Robert Cooe, Sen., the first in America, who is said to have been born in Suffolkshire, England, in 1596, sailed from Ipswich in the ship Frances in 1634 with his wife Anna, who was born in 1591, and three children. He was made freeman in Watertown, Mass., in 1634, and tarried there about two years, but was among the first at Hartford, Conn. (then called Newtown), where in 1636, at the first Court held there, he and others presented their certificates of dismission from the church at Watertown, dated in the March previous, to form anew in church covenant " on the River of Connecticot." He and others settled at Wethersfield, where he with others, after about four years, formed a company and bought of New Haven colony, the plantation of Ripowams (now Stamford), where they settled in 1641. For this territory they agreed to pay 100 bushels of corn, and Robert Cooe's proportion was four bushels and one peck. In 1644, Robert Coe, with other inhabitants, removed with their minister, Mr. Richard Denton, to Hempstead, L. I., at which date, Robert, Jr. was seventeen years of age. In 1652, Robert, Sen., removed to Middlebury, now Newtown, L. I., where he was made sheriff in 1669, which office he held until 1672.

27—Thomas Uffoot came from England in the ship Lion in 1632, with William Curtis; was made freeman in Boston that same year; may have lived in Roxbury; came, probably, in 1639 to Stratford, and may have been related to the Curtis family by marriage. His house lot was No. 16, which still remains in the family, yet his descendants are scattered far and wide, like those of many other families. He was a juryman at Hartford as early as 1643 and again in 1644; was in Milford in 1646, when he and his wife joined the church there, and is said to have been there in 1654. He died in 1660, and as the inventory of his property is at New Haven, he may have been residing at Milford at his decease.

28—Joseph Hawley was in Stratford a proprietor as early as 1650 and probably a few years earlier. His home lot was No. 37, which he purchased of Richard Miles in or before the year 1650. The tradition in Stratford has been and is that he married Catharine Birdseye, a niece of John Birdseye, her father residing first in New Haven and then in Wethersfield. He was prominent in the town and a more than usually energetic business man. He purchased of the Indians a large tract of land in Derby, of which that town allowed him to retain the old Indian planting field, and also another tract which joined it, including Great Hill. He was chosen Deputy in 1665 and many times thereafter until near his decease. He made his will in 1689 and died the next year. His descendants are numerous and a genealogy of them is largely collected and nearly ready for publication by Mr. Elias S. Hawley, of Buffalo, N. Y.

29—Sergt. Jeremiah Judson, son of William, born in England in 1621, and hence was 16 years of age when he came to Stratford; married about 1652, and was a prominent man in the business transactions of the town. He died in 1700, aged 79.

30—Joshua Judson, third son of William Judson, born in England in 1623, came to Stratford with his father; married Ann Porter of Windsor about 1656, and died in 1661, aged 38, leaving two sons and a widow, who married John Hurd, Jr.

31—Mr. Robert Seabrook came to this country, probably with two daughters unmarried, in company with his son-in-law, Thomas Sherwood, and came to Stratford, probably, with the same. One daughter married Thomas Fairchild, perhaps before they came to Stratford. In 1651 he must have been about 85 years of age or more. In 1634 his daughter Alice, who was the wife of Thomas Sherwood, was 47 years of age. He was also the father of William Preston's wife, of New Haven, and in his will gave his home lot in Stratford to his grandsons, Jehiel Preston of New Haven and Thomas Fairchild, Jr., of Stratford. He is also supposed to have been the father of Lieut. Thomas Wheeler's wife, who was married, probably, in this country.

32—Henry Gregory was in Stratford in 1647, when he is described in the New Haven Records as having sons Judah and John and a daughter who was the wife of William Crooker of Stratford.

The Probate Court, June 19, 1655, orders administration on Henry Gregorey's estate, giving the eldest son, John, a double portion and making him the distributer of the estate. It mentions the children, but names only John. In 1647 the son John testified that his father was old and that his sight had failed him. The descendants remained in the town many years, but were not numerous.

33—Richard Boothe, was born in England in 1607, for in an affidavit, March 15, 1687–8, he describes himself as about 81 years of age. From what part of England he came, or in what year is not fully known, nor is there certain evidence of his immediate ancestors, but his name—Richard—and those of John and Robert, are family names in the line of the Boothe families of Cheshire, England, an ancient house, connected also by marriage with several families of distinction. If, as is not improbable, Richard, of Stratford, were of that stock, the relationship, it is supposed, would be established through Richard, of Coggshill, and Baron in Cheshire, who was son of Sir William Boothe, by his wife Elizabeth, daughter of Sir John Warburton, and was born about 1570, and died in 1628.[10]

---

[10] See Booth Genealogy.

Richard Boothe's name and those of his descendants are prominent on Stratford records. His home lot, 29, indicates his settlement there among the earliest, but probably not before his marriage in 1640. He married, 1st, Elizabeth, the sister of Joseph Hawley,[11] for his son Ephraim, in his will styles Samuel Hawley (son of Joseph) cousin. He was one of the proprietors of the township and received divisions of land located in various parts of the town, as did also the other proprietors. He was probably married twice and had eight children. The latest mention of him extant is in March, 1688-9, in his 82d year.

34—" Mr. Waklin." Henry Wakelee, was, probably, an original proprietor of Stratford, and was there before 1650. His home lot was No. 15, indicating him to have been among the first settlers. In 1663 he was attorney before the General Court in behalf of his son James, but the matter was withdrawn from court.

Ebenezer Wakelee went from Stratford to Waterbury, the part of the town now Wolcott, where his descendants still reside. The name is now generally spelled Wakelee, but at first it was generally written Wakelyn, and sometimes Weaklin and Waklin. The family have not been numerous.

35—Widow Curtis was Elizabeth Curtis, the mother of William and John, with whom she came to Stratford, leaving, apparently, three of her children at Roxbury, Massachusetts. The reason for the separation of the members of the family may have been the fact that the father, now deceased, had acquired a considerable property in land at Roxbury which could not readily be disposed of to advantage, and hence three stayed to care for it and three came to Stratford. Widow Curtis's home lot was near or joining Rev. Mr. Blakeman's. She died in June, 1658, and her estate was apprised at £100, 3s. 6d. (See sketch of William Curtis.)

36—Thomas Sherwood came from England in the ship Frances from Ipswich, in 1634, aged 48 years, with wife

---

[11] Rev. B. L. Swan makes a note as follows: "There is more than a probability that Jane, wife of Rev. Adam Blakeman, Ann, wife of Philip Groves, and Miriam, wife of Moses Wheeler, were also sisters of Joseph Hawley.

Alice, aged 47 years, and four children. His wife Alice was the daughter of Robert Seabrook and sister of the wife of Thomas Fairchild, and hence in all probability these two families came in each other's company to Stratford.

In June, 1645, he had four suits for slander, in three of which he was plaintiff and in one defendant, and he gained the four with costs of the suits and thirty-nine pounds money as damages. He, in the autumn of the same year, was elected deputy with William Beardsly, the first sent from Stratford, to the General Court. In October, 1654, when a draft was made for an expected war with the Narraganset Indians, Thomas Sherwood and Thomas Fairchild were appointed with the constables to "press men and necessaries" for the war, from Stratford. In this same year, 1654, John Hurd and Thomas Sherwood received from the town of Stratford forty acres of land and three pieces of meadow in the New Pasture in consideration of the expenses of building a corn-mill "to grind the town's corn," at what is now the east end of Old Mill Green. The amount of toll they were to have for grinding was one-sixteenth of a bushel, and the town was to furnish a correct measure for the purpose of taking the exact amount. Thomas Sherwood did not remove to Fairfield, as stated by some, but died in Stratford in 1656, where his death is recorded.

In 1645, in his suits at law, he is called "Thomas Sherwood the elder," in every case, showing that there was then a Thomas Sherwood the younger. The story of the three brothers who came over has been historical in this family, and is true, for Thomas Sherwood, Jr., Stephen Sherwood and Matthew Sherwood, sons of Thomas Sherwood, Sen., were made freemen in the town of Fairfield in the year 1664, where they and their descendants were prominent, influential citizens for two hundred years. The family has been also considerably numerous in the interior towns and in New York State.

37—Francis Hall, a professional lawyer, was of New Haven, in 1639, and came to Stratford before 1651 ; his dwelling-house seems to have been west of Main street, on what was afterwards called Lundy's Lane, being the old road

through the village to Fairfield. He and his family removed
to Fairfield, where he purchased considerable land, and in
1687 a paper was recorded showing that his wife possessed a
house and lands in England when she was married, and
which he had sold and for which he gave the paper signed
by himself securing the amount to her from his property." In 1654 he and his wife bought of Thomas Wheeler,
of Fairfield, "all that mesuage or tenement with ye appertenances," or a house and lot, and he may have resided in it
thereafter a part of the time, for his residence was in Stratford years after. His wife Elizabeth died July 6, 1665, and
he being an attorney at law was employed by Mrs. Jane,
widow of Rev. Adam Blakeman, against her daughter-in-law,
then widow Dorothy, and became charmed with his opponent in the case, and married her Oct. 31, 1665, just twenty-
one days after the suit was tried in court, and six days less
than four months after the decease of his first wife. Francis
Hall died March 5, 1689-90. His widow, Dorothy, married
3d Mark Sension, of Norwalk, who died in 1693, after which
she married 4th, Dea. Isaac Moore, of Farmington.

38—William Beardsley came from England in the
ship Planter," Capt. Travice commander, he being then 30

---

11 *Isaac Hall's Caveat against his father's property.*

"Whereas my Honored Father Francis Hall hath formerly sould a house
and land in England which was my mother's at her marriage with him and for
which he hath acknowledged himself Ingaged to make her as good a right in ye
like kind in sum other place by a writing under his hand bearing date ye 9th day
of March, 1664, may more fully appear and for ye performance of sd. Ingagement
hee hath nominated all ye housing and land he hass had in the liberties of Fairfield as in ye sd writing is expressed.

I Isaac Hall as heir to my Honoured Mother Elizabeth Hall deceased enter
Caveate against ye sd housing and lands yt they may be responsible to ye aforesd
Ingagement and for yt time this cavet is to stand according as ye law directs in
such cas.

Dated Fayrfeild This 27 of Septem. 1687."

18 *The following is the list of the vessel in which William Willcoxson and several other
families came to America who settled in Stratford, and it is given here to show the
method of emigration.*

"2 Aprilis 1635. These under written names are to be transported to New England imbarqued in the Planter, Nico : Travice Mr. bound thither the parties have

years of age, his wife Marie 26, his daughter Marie 4, son John 2, and Joseph 6 months. They embarked in April, 1635, on the same vessel with Richard Harvie and William Wilcoxson, both of whom settled in Stratford. He was a mason by trade and it is claimed very emphatically by his descendants that he was also a Freemason—a remarkable fact, if true—and that he came from Stratford on the river Avon, in Warwickshire, the birth-place of William Shakespeare. This tradition has been confirmed (it is said by good authority), by some of the Beardsley family, residing at Avon, N. Y., who have visited England and Stratford-on-Avon, and made a careful search for the facts, and which were satisfactory to this effect. The town of Avon, N. Y., was named by descendants of William Beardsley of Stratford, Conn., and thus named in honor of the old river in England. Some of the members of the Avon, N. Y., family have been very distinguished, specially Judge Samuel Beardsley, many years Chief Justice of the State of New York. The Beardsley family have claimed the honor of securing to the town of

---

brought Certificates from the minister of St. Albons in Hertfordshire and attestations from the justice of the peace according to the Lord's order.

	years.		years.
A Mercer, Jo: Tuttell,	39	Tho: Savage, a Taylor,	20
John Tuttell,	42	A Taylor, Richard Harvie,	22
John Lawrence,	17	Husbandman, Francis Pebody,	21
Wm. Lawrence,	12	Lynen Weaver, Wm. Wilcockson,	34
Marie Lawrence,	9	Margaret Wilcockson,	24
Abegall Tuttell,	6	Jo: Willcockson,	2
Symon Tuttell,	4	Ann Harvie,	22
Sarah Tuttell,	2	A Mason, Wm. Beardsley,	30
Jo: Tuttell,	1	Marie Beardsley,	26
Joan Antrobuss,	65	Marie Beardslie,	4
Marie Wrast,	24	John Beardslie,	2
Tho: Green,	15	Joseph Beardslie,	6 mo.
Nathan Heford, } servant to Jo: Tuttell,	16	Husbandman, Allin Perley,	27
		Shoemaker, Willm Felloe,	24
Marie Chittwood,	24	A Taylor, Francis Baker,	24
Shoemaker, Tho: Olney,	35	Tho: Carter, 25 } servants to
Marie Olney,	30	Michell Williamson, 30 } George
Tho: Olney,	3	Elizabeth Morrison, 12 } Giddins."
Epenetus Olney,	1	
Husbandman, Geo: Giddins,	20	See Hotten's *List of Emigrants.*

Stratford, Conn., its name, in honor of their old native place in their mother country, with much credible evidence.

William Beardsley was among the first settlers of Stratford in 1639. He was made freeman in Massachusetts, Dec. 7, 1636, but where he then resided is not known. He was a substantial, prominent man in the new plantation, but died in 1660 at the early age of 56, leaving property inventoried at £333, 15s.

He was elected deputy for Stratford in 1645, with Thomas Sherwood. In 1649 he was appointed with Mr. Hull, of Fairfield, to assist Roger Ludlow in securing provisions for the soldiers then drafted for the war against the Dutch at New York; and in 1651 he was propounded for an "Assistant to join with the magistrates for the execution of justice in the towns by the sea side."

There was a Thomas Beardsley who died in Stratford in 1667, who is said to have been son of Thomas, of Milford. He had a home lot near William Burritt.

39—John Curtis. The Curtis family in Stratford has been curiously represented as to the first settlers, in which confusion rather than history has prevailed.

John and William Curtis, with their mother Elizabeth, appear at Stratford among the first settlers; the brothers have each the birth of a child recorded in 1642, but that does not prove that the children were born in Stratford, since such records were sometimes transferred from one town to another; but these brothers probably came here in 1639, or with those who came in company with Mr. Blakeman, and the record shows that at that time, 1642, they were of age, and married, which could not have been the case according to the account given in the Woodbury History, which makes William at that time not more than ten years of age. The Curtises of Scituate and Roxbury, Mass., were different families, and remained with their descendants in and about each of those places except those who came to Stratford.

William Curtis, who came in the ship Lion in 1632, was the settler at Roxbury and father of William and John who settled in Stratford, and he died at Roxbury near the end of the year 1634. He came to America, leaving his family for the time, as did many others, in England, and in the spring of 1634 they came and joined him at Roxbury, where his name appears frequently in the records as a land holder, and he died about eight months after they came. His children were William, Thomas, Mary, John and Philip; William and John with their mother Elizabeth, came to Stratford, the others appear to have remained at Roxbury, where are still their descendants.

Thomas Uffoot came in the ship Lion in 1632, with William Curtis, Sen., and he and the Curtises probably came in company to Stratford.

John Curtis was made freeman in 1658; had his home, perhaps, with his mother, bought the shares of the other heirs after her death, and gave it to his son Israel in 1660. John and William Curtis had each a home lot at No. 69 (on diagram). William had the east half, John the west. This was before 1660.

John Curtis was prominent as a citizen and in the work of settling the township, but he was not as much in public life as his brother William.

William Curtis, son of William, came to Stratford with his widowed mother Elizabeth, and his brother John Curtis, probably in the spring of the year, 1640, where he died in 1702, full of years and honors.

Much effort has been made to ascertain the relation of several families of this name at Roxbury, Mass., and Stratford, Conn., with little success, except by the Rev. B. L. Swan, who succeeded finely.

A paper has come to light since the commencement of this book, which has been preserved with great care about 200 years, which makes the matter quite definite. This paper reads: " William Curtis came to this land in the year 1632, and soon after joined the church; he brought four children with him—Thomas, Mary, John and Philip, and his eldest son William came the year before; he was a hopeful scholar, but God took him in the end of the year 1634. Sarah Curtis, wife of William Curtis." This is all there was on the original paper except a description of the coat-of-arms, a painted copy of which has been preserved with the paper, both being the property of the late Samuel Curtis Trubee, of Fairfield, and which had been preserved very carefully by his mother Elizabeth (Curtis) Trubee, who was born in Stratford Dec. 25, 1788.

This paper was evidently written by some member of the family at Stratford about the year 1700, or earlier, for it must have been William Curtis the father who died at Roxbury in 1634, since the five children of that family were then born, and the William Curtis of Stratford had a family of nine children, all born after 1641, and also since Elizabeth Curtis, widow, and mother of William and John, came to Stratford with the first settlers, probably, in 1639, and died there. And also the Sarah Curtis mentioned on the old paper was the second wife of the second William Curtis, or the one who came to Stratford.

Further: The high standing of William Curtis of Stratfort as a military officer corresponds to the description given: "he was a hopeful scholar;" for education above the ordinary ability to read and write was greatly appreciated and honored in those days. His standing in this respect, having been Sergeant as early as 1650, as well as the military affairs of Stratford, are somewhat revealed in the following extracts and facts: "June, 1672. This Court confirms William Curtis, Captain, and Joseph Judson, Lieutenant, and Stephen Burritt, Ensign, of the Train Band of Stratford."

At the same time the General Court declared that "until further order be taken, Capt. Nathan Gold [of Fairfield] shall be deemed chief military officer of the county of Fairfield, and Capt. William Curtis, his second."

In August, 1672, Capt. William Curtis was appointed by the General Court one of six commissioners, with the Governor, Deputy Governor and Assistants, as a war council against the Dutch at New York, "to act as the Grand Committee of the Colony in establishing and commissionating military officers, in pressing men, horses, ships, barques or other vessels, arms, ammunition, provision, carriages or whatever they judge needful for our defence, and to manage, order and dispose of the militia of the Colony in the best way and manner they can for our defence and safety."

In the next November, Captain Curtis was appointed Captain "for such forces as shall be sent from Fairfield County" against the Dutch at New York, and in 1675 his commission in the same position was renewed; this showing that he stood the highest in the county as a military officer, except field officers.

While he was thus engaged in military affairs he was for some years regularly elected Deputy to the General Court, his election being repeated, sometimes after intervals, sixteen times.

His home lot was No. 34, but he owned a part of No. 69, and his name does not occur on the list of fence about the old field, probably because his cultivated land was in or nearer the village or in the new field. Several of these planters had land to cultivate, at first, from two to six acres, near or adjoining their home lots.

40—John Birdseye came to Stratford among the earliest settlers. According to his age at death, he was born in 1616, since he died in 1690, aged 74 years. The Rev. Samuel Peters, who married into the family, says he came from Reading in Berkshire, England, emigrated to America in 1636; came to New Haven, thence to Milford in 1639, and thence to Stratford. Mr. Peters says, also, he came to New Haven with his two sons, and one of them settled in Middletown and the other in Stratford. This is an error, for Middletown was not commenced as a settlement until 1650, and this John Birdseye's children were not born when he came to America. If this tradition is true, it must have been another John Birdseye, father of this John, which may have been the case. The tradition still in the family is that two brothers came to New Haven, one settled in Wethersfield, who had a family of daughters, and that Joseph Hawley, the first of the name at Stratford, married Catharine, one of those daughters; and that John came to Milford and thence to Stratford, but the precise year is not known. The births of his only children are recorded in Stratford, John in 1641 and Joanna in 1642, but their baptisms are recorded in Milford; and he and his wife Phillis (Phillipa) were dismissed from the Milford church to Stratford church in 1649.

It seems very improbable that he would, under the circumstances and customs of those days, remain at Stratford eight years and continue his membership at Milford, and therefore it is more probable that he remained at Milford until 1649 and had his children's births recorded in Stratford after he came here. The time of her death is not known, but he married a second wife, Alice, widow of Robert Tomlinson, about 1688. An agreement between himself and her in 1688 respecting property is on the probate records.

Both of his children survived him. Joanna married Timothy, son of William Willcoxson; the latter in his will in 1651 refers to his "brother Birdseye," whence it may be inferred that either William Willcoxson's wife was Birdseye's sister or Birdseye's wife was Phillis Willcoxson, and in either case John Birdseye's children married their cousins, for John Birdseye, Jr., married Phebe, daughter of William Willcoxson.

John Birdseye is said to have been one of the first deacons in the Congregational Church of Stratford. His descendants have been considerably numerous, widely scattered and of honorable position and standing as citizens. Victory Birdseye of Onondaga county, N. Y., son of the Rev. Nathan Birdseye, became a member of the Congress of the United States.

John Birdseye seems to have married Phillipa, daughter of Rev. Henry Smith of Wethersfield, for John Blakeman, Jr., who married Dorothy, daughter of Rev. Henry Smith, called Birdseye "brother." It is true that the term "brother" was used in those times familiarly in public documents, among the members of the church, to designate, simply, that relation, but it is not certain that it was used in this sense in wills, where definite terms are supposed to have been used.

41—Isaac Nichols, son of Francis, one of the first company of settlers in Stratford, came from England with his father and became a prominent citizen in the town, where he died in 1695. He was a deputy to the General Court three sessions in 1662 and 1665. He was a farmer but seems to have dealt somewhat in merchandise. In his will he says: "Concerning my Indian servant George, I give him to my wife during her natural life." His descendants are scattered far and wide in the land of freedom and prosperity. Of the brothers Caleb and John a notice will be made further on in this book.

Francis Nichols from England was in Stratford among the very first settlers. The General Court, on October 10, 1639, directed " Mr. Governor and Mr. Wells to confer with the planters at Pequannocke [Stratford], to give them the oath of Fidelity, make such free as they see fit, order them to send one or two deputies to the General Courts in September and April, and for deciding of differences and controversies under 40 s. among them, to propound to them and give them power to choose 7 men from among themselves, with liberty of appeal to the Court here; as also to assign Sergeant Nicholls for the present to train the men and exercise them in military discipline." This establishes the fact that Francis Nichols was in Stratford with several other families in 1639, and that he was the first military officer in the plantation, which was a matter of considerable distinction in those days, and it indicates that he had become somewhat acquainted with military matters before coming to this country.

He died in 1650 and the inventory of his estate in 1655, on Stratford records, was £29, 9s. His sons were Isaac, Caleb and John, all born in England. His widow Anne was the daughter of Barnabas Wines of Southold, L. I., and she married, 2d, John Elton of that place, and found a home on one of the most healthy islands, with the most charming climate in the world.

Thomas Alsop, born in 1615, came to America in the Elizabeth and Ann in 1635, aged 20 years, and evidently was one of the first settlers in Stratford, where he died 1650–1, leaving property which went to Joseph Alsop of New Haven, probably a brother. Judge Savage thinks that John Alsop, who is found on a tax-list with Edward Jackson and Thomas Child, who came to New England, and William Shakespeare, at Stratford on the river Avon, England, in 1598, was the father of Thomas Alsop of Stratford, and from this supposition it has been claimed that the new plantation in Connecticut received the name of *Stratford*.

9

William Hopkins was a resident in Stratford in 1640, and in 1641–2 was one of the magistrates at the General Court; then he disappears and nothing further is known of him.

Thomas Thornton was a business man early at Windsor and served on a jury at Hartford in 1643. In 1646 there was a motion before the General Court to excuse him and his men from training because " by having his men suddenly taken off" from work " he might sustain great loss;" but we have no information what his trade or business was. In the spring of 1651 he seems to have been at Stratford and become acquainted with business matters in Fairfield, for he " affirmed in court that it was reported there were a hundred beeves killed in Fairfield last year." He was on a committee for Stratford in 1653, with Goodman Groves to draft soldiers. Lands were granted to him by the town in September, 1651.

Robert Rose was of Wethersfield in 1639. He came from Ipswich, county Suffolk, in the ship Frances in 1634, aged 40, with wife Margery, aged 40; children, John, 15; Elizabeth, 13; Mary, 11; Samuel, 9; Sarah, 7; Daniel, 3; and Dorcas, 2. He was residing in Wethersfield in 1639, and was constable in 1640; representative in 1641, '42 and '43; removed, says Savage, before 1648 to Stratford, which is probable. He, and not his son Robert, purchased a home lot and several pieces of land in Stratford, April 3, 1668, of the town, which had been John Young's. Nov. 3, 1685, Robert Rose, of Stratford, gives his son-in-law Moses Johnson, of Woodbury, "fifty or sixty acres of land granted to me by the General Court for gratification for services done by me, the said Rose, in the Pequot wars." It is probable that his son, Robert Rose, settled at East Hampton, L. I., in 1650.

John Jenner had land recorded to him in 1652, in Stratford; a home lot, land in the Old field, New field, Nesumpaws and in the great meadow. Having land in the Old field it is a little surprising that his name does not appear among those who made the fence around that field. He soon disappeared from Stratford, but his name is found with others on a petition to the General Court from Cromwell

Bay, now Setauket, L. I., in 1659, asking to be admitted into Connecticut colony.

Moses Wheeler was at New Haven and had land proportioned to him in the first division that was made in that town, which occurred between 'the years 1641 and 1643. At that time his family consisted of two persons, which must have been himself and wife, and his estate was fifty-eight pounds.

There is nothing definite as to when he came to America or from what part of England, but the Wheeler family have been residents several hundred years in the county of Kent, southeast of and adjoining to London, and it would seem probable that he came with the New Haven Company which came from London; yet, if his sister married the Rev. Adam Blakeman, as believed, it would indicate that possibly he may have come from another county than that of Kent.

In May, 1648, Moses Wheeler was an inhabitant of Stratford, for at that time Roger Ludlow presented to the General Court a request that Mr. Wheeler should be allowed to keep a ferry at Stratford, and the decision of the matter being referred to the next Fairfield Court, the request was granted. It appears from these records that the ferry was then already established, and the application to the court was to secure the privilege as legal property.

What the conditions for the privilege of the ferry were is not stated, but seventeen years later, Nov. 21, 1670, the town saw fit to lease to "Moses Wheeler, ship carpenter, the ferry with thirty or forty acres of upland and six of meadow joining to the ferry for twenty-one years, without tax or rate except six pence per annum during said lease." The inhabitants were to be "ferried over for one half-penny per person, two pence per horse or beast." If he should leave the ferry at the end of twenty-one years, the town agreed to pay him for his improvements and take the property. By the will of Moses Wheeler, Jr., proved Jan. 23, 1724-5, it is ascertained that he received the ferry from his father and left it to his own son Elnathan Wheeler, and therefore the ferry continued in the same family, at least three generations, or nearly one hundred years.

It is probable that Moses Wheeler was the first ship-carpenter in Stratford, and that he continued to work at his trade, then much needed, and to cultivate his forty-six acres or more of land, while he attended the duties of the ferry many years. He died in 1698; having been born in 1598, therefore may have been the first centenarian white man in New England.

Mr. Samuel Sherman purchased in Stratford of Caleb Nichols a house and lot and other land in about 1650, and became one of the substantial, prominent men of the town. The family is traced back into England by the Rev. Henry Beers Sherman, of Esopus, N. Y., and the Rev. David Sherman, D.D.,[1] of Hopkinton, Mass., in regular succession, to the beginning of the sixteenth century, with interesting notes of the family a number of generations anterior to that.

"The family is of German extraction. In the fatherland the name Sherman, Schurman, Schearmaun, Scherman often occurs, and was doubtless transferred, many centuries ago, to the vicinity of London by the Saxon emigration, where it still remains. From this metropolitan stock a scion was transplanted to Dedham, county of Essex, England, which long flourished and sent forth other shoots. The name is derived from the original occupation of the family, for they were cloth dressers, or shearers of cloth. The family at Dedham retained the same occupation and also the same coat-of-arms as worn by those in and about London.

"There are found in New England two distinct families, one of them descending from William Sherman, who came to Plymouth with the Pilgrims about 1630, and settled at Marshfield, where some of his descendants still remain, but of his place of birth or immediate ancestry nothing is known.

"The other is the Dedham family, a branch of which emigrated to America and settled in the vicinity of Boston. Of this family, the first in the line, and perhaps the one who emigrated to Dedham, was Henry Sherman, of whom but few dates or facts are known, except that he bore the Suffolk

---

[1] See New England Genealogical Register for January and May, 1870.

coat-of-arms and died in 1589. His son Henry was the father of Edmund, the first emigrant of this line to America. He was born in Dedham, and married in England, in 1611, Judith Angier, and came to America about 1632, and settled in Watertown, Mass., whence they removed to Wethersfield, Conn., and thence to New Haven, where he died."

Samuel Sherman, born in Dedham, England, in 1618, son of the above Edward, came to this country with his father and was in Wethersfield as early as 1637, for in May of that year he was a member of the Committee which acted as the Court when war was declared against the Pequots, before the General Court was organized. The position he thus occupied was that afterwards denominated an assistant, and now a senator; the title he bore was that of " Mr." and this when, according to the dates given, he was only nineteen years of age; but he was probably twenty-one, and his being elected or appointed to that office even at twenty-one, assures that he possessed superior education, or he would not have been so selected from a score of others capable and older, his own father among the number.

Mr. Samuel Sherman was elected an assistant three successive years from 1662, and he served the State in this or some other capacity so profitably that the court granted him "a farm of two hundred and fifty acres of land upon New Haven river whereof fifty acres may be meadow, so it be out of the bounds of the town."

His next service was upon an important war committee consisting of Mr. Gould, Mr. Camfield, Ens. Judson, Mr. Lawes, Lt. Olmstead or any three of them, for, war between England and the Dutch States general having been declared Feb. 22, 1665, and the news of it having reached the colonies in June of that year with the information that DeRuyter, the Dutch admiral, with a considerable force was to visit New York City, the coast on Long Island Sound was divided into three districts for self-defence. But the Dutch admiral did not come. This news of war dangers produced great excitement among the people on the coast.

Liberty was granted by the General Court May 9, 1672, to "Mr. Samuel Sherman, Lt. Wm. Curtis, Ens. Joseph Judson and John Minor, themselves and their associates, to erect a plantation at Pomperaug," which grant eventuated in the settlement of Woodbury.

Mr. Sherman was thus a valuable as well as a prominent member of the early township of Stratford. He died in the year 1700.

Henry Tomlinson was in Milford as early as 1652; removed to Stratford in the autumn of 1656, where, April 1, 1657, he purchased of Joshua Atwater a house and lot and several pieces of land and became a permanent inhabitant. Before coming to Stratford, in June, 1656, the town of Milford brought a complaint against him and he against it, as to the ownership of a house, both claiming it, as an ordinary or tavern which he had conducted one or more years as a town officer, and the town charged him with "breaking the jurisdiction order in selling strong water at a greater price than is allowed, and wine and dyet at (as is conceived) immoderate prices, whereby the town suffers, and some have said they never came at the like place for dearness." Soon after this Mr. Tomlinson removed to Stratford, but the suit was brought in court several times until the spring of 1659, when it was again put over until the next October, and that is the last that is recorded concerning it except as it came up in another form. The Governor of New Haven had rendered a decision of small penalty against Mr. Tomlinson, and he in turn arrested the governor, by legal process, as having done him a personal injury. This arrest of the chief magistrate of the colony created much excitement, and after two hearings in court Mr. Tomlinson was fined £100, and required to give bonds in that sum with the assurance that the court would "call for the £100 when it should see cause," and there the matter stands to the present time, so far as the records show. In Milford he was not a member of the church and hence not a voter, and this may have had something to do with the lawsuit.

Henry Tomlinson came from England with a wife, two sons, Jonas and Abraham, and several daughters. His son Abraham died on the passage hither, and his son Agur was born in Stratford. The tradition is that his nephew came with him to this country, and there was a Robert Tomlinson in Milford whose wife was dismissed from the church in Milford to Stratford Church in 1653, and who died in Stratford, and his widow married John Birdsey, Sen., about 1688.

William Tomlinson was accepted an inhabitant in Derby in December, 1677, who is supposed, in consequence of several favoring facts, to have been the son of this Robert of Milford and Stratford.

Henry Tomlinson was one of the most active business men of Stratford and known as such in the Colony. He was not a military man; he had no title to his name, but was a farmer, buying, selling and cultivating land. In 1668 he and Joseph Hawley—another land buyer—purchased a large tract of land in Derby—"all that tract of land lying upon the Great Neck near unto Pawgassett, ... for the consideration of £6. 10s.,"[1] and in 1671 he and others by permission of the General Court purchased a large tract of land of the Indians of Weantinock—New Milford.

His will was dated in the winter of 1680–81 and proved April 28, 1681, and his inventory amounted to £518 16s. 2d., besides his tract of land at Weantinock, which he gave to his "two sons," Jonas and Agur.

The old Bible, printed in 1599, which Henry Tomlinson brought to this country, is still preserved, although it has removed west to the state of Michigan. The coat-of-arms in a painting of the family has been preserved many years through the care of Governor Gideon Tomlinson and his descendants.

The descendants of Henry Tomlinson have been prominent in business enterprises and professions in many parts of the country.

Hugh Griffin became an inhabitant probably about 1654, and purchased of the town a house and lot.

John Ferguson purchased land in Stratford of James Blakeman, Nov. 28, 1660, and appears to have been a resident, and in October, 1664, sold his estate to Abraham Wakeman and removed from the town.

---

[1] Col. Rec., ii. 303.

Thomas Beardsley purchased in Stratford, Feb. 7, 1661, a house and lot of land amounting to ten acres or more, became an inhabitant, and died Feb. 13, 1688. How he was related to the other Beardsley family, if at all, has not been ascertained.

John Beach, son of Richard of New Haven (says Savage), perhaps a brother, came to Stratford and bought his first land here May 21, 1660, of Ens. Bryan of Milford, "one house lot 2 acres." He had then a wife and four children.

In January, 1671, he was made an auctioneer by the following vote: "John Beach was chosen crier for the town, and to be allowed four pence for every thing he cries; that is to say for all sorts of cattle and all other things of smaller value, two years."

Benjamin Beach, son of Richard of New Haven, came to Stratford a single man.

Thomas Quenby may have been a son of William Quenby, had a home lot and was a land owner in Stratford about 1660, and removed to West Chester, N. Y., about 1664.

Francis Jacockes had a home lot in Stratford about 1660, but disappeared soon. He may have been the father of William and Joshua, who were in Hempstead, L. I., in 1682. His descendants are said to be still in New Haven, Conn.

Jonas Halstead was among the early dwellers of Stratford, went to Jamaica, L. I., before 1660.

Edward Higbee had a home lot in Stratford, but removed to Jamaica, L. I., before 1660.

John Barlow had a home lot in Stratford about 1660 and removed to Fairfield.

CHAPTER VII.

CONFLICTS, WARS, WITCHCRAFT.

ONCERNING the toil, endurances and hope through which the settlers of Stratford, as well as those of neighboring plantations, passed the first stage of their progress, it is difficult to write without commiseration, gloom and indignation. Commiseration for them as separated from their native land and kindred, the greatness of their privations and toils, and the enmity with which they were watched by the natives around them; gloom in view of their early dead, and general want of knowledge in order to adapt themselves to the untried conditions of life to which they were subject; and of indignation at the outrage of the civil and ecclesiastical governments which drove them to renounce their manhood as to conscience and reason, or flee from their native land into an untried, unsettled and uncivilized wilderness; and finally, indignation that these commonly intelligent and Christianized men should have brought with them so much of the superstition, bigotry and stupid foolishness of the old country as they did, by which they were lead to treat the natives of the land in a barbarous manner, and to hang poor innocent old women as supposed witches. However execrable some of their beliefs and practices were, they brought them all with them from Old England with the exception of a very few items taken up anew from the law of Moses. They came here with the same minds and principles with which they and their neighbors were possessed in England, with one grand and noble ex-

ception, which was that they had scarcely put their feet upon
American soil before a great light of freedom shone around
them and at once transformed them into independent republics: the like of which had never yet been conceived by
mortal man.   Suddenly, as the comet dashes into sight from its
trackless journey, the new earth spread its wide and fertile
domain to a coming nation of liberated and enlightened freemen; and such was the amazement to the awakened mind
that they scarcely dreamed to what end it would come, only
that they were defiant to tyrants, and pledged to the
improvement of the grand opportunities spread before them
until "*further light should come.*"

With such a comprehensive view of practical life, destiny
spread before them the grand achievements which they in
due time organized and established, and into the glory of
which we have already in part, entered.   Hence; in view of
the reward we now possess as to a largely enlightened nation,
it is unfitting that we should cast a disparaging reflection
upon those through whom we possess so advantageous an
inheritance.   No greater eulogy can be set forth concerning
any one than the actualities of life, for anything beyond this
dwindles into insignificance.   Therefore we proceed to
gather the items now scattered far and wide in hundreds of
family Bibles, stacks of town records and personal manuscripts, and place them in book form for the perusal of
thousands of interested readers, and as the starting point for
future and further research and collections.

How, then, did these wilderness planters make such
steady and marvelous progress under the new, varied and
difficult, as well as discouraging circumstances around them,
during the first twenty years of their Stratford plantation?

Wars and Rumors of Wars.

In a preceding chapter, pages 55-60, the effects upon
Stratford and neighboring towns of the Indian war with the
Dutch at New York, which began in 1643, has been carefully
narrated, and only a few things remain to be written.   The
settlers did not come to this country prepared for war, but
were almost wholly without implements and materials for

such a conflict. Neither had they the means or necessary appliances for making war materials to any considerable extent, and therefore they were to a great degree defenceless. One of the first things they did in Stratford, after fitting up the few guns they possessed, was, according to tradition, the fortifying the village against the Indians, by building palisades. This was done by setting into the ground wide slab-like stakes or split logs and posts close together, from eight to twelve feet high, making a palisade fence, from the Housatonic river across the north part of what was soon afterwards known as Watch-house Hill, and still later Academy Hill, to the swamp on the west side of the village, and then southward as far as was necessary to secure the settlers from a sudden attack by the Indians. In later years these palisades were renewed and the place further secured as directed by the General Court and attended to by a Stratford town vote.

In providing for the safety of the community, soldiers were drafted and placed on watch during the nights, and at particularly alarming times, during the day, and for the convenience of these soldiers a house was built on the hill, and hence the name Watch-house Hill. From this hill, when the trees were not half or a quarter as numerous as now, the whole village and far beyond it, could be overlooked and a careful watch kept by a few men.

It is possible that as early as 1643 the palisades were built so as to inclose a small territory at the mouth of the creek where the first meeting-house stood, for the hill a little to the east was called Guard Hill because of the soldiers keeping guard there at a very early period. From this hill, in 1643, a careful watch could have been kept over a few families —perhaps twenty or twenty-five—who were then dwelling there.

In 1649, new difficulties arose with Indians about Stamford and adjoining plantations. Forty-five soldiers were ordered by the General Court to be drafted and placed under Roger Ludlow, with William Hull and William Beardsley to assist, but the war passed off without bloodshed, although with a great fright to the people.

Added to this at this time was the great Revolution in
England which resulted in the execution of Charles I. and
the military dictatorship of Cromwell, which in effect threw
the Colonies upon their own resources of sustenance and
military defence, and furthered their ideas of personal and
Colonial freedom, although they had not the least thought of
independency from the mother country. Stratford above all
the plantations was loyal although some of its citizens were
among the most pronounced opponents to the political
claim that none but church members should be freemen so
far as to be allowed to vote; for, in 1663, after the restoration
of Charles II. to the throne and the officers were sent to this
colony to arrest Messrs. Goff and Whalley, the Regicides,
Stratford Constables obeyed the order of search, while other
towns refused, and presented a bill to the General Court for
£6. 17ˢ 1ᵈ, which the Court refused to allow,[1] and probably
the bill is still unpaid.

In the year 1652 war broke out between England and
Holland, and it at once was expected that the conflict would
be extended to America and prosecuted between the Dutch
possessions at New Amsterdam, afterwards New York, and
the New England Colonies. Trumbull says: "The commencement of hostilities this year between England and
Holland, the perfidious management of the Dutch Governor,
with apprehensions of the rising of the Indians, spread a
general alarm through the Colony."[2]

In May, 1653, "the Commissioners of the United Colonies, who were at this time in session at Boston, having
'considered what number of soldiers might be requisite if
God call the Colonies to make war against the Dutch, concluded that five hundred for the first expedition shall be
the number out of the four jurisdictions, and apportioned
this number to the several Colonies as follows: to Massachusetts, 333; to Plymouth, 60; to Connecticut, 65; to New
Haven, 42."[3] At this time also England sent over "a parcel of arms and ammunition, as a supply, and for the convenience of the United Colonies, and ordered "that the

---

[1] Col. Rec. i. 393.   [2] Trumbull, i. 201.   [3] Col. Rec., i. 241.

same should be divided as follows: to the Massachusetts, £309, 17ˢ, 8ᵈ; to Plymouth, £57, 14ˢ, 10ᵈ; to Connecticut, £60, 6ˢ, 10ᵈ; and to New Haven, £50, 4ˢ," the division being made according to tax lists of the several Colonies.

The part which Connecticut was to bear in this campaign is indicated by the record of the General Court, May 21, 1653. "The Court having received orders from the Commissioners that there are to be sixty-five men to be prepared forthwith, to be at a day's warning with provisions suitable; the Court raiseth the men out of the several towns of this Jurisdiction as followeth, who are to be forthwith impressed to be at a day's warning or call, as also that suitable provisions and ammunition shall be forthwith prepared :—

Windsor, 12	Norwack, 1	Farmington, 5
Pequett, 5	Hartford, 15	Seabrook, 5
Mattebezek, 1	Wethersfield, 8	Fairfield, 8
		Stratford, 6 = 64.[4]

"The officers of this Company that the Court requires to be over them, are as follows: Lieut. Cooke is to be Commander in Chief; Lieut. Bull to be their Lieutenant; Lieut. Thomas Wheeler, of Fairfield, to be their Ensign; Richard Olmstead, of Norwocke, to be a Sergeant; and the other is to be chosen by the officers of this Company; Hugh Wells to be their drummer."

In drafting men for this war a committee was appointed in each town to act with the constable, to fill which Goodman Groves and Goodman Thornton were appointed for Stratford.

The tax list for Stratford for the year 1654, only one year later, as rendered to the General Court, contained seventy-four tax payers, who were the owners of land or heads of families, but not the entire number of the inhabitants. Hence this draft took one in twelve of the men, and this while a home guard or watch was kept for self-defence, just in planting time in the spring. The calamity of the time is indicated by the General Court, June 25, 1653, thus: "It is ordered by this Court that there shall forthwith be presented to the Bay the present distresses, fears and dangers that the English

---

[4] Ibid, 242.

bordering upon the Dutch, both upon the Main [land] and Long Island are in."

After these preparations for war had continued from May until September, the news came that Massachusetts would take no part in the proposed war against the Dutch, which decision gave great offense to Connecticut and New Haven, because they were greatly exposed to injury by the Dutch, and had already made large expenditures for the war, while Massachusetts was not, and had not. The Court of New Haven convened October 12, and that of Connecticut November 25, both considering that the Court of Massachusetts had willfully violated the articles of union. The people at Stamford and Fairfield became much agitated and Capt. Underhill, of Greenwich, sent to his friends at Rhode Island for assistance "and with such Englishmen as he could obtain made the best defence in his power."[1]

Trumbull says: "The Dutch at New Netherlands waited only for a reinforcement from Holland to attack and reduce the English colonies. Of this both they and the English were in constant expectation. It was reported and feared that when the signals should be given from the Dutch ships the Indians would rise, fire the English buildings and make destructive work." If such had been the case no plantations would have suffered more than Stratford, Fairfield and Derby, for here were by far the greatest number of Indians except east of New London. But fortunately the Dutch fleet of reinforcement was defeated by the English at sea, and the Indians remained friends to the settlers.

It was from the midst of these times of peril that some trouble arose concerning Mr. Roger Ludlow, the staunchest and ablest man as a lawyer and statesman that was at the time in Connecticut. Trumbull says: "Stamford complained that the government was bad, and the charges unreasonable, and that they were neglected and deprived of their just privileges. They sent to the General Court at New Haven desiring them to prosecute the war against the Dutch, resolved to raise a number of men among themselves, and prayed for permission to enlist volunters in the several towns.

---

[1] Trumbull, i. 213.

"The town of Fairfield held a meeting on the subject, and determined to prosecute the war. They appointed Mr. Ludlow commander-in-chief. He was in the centre of the evidence against the Dutch, had been one of the commissioners at the several meetings at Boston relative to the affair, had been zealous and active for the war, and conceiving himself and the town in imminent danger unless the Dutch could be removed from the neighborhood, too hastily accepted of the appointment. Robert Bassett and John Chapman were at the head of this party. They attempted to foment insurrections and, without any instructions from authority, to raise volunteers for an expedition against the Netherlands."

This insurrection business was moonshine in the eye of the historian, of which there probably never was a particle of evidence. Robert Bassett and John Chapman with the others had been arraigned before the New Haven Court about eight months previous for speaking against the New Haven Colony law that none should vote except church members, which was, in the minds of some of those in authority at that time, a terrible wickedness, and now, when they again moved with energy to protect the plantations to which they belonged from slaughter, after Massachusetts had broken its agreement and left these towns to take care of themselves or be annihilated, it was thought noble to make Roger Ludlow, Robert Bassett and John Chapman the scapegoats for the perfidy of others, who, although vested with authority to protect the people and ordered to it by the home government with war material furnished to hand, saw fit to sit down in their chairs of state and take their ease at the peril of the whole coast of Long Island Sound. Had the Dutch fleet escaped the English on the ocean, as was intended, there might not have been left a living man on the coast from Rhode Island to the New Netherlands.

No wonder Mr. Ludlow sailed the next spring for Virginia, and Robert Bassett soon removed to Hempstead, L. I.

All these things added to the calamities which hindered the toiling planters at Stratford as well as elsewhere throughout one whole year, during which fortifications were established along the Sound at considerable expense of money and time, worked discouragement in the minds of the people, when in September, 1654, the Commissioners resolved on war with the Indian Chief Ninigret, or the Narraganset nation, and for this expedition soldiers were drafted from the several plantations in the following October: Windsor, 8; Pequot, 4; Mattabeseck, 1 ;[6] Norwalk, 0; Hartford, 9; Wethersfield, 6; Farmington, 2; Seabrook, 4; Fairfield, 6; Stratford, 5 = 45. The other colonies were to provide as follows: "Massachusetts, 40 horsemen and 153 foot; Plymouth, 41; and New Haven, 31." A part of this force was to be "dispatched with all expedition to the Niantic country, and the remainder to hold themselves in readiness to march on notice from the commander in chief." But as in the previous case the Massachusetts General Court when it came together, refused to take any part in this war. The committee to draft the men in Stratford to fill this order was Thomas Sherwood and Thomas Fairchild, with the Assistant and Constables.

At this time (October, 1654) Connecticut and New Haven fitted a frigate of ten or twelve guns with forty men, to defend the coast against the Dutch (whom they had so deferentially declined to fight the year before), and to prevent Ninigret and his Indians from crossing the Sound to prosecute his hostile designs against the Indians in alliance with Connecticut. After considerable playing war by the Massachusetts Major Willard, who finally came with troops as commanding general in this expedition, the whole display ended without so much as any smoke of battle, and the brave troops returned home, while Ninigret flaunted his colors more lively than ever.

The Connecticut Court allowed its soldiers in this expedition pay as follows: common soldiers, 16[d] per day; drummers, 20[d]; sergeants, 2[s]; ensigns, 2[s], 6[d]; lieutenants, 3[s]; and stewards, 2[s] per day.[7]

This proposed Indian war again awakened fear of a rising or at least hostile conduct of the Indians still residing in for-

---

[6] Middletown.   [7] Col. Rec., i. 273.

midable numbers in and near Stratford. Probably not less than one thousand Indians were residing in Stratford, Milford, Fairfield and Derby, if not fifteen hundred; and it was not an infrequent thing for individuals and families to have some difficulty with the Indians.

Thus matters continued as to the outside world with only now and then a report of trouble with Ninigret's people, until into the year 1656, when "The Protector, Oliver Cromwell, having conquered Jamaica, made it a favorite object to remove the people of New England to that island; but while this proposition made some commotion as to its importance and desirability and the contrary, it soon ceased to excite interest, and the people remained on their several plantations to improve them as best they could.

Witches and Witchcraft.

Historically speaking, the topics of witches and witchcraft are to-day treated as questions of undoubted absurdity, demanding only pity for their unfortunate victims. They are also often ignorantly spoken of as the inventions of the early settlers of New England, whereas they had been more strongly believed and cherished in England hundreds of years before New England was discovered. and always maintained as doctrines taught in the Bible. The New England people revived a few old Mosaic laws and teachings, but witches and witchcraft were none of them. Two eras for the mania of treating these matters by severe penalties of law, passed over New England, but suddenly disappeared; the one about 1650, the other in 1692; but the influence of a sentiment or legendary stories of witches, still lives throughout the United States as well as England, Germany and other countries on the globe. Among the first impressions of fear produced upon the mind of the author of this book, were those resulting from seeing "witch marks" in the unfinished chambers of dwellings in the western part of Albany county, N. Y.—his native place—which region was settled first by the Dutch, and afterwards by New England people, in the latter part of the seventeenth century. He does not remember having ever seen a dwelling (and he saw many) built by

10

the Dutch, that had not these marks on the inside of the roof to prevent witches from troubling the family ; and the witch stories of his boyhood days. represented as actual transactions in that region, were almost without number. This belief as developed in that part of the country did not originate in New England but came with the Dutch from their native land. The following is one of those stories related about fifty years ago, as stated above, and is given as illustrative of the beliefs of those times, and also as showing that witch troubles existed elsewhere besides in Connecticut and Massachusetts.

A farmer's wife in churning cream to secure butter, spent several hours without success, and gave up the effort as useless. Upon her husband coming into the house, she related her fruitless toil of the morning, when he, being strongly impressed with the thought that some one had bewitched the cream out of envy toward his family, took his old musket and fired a full charge through the cream and the bottom of the churn. He then stopped the hole made through the bottom of the churn and his wife with a few minutes' labor finished the churning, securing the proper amount of butter ; but that day, at the time of the shooting an old woman of the place was taken suddenly with a fit and died without any apparent cause, and the matter was talked of as though the community was rid of one witch. Many stories were told, particularly to the effect, that children and young people were prostrated by sickness for weeks and years by the envy and spite of witches, who were always represented as being old women.

The following account of witch troubles in Fairfield County having been collected with great carefulness and expense of time by Major W. B. Hinks and the Rev. B. L. Swan in some " Historical Sketches," printed in 1871, is so complete that it is here given as a proper historical summary of this lamentable delusion.

" It will doubtless be a matter of surprise to many to learn that any trials and executions for this imaginary crime ever took place outside of the State of Massachusetts, and particularly in this vicinity, historians generally being silent upon the subject. Dr. Trumbull indeed, in the preface to his history of Connecticut, says that one or two executions at Stratford were reported by an obscure tradition, and that this tradition together with a minute in Goff's Journal by Governor Hutchinson, respecting the execution of Ann Coles,[1] 'is all the information to be found' on this subject. He also adds that 'after the most careful research, no indictment of any person for that crime nor any process' relative thereto can be found.

Omitting all mention of cases in other parts of the State, let us inquire respecting the executions stated by Dr. Trumbull, to have taken place in Stratford.

We have here something more trustworthy than obscure tradition to guide us, for in the month of May, 1651, the following order was passed by the General Court, in session at Hartford:

"The Governor, Mr. Cullick and Mr. Clarke, are desired to goe down to Stratford to keep Courte upon the tryal of Goody Bassett for her life, and if the Governor cannott goe, then Mr. Wells is to go in his room."

That the Goody Bassett mentioned in this entry was put to death as a witch, cannot perhaps be positively demonstrated; but there is strong indirect evidence to show that such was the case, contained in the minutes of a trial preserved in the New Haven records. In this trial, which took place in 1651, one of the witnesses in the course of her testimony referred to a goodwife Bassett who had been condemned for witchcraft at Stratford, and another alluded to the confession of the witch at that place.[2]

"The place of her execution is pointed by tradition to this day, and would seem to be determined by the names "Gallows Brook" and "Gallows Swamp" in the first volume of Stratford town records. The former was a small

---

[1] Ann Coles, is the case supposed to be referred to in Mather's Magnalia, book vi. ch. vii.

[2] Col. Rec. i. 220.   [3] New Haven Col. Rec. ii. 77–88.

stream, long since dried up or diverted into another channel, emptying into the swamp, a portion of which yet remains, a little south of the present railroad depot. A rude bridge stoned up at the sides, crossed this brook, just where the Old Mill road and the railway intersect. The remains of the bridge were exhumed by the workmen about thirty years since, when the railroad was graded at that point. At that bridge, uniform tradition states the execution of the witch by hanging to have taken place. Near by where the street from the village turns off toward the depot, was, until quite recently, a small quartz boulder, with hornblende streaks like finger marks upon it, which was connected with the fate of Goody Bassett, by an ancient and superstitious tradition. The story was, that on her way to the place of execution, while struggling against the officers of the law, the witch grasped this stone and left these finger marks upon it. The stone, with its legend, came down to our day, but a few years since an unromantic individual used it in building a cellar wall, not far from the place where it had been lying.

"In October, 1653, about two and a half years after the event just narrated, the General Court passed another resolution in the following words: " Mr. Ludlow, Mr. Wells, Mr. Westwood and Mr. Hull, are desired to keep a perticulier Courte at Fairfield, before winter to execute justice there as cause shall require.[4]

"The unfortunate person on whose account justice was to be executed was, as before, a woman, charged with witchcraft. She is designated simply as ' Knapp's wife,' or ' goodwife Knapp,' in the only account we have of the proceedings; namely, a number of depositions in the case of Thomas Staples of Fairfield, who in the spring of 1654, sued Roger Ludlow of that place, for calling his wife a witch. It is not impossible that goody Knapp may have been the wife of Roger Knapp of New Haven, who removed to Fairfield, although his name is not mentioned among the residents there until 1656. His son, Nathaniel, lived in Pequannock in 1690, and joined the church afterwards organized there, his name occur-

---

[4] Col. Rec., i. 249.

ring frequently upon the early records of the North Church in Bridgeport.

"The trial took place in the autumn of 1653, before a jury and several 'godly magistrates' (the same probably that are named in the order of the General Court), and doubtless lasted several days. There were many witnesses, but the indictment and the substance of the greater part of their testimony are wanting. We learn, however, that a strong and perhaps decisive point against the accused, was the evidence of Mrs. Lucy Pell and Goody Odell, the midwife, who by direction of the Court had examined the person of the prisoner, and testified to finding upon it certain witch marks, which were regarded as proof positive of intimacies. Mrs. Jones, wife of the Fairfield minister, was also present at this examination, but whether as a spectator or as one of the examiners, is not clearly stated.

"The jury brought in a verdict of guilty, and goodwife Knapp was sentenced to death. After her condemnation she was visited by numbers of the towns-people, who constantly urged her to confess herself a witch and betray her accomplices, on the ground that it would be for the benefit of her soul; and that while there might have been some reason for her silence before the trial, since a confession then might have prejudiced her case, there could be none now, for the reason that she was sure to die in any event. The pains of perdition were held up to her as sure to be her portion, in case of a refusal.

"Upon one of these occasions, the minister and a number of the towns-people being present, the poor woman replied to her well-meaning tormentors that she 'must not say anything that was not true,' she 'must not wrong anybody,' but that if she had anything to say before she went out of the world she would reveal it to Mr. Ludlow, at the gallows. Elizabeth Brewster, a bystander, answered coarsely, 'if you keep it a little longer till you come to the ladder, the devil will have you quick, if you reveal it not till then.' 'Take care,' replied the prisoner indignantly, 'that the devil have not you; for you cannot tell how soon you may be my companion.' 'The truth is,' she added, 'you would have me to say that good-wife Staples is a witch, but I have sins enough to answer for already, and I hope that I shall not add to my condemnation; I know nothing against goodwife Staples, and I hope she is an honest woman.' She was sharply rebuked by Richard Lyon, one of her keepers, for this language, as tending to create discord between neighbors after she should be dead, but she answered, 'goodman Lyon, hold your tongue, you know not what I know; I have been fished withall in private more than you are aware of. I apprehend that goodwife Staples hath done me wrong in her testimony, but I must not return evil for evil.' When further urged, and reminded that she was now to die, and therefore should deal truly, she burst into tears, and desired her persecutors to cease, saying, in words that must have lingered long in the memory of those who heard, and which it is impossible now to read without emotion,—' never, never, poor creature was tempted as I am tempted; pray, pray for me.'

Yet it appears that her fortitude sometimes gave way, and that she was induced to make a frivolous confession to the effect that Mrs. Staples once told her that an Indian had brought to her several little objects brighter than the light of day, telling her that they were Indian gods, and would certainly render their possessor rich and powerful; but that Mrs. Staples had refused to receive them. This story she subsequently retracted.

"The procession to the place of execution, which is stated by an eye-witness to have been 'between the house of Michael Try and the mill,' or a little west of Stratfield boundary, included magistrates and ministers, young persons and those of maturer years, doubtless nearly the entire population of Fairfield. On the way to the fatal spot the clergyman[1] again exhorted the poor woman to confess, but was rebuked by her companion Mrs. Staples, who cried, 'Why bid her confess what she is not? I make no doubt, but that if she were a witch she would confess."

"Under the shadow of the gallows the heart of Goody Knapp must again have failed her, for being allowed a

---

[1] Rev. John Jones, who came from England in 1635.

moment's grace after she had mounted the ladder, she descended and repeated her former trifling story respecting Mrs. Staples, in the ear of Mr. Ludlow, her magistrate. If this was done in hope of obtaining a reprieve, as seems likely, the poor creature was disappointed, for she was speedily turned off by the executioner, and hung suspended until life was extinct.

"When the body had been cut down and laid upon the green turf beside the grave, a number of women crowded about it eager to examine the witch signs. In the foreground we see Mrs. Staples kneeling beside the corpse, and in the language of one of the witnesses, 'wringing her hands and taking ye Lord's name in her mouth,' as she asseverates the innocence of the murdered woman. Calling upon her companions to look at the supposed witch-marks, she declares that they were naught but such as she herself or any woman had. 'Aye, and be hanged for them, and deserve it too,' was the reply of one of the older women present. Whereupon a general clamor ensued, and seeing that there was now nothing to be gained, and much to be apprehended if she persisted, Mrs. Staples yielded, and returned home.

Among the names occurring in that narrative are some like Gould, Buckly and Lyon, that are common in Fairfield to this day. The Odells and Sherwoods may have been residents of Pequannock.' Mr. Ludlow saw fit to repeat the story told him by the dying woman, and to further assert that Mrs. Staples had not only laid herself under the suspicion of being a witch, but "made a trade of lying." Hence the suit already mentioned, in which the New Haven Court had the good sense to give a decision in favor of the plaintiff, and allow him fifteen pounds damages.

The last trial in the State of Connecticut for the crime of witchcraft took place in Fairfield in 1692, the same year in which the delusion rose to such a fearful height in Salem, Massachusetts. Capt. John Burr, one of the magistrates in this trial, was the father of the principal founder of St. John's Church, Bridgeport, and the name of Isaac Wheeler, a jury-

---

* There were no settlers at Pequannock as early as 1654.

man, may be seen upon the records of the North Congregational Church in Bridgeport.

Mercy Disborough, one of the accused persons was
from Compo or Westport. Three others, Elizabeth Clawson,
goody Miller, and the widow Staples were indicted at the
same time. The last named may have been the same person
who, as we have seen, was suspected of being a witch nearly
forty years before. The following extracts show the compo-
sition of the Court, and the manner of conducting the trial.

" At a special court of Oyer and Terminer, held at Fayre-
field, September 19th, 1692. Present, Robert Treat, Esq.,
Govenour, William Jones, Esq., Deputy Govenour, John
Allyn, Secretary, Mr. Andrew Leete, Capt. John Bur, Mr.
William Pitkin, Capt. Moses Mansfield, (composing the
Court.)

" 'The Grand Jurors impaneled were Mr. Joseph Bay-.
ard, Sam'l Ward, Edward Hayward, Peter Ferris, Jonas
Waterbury, John Bowers, Samuel Sherman, Samuel Galpin,
Ebenezer Booth, John Platt, Christopher Comstock, Wm.
Reed ; who presented a bill of indictment against Mercy Dis-
borough, in the words following, to wit :

" ' A bill exhibited against Mercy Disborough, wife of
Thomas Disborough, of Compo, in county of Fayrefield, in
colony of Connecticut.

" ' Mercy Disborough, wife of Thomas Disborough, of
Compo in Fayrefield, thou art here indicted by the name of
Mercy Disborough, that not having the fear of God before
thine eyes, thou hast had familiarity with Satan the grand
enemy of God and man, and that by his instigation and help,
thou hast in a preternatural way afflicted and done harm to
the bodyes and estates of sundry of their Majestie's Subjects,
or to some of them, contrary to the peace of our sovereign
Lord and Ladie, the King and Queen, their crown and digni-
tie ; and on the 25th of April of their majestie's reigns, and at
sundry other times, for which by the laws of God and this
colony, thou deservest to die.'   JOHN ALLYN, Secretary.

Fayrefield, 15th September, 1662.

"'The indictment having been read, the prisoner pleaded not guilty; and referred herself to tryal by God and her countrie, which countrie was the jury after written.'

Names of the petit jury:—James Beers, Isaac Wheeler, John Osborn, John Miles, Ambrose Thompson, John Hubby, John Bowton, Samuel Hayes, Eleazer Slawson, John Belden, John Wakeman, Joseph Rowland,'

The depositions of nearly two hundred witnesses were taken in this case. That their evidence was of trifling character, will be inferred from the annexed specimens, and these clearly show the excited state of public feeling at the time, that such accusations were the means of putting in jeopardy the lives of several innocent persons, and of causing the sentence of death to be passed upon one. Two of the depositions copied here relate to the water ordeal, and there is also evidence to show that the persons of the accused were examined for proofs of guilt.'

"'At a Court held at Fayrefield ye 15th day of September, 1692. The testimony of Hester Groment, aged thirty-five years or thereabouts, testifieth; that when she lay sick some time in May last she saw, about midnight or past, the widow Staples, that is, the shape of her person, and the shape of Mercy Disborough, sitting upon the floor by the two chests that stand by the side of the house in the iner rume, and Mrs. Staples' shape dancing upon the bed's feet with a white cup in her hand, and performed some three times. Sworn in Court, September 15th, 1692.

Attest: JOHN ALLYN, Secretary.

"'Edward Jesop, aged about twenty-nine years, testifieth; that being at Thomas Disburow's house at Compoh, sometime in ye beginnihg of last winter in the evening, he asked me to tarry and sup with him; and there I saw a pig roasted that looked very well, but when it came to ye table (where we had a very good lite) it seemed to me to have no skin upon it, and looked very strangely; but when ye sd. Dis-

---

¹ Conn. Col. Rec., iv. 76, note. Samuel Sherman and Samuel Galpin of Stratford were on the Grand Jury which found a true bill for witchcraft against Mercy Disborough in September, 1692.

burrow began to eat it, ye skin (to my apprehension) came upon it, and it seemed to be as it was when it was upon the spit, at which strange alteration of ye pigg I was much concerned. However, fearing to displease his wife by refusing to eat, I did eat some of ye pig ; and the same time Isaac Sherwood being there, and Disburrow's wife and he discoursing concerning a certain place of Scripture, and I being of ye same minde that Sherwood was concerning ye place of Scripture, and Sherwood telling her where ye place of Scripture was, she brought a bible (that was of very large print,) but though I had a good light and looked directly upon the book I could not see one letter; but looking upon it while in her hands, after she had turned over a few leaves, I could see to read it above a yard off.

"Ye same night going home, and coming to Compoh creek, it seemed to be high water, whereupon I went to a cannooe that was about ten rods off (which lay upon such a bank as ordinarily I could have shoved it into ye creek with ease), though I lifted with all my might and lifted one end from the ground, I could by no means push it into ye creek ; and then the water seemed so loe y^t I might ride over, whereupon I went again to the water side, but then it appeared as at first, very high ; and then going to ye canooe again, and finding I could not get it into ye creek I thought to ride round to where I had often been, and knew ye way as well as before my own dore, and had my old cart horse : yet I could not keep him in ye road, do what I could, but he often turned aside into ye bushes, and then went backwards, so that though I kept upon my horse and did my best endeavour to get home, I was ye greater part of ye night wandering before I got home, altho' it was not much more than two miles.

Fayrefield, September 15th, 1692. Sworn in Court September 15, 1692.

Attest: JOHN ALLYN, Secretary.

"Mr. John Wakeman, aged thirty-two years, and Samuel Squire, made oath that they saw Mercy Disburrow put into the water, and that she swam upon the water. This done, in Court, September 15th, 1692.

Test: JOHN ALLYN, Secretary.

"The testimony of Abraham Adams and Jonathan Squire also is, that when Mercy Disburrow and Elizabeth Clawson were bound hand and foot and put into the water, they swam like cork; and one labored to press them into the water, and they buoyed up like cork.*

Sworn in Court, September 15th, 1692.

Attest: JOHN ALLYN, Secretary.

"Catharine Beach, aged seventeen years or thereabouts, testifieth and saith, that sometime this last Somer She saw and felt goodwife Clawson and Mercy Disborough afflict her, not together, but apart, by scratching and pinching and wringing her body ; and farther, saith that goodwife Clawson was the first that did afflict her, and afterward Mercy Disborough; and after that sometimes one of them, and sometimes the other of them ; and in her afflictions though it was night, yet it appeared as light as noone day.

Sworn in Court, September 19th, 1692.

Attest: JOHN ALLYN, Secretary.

"Having taken this testimony and much more of a similar character, the court adjourned for several weeks. On the 28th of October, 1692, it assembled again at the same place, and after taking further evidence, the case was submitted to the jury. Elizabeth Clawson, goody Miller, and the widow Staples were acquitted, but a verdict was returned against Mercy Disborough of 'guilty,' according to the indictment, of familiarity with Satan. Being sent forth to consider their verdict, the jury returned saying they saw no cause to alter it, but found her guilty as before. Their verdict was approved by the court, and sentence of death passed upon the prisoner by the Governor. It seems probable, however, that she escaped this fate, and was pardoned, with the return to reason which followed the collapse of the Salem delusion, for a woman named Mercy Disborough was living

---

*The water test was the process of binding the hands and feet and putting them in sufficient water upon the supposition that if they were witches they would float upon the water, but if they were not witches they would sink, and thus prove their innocence.

in Fairfield in 1707, and is named as one of the executors upon the estate of her husband Thomas."

Witchcraft in Connecticut.—Authentic Records.

1648-9. Mary Johnson of Windsor was executed at Hartford, which was the first case in New England.[a]

1651. Goody Bassett executed at Stratford.[b]

1653. Goodwife Knapp executed at Fairfield.[c]

1653. Elizabeth Goodman of New Haven accused.[d]

1657. Thomas Mullener of New Haven accused.[e]

1658. Goodwife Garlick of East Hampton, L. I. was tried at that place and sent to and tried at Hartford and acquitted.[f]

1659. Mr. Willis and Dept. Governor Mason are ordered by the Court to investigate a case of " witchery " at Saybrook.[g]

1662. Greensmith and his wife executed at Hartford and two others fly from the country.[h]

1663. Elizabeth Seager was indicted in Hartford for witchcraft, but convicted of adultery on another count in the indictment. She was tried again in June, 1665, and found guilty, but the court set aside the verdict, for informality.[i]

1670. Catharine Harrison of Wethersfield tried and convicted of witchcraft at Hartford, but allowed to pay costs and leave the town.[k]

---

[a] Winthrop, vol. ii. 374. Col. Rec. i. 143, 171, and Savage's Genealogical Dictionary, article Johnson.

[b] Conn. Col. Rec., i. 220. New Haven Col. Rec., ii. 81.

[c] New Haven Col. Rec., ii. 77-84. Conn. Col. Rec., i. 249. Kingsley's Hist. Discourse.

[d] New Haven Col. Rec., ii. 29, 151.

[e] New Haven Col. Rec., ii. 224.

[f] Conn. Col. Rec., i. 573. Doc. Hist. of New York, i. 683.

[g] Conn. Col. Rec., i. 338.

[h] Mather's Magnalia, ii. book 6, p. 390 ; Remark Prov. Chap. 5.

[i] Winthrop, ii. 374.

[k] Conn. Col. Rec., ii. 132, note.

1671. False accusations made by Elizabeth Knapp of Groton.[1]

1692. Trial of Disborough, Clason, Miller and Staples at Fairfield, and the first convicted and sentenced.[m]

1694. "Winfield Benham, Sen. and his son Winfield Benham, Jr. were charged with witchcraft at Wallingford, but the Grand Jury refused to find an inditement."[n]

Improvements for the Public.

Public improvements, in the early settlement were confined more strictly to the things absolutely needful for the general success and advantage, and this not because the settlers could not appreciate the artistic and beautiful but because of the straitened circumstances in which they were placed. Of their ability to appreciate elegance and cultivated taste there is sufficient evidence in the laying out the village plot and its subsequent improvement. The first location of the company which came from Wethersfield, consisting according to tradition, of fourteen or fifteen families, was around or near Sandy Hollow where the first meeting-house was erected; then with much deliberation, apparently, they arranged and laid out the plan of the village by opening the highways, very much as they are to-day, only the streets at first were somewhat wider; especially Front street, now Elm.

The first record found in regard to public convenience, is concerning a ferry: "The motion made by Mr. Ludlow, concerning Moses Wheeler for keeping the Ferry at Stratford, is referred to such as shall keep the next court at Fayerfield, both in the behalf of the Country and the Town of Stratford."[o] The Fairfield Court gave a favorable order, for the ferry was established, and running as appears by the fol-

---

[1] Mather's Magnalia, ii. book 6, p. 390.

[m] Conn. Col. Rec. iv. 76 note, and 79. T. Lord's Scrap-book.

[n] The authority for this reported case has not been seen. Mr. C. H. Hoadly, in preface to Col. Rec., vol. vi. says, there was but one subsequent indictment, namely, that of two females in Wallingford in October, 1697, upon which the Grand Jury returned, "ignoramus."

[o] Col. Rec., i. 163.

lowing town record: "April 14, 1653. In consideration that the passage to the ferry was stopped up the town gave order to the townsmen to pull up the fence and make way for passengers where they had laid out the way formerly and they promised to bear them out in that act." The ferry continued in the Wheeler family three generations at least.

A mill to grind grains was one of the first public improvements, and being attended to before the year 1650, the present records contain no account of the time, or manner of building it, but a record of Nov. 7, 1671, informs us that it was in existence, for a division of the land between the mile-path and the fence " was ordered. The mill was a tidewater mill and stood on Nesumpaws creek, southwest of the village of Stratford, probably, on the east side of the creek.

In 1652, the town by vote made a proposition for another mill, and John Hurd and Thomas Sherwood entered upon the work, and two years later the enterprise was established as follows: " Jan. 5, 1654. John Hurd and Thomas Sherwood in consideration of the expense laid out for the making and keeping a mill to grind the town's corn, do require the town to give them forty acres of upland lying as near the mill as may be, bounded as followeth; the creek eastward of it, the common highway on the north, the commons west and southward; and three spots of meadow a little below the mill; all which is granted by the said townsmen.

PHILIP GROVES,		JOHN HURD,
THOMAS FAIRCHILD,	*Townsmen.*	THOMAS SHERWOOD."
RICHARD BUTLER,		
JOHN WELLS.		

These items were all according to the proposition made by the town, in 1652, and the mill stood at what is now the east end of Old Mill Green. The town required that the land should not be sold from the mill; that if either partner desired to sell the property, he should give the town the first chance to buy; and that the millers who were to have the sixteenth part of the corn they should grind, should use a measure provided by the town—" an even and just measure," so that " when it was stricken it may be just the sixteenth part of a bushel."

Public School was another enterprise entered upon by town vote to the following effect:

"1650. It was agreed by the town that they would give £36 by the year to a schoolmaster, the town to bear one-half and the parents of the children the other half." The same vote was passed the next year, and the same enterprise has characterized the township to the present day.

A proposition having been presented to the Commissioners of the United Colonies in 1644 to take collections yearly for the "poor scholars at Cambridge," it was approved by all, and committees were appointed for each town in Connecticut, and that for Stratford consisted of William Judson and John Hurd. Thus early and benevolently did the plantations unite in efforts for general education; and the higher, classical schools as well, for where these latter are neglected .the others are.

The first select school of the place was inaugurated, probably, in obedience to a town vote, March 17, 1670, "that the present townsmen shall endeavor by inquiry to see if there be children sufficient in the town whose parents are free to place them to school, that there may be encouragement to endeavor the obtaining a schoolmaster and endeavor to procure either Mr. Mitchell, Mr. Benj. Blakeman, John Minor, or any other suitable person."

Taxes were of small amount compared with those of the present day, but were very burdensome at the time'; and were paid in produce and not in money; the produce was shipped to Boston, New York, Barbados and the West Indies. Barbados was the principal market for grains outside of the coast, and Alexander Bryan, of Milford, was the great shipping merchant for thirty or more years from the settlement of Milford in 1639. There was no leading shipping merchant at Stratford; the man who approached nearest to it was Joseph Hawley, followed more prominently by his son, Samuel Hawley, a few years later.

The taxes were accepted in grains, and hence the government fixed the price of each yearly, and that price was the standard for exchange and private dealings.

Stratford was not taxed, probably, for the general government until 1645, and for several years afterwards Stratford
and Fairfield rates were collected together, or as of one plantation. The General Court order in 1646, that the rates of
Stratford and Fairfield should be divided, but they were
reported together after that.[1]

The assessment for Taxes by the Connecticut Colony, May 9, 1647, was for
£150, and Hartford, Windsor, Wethersfield. Seabrook and Farmington, only, are
mentioned in the list.

Grand List of Connecticut, Jan. 25, 1648.

Hartford,	£35 : 10	Farmington,	£ 8 : 00
Windsor,	24 : 10	Long Island,	5 : 00
Wethersfield,	24 : 00	Fairfield and Stratford,	20 : 00
Seabrook,	8 : 00		

Grand List of Connecticut, October, 1651.

Hartford,	£22404 : 19	Seabrooke,	£4150.
Windsor,	15435	Fairfield,	8895 : 3
Wethersfield,	12748	Stratford,	7118 : 8 : 6
Farmington,	4741		
			£75492 : 10 : 6

Grand List of Connecticut for the year 1652, October.

Hartford,	£19733 : 19	Seabrooke,	£3630 : 00
Wyndsor,	14093 : 00	Stratford,	7040 : 19
Wethersfield,	11499 : 00	Fairfield,	8850 : 15
Farmington,	5164 : 00		
			£70011 : 13

Grand List of Connecticut for October, 1653.

Hartford,	£19749	Norwake,	£1968
Windsor,	15084	Matabezek,	1501
Wethersfield,	12243	Pequet,	3334
Farmington,	5157	Fairfield,	8822
Seabrook,	4268	Stratford,	7450 : 19

Stratford Harbor, or, according to the more recent
name, Mack's Creek, from a negro of that name who made it his
business to gather and sell oyster shells to make lime—there
being no stone lime in that place at that time. His daily
work was to go down the harbor and obtain a canoe load of
shells and return, and in this way keep a supply for sale on

[1] For comparison, the Grand Lists of Connecticut for a few years are here
given.

the north point at the mouth of this creek, and hence the name Shellkeep Point, as the locality is still called.

At first there was deep water at the mouth of this creek, but the building of the wharf into the channel of the river, a quarter of a mile north, turned the current so that it became muddy south of the wharf down to the mouth of the creek, and hence all the sedge grass land at that place has been made since the settlement began. This creek was once so deep that Capt. Gorham used to winter his schooner of 200 tons burthen in it. He lived on the corner of the high ground a few rods north of the creek, the point now called Prospect Hill. On this site Mr. Nathan B. McEwen,[10] a descendant of Capt. Gorham, was born April 23, 1806, and from whom a number of interesting facts and historical narratives have been obtained.

Sometime before the year 1800 a dyke was made across this creek so that the water could not pass, but so much sickness of dysentery and typhus fever followed, that in 1805 the town voted to remove it, and leave the creek open. After it was opened and the salt water let in, there came to the surface out of this ground great quantities of worms, and their decay caused more sickness than had been before, but after that year the sickness ceased. In 1860 the dyke was again built and afterwards in dry summers there was considerable sickness as before, for a few years, along the line of the creek.

This harbor was a place of great importance for many years, it being the only place along the river where vessels could find a safe retreat in an easterly storm. The Housatonic river (Indian name was Pootatuck) was a broad sheet of water, with very little if any meadow or sedge grass along its banks, and one island in it, which was granted by the town to Nicholas Knell, for meadow, in about 1650, and which still bears his name, but it was then much smaller than now, according to tradition. It has been stated that the island was not there when the whites first came, but that is sufficiently refuted by the town record of its grant to Mr. Knell.

---

[10] Manuscript of Mr. Nathan B. McEwen.

11

This harbor was particularly advantageous in consequence of the small sized boats used at first and for nearly two hundred years. Boats were very few for many years, but canoes were common, being made of one pine log, the inside being cut out, sometimes three feet wide and from fifteen to thirty feet in length. These canoes were quite convenient as oyster boats and for fishing, and were in demand until fifty years ago. As late as 1825 many were made in the northern and western part of the State of New York and floated down the Erie canal and Hudson river and brought to New Haven where they brought from sixty to one hundred dollars each, some of them being thirty feet in length and without a knot in them. The oysters were very plenty in the Housatonic river from where the old Washington bridge stood to the Sound, in water from twelve to twenty feet deep, the longest handles to the rakes being twenty-two feet, and the number of bushels taken out in a day being sometimes fifty. Mr. Nathan B. McEwen remembers that one man made a bet that he could take out, in twelve feet of water, in a day, one hundred bushels, but lost his bet by only a few bushels. The oysters then were very large and of rare quality. The shells still dug up from two feet under ground, where they were deposited by the Indians, show their very large size and the gravelly bottom on which they grew, for some of them are very rough or full of indentures made by growing on a gravelly bed. The oysters from here were sold in Boston, New York and other cities as of the best quality. The immense quantities of shells left by the Indians in the fields a little back from the western shore near the mouth of the river indicate the Indian's appreciation of oysters for many generations, but the oysters now opened in one year at Stratford leave more shells, probably, than all left in all past time by the Indians.

Sandy Hollow, near Mack's Creek, was quite a hollow extending west some distance, which is called Sandy Hollow because the sand was deep, at first, and the tide came up the hollow, frequently, some distance. This has been filled by taking off the hill east during the many years that have passed since the first settlement.

Guard Hill, directly in front of South avenue, on the east side of Front, or Elm street, was quite a hill, higher than at present, which was called Guard Hill at the time of the first settlement because it was the parade ground or rendezvous for the guards or soldiers on watch against any attacks by the Indians. The hill extended north some distance from the creek, forming quite a plateau, terminating at the creek in a high bluff of soft sand, which was a noted place for athletic sports, specially of running and jumping, and for children to ride down on sleds. The first meeting house stood at the west end of this high bank, as elsewhere described.

Little Neck lay at the south of Mack's Creek, and was formed by a tide creek on the west which was originally of considerable depth. The north end of this neck was owned, at first, so far as the records now show, by Thomas Uffoot and by him was sold in 1661 to Nicholas Gray, from Flushing, Long Island, who had a tide-mill where the lane or highway crosses Little Neck creek, and to him the town granted, in 1671, another piece of land adjoining on the south if he should maintain his dam wide enough for a passable highway.

CHAPTER VIII.

THE CHURCH OF CHRIST IN

STRATFORD.

HE earliest mention of this Church now discoverable is in a vote by the Milford Church to invite the attendance of the Stratford Church and its aid on the occasion of ordaining "Bro. Whitman" as a ruling elder. The elders of the Church in New Haven were also invited and were present at the ordination, June 26, 1645, at which time Stratford Church was represented by its "pastor and another messenger." It is most probable that this Church was organized in the summer of 1639, the year when Mr. Blakeman and his followers came to the place, and if not, they began their work that year as a company of believers devoted to the Christian cause. The Rev. Adam Blakeman, who had labored as an ordained minister in England, was their pastor and served them about twenty-six years. Whatever church records he kept must have remained among his private papers, and are lost, and the same was true with the Rev. Israel Chauncey's records until 1675, with which year the existing volume commences. Nothing of Mr. Blakeman's writing is known to be extant except a paper drawn in 1665 by the Rev. Israel Chauncey as his assistant minister, which he subscribed.

No list of the membership, nor of the officers are found but the following names as the Deacons have been ascertained.

The Ruling Elder and Deacons[1] of the Congregational Church of Stratford.

Philip Groves was the first and only Ruling Elder in this Church from 1640 to his death in 1675.

Deacons:

John Birdseye.	Ebenezer Coe.
John Wilcoxson.	Nathan McEwen.
Thomas Wells.	Samuel Uffoot.
Robert Walker.	Agur Curtis.
John Thompson.	Philo Curtis.
Ephraim Judson.	Agur Curtis 2d.
—— Peat.	David P. Judson.
Elnathan Wheeler.	Agur Treat Curtis.
Israbiah Brown.	Lewis Beers.

The first sexton and bell-ringer was John Peat, the first of the name in Stratford, called in those days in a friendly way Goodman Peat. He held this office until 1660, when John Pickett was elected by the town to fill the place.

The First Meeting house stood on the east side of Front, now Elm street, at Sandy Hollow, on the southeast corner. This house must have been very plain, and of small dimensions, but there are no records by which its size or height can be ascertained. It was built without a gallery at first, for the following vote is recorded: " Feb. 4, 1661. It was agreed that there shall be a gallery builded in the meeting house in the convenient place."

The first burial ground was adjoining the meeting house and burials were probably made there until the new ground, which was laid by the town in 1677, was opened where it now is, in 1678, west of Main street. The grave stones standing at the old place were removed to the new. In the excavations made at the old ground since it was abandoned several skeletons have been exhumed. Quite many graves were made without head stones and no traces of them were to be seen when the removals were made, and hence after more than a hundred years some bones were found in digging a well that is still in existence near the barn standing on the old site.

---

[1] Manuscript of the Rev. B. L. Swan.

12

The almost total obliteration of this burying place is symbolical of the life of man, and our reflections, while melancholy, may be instructive. In the graveyard are still a few plain stones which were removed from the old ground, with rude inscriptions, consisting simply of initials of a name with a date such as, " E. B., March 9, 1652." Whom did men bear to his lowly rest beneath this monument, two hundred and fifty-two years ago? Was it a stranger, or did he or she belong to one of the families of Blakeman, Burritt, Booth, Bostwick, Beardsley, or Beach? Another is " J. H. 1690, Æ. 100." Who was this, born in 1590, somewhere amid the troublous times of the Mother Country, when the fires around the martyrs' stake had but just gone out? And yet another —" J. H., June 25, 1691," without the age. Others have no monumental letters,—only the date, as : " March, 1684," and " January, 1691 ;" and others there were, barely a stone, weather-chafed, shapeless, and yielding to most curious inquisition only defaced particles of an inscription, in which no letter or figure can be determined.' How much is it to be regretted that these stones do not tell us more about those who fell in a strange land, the first sacrifices for a liberated conscience and an enlarged freedom. How pleasing the thought that man but begins, in this life the high and noble purpose for which he is created, and looks forward to a larger sphere of activities and enjoyments, as set forth in the beautiful words of Everett in his commemoration of the decease of the great Webster : " The wakeful eyes are closed, the feverish pulse is still, the tired and trembling limbs are relieved from their labors, and the aching head is laid to rest upon the lap of its Mother Earth, like a play-worn child at the close of a summer's day ; but all that we honored and loved in the living man begins to live again in a new and higher being of influence and fame."

What Happened in the first Meeting House.

The first sexton, so far as known, was John Peat, called " Goodman Peake," and " Goodman Pickett " was elected by

---

' Manuscript of the Rev. B. L. Swan.

the town in 1660, to fill the place which Mr. Peat had resigned and a part of the instructions given him, besides ringing the bell, were these: " And also to watch over the disorderly persons in the meeting and use his discretion in striking any person whom he finds so disorderly." In this they had con- ferred two offices upon him, for in November the year before the town appointed Henry Wakelee to "watch over the youths or any disorderly carriages in the time of public exer- cises on the Lord's day or other times and see that they behave themselves comely, and note any disorderly persons by such raps or blows as he in his discretion shall see meet."

In 1666, Hugh Griffin was appointed to oversee the youth in the gallery or without doors," and if any did con- duct disorderly he was to report the same "to the parents and masters;" and the next year Esbon Wakeman was appointed to this difficult office.

In December, 1678, when they had commenced to build a new meeting house Thomas Jefery was chosen to keep order in the time of public service.

The bell spoken of above was in use in 1660, but how much earlier is not known. It is said to have been the first church bell in the State, and must have been brought from England, since it could not have been made at that day in this country. It would be an item of history of much interest and some curiosity to know how it was secured and when brought here.

Progress in the Settlement of the Township.

After the settlement of the right to the soil in the town in 1659, and some satisfaction made to the Indians the next year, the settlers of Stratford extended their work of division, laying out and settlement of the township with, apparently, new energy and enterprise. In view of this a town meeting was called and the following was a part of its doing:

"Jan. 3, 1661. It was voted that all the inhabitants shall have liberty to take up a whole division of land in the woods for planting land anywhere within the bounds of Stratford where he can find fit land, provided it be not within two miles of the town, and also all such who do take up land in this way are prohibited from making it their dwelling place, but by the consent of the town; and they have chosen by a vote Philip Groves, William Curtis and Joseph Judson to lay it out unto particular men according as they desire it."

It is probable that at this time there were no families residing two miles from the village of Stratford, in the town, unless it was at Farmill river, and it is quite uncertain if any were there. The hop garden had been cultivated in that vicinity but probably by persons residing in the village.

Neither were there any residents at Pequannock, or Stratford land on the west side of the Pequannock river. A family or two were residing probably at the mill at what is now the east end of Old Mill Green, and also at the tide mill at the Eagle's Nest, or as it was frequently called in those days, Old Squaws. There may have been, also, a few families residing out of the village a short distance north or upon Clapboard Oak Hill, but it is quite doubtful; yet within eight or nine years after 1661, the residences beyond two miles from the village had become quite numerous.

In January, 1664, the town voted that the "land between Pequannock river and the bounds between Fairfield and Stratford shall be laid out by division to the inhabitants of the town, fronting on the country highway." This highway was on the line, now Park avenue and the road up Toilsome Hill; and it is said "the lots to run three or four miles;" that is, extend along the road northward that distance. Previous to this there had been many pieces of land laid out to different men in the Pequannock field which lay south of Golden Hill, there having been a fence made along the boundary line, and hence the above division was largely if not wholly northward of what is now Fairfield avenue. Parcels of land had been laid to a number of individuals before 1661, at Oronoke and at Farmill river, but very few if any residences had been erected upon them.

The town having had considerable prosperity, and having made good progress as to the laying out and clearing up land, and establishing additional settlers, turned its attention to the needs of the Church, in the winter of 1665–6.

" March 5, 1665-5. The town being together at a lawful meeting, propounded whether or no the town will lay out a house lot out of the sequestered land, and fence it and build a comfortable house upon it and lay a considerable quantity of meadow and upland to it, as need shall require, for the use of the ministry to continue for ever for that end and use ; and this was the vote of the town that it should be so performed."

An entry, afterwards erased, adds "there was a clear vote, for there was not one blank, yet a considerable part of the town would not vote, not that they were against the ministry but the ambiguousness of the vote."

Since Mr. Blakeman had his house and land, which he had possessed more than twenty years, this vote could have no purpose but that of obtaining another minister, although as yet they had not voted to secure one.

This parsonage lot was taken out of the highway or public green at the southeast corner of Watchhouse Hill, near the site afterwards of the second meeting house. .

The Rev. Adam Blakeman had served this church from its settlement here in 1639. until the end of the year 1665—a pastorate of 26 years—without intermission or failure of health, apparently, unless just at the last, and without difficulty or trouble in his office. At this time the town saw fit to move in the direction of relief to their aged minister and a more ample supply of their needs as a parish or society. It was the movement of the town and not the Church, and hence the following vote :

" April 20, 1665. At a lawful meeting the town did consider the giving Mr. Chauncey a call to help Mr. Blackman in the ministry for a year ; and they agreed by vote. The word given was to draw to the west side of the meeting house, and it was clearly manifest to be the major part to give him a call for a year."

There is no evidence that he had been in the place before this vote, or that anything had been done previously to secure any other man as a supply. Mr. Chauncey was obtained and after about two months we find another record :

" June 1, 1666. At a lawful town meeting, the inhabitants being generally present, a paper was offered containing divers propositions to Mr. Israel Chauncy in order to a mutual agreement for his settling amongst us in Stratford ; the paper being dated with this present meeting, June 1, 1666. It was voted and agreed that the said paper should by the townsmen of Stratford be subscribed in the name of the town and presented to Mr. Chauncy."

This proceeding was in perfect harmony with the practice of other towns at that time, for the town employed and paid the ministers. If the records of this Church were preserved, we should find a vote by it, on the question of settling a pastor but not as to hiring him as a supply.

The paper addressed to Mr. Chauncey by the town, signed by the selectmen, is as follows:[1]

"Mr. Chancy: We, a Christian people, by the providence of God settled together in this plantation of Stratford, judging it our duty, as from the command of God, so from our own necessary spiritual and eternal good, to endeavor after, maintain and uphold a minister orthodox in doctrine and practice that the word of life and salvation may be held forth unto us, and all the ordinance of God dispensed among us: and whereas you have been some time amongst us, we accounting it reasonable, very necessary, and equal that some mutual agreement be made in a Christian way between you and us, we hereupon think to propound to you for your settling and continuing with us as followeth. We desire that you would perform the work of a minister of the gospel unto us in the preaching of the word and administering of the sacraments. More particularly we desire if all they that profess faith and obedience to the rules of Christ, not scandalous in life, and do present themselves in owning the Covenant, when they have given themselves unto the Lord in baptism, may be admitted and accounted members of the church, and under the care and discipline thereof as other members, and have their children baptized. Notwithstanding we desire not that any thus admitted may approach unto the Lord's Table till on and by examination and due trial they make testimony unto the judgment of Charity of their fitness thereunto. Moreover as God owneth the infant children of believers of the Covenant of Grace, neither doth exclude the same children when grown up from having their standing in the Covenant while they do so walk as they do not reject it. God owneth them and would not have the grace of His Covenant shortened or straightened nor put them from under the dispensation of His grace, giving His ministers a solemn charge to take care of and train up such as a part of their flock: We desiring also that the children of Church members may be accounted Church members as well as their parents, and that they do not cease to be members by being grown up, but that they do still continue in the Church successively until, according to the rules of Christ, they be cast out; and that they are the subjects

---

[1] In the Woodbury History, i. 119, the date of this paper is given as 1669, whereas on the town record it is plainly written as here rendered, 1666. But what is still more surprising is that this paper is used in that work to prove that the Stratford Church did not practice the Halfway Covenant, yet that was the very *one particular thing* it bound Mr. Chauncey to do. The labored effort made in that book to show that Stratford Church had a very wicked feud between 1666 and 1670, would have been commendable, if the author had possessed genius enough to have known or comprehended what the real questions of division were, but as it was, nothing is left to us but simple astonishment.

of Church discipline even as other members, and they should have their children baptized, notwithstanding their present unfitness for partaking of the Lord's Supper.

And further we assure you that without the least suspicion you may credit us that upon your accepting said propositions and granting them unto us we shall, according to our abilities, contribute to your comfortable subsistence amongst us. Expecting an answer from you in time convenient (we) " Subscribe " in the name of the town.

THOMAS FAYRECHILDE,
JOSEPH JUDSON,
HENRY WAKELYN,'
THOMAS UFFOOT."

" This is a true copy taken out of the original and compared this 25th June, 1666, by me. JOHN MINOR, *Recorder."*

It may be observed that this proposition to Mr. Chauncey was made after he had been hired two months and five days; that, by town vote—apparently without dissent—it was ordered to be signed by the selectmen and presented to him; and that it stated plainly the methods of church work and discipline which would be expected of him; and upon this Mr. Chauncey was settled in the town and church as pastor.

The letter shows definitely that the church practiced the Half-way Covenant and intended so to practice. This method of discipline arose thus: The Puritans in England had adopted the principle not to baptize children unless one or both of the parents were members of the church. Soon after settlement at Windsor, Conn., parents were found there who were not members of that church, but were members of the Episcopal Church in England, who desired to have their children baptized here since they could not go to England for it. This question came before the court at Hartford, and finally the practice was adopted to allow persons who were not members of these churches or any others, to have their children baptized upon certain conditions. These were, as stated in this paper to Mr. Chauncey, " not scandalous in life," and who believed the doctrines of these churches—" professed faith and obedience to the rules of Christ." Such parents and their children were taken under the " watch and care of the church," and the children were baptized; but the parents were not to partake of the Communion. Two sacraments were acknowledged—Baptism and the Lord's Supper, and as in this covenant one only was included, the church relation was expressed by the words "Half-way Covenant." In this relation all that was prohibited from such persons was the Lord's Supper, as is evident from the following, in this paper from the parish to Mr. Chauncey, viz: "Notwithstanding we desire not that any thus admitted may approach unto the Lord's Table till on and by examination and due trial they make testimony unto the judgment of Charity of their fitness thereto." That is, until by examination and a knowledge of their lives it should be evident that they were proper persons to come to the Lord's Table.

This Half-way Covenant method of membership, then, was in practice and had been for years in the Stratford church when Mr. Chauncey came here, and the whole expression of the church and the town so far as appears in any record or intimation, was to have it continued.

Soon after Mr. Chauncey was settled as pastor a question of difference arose in his parish which eventuated in the formation of a second church in the town and that church, largely, removed afterwards and settled at Woodbury. The inquiry is, what were the questions which caused the division and trouble? Evidently these, and only these, that the Half-way Covenant members should be allowed to come to the Lord's Table, and that the minister alone should examine the candidates, and receive them into the church. The church hitherto refused these. A small minority now demanded them. The minority were all members in Half-way Covenant, and hence were denied but *one privilege*, and therefore could complain of nothing else, for in their letter to Mr. Chauncey and the Church they say, speaking of what God had done for them,' "and hath given us an interest in himself to be our God, and taken us to be his own, giving us his own discipline and ordinances for our spiritual and eternal good, and owning us hath given us equal right with yourselves in all his ordinances."

' See Woodbury History, vol. i, 115-118.

This letter not being answered as the parties desired, they wrote another in which they say :[4]

"Whereas we have formerly made known our minds unto you in writing, as concerning our desire of communion in all God's ordinances with you, holding forth unto you by way of preface, our right unto them, from the free grace of God owning us externally sealing the privileges of the Cove-

---

[4] *The Minority's First Letter.*

"To Mr. Chancy and the rest of the Church at Stratford.

"Loving brethren and friends, God by his good providence having brought us hither, who are of his church and people, and separated us from the world, and of his free and abundant grace hath taken us and our seed into covenant with himself and with his church and people, and hath given us an interest in himself to be our God, and taken us to be his own, giving us his own discipline and ordinances for our spiritual and eternal good, and owning us hath given us equal right with yourselves in all his ordinances, his providence also having setled us together in this plantation that we might jointly together worshipp him in all his ordinances, and that we should be mutuall helpers of one another in our Christian race. These few lines are to informe you that wee whose names are underwritten doo declare to you our earnest desire to enjoy communion in all God's ordinances with you, that we may together worshipp him according to his holy will ; desiring also that wee and our posterity may be owned as immediate members of the Church of Christ by you ; as Christ owneth us and ours by his own institution, taking us into covenant, and solemnly setting his own seal upon us. We further declare, that owning it to be our duty, and hoping it to be our desire to account you our best friends, who shall use means to convince us wherein we have sinned, and bring us to the sight of our evils ; we desire that if any man being converted according to God's rules, and do not hold forth repentance, then no such person so remaining may be admitted to communion, till he hold forth repentance. And whereas there hath beene difference about the calling of Mr. Chancy, and severall of us have declared our objections against his setling amongst us till those objections were answered, and we judge they never were unto satisfaction ; yet if you shall see cause to answer our earnest and reall desires in the premises, as we hope you will, wee shall pass by what hath been, and endeavor lovingly to close together and walke together according to the rules of God's holy word, hoping and desiring you will so farr respect us as to give us an answer hereunto in writing as soon as you conveniently can.

"Yours in all due respects and desireous of unity according to the rules of Christ.

January 16, 1665-6.

JOSEPH JUDSON,	JOHN MINOR,
RICHARD BUTLER,	JAMES BLACKMAN,
DAVID MITCHELL,	SAMUEL SHERMAN,
HENRY WAKELYN,	DANIEL TITTERTON."

Woodbury History, i. 115.

nant unto us." Thus, clearly, they state the question to be " communion in all God's ordinances with you." In the second letter they state another point, not introduced in the first, thus:

" And if anything did on our part lie in the way, have seriously appointed us a time for examining of us in respect of our faith and knowledge: accounting it requisite that the Minister may take particular knowledge of all those that are to have Communion in the whole worship of God: And herein (to deal *plainly*) that nothing may hereafter be laid as a block in our way, we desire that in this examination by the Minister or Ministers and Elder we may issue in their questioning and examining only."[1]

---

[1] *The Minority's Second Letter.*

"Whereas we have formerly made known our mindes unto you in writing, as concerning our desire of communion in all God's ordinances with you ; holding forth unto you by way of preface, our right unto them, from the free grace of God owning us and externally sealing the privileges of y⁰ Covenant unto us ; have also declared our mindes concerning such letts as may hinder us from proceeding unto such attaynments mentioned in some clauses thereof ; and comeing together to know how you stood affected to our desires, hoped you might have seen good soe farr to have betrusted those yᵗ were to declare your minde unto us as in con-feering with us to take farther knowledge of our desire propounded ; and to putt us in a way of farther proceeding ; should have bin glad soe farr to have bin ten-der by you that they might have took it into consideration. And if anything did on our part lye in y⁰ way, have seriously appointed us a time for examining of us in respect of our fayth and knowledge : Accounting it requisite yᵗ y⁰ Minister may take particular knowledge of all those yᵗ are to have communion in the whole worshipp of God ; And herein (to deal *plainly*) yᵗ nothing may hereafter bee laid as a block in our way ; we desire that in this examination by y⁰ Minister or Ministers and Elder wee may issue in their questioning and examining only. And whereas we have openly, solemnly, wholly and only ingaged ourselves to be the Lord's, who hath graciously taken us into Covenant with himself and *his faithful* people ; we desire, yᵗ in the owning hereof, wee may not be further trouble with any imposition of that nature. The exercise of your tenderness unto us wee cannot but hope for, according as you are allowed. Ro. 14:1.

February 9th, 1665–6.

Joseph Judson,   John Minor,
Richard Butler,   James Blackman,
David Mitchell,   Samuel Sherman,
Henry Wakelyn,   Daniel Titterton."

Woodbury History, i. 116.

Here they make a condition or demand, that in owning the Covenant the minister or ministers and elder shall be the only parties admitted to the examination. They go further and with scorn stigmatize the examination before the Church, which was the custom then, an "imposition," thus:

"And whereas we have openly, solemnly, wholly and only engaged ourselves to be the Lord's, who hath graciously taken us into Covenant with himself and *his faithful* people; we desire that in the owning hereof, we may not be further troubled with any imposition of that nature."[4]

These letters were written in January, 1665-6, a short time after Mr. Chauncey's settlement, and to them a reply was sent the next April which shows that the particular questions at issue were the communion and examination of candidates by the minister alone:

"Whereas we received from you two writings, the sum of both which was to hold forth your earnest desire as to communion in all the ordinances of Christ with us, These are to give you to understand that our apprehension concerning the order of discipline is the same that we have formerly manifested it to be, both by our practice and answer to your proposals. And whereas you apprehend you have equal right with ourselves in all the ordinances of Christ in this place, these may certify you at present that we are of a different apprehension from you in that matter."[5]

---

[4] The italics are in the original.

[5] "*Church Answer to the Men.*"

"Neighbors, whereas wee received from you two writings the sum of both which was to hold forth your earnest desire as to communion in all the ordinances of Christ with us, These are to give you to understand that our apprehension concerning the order of discipline is the same that we have formerly manifested it to bee, both by our practice, and answer to your proposalls. And whereas you apprehend you have equall right with ourselves in all the ordinances of Christ in this place, these may certifie you at present that we are of a different apprehension from you in that matter. And whereas you desire that your posterity may: etc wee would put you in mind that as yet the matter is in controversie among the learned and godly. Likewise whereas you seem to intimate in the close of your first page that you have taken offence at our late proceedings, but as you say upon the granting of the premises are willing to pass it by; we return no more at pres-

The minority mention only one condition as ground of reception, viz: that of repentance, in their first letter, but claim membership by virtue of birth-right: "desiring also that wee and our posterity may be owned as immediate members of the Church of Christ by you."

Hence their views of membership were those, very nearly, of the Episcopal Church, except as to confirmation, and this they doubtless would have accepted very readily at the hands of a Bishop.

The Rev. Adam Blakeman died somewhere between April, 1665, and the next January, and hence Mr. Israel Chauncey was installed that year as pastor, and on Dec. 18, 1666, by town vote, his salary was fixed at sixty pounds per annum.

At the same time the town voted to divide the parsonage lot which had been appropriated according to a previous vote

---

ent but this, viz: wee hope if you had sufficient ground so to doo, the godly and learned would have spied it out, and have endeavored to convince us of our evills herein. Lastly, whereas in your latter page you prescribe the way wherein you desired to be attended: viz: you account it requisite: etc: To which we answer in the words of Paul in another case, wee have no such custom nor the churches of Christ with whom we hold communion, and moreover it is practised you know by those whose principles in discipline are farr different from ours. And truly neighbours, as it relates to your case, (notwithstanding wee gladly and heartily desire ye increase and enlargement of yᵉ Church when it may be attained in a rulable and satisfactory way yet) we must plainly tell you that we cannot at present see how it will stand with the glory of God, the peace of yᵉ Church and our and your mutuall edification (which ought to bee deare unto us, and earnestly sought by us) for you t⸴ embody with us in this society: The Apostle Paule exhorts the Corinthians, and so all that walk together in church fellowship: 1 Romans 10, to avoid divisions and to be perfectly joined together in the same mind and in the same judgment, otherwise it is not likely we should keepe the unity of the spirit in the bond of peace, to which we are exhorted, Eph. 4:3. And notwithstanding wee give this answer in generall to you all that were concerned in the pages presented to us; yet you may easily imagine that we have particular exertions as it relates to particular persons whereof we find that we are thereunto called, wee shall manage and desire satisfaction in before they are admitted to communion in all the ordinances.

April 16, 1666.

This is a true Coppe of yᵉ answer
given unto us as it was tryed by both papers.
Church Answer to the men."

Woodbury History, i. 117.

and to give "one quarter part of it to Mr. Chauncey and a quarter part of it to Mr. Peter Bulkley or any other man by that party obtained that now endeavors for Mr. Bulkley."

This is the first record that indicates a division of effort, in the form of another or second church; but the further statement of the vote at this time shows that the matter had matured to a large degree, for it says:

"And that which shall be laid out to Mr. Chauncy, shall by him be improved as his during his life or continuance in Stratford, and in case of removal the said land is to return to the town again. . . . . . It is also agreed in case Mr. Bulkley or any other minister be obtained, he shall have, hold and enjoy his part in every respect as Mr. Chauncy doth.

"It is further agreed respecting a house lot, the reserved land for that purpose shall be equally divided into two lots and Mr. Chauncy is to have his choice which of the two he will please to have."

Upon this agreement of the two parties application was made to the General Court to sanction the division, if there was nothing in the law against it; and the Court granted the request, and directed that "from henceforth they shall all jointly make payment of their proportions towards the maintenance of Mr. Chauncy till there be another minister at Stratford there cohabiting."

During the year 1667 the division made further progress, but as far as any records show took no new form, no violent conflict, other than that given above; and the representations other than here given seem wholly gratuitous. There was a division of sentiment as to church relations and privileges, brought out upon the settlement of Mr. Chauncey and at the decease of their former minister, and it took the form of a separate church within one year, but no legal organization was secured. Had there been any way for the dissenting party to have connected themselves with the Episcopal Church there can be no doubt but they would have done so, for their views were in accord with that Church, and it is probable that something of these views, after this discussion, remained in the community until 1706, when they began to secure services by the Episcopal Church.

The matter of dissention having been brought before the General Court, the advice of that body was rendered, probably, in the latter part of the year 1667, and on March 27, 1668, at a lawful town meeting the advice was "in every particular voted and accepted," and ordered recorded. It had reference not only to Church matters but also to civil rights and liberties ; and occurring as it did directly after the union of the New Haven and Connecticut Colonies, it was of importance to the whole united Colony.

Early in the year 1668, the minority engaged Mr. Zechariah Walker of Jamaica, L. I., to preach to them ; and as Mr. Israel Chauncey had signed a paper accepting the land proffered by the town upon the conditions stipulated ; Mr. Walker also signed a like agreement and acceptance.

These facts placed the two ministers and their parties on equal rights and privileges in law and worship ; but they were very differently situated as to advantages, for the minority had no organization and no meeting house.

The next trouble arose from the application of Mr. Walker and his adherents, for the use of the meeting house during some portion of each Sabbath day, as a place of worship, under the proposition that the two congregations should use the same house, but meet at different hours on the same day. This created more division and excited feeling, apparently, than had been experienced before, for the old congregation declined to grant the request, and that apparently by a large majority.

In accordance with the recommendation of the Court, a complete list of the proprietors of the town was made, on the 27th of March, 1668, just in the midst of these difficulties, and by it and Mr. Walker's report of the organization of his church the relative strength of the parties may be seen.

The Inhabitants of Stratford in 1668.

"*A list of the Inhabitants of Stratford,* drawn up by the townsmen and recorded by order from the Govenor and Mr. Jones and Mr. Stowe 27th March, 1668, as followeth and diligently recorded by order from the present townsmen this 28th March, 1668 :

1. Mr. [Samuel] Sherman.
2. Mr. [Thomas] Fairchild.
3. Mr. [Israel] Chauncey.
4. Mr. [Zech.] Walker.
5. Lieut. Wm. Curtis.
6. Elder [Philip] Graves.
7. Ensign Jos. Judson.
8. John Birdseye, Senʳ.
9. John Minor.
10. Nathˡ Porter.
11. John Birdseye, Junʳ.
12. Henry Wakelyn.
13. Jehiel Preston.
14. Mr. Nicholas Knell.
15. John Brinsmayd, Senʳ.
16. Richard Butler.
17. Benjamin Peak.
18. John Curtis.
19. John Peck, Jr.
20. Timothy Wilcockson.
21. Joseph Bearslye
22. Israel Curtis.
23. Arthur Bostick.
24. Caleb Nichols.
25. John Beach.
26. John Wells.
27. James Blackman.
28. John Pickett, Jr.
29. Robert Lane.
30. John Hull.
31. Jabez Harger.
32. Daniel Titterton.
33. Robert Rose.
34. Robert Clark.
35. John Wilcockson.
36. Hugh Griffin.
37. Richard Hurd.
38. Edward Hinman.
39. John Thompson, Senʳ.
40. John Thompson, Jr.
41. Moses Wheeler.
42. Francis Hall.
43. Esbon Wakeman.
44. Samuel Sherman.
45. Joseph Hawley.
46. Adam Hurd.
47. Henry Tomlinson.
48. Richard Boothe.

49. John Hurd, Jr.
50. Isaac Nichols.
51. Sergᵗ. Jeremie Judson.
52. Sámuel Bearslye.
53. John Pickett, Senʳ.
54. Thomas Uffoot.
55. James Clark.
56. John Peacock.
57. John Hurd, Senʳ.
58. Mr. David Mitchell.
59. Stephen Burritt.
60. Samuel Blackman.
61. John Bearslye.
62. Samuel Stiles.
63. Ephraim Stiles.
64. Thoˢ. Sherwood's children.
65. Thomas Wells.
66. John Wheeler, ⎫
67. Obadiah Wheeler, ⎪ *Outlivers,*
68. Hope Washburn, ⎬ *i. e. out*
69. Theophilus Sherman, ⎪ *of the*
70. Matt. Sherman, ⎭ *village.*

Admitted freeholders Jan. 1, 1668.
71. Thomas Kimberly.
72. Samuel Fairchild.
73. Thoˢ. Fairchild, Jr.
74. John Brinsmade, Jr.
75. Daniel Bearslye.
76. Jonathan Curtis.
77. John Judson.
Were by the townsmen ordered
to be recorded Outlivers,
March 3, 16⅞⅞.
78. Samuel Gregory.
79. James Pickett.
80. Benjamin Beach.
81. John Bostick.
82. Henry Summers.
83. Jonas Tomlinson.
84. Danˡ. Brinsmade.
85. John Burritt.
86. Widow Bearsley wife of Thomas B.
87. Mrs. [Adam] Blackman.
88. Widow Titterton.
89. Widow Bearslye, wife of William,
half proprietor of house lot
and accommodations."

This list gives 85 men, and if all were allowed to vote in a Society meeting, then the list includes both parties as to legal votes.

In the Woodbury History is an account given by the Rev. Mr. Walker of the organization of his Church at Stratford, May 1, 1670, and according to it the Covenant was taken that day by 20 persons, to whom 7 were added in a few days, making 27 in all, and omitting Mr. Walker himself, 26. Of the whole number 7 were not inhabitants, and could not vote in town meeting. Hence the number of Mr. Walker's voters to those opposed was 19 to 65.

Two years Mr. Walker and his people continued their work in Stratford under great difficulties, when the project of colonization to Woodbury arose and was soon after effected in a very commendable and successful manner. When settled in Woodbury they adopted the Halfway Covenant system of church relations and government, the same as the Stratford Church had pursued, probably, all the years of its existence before 1670, and which it followed, probably, about one hundred years later.

CHAPTER IX.

PROGRESS AMIDST DIFFICULTIES.

URING the years from 1650 to 1670, great changes took place in the town of Stratford. The purchasing of the lands from the Indians and the consequent proposition for extending the settlement; the decease of several prominent men and the incoming of new settlers; the differences which arose as to the privileges of the halfway covenant church members, resulting in the organiza-tion of a second society for public worship; the union of Connecticut and New Haven Colonies, and the taking of New York from the Dutch ;—all these had placed the community upon a new stage of social, religious and civil life.

The territory opened for settlement by paying the Indians for various tracts of land extended north into what is now Huntington and Trumbull, and west to Fairfield bounds. Different parties had become interested in these purchases by paying the Indians, in behalf of the town, and they desired to secure the return of their money by the division and sale of the land to old and new settlers, and this awakened a spirit of enterprise and progress to the extent that new settlers were not only made welcome but invited to come in, and the territory seemed so large that a proposition was made in 1670, and a petition presented to the General Court, to organize a separate plantation at Farmill river within the bounds of Stratford.[1]

---

[1] "October, 1670. Whereas, Mr. Sherman hath motioned to this Court in the behalf of some of the inhabitants of Stratford, that they might have liberty and

13

The Stratford company was organized at Wethersfield and Hartford in the beginning of the year 1639, and tradition says it contained fifteen or seventeen families. They began the settlement that Spring at what was afterwards called the harbor, in Stratford village, and in the Autumn of that year military drill was established under the command of Francis Nichols, acting as captain.

The land records as they now exist were commenced, probably, in 1652, and all dates prior to that were entered at that time or later. It is quite doubtful as to there having been any records in this town previous to that date, but if there were they have been lost or destroyed.

The law providing for such records and a town clerk to keep them was enacted in 1639, and provided such penalties as to make it hazardous for any town to neglect the matter twelve years, as must have been the case if Stratford made none but those now possessed.

The record of each proprietor's surveyed land, being entered in 1652, there are two forms of expression used which designate the first proprietors from those who came after. Of the first of these it is said he " hath a home lot," but of the second it is said, " hath purchased a home lot." Hence when the town clerk recorded his own lot, probably in 1652, he said: "Joseph Hawley hath purchased of Richard Mills, a home lot, 2 acres, bounded with the street on the east, John Blakeman west, Adam Hurd on the south, and a highway north." In this case Mr. Hawley appears to have purchased the whole Right of Mr. Mills as well as the home lot.

This was the only form of land records in the early settlement of the place.

Besides the above evidence as to the first families, nearly

---

encouragement to erect a plantation at or near a river called the Farmill river, and the lands adjacent, this Court refers the consideration of this motion to Capt. Nathan Gold, Mr. James Bishop, Mr. Thomas Fitch, and Mr. John Holly, and they are desired and appointed to view the said lands, and to meet sometime in November next, to consider of the aforesaid motion, and to labor to work a compliance between those two parties in Stratford; and if their endeavors prove unsuccessful then they are desired and ordered to make return to the Court in May next what they judge expedient to be attended in the case." Col. Rec., ii. 141.

all other early settlers in this town are found residing elsewhere in the year 1639. In a previous part of this book, all settlers before 1651 are spoken of as first settlers, but those included more than the first company formed at Wethersfield.

Most of these seventeen families had been in America four or five years, looking for a final location as a home for life, and it must have afforded a sense of rest and satisfaction when they planted themselves on the western shore of the great river, then known only as the Pootatuck, as their final earthly home. And yet it was not like home to them, but as unlike as was possible to be.

Apparently they had all left many friends and kindred whose faces they would have been glad to have seen after these several years of wandering in the new world instead of stopping among the Indians. Some of them, if not all had relinquished comfortable homes and possessions, but when landed at Stratford they had not a shelter nor a covering for the night, probably, unless they accepted hospitality in the Indian wigwams, of which there is no tradition. They may have sent on a part of their company early in the Spring to prepare some houses or places for temporary dwelling, but the company was organized so late in the winter that there was but little time before the important work of planting demanded all their labor and skill, and therefore but small preparations could have been made, however diligent and energetic their efforts.

And all this, for what? To escape religious oppression. Much has been written with a purpose to indicate that that oppression was of little consequence—largely imaginary, and soon forgotten, but no unprejudiced mind can read a tenth part of the historical proof of the trerribleness of that oppression without a shudder of horror and wonder.

But in their minds at least there must have been a great pressure, to drive them 3000 miles across a mighty ocean, with families of children, into a wilderness country such as they knew this was. If the emigrating companies had consisted only of men, as in the recent exodus to California in 1849, the case would have been very different and might have been stimulated solely for gain.

Fortunately, however, for the world, whatever the sad or hopeful experiences through which they had previously passed, they came, and through them the nations have been and are honored.

The First Families of Stratford, Connecticut.

1 Rev. Adam Blakeman.	*10 William Judson.*
2 William Beardsley.	*11 Francis Nichols.*
3 William Willcoxson.	*12 John Peat.*
4 Richard Harvey.	*13 Robert Seabrook.*
5 Elizabeth Curtiss.	*14 Thomas Sherwood.*
6 Thomas Fairchild.	*15 William Crooker.*
7 Philip Groves.	*16 William Quemby.*
8 John Hurd.	*17 Arthur Bostwick.*
9 Richard Mills.	

It is possible that this list should be varied a little, but from the best light after very close study, it seems to be correct.

There were no settlers here in 1638, as supposed by Dr. Trumbull.

These seventeen families consisted of the following persons:

1 Rev. Adam Blakeman, his wife and six children,	8 persons.
2 William Beardsley, his wife and four young children,	6 persons.
3 Wiliam Willcoxson, his wife and three young children,	5 persons.
4 Richard Harvey and his wife,	2 persons.
5 Widow Elizabeth Curtiss and two sons, young men,	3 persons.
6 Thomas Fairchild and his young wife,	2 persons.
7 Philip Groves and wife,	2 persons.
8 John Hurd, probably his wife and son Adam,	3 persons.
9 Richard Mills, his wife, sister of Caleb Nichols, and son Samuel,	3 persons.
10 William Judson, his wife and three sons.	5 persons.
11 Francis Nichols and his three sons,	4 persons.
12 John Peat, his wife and two children,	4 persons.
13 Robert Seabrook, probably no wife,	1 person.
14 Thomas Sherwood, his wife and six children,	8 persons.
15 William Crooker and wife, perhaps children,	2 persons.
16 William Quemby, his wife, two children, perhaps others,	4 persons.
17 Arthur Bostwick, probably his wife and one son,	3 persons.

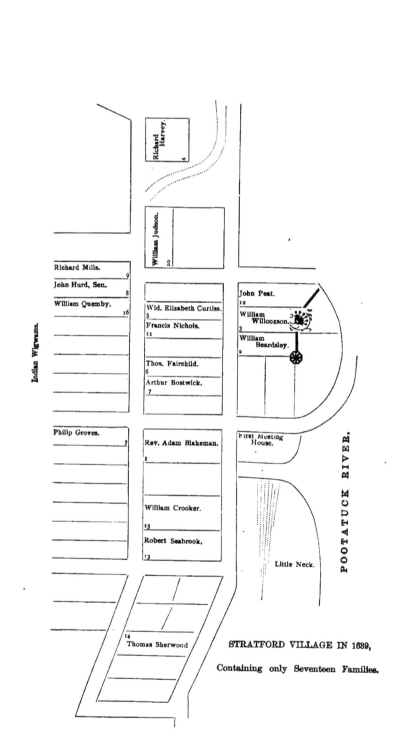

STRATFORD VILLAGE IN 1639,

Containing only Seventeen Families.

This was the company that came from Wethersfield through the wilderness to Stratford on foot and horseback, and tradition says, forded the Housatonic river somewhere above Stratford village. What few articles of household goods, if any, which were too heavy to bring on horseback were doubtless sent around by water.

Their encampment on the plain—then an Indian field— near the harbor must have been picturesque as compared with the present. Possibly they had some tents for temporary shelter and then built themselves wigwams or log houses. What they suffered in the chilly Spring winds and rains has not been recorded although, no doubt, it was often repeated to their successors for many years following.

Probably new planters came the next year; and thereafter, nearly every year, until 1675. In 1650 there were about fifty families in the town, several others having come and removed.

These families were all, probably communicants in the English or Episcopal Church when they left their native land, and brought their certificates as such, with them to America. In the list of the ship that brought three families that settled in Stratford—William Beardsley, William Willcoxson and Richard Harvie, it is said : " the parties have certificates from the minister of St. Albans in Hertfordshire, and attestations from the justice of the peace according to the Lord's order." [1] These certificates as communicants, and attestations of loyalty—they having taken the oath of loyalty— by the justice, were a prerequisite to the privilege of emigration. The Rev. Adam Blakeman himself was not only a communicant, but a regularly ordained minister of the English Church in good standing, having been suspended from officiating as a clergyman, for *nonconformity* to a few particular forms of service, then not in the prayer-book. One of these was the requirement that persons while partaking of the sacrament should be in a kneeling position. This kneeling was the form of the Roman Catholic Church in which they taught

---

[1] Page 122 of this book.

the "Worshiping of the Host." This form, the Puritans thought, was idolatry, and therefore refused to observe it.

There were no Presbyterians in Stratford, not even in 1708, when the Saybrook Platform was adopted, so far as any indications set forth.

When, therefore, these first families reached Stratford they organized themselves into a Church with the recognition of neighboring Churches, and called themselves, as did their neighbors also, "a Church of Christ," and these bodies worshiping together as congregations separate from each other, were after about thirty years, in 1669, styled "Congregational Churches." [4]

Richard Booth is not included as one of the first company, because the indications are that he came with his brother-in-law, Joseph Hawley, who came and purchased his first land here about 1650.

William Burritt seems not to have been among the first settlers, in 1639.

Richard Butler, the brother of William, of Hartford, as given on page 108, in this book, lived and died at Hartford, and the Richard Butler of Stratford, was here probably several years before 1651, and was another person than Richard of Hartford.

John Birdseye, in all probability, did not come to Stratford until 1649, as stated in Barber's Historical Collections, since he did not become a land holder here until 1654.

The list of deaths and removals between 1650 and 1670, is as follows, nearly, there having been some deaths, doubtless, before 1650, of which there are no records.

Francis Nichols, William Burritt, John Alsop and William Willcoxson died in 1650 and 1651. Henry Gregory died in 1655, Thomas Sherwood, Sen., in 1655, Robert Coe, Jr., in 1659, William Beardsley in 1660, John Wells, Sen., in 1660 or 1661, Joshua Judson, in 1661. Thomas Uffoot removed to Milford and died in 1660; William Judson removed to New Haven and died in 1662. The Rev. Adam Blakeman died in 1665; Samuel Blakeman died in 1668; Thomas Fairchild,

---

[4] Col. Rec., ii, 109.

Sen., and John Peacock, Hugh Griffin and his wife Dorothy Griffin, died in 1670.

Edmund Harvey from Milford, resided a short time in Stratford and removed to Fairfield, where he died in 1648. John Pettit, probably from Roxbury, Mass., was here about 1651, removed to Fairfield, and he and his wife were deceased in 1684, leaving children, Sarah, John and three younger. Edward Higby was a resident here a short time about 1654, and soon removed. John Reader, John Ferguson, William Read, and John Blakeman, were here but soon removed.

Some sketches of new settlers will be found in the next chapter of this book, the number being about 30 before 1680.

The difficulties which arose in the first church in Stratford, in 1666, in regard to the privileges of the halfway covenant members, resulted in the organization of a second ecclesiastical society in 1668, and a second Church in March, 1670.

The question as to a second ecclesiastical society and church was settled in a most generous and Christian manner by the old society, which was a large majority of the voters of the town, notwithstanding all that has been published to the contrary.

The law of the Colony did not allow an ecclesiastical society to be organized in any plantation, except by permission of the General Court. When the difference of opinion had continued in Stratford a little more than a year, the voters of the town, being most of them members of or in covenant with the old church, made a proposition for settlement with the minority, or those who proposed a second society, which was accepted, and was to take effect at once if the General Court should approve it, and this they did promptly."* It gave one fourth of the sequestered ministry

---

* "Dec. 18, 1666, Voted and agreed that there shall be (in case it be found no ways contradictory to a Court order to have another minister here in Stratford) a laying out of the sequestered land reserved for the ministry—viz: one-quarter part of it to Mr. Chauncy and a quarter part of it to Mr. Peter Bulkley or any other man by that party obtained that now endeavors for Mr. Bulkley ; and that which shall be laid out to Mr. Chauncey shall by him be improved as his during his life or continuance in Stratford ; and in case of removal the said land is to return to the town again ; provided always that the town pay him for what it is bettered by

land to Mr. Chauncey and the other fourth to the minister, whoever he might be,—for one had not then been secured,—of the second society, and that, too, when the voters of that society numbered 19, and those of the old society 65.

All this was done by the parties interested, without any governmental authority whatever.

The Woodbury History opens one of its chapters thus: "The settlement of Woodbury was the result of difference in religious opinions, among the inhabitants of Stratford. It was ushered in by 'thunderings and lightnings, and earthquakes ecclesiastical.'"

There were no "thunderings and lightnings" nor "earthquakes ecclesiastical," in the matter, except such as may have occurred in Woodbury years after.

There were no ecclesiastical or General Court threatenings or fulminations heard of in those days, for the whole arrangement was completed by amicable vote in the town meeting without any outside force or urgency whatever; and was fully settled before Mr. Zecharia Walker preached a sermon in Stratford.

The Woodbury History says Mr. Chauncey "was ordained in the independent mode," which means, if anything, that he rejected the advice and aid of the Association of Ministers, which was then the only ecclesiastical body known in the Colony except the local churches. This statement is wholly without foundation, as is shown by his own letter to the minority, April 16, 1666, in these words: "We have no such custom nor the churches of Christ *with whom we hold communion*," thus showing that he held in highest estimation his relation to the Association, which was the only formal communion of the "Churches of Christ" at that day.

---

his improvement, according as ye town and Mr. Chauncey shall agree, . . . and in case of decease the town is to pay Mr. Chauncy, his heirs, what the whole accommodation, together with the improvement shall be judged, at his decease.

It is further agreed on, in case Mr. Buckley or any other minister be obtained he shall have, hold and enjoy his part in every respect the same as Mr. Chauncy.

It is further agreed on that as respecting a houselot, the reserved land for that purpose shall be equally divided into two lots, and Mr. Chauncy is to have his choice which of the two he will please to have."

It is quite evident that after this arrangement had been made and the minority had secured half of the ministerial lands and the sanction of the Court to be a separate society, that their demand to occupy the meeting house as well as the old society some portion of Sunday, increased very decidedly the difficulties and controversies in the town.

In the next March, 1668, the town "Voted and unanimously agreed on the advice presented to us by our Honored Governor, the Worshipful Mr. Jones [an Assistant], and Mr. Stone, and our respected friends, Mr. Jehu Burr and Mr. John Burr, bearing date the 26th of March, 1668, for our present and future direction, as to inhabitants and their privileges (as also their explication of the first particular, subscribed by the honored Governor and Mr. Jones), every particular being particularly voted and agreed on, every particular was accepted and should be recorded.

John Minor, Recorder."

This advice, given[*] the day before this town meeting was held, consisted of four items and an after explanation, the

---

* *Advice of the Governor and his Associates.*

"1. That the present freeholders, dwelling upon or possessing allowed home lots in propriety be allowed as free planters, and have the privilege of vote in all town affairs ; and the present outlivers on propriety, have the like liberty of vote so far as may properly concern them in point of interest in town affairs, as choice of constable and townsmen, &c., but not in granting of home lots and receiving inhabitants, or the like where they are not concerned.

"2. That for the future none be admitted to privilege of vote as free planters but such as shall be orderly admitted by the town's consent upon certificate and testimony according to law.

"3. That the sons of settled and approved planters be not capable of vote in town affairs until of lawful age and distinct proprietors and planters themselves.

"4. That no transient person or persons, admitted for habitation only or mere tenantship be allowed the privilege of vote in the plantation until orderly approved to be free planters by the town's consent.

"And whereas persons have built upon division land contrary to the town's order, it is not our intent in any thing by us propounded to justify their so doing, but leave the case to the town's consideration, to provide for their own good and to add such penalty for the future to their above said confirmation thereof as they shall see cause.

"26th March, 1668. The contents of this writing we present as our advice to

whole established certain rules to settle the question of legal voters in town matters, and as proprietors in the township. One of these had become an important question in view of the voting in ecclesiastical or society matters, and the other from the fact that some persons had settled on lands which were not yet divided or if divided were not their own.

By these rules some persons were allowed, apparently, to vote in ecclesiastical matters who could not vote in receiving inhabitants or disposing of land.

The practical illustration of these rules may be seen in the following town acts:

" Nov. 22, 1667. Voted and agreed that Thomas Kimberly, sen., may come and dwell in said town after the manner of a sojourner."

" Feb. 5, 1671, William Roberts, by a certificate under the townsmen's hands is ordered to be enrolled as an inhabitant."

" Whereas, John Wheeler hath let his accommodations in Stratford, unto John Levens, and presenting his desire to ye town this 1st January, 1674, that the said Levens be accepted, presenting also a certificate of his blameless conversation according to law; The town voted and consented the same day to his admittance as a tenant."

Soon after or about the time this advice of the Governor and his associates was accepted, the second society secured

---

the inhabitants for their future settlement and peace, and to that end to be confirmed by vote at their next town meeting.

> John Winthrop,
> Wm. Jones,
> Benjamin Stone,
> Jehu Burr,
> John Burr.

" An explication added to the paper of advice, &c.

" It is declared that the inhabitants of the Mill lots are to be accounted and enrolled in the number of the freeholders and not to be looked upon as those who are named outlivers, in the paper presented to the town; and those that are of the outlivers who have also other town proprietors are to be also looked upon and esteemed freeholders.

> John Winthrop,
> William Jones.

March 27, 1668.

the services of Mr. Zecharia Walker as their preacher and established regular services; and having no meeting house, they applied to the first society for the use of their house some part of each Sunday. This was the first house of worship which stood at the Harbor.

The request was rejected at first, and the division in the community became greater than ever; but afterward it was granted, and in 1669, still further granted.[7]

In May, 1669, one year later, the matter went to the General Court by petition, and the Court requested that "till October Court there may be liberty for Mr. Walker to preach once in the day, as they have hitherto done by their agreement, the Church allowing him full three hours between the Church two meetings for the same;"[8] and at the October meeting of the Court the same recommendation was continued, but liberty given for Mr. Walker's people to provide · another place for meeting if it should be found necessary.

Connecticut and *New Haven Colonies* were united in one by a new charter granted by King Charles II. dated April 23, 1662; under which the freemen of the jurisdiction, the "one body corporate and politic in fact and in name," by their representatives, were "annually to hold two general assemblies—one on the second Thursday in May, and the other on the second Thursday in October—to consist of the governor, deputy governor and twelve assistants, with the more popular element of two deputies from every town or city."[9]

---

[7] "May, 1669, Genl Court. Upon the petition of the church at Stratford, this court doth declare that whereas ye church have settled Mr. Chauncey their officer and doe desire that they may peaceably injoy the full improvement of their minister and administrations without hindrance or disturbance, the Court grants their petition therein, only the Court seriously adviseth both parties to choose some indifferent persons of piety and learning to compose their differences and settle an agreement among them, and that till October Court there may be liberty for Mr. Walker to preach once in the day, as they have hitherto done by their agreement, the church allowing him full three hours between the church two meetings for the same."

[8] Conn. Col. Rec., i. 111.

[9] Hollister's Conn. History, i. 209.

This established the General Assembly in place of the old General Court, and constituted a popular government of great constructive force and executive ability ; and was the second "key note " to the government afterwards established for the United States; Ludlow's first constitution of Connecticut being the first. This union affected Stratford but little, since it had been under the Connecticut Colony from the first, but it created some considerable excitement and trouble in New Haven and the plantations in union with it.

New Amsterdam—now New York—had been a troublesome neighbor to the Connecticut and New Haven people, and whoever was most in fault, it is certain that the needless Dutch and Indian war in 1643, was the cause of great excitement, some loss of life and much expense to these two Colonies. This old calamity had not been forgotten in 1653, when by the irritating conduct of the Dutch Governor, the Commissioners of the United Colonies determined on an expedition with 500 soldiers against that government, and of this number of men Stratford was to furnish six and Fairfield eight. After the Commissioners had voted for the war and ordered and proportioned the men and war provisions among the Colonies, the Massachusetts General Court refused to coöperate in prosecuting the war, and the expedition was delayed and finally failed. This was the occasion of some irruption between Stamford and New Haven, because of this delay and failure, and because only church members were allowed to vote in those plantations; and also when Mr. Ludlow—by far the most capable statesman then within the two Colonies, determined to leave the jurisdictions.

When King Charles II. was restored, he gave to his brother, the Duke of York, large possessions in America, and the Duke proceeded to secure possession of his territory by sending in the summer of 1664, Col. Richard Nicolls to take possession of them, and his appearance at Boston created great excitement, the colonists fearing there might be some new trouble, but the only demand that was made was for soldiers to go against New Amsterdam. Col. Nicolls, however, proceeded to his place of destination, and in August of that year the city surrendered, without bloodshed, and it was named New York in honor of the Duke of York."[10]

Woodbury Plantation was settled by a company organized for the purpose at Stratford in the year 1672. The Woodbury History says this settlement " was the result of difference in religious opinions among the inhabitants of Stratford," but it seems to have been the result rather of a spirit of enterprise, progress and ambition to secure comfortable homes and inheritances for their descendants.

The plantation at Derby had been commenced in 1654 by Milford people, and several men in Stratford, namely : Joseph Hawley, Henry Tomlinson, Ebenezer Johnson, Doct. John Hull and Jabez Harger, had become interested in the settlement of that place, by purchases of land from the Indians of the Paugasset tribe.

In 1666, a company had been organized, principally from Milford and Branford, for a settlement at Newark, N. J., and with this movement some of the inhabitants of Stratford had joined.

Individual families had removed at various times from Stratford to Fairfield, Long Island, Westchester, N. Y., New London, Durham and Stonington.

In 1667, Mr. Samuel Sherman, Mr. Thomas Fairchild, Lieut. William Curtis, Ens. Joseph Judson, Mr. Joseph Hawley, John Minor and others had received liberty to establish a plantation at Potatuck, afterwards Newtown, but the enterprise was soon abandoned, for in 1670, the same parties nearly, led by the then comparatively wealthy Mr. Samuel Sherman, petitioned the General Court for liberty to make a plantation at Farmill river, then within the territory of Stratford, which failed, apparently, for want of room.

In 1671, Mr. Henry Tomlinson and others of Stratford, purchased, under a grant from the General Court, territory of nearly 30,000 acres of land for a plantation, at what afterwards became the town of New Milford.

The next plantation proposition was a grant by the General Court, in May, 1672, to " Mr. Samuel Sherman, Lt. Wm.

---

[10] See Hollister's History, i. 228.

Curtice, Ens. Joseph Judson and John Minor, themselves and associates, liberty to erect a plantation at Pomperoage," which was made a grand success in a very short time.

"Early the next spring," fifteen of Mr. Walker's congregation started with their families for the wilderness of Pomperaug." Seventeen had signed the " Fundamental Articles " for the settlement, but two, Mr. Samuel Sherman and Thomas Fairchild, did not remove thither.

The signers were:

SAMUEL SHERMAN, SEN.,   SAMUEL STYLES,
JOSEPH JUDSON, SEN.,   TITUS HINMAN,
JOHN MINOR,   DAVID JENKINS,
ISRAEL CURTISS,   MOSES JOHNSON,
JOHN WHEELER,   SAMUEL MUNN,
JOHN WYATT,   ROGER TERRILL,
JOHN SHERMAN,   ELEAZER KNOWLES,
JOHN JUDSON,   THOMAS FAIRCHILD.
JOSHUA CURTISS,

By this list it may be seen that only two of the original minority of eight" who inaugurated the division of the church at Stratford—Joseph Judson and John Minor—removed to Woodbury, and hence that the removal was more a question of personal interest and civil advantage than of church division.

Other families soon removed from Stratford to Woodbury, and the emigration continued many years. In King Philip's and the Narragansett war, several of the families returned to Stratford for temporary protection until the close of the war, when they again took possession of their homesteads in Woodbury.

This temporary return is proved by a town vote of Stratford in the autumn of 1675, when several of the leading Woodbury men were appointed on the committee to attend

---

11 Woodbury History, i. 35.

12 See page 173 of this book.

to the fortification of the village of Stratford." These men—
Lt. Joseph Judson and Sergt. John Minor, who was reëlected
town clerk and served two years, were among the most
prominent of the Woodbury company, and they with others
of their number were here in Stratford in the autumn of 1675,
and doubtless remained all winter and the next summer, for
in October, 1676, Rev. Zechariah Walker himself being then
at Stratford, with several other of his parishioners addressed
a letter to the General Court seeking special protection if
they should at that time return to Woodbury ; but they did
not all return that year, for some of them remained until into
the year 1678."

King Philip's War, which became largely a war
with the Narragansett Indians, then much the most numerous
tribe in Connecticut and Rhode Island, if not in all New
England, broke out in July, 1675, and continued one year or
a little more.

It was fortunate that the military forces of the Colony
had been well organized during the previous nine years, for
otherwise there probably would have been great slaughter of
the whites in New England.

In May, 1666, the General Court organized the four
counties of Hartford, New London, New Haven and Fairfield, they being the first in the Colony."

---

[13] " Nov. 1, 1675. At a lawful town meeting at Stratford, It was voted and
agreed to, and Capt. [Wm.] Curtiss, Left. Joseph Judson, Sergt. Jere. Judson,
Sergt. John Minor, Sergt. Jehiel Preston, Robert Clark, John Pickett, Sen., were
chosen a Committee to act according to ye order of ye General Court respecting
fortification.　　　　　　　　　　　　　　　　　　　　John Minor, Recorder."

[14] " Nov. 18, 1678. It was voted that that socioty formerly contributing to ye
maintaining of Mr. Chauncey should as formerly allow him seventy pounds, the
other inhabitants that have neglected to contribute to the maintenance of the ministry should pay to Mr. Chauncey in proportion with the rest of that society, to be
aded to the seventy pounds, the others that have yearly payed to Mr. Walker have
their liberty to pay to Mr. Chauncey as much as they please for the year past."

[15] " May, 1666. This Court orders that from the east bounds of Stratford to
the west bounds of Rye shall be for future one County which shall be called the
County of Fairfield. And it is ordered that the County Court shall be held at
Fairfield on the Second Tuesday in March, and the first Tuesday in November
yearly." Col. Rec., ii. 35.

In May, 1673, the militia companies of the towns were placed into county organizations, and a Major appointed for each county, and these were the highest officers in the military ranks at the time, except the Governor. Capt. Robert Treat of Milford, was chosen Major of New Haven county and Capt. Nathan Gold, of Fairfield, Major for Fairfield county.

The train band of Stratford had officers appointed June, 1672, as follows: William Curtiss, Captain; Joseph Judson, Lieutenant, and Stephen Burritt, Ensign; and at the same Court William Curtiss was appointed one of the "Committee for the well ordering of the militia in case of any sudden exigency," for the Colony.

At the same Court it was "hereby declared that till farther order be taken, Captain Nathan Gold shall be deemed chief military officer of the county of Fairfield, and Capt. William Curtice his second."

Also, at the same time, the Court "ordered that 500 dragoons should be forthwith raised; the proportion for Fairfield county was fixed at 120, thus: Fairfield, 38; Stratford, 33; Stamford, 24; Greenwich, 8; Norwalk, 7; Rye being near" is excused; the officers being Thomas Fitch, Captain; Jehu Burr, Lieutenant; Matthew Sherwood, Ensign. Each dragoon was provided with a sword and belt, a "serviceable musket with a shott powch and powder and bullitts."

All these military organizations were preparatory in view of self-defence against any emergency. During the last few days of July, 1675, the disturbances by King Philip's men which had commenced in Massachusetts in the early part of the month, rapidly increased, and on the 6th of August the first draft of soldiers was made—one hundred dragoons from Hartford, sixty from New Haven, and seventy from Fairfield counties, to be ready "at an hour's warning." Drafting men for the militia and collecting provisions, ammunition and arms was continued from this time forward for several weeks. Confusing reports of the hostile movements and the depredations of the Indians near Norwich, Connecticut, and up the

---

[16] This is obscure.

14

Connecticut river, reached the war council, and small parties of soldiers were sent in different directions. Major Treat, with an army of about two hundred men was sent into Massachusetts to aid the forces in that Colony, when an alarming report was circulated that the Paugasset Indians at Derby " were with their arms prepared in a hostile manner," and Mr. Alexander Bryan, of Milford, sent to Hartford for protection, in consequence of which Major Treat was recalled from Massachusetts.

At this time the greatest alarm prevailed throughout the Colonies, and great military exertions were made.

The war Council, Sept. 3, 1675, ordered, "that in the several plantations of this Colony there be kept a sufficient watch in the night, which watch is to be continued from the shutting in of the evening till the sun rise; and that one-fourth part of each town be in arms every day by turns, to be a guard in their respective plantations; to be ordered and disposed as the chief military officers shall appoint; and all soldiers from sixteen to seventy years of age (magistrates, commissioners, ministers, commission officers, school masters, physicians and millers excepted) are to attend their course of watch and ward as they shall be appointed. It is also ordered that, during these present commotions with the Indians, such persons as have occasion to work in the fields shall work in companies; if they be half a mile from the town, not less than six in a company, with their armes and ammunition well fixed and fitted for service." [11]

This put all the capable men of the Colony into the ranks and into the service, and the excitement and calamity were great. One event of war followed another in quick succession. On the 19th of September, the Fairfield dragoons, under Ens. Stephen Burritt of Stratford reported at Hartford and were sent north, the regular army having preceded them; and about fifteen days later while Major Treat and his army were at Westfield, Mass., Springfield was attacked by the Indians, but the Major and his forces arrived in time to save the lives of the people and about half of the buildings of the town; the rest were burned.

---

[11] Conn. Col. Record, ii. 361.

Thus continued the war, the troops marching to New London and Norwich and back, and into Massachusetts and back, great fear and startling reports prevailing. Simsbury was burned, private houses were burned and the families killed, and companies of white people while traveling were massacred in the eastern part of the Colony and in Massachusetts.

Frequent drafts were made for wheat in quantities of one and two hundred bushels from a county; and for January and February, 1676, the amount for Fairfield county was 120 bushels each month.

In October, 1675, upon the reports of the Indians being ready at Narragansett to attack Connecticut, Major Treat was sent in haste to Norwich to take charge of the forces raised in that vicinity and act in defence of the people until other troops should arrive; and each county was required to " raise sixty soldiers, well fitted with horses, arms and ammunition, as dragoons who shall be imbodied for motion in their several counties for the defence of the Colony;" and Capt. Wm. Curtiss was to command those raised in Fairfield, and appoint his inferior officers.

At this time the war cloud thickened fast over the Narragansett Indians, they having, after some hesitancy concluded to join King Philip, and venture their all on the field of war.

On the 23d of November the draft from Fairfield county was 100 bushels of wheat, and 72 soldiers, to be at New London before the 10th of December, the plan being to make an attack on the Narragansett fort in the winter, and thereby make a more complete destruction of the enemy than could be effected at any other season.

The Narragansett "swamp fight" or "fort fight," occurred on the 19th day of December, 1675, when there had just been a great snow fall and the weather was severely cold. The Indian fort was situated in the midst of a dense swamp, but it was finally reached and entered, captured and burned, and 1000 Indians and 200 English were killed and wounded. The Connecticut troops suffered more than the Massachusetts because they entered the fort at the place of the greatest resistance. Of these forces three of their five captains, Seeley, Marshall and Gallop were killed and one other, Mason, mortally wounded; and 40 men were killed or died of their wounds.

The next month a new army was raised and Fairfield county was called upon for 37 men, which were sent forward; and the next May, of an army of 300 soldiers, Fairfield was required to furnish 82, and of wheat 400 bushels.

The draft for meats was in proportion; and the taxes were raised from a penny and a half to twelve pence on the pound throughout the Colony.

Fortunately the war terminated in June and July of that year, king Philip and his brave, terrible warriors having been exterminated.[18]

Of those who distinguished themselves as officers from Stratford, in this Indian War, were Capt. William Curtiss, a faithful, reliable officer; Lieut. Joseph Joudson, mentioned specially as a capable field officer; and Ensign, afterwards Lieutenant Stephen Burritt, who became a distinguished Indian fighter, and was kept much of the time in the saddle with small squads of men hunting roving parties of Indians intent on depredations, along the Connecticut river.

The calamity of such a war falling upon new settlements in a wilderness country may be estimated somewhat from the number of freemen in the Colony. This, in 1669, was only 790.[19] Besides these the number of men from 16 years of age

---

[18] For a carefully prepared, although abbreviated and beautifully written account of King Philip's War, see Hollister's History of Connecticut, vol. i. 253.

[19] The number of Freemen in each of the towns of Connecticut, then incorporated, reported in October, 1669, except Middletown, Lyme and Rye, from which no report is recorded. Col. Rec., ii. 518.

Branford,	8	Killingworth,	19	Stamford,	8
Fairfield,	45	Milford,	46	Stonington,	17
Farmington,	43	New London,	21	Stratford,	64
Guilford,	36	New Haven,	91	Wethersfield,	58
Haddam,	9	Norwalk,	33	Windsor,	126
Hartford,	118	Norwich,	25		——790
		Saybrook,	23		

to 70, subject to military duty who were not yet made freemen, may have been equal to this, but then á draft of 300
would be a very serious matter from 1600 men, but there
were more than double that number called out within the
year the war continued; probably more than 1000 different
men went out in the service.

But this was six years before the war. The list for Oct.,
1676, gives 2303, which was a prosperous increase, notwithstanding the war," and by the grand list for that year it may
be seen how burdensome a tax of 12 pence on the pound
must have been.

Such were some of the interests and calamities which
occupied the attention of the people of Stratford for twenty
years previous to 1680, during which, notwithstanding all the
depletions from various causes, the numbers increased, and
general prosperity attended their labors.

A New Meeting-house was resolved upon only two
years after the close of the Narragansett war, by a town
vote, Nov. 18, 1678, "as soon as may be, for the use of the
town." Several sites were proposed," and at a meeting one

---

⁹⁰ The list of persons and estates for purposes of taxation in each town, in
October, 1676, was as follows:

	Persons.	Estates.		Persons.	Estates.
Hartford,	241	14559	New Haven,	237	12993
Farmington,	102	6128	Milford,	151	8524
Wethersfield,	141	10082	Branford,	48	2579
Windsor,	204	13053	Guilford,	98	6215
Middletown,	94	4811	Wallingford,	43	1660
Haddam,	29	1690	Fayrefield,	152	9428
New London,	153	9061	Stratford,	78	5522
Norwich,	71	4598	Norwalke,	65	4073
Stonington,	79	6016	Stanford,	,81	4673
Lyme,	45	2846	Greenwich,	36	1719
Saybrook,	85	5041	Rye,	32	1591
Kenilworth,	38	2342		Col. Rec., ii. 518.	

⁹¹ "Nov. 18, 1678. Voted that there should be a new meeting-house built as
soon as may be, for ye use of ye town." Five places were mentioned "for ye setting of the meeting-house upon." First, in the street by the pond; 2dly, in the
street by the north-west corner of widow Peat's lot; 3dly, in the street between
"Mr. Hawley and John Beach, their home lots; 4ly, in ye street between Caleb
Nichols and Daniel Beardsley; 5th, upon the hill called Watch-house hill."

The same day it was voted that these places should be decided by lot.

year later, Nov. 25, 1679, they settled the question to build it
on Watch-house hill, facing South down Front street, as then
called. This site was, as it is still, on the public commons.
The dimensions of the house were voted to be "48 feet in
length, 42 feet in breadth and 16 feet between joints;" and
the building committee were "Capt. [Wm.] Curtiss, Sergt.
Jerem. Judson, John Curtiss, Sergt. Jehiel Preston and John
Birdsey, Jr."

On the 10th of December, 1678, they voted to raise a tax
of one hundred pounds "to pay charges about the building of
a new meeting-house."

This meeting-house was built in the summer of 1680, for
the site was not established until November, 1679,[13] and in
September, 1680, it was approaching completion so far that
they proceeded to fix the rules by which it should be seated
as follows:

First, that "every inhabitant in Stratford, both men and
women, shall be seated and placed in the proper seats in the
new meeting-house," and Mr. Samuel Sherman, Sen., Capt.
Wm. Curtiss and Mr. Joseph Hawley, were appointed to seat
the inhabitants. The rules of dignity were established:

"First, Magistrates and Commission officers according
to their place of dignity.

"2ly, that all persons past the age of sixty years should
be accounted honorable, notwithstanding their payments and
be seated accordingly.

3ly, that all other persons under the age of sixty years
should be seated according to their disbursements and payments to the new meeting-house which has been according to
law."

It was, however, nearly three months before the place of

---

[13] "Nov. 25, 1678. It was voted that the new meeting-house should be built
and settled upon the hill commonly called the Watch-house hill.

"At the same time Mr. Israel Chauncey's proposal to the town was that if
they sett the meeting-house upon the hill hee would consent thereto with this pro-
visal that they would allow him one hundred pounds within the compass of two
years after the first meeting in the new meeting-house, and there was good encouragement given him by the town in answer to his proposal." Since Mr. Chauncey's
yearly salary was £80 or more, he contributed so much to the building of the
meeting-house.

worship could be seated, there being some delay in finishing the work.

As to the expenses of the house of worship, there is a bill of items entered upon the town records which includes only a part of its cost, the full sum not being found. The items consist mostly of an account of days' work rendered and wheat received on account. One entry is made that was one of the heavy items at the time: " Due to Mr. Richard Bryan for glass and box £19–14–8."

Wheat was received at the time at five shillings a bushel, and the work of a man was credited two shillings and six pence and three shillings a day.

This meeting-house was afterwards prepared for other purposes than those of worship, as indicated by the following town meeting record:

" Feb. 19, 1689. Voted that the present meeting-house shall be fortified for use as a place of security for women and children in all times of danger by any enemy." This was in obedience to the direction of the General Court the previous year.

Burying-places. — Before the second meeting-house was built or any action taken to secure that end, it became apparent to the people of the town that the first burying-ground was in the wrong place,—could not be extended to meet the wants of the community and that another must be secured. Hence in 1676, the town appointed a committee to select and lay out such a place, but the work was delayed until February, 1677–8, when it was completed.

Of those who died before the new ground began to be occupied, the town records furnish only the following list:

John Knell, son of Nicholas, died Jan. 16, 1651.
[Thomas Sherwood died in 1656.][28]
John Young departed this life Apr. 7, 1661.
Samuel Blakeman (an infant) died January, 1661.
Samuel Blackeman died Nov. 27, 1668.
Abram Tomlinson, son of Henry, died May 30, 1662.

---

[28] This has been placed on record not by the town clerk of that time.

Samuel Blackeman's infant buried January, 1664.

Hannah Griffin, dau. of Hugh, Sen., was buried Apr. 30, 1670.

Dorothy Griffin, wife of Hugh, Sen., was buried Apr. 30, 1670.

Robert Lane, son of Robert and Sarah Lane, died 17th, 1st, 1673-4.

Mary Harger, dau. of Jabez, died Apr. 17, 1673.

Mr. Nicholas Knell died April 2, 1675.

Mr. Thomas Fairchild died Dec. 14, 1670.

Mr. Philip Groves died 10th Feb., 1675.

Joseph Judson, son of Joseph, died Feb. 1, 1677.

James Levens, son of John, died Apr. 23, 1678.

John Peat, Jr., died January 28, 1677-8.

Esther Gelpin, wife of Samuel, died Aug. 27, 1678.

Sarah Birdsey, dau. of John, Jr., died Jan. 21, 1678.

Sergt. Nathaniel Porter died Jan. 14, 1679.

Henry Tomlinson died March 16, 1680-1.

Elizabeth Curtiss, wife of John, Jr., died March 9, 1681-2.

John Hurd, Sen., died Feb. 4, 1681-2.

Elizabeth Porter died Feb. 6, 1683.

" Feb. 13, 1677-8. The townsmen according to town act Feb. 12, 1676, and by town order have laid out. one acre of land on the west end of John Beers his home lot for the use of a burying place, bounded east with John Beers, his home lot and common land, South, West, and North with common land."

This was the place which is now, and for more than a hundred years, has been commonly called the Congregational burying ground. When laid out it was, doubtless, intended for all the people of the town, but many years afterward, when the Episcopal Church was established, another place was laid out which has always been called the Episcopal Burying Ground. Both of these grounds are well filled, and but seldom in these days is a new grave made in them. To walk through them and read the inscriptions is something like a visit to the hearthstones of long remembered kindred, where the house is left vacant. There is a melancholy sadness, and yet a pathetic loveliness about the places where kindred dust sleeps its long and peaceful sleep; and it is not the purpose in transcribing these records, to keep any from these sacred inclosures where lessons of wisdom may be learned, but to place them where they may be the more frequently consulted, and where the rain drops will not obliterate forever the record. Already some of them cannot be wholly read, while others have been deciphered by the assistance of various methods, at the expense of half an hour's time on a single stone.

What a pity there is not a grave-stone for every person that ever died in the town. What a pity, and a shame that such matters are, and have been·neglected, as demonstration now proclaims.

Much ridicule has been made of eulogistic epitaphs, but how much more to be commended such pathetic praise, as if the memory of the departed was not at once forgotten, than not even to mark the place where kindred bodies have been laid.

"Honor thy father and mother," being a precept sufficiently ancient and authoritative, why should children consign to oblivion the names of once fond and idolizing parents?

In the following record very great care has been exercised in going over the whole ground three times, with the intention and diligent effort to present the *lettering* of *every inscription* just as it is on the stone. The record may not be perfect but is very nearly so.

Inscriptions in the Congregational Burying-place in Stratford.

Alice Ambler died 1851.

Elizur Andrews died May 30, 1753, Æ. 83.

Sarah Morton, Wife of Elezer Andrews, Died Oct. 24, 1868, Æ. 95 yrs.

Hortensia E. Armstrong, died Sept. 5, 1854, Æ. 45.

In Memory of
Mrs. Elizabeth Baldwin, Relict of Nathaniel Baldwin, who died July 30, 1821, aged 52.

In calm repose her body lies,
When Christ appears her dust shall rise.

Laura Maria, Wife of Charles Barker and daughter of Thomas M. and Harriet M. Rogers. Born at Stratford, Ct., Sept. 20, 1822. Died at West Farms, N. Y., Dec. 18, 1853, Aged 31 years 2 months and 26 days.

The memory of other days
When thy loved form was by,
Will guide thy dear ones to thee,
In thy house beyond the sky.

In Memory of
Capt. John Barlow, who died May the 4, 1786, in the 37th year of his Age.

Tho' Borea's Blasts and Neptune's Waves
Have tossed me to and fro
In spite of Death by God's Decree
I harbor here below.

Where I do now at anchor ride,
With many of our fleet,
Yet once again I must make sail
Our admiral Christ to meet.

In Memory of
Capt. David Barlow, who died Oct. 6, 1820, aged 59 years.

Helen T., wife of Edward Batterson, died Feb. 5, 1848, Æ. 21 yrs. and 6 mo. Also their

Infant daughter, died Jan. 31, 1848, Æ. 2 ds.

Hiram, son of Sillick & Emma Batterson, died, Sept. 6, 1814, Æ. 1 yr. 1 mo. & 2 ds.

Isabella and Helen J., daughters of Edward & Mary H. Batterson, Æ. 5½ mos. Died Feb. 5, 1848.

Here Lyes Buried the Body of
Ephraim Beach, Who Deceas⁴ March the 15ᵗʰ, 1716–17 in yᵉ 30ᵗʰ year of his age.

Here lies Buried ye Body of
Mr. Isaac Beach, Who Died April 30ᵗʰ, Anno Domⁿⁱ, 1741, Aged 71 years & 10 mos.

Here lies Buried the Body of
Lieut. James Beach, he died September ye 16, 1752, aged 44 years.

Here lyes ye Body of
Jerusha Beach, Daug. of Mr. Jeames Beach & Mr. Sarah his wife, who died Jany, yᵉ 20, 1760, in yᵉ 19 year of her age.

Here Lyes ye Body of
Jerusha Beach, Dauᵘ of Mr. James and Mrs. Sarah Beach, who died Augᵗ 27ᵗʰ, 1738, Aged 5 years, 10 months & 11 Days.

Here lyes ye Body of
Nehemiah Beach, Son of Mr. James and Mrs. Sarah Beach, Who Died Augᵗ 7ᵗʰ, 1738, Aged 5 years 10 mos. & 11 Days.

Here lyes yᵉ Body of
Lieut. Joseph Beach, Who Departed this life December ye 17ᵗʰ, Anno Domⁿⁱ 1737 in yᵉ 66ᵗʰ Year of His Age.

Here Lyes Buried yᵉ Body of
Mr. Nathaniel Beach, Who Died Aug. 20ᵗʰ, Ann. Dom. 1734 in ye 38th Year of his age.

Here lyes Buried the Body of
Mr. Nathaniel Beach, Who Departed this life July 24ᵗʰ, Anno Domⁿⁱ 1747. Aged 84 years & 3 mos.

Here lyes Buried ye Body of
Mrs. Sarah Beach, Wife to Mʳ Nathaniel Beach, Who Died March yᵉ 25ᵗʰ, A.D. 1738, Aged 70 years.

Here lyes Buried the Body of
Mr. Nehemiah Beach, Who departed this life March ye 5ᵗʰ, 1770, in yᵉ 30ᵗʰ year of His Age.

In Memory of
Eunica Beach, Wife of Mr. Nehemiah Beach, who departed this Life November 11th, A. D. 17—, in the 4— year of her Age. [This stone is broken and two dates destroyed.]

In Memory of
Eunica Beach, Daughter of Mr. Nehemiah and Mrs. Eunica Beach, who departed this Life Aug. 24th, A. D. 1775 in the 6th year of Her Age.

In Memory of
Sarah, Daut^r of Mr. Nehemiah Beach Who died May 2, 1770 in ye 3^d year of Her Age.

Ransom Beach, Died Oct. 4, 1859, Aged 75.

Susan Beach, Daughter of Ransom & Lucy F. Beach, Died July 28, 1882, Aged 74.

Lucy Frost, Wife of Ransom Beach, died Aug. 17, 1849, Æ. 63.

Elijah W., Son of Ransom & Lucy F. Beach, died July 25, 1832, Æ. 22.

Here lyes ye Body of
Ruth Beardslee, Relict of Daniel Beardslee, Died May ye 4th, 1732 in ye 71 year of her age.

Here lyes ye Body of
Mr. Daniel Beardslee, died Octr ye 7. 1730, in ye 86 year of his age.

Here lyes ye Body of
Mr. John Beardsley, Died November 17th, 1739, in ye 52 Year of his age.

Here lyes r^e Body of
Mr. John Beardslee, Died November ye 7, 1702 in ye 52^d year of his age.

John Beardsley, Died Nov. 20, 1833, aged 30 years.

Sidney J. Beardsley, Died May 19, 1852, Æ. 54.

Mary Ann Thompson, Wife of Sidney J. Beardsley, Died Aug. 16, 1844, Æ. 45.

In Memory of
Helen Judson, who died May 26, 1825, aged 26 years.

Also of
Edwin Judson, son of Sidney J. & Mary Ann Beardsley, who died Sept. 25, 1825, aged 5 months.

Charles P. Beers, Died Oct. 7, 1850, Æ. 27 yrs.

Josiah, son of Nathan and Hannah Beers, died June 22^d 1752 aged 13 mos. & 4 ds.

Josiah Beers, son of Ensn. Josiah and Mrs. Elizabeth Beers, died Janry. ye 7th, 1750–51, aged 27 years.

Lewis Beers, Died April 12, 1851, Æ. 52 Yrs.

Susan, Wife of Lewis Beers, Died Dec. 23, 1881, Æ. 80.

Margaret, daughter of Lewis & Susan Beers, died June 30, 1831, aged 1 year and 11 months.

The Remains of
Samuel Beers, who departed this life October 17, 1798, aged 70 years & 4 months.

In Memory of
John Bell, from London, late merchant of the City of New York ; who died Septr 21st, 1798 in the 44 year of his age. He was son-in-law to John Brooks, Esquire, of Stratford.

(Our Father & Mother)
Wm. H. Benjamin, Died Feb. 10, 1860, Æ. 63. Also
Cynthia A., His Wife, Died Sept. 28, 1866, Æ. 60.

George F., Son of William H. & Cynthia A. Benjamin, died Oct. 13, 1848, Æ. 3 yrs. & 6 mo.

George, son of William H. & Cynthia A. Benjamin, died Feb. 14, 1838, aged 5 yrs. & 2 mo's.

In Memory of
Mrs. Hannah Betts, the Wife of Mr. Moses Betts, who died December 24th A.D. 1782, in ye 22 year of her Age.

Sacred to the memory of
Benjamin Bigelow, who died, Sept. 25, 1815, aged 70 years.

Sacred to the memory of
Catharine Bigelow, who died Aug. 1, 1821, aged 73.

Here lyes Buried the Body of
Lieut. Abel Birdsey, who departed this life May 14th, Anno Domni, 1747, in ye 68th year of His Age.

In Memory of
Nathan Birdsey, who died Aug. 5, 1832, aged 88 years, & 3 mo.

In memory of
Abigail Birdseye, who died May 4, 1827, aged 72 years.

Sacred to the memory of the
Rev. Nathan Birdseye, A.M. He was born Aug. 19, 1714 ; Graduated at Yale College, 1736. Ordained at West Haven, 1742 ; Dismissed & recommended by the Consociation, 1758, and departed this life Jan. 28, 1818, aged 103 years 5 months & 9 days.

The memory of the just is blessed.

Sacred to the memory of
Mrs. Dorothy Birdseye, Consort of the Rev. Nathaniel Birdseye, who died Sept. 21st, 1807, In the 88th year of her age.

In memory of
Miss Lucy, daughter of the Rev. Nathan Birdsey, who died much lamented, Dec. 24, 1823 ; aged 64 years.

In memory of
Mr. Philo Birdseye, who died Jan. 6, 1814, in the 30 year of his age. He was intered in Masonic Order.

Mrs. Betsey Birdsey, His Relict Died Feb. 1, 1814 ; in the 27 year of her age.

This stone was erected by Mrs. Helen Birdseye in memory of her husband,
Mr. Thadeus Birdseye, who died Feb. 23, 1800 in the 47th year of his Age.

Helen, Widow of Thaddeus Birdseye, Died April 26, 1856, Æ. 94 yrs. 11 mo. & 13 Days.

Here Lyes the Body of
Richard Blackleach, Esq., Decd. Sept. the 4th 1731, jn the 78th year of his Age.

Here Lyes Body of
Mrs. Abigail Blackleach, Wife to Richard Blachleach, Esq. Aged 60 years. Died March yᵉ 10, 1712-13.

Frederick, son of James & Fanny Blackman, was drowned Aug. 10, 1826, aged 19.

In Memory of
Capt. Abijah Blakeman, Who was lost at Sea on his passage from Bermuda to Newprovidence, In August 1807, aged 29 years.

Here lyes the Body of
Anna, Wife of Zachariah Blakeman, who departed this life March 23ᵈ 1789, in the 32ᵈ year of her age.

Here lyes yᵉ Body of
Mrs. Elizabeth Blekman, Wife to Mr. Zechariah Blekman, Who Died March 23ᵈ, 1732, in yᵉ 52ᵈ year of her age.

Miss Anne Blakeman, Daughter of Mr. James & Mrs. Anne Blakeman, died March 3, 1809, in the 22 year of her age.

In Memory of
Mr. James Blakeman, who died November 12th, 1791, In the 79th year of his age. Also,

Mrs. Sarah, his Wife, died Decemᵇʳ 15th, 1793, In the 73ʳᵈ year of her age.

In memory of
Sarah, the wife of Mr. James Blakeman, Junʳ, Who Died December the 12 A.D. 1775, in the 26 year of her age.

In Memory of
Miller Blakeman, son of James Blakeman, Junʳ, who departed this Life, May 27, 1781, in the 8th year of his age.

In Memory of
Capt. Agur Booth, who died Oct. 29, 1818, aged 70 years.
Mrs. Anna, his relict, died Nov. 26, 1818, aged 66.

In Memory of
Daniel Booth, who departed this Life May 8, 1801 In the 77 year of his Age.

Here lieth the Body of
Mrs. Elizabeth Booth, Who died in the 21st year of her age, July 29, 1702.

[MONUMENT.]
Elizabeth Pratt, wife of Charles H. Booth, Died in New York, Dec. 29, 1844, Æ. 33 yrs.
"For if we believe that Jesus died and rose again, even so them also which sleep in Jesus will God bring with him."

Charles E., son of Charles H. & Elizabeth P. Booth, Born March 27, 1843, Died Sept. 18, 1870.
"We know that when he shall appear we shall be like him; for we shall see Him as he is."

In Memory of
Edward Wainwright, infant son of Charles H. & Elizabeth P. Booth, who died July 17, 1835, aged 6 months.

In Memory of
Eli Booth, son of Abijah L. & Abby B. Booth, who was killed by fall of a tree April 15, 1823, aged 14 years.

Eli Booth, Died Feb. 1, 1864, Æ. 76 yrs. & 10 mos.
Blessed are the dead which die in the Lord.

Mary, Wife of Eli Booth, Died Sept. 12, 1865, Æ. 78.
For they rest from their labors and their works do follow them.

Frederick Leavenworth, son of John C. & Margaret J. Booth, died Dec. 29, 1852, Æ. 7 months.

In Memory of
Capt. James Booth, who died March 19, 1809, In the 75th year of his age.

Here lyes Buried the Body of
Mr. James Booth, Who departed this life, August the 20, 1766, Aged 78 years.

In Memory of
Mrs. Abigail, wife of Mr. James Booth, who died Aug. 10, 1817, Æ. 79.

In Memory of the Children of Capt. James & Mrs. Abigail Booth.
Abel Booth, who died April 15, 1777, in the 20th year of his Age.
James Booth, who died March 30th, 1766, in the 2d year of his Age.

Here lyes Buried the Body of
Mrs. Martha Booth, 2d wife to Mr. James Booth, Who Departed this Life Decem. 3d, 1747, in 52d Year of Her Age.

In Memory of
Mr. John Booth, who died Dec. 2, 1822, aged 86 years.

In Memory of
Mrs. Lucy Booth, wife of Mr. John Booth, who died Sept. 17, A. D. 1817, in the 77 year of her age.

In Memory of
Mary Booth, who died Nov. 24, 1772, in ye 3d year of her age.

In memory of
Josiah Booth, who died Dec. 30th, 1772, in ye 5 year of his age.
The Children of John and Mrs. Lucy Booth.

In Memory of
John Booth, who died Aug. 10, 1825, aged 61 years.

In Memory of
Mrs. Sarah Booth, the wife of John Booth, who died March 24, 1826, aged 60 years.

In memory of
Mrs. Jerusha Booth & her two babies, Wife of Mr. John Booth, Jur. & Daughter of Mr. Eli Lewis, who died Novr 10, 1796, Aged 31 years.

[A MONUMENT. West Side.]
Erected over the graves of
Joseph Booth, Son of Richard Booth, who died Sept. 1, 1703, Æ. 46. And
Hannah, Wife of Joseph Booth & daughter of John & Elizabeth Willcoxson, who died July 10, 1701, Æ. 38.

Their Children were :
James, Born 1688, Died 1766.
Joseph, Born 1687, Died 1763.
Robert, Born ——, Died ——.
Nathan, Born ——, Died ——.
Zechariah, Born ——, Died 1762.

David, Born 1679, Died 1753.
Hannah, Born ——, Died ——.
[North Side.]
James Booth, son of Joseph Booth, died Aug. 20, 1766, Æ. 78.
Martha Clark, wife of James Booth, died Dec. 3, 1747, Æ. 52.

Their Children were :
Sarah, Born 1732, Died 1786.
James, Born 1735, Died 1809.
John, Born 1736, Died 1822.
Hezekiah, Born 1739, Died 1761.
Josiah, Born 1742, Died 1767.
James Booth, son of James Booth, died March 19, 1809, Æ. 75.
Abigail Ann, wife of James Booth, died August 11, 1817, Æ. 78.

Their Children were :
Abel, Born 1757, Died 1777.
Sarah, Born 1759, Died 1841.
Hezekiah, Born 1762, Died 1814.
Silas, Born 1763, Died 1819.
James, Born 1765, Died 1766.
Abigail Ann, Born 1766, Died ——.
Betsey, Born, 1768, Died 1825.
Charity, Born 1771, Died 1810.
Amy, Born 1773, Died 1844.
James, Born 1776, Died ——.
Abel, Born 1780, Died ——.
[South Side.]
John Booth, son of James Booth, Born Aug. 3, 1736, Died Dec. 2, 1822.
Lucy, Wife of John Booth, & Daughter of Henry & Ann Curtiss, Born March 1, 1741, Died Sept. 17, 1817.

Their Children were :
John, Born 1764, Died 1825.
William, Born 1765, Drowned 1810.
Josiah, Born 1768, Died 1772.
Mary, Born 1770, Died 1772.
David, Born 1771, Died 1792.
Josiah, Born 1773, Died 1852.
Elijah, Born 1776.
Isaac, Born 1783, Drowned 1810.
[East Side.]
Richard Booth, From England, one of the first settlers in this town in 1639, Born 1606, Aged 82 years in 1688. Date of death unknown.

Their Children were :
Elizabeth, Born 1641.
Ann, Born 1643.
Ephraim, Born 1648.
Ebenezer, Born 1651.
John, Born 1653.
Joseph, Born 1656.
Bethya, Born 1658.
Johanna, Born 1661.
Sarah A., The Wife of John C. Booth, died March 8, 1849, Æ. 39 yrs.

John Henry, the son of John C. & Sarah A. Booth, died Dec. 6, 1848, Æ. 2 yrs. & 7 mo.

[A Monument].

Capt. William Booth, was drowned off Cape Cod, Oct. 18, 1810, aged 45 yrs.

Mary Ann, Wife of Capt. Wm. Booth, Died July 22, 1851, aged 83 yrs.

David, son of Wm. & Mary Ann Booth, was drowned off Cape Cod, Oct. 18, 1810, aged 18 yrs.

In Memory of

Capt. William Booth, aged 45 years, and his son

David Booth, Aged 17 years; and of *Isaac Booth,* Aged 27 years, Who were all drowned in Boston-Bay on the 18th day of Oct. A.D. 1810.

Also in memory of

David Booth, who died at New York, Dec. 23d, 1792, Aged 21 years.

Mr. Zechariah Booth, 1762. [This is the foot-stone, of fine slate. The head-stone has been broken off at the ground, and is not to be found.

Here lyes ye Body of

Mrs. Ann Booth, Wife to Mr. Zechariah Booth, Who died May 18th, 1733, in yᵉ 37 Year of her Age.

In Memory of

Zechariah Brinsmade, died November yᵉ 22d 1741 in yᵉ 56 year of his age.

Here lyes yᵉ Body of

Sarah Brinsmade, Wife to Mr. Zechariah Brinsmade, Aged 48 Years 6 months. Died June ye 9, 1736.

Hannah Brinsmade, Dau. to Mr. Zechariah & Hannah Brinsmade, Aged 3 years & 4 mo. Died Sept. ye 2d, 1736.

Here lyes Buried ye Body of

Mr. Benjamin Brooks; Who Departed this life Dec. 30, Anno Domini, 1745, in yᵉ 61st Year of His age.

Here lyes Buried yᵉ Body of

Mrs. Mary Brooks, Wife to Mr. Benjamin Brooks, Who died Novʳ 2ⁿᵈ, A.D. 1740, in yᵉ 49ᵗʰ Year of Her Age.

Here lyes yᵉ Body of

Huldah Brooks, Dautʳ of Mr. Benjamin & Mrˢ Mary Brooks, Who Died Januaʳʸ 2ⁿᵈ 1737 in yᵉ 12ᵗʰ Year of her Age.

Sacred to the memory of

Capt. N. Birdsey Brooks, who with his Crew was lost at Sea, Sept. 1789; In the 22d year of his Age.

Stern Neptune nods, the billows rise,
In vain the Seamen raise their cries;
Each in a moment know their dom,
And share alike a watery tomb.

David Brooks, died Mar. 16, 1862, aged 65 years.

Anna, Daughter of David & Anna Brooks, died February ye 13, 1755, Aged 16ᵐᵒ.

In memory of

David Brooks, who died Apr. 26, 1860, Æ. 87 yrs. & 11 mo's.

In memory of

Abigail Brooks, wife of David Brooks, Esq., who died Feb. 13, 1839, aged 66 years.

Sacred to the memory of

Edward Brooks, son of David & Abigail Brooks, who died Apr. 1, 1822, aged 7 years and 7 days.

Here lies inter'd the Remains of

Eli Brooks, Esq., son of John Brooks & Anna his Wife who Departed this Life Octbʳ 25ᵗʰ, 1775, Ætat 19.

A youth of a promising genius & an obliging disposition, desirous of making all around him happy. Just as he had entered upon his Collegiate studies, and given his Friends and Acquaintance rais'd Expectations of his future usefulness, Death marked him for his Prey, & in the morning of Life called him to the grave.

Here lies entered the Body of

Eli, son of Capt. Benjamin & Rebekah Brooks, who died March 4ᵗʰ, 1777 in the 2d Year of his age.

Here lies Buried the Body of

Isaac Brooks, son of Mʳ. Isaac & Mrs. Temperance Brooks who departed this life, July 23d, 1777, Aged 1 year & 7 months.

Sleep lovely Babe and take thy peaceful Rest, God called the hence Because he thought it best.

In memory of

Maria Brooks, daughter of David & Abigail Brooks, who died Jan. 12, 1834, aged 22 years & 8 mo.

John Brooks, Son of John & Polly Brooks, died Aug. 22, 1794, in his 4ᵗʰ year.

Here lies intered the Body of

John Brooks, Esq., who departed this Life March 7ᵗʰ, A.D. 1777 in the 63d year of his age.

In Memory of
Anna Brooks, Relict of John Brooks
Esq., who died March 19, 1804, aged
89 years.

Here lies the remains of
John Brooks, Esq., who departed
this Life October 22⁴, 1788, Aged 49
Years.

Farewell bright soul a short farewell
Till we shall meet again Above,
In the sweet groves where pleasures dwell
And tears of life bear fruits of love,
There glory sits on every face,
There friendship smiles in every eye.
There shall our tongues relate the grace
That led us homeward to the sky.

John Brooks, Esqr. and Mrs. Dorothy
Brooks, his Wife, have erected this
stone in memory of their Son
Eli, who died August 29, 1783, Aged
4 Years 4 months & 25 days.
Likewise in memory of another infant
son, named also
Eli, who died the 11 of August, 1785
aged 1 week & 7 hours.

In memory of
Theodosia Brooks, Daur. of Mr.
John Brooks, Junr & Mrs. Dorothy
his wife; who died Nov. 15th, 1773,
Aged 4 years & 22 Days.

Beneath this scattered dust here's silent laid
the Father's Comfort & Mothers Aid.
Cropt like a flower she fell a victim soon
tho flattering life had promised years to come.

Nathan Brooks, Son of Mr. David
& Mrs. Ann Brooks, who Died Novᵇʳ
2ᵈ, 1746 Aged 13 months and 7 Days.

In memory of
William Brooks, who departed
this life August 11, 1804, in the 50
year of his age.

In Memory of
Phebe, relect of William Brooks, who
died July 6, 1822, aged 66.

Sacred to the Memory of
William Brooks, who departed this
life July 24th, 1809, aged 30 years.

Nathan, son of Cap. Isaiah & Mrs.
Ann Brown, died Nov. 23ʳᵈ, 1753,
aged 4 months.

Rhoda, Daughter of Capt. Isaiah &
Mrs. Ann Brown, died Jany 24, A. D.
1754, aged 3 years.

John Bruce, Died May 10, 1870,
Æ. 82 yrs. 8 mo.

In memory of
Comphy, Wife of John Bruce, died
Sept. 17, 1849, Æ. 60.

Sarah Burch, Daughter of Mr.
Jeremiah & Mrs. Sarah Burch, Died
May ye 14th, 1738, aged 2 years 9 mo.
& 12 Da.

In Memory of
Hezekiah Burritt, who departed
this Life, June 1, 1809; In the 70th
year of his Age.

In Memory of
Mr. John Burritt, Who departed
this Life, June 29, 1787, in yᵉ 77 Year
of his Age.

Redeemed from Earth and Pain
Oh when shall we assend
And all in Jesus presence reign
With our departed Friends.

Here lyes the body of
Mrs. Phebe Burritt, formerly Wife
to Mr. John Burritt, who departed
this Life, March 22, 1789, in yᵉ 83
Year of her Age.

Redeemed from Earth and Pain
And all in Jesus presence reign
With our departed friends.

In memory of
Nathan W. Burritt, who died,
Aug. 4, 1838 ; Æ. 40 years.

In memory of
Robert, Son of Nathan & Sarah Burritt, who died Augˢᵗ 18, 1803, aged 3
years.

Here lieth the Body of
Capt. Stephen Burritt, who departed this Life in the 57 year of his
age, January 24th, 169⅘.*

In memory of
Mrs. Mary, the Wife of Mr. Charles
Burroughs, Who departed this life
April the 13, A. D. 1777, With the
small pox in the 62 Year of her age.

In Memory of
Mrs. Bette Burton, Wife to Mr.
Ephriam Burton, departed this life,
Aug. 10, 1783 in the 55 Year of Her
Age.

Erected by Robert Coldwell, in mem-
ory of his mother,
Jane Coldwell, and sister of Joseph
Jamieson, who died Mar. 23, 1851,
Æ. 53.

* Mr. Robert H. Russell found this stone,
recently, in the foot-path from his house to his
garden. It was several inches under the surface of the ground, and about 200 feet from the
southeast corner of the cemetery. There is no
knowledge of, nor conjecture how it came
there. It was probably first erected at the old
cemetery.

Here lyes interred the Body of
Samuel Casrell, who died April ye
2ᵈ, 1707, in yᵉ 29 year of his age.

Here lyeth yᵉ body of
Mr. Israell Chauncey, Who was
minister of yᵉ Gospell in this place
upwards of 38 years & dyed March
yᵉ 14ᵗʰ 170½ in ye 59ᵗʰ year of his age.

Here lyes ye Body of
Sarah Clark, Wife to David Clark,
Aged 18 years & 12 Ds. Died March
ye 12, 1743.

Carrie Clark, daughter of Myron
& Jane E. Jurson.

Here lyeth the Body of
Deborah Clarke, Wife to J. C. Senr.
who departed this life in the 61ˢᵗ year
of her Age, December 14, 1705.

In Memory of
Edward Lawarence, Son of John
W. and Susana A. Close, who died
May 12ᵗʰ 1843, aged 6 months and 14
days.

David Coe, Died Oct. 6, 1842, aged
30 years.

Blessed are the dead who die in the Lord.

Mary Elizabeth, Wife of David
Coe, Died Aug. 27, 1849, Æ. 37 yrs.

Into thy hand I commit my spirit; thou hast
redeemed me, O Lord God of Israel.

In Memory of
Capt. Ebenezer Coe, Who departed this life March the 26ᵗʰ 1766, Aged
62 years.

In Memory of
Mrs. Mary Coe, Wife of Capt.
Ebenezer Coe, who departed this life,
May the 23ᵈ 1773, in ye 68 year of Her
Age.

In Memory of
Deac. Ebenezer Coe, who died
Aug. 1ˢᵗ, 1820, Aged 85 years.

In Memory of
Mrs. Sarah Coe, Wife of Deacⁿ
Ebenezer Coe, who died Oct. 15ᵗʰ
1802, aged 67 years.

In Memory of
Sarah Coe, Dautr. of Mr. Ebenezer
& Mrs. Sarah Coe, who died Nov. 29ᵗʰ,
1772 in yᵉ 6ᵗʰ year of her age.

In Memory of
Mrs. Esther Coe, Wife of Mr. Josiah
Coe, who departed this life, Octʳ 16ᵗʰ,
1794, In the 26ᵗʰ year of her age.

Isaac Thompson, son of James and
Sally Coe, died Dec. 6, 1822; aged 12
yrs.

In Memory of
James Coe, Who died May 12, 1851,
Æ. 70.

Sarah T., wife of James Coe, Died
Oct. 5, 1868, Aged 87.

In Memory of
James Coe, Jr., who died, Dec. 18,
1848, Æ. 33 yrs.

The sweet rememberence of the just
Shall flourish when they sleep in dust.

James R., son of James & Helen
Coe, died Sept. 10, 1852, aged 4 yrs
& 9 mos.

Suffer little children to come unto me.

In Memory of
Mr. James Coe, Who departed this
life July 31, 1790, In the 50ᵗʰ Year of
his age.

In Memory of
Huldah Coe, wife of James Coe,
who died Nov. 10, 1814, aged 75 years.

In Memory of
James Coe, the son of James & Huldah Coe, who Departed this Life September 18, A. D. 1778, Aged 6 months
& 9 days.

Here lyes Buried yᵉ Body of
Capt. John Coe, Who Died April
19, Anno Domni 1741, in yᵉ 83ᵈ year
of His Age.

Here lies Buried yᵉ Body of
Mrs. Mary Coe, Wife to Capt. John
Coe, Who died September yᵉ 9ᵗʰ, 1731,
in yᵉ 69ᵗʰ year of Her Age.

In Memory of
John E. Coe, who died Nov. 8, 1827,
aged 59 years.

In Memory of
Mrs. Eunica Coe, Wife of Mr.
John E. Coe, who died Aug. 3, 1815;
Aged 43 years.

In Memory of three children of John
Ebenezer & Eunice Coe,

Sally Coe, died Oct. 31ˢᵗ, 180– [1801
or 2], aged 6 years.

Mary Coe, died Oct. 10ᵗʰ, 1802, aged
2 years & 6 months.

Robert Coe, died April 4ᵗʰ, 179– [per-
haps 1796] aged 3 months.

John Wm., son of John & Anna Coe,
died Aug. 4, 1826, aged 6 months.

Sacred to the memory of
Deacon Zechariah Coe, Who died
Aug. 8ᵗʰ, 1805, Æ. 73.

Also of his wife
Levinia Coe, who died July 10th,
1805, Æ. 71.

Charles Mortimer Cook, son of Joseph & Mary Cook, died June 4, 1809, aged 7 years & 25 days.

In Memory of
Helen Louisa, only child of Joseph H. and Susan T. Cowdry, who was born in New York, Feb. 26, 1839, and died in New York, Dec. 4, 1840, Aged 1 year 9 months and 18 days.

In Memory of
Helen Louisa, second child of Joseph H. and Susan T. Cowdry, who was born in New York, Oct. 16, 1842, and died in New York, Nov. 21, 1844, Aged 2 years 1 month and 5 days.

Here lyes Buried y⁰ Body of
Mrs. Abigail Curtis, Wife to Mʳ Ebenezer Curtis, Who Departed his life Novᵇʳ 29ᵗʰ, A. D. 1746, Aged 32 years 10 months & 25 Days.

In Memory of
Mr. Abner Curtiss, who departed this LIFE December 19ᵗʰ, 1779 in the 48ᵗʰ year of his age.
O reader stop and cast an eye
As thou art now so once was I.
As I am now soon thou must bee,
Prepare for death and follow me.

Here lies the Body of
Mr. Abram Curtiss, Who departed this Life September y⁰ 7ᵗʰ, A. D. 1779, Aged 79 years.

Here lyes ye Body of
Mrs. Elizabeth Curtiss, Wife to Mr. Abraham Curtiss, Who departed this Life, August y⁰ 31ˢᵗ, 1770 in y⁰ 68 year of her Age.

Anna Curtis, died Jan. 4, 1871, Æ. 86 yrs.

Sacred To the Memory of
Dea. Agur Curtis, who died April 22, 1844, in the 84ᵗʰ year of his age.

In memory of
Huldah Curtis, wife of Agur Curtis, & Mother of Lewis & Benjamin Curtis, who died on the 6ᵗʰ day of June, 1858, Aged 92.

In Memory of
Augur Curtiss, who died Nov. 10, 1838, aged 81 yrs.

In Memory of
Mercy, wife of Agur Curtiss, who died Dec. 17, 1850, Æ. 90 yrs. & 7 mo.

Agur Peck, son of David & Amy Curtiss, died Oct.1,1810,aged 2 yrs & 3 mo.

Here lyes y⁰ body of
Mrs. Bethsheba Curtiss, formerly wife to Mr. Ephriam Stiles, Aged 74 years. Died Febuary y⁰ 9ᵗʰ, 1735.

15

In memory of
Betsey Curtiss, who died March 21, 1843, aged 52 years.

Catharine, Wife of Marcus Curtiss, died June 17, 1855, Æ. 61 years.

In Memory of
Charlotte Curtis, who died Mar. 13, 1866, Æ. 67 yrs.

In Memory of
David Curtiss, who died Nov. 1, 1819, in his 81 year.

In Memory of
Mrs. Sarah Curtiss, Wife of Mr. David Curtiss, who departed this life, March 6ᵗʰ, 1801, in the 60ᵗʰ year of her age.

Agur, The son of Mr. David & Mrs. Sarah Curtiss, who died October ye 9, 1776, in y⁰ 5 year of his age.
Your moans fond parents cease
and let this hope suffice
Your babe shall sleep in peace
till Jesus bid it rise.

Dolly Curtis, died Feb. 27, 1875, Æ. 75 yrs. 10 mo.

In Memory of
Ebenezer Curtiss, who died, May 19, 1819, Æ. 42.

Here lyes y⁰ Body of
Mrs. Ruth Curtis, wife to Mr. Ebenezer Curtis, Departed this life, May y⁰ 28ᵗʰ, 1739 in y⁰ 70ᵗʰ year of her age.

In memory of
Mr. Elihu Curtiss, who died, Aug. 9, 1820, aged 79 years.

Elihu, son of Daniel Curtis, died Sept. 23, 1820, Æ. 73.

Aner, wife of Elihu Curtis & daughter of Lewis Nodine, died 1804, Æ. 47. This stone erected to their memory by their son Alfred.

In Memory of
Mr. Elijah Curtis, Son of Mr. Henry & Mrs. Anne Curtiss, who died Sept. 23ᵈ, A. D. 1776, in the 35ᵗʰ year of his Age.

Here lies inter'd the Body of
Ephraim Curtiss, Esqr., who departed this Life, May 9ᵗʰ, 1775, in the 92ᵈ Year of his Age, &
Elizabeth, his wife, who departed this Life, October 5ᵗʰ, in the 91ˢᵗ year of her age.*

* No year is given to the death of Mrs. Elizabeth; but probably she died in 1775.

Here lyes ye Body of
Ephraim Curtiss, son of Ephraim
Curtiss, Esq., & Mrs. Elizabeth his
Wife, Who Died Decembr 2, 1737,
Aged 20 years 3 months & 2 Days.

Here lyes y⁰ Body of
Elizabeth Curtiss, Daughter of
Ephraim Curtiss, Esq., & Mrs. Elizabeth his Wife, Who Died July 31, 1788,
aged 8 years 8 months & 15 Days.

In Memory of
Dr. Ezra Curtiss, who died & was
buried at Litchfield. Nov. 17, 1797, in
the 33d year of his age.

In Memory of
Hannah Curtis, wife of Samuel
Curtis, who died Jan. 7, 1822, aged 74
years & 1 month.

In Memory of
·**Hannah Curtis,** wife of Stiles Curtis, of Norwalk, & daughter of Seymour C. & Hannah Whiting, who
died Feb. 8, 1838 ; aged 35 years.

Here lyes y⁰ Body of
Mrs. Hannah Curtis, Wife to Mr.
Zechariah Curtis, Aged 73 years.
Died Feby 14ᵗʰ, 173⅔ [or 175⅜].

Henrietta Curtiss, Born Jan. 25,
1811. Died April 30, 1874.

In Memory of
Mr. Henry Curtiss, who departed
this life, May 23ᵈ, 1804, in the 95th
Year of his Age.

In Memory of
Mrs. Anne Curtiss, the wife of Mr.
Henry Curtiss, who Departed this
Life September 14ᵗʰ, A. D. 1783, in
the 68ᵗʰ Year of her Age.

In Memory of
Mr. Henry Curtiss, who died April
18, 1814, aged 63 years.

In Memory of
Phebe Curtiss, wife of Henry Curtiss, who died Feb. 5, 1826. Aged 67
years, also

George Curtis, their son, died in
the State of Illinois, Sept. 18, 1822,
Æ. 24.

Harriet, Daughter of Mr. Henry &
Mrs. Phebe Curtiss, died June 20ᵗʰ,
1793, aged 5 months.

Eliza, their Daughter, died March 7ᵗʰ,
1800, aged 15 days.

In Memory of
Mrs. Hepsy Curtis, who died, Feb.
10, 1832, aged 54.

Here lyes buried the Body of
Mr. Hezekiah Curtiss, Who departed this life Oct. y⁰ 9ᵗʰ, 1771, in y⁰
64ᵗʰ year of His Age.

Here lyes Buried the Body of
Mrs. Bulah Curtiss, Dau. of Mr.
Hezekiah Curtiss & Mrs. Mehetable
Curtiss, Who departed this life Sep-
tember y⁰ 16, 1771, in y⁰ 17ᵗʰ year of
her age.

In memory of
Mrs. Huldah, Late Consort of Mr.
Samuel Curtiss, who was born April
15ᵗʰ, 1738, & died April 28, 1765.

Huldah, Dau. of the above Parents,
who was born March 16ᵗʰ, 1765, &
died in July, A. D. 1765.

In calm repose
Their body lies
When Christ appears
Their dust shall rise.

In Memory of
Mr. Isaac Curtiss, Son of Mr. Sam-
uel & Mrs. Hannah Curtiss, who died
Jan. 17, 1796, Ætat, 21.

Behold and see as you pass by
As you are now so once was I
As I am now so you must be
Prepare for death and follow me.

Elezabeth Curtiss, wife of Isaac
Curtiss, died July 1, 1797, aged 26.

In Memory of
Mr. Jabez Curtiss, who departed
this life, Jan. 16ᵗʰ, 1829, in the 90ᵗʰ
year of his age.

In Memory of
Mrs. Betty Curtis, wife of Mr. Jabez
Curtis, who departed this life, Oct. 1,
1818, in the 75ᵗʰ year of her age.

In memory of
James Curtis, who died March 22,
1821, Aged 41 Years.

Here lyes Buried the Body of
Mrs. Jerusha Curtiss, Wife to Mr.
Stephen Curtiss, Who Departed this
Life Dec. 24ᵗʰ, A. D. 1747, in ye 21
Year of her Age.

Abraham Curtiss, Son of Mr. Stephen & Mrs. Jerusha Curtiss, Died
Janry 23ᵈ, 174⅞. Aged 2 months &
12 Ds.

In memory of
John Curtiss, who died Aug. 31,
1825, aged 80 years.

Also of
Mary, his wife, who died the same
day & hour, aged 78.
They were both deposited in the
same grave.

Mr. Joseph Curtiss, died Mar. 15, . 1801, aged 80 yrs.

Here lyes enter'd the Body of
Mr. Josiah Curtiss, who died May 26th, 1773, in the 71st year of his Age.

In Memory of
Miss Eunice Curtiss, daughter of Mr. Josiah Curtiss, who died Oct. 21–1817, in the 53 year of her age.

In Memory of
Mr. Josiah Curtiss, who departed this life, Feb. 6th, 1804, in the 70th year of his age.

In Memory of
Mrs. Mary Curtiss, Wife of Mr. Josiah Curtiss, who died May 20–1817, in the 80 year of her age.

In Memory of
Lewis Curtis, who died, March 5, 1834, Aged 89 years.

In Memory of
Mrs. Hepsa Curtiss, the wife of Mr. Lewis Curtiss, who died April 16, 1819, aged 71 years.

Mrs. Martha Curtiss, died Aug. 26, 1790, aged 77.

Mary, wife of Judson Curtiss, died Feb. 23, 1814 ; aged 42 years.

Judson Curtis, Son of Mr. Judson & Mrs. Mary Curtiss, was killed by a Cart wheel going over him Octo 4th, 1805, aged 5 years & 10 days.

In Memory of
Nehemiah Curtiss, who died May 13, 1810, aged 69 years.

Phebe Curtiss, Died Jan. 2, 1864, Æ. 76 yrs. & 7 mo.

Here lies intered the Body of
Mrs. Phebe, Wife to Mr. Nehemiah Curtiss, who departed this life, July 24, 1770, in the 32nd Year of her age.

No gift of nature, Art, or Grace,
Exempteth from the Burying place,
All must obey the solemn call
Before that Tyrant all must fall.

In Memory of
Polly, wife of Nehemiah Curtis, who died Sept. 17, 1817, aged 34 years.

Also of three Children of Nehemiah & Polly Curtis :

Stiles, died Sept. 15, 1808, aged 15 months.

Betsey Ann, died Sept. 11, 1813 ; aged 6 months.

Nehemiah, died Sept. 25, 1817 ; aged 17 months.

In memory of
Nehemiah Curtis, who departed this life, Sept. 30, 1835, Æ. 61.

Sacred to the Memory of
Anne Curtiss, Wife of Nehemiah Curtis, Junr., who died March 3, 1804, in the 22d year of her age,
And of their Infant.
She lived much esteemed
And died much lamented.

Peter Pixlee, Son of Mr. Daniel & Mrs. Betsey Curtiss, died May 10, 1817, aged 3 months.

Dea. Philo Curtis, Died May 5, 1852, Æ. 78.

In Memory of
Betsey Curtis, wife of Dea. Philo Curtis, who died Feb. 11, 1844, aged 68.

In memory of
Rebecca, Consort of William Curtiss, Deceased, Dec. 3, 1823, aged 41 years.

In Memory of
Rejoice Curtiss, who died Oct. 11, 1861, Æ. 74 y'rs.

In memory of
Sally Curtis, Who Died May 2, 1831, Aged 39 years.

Eliza Curtis, Died Jan. 11, 1831, aged 28 Yrs.

In Memory of
Capt. Samuel Curtiss, who died Feb. 15, 1833, aged 63 years.

In Memory of
Alice, Wife of Capt. Samuel Curtiss & daughter of Elisha & Sarah De Forest. Who died Dec. 13, 1859, Æ. 74.

Mary Ann, daughter of Capt. Samuel & Mrs. Alice Curtiss, died June 14, 1814, aged 5 months.

Erected by Capt. Curtiss In Memory of his Daughter
Henrietta, who died Augt 26th, 1803, in the 7th Year of her age, & of his son SAML. J., who died Augt 28th, 1803, aged 5 years.

Miss Mary Ann, daughter of Capt. Samuel & Mrs. Temperence A. Curtiss, died April 1, 1814, aged 19 years.

Erected by Capt. Saml Curtiss, In memory of his Wife.
Temperence Anna Curtiss, who departed this life, Augt 30th, A. D. 1800, aged 30 Years.

In Memory of
Mr. Samuel Curtiss, who died Sept. 8th, 1802, in the 68 year of his age.

In Memory of
Samuel Curtiss, who died May 19, 1826, aged 69 years.

In Memory of
Dolly Curtiss, wife of Samuel Curtis, who died, Sept. 19, 1829, Æ. 66 yrs.

In Memory of
Charles Curtiss, the beloved son of Mr. Samuel Curtiss, Jr., & Mrs. Dolly Curtiss, who died Janu^ry 8th, 1793, In the 4 year of his age.

Sleep, sweet Babe and take thy rest
God call'd thee Home he thought it best
Though to thy parents dear.

Sarah, Wife of Charles Curtiss, Died Nov. 25, 1877, Aged 85 yrs. 4 mo.

In memory of
Mary J., who died May 12, 1831, aged 3 yrs. Also
Samuel H., died April 16, 1831, aged 1 y. & 3 mo., daughter & son of Charles & Sarah Curtis.

As you stand by this grassy tomb
In silent sorrow weep,
For two sweet infants side by side
In death's cold slumbers sleep,
So fades the lovely blooming flower
Frail smilling solace of an hour
So soon our transient comforts fly
And pleasures only bloom to die.

Charles, son of Charles & Sarah Curtiss, died Sept. 3, 1833, aged 5 mo. & 23 ds.

Emily, daughter of Charles & Sarah Curtis, Died Feb. 11, 1832, Æ. 8 mos.

Adieu sweet baby thy stay was short
Just looked about and call'd away.

Roxana Peck, Adopted Daughter of Charles & Sarah Curtis, Died April 16, 1848, Æ. 23.

Blessed are the dead who die in the Lord.

In memory of
Sarah, Dr of Mr. Curtiss & Mrs. Mary.

In memory of
Mr. Silas Curtis, who died Aug. 5, 1822, Aged 72 years.

In memory of
Mr. Silas Curtiss, who died Jan. 15, 1816, in the 74 year of his age.

In memory of
Mary, wife of Silas Curtiss, who died April 11, 1805 ; in the 50 year of her age.

In Memory of
Mrs. Helen Curtiss, Wife of Silas Curtiss, Ters. Daughter of Stiles & Naomi Judson, who died April 2^d, 1801, Aged 21 years.

In Memory of
Hannah, Wife of Silas Curtiss, who died Nov. 25, 1811, in the 65 year of her age.

Sacred to the Memory of
Solomon Curtis, who departed this life, July 13, 1824, Æ. 76 years & 11 months.

Blessed are the dead who die in the Lord.

Sacred to the Memory of
Jerusha Curtis, relict of Solomon Curtis, who died Aug. 29, 1834, aged 76 years.

O Death ! where is thy sting ?
O Grave ! where is thy victory !

In Memory of
Jabez Curtis, son of Mr. Solomon & Mrs. Jerusha Curtis, who died Feb. 8, 1797, Ætat. 8 years.

Thy flesh disolv'd in sorrow must appear,
While here we drop ye sympathetic tear ;
The tomb shall safe retain its sacred trust,
Till life divine reanimates thy dust.

In memory of
Stephen Curtis, who died May 8th, 1806, aged 79 years.

In memory of
Mrs. Sarah Curtiss, Wife of Mr. Stephen Curtiss, who departed this Life, November 2^d, 1794, Aged 64 yrs.

Here lyes ye Body of
Stephen Jetson Curtiss, Son of Mr. Stephen & Mrs. Sarah Curtiss Who died June 17, 1760, Aged 3 Years.

Sarah Curtiss, died April 9, 1766, Aged 2 Years & 8 months.

Stephen Jetson Curtiss died April 18, 1766, Aged 5 years & 6 mos. Children of Mr. Stephen Curtis, Junr & Sarah his Wife.

In Remembrance of 2 Children of Mr. Stephen & Mrs. Sarah Curtiss :
Abram Curtiss, Departed this Life at New York, September 4th, A. D. 1776, & Buried in Harlem Burying place, in the 23rd year of his age.

Betty Curtiss Departed this Life, October 9th, A. D. 1777, in the 11th Year of her age.

In Memory of
Capt. Stiles Curtiss, who departed this Life the 22^d Day of April, A. D. 1785, in the 78 year of his age.

In Memory of
Mrs. Rebekah Curtiss, Relict of Capt. Stiles Curtiss, who departed this Life, July 1st, 1798, In the 89th Year of her Age.

In memory of
Mr. Thaddeus Curtis, Who died Septr. 23ᵈ. 1776, in the 30ᵗʰ Year of his age.

Mr. Thaddeus Curtiss, who died on his passage from Exuma and was buried in the Sea Dec. 25, 1801, in the 22ᵈ year of his age.

In memory of
Sally Curtis, Who Died, May 2, 1831, Aged 39 yrs.

Elizabeth Curtis Died Jan. 11, 1831, aged 28 yrs.

Andrew Dayton, died Feb. 11, 1807 ; aged 53.

Anna Dayton, Died March 23, 1869, Aged 81 yrs. & 8 Mos.

John Dayton, Died June 16, 1819, Æ. 35 years.

Betsey Dayton, died Sept. 9, 1815, æ 21 yrs.

Jerusha, widow of Andrew Dayton, died Jan. 7, 1847, Æ. 91 Yrs.

Robert Dayton died June 16, 1816, aged 24.

Mrs. Ruth Dayton, Wife of Mr. Brewster Dayton & Daughter of Mr. Abner Judson, died June 15, 1788, Aged 26 years & 11 months.

Sarah, Wife of Wm. S. DeForest, died March 16, 1848, Æ. 30 y'rs.

Our Little
Willie, only son of A. E. & M. L. Dudly, died Feb. 20, 1856, Æ. 3 mos. How many hopes lie buried here.

Here lyes the body of
Mr. Archable Dunlap, who deceased Septᵇʳ 24, 1713, in ye 35ᵗʰ year of his age.

Here lies Interr'd the Body of
Mrs. Sarah Easton, Widᵒ of Mʳ John Easton, of Hartford, who died March yᵉ 10ᵗʰ, 1750, In the 59 year of her age.

Charles S., son of Charles & Sarah M. Edmond, Died Oct. 1, 1843, Æ. 3 and a half mos.

Sarah M., Wife of Charles Edmond Died Sept. 1, 1881, aged 80 years.

Betsey, daughter of William & Hannah Edwards, died Nov. 13, 1825, Æt. 28.

Sacred to the Memory of
Anne Fairchild, Wife of Robert Fairchild, Esqr., who departed this Life, August 29ᵗʰ, 1796, in the 85ᵗʰ Year of her Age.

Benjamin Fairchild, Died April 14, 1865, Æ. 83 yrs. 9 mo.

Eunice Fairchild, Died Feb. 10, 1874, Æ. 88 yrs. 10 mo.

Charles C. Fairchild, Died April 30, 1849, Æ. 30 yrs. & 11 mo.

In Memory of
Cornelia, Daughter of Robert & Esther Fairchild, who died April 11, 1836, Æ. 22 yrs.

In Memory of
Frederick, son of Robert & Esther Fairchild, who died May 9, 1862, Æ. 50 yrs.

In Memory of
Mr. Hamlet Fairchild, Son of Capt. John Fairchild, of Durham, who departed this life, January the 13, 1773, in yᵉ 17ᵗʰ Year of His Age.

In Memory of
Jane Emeline, daughter of Robert & Esther Fairchild, who died, Nov. 25, 1835, Æ. 30 yrs. 10 mo. & 4 ds.

John C. Fairchild, Died Feb. 27, 1873, Æ. 67 Yrs.

Mabel, Wife of J. C. Fairchild, Died May 16, 1880, Æ. 77 Yrs.

Here lyes the Body of
Mr. Joseph Fairchild, Who Died April yᵉ 20ᵗʰ, 1727, in yᵉ 37ᵗʰ year of His Aged.

Julia A., Died July 10, 1809, Æ. 9 yrs.

Maria, Died Sept. 5, 1882, Æ. 83 yrs, Daughters of Robert & Esther Fairchild.

Esther Fairchild, wife of Robert Fairchild, Esq., died Dec. 19, 1819 ; aged 43.

In memory of
Lewis Fairchild, who died Sept. 4, 1826, aged 32.
Give joy or grief, give ease or pain,
Take life or friends away ;
But let me find them all again
In that eternal day.

Louisa, wife of Lewis Fairchild, Died Oct. 16, 1867, Aged 71.

Mariah, Daughter of Thomas & Susan Fairchild, Died May 19, 1849, Æ. 1 yr. & 11 mo.

In Memory of
Martha, wife of John Fairchild, who died Nov. 25, 1834, Æ. 79 yrs. 7 mo. & 24 days.

Here lyes yᵉ Body of
Mr. Nathan Fairchild, Who died Jany, yᵉ 9ᵗʰ, 1730-1, Aged 38 years.

In memory of
Philip Fairchild, who died, Nov. 8, 1830, aged 64 years.

Philip, son of Mr. Philip & Mrs. Charry Fairchild, died Jany 21st, 1803, Aged 9 months.

In Memory of
Robert Fairchild, Born Jan. 19, 1775, died July 11, 1835, Æ. 60 yrs. 5 mo. & 22 ds.
" Requiescat in pace."

Robert R. Fairchild, Died Nov. 1, 1849, Æ. 34 yrs. & 6 mo.

Sacred to the Memory of
Robert Fairchild, Esqr., who departed this Life January 20th, 1793, In the 90th year of his age.

In memory of
Mr. Robert Fairchild, only son of Robert Fairchild, Esq., and Mrs. Anne Fairchild, his wife, who deceasd, April 12th, 1765, in 17th year of his age.

In Memory of
Elizabeth Fairchild, the only daughter of the same Parents, who deceased July 19, 1745 in the 3d year of Her Age.

Sarah Fairchild, daughter of Curtis & Mary Fairchild, died Oct. 1756, aged 9 yrs.

In Memory of
Samuel A. Fairchild, who died Nov. 1, 1844, Æ. 24 y'rs & 10 mo.

Samuel William, son of Benjamin & Eunice Fairchild, Born in Stratford, March 30, 1811, Who was lost at sea, on his passage in Steam Ship Pacific, which left Liverpool for New York, Jan. 23, 1856.

Susan E., daughter of Robert & Sarah M. Fairchild, Born July 25, 1854, Died March 19, 1860.
He is fitting up my mansion,
Which eternally shall stand,
For my stay shall not be transient
In that holy, happy land.

Here lyes ye Body of
Timothy Fairchild, Aged 39 years, Died November 23, 1728.

Joseph Farrand, Died Sept. 26, 1860, Æ. 64.

Anna, His Wife, Died Aug. 19, 1863, Æ. 76.

In Memory of
Mr. Jehiel Foot, who died Novbr. 16, 1754, In His 31st Year.

Here lies the Body of
Mr. Jehiel Foot, who died Sept. y° 2d, 1740, in the 55 year of His Age.

Joseph Foot, son of Miller & Mary Foot; Decd March 26th, 1726, in y° 17th year of his age.

Here lies the Body of
Mr. Peter Foot, who died Decembr y° 8, 1753, in y° 56 year of His Age.

Sarah Foot, wife to D—— Foot, sen. died Mar. 26, 1704, in her 46th year.

Eugenia, daughter of John & Hannah Ford, Died Aug. 23, 1851, Æ. 12 yrs. 10 mo. & 17 ds.
Bud of promise early taken,
To a more congenial clime,
Oh ! how soon thou hast forsaken,
Those who loved thee here in time.

In memory of
Mr. Stephen Frost, who died Aug. 3, 1807, in the 61st year of his age.

In memory of
Eunice Frost, Wife of Stephen Frost, who died Jan. 14th, 1807, aged 63 years.

Joseph Frost, son of Miller & Mary Frost, Died March 26th, 1726, in y° 17th year of his Age.

Wheeler Frost, Died March 2, 1852, Æ. 79.

Here Lyes Interred the Body of
Samuel Gaskill, Who died April y° 2d, 1707, in y° 29 Year of his Age.

Christopher Godfree, aged 58, Died November 26, 1715.

Mrs. Amy Goodwin. [This is on the foot stone ; the head stone, a fine brown stone, is broken off and the inscription entirely gone.]

In Memory of the ·
Rev. Hezekiah Gold, Who departed this mortal Life April the 22d, A. D. 1761, in y° 67 Year of His Age.
He was the 4th Settled Minister in the first Society of Stratford of the Presbyterian & Congregational Denomination, & executed the Ministerial office in Sd Place for more than 30 years, which he performed with Diligance & an honest heart to the end of his Ministry.

Here lies Interr'd the Body of
Mrs. Mary Gold, Consort to the Revd. Mr. Hezekiah Gold, who Departed this Life July the 2d, 1750, In the 48th year of her Age.

Here lyes y° Body of
Anna Gold, Daughter to y° Rev. Mr. Hezekiah & Mary Gold, who died April 9th, Anno Dom. 1739, Aged about 4 years & 4 Mo.

Here lyes ye Body of
Catee Gold, Daughter of yᵉ Revd.
Mr. Hezekiah & Mrs. Mary Gold, who
died Sept. 30ᵗʰ, Anno Dom. 1742, in
ye 18 year of her Age.

Here lyes yᵉ Body of
Catharine Gold, Daughter of yᵉ
Revd Hezekiah & Mrs. Mary Gold,
Who died Oct. 23ᵈ, 1743, Aged 1 year
& 7 Ds.

Ann Gorham, Died May 2, 1878,
Aged 87.

Charles R. Gorham, Died Feb.
25, 1881, Aged 83 ycars & 4 mos.

Eliza B., Daughter of Charles R. &
Sarah Gorham, Died June 3, 1862. Æ.
25 yrs. & 6 mo.

In Memory of
Eliza, Wife of Charles R. Gorham, &
daughter of the late Isaac Brooks,
who died May 2, 1835, aged 27 years
& 10 months.

In memory of
Capt. Isaac Gorham, who died
Feb. 14, 1820, aged 81.

Capt. Nehemiah Gorham, died
Feb 17, 1836, aged 83.
He was an officer in the army of the
Revolution, and served his country
faithfully through the war which estab-
lished the Independence of his country.

Joseph Gorham, died April 24,
1742, aged 60 years.

Sarah, his wife, died April 18, 1822,
in yᵉ 37th year of her age.

Mary Gorham, Wife of Capt. Nehemiah Gorham, died Jan. 2, 1837,
aged 74.
Blessed are the dead who die in the Lord.

Lewis Walker, son of Lewis W. &
Louisa M. Gorham, died July 17, 1852,
Æ. 8 mos. & 16 d's.

In Memory of
Julia Elizabeth, wife of Judson
Gorham, who died Oct. 7, 1832, aged
26 years.

Judson Gorham, Died March 29,
1848. Æ. 44.
In midst of life we are in death.

Nancy Gorham, Relict of Judson
Gorham, Died Apr. 24, 1878, Æ. 65
y'rs.
In the midst of life we are in death.

In Memory of
Miss Mary Gorham, daughter of
Mr. George Gorham, who died Dec.
26, 1813, in the 70 year of her age.

In memory of
Phebe Gorham, who died July 6,
1824, Æ. 65.

Also
Charity Gorham, who died Dec.
14, 1833, Æ. 78 :

And
George Gorham, who died Oct. 21,
1837. Æ. 77.

Sally Gorham, Died April 28, 1872,
Aged 66.
Blessed Rest.

James, son of Jeremiah & Sarah
Greemman, died Mar. 29, 1726, Aged
1 year 7 mo. & 20 ds.

Here Lyes the Body of
Joseph Grimes, Died March yᵉ 4ᵗʰ,
1716, in yᵉ 25ᵗʰ Year of his age.

Here lyes the Body of
Hannah Grimes, Wife to Joseph
Grimes, Died January yᵉ 4ᵗʰ, 1715–6
in ye 22 Year of Her Age.
[A Monument.]

Merwin Hale, aged 58, Died at
Elizabethtown, N. J., Aug. 13, 1847,
From injuries received on the Rail
Road.

Mary, Wife of Merwin Hale, Died
Aug. 30, 1870, Aged 70.

In Memory of
Asael Hawley, who died Jan. 23,
1820, aged 25 years.

In Memory of
Mrs. Abigail Hawley, Relict of
Mr. Edward Hawley, who died Aug.
31ˢᵗ, 1803, in the 72ᵈ year of her age.

In Memory of
Mr. Edward Hawley, who de-
parted this Life January the 11ᵗʰ, A.
D. 1732, in the 62 Year of his Age.

Catrin Hawley, Daughter of Mr.
Samuel & Mrs. Patience Hawley, who
died in the 2ᵈ year of her age, February, 1696.

J. H., May 20, 1690.*
J. H., June 25, 1691.
M. Hawley, 1693.

Here Lyes Buried the Body of
Mr. Daniel Hawley, who departed
this life July yᵉ 28ᵗʰ, Anno Domini,
1750 in yᵉ 66ᵗʰ year of His Age.

Here lyes ye Body of
Mrs. Deborah Hawley, Wife to
John Hawley, Esq., Who died December 3ʳᵈ, Anno Domni, 1739, in ye 73ᵈ
year of Her Age.

---

* Probably the monument of Joseph Hawley,
the first of the name in Stratford.

In Memory of
Mr. Edmund Hawley, who died March 21st, 1810, Aged 55 years.

Here lyes ye Body of
Mrs. Elizabeth Hawley, Wife to Mr. Daniel Hawley, who departed this life, Jan. the 6, 1763, in ye 79th Year of Her Age.

Here lyes the Body of
John Hawley, Esq., aged 68 years and 1 mo. Died July 27, 1729.

In Memory of
Lucy Hawley, Relect of Edmund Hawley, who died Aug. 31, 1840, Æ. 82 years.
This stone is erected by her son Lewis Hawley.

Lucy, Daughter of Edmond & Lucy Hawley, Died Nov. 6, 1822, aged 25 yrs.

Here Lyes Buried the Body of
Mr. Nathaniel Hawley, Who Departed this Life, Janry 7th, Anno Dom. 1754 in ye 52d Year of His Age.

In Memory of
Pairson Hawley, who departed this Life, August 27, A. D. 1795, in the 65 year of his age.

In Memory of
Mrs. Abiah Hawley, widow and Relect of Mr. Pairson Hawley, who departed this Life, Oct. 10, A. D. 1795, in the 60th year of her age.

Here lyes Buried ye Body of
Mr. Samuel Hawley, Who Departed this Life, Aug. 24th, A. D. 1734 in ye 87th year of His Age.

Wm. Hawley, Killed Nov. 26, 1842, Æ. 22.

Charles Hill, son of Charles & Sarah Tomlinson, Died Jan. 19, 1814, Aged 5 months & 5 days.

Daniel Holmes, Son of Mr. Daniel & Mrs. Mary Holmes, Died May 3, A. D., 1738, Aged 1 year 6 months & 21 Days.

Here lyes ye Body of
Mary Holmes, Daur of Mr Daniel & Mrs. Mary Holmes, who Died May 5th, 1738, Aged 6 years 7 months 5 days.

Mehetabel Holmes, Daur of Mr. Daniel & Mrs. Mary Holmes, Died April 25th, 1738, Aged 4 years & 5 Days.

Here lieth ye Body of
Mr. Nathaniel Hodson, aged 27 years, Deceased May the 6th, 1701.

Mr. Eliakim Hough, died Jan. 3, 1822, aged 53 Years.

Sarah Lewis, widow of Eliakim Hough, Died Dec. 9, 1858, aged 88 yrs. 2 mos. & 24 days.

This stone is erected in memory of
Aner Howes, Wife of Ebenr Howes, who died Oct. 20th, 1803, in the 47th year of her Age.

In memory of
Ebenezer Howe, who died Jan. 16, 1832, aged 90 years.

Mary Howe, Died Sept. 5, 1863, Æ. 84.

Sarah Howe, Died Oct. 2, 1861, Æ. 85.

Emily Hoyt, Born Feb. 17, 1800, died Sept. 28, 1862.
"He giveth his beloved sleep."

In memory of
Mrs. Betsey Hubbell, Wife of Mr. David Hubbell, who died March 4th, 1811, aged 23 Years.

Hannah Hubbard, Widow of Daniel Hubbard, Died Aug. 1, 1855, Æ. 73.

In memory of
Mrs. Mary Hubbell, wife of Mr. Ebenezer Hubbell, who died Septr 18th, 1790, Æ. 67.

Sarah Mariah, daughter of Lewis S. & Julia Ann Hubbell, died July 22, 1835, aged 4 yrs. and 4 mos.

In Memory of
Lovisa, wife of Roswell Humiston, who died March 11, 1831, aged 29 years.
Sleep on dear wife & take thy rest,
Thy God has called, he thought it best,
Sleep calmly with the silent dead,
For thy blest spirit now has fled.
No joys on earth were worth thy stay,
They'll soon forever pass away,
But joys eternal now are thine
Far, far beyond the bounds of time
Lovisa I hope to meet you there
And in God's kingdom have a share
I hope to sing with you above
The notes of everlasting love.

Miss Sibel Huntington, of Norwich, Conn., Died April 11, 1820, Æ. 78.
Erected by Jedediah Huntington.

In Memory of
Josephine, daughtr of Frederick & Delia C. Hunt, who died July 7, 1834, Æ. 2 y'rs. & 1 mo. Also

Frederica, died July 20, 1834, Æ. 1 year.
Suffer little children to come unto me, and forbid them not, for of such is the Kingdom of Heaven.

In Memory of
Delia C. Hunt, widow of the late Capt. Frederick Hunt. of New Haven ; & dau^{tr} of John Thompson. dec'd ; who died April 16, 1842 ; aged 39 years.
In thee O Lord, do I put my trust ; let me never be ashamed ; deliver me in thy righteousness. Into thy hand I commit my spirit ; thou hast redeemed me, O Lord God of truth. I will be glad and rejoice in thy mercy ; for thou hast considered my trouble ; thou hast known my soul in adversities.

Here lyes ye body of
John Hurd, deceased in ye 68 year of his Age.

In memory of
Naomi, the wife of James Hurlburt and daughter of Stiles & Naomi Judson, who died, March 6, 1845, Aged 50 yrs.

In Memory of
Dorothy Ives, formerly wife of John Brooks, Esq., dec'd. and late widow of Thomas Ives, Esqr., who died Sept. 12, 1834, aged 92.

Here lyeth the Body of
Alice Jenkins, the Daughter of D. J., Who departed this life in the 20 year of her age. January 9th, 170$\frac{8}{9}$.

Abel Judeson, son to David & Phebe Judeson. Aged about 7 mo. Died Sept. y^e 18th, 1721.

Mr. Abner Judson, died July 16, 1814. Æt. 49.

Fanny Judson, daughter of Abner & Elizabeth A. Judson ; died Dec. 29, 1812, Æt. 14.

In memory of My beloved husband,
Abner Judson, who departed Nov. 22, 1867. Æ. 76 yrs. & 10 mo.

Maria, Wife of Abner Judson, Died July 31, 1881. Æ. 85 yrs. & 9 mo.

Here lies inter'd the Remains of
Mr. Abner Judson, who Departed this Life February ye 18th, A. D. 1774 in ye 43^d Year of his Age.

Here lyes the Body of
Mrs. Ann Judson, wife to Mr. Samuel Judson, Aged 19 Years & 6 months 14 days. Died March 14, 1729.

In Memory of
Aaron Judson, who died Jan. 31, 1835, aged 75 years.

In Memory of
Betty Judson, who died Oct. 2, 1815 ; in the 59. year of her age.

In Memory of
Clarissa, wife of Isaac Judson, who died Oct. 29, 1822, aged 39 years.

[A MONUMENT.]
David P. Judson, Died May 24, 1869, Æ. 60.

William Judson, Died Aug. 30, 1868. Æ. 55.

Kate Holden, Died Oct. 5, 1857, Æ. 5 mos.

William, Died Mar. 5, 1869, Æ. 7 mos.
Children of D. P. & E. S. Judson.

Here lyes Buried the Body of
Capt. David Judson, Who Departed this life May the 5th, 1761, Aged 67 years & 9 months.

Here lyes ye Body of
Mrs. Phebe Judson, formerly Wife to Capt. David Judson, Who departed this life May ye 20th, 1765, Aged 69 years & 2 months.

Daniel Judson, Esq., Deceased Nov. 4, 1813 ; in the 86 year of his age.

Daniel Judson, the son of Daniel & Sarah Judson ; died Sept. 14, 18·5 ; in the 14 year of his age.
Death called Daniel long before his hour ;
(How immature this sacred marble tells)
It called his tender soul, by break of bliss,
From the first blossom, from the buds of joy ;
To join the dull mass, increase the trodden soil,
And sleep till earth herself shall be no more.

Daniel, son of Daniel & Sarah Judson, died Dec. 6, 1823, aged 7 years.
So break our glittering shaddows, human joys,
The faithless morning smiled, he takes his leave.

[A MONUMENT.]
Daniel Judson, Died Oct. 4, 1847, Aged 84.

Sarah, Wife of Daniel Judson, Died Aug. 14, 1857, Aged 82.
The Children of Daniel and Sarah Judson.

Daniel, Died Sept. 7, 1815, Aged 14.

Daniel, Died Dec. 6, 1823, aged 7.

In memory of
Mrs. Elizabeth Abigail Judson, who died Aug. 31st, aged 38 years ;

Also their Daughter
Betsey Judson, who died Sept. 21st, aged 15 years ;

Also their Son
David Judson, who died Sept. 3^d, aged 8 months :
All in the year 1803.

Elizabeth Ann Mills Judson, daughter of Rosswell & Sarah Judson, died March 12th, 1806, Æ. 22 months & 11 days.
Alas ! how transient all our earthly store ;
To-day we bloom to-morrow are no more.

[MONUMENT.]
H. T. Judson, M.D., Died Feb. 23, 1851, Æ. 50.

Nancy T. Judson, died Sept. 27, 1864, Æ. 69.

Sarah Judson, died April 18, 1859, Æ. 83.

Miss Hannah Judson, Daughter of Mr. Abner & Mrs. Hannah Judson, died Septr 17, 1795, Aged 21 years & 5 months.

In Memory of
Mrs. Hannah Judson, formerly Wife to Mr. Abner Judson Who departed this Life May ye 15, A. D. 1777, in the 41 Year of her Age.

In Memory of
Helen Judson, wife of Aaron Judson, who died May 26, 1825, aged 56 years. Also of

Edwin Judson, son of Sidney I. & Mary Ann Beardsley, who died Sept. 25, 1825, aged 5 months.

In Memory of
Isaac Judson, son of Mr. Abner & Mrs. Hannah Judson; Who died July y[e] 26th, 1772. Aged 4 years & 6 months.

In memory of
Abner Judson, son of Mr. Abner & Mrs. Hannah Judson, Who died May 17, 1764. Aged 2 months & 17 Ds.

Here lyes Buried ye Body of
Joshua Judson, who departed this Life, Nov. 27, Anno Domni, 1735, in y[e] 58th year of his age.

Here lyes the Body of
Capt. James Judson, Esq., Who dyed Feby y[e] 25th, 1721, Aged 71 yrs.

Here lyes y[e] Body of
Mrs. Rebekah Judson, Who Dyed Nov. y[e] 5th, 1717, Aged 62 Years.

In Memory of
Isaac Judson, who died Nov. 5, 1831, Aged 46 years.

Here lyeth the Body of
Mr. Jeremiah Judson, Who died in the 79 year of His Age, May 15, 1700.

Here lyes Buried ye Body of
Mr. Jeremiah Judson, who departed this life, Decem. 11th, 1759, in ye 26 Year of His Age.

Here lyes Burried y[e] Body of
Capt. Jeremiah Judson, Who departed this life Feb. 9, 1734, aged 63 years.

Sacred to the memory of
Joseph Judson, and **Sarah,** his wife: Joseph died Oct. 8, 1690, aged 71 years.

Sarah died March 16, 1696, aged 70 years. Joseph came from England when 13 Years old in 1634 with his father Wm. and two brothers and resided in this Town :

The old monument being so effaced by time as to be scarcely ledgible his descendants have erected this to perpetuate his memory, in the year 1812.

In memory of
Lewis Judson, son of Stiles & Charry Judson, who died Mar. 25, 1837, aged 21.

In memory of
Charity Judson, daughter of Stiles & Naomi Judson, who died Feb. 26, 1817, aged 29 years.

In Memory of
Lewis Judson, Son of Stiles & Naomi Judson, who died July 9, 1815, aged 25 years.

In memory of
Naomi, wife of Stiles Judson, who died June 4, 1850, Æ. 91 yrs.

Stiles Judson, Died, March 10, 1834, aged 81 years.

Sacred to the memory of
Sarah Judson, Consort of Daniel Judson, Esq., Who died May 30th, A. D. 1808. Aged 77 years.

Here lyeth Burried the Body of
Mr. Isaac Knell, sen., who departed this life in the 57 year of his age, November 2, 1708.

Here lieth the Body of
Lieut. Thomas Knowles, Who Departed this Life, November ye 17th, in the 57th Year of his Age, 1705.

B. L., March 30, 1691.

Cornelia Augusta, Daughter of David & Laura Lacy, Died April 24, 1850. Æ. 18 Y'rs & 6 mo.

"Come, dear Saviour take me home."
I long to see thy blessed face,
To hear thy voice and wear thy crown,
The gift of thy free grace.

Short from the cradle to the grave.
Christine S., Daughter of Francis B. & Cathrine A. Lacy, Died Aug. 22, 1844, Æ. 17 mo. 2 da's.

David Lacy, Born Dec. 4, 1785, died Feb. 9, 1862, Æ. 76 Y'rs, 2 mo. & 5 d's.

D. Augustus Lacy, Died at Vicksburg, Miss., October 6, 1855, Æ. 26 y'rs & 4 mo.
His remains were removed to this place, Apr. 7, 1856.
Beneath this silent marble sweetly sleeps
A Farther, friend, and husband, loved.
The memory of whose bright virtues keeps
Fond hearts prepared to meet above.

Little
Laura, daughter of D. Augustus & Eliza D. Lacy, Born Aug. 22, 1852, Died Dec. 1, 1860, Æ. 8 Yrs. 3 mo. & 9 d's.
A flower transplanted.

In Memory of
Francis B. Lacy, who died Dec. 26, 1847, in the 29th Y'r of his age.

Mother
Laura Burr, Wife of David Lacy, Born Apr. 25, 1793, Died Nov. 5, 1869, Æ. 76 Y'rs 6 mo. 10 d's.

Peter Laboree, the son of James & Abigail Laboree, died March 11, 1721.

Here Lyes Buried y° Body of
Mary Lamson, Daughter of William & Elizabeth Lamson, Who Departed This life March the 30th, 1727, Aged 2 Years, 3 months & 20 Days.

Jacob Lattin, Son of Benjamin & Mary Lattin, Dec⁴ Novb⁺. y° 23, 1724, Aged 3 months & 25 Ds.

John Hooker, son of Rev. Jackson & Sarah Leavitt, died July 11, 1828, aged 3 yrs. 8 ds.

In memory of
Abram C. Lewis, who died Dec. 9, 1845, Æ. 68 Yrs.

In memory of
Elizabeth Lewis, Wife of Abram C. Lewis, who departed this life Oct. 30, 1804, aged 26 years.

In Memory of Two Children of Abram C. & Elizabeth Lewis,
Caty, died Sept. 12th, 1803, aged 3 years & 5 months.
Charles, died Sept. 5th, 1803, aged 1 year & 10 months.
Juliana, wife of Abram C. Lewis, died May 16, 1849, Æ. 65.
Edward C., Son of A. C. & J. Lewis, died in California, Sept. 29.

Here lyes Buried the Body of
Mr. Benjamin Lewis, who departed this life, July y° 7th, 1759, in y° 63d Year of His Age.

Here lyes ye Body of
Mrs. Sarah Lewis, Wife of Mr. Benjamin Lewis, Who departed this Life, June y° 8, 1765, in y° 66 Year of Her Age.

In Memory of
Mr. Benjamin Lewis, who departed this life, May 2, 1800, aged 71 years.
O! welcome, welcome Death.

In Memory of
Mrs. Elizabeth Lewis, Relict of Mr. Benjamin Lewis, who died Oct. 29th, 1802, aged 64 years.

Benjamin Birdsey Lewis, son of Mr. Agur & Mrs. Charity Lewis, died Sept. 13th, 1805, aged 11 months.
Youth's forward slips
Death soonest nips.

Here lies intered the Body of
Daniel Lewis, Son of Mr. Joseph Lewis, who departed this Life, April 9th, A. D. 1775, aged 21 years 11 months & 22 Days.
No gift of Nature, art or Grace,
Exempteth from the burying place,
All must obey the solemn Call,
Before that tyrant all must Fall.

In Memory of
Mr. George Lewis, who died Nov. 13, 1815, in the 81 Year of his age.

Mrs. Mary Lewis, wife of Mr. George Lewis, died May 24th, 1814. Aged 76 Years.

In Memory of
Jerusha Lewis, wife of Stephen Lewis, who died Feb. 12, 1838; in the 86 year of her age.

Jerusha, daughter of Mr. Stephen C. & Mrs. Hannah Lewis, died Nov. 4, 1814, aged 7 months.

Here lyeth y° Body of
Hannah Lewis, the Daughter of Mr. E. L., Who Departed this Life in y° 3 Year of her age, April 10, 1700.

In memory of
Mr. Joseph Lewis, who died Oct. 7, 1797, In y° 77 Year of His Age.

In memory of
Rebecca J., daughter of Abram C. & Juliana Lewis, who died Feb. 14, 1835, Æ. 9 years 8 months.

In memory of
Sarah Lewis, the beloved Consort of Mr. Joseph Lewis, who died Feb. 20th, 1789, in the 63 year of her age.

In memory of
Stephen Lewis, who died July 18, 1839, aged 91 yrs.

Charlotte A., only Daughter of Benedict & Marilla Lillingstone, Died July 6, 1861, Æ. 24 yrs. 3 mo. & 16 Ds.
This is ground
which no rude footstep should impress.

Mary H., Wife of David W. Lillingstone, Died Oct. 13, 1863. Æ. 22 yrs. 2 mo. & 11 Ds.
Tread softly stranger.

In memory of Four Infant children of *Ezekiel & Hannah Lovejoy.* They died in the year of 1793, 1794, 1795 & 1805.

Little Carrie

In memory of
Ezekiel Lovejoy, who died April 20, 1837 ; aged 77 years.

In memory of
Clarissa Lovejoy, relict of Ezekiel Lovejoy, who died March 31, 1839, aged 46 years.

Theodora, daughter of Ezekiel & Clarissa Lovejoy, died Sept. 27, 1824, aged 3 years & 7 months.

Mrs. Hannah Lovejoy, wife of Mr. Ezekiel Lovejoy ; died Dec. 15, 1813 ; aged 48 years.

In memory of
Mrs. Susannah Lovejoy, wife of Capt. Phineas Lovejoy, who departed this life, April 6th, A. D. 1806, Æt. 76.
Behold and see, you who pass by,
As you are now so once was I ;
As I am now so you must be,
Prepare for death and follow me.

Capt. Phineas Lovejoy, died Sept. 21, 1812, in the 81 year of his age.
Farewell, my offspring, left on shore,
You soon must pass this dangerous deep ;
Where all our ancestors are gone before ;
I hope in heaven we all shall meet.

The Grave of two sisters, only children of DeForest and Catharine Maria Manice, died in New York of scarlet fever.

Catharine Maria, born in New York, Jan. 26, 1828, died Feb. 11, 1830, aged 2 years & 16 days.

Mary Anne, born in Hartford, Jan. 6, 1826, died March 8, 1830, aged 4 years 2 months & 2 days.

In Memory of
Samuel McAlister, Born 1803, Died May 12, 1852.
And also
Harriet, his wife, Born 1783, Died Sept. 13, 1863.

Samuel Ufford McAlister, Aged 10 yrs. 1843.
A blighted flower,
A bud of fairest promise nipped
In early morning hour.

Abijah McEwen, Esq., died Dec. 1, 1812, aged 70.

In memory of
Mrs. Catee, the virtuous and beloved Consort of Abijah McEwen, & Daughter of Agur Tomlinson, Esqr., who departed this Life in a glorious prospect of a better ; December 28th, A. D., 1774, Æiat. 28.
O just beloved and lost, O ever dear !
Thy memory still shall prompt the tender tear
With every virtue, every Grace adorn'd
Whatever in life is Loved, in Death is mourned.

Charles McEwen, Died January 6th, 1836, Aged 56.

Sarah McEwen, wife of Charles McEwen, died Sept. 17, 1847, aged 68.

Wm. Wallace, son of Charles & Sally McEwen, died Aug. 25, 1815, aged 4 years.

George V. T. McEwen, Died Sept. 10, 1882, Aged 63 years.

Jane Elizabeth, daughter of Charles and Sally McEwan, died Novbr 16th, 1804, aged 10 months.

Jerusha McEwen, Died April 6, 1839, Aged 82 years and 7 months.

Dr. John Betts McEwen, born in Stratford, March 31, 1808, and died in New York October 7, 1867.

Maria Catharine McEwen, Died Dec. 16, 1843, Aged 62.

In Memory of
Mary Alice McEwen, Daur of Mr. Abijah & Mrs. Catey McEwen, who died April 7th, 1772, Aged 5 months.

In Memory of
Ruth McEwen, wife of Samuel McEwen, who died June 22d, 1836, Aged 55.

Sacred to the Memory of
Sally McEuen, Wife of Samuel McEuen, who died Oct. 20, 1802, Æt. 23, and of their
Daughter, who died Oct. 17th, 1802, Æt. 17 hours.

In memory of
Samuel McEwen, who died March 2, 1849, Æ. 74.

In Memory of
Mr. Timothy McEuen, who died Feby 9th, 1788, aged 84 years.

In Memory of
William S. W. McEwen, who died
Aug. 17, 1833. Aged 34.

In Memory of
Caroline Elizabeth, daughter of
William S. & Sarah M. McEwen, Who
died Sept. 4, 1828, Æ 13 Months.
This lovely bird so young and fair,
Called hence by early doom,
Just come to show how sweet a flower,
In Paridise would bloom.

In Memory of
Samuel Curtiss, son of William S.
& Sarah M. McEwen, who died July
6, 1836, Æ 7 yrs.

Wm. Samuel, son of Abijah & Mary
Ann McEwen, died Oct. 14, 1845,
aged 7 years.

In Memory
George McCune, Son of Mr. Timothy & Mrs. Abigail McCune, who
Departed this Life April yᵉ 6ᵗʰ, 1768,
in yᵉ 16ᵗʰ year of His Age.

Here lies inter'd the Body of
Mrs. Abigail Mc eune, Wife of
Mr. Timothy McEune, Who died Aut.
17ᵗʰ, 1775, in the 66ᵗʰ year of Her Age.

Jane Mills, Died April 12, 1849, Æ
37.

Mr. William Morehouse, died of
consumption, Sept. 11, 1832, aged 34
years.
Farewell my dear husband, he's gone
And we are destined for a while to part
I am left for to weep and to mourn—
The wound has sunk deep in my heart.

To the Memory of
Mary Mumford, daughter of B M.
& Harriet Mumford, of New York,
died 31 July, 1814, aged 1 year & 29
days.

Here lyes Buried the Body of
Mr. Howkins Nichols, Who De-
parted this Life Sept. yᵉ 13ᵗʰ, 1757,
Aged 29 Years, 11 months & 29 Days.

Here lyes Buried the Body of
Mr. Jonathan Nichols, Who departed this Life November yᵉ 6ᵗʰ, 1760,
in yᵉ 73 year of His Age.

In Memory of
Mrs. Susan Nichols, who departed
this life, Janʳʸ 13ᵗʰ, 1792, In the 35ᵗʰ
year of her Age.

Josiah Nicols, June 25, 1692, [Aged]
39 y.

Here lyes Buried the Body of
Richard Nichols, Who departed
this life, Sept. yᵉ 20, 1756, in yᵉ 78
of His Age.

In Memory of
Mr. Silas Nichols, who departed
this Life Janʸ. 13, 1792, in the 55 Year
of his age.

[A Monument.]
Sacred to the Memory of
Mrs. Ann Nichols, wife of George
K. Nichols, and daughter of Jabez H.
Tomlinson, Esqr., born on the 23ᵈ
day of January, 1785. She died deeply lamented, on the 26 day of February, 1812, aged XXVII.
She was a dutiful Child, an affectionate Sister, a constant Friend, a loving Wife, and a tender Mother.
Possessing an elevating and descriminating
mind, She gratefully embraced the religion of
Jesus, and living in the exercise of the Christian
Faith, she resigned this life with a well founded hope of a blessed immortality, through the
divine Redeemer.

In Memory of
Mr. George K. Nichols, who was
born Dec. 26, 1776; died Sept. 1,
1821, near Natchez, where his remains
were buried.
An amiable and generous heart, enlivened by
the love of the divine Redeemer, endeared
himself to his numerous friends and relatives.

Elizabeth Huntington Nichols
was born on the 3ᵈ day of February,
1809, and died on the 9ᵗʰ day of July,
1812.
She was a lovely child. She was committed
to our care, and we watched over her with the
tenderest affection, but we loved her, perhaps,
too well, and she was taken from us in mercy.

Here lies the body of
Josiah, Son to Mr. Thomas & Mʳˢ
Sarah Olcott, who died May yᵉ 3ʳᵈ,
1747, in the 10 year of his Age.

Sarah Olcott, wife of Thomas Olcott,
died May 11, 1811, in the 89 year of
her age.

In Memory of
Mr. Thomas Olcott, who died May
3, 1795; In yᵉ 82 year of his Age.

Here lies Interred the Body of
Mrs. Sarah Ollcott, wife of Mr.
Thomas Ollcott, who Departed this
Life March yᵉ 30ᵗʰ, A.D. 1756, In yᵉ
40ᵗʰ Year of Her Age.

In Memory of
Frederick Olmstead, who died
Nov. 9, 1826, aged 39 years.

In Memory of
Mary J. wife of Frederick Olmstead,
Born Nov. 20, 1792, Died Jan. 10,
1882.

William Pixlee, son of Frederick
and Mary J. Olmstead, died Jan. 21,
1823, aged 17 months.

Mr. *Normand Olmstead*, died March 28, 1819 ; aged 43 years.

In Memory of
Marther Osborn, wife of Nathan Osborn, who died Oct. 5th, 1803, aged 54.

Here lyes Buried yᵉ Body of
Mr. *Andrew Patterson*, Who departed this Life December yᵉ 2ᵈ, Anno Domni 1746, Aged 87 years.

Isaac Patterson, Son of Mᵣ John & Mᵣˢ Mary Patterson : Died Febʳʸ 13th, A.D. 1749, aged 1 year & 8 Months.

Helen T., wife of Edward Patterson, died Feb. 5, 1848. Æ 21 yʳˢ & 6 Mo. Also their Infant daughter died Jan. 31, 1848, Æ 2 ds.

Isabella & Helen T., Daughters of Edward and Mary H. Patterson, Æ 5½ mo.

Here lyes yᵉ body of
Parthenia Patterson, Daughᵣ of Mᵣ John & Mᵣˢ Mary Patterson, Who Died Janʳʸ 26th, 174⅞, Aged 16 Years 1 mo. & 27 dˢ.

Here lies Interr'd the Body of
Lieut. Samuel Peat, who Dec'd Septᵣ the 14th, 1747, in the 84th Year of his age.

In Memory of two Children of Capt. John & Mrs. Mary Peck.

Elizabeth Peck, departed this Life, Janry 30th, 1785, in the 5 Year of her age.

David Brooks Peck, departed this Life, Febry 4th. 1785, in the 2 year of his Age.
Your moans fond parents cease & Let this hope suffice.
Your babies shall sleep in peace till Jesus bids them rise.

In memory of
Hannah, wife of Thaddeus Peck, who died Oct. 5, 1815, aged 33 years.

In memory of
James Peck, Son of Dean Job & Mrs. Bettee Peck, Who died Octᵇʳ. 8, A.D. 1776, in the 18th Year of his Age.

In memory of
Deacon Job Peck, who departed this Life, September the 9th, A.D. 1782, in the 62ᵈ Year of his Age, and also of
Betty Peck, his wife, who departed this Life, december the 21ˢᵗ, A.D. 1780, in the 56th Year of her Age.
Redeemed from Earth & pain
Ah when shall we ascend
And all in Jesus presence reign
With our departed friends.

In Memory of
Mr. Job Peck, who died Feby 3, 1797, in the 44th Year of his age.
Redeemed from earth and pain
O when shall we assend
And all in Jesus presence reign
With our departed friends.

In memory of
Mrs. Martha Peck, Wife of Mr. Job Peck.   She died Sept. 13, 1798, Ætat. 42.

In memory of
Josiah Peck, Junᵣ, who died at St. Christopher's August 27th, 1809, In the 23ᵈ year of his age,
Also,
Sally Peck, Daughter of Mr. Joseph Peck, who died Sept. 17th, 1809. In the 17th year of her age.
While our departed friends are gone,
To join the Church above,
May We Prepare to follow them,
And sing Redeeming Love.

In memory of
Lewis Peck, Son to Mr. Job & Mrs. Martha Peck, who died June 3, 1796, in the 12 year of his Age.

Alice, widow of Isaac Pendleton. Died Dec. 10, 1868 ; Aged 88 yrs.

Isaac Pendleton, deceased, Nov. 10, 1824, aged 46 years.

William Pendleton, Died Sept. 14, 1883, æ 78 yrs. 9 mos.

J. P., S. P.

Here lyes Buried yᵉ Body of
Mr. David Pixley, Who Died August yᵉ 1ˢᵗ, A.D. 1742, in yᵉ 38th year of his Age.

Memory of
Mr. Peter Pixlee, Who Departed this Life, Aug. 2ᵈ, 1788, In the 86th Year of his age.

David Pixlee, son of Peter & Mary Pixlee, died Sept. yᵉ 18, 1751, in his 9th year.

In memory of
Mrs. Mary Pixlee, Relict of Mr. Peter Pixlee, who died June 13, 1799, aged 92 Years.

In Memory of
Mr. William Pixlee, who died May 8th, 1800, aged 66 years.

In memory of
Bette Pixlee, Wife of Mr. William Pixlee, who died Septᵣ 27th, 1776, in the 40th Year of her Age.
And also two Children.

Bette, died Sept. 28, 1776, in the 8th Year of her Age.

William, died Octᵣ 16, 1776, in the 6th Year of his Age.

Sacred to the Memory of
Mrs. Bathshebah Plant, Relict of Mr. James Plant, late of Branford, who died Jany 5th, 1803, in the 87th year of her age.

In Memory of
Cathrine, wife of David Plant & Daughter of William & Phebe Tomlinson, who was born Oct. 9, 1787, & died June 2, 1835.

David Plant, born March 29, 1783, died Oct. 18, 1851.

Edward, son of David & Cathrine Plant, died May 14, 1826, æ 10 months.

Mary, Wife of Henry Plant, Died Nov. 7, 1860, aged 38 years.

Mary B., Wife of Henry Plant, Died Nov. 7, 1862, aged 38 years.

John Henry, son of David & Cathrine Plant, died Sept. 7th, 1815, aged 1 year & 7 months.

In Memory of
Sarah, wife of Solomon Plant, who died Sept. 15th, 1815 ; aged 68 years.

In Memory of
Mr. Solomon Plant, who died, May 20, 1822, aged 81 years.

Justus Plumb, Died March 17, 1845, Aged 81.

Huldah, His Wife, Died Sept. 19, 1853, Aged 88.

In memory of
Rebecca Poore, wife of Dr. Joshua Poore, who died July 8, 1838, aged 81 years.

Joshua Poor, M.D., Died 1792, Aged 42.

Catharine, Daughter of Joshua & Rebecca Poor, Died Sept. 7, 1868, Aged 80.

In Memory of
Mrs. Charity Porter, wife of Stephen Porter, who died Oct. 12, 1817, aged 63 Years.

In Memory of
Mr. Stephen Porter, who died September 7, 1817, aged 81 years.

In Memory of
Charlotte Prince, widow of William Prince, who died Dec. 17, 1841, aged 79 years.

James Prince, Son of William & Grandson of Joseph Prince, of Stratford, Died Aug. 4, 1876, Æ. 88 y'rs, 6 mo.

Jerusha, Wife of James Prince, Died Dec. 29, 1873, Æ. 82 yrs. 5 mo.

Charlotte Augusta, Daughter of James & Jerusha Prince, Born May 17, 1829, Died July 10, 1833.
Love to her Savior, love to all
She knew, were her last accents.

To the lovely and much lamented
Mary Abigail, Daughter of James and Jerusha Prince, who died September 12th, 1827, aged 3 months and 8 days.

John Prince, Son of Mr. Joseph & Mrs. Hannah Prince, Died Feb. 13, 1740-1. Aged 4 Years 4 months & 8 Days.

Here lie the Remains of
Mr. Joseph Prince, 4th Son of Samuel Prince, Esqr., by Mary his 2d Wife of Sandwich, where he was born April 1st, 1695, and Died here Decemr 4, 1747, in the 53rd year of his Age, Much beloved and lamented.

Here lyes the Body of
Samuel Pitman, Son of Mr. Jonathan Pitman, Deceased, May ye 18th, 1717, Aged 25 years, 3 Mo. & 13 Ds.

Mary Rexford, daughter of Hezekiah & Maria Rudd, died Aug. 17, 1817, Aged 1 year 8 mo.

Mary L. Rexford, died Jan. 18, 1869, aged 80 y'rs.

Mrs. Sarah Rexford, died Aug. 11, 1831, aged 80 years.

Charles H. Rogers, Died March 10, 1864, Æ. 48 yrs. 3 mos.

Harriet Maria Rogers, relict of T. M. Rogers, daughter of Robert died Mar. 19, 1847, aged 60 years.

Laura M. Rogers, Born Oct. 13, 1855, Died, Dec. 25, 1880.

Sophronia E. Rogers, Born June 14, 1854, Died June 9, 1875.

Thomas Mumford Rogers, aged 63 Years.

Here Lyes Burried ye Body of
Abigail Rumsey, Daughter of Mr. Benjmn & Mrs. Rebecka Rumsey, of Fairfield, Who Died Octbr 14, 1743, Aged 16 years & 7 months.
Wasting sickness spoiled ye beauteous form
And Death Consigned her to her kindred Worm.
The Day Advances When ye saints shall Rise
With Sparkling Glory & Ascend ye skyes.

Alden Russell, Died Dec. 26, 1863, Aged 77 years.

Sarah A., Wife of Alden Russell, Died Feb. 21, 1865, Æ. 70.
" The morning cometh."

Julia E. Russell, Died Oct. 26, 1860, Aged 21 yrs. 4 mos. & 15 ds.

In Memory of
Eliphalet Russell, son of Doct. Wm. & Hannah Russell who departed this Life Mrch 26, 1776, in the 21 year of his age.

In memory of
Betsy Russell, Daughter of Mr. William & Mrs. Jerusha Russell, who died Sept. 28, 1790, aged 1 year & 11 mo.

In memory of
William Russell, son of Mr. William & Jerusha Russell, who died Dec. 2, 1792, aged 1 year & 3 months.
Sleep, lovely Babe and take thy rest
God called thee home as he thought best,
Though to thy Parents dear.

From the affectionate desire of a Father let this Stone remain Sacred to the memory of his son,
James Saidler, Jun., Student of Columbia College, New York, Aged 14 Years & 9 months, who, after three days' illness, died on his arrival here from that city of the Pestilential disdisease on the 11th day of August, 1798.

Here lieth The Body of
Sarah Foot, Wife to D. F. Senior, Who died in the 46th year of her age, March 26, 1704.

Elijah Sharman, died August ye 15th, 1751, aged 9 months.

Mr. Benjamin Sherman.

Mrs. Rebeckah Sherman.

Walker, the Son of Mr. Enos & Mrs. Abigail Sharman, April ye 6, 1751 in the 19th year of his age.

In Memory of
Charles R. Smith, who died Nov. 3, 1822, Æ. 29.

In Memory of
George Smith, who died Oct. 13, 1822, Æ. 73.

Sacred to the Memory of
Lucy Smith, wife of George Smith, deceased June 26, 1813; Ætat. 53 years.

And of
Sarah Anna, their daughter, who died at Huntington, Long Island, Feb. 19, 1785; Æt. 6 months & 4 dys.
Here silence dwells with all her solemn train
And secrecy holds her Court explored by man in vain.

George B. Smith, son of George & Lucy Smith, was killed at Stratford tide mill, Nov. 17, 1796, Æ. 15.

Grace, Daughter of L. D. & Julia E. Smith, Died Apr. 20, 1882, Aged 4 years.

Here lies Buried the Body of
Mrs. Charity, wife of Mr. William Southworth, who departed this Life, August 15th, 1773, in the 39th year of her age.
In calm repose her Body lies,
When Christ appears, her dust shall rise.

In Memory of
Mercy, widow of Samuel W. Southworth, who died Dec. 24, 1842, Æ. 80 yrs.

In Memory of
Samuel Wells Southworth, who died Aug. 17, 1837, aged 80 yrs.
Also his son
Samuel Wells Southworth, Jr., who died at sea, A. D. 1818, aged 30 yrs.

Sacred to the Memory of
Robert Southworth, who died May 17, 1814; aged 29 years.
Also of
Edward Southworth, who died Sept. 18, 1815, aged 8 years & 6 months.

In Memory of
Mr. Robert Southworth, who died October 23d, A. D. 1770 in the 22d year of his Age.

Miss Abigail Southworth, daughter of Mr. Samuel W. Southworth, died May 5, 1817; Aged 22 years.

In memory of
Phebe Spratt, wife of Capt. Wm. Spratt, formerly the wife of Abijah Curtiss, who died June 28, 1834, aged 79.

Eunecia, daughter of Revd. Stephen W. & Mrs. Eunecia Stebbins; departed this life July 4, 1811; in the 27 year of her age.
Let me but hear my Saviour say
Strength shall be equal to the day
Then I rejoice in deep distress
Leaning on all sufficient grace.
I glory in infirmity
That Christs own power may rest on me.
When I am weak, then am I strong,
Grace is my shield & Christ my song.

Eunice Sophia, Daughter of Revd. Stephen W. & Mrs. Eunecia Stebbins, departed this life May 4th, 1806, in the 19th year of her age.
To a tender and benevolent heart, expanding with those virtues which endear & strengthen every social tie; She united an apparent submission to God, & an humble trust in Jesus Christ, which cherish in surviving friends, the hopes of her blessed immortality.

[A Monument.]

John W. Sterling, Born Sept. 4, 1796, Died Feb. 13, 1866, Æ. 69.

[A Monument.]

Mary R. Sterling, wife of John W. Sterling and daughter of Daniel & Sarah Judson, Died June 2ᵈ, 1838, aged 31 years.

Mary Judson, daughter of John W. & Mary R. Sterling, Died Sept. 14, 1838, Æ. 7 months.

Here lyes yᵉ body of
Mr. Ephraim Stiles, Aged 69 years, died June yᵉ 21, 1745.

Frances Ives, Daughter of G. W. & S. A. Stow, Died Mar. 1, 1859, Æ. 8 mos. 23 Ds.

Frederick H. Stow, Died July 18, 1872, Æ. 58 yrs.

Susan A. Fairchild, Wife of George W. Stow, Born Aug. 12, 1823, Died Dec. 6, 1873.

Susan Fairchild, Daughter of F. H. & S. B. Stow. Died June 11, 1858, Æ. 11 Years, 3 mos. & 20 Days.

Here lyes Buried yᵉ Body of
Mr. Joseph Strong, Who departed this Life Sept. 22. Ann Domni, 1741, Aged 24 Years.

Mrs. Priscilla Stratton, died April 11, 1738, aged 86 years.

In memory of two Children of Mr. John & Mrs. Mehetable Thacher.

Anthony, died the 3ᵈ of February, 1779, aged 7 days.

Mehetable, died the 16ᵗʰ of July, 1780, aged 30 hours.

Solomon Thomas, Aged about 61 years, Died April 16, 1729.

In Memory of
Mr. Abijah Thompson, who died Oct. 5, 1799, in the 61ˢᵗ year of his age.

In Memory of
John Thompson, Who died July 16, 1836, Æ. 73 y'rs.

In Memory of
Alice Thompson, relict of John Thompson, who died May 14, 1862, Æ. 97 y'rs & 8 mo.

Here lyes Burried yᵉ Body of
Mr. Ambrose Thompson, Who Departed this Life, Sept. 7ᵗʰ, Anno Dom. 1742, in the 92ⁿᵈ Year of his age.
Precious in ye sight of ye Lord is ye death of his saints.

In Memory of
Mr. Ambrose Thompson, who departed this Life the 3ᵈ day of May, 1768, In the 86ᵗʰ Year of his age.

In Memory of
Mrs. Ann Thompson, Wife of Mr. Ambrose Thompson, who departed this Life, Sept. 22, 1774, in the 86 Year of her age.

Mrs. Bathsheba Thompson, relict of Mr. Abijah Thompson, died Feb. 12, 1814, in the 70 year of her age.

Bathsheba Thompson, died Aug. 27, 1815, aged 87.

In Memory of
Mrs. Betty Thompson, wife of Mr. David Thompson, who died Jan. 18, 1800, Aged 44 Years.

In Memory of
Mr. David Thompson, who died April 8, 1800, In yᵉ 82 Year of his age.
Blessed are the dead that die in the Lord.

David Thompson died Aug. 4, 1817, Aged 67 years,
And his wife,
Sarah, died Dec. 12, 1815; aged 64 years.

Sacred to in the Memory of
Delia Thompson, Daughter of John & Ellis Thompson, who died Oct. 5ᵗʰ, 1790, aged 12 years.
She is not lost, but only gone;
To realms of Glory & celestial peace.

Harriet Thompson, Died Sept. 21, 1874, Æ. 89 Y'rs.

Jonathan, son of Ambrose Thompson, Junr., & Ann, his wife, Decᵈ June yᵉ 28, 1726, Aged 3 years & 5 mo.

Here lies the Body of
Mrs. Elizabeth, Wife of Mr. Ebenezer Thompson, who died Nov. 28ᵗʰ, 1747, in her 40ᵗʰ year.

Here lyes Burried yᵉ Body of
Mr. Ephraim Thompson, Who departed this Life June 18, Anno Domni, 1746, Aged 26 years.

Maria Thompson, widow of the late Enoch St. John, of New Canaan, Died March 3, 1873, Æ. 83 Y'rs.

In Memory of
Mrs. Martha Thompson, the Beloved wife of Mr. David Thompson, who departed this Life January 26ᵗʰ, 1792, In the 74ᵗʰ Year of her age.
She lived much esteemed and died much lamented.

16

Here lyes Buried y* Body of
Mrs. Martha Thompson, wife to
Dea*con* John Thompson, who departed
this life Feb*ry* 7th Anno Dom[l], 1740,
in ye 63[d] Year of his age.

Here lyes buried the Body of
Deacon John Thompson, Esq.,
who departed this life July y* 20th,
1765, in y* 85 Year of His Age.

Here lyes y* Body of
Samuel Tompson, Son of Mr. Ambrose & Mrs. Anne Tompson, Who
Departed this life, Feby 19th, Anno
Dom 1749-50, in y* 29th Year of his
age.

Here lyes y* Body of
Mrs. Sarah Thompson, Wife to
Mr. Ambrose Thompson, Who Departed this Life Mar. 23[d], 1730, Aged
About 71 Years.

Sacred To the Memory of
Lieut. William Thompson, Who
fell in battle, bravly fighting for the
liberties of his country, in the memorable action at Ridgefield, on the
27th of April, 1777, where a handful
of entrepid Americans withstood some
thousands of British troop till overpowered by numbers, he fell a victim
to the British tyranny, and more than
savage cruelty in the 35th year of his
age. He lived greatly beloved, and
died universally lamented, and his
body being removed from the place of
action, was here deposited with military honors.
Relettered in 1864.

In Memory of
Capt. William Thompson, who
died at sea. Dec. 14, 1812, aged 47
years. Also of
Edward, son of Capt. William & Mrs.
Phebe Thompson, died, Sept. 30, 1815,
aged 10 years.

Isaac, son of Mr. William & Mrs.
Mehetable Thompson, who departed
this Life Aug. 20th, A.D. 1775, aged
7 years 5 months.
Ye Young, ye gay, attend this speaking stone,
Think on his fate and tremble at your own.

In memory of
Phebe, widow of the late Capt. William Thompson, who died April 27,
1844, in the 80th yr. of her age.

Mary Thompson, daughter of William & Phebe Thompson, died Oct.
28, 1860, Æ. 69.

Miss Huldah Tibbals, died Oct.
22, 1823, aged 58 years.
The soul of a sister is gone
To brighten the triumph above;
Exalted to Jesus' throne,
And clasped in the arms of his love.

Abraham Tomlinson, died April,
1821, aged 88 Years.

Anna Tomlinson, relect of Abraham Tomlinson, died May 5, 1827,
Aged 85.

In Memory of
Anna Tomlinson, daughter of
Abraham & Anna Tomlinson, who
died July 28, 1799, aged 17 years.

In Memory of
Sarah Tomlinson, daughter of
Abraham & Rebecca Tomlinson, who
died March 24, 1813, in the 53 year of
her age.

Bathsheba Tomlinson, died Aug.
27, 1815, aged 87.

Here lyes Buried y* Body of
Lieut. Agur Tomlinson, Died
March 5, 172⅞ in y* 70 year of his age.

Here lies Intered the Remains of
Agur Tomlinson, Esq., who departed this Life, February the 15th,
A. D. 1774, in the 53[d] year of his age.
You pass with melancholy state
By all these solemn heaps of fate,
And think as soft as sad you tread above
the Venerable Dead,
Time was like you Life possess'd
And time will be when you shall rest.

Doct. Charles Tomlinson, died
July 10, 1830, aged 55.

Sarah H. Tomlinson, Wife of Dr.
Charles Tomlinson, Died March 1,
1858, aged 77.

Charles Hill, son of Charles & Sarah
Tomlinson, died Jan. 19, 1814, aged 5
mos. & 5 ds.

In Memory of
Mr. George Tomlinson, who was
born June 29, 1796, and died June 19,
1824.

Gideon Tomlinson, was born in
Stratford, December 31, 1780, and
died at Greenfield, October 8, 1854.
He was admitted to the Bar and commenced
the practice of Law at Greenfield in 1807; was
successively a member of the State Legislature;
Speaker of the House of Representatives;
Member of Congress, Governor of the State of
Connecticut, and United States Senator; at the
close of the last named term of office he voluntarily retired to private life. Amiable and upright, an affectionate husband and fond father,
happily exemplifying Christian piety in life,
and dying, supported by the hope which it inspired.

Sarah, the beloved wife of Gideon Tomlinson, died December 25, 1842, in the 56 year of her age.
Her affectionate kindness, enlightened mind, good principals, sincerity & many endearments & virtues, made her worthy of love, respect & confidence. The loss of her endeared society was deeply felt and lamented by her bereaved husband, but he derived comfort from the hope and evidence that, while she realized the decay of her body & mourned for their darling son, in devout submission to the will of God, she was mercifully brought to exercise faith & trust in Christ.

Jabez Huntington Tomlinson, the beloved, loving & only son of Gideon and Sarah Tomlinson, was born June 28, 1818, and died of consumption, April 21, 1838 in New York, where he had recently arrived from Charleston with his deeply afflicted parents.
The remembrance of his promising and improved talents amiable disposition, sound judgment, exemplary virtues and endearing deportment, is warmly cherished, while his patience in a long sickness and the disappointment of earthly expectations, his solicitude for the happiness of others; penitence and faith, hope and trust in God afford consolation, under the mournful & trying dispensation of an all-wise just, merciful and holy Providence.

In Memory of
Mrs. Hannah Tomlinson, Consort of Capt. Gideon Tomlinson, & Dautr. of Colo. Jabez Huntington, of Windham, Who departed this Life, December ye 26, 1762, in ye 27th Year of Her Age.

In Memory of
Capt. Gideon Tomlinson, Who departed this Life January the 19th, 1766, in ye 35th Year of His Age. He was an officer in ye army & fought in ye battle at ye Narrows ; was at ye Taking Ticonderoga, Crown Point, La Callette and Montreal.

In Memory of
Miss Hannah Tomlinson, who was born Jan. 16, 1783, and Died April 2, 1827.

Huldah Tomlinson, Born May 1, 1766, Died Sept. 16, 1844.
Blessed are those servants whom the Lord when he cometh shall find watching.

In Memory of
Dr. Hez. Tomlinson, A.M., a learned and eminent Physician, who departed this Life on the 12th day of May, A. D. 1781, in the 34 year of his Age.
He lived much esteemed and died greatly lamented. Vain World, farewell to you. Heaven is my native Air, I bid my friends a short Adieu, impatient to be there.

In memory of
Anna, the Daughter of Dr. Hezekiah & Mrs. Sarah Tomlinson, who deceased July 2, 1781 in the 3^d year of her age.
Happy the Babe
Who's priviledged by Fate
To shorten labor
And lighten weight.

In memory of
Jabez H. Tomlinson, Esq., who died January 14, 1849, Æ. 89.
He was highly respected as a patriotic officer of the revolutionary army and an experienced, able and upright legislator and magistrate; and deservedly honored and beloved as a friend, husband, father & Christian.

In memory of
Rebecca Tomlinson, the Wife of Jabez H. Tomlinson, who was born on the 3 day of Dec. 1761, & died on the 1 day of Jan. 1823, deeply & justly lamented by her afflicted husband & bereaved children.
Let those who delight to cherish the remembrance of her unwearied and constant affection, imitate the pious example of one, whose active and unshaken faith, in the Divine Redeemer, affords just ground of confidence that she has gone to possess an inheritance incorruptible & eternal in the heavens.

In Memory of
Capt. Joseph Tomlinson, who departed this Life Oct. 5th, 1774. Aged 50 years.

In Memory of
Elizabeth Tomlinson, Relict of Capt. Joseph Tomlinson, who died July 28th, 1809, aged 80 years.

Mary Tomlinson, Born Jan. 27, 1772, Died Dec. 19, 1861, Ninty Years.
We know that when he shall appear, we shall be like him, for we shall see him as he is.

In memory of
Mrs. Mary Tomlinson, Consort of Capt. Gideon Tomlinson, Who Departed this Life, June ye 7th, 1758, in ye 26th Year of Her Age.

In Memory of
Mrs. Mary Tomlinson, Relict of Augur Tomlinson, Esq., who died June 23^d, 1802, in the 79 year of her age.

In Memory of
William Agur Tomlinson, an eminent Physician who Departed this Life on the 20th day of August, A. D. 1789 in the 27th Year of his Age. He lived much esteemed and greatly lamented.
Christ my Redeemer lives
And freely I can trust
My naked soul into his hands
When parted from its dust.

In Memory of

Mary Alace, the Daughter of Agur Tomlinson, Esqʳ and Mʳˢ Mary his Wife, who died October 8ᵗʰ, A. D. 1771, Aged 5 years and 1 month, & 5 other infant children of the above Parents, Who lie here interr'd.

Sleep lovely Babes and take your perfect rest.
God called you home because he thought it right.

In memory of

Phebe Tomlinson, widow of Dr. William Agur Tomlinson, who died March 11, 1842, Aged 76 years.

Here lies Hid in this Grave the Body of **Mrs. Rebekah,** the amiable Consort of Abraham Tomlinson, Esqr., who Departed this Life on the first Day of Novemᵇʳ, 1774, in the 39ᵗʰ year of her age.

I have been what thou art now, and are what thou shalt shortly be.
How Loved thou valued once, avail me not to whom Related or by whom begot, a heap of Drift alone
Remains of me, 'tis all I am, and all that you must be.

In memory of

Rachel E., widow of John Tomlinson, who died Sept. 21, 1841, aged 74.

Susan Tomlinson, wife of William A. Tomlinson, and daughter of Joseph & Susannah Walker, died May 5, 1826, aged 33 years.

In memory of

Mr. Stephen Tomlinson, son of Capt. Joseph & Mrs. E. Tomlinson, who departed this Life Oct. 27, 1774, Aged 25 Years.

Susan Walker, daughter of William A. & Susan Tomlinson, died Sept. 23, 1822, aged 1 year & 6 months.

[Monument.]

William A. Tomlinson, died in New York, Dec. 19, 1837, in the 49ᵗʰ Year of his age.

Mark the perfect man, and behold the upright, for the end of that man is peace.

Susan Walker, Wife of Wm. A. Tomlinson, died May 5, 1826, Æ. 33.

Susan Walker, daughter of W. A. & S. W. Tomlinson, died Sept. 23, 1822, Aged 1 y'r & 6 mo.

Eliza Russell, wife of Wm. A. Tomlinson, died Sept. 13, 1862, Æ. 74.

In Memory of

Mr. Zachariah Tomlinson, who Departed this Life on yᵉ 15ᵗʰ day of April, Anno Domni, 1768, in yᵉ 75ᵗʰ Year of His Age.

Here lyes yᵉ Body of

Mrs. Hannah Tomlinson, Wife of Mʳ Zachariah Tomlinson, who departed this life, Octoᵇʳ 5ᵗʰ, 1740 in yᵉ 37 year of her age.

Elijah Uffoot, died March 28, 1814, aged 68 years.

Here lies the Body of

Lieut. Samuel Uffoot, who died Decʳ yᵉ 30, A. D. 1746, in yᵉ 77 year of his Age.

In Memory of

Mrs. Abigail Ufford, wife of Mr. Samuel Ufford ; who died Dec. 3, 1817 ; aged 73 years.

In memory of

Anne, Wife of Elijah Ufford, Who died April 24, 1810, aged 62 years.

In memory of

Alice Ufford, wife of William Ufford, who died Oct. 27, 1819, aged 36 years.

In Memory of

Benjamin Ufford, who died March, 1810, aged 68 years,
And of his wife,

Elizabeth, who died July 1824, aged 78.

Betsey Ufford, Died August 20, 1837, Aged 25 years.

Catharine Ufford, Died Oct. 21, 1866, Aged 85 yrs & 6 mos.

In Memory of

Benjamin Ufford, who died July 12, 1844, Aged 73 yrs.

In Memory of

Caty, wife of Benjamin Ufford, who died Sept. 22, 1831, in her 61 year.

Henry Ufford, Died Nov. 30, 1831, Æ. 44 Yrs. 4 mo.

Hannah Jerome, His Wife, Died Feb. 2, 1879, Æ. 81 yrs. 5 Mo.

Rev. Hezekiah Gold Ufford, Died January 23, 1863, Aged 84 yrs.
"Be thou faithful unto death, and I will give thee a crown of life."

Julia, Wife of Hezekiah Gold Ufford, Died May 5, 1864, Æ. 76 yrs.
"Blessed are the pure in heart, for they shall see God."

Isaac Ufford, Died Dec. 18, 1836, Æ. 52 years.

Phebe Dayton, wife of Isaac Ufford, Born Aug. 8, 1785, Died Aug. 11, 1872.

Louisa J., Daughter of Henry J. &
Lucy L. Ufford, died April 13, 1863,
aged 15 yrs. & 6 mo.

Too fondly loved
Too early lost.

Lucy L., Wife of Henry J. Ufford,
Died April 8, 1861. Æ. 41.

O Mother dear thy pains are o'er
Thou ne'er shall sigh nor weep no more,
Thy spirit dwells among the blest,
In heaven thou shalt forever rest.

We've laid thee in thy narrow home,
Until the resurrection morn,
Till Christ shall bid the sleepers rise,
To dwell in mansions in the skies.

In memory of
Phebe, wife of Benjamin Ufford, who
died Sept. 21st, A. D. 1810, aged 37.

Caroline, their daughter, died Sept.
3d, 1803, aged 1 year & 8 months.

Catharine, Daughter of Benjamin &
Phebe Ufford, Born Dec. 9, 1801,
Died Mar. 21, 1880.

In memory of
Samuel Ufford, who died Dec. 21,
1824 ; in his 54 Year.

In memory of
Mrs. Susannah Ufford, wife of
Samuel Ufford. Jur., who died Dec.
29, 1817, Æt. 43.

In Memory of
Dea. Samuel Ufford, Who was
born Feb. 27, 1749, and deceased Dec.
10, 1822 ; in the 74 year of his age.

In Memory of
Sophia, Daughter of Elijah Ufford,
Jun., who died Sept. 18, 1803, aged 1
year & 4 months.

Susannah & Hezekiah. Children of
Samuel & Susanna Ufford.

Susannah, died Dec. 23, 1801, in
the 4th year of her age.

Hezekiah, died June 3, 1801, in the
4th day of his age.

In memory of
William Ufford, who died May 29,
1848, Æ. 70 yrs.

In Memory of
Abigail, wife of William Ufford, who
died Dec. 5, 1848, Æ. 62.

Here lyes the Remains of
Deliverance Waklin, who departed
this life in the 57 year of his age,
November 6, 1707.

Sacred to the memory of
Ann Brasher Walker, who departed this life Jan. 12, 1837, aged 46.

[A Monument.]
Joseph Walker, Died Aug. 12, 1810,
Aged 55 Years.

He entered the American Army in the year
1777, & served his country in the several grades
of office, from a Captain to a Major General.

Jonathan Otis Walker died Oct.
27, 1821, aged 36 years.

Mary Ann, Wife of Jonn. Otis Walker, Died Nov. 23, 1867, Aged 72.

Susanna, relict of Gen. Joseph Walker, died Oct. 20, 1822, aged 70 years.

Joseph Walker, son of Joseph &
Susannah Walker, died on the 18th of
March, 1803, in the 13th year of his
age, of a fracture in his scull, occasioned by a fall from a horse, Jan. 10th,
1803.

Here lyes Buried ye Body of
Mrs. Mary Walker, Wife to Mr.
Josiah Walker, who departed this Life
Jany ye 5th, A. D. 1745, or 6 in ye 24th
year of Her Age.

Mrs. Eunice, Relect of Capt. William Walker, died Dec. 28, 1832 aged
64 years.

Capt. William Walker, died Dec.
5th, 1830, aged 62 years.

[A Monument.]
Robert Walker, Esq., Died November 7. A. D. 1810, Aged 64 years.

In private life his deportment was in the highest degree exemplary. The urbanity of his
manners, the amiableness of his Disposition,
and the benovolence of his character, were pre-
eminently conspicuous. He was kind, courteous and charitable ; ardent in his friendships,
and forgiving in his resentments. To his strong
intellectual powers, were united a quick dis-
cernment and a discriminating judgment. He
was honored with many civil offices, the duties
of which he discharged with an unwavering
fidelity. He was a firm believer in Christianity
and a powerful advocate for good morals, An
affectionate Husband and tender Parent.

Here also lies mingled with the same
earth the dust of
Mrs. Margaret Walker, relict of
Robert Walker, Esq., who died Feb.
6, 1819, aged 66 years.

[A Tablet of sandstone with slatestone
inlaid.]
In Memory of the
Honble. Robert Walker, Esq.,
Who departed this Life, July 13, A.D.
1772, Ætat 68.

He sustained many important offices in civil
Life. For many Years before and at the time
of his Death, He was one of his Majesty's
Council for the Colony of Connecticut, one of
the Judges of the Superior Court, and a Colonel of the Militia ; all which offices he discharged with Fidelity and honor. He firmly believed
and Conscientiously Practiced the Christian
Religion ; was a kind Husband, a Tender Parent, and faithful Friend.

Mrs. Rebeckah Walker, Relict of Honble Robert Walker, Esqr., died Feby 28th, 1805, in the 89th Year of her age.

Robert Wm. Walker, Died May 8, 1852; Aged 59.

Here Lyes Buried Ye Body of
Mr. Robert Walker, Who Departed this Life, April ye 1st Anno Domni, 1743, in ye 75th Year of His Age.

In memory of
Mrs. Abigail Walker, the beloved Consort of Mr. Robert Walker, Junr., Who departed this Life June 25th, 1769 in the 25th year of her Age.

Joseph Walker, Son of Robert Walker, Esqr., by his wife Rebeckah, who died the 8th day of May, A. D. 1752, aged 9 years, five months & 27 Days.

Capt. William Walker, died in the service of the United States at Burlington, Vt., Dec. 31, 1812, aged 29.

In Memory of
Anna Wells, Wife of James Wells, who died April 9, 1831, aged 77 years.

Two Children, daughters of Nathan and Mary R. Wells.

Catharine Jane, died March 1, 1806, aged 16 days.

Mary Ruggles, died Sept. 2, 1813, aged 2 years & 5 months.

In Memory of
Mrs. Charity Wells, ye daugr of Mrs. Comfort Wells, and Sister to the wife of Jabez Curtis. She Departed this Life July 29th, 1783, in the 42d Year of her Age.

Here lyes Buried the Body of
Mr. David Wells, Who Departed this life April 25th, Anno Domni, 1742, Aged 43 Years.

In memory of
Hannah Wells, who died April 19, 1806, aged 55 years.

Mrs. Hepsa Wells, wife of Mr. John Wells, died Sept. 9, 1815, in the 26 year of her age.

Nathaniel B., their son, died August 30, 1815, Æt. 8 weeks.

In memory of
Mr. Isaac Judson Wells, Who Departed this Life, April 19th, 1772, in ye 62 Year of his Age.

Mr. Isaac Wells died Feb. 27, 1814, in the 62 year of his age.

In Memory of
James Wells, who died August 2, 1821, in his 74th year.

Here lyes Buried ye Body of
Capt. John Wells, Who Departed this Life February 17th, Anno Domni 1735, Aged 59 Years.

Here lyes Buried the Body of
Mr. John Wells, Who Departed this Life February ye 8th, Anno Domni, 1753, in ye 40 Year of his Age.

In Memory of
Mrs. Comfort Wells, Wife to Mr. John Wells, who departed this Life, February 9, 1790, In the 73 Year of her Age.

In memory of
Mr. John Wells, Son of Mrs. Comfort Wells and only Brother of the Wife of Jabez Gorham & beloved friend of Phebe Gorham, who Departed this Life, Jany 14th, A. D. 1789, in the 41st Year of his Age.

Here lyes Buried ye Body of
Mrs. May Wells, Widow of Capt. John Wells, Who Departed this life Jany 6th, Anno Domni 1743. Aged 64 Years.

In memory of
Mary Wells, Relict of Benjamin Wells, who died May 24, 1796, aged 68 Years.

Mrs. Molly Wells, wife of Mr. John Wells; died Jan. 29, 1814; aged 46.

In memory of
Nancy Wells, who died Nov. 29, 1835, in the 60 year of her age.

Mrs. Eunice Wells, relict of Mr. Nathan Wells, died April 12, 1816, aged 87 years.

In memory of
Lieut. Nathan Wells, Who Departed this mortal life on the 20th of May, Anno Dom. 1776, in the 49th year of his Age.

> Think of your friend lies buried here,
> And view your transient state;
> Bestow at least one pious Tear,
> And with Submission wait,
> E'er long this melancholy scene,
> Shall on your hearse attend;
> With haste employ the Space between,
> To make of God a Friend.

In Memory of
Miss Phebe, Daughtr of Mr. Stephen & Mrs. Mary Wells, Who Departed this Life, Sept. 9, 1775, in the 10th Year of her age.

In memory of
Mr. Samuel Wells, Jr., who departed this life, Sept. 9th, 1804, aged 39 years.

In memory of
Lieut. Stephen Wells, who departed this life April 4, 1799, in ye 58 year of his age.

In memory of
Mr. Thomas Wells, who departed this Life, Sept. 23d, 1791, In the 74th year of his Age.

Here lyes Buried ye Body of
Mr. William Wells, Who departed this life Nov. 1, Anno Domni, 1745, in ye 30th Year of his age.

[A MONUMENT.]
This monument, erected by Robert M. Welman, of New York.
Sacred to the memory of his much beloved wife,
Catharine Rebecca Welman, who left this sublunary sphere July 2d, 1804, Æ. 22 years, 7 months and 11 days.
Pause Gentle traveler,
    Was her matchless worth
To thee in happier moments known?
Then pour the tide of sorrow forth,
And in her fate lament thine own.
    But didst thou not her virtue know,
Still let thy tears her death attend
And mourn that midst a world of woe
Thou wert not lovely Catharine's friend.
Deep the sleep of death ! low the pillow of dust.

Catharine M. Wetmore, relict of Victory Wetmore, died Oct. 14, 1859, Æ. 86.

Sacred to the Memory of
Victory Wetmore, Esq., who Departed this life, March 10, 1817 ; Æt. 50.

In Memory of
Charles Joseph Wetmore, who died the 17 of July, A. D. 1816, in the 37 year of his age.

Rev. Izrahiah Wetmore, died Augt. 3d, 1798, in the 70th Year of his age, and 45th year of his ministry.

Mrs. Phebe Wetmore, Consort of Revd Izh. Wetmore, and Daughter of Robert Walker, Esq., died Septr. 12th, 1784, in the 45th year of her age.

In Memory of
Victory, son of the Revd Izrahiah Wetmore, and Phebe Wetmore, his wife, who Deceased Novemr 1762, in the 3d Year of his Age.

In Memory of
Rebecca, Daughter of the Revd. Izrahiah Wetmore, and Phebe Wetmore, his wife, who deceased Decr. 1, 1760, Aged about 10 months.
Light as the Summer's dust we take in air
A moment's giddy flight and fall again
Join the dull mass, increase the trodden soil,
And sleep till earth herself shall be no more.

In Memory of
Mrs. Tryphena Whetmore, Daur of Capt Hezekiah Wetmore, of Middletown (Deceas'd), Who departed this mortal life on the 11th day of July, 1772, in ye 22d year of her age.
The Souls the only thing we have
Worth an important thought.
The soul is of the immortal kind
Ne'er formed of Fire, or Earth, or Wind
outlives ye mouldering corpse & leaves
ye globe behind.

Mrs. Charity, relect of Mr. Elnathan Wheeler, died March 6, 1816, in 77 year of her age.

In Memory of
Miss Charity Wheeler, Daughter of Mr. Elnathan and Mrs. Charity Wheeler, Who died May 1st, 1797, in the 28th Year of her Age.

Charles H., died June 17, 1812, Æ. 7 years & 5 months.

Nelson, died June 28, 1817, Æ. 8 years, Sons of John & Avis Wheeler.

Elisha Wheeler, died May 5, 1853, Aged 81 years.

In memory of
Dorothy, Wife of Elisha Wheeler, who died Jan. 12, 1847, Æ. 71 Years.

Here lyes Buried ye Body of
Mrs. Elizabeth Wheeler, Wife to Nathan Wheeler, Who Died Jan. 22, Anno Domini, 1739–40, in ye 51st Year of Her Age.

In memory of
Elnathan Wheeler, Jr. He died Nov. 1st, 1805, aged 39 years.
The sweet memory of the just
Shall flourish when he sleeps in dust.

In Memory of
Mr. Elnathan Wheeler, who died Feb. 14, 1809, In the 69th year of his age.

Here lyes Buried the Body of
Deacon Elnathan Wheeler, Who Departed this Life, March the 14th, 1761, Aged 58 Years.

Emily Curtis, Daughter of Ezra & Emily Wheeler, Born Oct. 4, 1852, Died Aug. 28, 1872.

Edward, son of Ezra & Emily Wheeler, Died Nov. 10, 1865, Æ. 1 yr. & 6 mos.

George Wheeler, died July 16, 1835, aged 35, also,

Mary C., daughter of George & Betsey C. Wheeler, died July 29, 1833, Æ. 2 yrs. and 7 mo.

J. W., 1694. [Perhaps Joanna Wheeler, youngest dau. of the 1st Moses.]

In memory of

Mrs. Jennet, wife of Mr. David Wheeler and daughter of Capt.,Daniel and Mrs. Betsey Booth, who died Oct. 29, 1817, aged 23 years.

Here lyes intered The Body of *Mary Wheeler,* Who Departed this Life in March the 4th day in the year 1726, and in 17th year of her age.

Here lyes yᵉ Body of *Mrs. Martha Wheeler,* Wife to Mr. Elnathan Wheeler, Who departed this life August the 5th, 1764, Aged 64 Years.

In Memory of *Miss Martha Wheeler,* who died Aug. 14, 1827, aged 63.

1694
J. W.
February yᵉ 17.*

Nathaniel Wheeler, died May 19, 1819, Æ. 85.

Mrs. Rachel Wheeler, wife of Mr. Nathaniel Wheeler, Died Sept. 15, 1814 ; aged 81 years.

Here layes the Body of *Nathan Wheeler,* Who Departed this life, January the 31, 172¾, In 19 year of his Age.

Here lyes Buried the Body of *Mr. Nathan Wheeler,* Who departed this life Nov. yᵉ 7th, 1765, in yᵉ 86th Year of his Age.

In Memory of *Capt. Samuel Wheeler,* who died June 2, 1815, in the 57 year of his age.

Our Mother Rests. *Betsey Hawley Wheaton,* Died Aug. 17, 1872, In Her 85th year.

Anna M., Daughter of David & Jane E. Wheaton, died June 20, 1863, Æ. 16 yrs. & 1 mo.

---

* This Stone is at the left side of Moses Wheeler's.

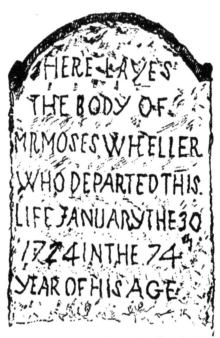

In memory of
Mary Whippo, who died Jan. 23,
1812, aged 53 years, and of her late
husband, **Isaac Whippo,** who
died in New York, July 6, 1807, aged
— years, also of their two sons John
& Charles.
John died in the Island of New Providence, June 30, 1799, aged 17.
Charles went to sea Aug. 1807, at 23
years of age and has not since been
heard from.

In Memory of
Mr. Ephraim Willcockson, Who
died July 21, 1806, Aged 78.

In memory of three Children of Elnathan & Sarah Willcoxson.

Isaac, died July 14, 1783, Æt. 5 years.
Elias, died July 3, 1783, Æt. 3 years.
Sarah, died July 12, 1783. Æt. 8
months.

Here Lyes Buried yͤ Body of
Lieut. John Willcockson, Who
Departed this Life, Sept. 12ᵗʰ, Anno
Domni, 1748, in yͤ 65ᵗʰ Year of His
Age.

Here lies the Body of
Lucy Willcockson, Daughter of
Lieut. Ephraim & Ruth Willcockson,
died June 9ᵗʰ, A.D. 1784, in the 28ᵗʰ
Year of her age.

Sacred to the Memory of
Mrs. Ruth Willcockson, Consort
of Lieut. Ephraim Willcockson, Who
departed this Life, July 30, 1801, In
the 74ᵗʰ Year of her Age.

In memory of
Ruth Ann, daughter of Col. Ephraim
J. & Mrs. Mary Wilcoxson, who died
Sept. 22, 1815, aged 6 years.

In memory of
Samuel O. Willcockson, who died
June 7, 1804, Æt. 34.

Here lies the Body of
Samuel Willcockson, who departed
this Life August 19, A. D. 1783, in
the 59th year of his Age.
The Woman's Seed shall bruise the Serpent's
Head,
And Christ shall raise his servants from the
Dead.

In Memory of
Chester G. Whiting, who died
Aug. 19, 1847, Æ. 25 yrs. & 6 ms.

Hannah, wife of Seymour Whiting,
Died Sept. 25, 1846, Æ. 78 yrs. & 3
mo.

Mrs. Mary Ann, widow of Ezra
C. Whiting, Died Dec. 16, 1866, Æ.
67 yrs. 11 mos.
"I shall be satisfied when I awake with thy
likeness."

In Memory of
Ezra C. Whiting, who died April
10, 1824, in his 32 year; And of 2 infant Children by his wife Mary Ann:

Elbert, died Sept. 7, 1819, aged 1 year
& 17 days.

Elbert, 2d, died Aug. 27, 1821, aged
1 year & 10 days.

In Memory of
Col. Samuel Whiting, who died
Feb. 15, 1803, aged 82 yrs.
Also of
Elizabeth, his wife, who died Dec. 5,
1793, aged 70 yrs.

In memory of
Seymour Conway Whiting, who
departed this life July 26, 1841, aged
74 years.

Here lies Interred the Body of
Mr. Samuel Whitney, who De-
parted this life December y[e] 6th, 1753,
in y[e] 66th Year of his Age.

Sacred to the memory of
Mrs. Abigail M. Woodbridge,
the amiable Consort of Samuel Woodbridge, Esqr., and eldest daughter of
Robert & Margaret Walker, who departed this life, Aug. 15, A. D. 1814,
Aged 34 Years.

In memory of
Ruth Wooster, widow of the late
Col. Joseph Wooster, who died March
23[d] 1801, aged 86 years.

ERRATA.

Peter Pixley, son of Mr. David &
Mrs. Betsey Curtiss, died May 10,
1817, aged 3 months.[*]

[*] This inscription should have been
in the Curtiss families, but was entered
in the wrong place.

The date of death of John Hurd on
page 221 was 1681, but it is not legible
on the grave-stone.

NOTE.—The author has had the privilege, after copying the above list from the
stones, of comparing it with the manuscript copy of these *names* and *dates,* made
with great care and labor by Mr. Abraham W. Morehouse, of Bridgeport, at the
request of the Fairfield County Historical Society, which has contributed much to
the present state of perfectness of the list.

CHAPTER X.

NEW SETTLERS AND ENTERPRISES.

 XCELLENCE of character is one of the most valuable qualities in the establishment of a new plantation in the wilderness. In the settlement of Stratford the planters possessed, not only this quality in a marked degree, but there was almost a complete absence of those of an opposite kind during the first fifty years, and largely so the next fifty.

The early settlers in all New England were a select class, from the best stock of England, France and Scotland, in the sense of a well-informed, thinking, energetic people. Many of them were of the homes of the commoners of England, sometimes termed Landed Gentry, and most of them were accustomed to honorable daily employment, although some of them could trace their ancestry back to royal blood. This pride in ancestry, although often the topic of ridicule, is nevertheless of much value and satisfaction, for, while royal blood—or any blood—may not always exhibit itself in the most perfect manner, nor prove itself worthy of the highest honor, yet it has represented the very best qualities of which the old nations can boast; and every child in America that can trace its line of inheritance back to such an origin, may well claim it as a high honor.

It has been a practice to laugh at those who, not being third-rate mechanics when they came to this country, pretended to be descended from royalty; but only

novices would indulge in such sourness of mind, for it is beyond controversy that quite a number of the planters were
not far enough removed from royalty and wealth to have had
need of mechanical trades, and therefore had not such
knowledge.

A large proportion of the settlers at Stratford were by
occupation farmers, called planters here because they were
of a company which established a plantation. A few had
other trades, as ship builders, tailors, stone masons, and merchants, or traders. Several had estates which they left in
England, but which they retained in their right and possession many years after leaving them.

The prominent object in these planters in coming here
was that they might enjoy church privileges in accord with
the teachings of the Bible, as they understood them, and this
they proposed to enjoy under the English Constitution.
They evidently had no thought of independency from that
constitution, and for one hundred years did not dream of
such a thing.

This company of seventeen, after becoming located, immediately invited others to join them upon certain liberal, but
substantial terms, and at the year 1650 about thirty-five had
accepted those terms.

The township, being twelve miles long and ten miles
wide, contained 120 square miles, or 76,000 acres of land ;
giving to each of the 17 families over four thousand acres.
The company disposed of their lands in various ways. A
few acres were sequestered for public use ; some for individual use and ownership. To new settlers they gave a home
lot, a piece for meadow and another piece of upland for cultivation, upon condition that the party should build a house
and improve the few acres thus donated during four years,
at the end of which the land became their own and was so
recorded. Individual proprietors sold fractional parts of
their Rights, so that at the end of about fifty years the proprietors numbered one hundred instead of seventeen, and in
1699 the number was 143.

The proprietors, for themselves, voted at first, to divide
to each Right a certain number of acres, and the owner

selected the land, or located it, wherever he pleased, subject to the sanction of the division committee, only that he could take up but 'a few acres in one place, about 18 or 20 at most.

After some years certain tracts of land were laid into plots one for each proprietor, and then they drew lots for them as the most impartial way of locating each man's land.

Having heretofore given some personal account or biographical sketches of nearly seventy persons, some further items in the same direction will illustrate the work of the settlement of the town.

Edward Katcham died in Stratford, and his will was proved June 17, 1655. The inventory of his estate amounted to £90–11–6. In his will, dated June 1655, he names three daughters, Mary, Hannah and Hester.

Richard Mills, to all appearance, was one of the first company at Stratford. He married the daughter of Francis Nichols, and probably came with the Nichols family to Stratford in 1639. He sold much, perhaps all of his estate to Joseph Hawley in 1650, and removed, it is said, to Westchester, N. Y.

It is in connection with his name that the term "Lordship" is first found, as applied to a meadow, on what is still known as the Lordship farm, It is said in the deeds of land—1650 to 1660—several times, "Mill's Lordship" and the "Lordship meadow."

No explanation of the term is found or known, but was doubtless wholly connected with Mr. Mills or his family; and hence the name did not originate with the Nicoll family who owned the Lordship farm many years. The term was at first applied to the salt meadow at that place.

Samuel Mills, believed to be the son of Richard, came to Stratford, and on Dec. 24, 1666, purchased land of Hope Washburn, and was one of the earliest settlers at Oronoke, soon after this purchase, where he resided nearly twenty years, being quite active as a citizen of the town. One record says, "Samuel Mills purchased from his uncle Caleb Nichols, six acres of land, 29th 10th month, 1668."

He sold his estate here in 1670, to "Hugh Makie," but

the next year he took it back and Mr. Makie removed from the town.

Samuel Mills died at Southampton, L. I., in 1685, leaving a widow and an only heir Richard Mills, who disposed of the Stratford property soon after.

David Mitchell, son of Matthew, and brother of the wife of Mr. Samuel Sherman, sen., came to Stratford and purchased the "accommodations" of John Reader, Feb. 26, 1659, consisting of a house lot and several pieces of land.

David Mitchell became quite prominent in the town as a land owner and farmer.

John Washburn was at Stratford and married Mary, daughter of Richard Butler, June 7, 1655, and probably removed to Hempstead, L. I., with his father, William Washburn.

Hope Washburn, son of William of Mass., and perhaps of Stratford a short time, was made a freeman here at or before 1669. He purchased land at Oronoke in 1666, and was one of the three earliest settlers at that place, probably the next year. He purchased several pieces of land at that place, but soon removed to Derby, where his descendants continued many years.

On the Stratford records is an agréement of the widow Mary and children, William, Samuel, Sarah and Jane, to divide the estate of Hope Washburn, dated Nov. 16, 1696.

James Clark, Jr., son of James of New Haven, came to Stratford and married Deborah, daughter of John Peacock, about 1662. He was a farmer and received considerable land by his wife; had a family of five sons and three daughters, and the descendants were quite numerous and active citizens for many years. He purchased land of Joseph Judson "near unto Nesumpaws creek," Nov. 25, 1667, and several other pieces soon after.

Jabez Harger, said to have been a Huguenot, from Westchester, N. Y., came to Stratford and married Margaret the daughter of Henry Tomlinson in 1662, and settled in Derby about 1670. He had a house lot recorded to him in

1669 in Stratford, and the same year seems to have had land recorded to him in Derby, where he lived, and died in 1678. He had a family of three sons and six daughters. He resided in Stratford several years and bought land of the Indians at Oronoke, on which one of his sons settled many years afterwards.

John Hull, son of Richard of Dorchester, Mass., and New Haven, came to Stratford, and received in 1662, the grant of a "home lot on the north side of Jabez Harger, provided he build on it and improve it three years." This was only a home lot without other land. He was accepted as an inhabitant at Derby in 1668, but seems to have resided at Stratford until 1675. He was successful at Derby in accumulating property, but removed to Wallingford in 1687, where he is called Doctor,—received a mile square of land from the town, and where he died Dec. 6, 1711, leaving a numerous family. Three of his sons remained in Derby and their descendants became greatly celebrated.

John Pickett was of Salem, Mass., in 1648, and came to Stratford in 1660, with a family of four sons and two daughters. He had a home lot granted him by the town, Apr. 1, 1665, and was a permanent citizen. His wife died Oct. 6, 1683, and he died Apr. 11, 1684. His son Daniel settled at Danbury about the year 1700, and Daniel, junior, was one of the early settlers in New Milford. John, sen., was constable at Stratford in 1667, townsman in 1669. and representative in 1673.

Robert Lane, from Derbyshire, England, first located at Killingworth, Conn., came to Stratford and was granted a home lot, two acres, April 1, 1665, "on the same terms as John Hull and Jabez Harger." On the 19th of December he married Sarah, the daughter of John Pickett, and became a successful farmer in the township. On February 21, 1676, he was chosen "burier," or sexton for the graveyard.

Robert Clark, from New Haven, married Sarah, the widow of Francis Stiles of Windsor some years before 1665, and probably after he came to Stratford.

He became an influential citizen; was successful as a farmer, and gave considerable land to each of the sons of his wife, Ephraim, Samuel and Thomas Stiles.

Nicholas Gray came from Flushing, L. I., and purchased land in Stratford in 1661; remained here 12 or 14 years and returned to Flushing. In 1676, he was in Flushing, and in 1678 he rented "his dwelling house, land and orchard in Stratford to Joseph Blakeman, but in 1680, his taxes remaining unpaid for several years the constable took possession of his estate, which matter he seems to have settled by the sale of the land.

John Cook seems to have come to Stratford as servant to Richard Butler, perhaps when quite young. His first land is thus: "John Cook by gift from his Master Richard Butler, two acres of upland in the Neck," and "by gift from the town two acres, Feb. 1, 1667."

Henry Summers came to Stratford, apparently in company with Samuel Gregory, who was his brother-in-law, before 1668. Whether they were just come from England or not has not been ascertained. The town records say that Samuel Summers purchased of his uncle Samuel Gregory, four acres of land, in 1696, near Golden Hill.

Henry Summers purchased his first land in Stratford, "27th of 1st month, 1668; land lying at Pequonnock, bounded east with the great river called Pequonnock river, and south with the Indians' land, north on common." This he sold the same day to Samuel Gregory.

In 1686, he was living at Pequonnock, his dwelling being located, as near as can be ascertained, a little way south of what is now the junction of Park and Washington avenues. Here he was residing, apparently, in 1707, but in 1710 he was residing in Milford, for at that time, he deeded, as he says: "to my son John Summers, one-half of my house lot in Stratfield, a dwelling house, barn and orchard," it being eleven acres, "the half of the home lot on which the building stands." He owned several pieces of land in the vicinity— one of 16 acres, purchased in 1686, "lying on a hill west of Ireland's brook between the wolf-pits."

Henry Gregory was in Stratford as early as 1647, as recorded in the New Haven records, where he is represented as having sons Judah and John and a daughter, the wife of William Crooker. Henry Gregory died before 1655.

Samuel Gregory, probably the son of the above Henry, was one of the first settlers at Pequonnock, now Bridgeport, where he was residing in 1686, at what is now the junction of Park and Washington avenues, for the highway now Washington avenue was laid out through the Indians' land, beginning at Samuel's Gregory's house. He settled at Pequonnock about 1665.

Richard Beach was of New Haven in 1639, and one of the original signers of the compact. He married there about 1640, and came to Stratford with a family of four children, where he purchased his first land February 6, 1660, of Thomas Wheeler; " one house lot with all the buildings upon it." In 1662, he purchased other pieces of land—one of five acres " on west point of the Neck, butted south upon the meadow called Mills' Lordship."

He and his descendants became substantial and influential inhabitants of the town.

Rev. Israel Chauncey, youngest son of the Rev. Charles Chauncey, president of Harvard College, was born in 1644, at Scituate, Massachusetts, where his father was then preaching. He was graduated at Harvard in 1661, in the class with his older brothers Nathaniel and Elnathan.

In 1663, he compiled and edited the New England Almanac, on the title page of which is, ISRAEL CHAUNCEY. On the last two pages he states " The Theory of Planetary Orbs and the natural portents of eclipses."

He preached in Stratford from April, 1665, to June, 1666, as assistant to the Rev. Adam Blakeman, when he received a call to settle as pastor over this church and society, and was soon after ordained as such, he being then but 22 years of age. He was made freeman in the town in 1667, and married Mary, the daughter of Isaac Nichols, senior, one of his most prominent parishioners. His first wife died and he married 2d Sarah Hodson of New Haven in 1684.

17

In 1666, upon his settlement as pastor, his salary was fixed at £60 per annum, and one-fourth of the sequestered ministry land was given him for his use, and a house soon after built on the home lot for him to reside in and improve as his own property, but in case of death or removal these were to revert to the town. In 1677, however, the house and land was fully deeded to him, as was a like estate to the Rev. Zechariah Walker, pastor of the Woodbury Church.

Mr. Israel Chauncey studied medicine and was a practicing physician of eminence as well as a divine, and hence he was an important personage in the Council of War, in the Narragansett Indian troubles.

On the 9th of March, 1675-6, the authority at Hartford make this record : " The Council also ordered the Secretary to write to Mr. Israel Chauncey to hasten up to Hartford to attend the Council's orders, with an order to impress men, horses, and accommodations for his coming up."[1]

Two days later a further record was made.

" March 11, 1675-6. The Council appointed Mr. Chauncey to be one of the Council of the army in room of Mr. Hooker, and also that he should now go forth with the army as their chirurgion," [surgeon].

Upon the breaking out of the King Philip or Narragansett War, in July, 1675, a " Council " of War was appointed by the General Court, consisting of the Governor, Lieut. Governor, Assistants and a few others named, and Mr. Israel Chauncey being appointed a member of that body shows the estimation in which he was held, but this act brought the calamity to the heart of Stratford by taking their minister from them a number of months, in the midst of the most distressing anxieties, for the war created great fear and excitement.

The destination of the army under Major Robert Treat, when Mr. Chauncey was ordered to go with them as their Surgeon, was Norwich, and if he went, he soon returned, for the burning of Simsbury, Connecticut, the following Sunday, caused the Council to recall Major Treat and a part of his forces and send them north, to protect the settlements in that direction.

---

[1] Conn. Col. Rec., ii. 415.

On the 27th of the same month, Mr. Chauncey being at Hartford as a member of the Council, having received intelligence "of the death of his child and the dangerous sickness of his wife, was permitted to return home; but before leaving he addressed a letter[1] to the Council which shows a little further his influence and public relations to the Commonwealth.

His brother, the Rev. Nathaniel Chauncey, was the pastor at Windsor, and had been with the army as chaplain, apparently, on its first expedition to Norwich, in this war.

His brother Bulkly, whom he mentions in his letter, was the Rev. Gershom Bulkley, pastor at Wethersfield, and had married Sarah, the eldest sister of Mr. Chauncey, and the occasion for his having an "easy horse" was from the fact that he had accompanied Major Treat's forces northward two weeks previous, and was wounded by a shot from the enemy, in a sudden assault made upon the English by a small party of Indians.

Mr. Chauncey was successful in his pastorate at Stratford, beginning in the Spring of 1665 and ending at his decease, March 14, 1702-3, a term of thirty-seven years. He conducted his church through the troublous time which resulted in the organization of a second church and its removal to Woodbury, with dignity of character in apparently a large Christian spirit, securing to himself great respect and honor during his subsequent life.

---

[1] Mr. Chauncey's letter.

"Much honoured: I am truly sorry that I am necessitated to trouble you. I have lately received a letter from some friends, who doe acquaint me with the afflicted state of my family; my wife being very lately delivered, the child dead, and my wife in danger of death, by reason of weakness prevailing upon her. I doe therefore humbly entreat your Worships to grant me a release to visit my afflicted family, and dear wife, if living. Excuse my boldness and troublesomeness, and consider my condition. I hope my brother Bulkly, provided he have an able and easy horse, will attend the army, upon their present motion; only, if it be expected, he doth desire care may be taken for an easy horse, and that it may be sent him this night. I have not further to adde but my hearty prayers for the presence of the great and wonderful Counsellor with you, in your solemne consultations, and to subscribe myselfe Your Worships reall servant,

Stratford, Mar. 27th, '76.   . Is: Chauncey.
(Conn. Col. Rec., ii. 424).

Notwithstanding the calamity of King Philip's War, two years later they commenced the building of a new meeting-house and completed it in 1680.

After the death of his brother, the Rev. Nathaniel Chauncey of Windsor and Hatfield, Mr. Chauncey took, in 1686, the son Nathaniel, of that brother, to bring up until of age, for the use of the Rev. Nathaniel's library during that time. This library was valued in the inventory of the estate at £85, and comprised, probably, says Prof. Fowler, a large part of Pres. Charles Chauncey's library.

Mr. Israel Chauncey was one of the founders of Yale College, and probably presided over the first meeting of its projectors, his name being first on the list of their names; and on November 11, 1701, he was chosen Rector, or President of the Institution, but declined the labor and honor, probably because of a sense of failing health, as he lived but about a year and a half after.

Dr. Charles Chauncey, a nephew, of Boston, said of him: "He spent his days among that people [Stratford] in great reputation as a physician as well as a divine."

Mrs. Sarah (Chauncey) Whittelsey, who lived in his family when a young woman, said, "he was one of the most hospitable, benevolent old gentlemen she ever knew."

Nathaniel Chauncey, nephew of the Rev. Israel Chauncey, was settled in Durham. He began preaching there in 1706, but was not ordained before 1711. In 1708, he was called with but one dissenting vote to become pastor of the Stratford Church. Five candidates had been previously tried without success. He declined and Mr. Cutler was secured.

Robert McEwen came from Dundee, Scotland. He early in life attached himself to the sect called from their leader, Cameronians, and at the age of eighteen, in 1679, was engaged in a battle against the King. In 1685 many of the persecuted Christians being in bonds and imprisonment, were sent by the government of Scotland on board of a ship of War of fifty guns, to colonize the isthmus of Darien. The commander of the ship dying a few days after they were at sea the passengers brought the ship toward New York and ran her ashore at Amboy, N. J.

Robert McEwen wrote in his account book the following: "In June 18, 1679, I was in one engagement in Scotland at Bothwell's Bridge, I then being the age of 18 years. The 5th of September, 1685, we set sail from Scotland to come to America, and we landed at Amboy the 18th of December. The 18th of February I came to Stratford in New England, 1686."

"June 30, 1695, I was married to Sarah Willcoxson in Stratford."

Robert McEwen died in 1740 aged 78 years. Tradition in the family says that after being landed at Amboy, eleven of the passengers having heard of the freedom of the people in Connecticut, came on foot to Stratford.

James Blakeman, son of the Rev. Adam Blakeman, married Mirriam, daughter of Moses Wheeler in 1657, and died in 1689. He and his brother Samuel married cousins. He was a farmer and miller, purchasing first the tide mill at the Eagle's Nest, next the one at Old Mill green, which he sold and went to the Near-Mill river and built the first mill there, receiving considerable land from the town to aid, or remunerate him in part for the expense of building the mill, at the place now called Peck's Mill. He was one of the most active business men in the town, in his day.

Rev. Benjamin Blakeman, son of the Rev. Adam Blakeman, after his father's decease chose to seek an education in accordance with his father's previous wishes, and was graduated at Harvard College in 1663. He resided at Stratford a few years as a teacher, then entered the ministry. In 1674, he removed to Malden, Massachusetts, and in 1675 married Rebecca, daughter of Joshua Scottow, merchant of Boston. He preached at Malden until 1678, and afterward he preached at Scarborough. He represented Saco in the General Court of Massachusetts, and was a large land holder in that town. He died before 1698.

Thomas Kimberly was received in Stratford as an outliver in 1667. He was probably Thomas of New Haven in 1643, and purchased land of Joseph Hawley on "18th, 10th, 1668," and in 1670–71 he bought a part of a house lot of James

Blakeman, and died about one year afterward. Some of his sons were quite influential, successful men in after years.

Jeremiah Judson, son of William 1st, born in England, came with his father to Stratford in 1639, when eighteen years of age, and soon became a land owner and prominent citizen. He married, 1st, in 1652, Sarah, daughter of Nathaniel Foot then of Stratford, who died about 1672, and he married Catharine, the widow of Thomas Fairchild, senior.

He mas made a freeman in May, 1658, was a Sergeant in the Militia ; a justice of the peace, a large land owner and farmer, and died May 15, 1700, in his 79th year. He made one mistake in business transaction, as indicated and explained in the following record :

"General Court, May, 1669. This Court remitts Jeremy Judson the remaynder of the fine that is unpayd, which fine was imposed upon him by the County Court, March last, at Fayrefield, for selling Cider to the Indians."

His son, Jeremiah, when sixteen years of age, with William Hunnywell, had a little court business, which indicates that they were like some other young men since that day.

" These lads, with two others, were prosecuted at the Fairfield county court, August, 1685, for 'stealing water milions, the last Thursday in the night about the going down of the mone,' from Benjamin Lewis's yard. They confessed having taken two melons,—for which they were fined eleven shillings, cost and damage; and for 'night walking' were fined in addition, ten shillings each, or in default of payment, to sit in the stocks. They petitioned for a remission of the latter penalty, which was granted.'"

Lieut. Joseph Judson, son of William 1st, born in England in 1619, came with his father and two brothers to America, at the age of 15 years, in 1634. The family remained at Roxbury, Massachusetts, four years, came to Hartford or Wethersfield in 1638, and, with Mr. Blakeman's company, to Stratford in the spring of 1639.'

Joseph Judson was made a freeman in May, 1658, when

---

⁸ Col. Rec., iii. 197.

⁴ See inscription on his tombstone, p.

39 years of age, and was elected a representative the next October.

He was made a Lieutenant of the Train Band of Stratford in June, 1672, and was engaged in the Narragansett War in 1676.

In his time he was one of the most active, and well-known business men in the county, but was not the highest military officer, as stated on page 110.

In May, 1673, a petition was presented by Stratford townsmen to the General Court, to confirm the bounds of their plantation, and " for adjudication of the claim of Lieut. Joseph Judson to a large tract of land alleged to be within Stratford bounds."[3]

This was a tract of land purchased by Joseph Judson of the Indians in 1661, twelve years before the petition, called Mohegan Hills, and contained over 5,000 acres of land, lying between the two branches of the Farmill river, including the present Walnut Tree Hill School district of Huntington, a part of two other districts and extending into Monroe, nearly to the place called East Village;[4] it being a territory averaging about two miles wide and five in length. This land was wholly within the township of Stratford, and they could claim it under their grant, but Joseph Judson had paid the Indians for it and hence he had a good claim. No record has been seen as to how the matter was settled, but it was doubtless done, as in several other cases in which the individual parties retained land sufficient to remunerate them fully, and the town took the remainder.

Joseph Judson removed with the Woodbury company to that town, where he was a leader among the people, a deputy to the General Assembly a number of years, and also a commissioner of the town, but he was buried in Stratford.

Francis Hall was of New Haven in 1639. He purchased land in Fairfield in 1654, where he seems to have resided a number of years. He bought of James Rogers of New London, as the agreement says: " All my debts that appear

[3] Col. Rec., ii. 195.

[4] See Indian deed on page 22 of this book.

by account, or otherwise due to me, that is to say at Nor-
wolke, Fayrfeyld, Stratford, Milford and New Haven, with
my lands at Stratford, houses, commons belonging to those
lands, with a little house by the water's side at Milford, August 1, 1659." Not long after this he settled in Stratford,
where he died; his will being proved March 14, 1689–90. He
was a practicing lawyer while in Stratford; was employed
quite a number of times by the town, and by the proprietors
of the common lands. He was influential in ecclesiastical
affairs. and appears to have been a useful, good, and honored
citizen.

Ephraim Stiles, whose mother married Robert Clarke,
came to Stratford about 1660, received land from his step-
father in 1667, at Oronoke, where he settled and became a
thriving, valuable citizen. He was considerably active in
town matters, had a gristmill at Farmill river, "a little below
Black Brook, near the place called the Plum trees," and in
character and standing appears to have been among the first
of the town. His children being three, and all daughters, his
family name ceased. with himself when he departed this life.

Samuel Stiles, brother of Ephraim, was equally fortunate in receiving land by gift from his step-father Robert
Clark, and thus had a more advantageous start in the world
than many others. All persons of this name have disappeared from the old town of Stratford some years ago, but
there are a few in Bridgeport.

"June 11, 1667, Samuel Stiles, by way of gift from his
father Robert Clarke, hath a dwelling house and the home
lot thereto adjoining, lying at Woronoke, bounded east with
the great river, south with the land of John Wheeler, north
with the Farmill river, and west with a creek."

He and his brother Ephraim received twenty acres to be
divided between them, from Mr. Clark.

Thomas Stiles, brother of Ephraim and Samuel, received land from his step-father Robert Clark, "fifteen acres
in the woods by the river called Stratford river on the south
side of Joseph brook."

Considerable search has been made by different parties

to ascertain if Francis Stiles, the father of the above three sons, came to Stratford with his family before his decease, without success, but the following record seems to give some light on the question, and is the only item of the kind that has been seen.

" Caleb Nichols purchased of Mr. Stilles one house lot, one acre and a quarter, bounded with Mr. Fayrechild on the south, Isaac Nichols on the west, my own lot, that was Francis Nichols' on the north, and the street on the east." No date is given to this purchase, but it being in the hand-writing of the town clerk, Joseph Hawley, it must have been made before 1666, and was probably made about 1660. Mr. Stiles' purchase of it was not recorded, as far as can be ascertained. The record of this sale was made in 1664.

Besides this, the fact that Robert Clark gave to the three sons of his wife, formerly widow of Francis Stiles, about fifty acres of land, when he had several children of his own, indicates that he received this land from his wife, and deeded it to its rightful owners, her three sons. By these items it seems quite evident that Francis Stiles resided here several years, was the owner of considerable land and a homestead. Also no record is found showing that Robert Clark purchased the land he gave to his step-sons.

Captain John Minor was a valuable inhabitant of Stratford nearly twenty years. He was a native of New London or that vicinity ; was educated at Hartford at the expense of the Colony for an interpreter to the Indians, and came to Stratford in 1659, or before. He was town clerk ten or twelve years from 1666 until his final removal to Woodbury in 1677. He was in demand as interpreter very frequently during most of his life. After settlement in Woodbury he was appointed captain of the train band, served many years as representative and departed this life with many honors, September 17, 1719, aged 85 years.

Samuel Galpin, from New Haven, came to Stratford about 1675, bought land here September 6, 1681, which was laid out in the Newpasture in 1682, and he may have made his home at Old Mill green. He married Esther, the daughter of John Thompson, in 1676–7, and died before 1701, leaving several children, two sons, whose descendants soon disappeared from the town.

John Pryor, became a land owner and inhabitant in Stratford in 1686, but soon removed.

Richard Rounesfall became a proprietor and inhabitant in 1687, but remained but a short time.

Jacob Walker, son of Robert of Boston and brother of the Rev. Zechariah, came to Stratford about 1667, and married Elizabeth, widow of Samuel Blakeman, December 6, 1670. He is said to have been a weaver by trade, and his wife had considerable property left her by her husband at Old Mill Green. They prospered, accumulated property and became prominent citizens, but his descendants of his name soon became extinct in Stratford. His daughter Mary married Abraham Wooster and was the mother of General David Wooster, of imperishable fame.

Joseph Walker, son of Robert of Boston, and brother, also, of the Rev. Zechariah and Jacob, came to Stratford about 1667. He married Abigail, daughter of the Rev. Peter Prudden of Milford in 1667. His life work in Stratford was soon finished, for he died in 1687, leaving one son and four daughters. His son Robert was deacon of the church eleven years, and died, aged 75 years. The grand-son, Robert, became Judge of the Superior Court of Connecticut, and is reported as one of the most capable men, of irreproachable character, that Connecticut had produced to that day. He is said to have been the equal of Hon. William Samuel Johnson, in many respects. The name of Walker has been celebrated above most names in Fairfield County.

John Brooks, a young man from New Haven, bought his first land in Stratford March 18, 1679–80. He married here and had one son. His wife, who was widow of John Peat, died in 1694, and he in 1695.

This Brooks family became quite numerous in the west ern part of the town, in Stratfield Society.

William Roberts became a land owner and inhabitant of this town in 1668. His family, consisting of one daughter and two sons, seems to have left the town about the year 1700.

Benjamin Lewis was first in New Haven, from which place he removed to Wallingford and thence to Stratford, where he purchased his first land March 1, 1679, a house and lot bounded west with the Congregational burying place, and east on Main street. This has been a numerous, successful and influential family—several descendants still residing in the town.

Rev. Zechariah Walker, son of Robert of Boston, was preaching at Jamaica, L. I., from 1663 to 1668. He was ordained pastor over the second church in Stratford May 5, 1670; went with the company to Woodbury, whither he removed his family in 1678. He, after a laborious and successful pastorate at that place, died January 20, 1699–1700.

The coming of this man to Stratford was of great honor, for although he soon removed to Woodbury, yet, through his being here for a time, probably, his brothers became inhabitants here and their descendants, some of them, were among the most noted persons in the State.

Robert Bassett, son of John the first, was in New Haven with his fathar in 1643. He was a shoemaker, and served the plantation as drummer a number of years. He removed to, and was an inhabitant at Stamford, in March, 1653.

While in Stamford Robert Bassett had a difficulty with the civil authority, which made a great commotion, with considerable remarks against himself.

The difficulty arose out of the proposition to go to war against the Dutch, in 1653; and in this matter Roger Ludlow and several others were involved. What were the facts?

In the spring of 1653, while the Commissioners of the United Colonies were in session at Boston, they decided that 500 soldiers should be raised for an expedition against the Dutch at New Amsterdam, and proportioned the soldiers to be drafted, to the Colonies as follows: Massachusetts, 333; Plymouth, 60; Connecticut, 65; New Haven, 42.[1]

---

[1] Conn. Col. Rec., i. 241.

Upon the receipt of this action, Connecticut proportioned her number among her plantations: "Windsor, 12; Pequett, 5; Mattabezek, 1; Norwalk, 1; Hartford, 15; Wethersfield, 8; Farmington, 3; Seabrook 5; Fairfield, 8; Stratford, 6." The order of the General Court, May 21, 1653, was, that these soldiers should "be forthwith impressed, to be at a day's warning, or call, as also that suitable provisions and amunition shall be forthwith prepared."

The colony of New Haven took favorable action in regard to the war and sent commissioners special to urge upon Massachusetts the necessity of united and energetic action; the 42 soldiers were proportioned, and in June of that year Stamford, then under the jurisdiction of New Haven, reported her soldiers raised and under pay, and that they were put to the service of watching for the protection of the town until ordered forward.

Immediately after the act of the Commissioners inaugurating the war, Massachusetts as a colony declined to be governed by that act, pretending that the Commissioners had not power to such an extent.

Roger Ludlow was one of the Commissioners when the expedition was decided upon, and the trouble which arose out of this proposed expedition, in addition to some other matters, is said to have led him to leave the country in disgust; and it is not much wonder; for, after the soldiers had been in arms drilling and wasting their time some months at a heavy cost to the plantations along the Sound, and the Dutch, meanwhile making their trespasses at Greenwich and threatening Stamford and Norwalk, the expedition was delayed by Connecticut and New Haven until late in the autumn of that year, in consequence of the inaction of Massachusetts. Then it was that Stamford men, with other plantations, proposed to go against the Dutch, without Massachusetts.

It was at this point that Robert Bassett was brought before the agents sent to Stamford from New Haven to settle these difficulties, charged as the leader of the disturbances.

The particular items in this matter are revealed in the record of the New Haven Court, November 22, 1653:

" The Governor acquainted the court with a letter he had received which had been sent to Robert Bassett without date or name subscribed, which is to stir up to stand for the State of England, as they pretend, and to stand for their liberties, that they may all have their votes and shake off the yoke of government they have been under in this jurisdiction; also with a letter from the town of Stamford, making complaints of their rates and other grievances as they pretend; also another writing from Stamford, stirring up to raise volunteers to go against the Dutch, and that themselves will send forth ten men well furnished for the war; also a letter from Mr. Ludlow, informing of a meeting they have had at Fairfield, at which they have concluded to go against the Dutch, and have chosen him for their chief, and he hath accepted it; all which writings were read to the Court, after which the Court considered whether they were called at this time to send forth men against the Dutch, and after much debate and consultation had with most of the elders in the jurisdiction, the issue was, which the Court by vote declared, that considering the hazards and danger attending such a design, especially now, it being so near winter, and the want of suitable vessels and the like, they see not themselves called to vote for a present war, but to suspend a full issue till Connecticut jurisdiction be acquainted with it and give notice what they will do; but if they agree to carry it on now, then this Court agrees to join with them and to meet again to consider and order, as the case may require."[8]

It may be seen that all the above items enumerated were in harmony with the laws and usage of the times and the proceedings of the General Courts except the opposition of Stamford men to the law of New Haven Colony that none should vote but—members of the church; and this they—the Stamford men—claimed a violation of the English Constitution.

These plantations, west of Milford, had raised the number of soldiers proportioned to them, and kept them in readiness at a day's call, nothing more, except they now proposed to raise and equip more than the number called for. The

[8] New Haven Col. Rec., ii. 47–48.

nomination or choice of Mr. Ludlow at Fairfield was in harmony with both, the Connecticut and New Haven Courts. Twenty years later the General Court refused twice to confirm John Beardsley of Stratford as lieutenant until every voter of the town had had an opportunity to vote in his nomination.

During this delay of the expedition, Stamford, having promptly equiped its soldiers at considerable expense, seeing that the whole expense was likely to fall on that town, if the war did not go on, demanded that those expenses,[1] even some damage to the meeting house (probably in consequence of the soldiers having occupied it), should be borne by the Colony of New Haven; "and that they might have twelve men sent them at the jurisdiction charge to lie there all winter for their defence." "Defence" against the Dutch, whose trespasses and depredations had been going on all summer, and for years; and this request was according to the pledge of the New Haven Colony, to protect the plantations under its jurisdiction.

Under these circumstances Mr. Goodyear and Mr. Newman were sent by New Haven Court to quiet matters at Stamford, but finding much more commotion than they expected, they called the whole town together; and at this meeting Robert Bassett and John Chapman were the chief speakers against the proceedings of the New Haven Court, and in consequence of it Robert Bassett was summoned before the New Haven Court to answer. On his way to Court he said: "This is the thing that troubles me, that we have not our vote in our jurisdiction [New Haven] as others have, and instanced Connecticut jurisdiction."

Connecticut Colony never had any law excluding persons from voting because they were not members of the churches, but New Haven Colony always had.

Here, then, in Stamford, in the person of Robert Bassett, was the second contest held in New England in favor of *civil* liberty against *church* dictation and control; the first having taken place in Massachusetts with Roger Williams, who fled to Rhode Island.

---

[1] New Haven Col. Rec., i. 48.

In this conflict Robert Bassett made one speech worthy of the American Revolution which occurred one hundred and twenty years later, and sounds very much like Patrick Henry and other of his associates. In a town meeting in Stamford March 7, 1653, after he had been once before the Court at New Haven to answer in this matter, the record says:[10]

"Robert Bassett stood up and asked what the meeting was for, Richard Law, the constable, answered there was a general court to be at New Haven, and deputies were sent to go thither; Robert Bassett replied, they would obey no authority but that which was from the State of England; the constable answered, this authority is the authority of England; that he denied and said, then let us have English laws, for England does not prohibit us from our votes and liberties, and here we are cut off from all appeals to England, and we can have no justice here. Further, he said, they were made asses of, and their backs were almost broke, and it is time for them to look to themselves and to throw their burden off, for they shall be made very fools. And he spake against the justice of the authority of this jurisdiction; a reply being by some in defence thereof, he said, is that authority just, that makes what laws they please, executes them as they please, calls for rates when they please, and never so much as give them a reason?" Francis Bell told him that this should be declared at the Court; he answered, yes, it was his mind it should be, and therefore saith he I will say it again, is that authority just that makes what laws they please, executes them as they please, calls for rates when they please and never so much as give them a reason."

For these things Robert Bassett was imprisoned nearly two months, then again brought before the Court, and under the pressure of the courts, prisons and public sentiment largely against him, he confessed, not only that he had done these things, with one exception, but that he had done wrong and the Court released him on bonds of "one hundred pounds sterling."

Three other men as leaders in this contest for the right

---

[10] New Haven Col. Rec., i. 59.

to vote, were arrested, tried, fined and placed under bonds of fidelity to the New Haven Court.

Roger Ludlow's part in this matter seems to have been perfectly honorable and loyal so far as he acted in it; and this contrary to the generally received opinion of him. So far as any and all records show, no soldiers were raised in Fairfield but those ordered to be raised by Connecticut General Court. The vote to nominate him as their chief or captain, by the town, was in perfect keeping with the usage of the Court; and all of these things were done while the New Haven Court itself was preparing for the war and urging Massachusetts to fulfill her engagements in the same direction. That Ludlow, Fairfield and Stamford had no idea of going to war without New Haven and Connecticut is evidenced by the fact that as soon as the report of the proposed additional volunteers was offered, the New Haven Court at once—November 22, 1653,—took counsel as to " whether they were called at this time to send forth men against the Dutch, [that is, without Massachusetts], and after much debate and consultation had with most of the elders in the jurisdiction," the decision was against it, but even then they voted that if Connecticut would go, New Haven would.

Immediately upon this decision Fairfield and Stamford acquiesced, without a word of complaint, except as to paying the bill of expenses caused by raising the soldiers and keeping them all summer, as ordered by the Court; and the question as to the right of voting.

Such, in brief, were the doings in this matter, and such the result.

The particular offence, as claimed by the New Haven authorities, was, that the New Haven government being a government of God, any person opposing it as a government, sinned against God, his own soul, and the authority, a claim as arbitrary and self-conceited as Arch Bishop Laud, of England, ever proclaimed or acted upon.

The above items are taken from the New Haven records, they being the only authority as to the trial of these persons.

Robert Bassett came to Stratford and purchased his first land here November 10, 1681; and the next February he purchased a home lot of John Wells, and the next year he built a house on this lot, placing a stone over the mantel piece in the cellar with the following letters and figures: " R. B. 1683." These were cut in large size. When that house was torn down by John McEwen and another built on the same site in 1723, or soon after, this stone was placed in the cellar wall, where it may still be seen, the house having been owned and occupied many years by the late Nathan B. McEwen.

Robert Bassett was a peaceable, acceptable inhabitant in Stratford; was quite prosperous in worldly things, especially in possessing lands.

It was his grand-son Samuel, son of Robert, Jr., who settled in Derby in 1716 and became one of the most prominent citizens of that town.

No near relation existed between this Robert Bassett and the Goody Bassett executed at Stratford in 1651, for the wills of both his father and mother, John and Mary Bassett, were dated one and two years after the execution.

Arthur Perry came to Stratford and married Anna, only daughter of Joshua Judson, about 1675. He had a large family, but most of his children removed early from the town. It is possible that he traded somewhat as a merchant, for there is a due bill recorded, signed by him in 1678, and secured by sixteen acres of land, to Henry Powning of Boston, which bill was to be paid in money or merchantable provision, at Boston. It is difficult to imagine the reason or cause of such a debt, unless he was a trader in some way.

Samuel Blagge came from New York to Stratford with a family about 1685, and continued here as a merchant ten or twelve years. He had a number of children, several sons, but the name disappears from the town after about fifty years.

Richard Blacklach from Guilford, came to Stratford, probably in the spring of 1686, and established himself as a merchant, and thus continued about thirty years. He was successful, and became very prominent as a business man; bought considerable land, leased the Stratford ferry some years, interested himself in public matters; was the first one to build a box pew in the meeting house, which he did about 1710, at his own expense, upon a vote of permission by the town.

Upon his first coming here the town passed the following: "May 6, 1686. It was voted and granted unto Mr. Richard Blacklach and Mr. Daniel Shilton to build each of them a warehouse and wharf in some convenient place where it is judged most suitable by the selectmen of the town, provided the proprietors of Stratford forever have free wharfage."

Daniel Shelton having received permission in May, 1686, to build a ware house and wharf, as well as Richard Blacklach, he went forward with much success as a merchant, about twenty years, when he had not only married a fine young lady, but changed his business to farming and buying and selling land. After some years he removed to Ripton, where he died. A further account of him will be found in the history of the town of Huntington in this book.

Joseph Curtiss, son of the first John, was among the most prominent citizens of Stratford for many years. He was town clerk fifty successive years, and did the work in a creditable manner, to himself and the town. He always wrote the name Curtiss with two esses, and another name he always wrote Blakeman and never Blackman.

Mr. Curtiss was elected an Assistant, an office now called Senator, of the State, first in May, 1698, and elected after that 22 successive years, making in all 23 years. He was several years Judge of the County Court ; and was appointed on several state committees of importance ; one in 1710 with Hon. Nathan Gold and Peter Burr with a committee of New York State to locate the boundary line between these States, as settled by the authorities in 1700.

He is reported to have secured the slip of paper and coat of arms referred to in this book on page 125, which paper was an exact copy of the church record at Roxbury, Massachusetts, and he had the opportunity to know whether he belonged to that family or not. He was cotemporary with his father, John, thirty years, and with his uncle William fifty years, and therefore he knew whether Thomas, Philip and Mary Curtiss of Roxbury, Massachusetts, were his uncles and aunt, or not.

Further, it is possible that this slip of paper was not secure until about 1760, thirty years after Joseph Curtiss died, but there were living then from twenty to fifty persons in Stratford, if not many more, who knew what William and John Curtiss had told as to the family in Massachusetts.

The same is true in regard to several families of Stratford, who made records one way and another about 1760, when a number of persons obtained samples of the coat-of-arms belonging to their family in England.

Joseph Curtiss, in 1727 declined to serve longer as town clerk and another was appointed, and soon after he departed this life. For many years his descendants gloried in the honorable title applied to him frequently while living—"the Worshipful Joseph Curtiss."

Capt. William Curtis, sketched somewhat on pages 125–6, was the most prominent military man in Stratford until 1700. Next to him were Capt. Stephen Burritt and Lieut. Joseph Judson, but both of these were younger, not less noted. He served the town in many offices, on many committees; and for eighteen years he was representative with only one or two exceptions.

A List of the proprietors of all common or undivided lands in the township was recorded in 1699, and is valuable as showing who were proprietors and what their relative proportioned interest was. The list does not show how many acres each owned but simply his proportion; that is, as often as Jere Judson had 48 acres, Joseph Hawley had 14, Jonathan Smith 15, and so to the end of the list.[11] Also, it does not show the relative wealth of the families named.

[11] "A record of each and every particular proprietor's Rights in future commonage in Stratford adjusted by the Committee Chosen and appointed for that work and by them ordered to be Recorded for the future benefit and peace of the town, January 13, 1699, by which Rule all future Divisions are to be laid out.

Mr. Jere Judson, sen.	48 acres.	Samuel Judson	24½ acres.
Joseph Hawley	14 "	Jacob Walker	12 "
Jonathan Smith	15 "	Isaac Judson's heirs	12 "
Eben' Booth	18½ "	Abraham Kimberly	6 "
John Booth	18½ "	Mr. Samuel Blagg	6 "
Ephraim Booth's heirs	14 "	Joseph Blakeman	6 "

Various Items Worth Recording.

"At about the latter end of July, 1671, there being four Indians complained of for being drunk and disorderly, they were brought before ye authority in ye Town and there fined tenn shillings apiece.

Item. Ye charges in apprehending them and keeping them in Custody till a hearing and ye tryall, five and twenty shillings. This entered for memoranda. Jno. Minor, recorder. To Left[enant] 6ˢ; To ye Constable 12ˢ; To Interpreter 7ˢ."

John Blakeman, deceased..20	acres.	John Peat................ 7	acres.
Daniel Foot..... 6	"	Jacob Weaklin 18	"
Samuel Galpin, deceased...12	"	Edmon Sherman's heirs 12	"
Samuel Mil 14	"	John Hurd, junr. 6	"
Benjⁿ Nicolls................19½	"	Capt. Jon. Beardslee.......22	"
Jonathan Nicolls 8½	"	Zechariah Fairchild........20	"
Josiah Nicolls, sen. 17	"	Capt. James Judson 32½	"
John Hawley................21	"	Mr. John Judson 34¼	"
Mr. Samuel Hawley 39	"	John Curtiss, sen. 12½	"
Ephraim Hawley 21	"	Benjⁿ Curtiss 9½	"
Ebenʳ Hawley's heirs 5½	"	Lieut. Israel Curtiss 14	"
Samuel Beacher............ 6	"	Richard Butler's heirs......22	"
Benjⁿ Lewis................24	"	Caleb Nicholls, deceased...24	"
John Wilcoxson............39¼	"	Abraham Nicolls 6	"
Timothy Titharton.........18½	"	Joseph Fairechild 4	"
Joseph Booth............... 6	"	Mist. Katharine Judson 18	"
Daniel Curtiss 6	"	Sergt. Samuel Fairechild ...14	"
Daniel Titharton 14	"	Edward Hinman 18	"
Ebenʳ Blakeman 6	"	John Gilbert 6	"
Samuel Titharton..........15½	"	Isaac Stiles................ 6	"
Jonathan Curtiss 14	"	Arthur Perry..............12¼	"
Nicolas Huse 6	"	Mr. Benjⁿ Blakeman.......14	"
Jon. Bostick, deceased 19½	"	Mrs. Jane Blakeman.......18½	"
Benjⁿ Sherman 6	"	Isaac Bennit 6	"
Joseph Watkins 10	"	Robert Rose 12	"
James Phippeny............ 6	"	Francis Griffin............. 7	"
Mr. D. Mitchell, deceased ..47	"	Hugh Griffin 7	"
Abraham Mitchell 6	"	Thomas Griffin 6	"
Nathaniel Sherman 6	"	James Blakeman 18	"
Samuel Beardslee, sen......14	"	Capt. John Minor..........14	"
John Hurd, senr's heirs 36	"	John Wheeler 15	"
Henery Summers...........14	"	Joshua Curtiss 14	"
Samuel Wells 16½	"	Samuel Gregory 14	"
and 8 acres 6 miles distant		Samuel Stiles 20	"

Four pounds and a half, money, for Indians to pay, who probably had not a penny in possession, was a costly drunk, but white people can throw such a spree all into the shade.

Selling their services for a passage to America.

" Be it known to all men by these presents that I, Andrew Alexander now of new east Jersey in America have bargained and sold and do hereby sell and alienate unto Andrew Winton of Fairfield in New England, his heirs and assigns, two servants called Duncan Garnoch and Margaret his wife lately come out of Scotland, which are indebted to me for indenture;

John Brooks	6	acres.	Lieut. John Hubbel's heirs .18	acres.
Robert Lane	14	"	Mr. Zecheriah Walker	30	"
John Burroughs	6	"	Mr. Elizer Kimberly	12	"
John Porter	15	"	Mr. Alex{dr} Bryan	14	"
Isaac Knell	35½	"	John Hurd Woodbery	28	"
John Johnson	6	"	Mr. Samuel Preston	22	"
Mr. Jonath. Pitman	20	"	Ambrose Tompson and	} 44	"
Daniel Weaklin	20¼	"	John Tompson	
John Sherwood	28	"	Francis Hall, deceased	18	"
Robert Basset	6	"	Mr. Daniel Shelton	28	"
Deacon Wells	31	"	Mr. Richard Blacklack	50¼	"
Samll Peat, senr	14	"	Mr. Joseph Curtiss	34	"
Joseph Beardslee	19½	"	Mr. Ephraim Stiles	30	"
Daniel Beardslee	36¼	"	Mr. Samuel Sherman, jun...	20	"
Robert Walker	12	"	Capt. Stephen Burritt	20	"
Samll Peat, junr	6	"	Mr. Israel Chancey	32	"
John Beach	12	"	Mr. John Wells	30	"
and 8 acres within 5 miles			Benjn Peat, senr.	8	"
George Searles	6	"	Deacon Tim.ºWilcoxson	29½	"
Robert Clarke	28	"	Daniel Brinsmead's heirs...	28¼	"
Nathaniel Beach	6½	"	Capt. Wm Curtiss	26	"
Serg{t} Ebenr Curtiss	12½	"	Josiah Curtiss	6	"
Zechariah Curtiss	15½	"	Lieut. Thomas Knowles	12	"
Benjn Beach	14	"	Lieut Agur Tomlinson	14	"
Sergt. Daniel Picket	12	"	Ensign John Coe	21	"
John Picket's heirs	12	"	James Clarke, senr	14	"
Nathaniel Porter	6	"	Saml{l} Uffoott	35	"
John Peacock's heirs	14	"	John Birdsey, senr.	21	"
Jonas Tomlinson	14	"	John Birdsey, junr.	12	"
Mr Samuel Wheeler, deceased	27½	"	John Burritt	19	"
Moses Wheeler	31½	"	James Weaklin	20¼	"
Mr Saml Sherman, senr.	17½	"	Samuel Beers in Right of his	
Matthew Sherman's heirs...	12	"	farther John Beers, deceased 6	"

and assigned by George Tomson to John Swinton, by John Swinton to Mr. Francis Scott, by Mr. Scott to Mr. George Alexander, and by Mr. George Alexander to me the said Andrew Alexander by facture and his full power whereby I the said Andrew Alexander do dispose and sell the two servants, my full power, title and right as is above expressed to the said Andrew Winton his heirs and asigns and obliged me to warrant the said Andrew Winton at the house of the forenamed persons that they shall not molest nor trouble the said Duncan or his master Andrew Winton through my seal of this indenture being made at Edinburgh the 29 day of May 1684, which remains for the space of four years after their arrival at east Jersey being the first of November, 1684, and from that time they are to serve the said Andrew according to the time of said indenture, and I oblige also me to warrant this indenture from the above named persons, George Tomson, Mr. Francis Scott, John Swinton and the said George Alexander.

In witness hereof I have written and subscribed obligatory with my hand before these witnesses, Josiah Harvey, Thomas Murrin indweller in Fairfield."

Ye 13ᵗʰ April, 1684.　　　　ANDREW ALEXANDER.
　　　Signed in presence of us　　⎱
JOSIAH HARVEY, THOMAS MURRIN. ⎰

"These may certify whom it shall or may concern that I Andrew Winton doth discharge and set at liberty to their own will and pleasure the within mentioned Dunkin Gardner and Margaret Gardner of and from the within servitude and time within expressed and from all dues, debts and demands, as witness my hand this 2ᵈ day of July, Anoque Dom. 1685."

A Ladder Company.

1686. "It was voted that every householder in Stratford shall provide a suitable lather to his house that will reach the top of his house at least within — feet of the top, and whatsoever householder shall neglect providing a suitable lather as aforesaid, above one month from this date, shall forfeit five shillings, the one half to the complainer, the other half to the town treasurer."

Modlin, the French girl. "This indenture made the 24th of June, 1662, witnesseth that we the townsmen of Stratford upon good and serious considerations moving us thereunto doe bind out one Modlin a little girl about six years of age, that formerly did belong to a Frenchman that was in necessity upon the town of Stratford; we say, to John Minor of Stratford, to him, his heirs and assigns, till the aforesaid girl shall attayne the age of twenty-one years; we say we bind her with her father's consent; also a lawful apprentice to the aforesaid John Minor till the aforesaid term of tyme shall be fully and completely ended.

The aforesaid John Minor engages to provide her with apparel and diet and bedding as may be suitable for such an apprentice.

That this is our act and deed, and witnessed by subscribing the day and date above written.

RICHARD BOOTH,   JOHN BRINSMADE, ⎫
WILLIAM CURTIS,   CALEB NICHOLS, ⎬ Townsmen."
        JEREMIAH JUDSON.   ⎭

"***Memoranda,*** that upon the 29th day of September, 1679, Sergt. Jeremiah Judson, constable, by order of the selectmen was sent and forewarned Phillip Denman and his mate Collins out of the town or from settling or abiding in any part of our bounds.

And upon the 12th of November, 1679, Phillip Denman and Daniel Collins by the townsmen, were warned as above."

Herders were employed to take care of the cattle which were pastured in the woods. It was employment without as much amusement, even as working in the harvest field afforded, and hence men sometimes played truants.

"February 18, 1662. Samuel Fayrechild and Robert Lane, Cow keepers for the year 1662, being detected of unfaithfulness in keeping the heard, the sayed Samuel and Robert doe owne they did leave the heard in the woods and come home several days. This was owned in a public town meeting before Mr. Sharman, February 18, 1662. Mr. Sharman hath adjudged the above said Robert Lane and Samuel Fayrchild to pay to the townsmen twenty shillings use."

Town Boundaries were intelligible to those who established them, but are now a little indefinite and amusing. The following is a sample.

"An agreement of ye agents of ye two towns of Stratford and Fairfield this 24th of Aprill 1679, about ye bound between ye two towns from ye Cheritree Southerly to ye Sea as itt used to bee, and northerly from ye Cherytree to a stone whereabouts a walnut tree growed, and from thence to a rock by Henry Summer's fence, from thence to a tree near ye path marked of ould with a cross south and north, from thence to a heap of stones nearer ye path upon ye hill of rocks in sight of ye rode, and from thence to the next marked bound and so to Continue ye ould marked bound to ye extent of our twelve miles. That this is our agreement wee attest by subscribing our names, Joseph Hawley, Jehu Burr, Francis Hall, John Wheeler, Samuel Morehouse."

This cherry tree stood in what is now Park Avenue near the junction of that and Fairfield Avenue.

CHAPTER XI.

PUSHING INTO THE WILDERNESS.

ROM cultivated fields to the wilderness was the change in the lives of the first settlers when they came to Stratford, and their children, while yet some of the fathers were living, pushed into the wilderness with a courage and heroism equal to that which the fathers themselves had shown. The spirit of enterprise sent the planters to Stratford, as well as to all New England, and when once these planters had secured the proprietorship in something near 75,000 acres of land, called Stratford township, there was no diminution of the spirit of enterprise; and following them, their sons and daughters moved forward in the laborious work of settling a great country in the rights and privileges of freedom.

These men took great care to secure the right to the soil by fair, impartial, and even generous purchase from the native owners. This done, they proceeded to divide, fairly, and even benevolently the domain thus equitably obtained.

When the company took possession of this territory they evidently believed that the Connecticut Colony had secured the right of soil as well as title to it, and proceeded upon that understanding to divide the same to themselves and new settlers as they came in. But after twelve or fifteen years, when the settlement had assumed formidable proportions, the Indians began to clamor for pay for the land which lay north of an east and west line about six miles from the Sound, to which the inhabitants agreed, and hence the several different purchases made, as heretofore represented by the Indian deeds, on page 22, and following.

Ansantaway,[1] the chief of Milford, presenting a claim, it was payed in 1658, and then followed several others. Bray Rossiter, of Guilford, secured 100 acres in payment of a debt.

In 1661 Joseph Judson made a purchase of a large tract known as the Mohegan Hills, lying between the two branches of the Farmill river, containing about 5,000 acres. In 1673 the townsmen applied to the General Court to settle the differences between the town and Joseph Judson as to the ownership of this land. The Court appointed a time for hearing the claims in the matter, but it seems to have been amicably settled without the help of the Court; probably about as the town had agreed before,[2] and a division of this tract was some years later made among the proprietors, Joseph Judson retaining such a proportion as satisfied him for the outlay in the purchase.

Another purchase was made in 1661, "a large tract of land lying west from the Farmill river at Woronoke," it being made by Joseph Judson, but probably in behalf of the town.

The tract of land between the Nearmill and Farmill rivers was purchased in December, 1661, by Mr. Samuel Sherman, John Hurd and Caleb Nichols—townsmen for the town, and all proprietors had their proportion of it, in after years.

On the 22d of April, 1662, was received a deed for the territory of a considerable part of what is now the townships of Trumbull, Monroe and Easton, " lying west of the land which the town of Stratford had previously purchased," or west of

---

[1] The frame of a house spoken of in a foot note on page 12 of this book as being at Milford when the whites first came, was the frame of Ansantaway's large wigwam. In the summer the old chief occupied this tent, covering it with bark and matting. The matting he took off and carried with him to his residence at Paugasset for the winter.

[2] " The Town uppon yᵉ 6th December, 1672, sufficient consideration moving thereunto doe give grant and allow to Leiftᵗ Joseph Judson the peacable improvement of so much land, good and bad altogether lying at yᵉ place commonly called yᵉ Mohegin Hills, ye hop-garden, meadow and lowland on both sides yᵉ East Spraine of yᵉ Far Mill River as high on that Sprayne as this accommodation reacheth, as is the proportion of an eight acre meadowed inhabitant to yᵉ whole bounds, with this proviso yᵗ it shall not be expected to be all laid out at present but successively as other proprietors."

the Pequonnock river, extending to Fairfield line and from a line crossing the township east and west about at the Trumbull Church, or possibly a little further south, north to Newtown. This was the Long Hill purchase.

The last large tract was bought May 25, 1671, called the White Hills purchase, and the agreement with the Indians was, that this purchase should cover "all lands within the bounds of Stratford," and no reservations whatever were made—not even the usual "hunting and fishing."

There was no exceptions, not even the reservations at Golden Hill or Coram, which had in all other deeds been made, and there is reason for supposing that the inhabitants believed these reservations were included, so that when the Indians died or deserted them, there would be no more purchasing of Indian claims. This is evident from the amount paid—£50-14-6—and the specific terms of the deed in which the boundaries of the territory included are definitely given; —"Stratford river on the east, Fairfield on the west, and from the sea twelve miles northward, as it is now settled by the Court; . . . with all rights, titles, privileges, and appertenances thereunto belonging or in any manner of ways appertaining, which we do freely and absolutely resign and make over unto the aforesaid inhabitants."

A tax was levied on the inhabitants of the town to raise this purchase money and the record of it specifies that it was for the "White Hills purchase, together with the expenses, both to English and Indians, in and to the sale of all land within the bounds of Stratford." In another record, as to the expenses of this transaction, it is said : "all the charges and expense of the White Hills and the confirmation of lands within the bounds of Stratford."[1]

---

[1] "A memorandum of all the Charges and Expenses about ye purchase of ye White Hills and ye Confirmation of all lands within ye Bounds of Stratford :

To Mr. Richard Bryan for cloth coats, . . .	£16-00-00
Mr. Alexander Bryan for goods to ye Indians for ye same land, ...	2-11-00
Mr. Hawley for goods to ye Indians for ye White Hills purchase, ...	3-10-00
Mr. Hawley for entertainment of ye Indians at y' time with his own time, ...	1-00-00

This tax list is interesting, not only as showing the proportion of each man's proprietorship—not each man's wealth—but the number of, and who were the inhabitants of the town at the time, it being just two years before the Woodbury company removed.

It is further evident that the inhabitants supposed they settled all claims from the Indians, on the reservations, from the fact that the town voted, February 8, 1674, to lay out Golden Hill "by way of division to every proprietor according to his proportion," and appointed a committee to do the work; and in 1677, this reservation was divided to the proprietors of the town, then numbering just 100, and they " drew lots " to effect an impartial distribution.

This is not all, for in the settlement of the question of the support or location of the Indians in 1659, on the 80 acres on Golden Hill, the Court directed, " that in case these Indians shall wholly, at any time, relinquish and desert Gold Hill, that then it shall remain to Stratford plantation, they repaying to Fairfield the one-half of that which they received in consideration of the said land. They had received from Fairfield twenty pounds and therefore should have paid ten pounds only.

The next year, 1678, the Indians—there being a few left—made complaint, or some whites for them, to the General Court, and that authority prohibited the Stratford men from taking or using any of the 80 acres or reservation. Thus the

Mr. Fayrechild for his entertainment of ye Indians at ye same time with his own time, ...	£ 0–10–00
Ensign Judson for his time about that purchase, . .	0–18–00
Thos. Uffoot for expenses to ye Indians, . . .	0–10–00
John Minor for interpreting, and his time about Pequonnuck Indians in order to what was done at ye General Court, Surveying whole Bounds of ye town May. '71, . .	8–08–08
To Mr. East for trading cloth, ...	7–13–00
To Mr. Bryan for goods upon ye same account, . .	1–12–06
To Mr. Hawley for one coat upon that account, . .	1–00–00
To Mr. Benjamin Black for goods to pay ye Indians, .	2–10–00
To Mr. Henman credit for his time, . . .	0–05–00
[Records effaced]	1–16–00
" "	3–13–06
" "	2–06–00"

matter was left nearly one hundred years, until 1765, when 70 acres of this land cost the town of Stratford nearly one hundred pounds, a part of which was placed as a fund for the support of the three Indian claimants, then the only remaining ones known.

The equity of this cost is doubtful, since the land had, in fact, been paid for one hundred years before, as all the people of Stratford understood the matter; but it is probable that some persons outside of the town of Stratford feared that these Indians might need support from the state, and if a fund could be raised by Stratford paying twice, or thrice, for this land it would save other people from bearing the expense.

From this time—1671—foward the proprietors proceeded to divide their entire territory, except the two Indian reservations, and clear and improve the same with great rapidity, securing abundant remuneration. The soil was rich, the produce abundant, and although money was scarce, nobody suffered for want of food, unless they deserved it, because too lazy to work; but now days it is not so, for often hard-working persons do suffer because of want.

During all this time, and the work of extending the purchased territory, most of the inhabitants were residing in the village of Stratford, within a distance of two miles from the meeting-house.[4]

In the list of the inhabitants for March,[5] 1668, there were recorded five " outlivers," or persons living beyond the two mile limits.

These were John Wheeler, Obadiah Wheeler and Hope Washburn, at Oronoke, and Theophilus Sherman and Matthew Sherman, at the east end of Old Mill Green.

It is quite certain that the three families were at Oronoke, for Hope Washburn sold, in 1668, to Samuel Mills, a

---

[4] January, 1685. Whereas, several town acts have been passed for granting lands to the proprietors, but not to come within two miles of the town, and there being no particular place stated where to begin the measure for the two miles, it is, therefore, voted that the meeting-house shall be the place stated to begin at for the future,"

[5] See page 179 of this book.

new man in the town, three acres of land, and in 1670, Samuel Mills sold his " house, barn and home lot lying at Woronoke," to Hugh Makie.

On the 24th of June, 1678, Nathaniel Foot, another new man, received liberty from the town to settle at Oronoke.

At that time there were probably scattering settlers along the main road from Stratford village northward as far as Peck's Mills, and a few at Oronoke, and six years later—February, 1684,—an agreement was made by James Blakeman, with a committee of the town, to build "a corn mill at the mouth of the Nearmill river, and he doth engage to grind their wheat and rye for a sixteenth part, and their corn for a twelfth part, and all malt for a thirtieth part, provided there is brought five bushels at a time. He also engageth to bring the black brook to run into the Nearmill river to feed it, if it may be done with three pounds charges.

" For which the committee gave the stream and 15 acres of land to build on, as near the mill as may be."

James Blakeman, in 1660, was the miller, and owned the property at the tide mill near the eagle's nest, and in 1663 he sold the mill property at Old Mill Green to Mr. Samuel Sherman, having conducted it, probably, three or four years; and hence the town knew the man they trusted to build a new mill at the place now called Peck's Mills.

In 1676 the town gave liberty to James Blakeman to build a saw mill at the mouth of Farmill river, which was, probably, the first mill there.

Pequonnock[1] was the Indian name applied by the English to the territory where the city of Bridgeport now stands. The township of Stratford was bounded on the west by the Fairfield line, and that line was to be the center of a highway, and this road to be eight rods wide, for in some of the deeds of land given by the town, it specified carefully that four rods on the Stratford side should be reserved for a highway, and the same reservation was made by the town of Fairfield on its side of the line. It is a misfortune that that

---

[1] This spelling has become established by use in the locality and hence is here continued.

highway, now the magnificent Park Avenue of Bridgeport, had not been retained 132 feet wide.

As the Indian name Pequonnock indicates, there was a large cleared field or fields in the western and northern parts of this territory when the English first came here. The cleared land southwest of Golden Hill was called Pequonnock field, and was divided by the boundary line between Fairfield and Stratford, and that part of it belonging to Stratford was fenced, in one enclosure, and still called Pequonnock field, and was used for raising grain. In 1657 it was laid out to the proprietors in such a manner that each proprietor's proportion is said to have been "two-thirds of a division, and in William Beardsley's case and others, amounted to eighteen acres for each.

The Indian reservation contained 80 acres laying in nearly a square plot, the boundary line passing from the river west nearly on the present Elm street to Courtland street, or a little further west and thence northward about 150 rods, thence east crossing Main street about where now Washington avenue crosses it.

North of this reservation were two plains, called frequently the upper and lower plains, but the upper one was more frequently called the Calf-pens plain, because the cattle were pastured in that region and the calves put in pens while young. These two plains were early—from 1657 to 1665— divided into plots for meadow and farming, and in several of the deeds occurs the name "Ireland's Brook"—now degraded to Island Brook—but whence the name is not known, indicating that the first settlers may have located in that vicinity.

The first settlers west of Pequonnock river, in Stratford, were Henry Summers, Sen., and his two sons Henry and Samuel, and Samuel Gregory; and they seem to have come here in the year 1665, and some years later Samuel Gregory's house stood near the junction of the present Washington and Park avenues.

Soon after these came John Beardsley and his brother Samuel Beardsley, and Henry Summers, Sen., removed to Milford, but his two sons remained here on the homestead, it being divided to them.

Slowly the settlement increased, spreading northward along what was afterwards known far and near as Toilsome Hill road, the land having been laid out for the distance of three miles at one time, which probably reached nearly to the long hill purchase. The name Toilsome Hill, arose from the steepness of several portions of it, and the winding of the road in order to effect the ascent. When the height is reached it affords a beautiful and extensive view over the Sound and along the Long Island coast.

When the settlers first made their dwellings here there were several hundred Indians resident on the reservation, for it is said by Dea. Isaac Sherman in his manuscript notes, that the wigwams numbered at least one hundred when the whites began to settle here, that is, about 1670. There may have been three or four families here as early as 1665.

Gradually the settlement grew and prospered, the inhabitants attending church at Stratford, a distance of three miles, nearly thirty years, when in 1695 the ecclesiastical society of Stratfield was organized and a church established.

Old Mill Green was a flourishing and an aristocratic part of the town of Stratford from about the year 1700 until after 1800. It is at the present time a beautiful part of the city of Bridgeport, but was a wild wilderness country when first traveled by white men. The land was a plain, and rich, and hence the trees were large and tall.

The first white persons who traveled through the forests here were in pursuit of the Pequots who fled from their burned forts near Norwich, Connecticut, and who doubtless were conducted by friendly Indians along an Indian path in the summer of 1637. This Indian path was continued, being used by the English at Stratford to reach their fields at Pequonnock, about forty years before it was made a legal highway; the path crossing the Pequonnock river about where the Old Mill Green road does now.

In 1679 the General Court ordered certain roads to be constructed in the Colony, as "Country roads or King's highways;"[8] and such ways were for more than a hundred

---

[8] "May, 1679. This Court orders that the present roads from plantation to

years known by these names. The town act establishing this
as a' highway, was passed in 1685, in the following words:
"All the uplands and marshes lying southward of the road
leading to Fairfield, between the physicall spring and the
uppermost cartway over ―――― Brook shall be left for a perpetual common,' and twenty rods in breadth shall be left for
a road to Fairfield bounds."

The "physical spring" is that lately called the sulphur
springs, about which some considerable excitement was
raised a few years since, but no successful effort has been
made to make a medical resort.

The intention of the above vote, doubtless, was to have
the highway twenty rods wide from its commencement to
Fairfield line, and it was probably so laid out in 1687, as they
were that year required to do it by the Court; but some
years later the proprietors of the town sold much of the land
in the wide highways and reduced their width. It is also
said that Theophilus Nichols, a little after 1700, then living
at Old Mill Green, was largely influential in preserving the
green at its present width, which is twelve rods at the west
end and fifteen at the school house. The road was continued
in Fairfield at an unusual width as it still remains. It has
been known in name as the Old King's highway just two
hundred years, but is in danger of losing its monarchical title
for one more in harmony with the government of the country
in which it is located.

This Old Mill Green is the part of the Old King's highway from Mill brook, westward to the Pequonnock river, and
was so called from the mill which was built on Mill brook in
1654, by John Hurd, Sen., and Thomas Sherwood, Sen., and
by the time there were such a number of settlers along this

―――――――――――――――――――――――――――

plantation shall be reputed the country roads or King's highway, and so to remain
until the Court do see good reason to make alteration of the same. And whereas,
each plantation is by law required once a year to work a day in clearing the brush,
it is by this Court recommended to the townsmen of the several plantations to
improve their inhabitants in clearing the common roads, in the first place, that lie
between town and town, until the said roads are cleared at least one rod wide."
Coll. Rec., iii. 30.

' This included a large part of Clapboar Hill.

19

road as to form a community of social life, the first mill had become old, and hence the name, Old Mill Hill and Old Mill Green.

The old mill was called a corn mill, but all kinds of grain were ground by it. It had several owners. Thomas Sherwood, who was partner in building it, soon sold his share to John Hurd, who sold it to Alexander Bryan of Milford, and he to James Blakeman, who sold half of it to his brother, Samuel Blakeman, in 1662, who settled here, probably in the house, or built him a house on the south side of the highway near the brook, as this land with quite a number of acres, belonged to the mill property. Here he died in 1668, and his widow afterwards married Jacob Walker. She had only two children living, both daughters, one five years of age and the other, one, when her husband died, but had considerable property. Her mother-in-law, Mrs. Jane Blakeman, resided with her in March, 1668–9, and hence she is recorded that year as an "outliver."[10]

James Blakeman sold his half of the old mill Dec. 4, 1663, with considerable land, to Samuel Sherman, Sen., who soon purchased more land here, and placed his three sons, Edward, Matthew and Samuel as residents in this vicinity. In 1680 Edward and Matthew were living on the east side of the brook, north of the highway, and Samuel west of the brook, south of the highway.

Various mills have been in use at this old mill place, the first one standing probably on the north side of the highway. For some years before 1800, a bark mill and tannery were in operation here. The last was a wool carding mill in 1818.[11]

---

[10] See page 179 of this book.

[11] From the *Republican Farmer*, Oct. 17, 1818.

"WOOL CARDING."

The subscribers have their machine in complete operation. Wool brought to the machine will meet with immediate despatch, and wool left at Burritt's and Sherman's, Bridgeport and at Daniel DeForest's, Stratford, will be attended to once or twice a week. The subscribers feel thankful for past favors and solicit a continuance of them.

B. & M. SILLIMAN & CO.

Old Mill, 8th June, 1818."

The point of land south of Old Mill Green, reaching to the Sound, lying between Mill brook on the east, and the Pequonnock river west was known from about 1650, for two hundred years, as New Pasture field, and the southern end of it New Pasture point. It was fenced into one field for a pasture, but not long after became a field for raising grain, in which case the cattle were excluded by the fence which had before kept them in. When used as a pasture it may have been much smaller, the fence crossing the neck further south, but later, the fence ran on the south side of the green, apparently, and was divided anew in 1692, into 46 sections in proportion to the number of acres each person owned within the inclosure,[12] but these owners did not all nor half of them, reside at the green.

The first movement made, that finally resulted in a mill

---

[12] "A record of the general fence for the new pasture from ye mill brook to Paquanock river being just eleven foott to one acre of land; the first lot begining at ye sd mill brook, and being measured by a pole eleven foott long which is for one Acre of land—first lott Daniell Mitchell for 22 acres 22 pole.

1	Daniell Mitchell	22	pole.	24 John Hubbell	06	pole.
2	Ebenezer Booth	24½	"	25 The Hawleys	36	"
3	Nathaniel Sherman	21	"	26 Agur Tomlinson	11	"
4	Benjamin Sherman	21	"	27 Daniel Brinsmead	07½	"
5	John Bostick	04	"	28 Paul Brinsmead	10½	"
6	Stephen and John Burritt	11	"	29 John Hurd	18	"
7	Samuel Sherman	05	"	30 Joseph Curtiss	04½	"
8	Ebenezer Blakeman	06	"	31 Isaac Hurd	03	"
9	Thomas Knowles	04	"	32 Benjn and Hannah Nicolls	07½	"
10	Ebenezer Hubbell	10½	"	33 William Piglee [Pixlee]	15	"
11	Widow Rayner	12	"	34 Charles Dugles	12½	"
12	Samuel Peat	07	"	35 Capt. Curtiss	12	"
13	Samuel Galpin	09	"	36 John Birdsey	04	"
14	John Wells	02½	"	37 Joseph Blakeman	06	"
15	Jonathan Nicolls	06	"	38 Joseph Watkins	13	"
16	Mr. Samuel Sherman, sen.	13½	"	39 Nicolas Huse	10	"
17	Daniell Pickett	03½	"	40 Joseph Booth	04	"
18	Deacon Wilcockson	05	"	41 Weaklins, Dil and James	05½	"
19	James Judson	03	"	42 Benjamin Curtiss	04½	"
20	John Brooks	04	"	43 Thomas Wells	08	"
21	John Pickett	03½	"	44 John Coe	03	"
22	Thomas Pickett	03	"	45 Ephraim Booth	04	"
23	Ambross Thompson	20	"	46 Thomas Pickett	03	"

Recorded April 28, 1692."

on the Pequonnock river a little way above the old King's highway, began in May, 1691, when the town granted liberty to Matthew Sherwood, John and Matthew Sherwood, Jr., "to set up a gristmill and sawmill on Pequonnock river above the road where it may be thought most convenient;" but the mill was not built until a number of years after that time. The next grant was to John Seeley in 1697.

The river at this place was without a bridge, at least, until the date of the following town vote :

"Third Tuesday, Dec. 1736. Sergt. Richard Nicolls, Nathaniel Sherman and Peter Pixlee were chosen a committee to endeavor that a cart bridge be built over Pequonnock river in the Grand Country Road at the town's charge, provided that particular persons do appear to build the butments, in the whole, thirty feet free of any town charge."

The committee to take the oversight of the New pasture field in 1718, consisted of Capt. John Hawley, Mr. Benjamin Sherman and Sergt. Richard Nichols, and the pound keeper was John Hurd, all residing at Old Mill Green.

The large rude mile-stone standing on this green, was set there by the direction of Benjamin Franklin, while he was Colonial Postmaster, between the years 1753 and 1774, a most interesting monument of the days when public improvements began at a great venture as well as enterprise. Many of these stones are still standing along this ancient highway between New York and New Haven.

The beginning of a separate school in this locality was inaugurated by a town vote in 1717, to allow them " their part of the 40 shillings per thousand allowed by law and the appointment of Sergt. John Hurd, and Sergt. Andrew Patterson, as committee. This seems to be the first occurrence of the name Pembroke, spelled then Pembrook.

Oronoke began to be settled about 1665, the first inhabitants, John Wheeler, Obadiah Wheeler and Hope Washburn settled at Farmill river, and a little way south of it. In 1666 Samuel Mills settled there, and in 1667 Ephraim Stiles and Samuel Stiles became land owners there and soon made it their place of residence.

Other inhabitants soon followed, and in January, 1705-6, the town granted Ephraim Stiles the privilege of setting up a gristmill at Farmill river, a little below Black brook, and granted liberty to Lt. Agur Tomlinson to maintain a fulling-mill there. At that time the inhabitants at that place had become quite numerous, and it was an influential part of the town.

General David Wooster was born there in 1710, and in the Revolution it was a center of much public influence and activity, while for fifty or more years afterwards some of the most noted families of the town resided there. It is still a most beautiful locality, even from Stratford village to Farmill river; the residences are beautifully located along the river banks, and are kept in fine style, so that a five mile drive along the old Oronoke road is one of the most attractive of which the town can boast.

The spirit of Education began to be fostered at that place by the following vote :

" January 11, 1716-17. Voted, that the farmers at Long hill, Oronoke, Putnee, Mohegin hill, Trap falls, Fairchilds and Nichols lakes and Pambrook, shall have the use of their part of the 40 shillings per thousand allowed by law for seven years ensuing, providing they educate their children accor-ding to law."

Several men raised at this place—including what is now Oronoke and Putney school districts—were graduated at college and did honor to the world and their day and gene-ration. One, David Wooster, became a General in the United States army; another, Gideon Tomlinson, became a Governor of the State and then a Representative and also a Senator in Congress; another, Nathan Birdseye, became a clergyman and lived to be over one hundred years of age ; several be-came officers in the militia and served in the French War and in the Revolution.

" May, 1727. Upon the petition to Thomas Gilbert of Oronoque in the township of Stratford, for liberty to set up a ferry at the said Oronoque, about four miles northward of the ferry called Stratford ferry: This Court grant unto the said Thomas Gilbert the liberty or privilege of setting up a ferry for the transportation of passengers across the river called Oronoque River, during the pleasure of this Court, and order that the fare shall be the same with the fare appointed for Stratford ferry."[11]

In 1759 the like privilege was granted by the same authority to Zechariah Blakeman, Jr.

Division of the common lands was a matter of great difficulty, expense and dissatisfaction in Stratford, which continued until after the year 1800.

Up to about 1670 persons selected their lands wherever they desired, subject to the sanction of the committee or townsmen. In the Spring of 1680, "the town agreed to lay out all lands within six miles of the town" [meeting house], and appointed a committee to do it. In the autumn of the same year "the town voted to lay out one hundred or one hundred and six score acres, as may be found convenient, at the north and northwest end of the town," and appointed a committee to ascertain " what land might be convenient for such a division."

In 1687, a tract of land within two miles of the meeting house, lying, apparently, north of the Fairfield road, was ordered to be laid in lots, yet kept in common, " in a general way only for herbage for the proper use and benefit of the town in general and poor of the place, for them and their heirs forever; timber, wood, clay and stone to be free for each inhabitant, to be taken off the land without molestation from any person. Also, it is voted that the land lying southward of Fairfield road between the place called Ireland's Brook and Snake Brook hill, shall be laid out and improved in the same way and manner.

The lots north of the Fairfield road were laid in strips the whole length of the tract, and hence was called the "Slip, or pasture division." After many years it was also called the Farm, for in remeasuring the lots in 1711, many of them are said to be bounded on the " Farm Highway."

The acts of the proprietors of common lands were performed in the town meetings, non-proprietors not being

---

[11] Col. Rec., vii. 102.

allowed to vote until March, 1723-4, when the proprietors met according to notification and organized into a separate body; appointed a committee to ascertain all the claimants of these lands in order to a complete adjustment of all rights in the matter. They voted, also, to lay out a division of all their undivided lands in the township, six miles from town,"[19] with the allowance of sufficient highways and commons; and appointed a committee to do it.

This placed the whole north end of the township, beyond six miles, into one plot to be divided, and on May 18, 1724, having ascertained, as they supposed, the names of all parties, they voted to divide the whole plot into 144 lots, that being the whole number; drew a plan of every lot and placed it on record in the town book. In this plan there are twelve ranges of lots, each range 160 rods wide, running north and south, six miles long, and the lots running east and west across the range of lots.

The peculiarity of this proposition is that they voted to have "a highway twenty rods wide between each range of lots;" with cross highways in every range eight rods wide. This would have been a picturesque township—eleven highways, six miles long, twenty rods wide, within the distance of about ten miles. But the early settlers were not accustomed to such an estimate of the picturesque as to throw away 440 acres of land in half a township, not by a very great difference. What, then, was the idea in making such wide highways? One and only one: common pasturage for sheep and cattle.

But this plan of this great "North Division" was not carried into effect, although the lots were actually drawn for 144 proprietors, on the 18th of May, 1724, by Capt. Edmund Lewis; for it was soon found that the number of proprietors was considerably larger than had been obtained, and that other obstacles were more effectual against it than had been supposed, especially that a considerable portion of this land had been already taken up and some of it occupied by actual settlers.

Thus the matter stood until Jan., 1732-3, when "the

---

[19] The word town was often used to designate the village.

proprietors voted to lay out first the highways in the land six miles distant from the old meeting house," these highways "running northerly and southerly from the end of six miles to the northerly part of Stratford bounds, as wide as by said committee may be thought needful," and the cross highways the same. In this final draft there were 199 claimants, and Capt. Edmund Lewis drew the lots."

---

[18] " At a Proprietors meeting of yᵉ proprietors of Common undivided Land in Stratford held by adjournment on the last Monday of November A. D. 1738.

Here followeth an account of yᵉ draught of yᵉ Lots voted to be drawn at the proprietors meeting October 3 Monday 1738."

1 Nathan Hawley.	35 Timothy Titharton.
2 Heirs of Samuel Wheeler.	36 Zach. Beardslee.
3 Elisebeth Curtiss.	37 Thaddeus Gregory.
4 Heirs of Benj. Blakeman.	38 Thomas Beardslee.
5 Zachariah Curtiss, Jr.	39 Zach. Booth.
6 Nathan Beach.	40 Joseph Nichols, Jr.
7 James Booth.	41 Robert Walker.
8 Heirs of Wᵐ Jeans.	42 Benjamin Lewis.
9 Jonathan Beardslee.	43 Mr. Ephᵐ Curtiss and wife.
10 Sarah Beach.	44 Heirs of Jose Blakeman.
11 Heirs of Joseph Fairchild.	45 Jonathan Curtiss.
12 Israel Beardslee.	46 Caleb Beardslee.
13 Capt. Richard Hubbell.	47 Tim. Wheler.
14 Samuel French, Joiner.	48 Ephraim Bennett.
15 Eben. Hurd.	49 John Curtiss.
16 Capt. John Coe.	50 Heirs of Jose Beardslee.
17 William Standard and wife.	51 Samuel Uffoot.
18 Nathan Curtis and Eunice his wife.	52 Ens. Jonas Wooster.
19 Heirs of Isaac Stiles.	53 Enoch Gregory.
20 David Hubbell.	54 Heirs of David Wakelin.
21 Samuel Hall.	55 Zachariah Tomlinson.
22 John Oatman.	56 Samuel French, Jr.
23 Ephraim Clark.	57 James Hubbell.
24 Nathaniel Hawley.	58 Heirs of Daniel Beardslee, Stratfield.
25 Samuèl DeForest.	59 Josiah Gilbert.
26 Capt. David Sherman.	60 Heirs of Abel Curtiss.
27 Daniel Shelton's heirs.	61 David Sherman, Jr.
28 Jonadab Bassett.	62 Mary and Jeremiah Judson.
29 Jose Seele.	63 Samuel Hawley and wife.
30 Samuel Blagge.	64 Heirs of Arthur Perry.
31 Elnathan Wheeler.	65 Jose Hawley.
32 Dea. Ephraim Judson.	66 John Fairchild.
33 Wid. Joanna Hawley.	67 Joseph Booth.
34 James Fairchild.	68 Daniel Hyde.

Sequestered lands, so called, were laid out at various times for pasture lands, and when the plan of wide highways failed at the north end of the town, they then set apart several hundred acres for the purpose of pasturage for sheep.

"March, 1734–5. Voted that all the common lands within two miles distance from the old society meeting-house shall be, and is, sequestered a perpetual common for the use

69 William Peat,	108 John Hubbell.
70 Mrs. Theophilus Nichols.	109 Nathan Curtiss and wife.
71 Zachariah Blakeman.	110 David Beardslee.
72 Benjamin Burton.	111 Edward Lacee.
73 Heirs of Timothy Fairchild.	112 John Nichols.
74 Nathaniel Sherman.	113 Heirs of Nat. Shearman.
75 Daniel Brinsmade.	114 Capt. Jose Judson.
76 Enos Sherman.	115 Seign' Lewis.
77 John Levensworth.	116 Daniel Porter.
78 Nath¹ Wakelee.	117 Heirs of Nathan Porter.
79 Edward Lacee and wife.	118 John Patterson.
80 John Clark, Jr.	119 Charles Burritt.
81 Gideon Hawley's heirs.	120 Capt. Jose Nichols.
82 John Thompson.	121 Thomas Latten.
83 Josiah Beardslee.	122 Daniel Pickett.
84 Richard Nichols.	123 Capt. James Judson.
85 Matthew Curtiss.	124 Thomas Wells and wife.
86 Ebenezer Beach.	125 Daniel Hawley.
87 Daniel Curtiss.	126 James Laboree.
88 Nathan Bennett,	127 Benjamin Booth.
89 Mr. John Edwards.	128 Capt. James Lewis.
90 Ens. Samuel Gregory.	129 Heirs of Thomas Knowles.
91 Robert McEwen.	130 Jonathan Nichols.
92 Heirs of John Cluckstone.	131 Samuel Osborn's heirs.
93 Heirs of Marcy Rose.	132 Mr. Samuel Cook,
94 Nathan Wheeler.	133 Heirs of Mr. Joseph Blacklach.
95 Stephen Burroughs.	134 Robert Walker, Jr.
96 Heirs of James Selee.	135 Jose Birdsey.
97 Hezekiah Gold.	136 Jose Beardslee.
98 Thomas Gilbert.	137 Ebenezer Blackman.
99 Comfort wife of David Latten.	138 Nathan Blackman.
100 James Levensworth.	139 Heirs of Samuel Judson.
101 Jonathan Nichols.	140 Ebenezer Thompson.
102 Henry Hawley.	141 Mr. Jedidiah Mills.
103 Heirs of Capt. John Wells.	142 Joseph Burritt.
104 Stiles Curtiss.	143 Heirs of Thomas Hawley.
105 Heirs of Jacob Wakelee.	144 Zachariah Curtiss, sen.
106 William Fanton.	145 Jose Lewis.
107 Heirs of Nathan Fairchild.	146 Ephraim Watkins.

and benefit of the proprietors according to their propriety, as formerly fixed by the selectmen in 1689; and also 100 acres in Bear Swamp Rocks, 100 acres near Broad Bridge. Voted that 800 acres of ruff land be surveyed, and is sequestered ... in the parish of Ripton for a perpetual common ... at the places hereafter named: by the Farmill river, at Corum burying place, Knell's Rocks, Quimbie's Hill, about Moose hill, by Barn hill, north by Bagburn, by the Great river south of Pine Swamp on both sides the east Sprain of the far mill river.

"Voted that three hundred acres of Ruff land are sequestered in the parish of Unity—by Turkey meadow Sprains, by saw mill, by Butternut swamp, by Walker's hill west of Daniel's Farm.

"Voted that 300 acres in the parish of Stratfield—at the place below Ox hill, west of Rocky hill near Canoe brook.

147	David Booth.	174	Capt. Abraham Wooster.
148	John Willcockson and wife.	175	Sarah, Jon. Clark's wife.
149	Capt. David Judson and wife.	176	Heirs of Samuel Summers.
150	Nathan Beardsley of Stratfield.	177	Samuel Sherman.
151	Ens. Samuel Fairchild.	178	Heirs of John Blackman.
152	Joseph Wells.	179	Lt. Abel Birdsey.
153	Peter Pixlee.	180	Zechariah Brinsmade.
154	John Hawley.	181	Eben. Curtis.
155	Zach. Clark.	182	Joshua Judson's heirs.
156	Benjamin Beach.	183	Heirs of Theoph. Sherman.
157	Nathan Wheeler.	184	Joseph Curtiss.
158	Heirs of John Bostwick.	185	Edmund Lewis, Esq.
159	Heirs of George Searls.	186	Sarah Everitt.
160	Ens. John Porter.	187	Ambrose Thompson, Jr.
161	Peter Curtiss.	188	Andrew Patterson.
162	Robert Wells.	189	Jonas Curtiss.
163	Heirs of Jose Beach.	190	William Patterson.
164	James Sherman.	191	Abram Nichols, Jr.
165	Jonathan Wakelee and wife.	192	John Beardsle of Stratfield.
166	David and Sarah Wells.	193	William Beach.
167	William Curtiss.	194	Benjamin Brooks.
168	Timo. Sherman.	195	Daniel Nichols.
169	Heirs of Jacob Walker.	196	Judson Burton.
170	Ebenezer Gregory.	197	Heirs of Robert Wells.
171	James Wakelee.	198	Heirs of Eben. Hawley.
172	John Beardslee's heirs.	199	Elisha Blagge.
173	Heirs of Thomas Sherwood.		

Town Acts, B. i. 78.

"The whole to remain common until the proprietors agree to the contrary."

In October, 1738, they voted that the sequestered lands should "lie in common for the use of the proprietors so long as the neat [net] earnings of the flock or flocks of sheep in Stratford going and feeding thereon, shall be paid to the proprietors of the said land."

Local names are mentioned in laying out highways, in deeds of land, in wills, and divisions of land.

"January, 1691. Richard Blacklach hath a parcel of land in the woods at Ocquanquage, bounded on the south with the west sprain of the Farmill river, on the east with a highway that runs on the easterly side of Ocquanquage plains, on the west with a rock at the southwest corner, and on the west with a high hill." And in March, 1723, a highway laid out "the whole length of Ocquanquage plain, on the easterly side of it, beginning by the side of the west sprain of the Farmill river, northward, full 16 rods wide, then east full 18 rods wide."

"In June, 1727, a highway was recorded as lying "upon Pissepunk hill; and about 1710, John Pickett had land laid to him 'lying on the southwesterly side of Pissepunk brook.'" Pissepunk is an Indian name. "It doubtless came from an Indian 'hot house,' somewhere on or near this hill. 'This hot house is a kind of little cell or cave, six or eight feet over, round, made on the side of the hill, commonly by some rivulet or brook; into this frequently the men enter after they have exceedingly heated it with store of wood, laid upon an heap of stones in the middle.'"[14]

"1676. Thomas Clark hath 4 acres near the nearmill river commonly called Scutt's spring."

"April, 1711. A lot of land was laid to Josiah Curtiss lying on Wigwam hill."

About 1714, land was laid to John Hurd "on the plain called Weeping plain, part on both sides of the west sprain of the Farmill river, on the west side of the Hundred hills . . .

---

[14] J. H. Trumbull's Indian Names.

lying on the west side of the hundred hills on the east side of a swamp called weeping plain swamp."

April, 1714, "a lot of land, originally laid out to Mr. Samuel Sherman, sen., 55 acres, at a place called tilesom, bounded southwest with highway between Fairfield and Stratford." This "Tilesom" was afterwards written and pronounced Toilsome.

" 1714, one piece of land southward of Castle hill."

In February, 1691–2, Robert Bassett bought land on Turkey Hill at Coram; and the next June he had laid out " 100 acres, by way of division, lying in the woods on the east of Paquannock river against Mount Moriah, bounded on the west with that sprain of Paquannock river that runs east of Rock-house Hill and a great plain on the east side of Paquannock river that lyeth southward of the sprain of said river."

Tanneries for making leather were not numerous during the first fifty years of plantation life at Stratford. No record of any has been seen before 1690, except the name Tanner's brook in the northern part of Stratford village, which name implies that some tanning enterprise may have been conducted upon it at a very early period, as the name occurs early, about 1660.

The following are town records on this subject :

" January 20, 1691. The town, by vote, gave unto Joseph Booth three rods square of land for a tan-yard, lying on both sides the run of water near his dwelling house to be for him the said Booth, his heirs and assigns, so long as they shall keep and maintain the trade of tanning."

" January 13, 1696. Mr. Ephraim Stiles requested the town that they would be pleased to grant him about forty feet of ground at Woronock, lying between the home that was Hope Washborn's, and the house belonging to the heirs of James Blakeman, in order for the setting up of tan-fats, and the town granted his request."

Another enterprise, the first of the kind that has been seen as recorded in the town books explains itself.

Wolves were a great annoyance and an expensive creature in the vicinity of Stratford. Premiums of various amounts were offered by the town, at different times, in addition to the premiums offered by the Colony or county ; yet the animals rather increased than diminished.

In 1687 the premium stood at thirty-two shillings for each one killed, and that figure seeming too expensive, it was reduced to twelve shillings.

Thus it seems to have stood a number of years, when the creatures so increased that a monster wolf hunt was organized.

"April 17, 1693. Voted that all persons ratable should be allowed for man and horse in this service of destroying wolves, three shillings per day out of the town treasury."

"It was voted and agreed that the next Thursday shall be the day to goe upon this business of killing wolves, if the weather permit, or the next fair day ; all persons to be ready by seven of the clock in the morning, and meet upon the hill at the meeting-house, by the beat of the drum.

"The town, by vote, made choice of Captain Burritt, Lieut. Beardslee, Ens. Judson, Mr. Samuel Sherman [Jr.], Ephraim Stiles, Daniel Beardslee, Daniel Curtiss, Ebenezer Curtiss, Sergt. Knowles, Joseph Curtiss, Benjamin Curtiss, Lieut. Tomlinson, Nathaniel Sherman and Joseph Curtiss to be overseers of this affayre, and authorized them with full power to order, dispose and direct all and every person that shall goe upon this work from time to time, and all persons are to observe and attend their directions."

How much this expedition cost the town, or how many wolves were killed, has not been ascertained, but it must have been such an imposing, formidable war-like demonstration as to indicate considerable vengeance on the wolves. By another vote in 1696, when each person was to receive only six pence every time he went out in a certain expedition, the cost to the town was fourteen pound, nineteen shillings and six pence.

Hence, the expense of killing wolves, and the value of the creatures destroyed by the wolves, was quite an item of yearly loss to the toiling citizens of those early days.

Between 1690 and 1700, specially, and largely thereafter for many years, town meetings were held frequently, transactions of much importance in the settlement of the township enacted and a list of officers elected." The business of the town meetings occupied so much time that often the meeting was adjourned to a second day.

The town clerks, in recording the proceedings of the meetings, were very careful to give the title to every man's name as regularly as the name occurred. The list of town officers was, at first, very short, but it had the energy of increase to marvelous proportions. When the law giving ecclesiastical societies separate offices and officers, the town list was somewhat shortened, but if there was more than one such society within a township, the list was kept about the same. In Stratford, for some years, there were four Congregational societies and three, if not four, Episcopal.

A Town-house for the accommodation of the town meetings was built between the years 1752 and 1758; for the town meeting of December, 1758 was held in the new town house.

The movement began January, 1749-50. "Voted to build a town house, and that the same shall not, any part thereof, be used for a school house, under any pretence whatsoever, and to set the house upon the hill just south of Tanner's brook, called the Smith shop hill; the house to be 45 feet long, 32 feet wide, and ten feet between joints.

"Voted the same to be furnished with seats and chimney." This they proposed to build by subscription, but they

---

"John Minor, } Constables.
Jehiel Preston, }

Thomas Uffoot, ⎫
John Wells, ⎪
Sergt. John Curtiss, ⎬ townsmen.
Henry Wakelyn, ⎪
John Pickett, sen., ⎭

John Minor, recorder.

Sergt. John Curtiss, town treasurer.

Thomas Fayrechild, } Haywardens.
Ell. Knowles, }

Robert Lane, } fence viewers.
Benjamin Beach, }

Edward Hinman, packer.

John Peak, Jr., marshal.

Nathaniel Parker, } surveyors of high-
James Clark, } ways.

Mr. Hawley, ordinary keeper.

John Pickett, Jr., sealer of weights and measures.

James Clark, pound keeper.

John Peck, custom master.

Robert Rose, cryer.

Capt. Curtiss, Mr. Mitchell, Jehiel Preston and John Minor to audit the town's accounts."

also voted a tax for the same purpose, and, although they appointed a committee to do the work, yet it was delayed.

In 1752 they appointed a committee, consisting of one man from each society in the town, to consult about the best way to build the town house ; and the town meeting was held in it in December, 1758.

Previous to this the town meeting is mentioned several times as having been held in the school house.

A Pest-house was voted to be built in December, 1760. The year previous to this Daniel Nichols had the small-pox and the town voted him four pounds, if he recovered of his distemper.

CHAPTER XII.

BEGINNING THE EIGHTEENTH
CENTURY.

GREAT was the spirit of enterprise in Stratford when the eighteenth century was introduced by the opening of the year 1701.
Sixty-one years had passed since the first
seventeen families established the plantation
as new settlers in the wilderness. At the
end of the first age, of thirty years, many of
the persons in these families, and of all the
families that came before 1650, had passed
away, and only a few dwellings—perhaps
a half dozen—had been extended beyond
the limits of the village of Stratford; while
the families had reached the number of a
little over one hundred, in 1677; the proprietors of the township being just one hundred.

During the second age, thirty years, great progress had
been made in laying out the lands northward into the wilderness preparatory to their occupancy by resident farmers;
and quite a number of the young men had established their
homes on these farms. The monotony and loneliness of their
locations were greatly relieved by the animation of the natural scenery and the spirit of enterprise and progress in the
further settlement of the country. The woods were full of
birds and animals—quite too much so, as to wolves and bears
—and the courage and ambition of the young people were
exercised, equally, with any succeeding age.

In 1699, the proprietors or owners of the undivided land,
numbered one hundred and forty-three, and the families, about
two hundred.

An ecclesiastical society and a church had been organized at Pequonnock, called Stratfield, which at first included twelve or fourteen of the Stratford families, and those all residing west of the Pequonnock river.

There may have been three or four families residing in what is now Huntington, but it is doubtful if there were more than two who were located at Shelton, unless there were others in the southeastern corner of that town.

There were about a dozen families in the vicinity of Oronoke, and as many more along Old Mill Green and on Old Mill hill.

Such was the field of operations, the center or headquarters being at Stratford village, which had become a place of considerable mercantile business and social enterprise. The meeting-house had been removed from the harbor and a new one built on Watch-house Hill. Two ware-houses had been built, one by Richard Blackleach, the other by Daniel Shelton,[1] perhaps one of them on the site of the old meeting-house at the harbor, for one was built there very early, the stone basement story of which is the foundation of the barn now standing upon it. The merchandise consisted largely of grains, beef and pork and live horses; the last for the West Indies, the others for Boston and New York. There was no trade in articles of wood, for in 1690 the town, by vote, forbid the transportation of any timber for clapboards, pipe staves, hoops, heading, rails or building lumber, from the place, because of its scarcity.

It has been difficult to ascertain in what hands the mercantile business was held previous to this time, except that, from the first, or about 1650, until 1680, or near that time, Joseph Hawley and Isaac Nichols, sen., had some, considerable, probably the leading part in such trade. Joseph Hawley built vessels, here and at Derby, and also sold foreign cloths and other mercantile goods. He was also, some of the time, the ordinary, or tavern keeper, and in those days, and

---

[1] "May 6, 1686. Voted and granted unto Mr. Richard Blacklach and Mr. Daniel Shilton to build each of them a warehouse in some convenient place where it may be judged most suitable by the selectmen of the town and the wharfe presented them as proprietors of Stratford, for ever, free wharfage."

20

many years later, not only liquors were sold, but teas, sugar, molasses, indigo, logwood, nails of all kinds, made in England and at home, at such places of public entertainment. Isaac Nichols, sen., seems, from certain records, to have conducted a like business, later, perhaps after Mr. Hawley retired.

Alexander Bryan, of Milford, was the great merchant for the whole region of country, and his son Richard with him for more than half a century. They bought and sold land in almost, or quite, every town from New London to New York. They furnished goods to pay the Indians for nearly all the townships in the region. Their vessels traded, not only at home, but in foreign ports, England, Holland and Spain. Their bills passed in exchange, in all parts of the country, and particularly in England. It is doubtful if there was another merchant, out of Boston, on the American coast, that did as large a business as Alexander Bryan from 1639 to 1670.

Isaac Nichols, sen., as seen by the records, obtained considerable supplies from Alexander Bryan, and hence the information as to his mercantile business.

Samuel Blagge, from New York, Richard Blacklach, from Guilford, and Daniel Shelton from England, came to Stratford, as merchants, about 1686; Samuel Blagge, perhaps, several years earlier than the other two.

The farmers of Stratford resided in the village, and went out to their farms, from one to three miles, in the true oriental style, to do the work of the farm. In the morning they were seen going out with their teams, many of them to the south, to the Old Field, and the Great Neck, all of which was put into one great field, about 1693, the fence crossing from the rocks on Little Neck, west to mill brook, and all the land south of it, being in the field. The Old Field, at first did not include the Great Neck. Other of the farmers went to the New Field, joining the village on the southwest, between it and the swamp. Then there was a field called Nesingpaws, on the west side of Mill brook, as called in the deeds about 1700, and after, or west of the swamp extending to Bruce's Brook; and from this field, or Bruce's Brook to the old yellow mill, was the Far-field; then the Newpasture field south of Old Mill Green, and Pequonnock field south of Golden Hill. There was also a common field—not very large—at Oronoke, besides what was called the great meadow at that place.

Gristmills, Sawmills, and Fullingmills.

As the families settled back into the wilderness, they needed mills of various kinds to facilitate the work and comfort of life. To build a small saw mill was an enterprise of venture, requiring much energy and considerable money, as then money was estimated. The town owned all the mill-sites, as well as the land around them, and therefore none of them could be used without a grant from the town. At first, besides granting the privilege of the mill, the town gave to the person who should build a gristmill several acres of land, upon condition that the party "should grind the town's corn," for a sixteenth or twelfth or an eighth part of the grain brought to the mill.

At this time, 1700, there had been two gristmills and two fulling mills built, and soon after several other mills were erected, as the following records show :

" January 26, 1702–3, the town granted liberty to Ebenezer Curtiss, James Lewis and Edmund Lewis, to erect a sawmill near Misha hill."

" December 25, 1704, Benjamin Sherman, John Williams, and John Seeley were granted liberty to erect a gristmill upon Pequonnock river at the narrows below Essay's pond." Upon securing this site they were to sign certain articles of agreement with the selectmen.

" January 11, 1705–6, the town granted liberty to Mr. Ephraim Stiles to set up a gristmill at Farmill river, a little below Black brook, near the place called the Plum-trees." At the same time the town granted full liberty to Lt. Tomlinson to maintain his fulling mill on Farmill river.

" February 14, 1721–2, Mr. John Edwards requested liberty to " erect a fulling mill upon the river on the west side of Ox hill," and in 1724 Mr. Edwards and Lt. Richard Hubbell, erected a fulling mill at the same place, then called Jackson's river, it being near Fairfield line.

"December 5, 1725. Upon the request of Zechariah Beardslee, Charles Lane and Ephraim Judson, to erect a saw-mill and make a dam for said mill at the south corner of Acquanquedy plain on the west sprain of the Farmill river, the town grants their request, with this proviso, that they satisfy for all damage that their dam may cause in any particular person's land."

"December 29, 1725. Liberty was granted Captain Josiah Curtiss and Mr. John Willcoxson, Jr., to erect a saw-mill on the halfway river," at the north end of the town.

Ecclesiastical Progress and Prosperity.

The Rev. Israel Chauncey died at Stratford March 14, 1702-3, in the 39th year of his ministry, and the 59th year of his age; which appears to have been an unexpected event without forewarning, as he was not aged, or in any way enfeebled. He had been a successful, faithful minister, and seems to have been very acceptable in the parish, his salary having been increased at several times, being the highest, and standing at £112, and his yearly allowance of wood, at his decease.

Two candidates for the supply of the pulpit were soon secured; Mr. Nathaniel Hubbard, of the class of Harvard, 1698, and Mr. Joseph Morgan. Upon this the town came together on May 7, 1703, and voted to buy a house "of Daniel Shelton for £100 cash, for the minister in Stratford," but "after the vote was recorded, Isaac Knell, Joseph Fairchild, Edward Hinman, Samuel Peat, sen., and Timothy Titharton, did protest against buying Mr. Shelton's house." This is the first intimation of trouble that the records afford, nor is there any reason stated for the opposition.

The next proceeding, at the same meeting, was to apply for Mr. Reed to preach, and "Nathaniel Sherman was by vote chosen as agent for the town, forthwith with all convenient speed to go to Hartford and endeavor, by all lawful means, the obtaining of Mr. Reed for the work above said." Mr.

Reed was secured and preached, and the August following the town voted him " £40 pay in provision and £6 for fire-wood for half a year, and Mr. Nathaniel Sherman, Sergt. John Hawley, Mr. Jeremiah Judson, were appointed a committee to " take care of transporting Mr. Reed's family from Hartford, and providing a suitable habitation for him." The next February—8, 1703-4—on a proposition for settling a minister, Mr. Reed received 96 votes; Mr. Hubbard, 18; and Mr. Morgan, 15.

Mr. Reed continued to preach regularly until November 14, 1704, when he received 70 votes, and there were " 14 votes to the contrary." On the 24th of April, 1705, "there being some persons dissatisfied with the former vote," another was taken, and Mr. Reed received 67, for settlement, there being " 43 otherwise," and 32 not voting. The last vote taken to settle him was on September 25, 1706, in which the whole number of votes was much smaller, he having 63 votes.

Very soon, following this last vote, perhaps before, some talk was indulged in by the public, which Mr. Reed resented and demanded inquiry, and hence the following action by the town:

" November 20, 1706. Whereas, the Revd. Elders in their advice to the town of Stratford, recommended to take all suitable care to purge and vindicate Mr. Reed from such scurrilous and abusive reflections (if any be) that such sentiments may reasonably be supposed to being upon him; and Mr. Reed in order thereto, having laid before the town his request that the town would be pleased to call a Council of Elders to hear what shall be proper to lay before them in order for a clearing of his name from those abusive reflections that he is apprehensive have been put upon him."

In harmony with this request choice was made of the " Revds. Mr. Andrews, Mr. Pierpont, Mr. Webb and Mr. Chauncey, by the town, to be a committee for that end;" and a day of fasting and prayer was appointed.

No indication as to what was said offensive to Mr. Reed or to his parish, has been found, except the intimation that he had made overtures to join the Episcopal Church; but what-

ever it was, it is certain that he declared the matter to be
"scurrilous and abusive reflections."

It has been represented, also, that Mr. Reed was unkindly
and almost uncivilly treated by his parish, in an effort to
deprive him of his salary; and that they were countenanced
in it by the neighboring ministers. This is a wholly gratuitous reflection, since his salary was continued regularly by
town vote at one hundred pounds a year—a salary nearly equal
to that of the preceding minister, and also to that of Mr.
Cutler, who followed him, and this salary was as regularly
paid, probably, as that of any minister in the Colony; as
exhibited in the records in the book of town acts for those current years of his service.[4] Mr. Reed regularly resigned his
ministerial relations to the town on the 27th of March, 1707,
and a full settlement was made with him.

Following Mr. Reed, Mr. Francis Goodhue was a candidate, and on July 18, 1707, he had 41 votes for settlement,
with quite a number of persons present not voting. The
meeting was adjourned one week when he had 42 votes, out
83 cast, and the town voted to allow him one hundred pounds
a year while he should preach here; but he continued only a
short time and Mr. James Hale preached for a time in the
latter part of the year 1707.

The next candidate for settlement seems to have been Mr.
Azariah Mather who, August 24, 1708, had a vote favorable

---

[4] "April 1, 1708.　Then upon the adjustment of accounts with Mr. Reed, wee
find as followeth :

"In ye year 1704, ye rate fell short of ye 100lbs.　Mr. Samuel
　　　Hawley collector,　.　　.　　.　　.　£00–17–9I
"In ye year 1705, ye rate fell short of the 100lbs, sundry per-
　　　sons being non-solvent,　.　　.　　.　　1–15–0I
"In ye year 1706 ye rate fell short of ye 100lbs, several per-
　　　sons being non-solvent, allowed,　.　　.　　2–00–00
　　　　　　　　　　　　　　　　　　　　　　　　　　　　─────
　　　　　　　　　　　　　　　　　　　　　　.　　4–12–2

"In 1702, due to Mr. Reed to a quarter of ye year 25lbs, agreed.
"Of which sums remains due from ye collector to Mr. Reed.　14–15–10
"Francis Griffin, Dr., upon arrears of his rate 1700 yet to
　　　see pay'd to Mr. Reed,　.　　.　　£3–00–01½
"Richard Nicolls, Dr. upon his arrears of his rate 1706, yet
　　　to see pay'd to Mr. Reed,　.　　.　　7–12–6½."

"not one vote against or for any other person, but the vote was so small that nothing was done further until January following, when he had 55 votes in favor, and 38 for others. The next June they voted to seek for a stranger, and appointed seven prominent men to obtain one; the result being that, on September 16, 1709, action of the town was taken "for the continuance of Mr. Cutler amongst us in the work of the ministry in order for a settlement, of 103 in favor and none against;" and he was offered £80, yearly salary, which was less than they had paid, during several years previous, but it was afterwards raised.

They next proposed a settlement, and September 30, 1709, "voted to give Mr. Cutler a home lot of one or two acres, to build a house on it of forty-two feet in length and twenty in breadth, a girt house, two story high with a suitable porch, every way well finished, and one hundred acres of land in the six-mile division, to be his own, his heirs, executors forever, provided he settle with us and continue in the work of the ministry, and to give him the use of eight acres pasture and four or five of meadow, and after two years to pay him yearly £140 country pay as salary. This amount was afterwards changed to £93-06-8, current money, instead of "produce at fixed prices." "All, provided his disciplining be agreeable with the way of the Colony or country at present or future."

During these years of progress from 1680, the meeting house, from which the old bell rang out a cheerful sound every day at nine o'clock in the evening,' became crowded, and on January 22, 1700-1, the town voted that there should be a gallery built in the meeting house, and a committee was appointed to proceed with the work, which they did, for the remaining expense of it was ordered paid the next January. This was an end gallery, for in 1715 "two side galleries" were built "at the charge of the town,"' and on March 2,

---

' "Dec. 29, 1691. The present townsmen by vote were impowered to hire some suitable person or persons to sweep the meeting house and ring the bell on all public days and at nine of the clock every evening.

' "January, 1715-16. The committee of the Meetinghouse gallery then agreed and bargained with Josiah Hubbell and Israel Burritt to build the flank galleries

1718, they "voted that the seats of each gallery shall be seated, the west side gallery with married men, the east gallery with married women, and antiant bachelors and antiant maides the second seats."

In May, 1713, the town voted liberty to Doctor Laboree to "erect and build a pew on the south side of the west door of the meeting house at his own expense." A few years previous to this, Richard Blackleach had made a pew for his family in this house, and these probably were all the pews then in the house; the other seats were high backed slips like other meeting houses at that day.

In 1715, "liberty was granted to the farmers to erect suitable shelter for their horses on all public days at some convenient place, with the advice of the selectmen."

The Rev. Timothy Cutler had preached in Stratford just ten years, when the trustees of Yale College invited him to become Rector of that institution, and Stratford reluctantly consented to the change. The town, in response to the desire of the trustees, communicated to it, July 31, 1719, appointed a committee to hear the propositions which might be made, and adjourned to a specified day, to hear the report; which was communicated at the time and action taken:

"At a town meeting in Stratford, September 7, 1719, several proposals presented by the Rev. Trustees Respecting Mr. Cutler's Remove from us to the Great work of a Rector of Yale College being laid before the town for further thought and consideration, and the town seriously considering thereof did unanimously signify their great grief and sorrow Respecting Mr. Cutler's Remove from us who under God hath been the happy instrument of uniting us in love and peace after so many years of contention. However, if the Rev^d Mr. Cutler and Trustees are fully satisfied that Mr. Cutler hath a warrantable Call of God to Remove from us, we desire passively to submit to Divine providence.

"And as to the proposals made by the Revd Trustees, the town for peace and to maintain their good affections to

---

of the meeting house—both the joiner's and the carpenter's work to be done well according to rule, and finish the said gallery by the first of June next, and for their labor the committee promises to pay them thirty-three pounds in money."

Mr. Cutler Do allow to him the hundred acres of woodland to be his own according to his desire; the said Mr. Cutler returning the house and home lott which he received of the town, to the town again in the capacity it now is, with all betterments, fences, &c.—always provided that the Rev. Trustees or General Court allow to the town of Stratford one hundred pounds money for and towards the charge of settling another minister among us.

Test, JOS. CURTISS, Town Clerk."

Mr. Cutler went to Yale College, but there was much trouble in settling money matters between him and the town of Stratford, for one or two years afterward.

The trouble anticipated by a town vote in settling another minister, when they consented to allow Mr. Cutler to remove, was more than realized. They soon found a candidate, Mr. Samuel Russell, and took a vote on his settlement, October 1, 1719, but the numbers present being small, the matter was deferred, although there were no votes against him. The next March—1720—the vote stood 83 for him and 41 against and 8 scattering. In the April following a council was called for advice, and the next month the matter went to the General Court, who advised a delegated council from all the ministerial assemblies of the State, if Stratford would pay the expense. This created much greater excitement and difficulty, and many names were entered on the records as protesting against making any expense in that way. Trouble increased during two years, Mr. Russell continuing to preach, until quite a number of inhabitants recorded their names as refusing to pay to his support, November 2, 1721, when it was concluded to seek another candidate.

The next February they held a day of fasting and prayer in view of their trouble in calling a minister, and they soon after found a preacher upon whom they could fully unite, as seen by the town record:

"April 16, 1722. Whereas, the society at a lawful meeting March 1, 1721-2, by a unanimous vote called Mr. Hezekiah Gold to the work of the ministry in Stratford in order for a settlement among us, and having ever since sat under his ministry with great satisfaction and delight; and for his incouragement to settle with us in the work of the ministry, it was this day voted and granted to allow him 130 pounds per annum as his yearly salary in money so long as the public good requires his labors among us. And for his settlement to give him the town house [probably the one built for Mr. Cutler] and home lot of one acre and a half to be his own forever, provided he settles with us and continue with us in the work till death; also the barn and half the land adjoining to the home lot."

To this he made the following reply:

"To ye old Society and Church of Christ in Stratford, to whom Grace and Peace be multiplied from God our father and from our Lord Jesus Christ. Dearly beloved, these may inform you of my greatful and thankful acceptance of your generous and honorable proposals for my incouragement in ye great work of ye ministry among you in which I purpose to continue as God in his providence shall permit, your faithful servant in Christ during life.   HEZ. GOLD."

Stratford April 23, 1722.

May 8, 1722. The Society appointed the first Wednesday in June next to be the day for the ordination of Mr. Gold.

Jan. 6, 1723-4. Mr. Gold's request of the town, "liberty to erect a pew at some convenient place in the meeting house for his family" was granted. A few years later his salary was fixed at one hundred and fifty pounds a year and so continued many years, but when the inflation of State bills went on a few years, his salary—about 1750—was considerably over two hundred pounds old tenor.

It is during the transactions for securing and settling Mr. Gold, that the distinction between the acts of the town and the ecclesiastical society, are first noticed on the records. The General Court in 1717 passed an act defining the powers and jurisdiction of such a society;' and in 1723 added the liqerty for each society in every town to have its own clerk.

' *An Act for the better Ordering and Regulating Parishes or Societies, and for their Supporting the Ministry and Schools there.*

That the settled and approved inhabitants in each respective parish or society within this Colony, shall annually meet together in December, at some time and place, according to the notice thereof to be given them at least five days before

During Mr. Cutler's pastorate, in 1717, when harmony and prosperity prevailed throughout the township, the movement began, which resulted in the organization of the parish or society of Ripton, of which a careful and full account will be given further on in this book in the history of the town of Huntington.

Timothy Cutler, D. D., son of Major John Cutler, of Charlestown, Massachusetts, was born June 1, 1684, and was graduated at Harvard College in 1701. A call was extended to him by the Stratford Church September 16, 1709, and near or in the following December he was ordained pastor of this Church and congregation.

He served the parish acceptably ten years, but without any marked success, except as a pleasing and entertaining preacher. He was held in high esteem by the parish, was " reputed as a man of profound and general learning," but his letter of resignation, herewith printed, if such it may' be

---

such meeting, by the committee for ordering the affairs of the society, or for want of such committee, by the clerk of the same. And the said inhabitants thus met and convened together are hereby fully impowered by their major vote, to choose a clerk for their society, and three or more discreet, able inhabitants to be a committee to order the affairs of the society for the year ensuing. And also the said inhabitants assembled as above, or the major part of them, shall have power to grant and levy such rates and taxes on the inhabitants for the advancing such sum or sums of money for the support of the ministry and school there, as the law directs, and to appoint a collector or collectors for gathering thereof, who are hereby ordered and impowered to proceed in collecting the same, according to the direction of the law to collectors chosen for gathering the town and minister's rates. And in case the collector or collectors shall not perform the trust hereby committed to him or them, he or they shall be accountable for such arrearages by him or them neglected to be gathered, to the committee of such society, who are impowered to demand or distrain for the same, according to the direction of said law.

To this was added, in October, 1723, "That where there are more societies than one in any town in this governmnent, every such society are enabled, and they hereby have full power, to choose their own clerk." Col. Records, vi. 33.

[1] Mr. Cutler's resignation was as follows, dated September 14, 1719:
" BRETHREN AND FRIENDS:

I hope I have, with seriousness and solemnity considered the invitation made to me for a removal from you to the Collegiate School at New Haven, and can look upon it as nothing less than a call of providence which I am obliged to obey.

I do, therefore, by these lines, give you this signification, giving you my hearty

called, does not sustain the reputation thus given him. A
brief letter of this description, in which the pronoun of the
first person nominative occurs nine times, and six times in the
possessive, is doubtless a literary production, but not of a
very highly cultivated style; and, instead of resigning his
office, he discharges the parish from further service to him,
in these words, " and discharging you from the date of this
letter forever."

In the summer of 1719 he accepted the presidency of
Yale College, which office he discharged acceptably three
years, when, professing a preference for the Church of England and renouncing his connection with the churches of the
Colony, he, upon request, resigned the presidency of the College; went to England in 1723, where he was ordained priest
and honored with the title of D. D., by Oxford University;
returned to America and became pastor of Christ Church
in Boston. He died in that city in 1765, aged 82 years.

Rev. Hezekiah Gold, son of Hon. Nathan Gold, Jr., of
Fairfield, was born in 1794; graduated at Harvard College in
1719, and was ordained pastor of the Stratford Church on the
first Wednesday in June, 1722. Within the first year of his
ministry his labors were honored by the accession of sixty
persons to membership of his Church; and from that time
forward a good degree of prosperity attended his ministra-

---

thanks for all that respect and kindness I have found with you and praying God abundantly to reward you for it—and discharging you from the date of this letter forever—and praying you to apply yourselves with all convenient speed to the settling of another minister with you.

I intend, if it be not unacceptable to you, to visit you and take my farewell of
you as soon as I can conveniently in some Lord's day after my return from Boston,
where I am now going, if it please God. When I am bodily absent from you my
affections shall persevere towards you and my hearty desires and prayers shall be
to God for you, that he would preserve you in his favour and in peace among
yourselves; direct your endeavours for the settlement of another to break the
bread of life with you and make your way prosperous, and abundantly make up
my removal from you by his gifts and his painful and successful endeavours for
the good of your souls and your children after you. Thus, I leave you to the care
of the Great Shepherd of the sheep always remaining an earnest well-wisher to
your souls and all your concerns.

                                        TIMOTHY CUTLER."

tions. From 1731 to 1746, 260 persons became members of his church; among whom were the Rev. Nathan Birdseye, who died in 1818, in his 104th year, and David Wooster, afterwards General in the army of the Revolution.

Mr. Gold was dismissed from the pastorate of the Stratford parish July 3, 1752, and died in 1761.[b]

Mr. Gold was placed in unusual circumstances in his ministry from 1740, to his dismission. From the beginning of his labors his zeal and spirit was in harmony with the gospel idea of saving sinners as well as to teach the church, and hence many were converted and added to the church. When in 1735 an unusual religious interest was developed under the Rev. Jonathan Edwards, at Northampton, Mass., it was in harmony with Mr. Gold's labors as much, probably, as those of any minister in Connecticut; and it was the same when the Rev. George Whitefield of England came.

The Rev. Benjamin L. Swan made the following notes concerning the Rev. George Whitefield's visit to Stratford.

" Mr. Whitefield preached here Monday afternoon October 27, 1740, on his way from New Haven, where he preached on Sunday the 26th, and on the three days preceding. He records an interview at New Haven with the Rev. Jedediah Mills of Ripton parish in Stratford, whom he calls a 'dear man of God. My soul was much united to him.'

"That Mr. Gold, then pastor in Stratford, was cordially interested in the work of grace attending Mr. Whitefield's preaching, is evident from his signature to the testimony of of the Fairfield County ministers in favor of the revival, given in October, 1743. Of the eleven signers of that paper, there were of ministers in Stratford, Mr. Cook, of Stratfield, Mr. Gold of Stratford, and Mr. Mills of Ripton.

"The sermon by Mr. Whitefield was heard by Mrs. Ann, wife of John Brooks, grand-daughter of post-master Daniel Brooks, who, herself, narrated the matter to Miss Polly Tomlinson, who related it to me in 1859, and she was so much interested that, with her infant in her arms, she went to Fairfield to hear him again the same day.

---

[b] Manual of the Stratford Congregational Church 9.

"Mrs. Brooks was probably a subject of grace on that occasion, for in the January following, she united with the church.

"Mr. Whitefield certainly had access to the Church, but a tradition preserved by Mrs. Victory Wetmore—daughter-in-law of the Rev. Izrahiah Wetmore, and given me by her in 1859, represents a Mrs. Burritt who lived on the wood end road below Main street, as being in the yard of her dwelling, farther down, than any house now stands, and a mile nearly from the Meeting House Hill, where she distinctly heard Mr. Whitfield name his text from Zechariah ix. 12 : 'Turn ye to the stronghold ye prisoners of hope;' and repeated it to her husband on his return home. Hence, it is probable that.this sermon was delivered in the open air.

"Mr. Whitefield, after preaching, was the guest of Mr. Gold, who lived on the spot now occupied by Captain Sterling's house.

"Dr. Johnson is said to have called on Mr. Whitefield here, and desired some account of his principles, but he declined any discussion, saying he had already announced his principles in his sermon, and speedily departed for Fairfield.

"Mrs. Wetmore relates that a daughter of Mr. Jeremiah Green, who lived on Old Mill road, just beyond the railroad crossing, heard Whitfield preach, was convicted, and in the overwhelming excitement of her mind, swooned and fell into a sort of trance, or insensible state, which lasted one or two days."

In the winter following, Mr. Gold's settlement in Stratford a movement commenced, which resulted in securing a parsonage for the first society, for the use of the minister. The deed for the property so purchased was dated February 8, 1722–3, and was in consideration of £67. The money was secured by voluntary subscription, the largest amount paid by one person being £1. 10s., there being 123 subscribers to the fund.'

' " Stratford, November, 1722. We, the subscribers hereunto being desirous to propagate the gospel by the Presbyterian ministry among us ; and in order thereunto, being sensible that it may be of great service to purchase a parsonage lot, and sequester it forever to remain a parsonage lot for the use of a Presbyterian

A New Meeting house was built during Mr. Gold's ministry according to the following directions of the society :

"Second Monday, February, 1742-3. Voted that it was necessary to ·build a meeting house for said society for the carrying on the public worship, by more than two-thirds of voters present.

"Voted, that Captain Theophilus Nichols, Mr. Robert Walker, Jr., Sergeant Daniel Porter, make application to the General Assembly in May next to appoint a committee to affix a place where the said society shall erect their meeting house."

"February 21, 1742-3. Voted that the meeting house shall be sixty feet in length, forty feet in width, and the posts twenty-six feet in length.

"Voted that the society will build a steeple, 130 feet high.

"June 27, 1743. Voted that Capt. David Judson, Lt. John Wilcockson and Sergt. Daniel Porter shall be the committee for building and furnishing the meeting-house on the place appointed by said society by the General Assembly in May last."

The location of this house was a few rods west of the old one, on the public green, where the academy afterwards stood, and was the one burned by lightning in 1785.

Mr. Gold's Dismission was a serious matter, although it had been sought by some parties in the church and parish several years.

Mrs. Nancy Wells, widow of John Wells, and previously of Doctor Ezra Curtis, was the daughter of Samuel Ufford, and born in 1772. She was living in 1862, in her 89th year, and gave to the Rev. B. L. Swan some ministerial reminiscences. "She was a grand-daughter of the Rev. Hezekiah Gold, but was born under Rev. Izrahiah Wetmore's ministry and baptized by him. She said Mr. Gold's first wife was a Ruggles, of Guilford, who died, and Mr. Gold married the widow

ministry in Stratford for the benefit of succeeding generations ; do freely give the particular sums prefixed to our names for the purchasing of Captain David Bostick's lot, called Harvey's lot, for the use aforesaid, and for no other."

of John Prynn, who came from the West Indies to Stratford,
where he resided some years [and died November 23, 1751,
æ. 51]. He brought some negroes with him and practiced
the breeding of them for sale.

"He and his wife were Episcopal Church people of very
high pretentions.

"After Mr. Gold married the widow Prynn, he was compelled to wait on her to the door of the Episcopal Church;
and after his own service in the Congregational Church was
out to return thither and receive her at the door, into his carriage again.

"This marriage and her conduct offended many in Mr.
Gold's church—among them Colonel Robert Walker—a man
who came to Stratford as a weaver, but married Rebecca
Lewis of Old Mill Green, who had property, and he soon
rose to be Justice of the Peace, then Judge of the County
Court, and became an influential man.

"Through his instrumentality Mr. Gold was dismissed
from the service of his church, and Mr. Wetmore became
pastor. He was a young man, and married Colonel Walker's
daughter. Mrs. Wells' remembrance of Mr. Wetmore was
very distinct. He was very tall, with colorless, inexpressive
eyes, red and close curling hair—the homeliest man, she said,
she ever saw. He was the tallest man, except one, in the
place.

"Mrs. Wells remembered well when wooden trenchers
and wooden tea-cups and saucers were used.

"A Miss Tomlinson living at the same time with Mrs.
Nancy Wells, said that the marriage of Mr. Gold, and the
aversion of a party to his evangelical preaching—in which
party Colonel Walker was prominent, were, together, the
occasion of his being dismissed. She said, also, that this dismission caused the elderly Mr. Hezekiah DeForest, and
others, to remove from Stratford to Huntington, New Haven,
and other places."

There is an error in the above statement concerning the
Walker family. Hon. Robert Walker, whose daughter Mr.
Wetmore married, was born in Stratford, in 1705, and was not
a weaver. It was his great uncle, Jacob Walker, brother of

the Rev. Zechariah, who married the widow Elizabeth Blakeman and who may have been a weaver, but became a large farmer in Stratford.

The excitement in Stratford, as well as throughout New England, was very great, for several years following Mr. Whitfield's preaching. That preaching was very severe as to true conversion. Those persons, members of any and all churches, who had not experienced definite and remarkable exercises at the time of their professed conversion were represented as never having been converted, and as having no assurance of heaven. Mr. Gold, who had had an unusual revival for those days, soon after his settlement here, the spirit of which still continued, received Mr. Whitfield as a brother minister, and favored the public interest taken in the revival of religious interests in New England in 1741, 2 and 3. This season of unusual religious interest has since been termed " The Great Awakening." Many persons became greatly interested in religion in the specific form of a wonderful, or miraculous conversion, claiming that it was directly accomplished by the invisible power of God; and that this power was exerted upon those only who were the elect. Hence, in this movement, there was the revival of the Calvinistic doctrines. There grew out of it, also, a strong sentiment against the union of church and state as it then existed in New England; and hence there were two parties in the Congregational Churches, which resulted a few years later in the organization of what were called New Light Churches, but these churches called themselves Strict Congregational Churches.

There was another influence which affected Mr. Gold's parish very seriously. The Rev. Richardson Miner, settled pastor at Unity (now Trumbull), was a very successful physician as well as pastor, and practiced throughout Stratford, and largely in Stratford village, and hence attained a large popular influence. He, it is said, and with corroborating evidences, held more to the old ways of religious life than Mr. Gold, and hence, a movement sprang up about 1742 and 3, to have Mr. Gold dismissed and Mr. Miner called to Stratford; but when, in 1744, Mr. Miner joined the Episcopal Church,

21

there was great disappointment and great excitement in this region of country, and quite a number of influential families withdrew from the Congregational communion and united with the Episcopal Church. The same was true in several adjoining parishes.

In the parish of Stratfield, although there was an Episcopal Church at Fairfield, some persons in 1751, under the New Light teachings, objecting to the levying of taxes to support the gospel, withdrew and organized a Baptist Church at Stratfield.

Some further notice of Mr. Gold's controversy with the Rev. Samuel Johnson, D.D., may be found in the next chapter of this book, in the biographical sketch of Dr. Johnson.

Presbyterians in Stratford.

As far as has been ascertained by careful search, Presbyterians have existed in Stratford only in the name as applied to Congregationalists, after the establishment of the Saybrook platform of ecclesiastical government.

When in October, 1666, the General Court of the Colony ordered all the ministers to meet in convention to discuss and settle a number of ecclesiastical matters, it gave the name ynod to that meeting, but this term was so unwelcome, as being a Presbyterian name, that the Court changed it the next May, and styled the meeting "an assembly of the ministers of this Colony."

The order of the Court in May, 1708, in decreeing the delegated convention at Saybrook to remedy "the defects of the discipline of the churches of this government," used no terms that were Presbyterian or that indicated that form of government ;' nor did the convention itself, except in the title

---

[1] "May, 1708. This Assembly, from their own observation and from the complaint of many others, being made sensible of the defects of the discipline of the churches of this government, arising from the want of more explicit asserting the rules given for that end in the holy scriptures, from which would rise a firm establishment amongst us, a good and regular issue in cases subject to ecclesiastical discipline, glory to Christ our head, and edification to his members, hath seen fit to ordain and require, and it is by authority of the same ordained and required, that the

given to the Articles of Discipline, in which it said the ministers were "formerly called Presbyterian and Congregational."

In 1679, the Governor of the Colony and his Assistants,
in answer to inquiries made by the King's Council Chamber
as to what persuasion in religious matters is most prevalent,"
said : "Our people in this Colony are, some strict Congregational men, others more large Congregational men, and some
moderate Presbyterians; and take the Congregational men of
both sorts they are the greatest part of the people in the
Colony."

Therefore, there were, probably, at that and up to 1708,
a few "Moderate Presbyterians" in the Colony of Connecticut.

The result of these conventions was the formation and
adoption of the Saybrook platform, or system of church government.

Upon the adoption of the Saybrook platform in 1708 it
became the custom to call these churches Presbyterian, which
term grew more and more acceptable until the New Light
movement began in 1741, when the name became objection-
able; quite a number of churches refusing to be known as
Presbyterian.

The Consociations established by the Saybrook Platform—being composed of ministers and laymen—and the
authority which they were intended to exercise, were the
only principles which conformed to the government of the
Presbyterian Church. The Halfway Covenant, which was

---

ministers of the churches in the several counties of this government shall meet
together at their respective countie towns, with such messengers as the churches to
which they belong shall see cause to send with them, on the last Monday in June
next, there to consider and agree upon those methods and rules for the management of ecclesiastical discipline, which by them shall be judged agreeable and
conformable to the word of God, and shall, at the same meeting, appoint two or
more of their number to be their delegates, who shall all meet together at Saybrook, at the next Commencement to be held there, where they shall compare the
results of the ministers of the several counties, and out of and from them to draw
a form of ecclesiastical discipline, which by two or more persons delegated by
them shall be offered to this Court at their sessions at New Haven in October
next, to be considered of and confirmed by them, and that the expenses of the
above mentioned meetings be defrayed out of the public treasury of this Colonie."

only confirmed, not instituted by that Platform, had nothing Presbyterian in it, but was clearly in harmony with the usages of the Episcopal Church, in as much as it opened the way for the baptism of all children, by the parents becoming sponsors for their own children, in the form denominated owning the covenant.

The specific object of the Saybrook convention was to establish a more thorough system of ecclesiastical government; or in the words of the call for that meeting, to remedy " the defects of the discipline of the churches of this government."

When the Consociations were organized under it, in the western part of the State, at least, this matter was carefully confirmed and authorized, so far as those bodies could do it.' This was the action taken by the ministers of Fairfield County, and the form of this Consociation government was strongly Presbyterian.'

ˢ "Sigillum Consociationis Fairfieldensis.

Present from yᵉ Chh. of Fairfield
The Revᵈ Mr. Joseph Webb.
Messengeʳˢ.
Deacon John Thomson
Mr. Samuel Cobbet.

From yᵉ Chh. of Stratford.
Messengeʳˢ.
Joseph Curtiss Esqr.
Mr. Samuel Sherman.

From yᵉ Chh. of Stratfield.
The Revd. Mr. Charles Cauncey
Messenger.
Lieut. James Bennet.

From yᵉ Chh. of Stamford.
The Revd. Mr. Jno. Davenport.
Messengers.
Deacon Samˡˡ Hoit
Mr. Jos. Bishop.

At a Consociation or meeting of the Elders and Messengers of the County of Fairfield at Stratfield March 16, 1708-9. The Revd. Mr. John Davenport chosen Moderator.

The Revd. Mr. Charles Chauncey Scribe.

After Solemn Seeking of God for divine guidance, direction and blessing the Councill convened.

The Acts of yᵉ Councill at Saybrook, September 9, 1708 were read the first time as also yᵉ general Assembly's approbation and sanction thereof, October 1708.

Voted in Council to adjourn till 8 of yᵉ clock in yᵉ morning.

The Consociation being met according to adjournment, after prayer made it was agreed

Imps. That all the Chhs. in yᵉ County of Fairfield be one Consociation.

2. That yᵉ Pastors met in our Consociation have power with yᵉ Consent of the Messengers of our Chhs. chosen and attending, Authoritatively Judicially and Decisively to determine ecclesiastically affairs brôt to their Cognizance according to the Word of God and that our Pastors with the concurrence and consent of the Messengers of our Chhes. to be chosen and that shall attend upon all future occasions, have like Authoritative, Judicial and Decisive power of Determination of affairs ecclesiasticall, and that in further

From yᵉ Chh. of Danbury.
The Revᵈ Mr. Seth Shove.
Messengers.
Lieut. James Beebee
Mr. James Benedict.

and fuller meetings of two Consociations together compliant with the conclusions of yᵈ sd Councill at Saybrook, there is the like Authoritative, Judiciall and Decisive power of Determination of Ecclesiastical affairs according to yᵉ word of God.

3. That by Elder or Elders of a particular Chh in said Saybrook conclusions mentioned in Paragraph yᵉ first is understood only in yᵉ teaching Elder or teaching Elders.

From yᵉ Chh. of Norwalk.
The Revᵈ Mr. Stephen Buckingham.
Messenger.
Deacon Zerubbabel Hoit.

4. That in yᵉ 6ᵗʰ Paragraph of sd Conclusions we do not hold ourselves obliged in our practice to use yᵉ phrase of yᵉ sentence of Non Communion but in yᵉ stead thereof to use yᵉ phrase of yᵉ sentence of Excommunication which may in our judgment be formally applied in yᵉ Cases expressed in said Paragraph.

From yᵉ Chh. of Woodbury.
The Revd. Mr. Anthony Stoddard.
Messengers.
Deacon John Sherman,
Deacon Matthew Mitchell.

The Councill adjourned till half an hour past two oclock in yᵉ afternoon.

5. That to yᵉ orderly begining of a case before a Councill of our Chhes. yᵉ aggrieved member shall make application unto yᵉ moderator of the Councill or Consociation for yᵉ time being or in case of yᵉ moderator's death to yᵉ free Senʳ Pastor of yᵉ Consociation who upon his desire shall receive attested copies of yᵉ Chhs. proceedings with yᵉ aggrieved member from their minister and yᵉ sd. Moderator with the two free senr. Pastors of yᵉ Circuit or in yᵉ Case premised of yᵉ death of yᵉ Moderator yᵉ sd 2 senr. pastors of yᵉ circuit being satisfied there is sufficient cause shall warn yᵉ convening of the Consociation.

6. That a Copy of a Warning to appear before yᵉ Councill the time and place being notified being read in the hearing or left in yᵉ house of the ordinary abode of a scandalous member or witness concerning the case depending before two members of the designation of the Scribe for yᵉ time being and signed by the sd Scribe be adjudged a regular notification.

7. That a copy of a Warning to appear before yᵉ Pastor or Chh. yᵉ place and time notified being read in yᵉ hearing or left in the ordinary abode of an offending member or witness needfull in the case before two members appointed by the pastor and signed by him shall be a fair notification yᵉ neglect whereof unless upon sufficient reason shall be reputed a scandalous contempt in our respective Chhes

8. That all persons that are known to be Baptized shall in yᵉ places where they dwell be subject to yᵉ Censures of admonition and excommunication in case of scandall committed and obstinately persisted in.

9. That the Moderator and Scribe now chosen be accounted to stand in yᵉ same respective capacities for yᵉ time being untill a new regular choice be made, and so for the future.

10. That yᵉ Judgment of yᵉ Consociation or Council be executed by any Pastor appointed thereto by yᵉ Councill when yᵉ Pastor that hath already dealt in yᵉ case hath not a freedome of Conscience to execute yᵉ same.

The above Acts and Conclusions of the present Consociation unanimously Voted March 17, 1708-9.

Signed   Charles Chauncey, Scribe.
The above and foregoing is a true Copy of the Originall Compared.

pr. Samuel Cooke."

CHAPTER XIII.

THE EIGHTEENTH CENTURY CONTINUED.

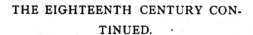

ISTORY in church matters for many years in Connecticut, is very largely the history of the people, socially and politically. There is no nation in which religion had a larger part in its formation than the American nation of the United States, and the ecclesiastical form in which this religious influence and teaching were prominently and successfully propagated for nearly one hundred years, was Congregational. Whether right or wrong, better or worse, or whatever the final result, this is historical fact, so widely recorded as to be beyond the possibility of change.

It is, therefore, proper, in the further delineations of history, to recognize the religious element, in its movings and effect, in such a degree as to show its force in the formation of the national life and character. In local history especially is this true, for in it is seen more directly the democratic elements of a free people.

Some notice of the churches in Connecticut, and especially as developed in Stratford, under the name of Congregational and Presbyterian has been given, as constituting largely the settlement and organization of the place.

The second denomination recognized by law and largely by the people of the state, was the Protestant Episcopal, at that day denominated the Church of England, and the place of its first organization in this State was Stratford.

The Episcopal Church in Stratford.

᛫ Stratford was settled by persons who had been communicants in the Church of England to the time of their sailing· for America. The Rev. Adam Blakeman had been regularly ordained in that church, and had served in it as priest for several years under the Bishop, but had been silenced for non-conformity. He and his associates dissented from several requirements of the Bishop; not from the doctrines or existing ritual of the Church;[1] and as regular members of that church received their certificates from the minister of the parish where they had resided and "attestations from the Justice of the Peace," according to the order of the government, upon which they were allowed to sail as emigrants to America.

They came to America with no other name than dissenting members of the Church of England, and as such were organized into a local body and called the "Church of Christ in Stratford."

It is not a supposable thing that these persons, although placed in church organization, without the approbation of a Bishop, could at once forget, or wholly forsake the religious training received, or their affection for the church and its usages, from which they were separated. Hence, in 1666, when some questions of church discipline arose there were found those who desired to maintain and be governed by rules which had been familiar to them in England.

The eight persons who were the minority in the division which finally went to Woodbury, were all born in England, with only one exception, if any, and four of them—Richard Butler, Henry Wakelyn, Samuel Sherman and Daniel Titharton, had been, probably, communicants in the Church of England before coming to this country. They desired, when received under the Halfway Covenant, to be examined

---

[1] Those who fled from England to this country were compelled to do so or observe certain rites and ceremonies of the English Church, which they believed unscriptural, and therefore wrong. They objected to the cap and surplice, the ring in marriage, the cross in baptism, the rite of confirmation, kneeling at the Lord's supper, etc."—New Haven Historical Society Papers, iii. 307.

alone by the minister—or minister and elder—and to be allowed to partake of the Lord's Supper, and their children,
when baptized, to be members of the church in the sense
entertained then in the English Church. Hence, this church
at Woodbury did admit the halfway covenant members to the
communion for many years after its organization.

Nor is it to be supposed that all kindly remembrances and
feelings of attachment for the Episcopal Church had died
out in Stratford at the year 1700, while their numbers had
been increased frequently by emigrants from the Church of
England, yet it is doubtful if before 1706 there were any families in Stratford who stood aloof from the Congregational
Church, claiming to be adherents of the Episcopal Church.
This is a conclusion, after careful examination, of every family name, as to births, baptisms, civil and social relations and
owners of property, to that date. It has been claimed that
Daniel Shelton was an Episcopalian from 1687, onward, but if
so, he was, as may hereafter be seen, a very good " pillar " in
the Congregational Society as late as 1717, for his name was
the first on the petition in that year for society privileges in
Ripton for the Congregational Church.

Isaac Knell has been represented by the Rev. Samuel
Peters as an Episcopalian as early as "about 1690," but he
was a Congregationalist and took an active part in that society's proceedings, in settling a minister in 1698; and ten
years later he was so much attached to Mr. John Reed when
he had closed his labors in Stratford, that the following deed
is found in the land records: " July 13, 1708, Isaac Knell and
John Clark for good will and affection," deeded to " Mr.
John Reed for the space of ten thousand years, the day of
this date forward . . . all our undivided lands in Stratford."
Mr. Peters calls him " Mr. Knell," but there was no other
Mr. Knell than Isaac, in the town, at that time ; and he died
only a few months later—November 2, 1708. He was a prominent, active man in the town, but probably was never an
Episcopalian.

Doctor James Laborie, son of the Rev. James Laborie,
an Episcopal clergyman and a physician, was born in 1691,
and settled in Stratford as a physician, where, in 1714, he

was granted liberty, by a town vote, to build a pew in the Congregational meeting-house, at his own expense, it being the second pew in that house, the other seats being high-back slips.

The Episcopal Church was introduced, in form, into Connecticut at Stratford in the summer of 1706, by the Rev. George Muirson, in the use of the church service, preaching, and the baptism of "about twenty-four, mostly grown people."[1] His visits, as a missionary for the Society for the Propagation of the Gospel in foreign parts, stationed at Rye, N. Y., were repeated, and the "churchmen of Stratford were organized into a parish, with Wardens and Vestrymen, at the visit of Mr. Muirson, in April, 1707."[2]

"Mr. Muirson died in October, 1708," and hence "the parish, with about thirty communicants and a respectable number of families, was left to the occasional services of missionaries who chanced to visit this and the neighboring towns."[3]

The circumstances in Stratford at Mr. Muirson's introduction of the church service were favorable for such an object. The community had been divided in sentiment, as to the settlement of a minister, nearly four years. Two candidates had preached, some months each, before Mr. Reed, who was called on probation in view of a settlement, with much enthusiasm, by about a two-thirds majority of voters in the town ; became a resident in the town, and held a fair majority until he resigned. The votes in opposition to him, at any time, were very few, but these, with those in favor of other candidates, ranged from thirty to fifty during his stay in the place. It was during his fourth year, in the summer of 1706, that Mr. Muirson first came to the place and held services, they being quite opportune under the unsettled state of religious sentiment as to the minister.

The same trouble occurred again just before the Rev. Samuel Johnson was appointed missionary to Stratford. The division as to the settlement of a minister after Mr. Cutler left, in

---

[1] Hist. of the Church in Connecticut by Rev. E. E. Beardsley, D.D., i. 20.
Ibid.

[2] Ibid, i. 23.

1719, was much greater than when Mr. Reed ministered here, until Mr. Gold became a candidate, and when he was settled, there were some apparently who were ready to go elsewhere as soon as opportunity favored, but the greatest accessions of substantial value to the Episcopal Church occurred between the years 1740 and 1750.

Another missionary, the Rev. Francis Philips, was sent to Stratford in 1712, who remained about five months and departed.

In the spring of 1714, the churchmen of Stratford began the work of building a church edifice, but discouragements were so many that only little progress was made.

The next missionary who visited them was the Rev. George Pigot, in the spring of 1722, he having been recently sent as missionary to New York. After his visits had continued about one year, proceedings were revived to build a church and the first important item was to secure a site on which to place it, and they made application to the town for a certain specified locality.

Very much has been said about the persecution they received in obtaining a site and erecting a house of worship, and it is probable that in a community entertaining some considerable conflicting religious sentiments, as was the case in Stratford at the time, some persons would do things of such a character, but that the general public sentiment favored such proceedings is not warranted by any reliable evidence, and is also refuted by the following town record :

"At a lawful town meeting in Stratford, June 21, 1723, voted : Whereas, Mr. George Pigott and his associates petitioned the town of Stratford to give them land to erect a church on and land for a church yard, and in their petition fixed upon two certain places, the one by Mr. Gold's house, and the other on the north side of the Town's meeting-house near widow Titharton's land, the town considering their proposals and the two places they had pitched upon, and found them clogged with great difficulties. and that it would be as they apprehend, greatly to the damage of the town in general, to build on either of those places, however nominated some other places which, as they thought, might be convenient for them; yet, notwithstanding, they went and purchased, of John Outman, thirty-six rods of land of his lot next to our meeting-house, within some four rods of said house, and gave, as appears of record, thirty pounds for the same where they designed to erect said church as they say, which, in the judgment of all thinking persons, may be very inconvenient and a great disturbance to each society, the houses being so near together, if erected there; the town, therefore, propose and offer to Mr. George Pigott and his associates aforesaid, to change with them, and for the thirty-six rods of land purchased of said Outman, and to allow them for it forty rods of land at the place they desired in their petition (namely, by the widow Titharton's) on the north side of the meeting-house; or in lieu of said thirty-six rods of land to let them have the forty rods aforesaid at a reasonable rate and price to erect their church on and church yard, and the town made choice of Mr. Joseph Curtis, Capt. John Hawley, Ens. Edmund Lewis and Ens. John Porter, or any of them, a committee in behalf of the town to present the above proposals and offers of the town to the said Mr. George Pigott and his associates, petitioners, etc.   Test, JOSEPH CURTISS, Town Clerk."

Five days after this meeting a record of opposition was made, it being the only one, although the accommodating town clerk left half a page blank for others, but it has not yet been filled:

"June 26, 1723. Lieut. Joseph Beach entered his dissent against the town disposing of any land of the commons on the north of the meeting-house hill by widow Titharton's, for the erecting of a church on, or church yard upon.

Test: JOSEPH CURTISS, Town Clerk."

The lot near the widow Titharton's was accepted, which was the one where the Episcopal burying place now is, and upon it was erected the first church edifice for this society, and the first for the Church of England in the Connecticut Colony; and the lot purchased of Mr. Outman was sold some years later.[4]

---

[4] Mr. George Pigot quit claimed this land to the church, March 14, 172⅜.

The Rev. Samuel Johnson arrived at Stratford November 4, 1723, being commissioned as a missionary to this place by the society in England, at which time the frame of the church edifice could scarcely have been set up, since the site was not determined upon until in July or August of that year, if as early as that time.

This building has been described as "a neat, small wooden building, forty-five feet and a half long, thirty and a half wide, and twenty-two between joints, or up to the roof," and was built, partly, at the expense of the members of the Church of England, in Stratford, and partly by the liberal contributions of several pious and generous gentlemen of the neighboring provinces, and sometimes of travelers who occasionally passed through the town."[5]

It was opened for divine service on Christmas day, 1724.

Mr. Johnson's missionary field was very large; for, besides occasional visits to a greater distance, his labors were distributed among the following places: Fairfield, Norwalk, Newtown, Ripton, West Haven, and New Haven.

Success to a good degree attended the labors of the missionaries in this place. At Mr, Muirson's death, in 1708, it is said: "The parish, with about thirty communicants and a respectable number of families, was now left to the occasional services of missionaries who chanced to visit this and the neighboring towns."[6]

The Vestry and Wardens quit claimed the same April 4, 1729.

Nehemiah Lorin,	Church
Richard Rogers,	Wardens.
William Smith,	
James Labore,	Vestry.
John Benjamin,	
Samuel French,	

This land was sold by quit claim to Mr. Joseph Brown, April 19, 1731, by
John Benjamin, Church Warden.
William Smith.
Thomas Latten.
John.Kee.
Francis Barlow.

[5] The Church in Conn., i.

[6] Dr. Beardsley's Hist. of the Church in Conn., i. 24.

In 1723, it is said: "The parish of Stratford, when he [Mr. Johnson] came to it, numbered about thirty families; and forty more—to say nothing of the few churchmen farther eastward—might be included in the neighboring towns and districts."' In 1727, Mr. Johnson, in writing to the Honorable Society, represented "that he had then in his parish fifty families, or about one-seventh of the whole number of families in the town."

The fact that the supporters of the Episcopal Church in Stratford and in Connecticut were required by law to pay taxes for the support of the Congregational churches, was the one most irritating and distressing difficulty with which they had to contend. It was a sore trial, and was all wrong, but was just what dissenting bodies were undergoing in England at the same time, and this is the only excuse, that a law had been established in this respect, in harmony with the law in England, and to it the English government made no objection. The law in Connecticut was in favor of the Congregational churches; the law in England was in favor of the Church of England.

The law in Connecticut was enforced, in regard to the organization of new Congregational parishes, in that the parties were required to pay to the old society until recognized by the General Court as a new society, for a part or the whole of the year.

A close examination of the record of town acts between 1706, and 1730, reveals no vote in Stratford to release the supporters of the Episcopal Church from paying taxes to the established church; and it would have been contrary to the law to pass such a vote.

In 1727, upon the petition of the Episcopal people of Fairfield, an act was passed by the legislature to relieve the members of the Episcopal Church from paying to the support of the Congregational churches.'

' Ibid, 54. Ibid, 60.

' "May, 1727. *Be it enacted by the Governor, Council and Representatives, in General Court assembled, and by the authority of the same.*

That all persons who are of the Church of England, and those who are of the churches established by the laws of this government, that live in the bounds of

After this, no vote of the town of Stratford has been seen, recognizing this act, until January, 1737-8, when, instead of saying, as usual, that the tax was for the salary of the minister, it says "to defray ministerial salaries and charges." Hence, the tax was laid on all persons alike, in the society, but that collected from Episcopalians was paid to the Episcopal minister or Church.

It further appears that the Episcopal Church and people of Stratford were treated in a friendly manner by the voters and proprietors of the common lands in the town.

Dr. Samuel Johnson was greatly in favor of education in higher branches as well as the lower. His influence at Yale College was decidedly helpful and notedly generous. The following record in Stratford was a movement projected by himself:

"At a town meeting 1st Monday in February, 1733-4, the Rev. Samuel Johnson, in behalf of the members of the Church of England in Stratford, requesting the liberty of erecting and setting up a School House on the Common, near the southeast corner of Lieut. Joseph Beach's house lot; on consideration thereof Edmund Lewis, John Thompson, Esq., and Captain John Wells were chosen a committee to view and consider the most important and convenient place, and where said committee shall fix the place that they shall

---

any parish allowed by this Assembly. shall be taxed by the parishioners of the said parish by the same rule and in the same proportion, for the support of the ministry in such parish : but if it so happen that there be a society of the Church of England, where there is a person in orders according to the canons of the Church of England, settled and abiding among them, and performing divine service, so near to any person that hath declared himself of the Church of England that he can conveniently and doth attend the public worship there, then the collectors. having first indifferently levied the tax as above said, shall deliver the taxes collected of such persons declaring themselves and attending aforesaid, unto the minister of the Church of England living near unto such persons ; which minister shall have full power to receive and recover the same, in order to his support in the place assigned to him. But if such proportion of taxes be not sufficient in any society of the Church of England, to support the incumbent there, then such society may levy and collect of them, who profess and attend as aforesaid, greater taxes at their own discretion, for the support of their minister. And the parishioners of the Church of England, attending as aforesaid, are hereby excused from paying any taxes for building meeting-houses for the present establisht churches of this government."

think most convenient, liberty is granted for said persons there to erect and set up said school house."

This was about seventy years before the building was erected on the green, still remembered as the Academy, and whether Dr. Johnson secured the erection of a school house as proposed, has not been ascertained.

Another item indicates this spirit of friendliness and also equity toward the members of the Episcopal Church, as well as all others; it was the granting of land to those members for their church or minister in proportion as the town or proprietors had granted to the Congregational ministers. When Mr. Chauncey was settled here, some land was given him, as a settlement. When Mr. Cutler was settled, one hundred acres, besides a house lot, were given to him, and one hundred acres were given to Mr. Jedediah Mills on his settlement at Ripton; and a number of acres were given to Mr. Richardson Minor, upon his settlement at Unity.

In the winter of 1735–6, the supporters of the Episcopal Church petitioned the proprietors of the common lands in the town to grant them land for their church in proportion to what had been granted to the Congregational ministers of the town, and a committee was appointed by the proprietors to ascertain how much land should in equity be thus sequestered. Upon that committee's report the following action was taken by the proprietors' meeting :

" March, 1736. Whereas, several persons belonging to the Church of England in Stratford for themselves and the rest of their brethren proprietors in said Stratford belonging to said Church of England, making request and desiring an equivalent of land may be allowed them for the lands formerly given to several Presbyterian ministers in fee and some given the use in said Stratford, in consideration whereof it was voted that our friends and neighbors in Stratford belonging to the Church of England, and being also proprietors in the common and undivided land in said Stratford, shall have the liberty of having laid out to them, collectively considered, ten acres of land in any of the common and undivided land six miles distant, provided it be in full satisfaction for their proportion in all lands formerly given to the Presbyterian

ministry in said Stratford, either for use or in fee, said land
to be taken up in one entire piece in the six-mile division, so
called. Said vote passed *nemine contradicente.*"[1]

Four years later another request made, was as readily
granted:

"To the moderator of the Proprietors' meeting in Stratford the 11th day of instant, February, A. D., 1739-40, and
the proprietors of Stratford of the common and undivided
land, the humble request of us, the subscribers for ourselves,
and on behalf of the rest of our brethren members of the
Episcopal Church of England in Stratford, that, whereas sundry persons have subscribed to an instrument of equal date
of these presents to give out of our rights of land in the last
six-mile division granted the first Tuesday of instant, February, for the proper use, benefit and behoof of the Episcopal
Church of England in Stratford, this is, therefore, to request
that we, the subscribers, may have the liberty to take up the
same land subscribed adjoining to a tract lately laid out [the
ten acres] for the use of the Church of England, or if that
cannot be, we may have liberty to take the whole of the subscription in one piece, if that may be found convenient.

Subscribed by Samuel Blagge.
Samuel French.
William Beach.
Francis Hawley.
Joseph Brown.

"Which above said request, at said meeting, was granted,
provided they lay not out above twenty acres, as aforesaid."
These petitioners were the officers of the church.

The restriction to twenty acres, limited only the laying
twenty acres in *one piece.* They might have given hundreds
of acres, in various places, if they had chosen.

---

[1] "*Church's land:*

Laid out ten acres by the proprietors' Committee—adjoining to the
South end of Menhantuck Swamp, so called—beginning at a pond of water on the
east side of Newtown road.

"May 6, 1736.   Edmund Lewis,
Jose Blacklach,
Theoph. Nicolls,
Proprietors' Com."

It should be remembered that proprietors of common, or undivided lands, were a different class from freeholders, for there were some freeholders who had no rights in common lands, but the number was small.

There were seventeen names attached to the paper referred to in the above petition, and the number of acres given are recorded, except in the case of the two last names, one of which the figures are not intelligible, the other has no figure attached, probably by the carelessness of the recorder.[19]

The owners of the common land, at this time, numbered 199, holding rights, claiming from a small fraction of an acre to nearly fifty acres, according as each held a greater or less proportion of one of the original seventeen rights. There were at this time a number of thousand acres of land undivided, but lying in smaller pieces in many portions or parts of the township.

So far then as the actions of the citizens, in town meeting assembled, and those of the proprietors of the common lands are concerned, there seems to have been a spirit of equity and neighborly conduct manifested, throughout, toward the supporters of the Episcopal Church in Stratford.

Some misapprehension seems to have been entertained as to the relation of the Connecticut government to other denominations than the legally established churches. The early settlers were very nearly unanimous in their religious prefer-

---

[19] "To all whom these presents shall come, Greeting—Know ye that we whose names are under written, Do give unto the Episcopal Church of England in Stratford, the several parcels of land affixed to our names . . . . for the only use, benefit, and behoof of ye s⁴ Church of England and their successors forever.

Feb. 11, 1739-40.

William Beach,	3 acres.		Elephalet Curtiss,	1 acres.
Samuel French,	1 "		Joseph Lewis,	½ "
Samuel French, Jr.,	¼ "		Benjamin Lewis,	½ "
Samuel Blagge,	½ "		Elisha Blagge,	⅛ "
Francis Hawley,	½ "		James Bears,	½ "
James Fairchild,	¼ "		Jonathan Curtiss, 60 Rods.	
Caleb Beardslee,	1 "		Richard Blacklach.	
Joseph Shelton,	3 "		Edmund Lewis."	
Israel Beardslee, ¼ and ½ quarter.				

Land Records, B. 9, page 132.

This land was laid next to Newtown line, April 4, 1743.

22

ences and ideas of church government; but soon persons began to settle here, holding different views in these matters, and as soon as these persons became sufficient in number to indicate the propriety of toleration, the General Court conceded the question, and acted accordingly.

The Connecticut Act of Toleration.

" General Court, May, 1669.

This Court having seriously considered the great divisions that arise amongst us about matters of church government, for the honor of God, wellfare of the churches, and preservation of the publique peace so greatly hazarded, doe declare that, whereas the Congregationall churches in these parts for the generall of their profession and practice, have hitherto been approved, we can doe no less than still approve and countenance the same to be without disturbance until better light in an orderly way doth appeare; but, yet, for as much as sundry persons of worth for prudence and piety amongst us are otherwise persuaded (whose wellfare and peaceable sattisfaction we desire to accommodate). This Court doth declare that all such persons being allso approved according to lawe as orthodox and sownd in the fundamentalls of [the] Christian religion may have allowance of their persuasion and profession in church wayes or assemblies without disturbance."[11]

This did not include Quakers, for they were regarded, in those days, as not orthodox, but light was springing as if from a hundred hamlets and spreading like the rays of the rising sun, and hence, six years later, in 1675, the Quakers were relieved from persecution, in the following act, although not allowed to meet in separate assemblies. " This Court being moved to consider of the law respecting Quakers, doe see cause at present to suspend the penalty for absence from our publique assemblies or imprisonment of those of that perswasion, provided they do not gather into assemblies in this Colony or make any disturbance."

---

[11] Col. Rec., ii. 109.

The act of 1669 allowed persons of every persuasion, if orthodox in faith, to hold public worship—or, in its own words, " that all such persons being also approved, according to law as orthodox, and sound in the fundamentals of [the] Christian religion, may have allowance of their persuasion and profession in church ways, or assemblies, without disturbance."

Although these acts did not secure full liberty of conscience—a thing then unknown to law in the world—yet, how great was the contrast between the religious liberties of Connecticut at that time, and those of England, the mother country whence the pilgrims came, where the Church of England was then in the ascendancy, and her Bishops held full sway. King Charles II. was restored to authority in 1660, and soon after a convocation of divines changed various parts of the Prayer Book, and added severe terms of conformity ; and it has been said it " was the study of the Bishops to make the terms of conformity as hard as possible ;" and, " on St. Bartholomew's day, August the twenty-fourth, in the year 1662, the act of uniformity expelled from the establishment [the English Church] all ministers who would not swear their unfeigned assent and consent to everything in the Book of Common Prayer. In many parts of the kingdom, the ministers could not procure the book before the time within which the law required them to swear to it or resign their livings, so that, in their farewell sermons, they told their flocks, that they were obliged to leave them for not swearing to a book which they had not been able to see.

" Two thousand ministers resigned their livings in the establishment, and exposed themselves to the loss of all things, rather than submit to these new terms of conformity, which their consciences condemned.

" The great Mr. Locke styled these two thousand ejected ministers, learned, pious, orthodox divines."

But this was not the severest part of the persecutions which then reigned with a high and severe hand.

" The conventicle act was passed, decreeing, that if any person, above the age of sixteen years be present at any meeting for worship, different from the Church of England, where there shall be more than five persons more than the household, they shall, for the first offence, suffer three months imprisonment, or pay five pounds; for the second, the punishment was doubled; and for the third, they shall be banished to America, or pay a hundred pounds; and if they return from banishment, suffer death."

" The oath of an informer was sufficient to inflict all the severity of this statute, and thus, while many of the best men filled the jails, the vilest of the human race rioted in debauchery by informing for the sake of the reward.""

A few years later and further measures were taken against the non-conforming ministers. " An act of passive obedience, and non-resistance was enacted ; and all who refused it, were prohibited from coming within five miles of any corporate town where they formerly preached ; or from keeping schools, or taking boarders, under a penalty of forty pounds. Thus, though they were not actually burnt alive, they were intentionally starved to death.""

Twenty years did these proceedings continue under the reign of Charles II., even until his death in 1680.

Such is the contrast between England and the Connecticut Colony, from 1660 to 1680. Connecticut, it is true, did enact a severe law against the Quakers, Ranters, Adamites and such like notorious Heretics," as styled in the language of that day; and did hang a few witches, which is, and ever will be, greatly to her dishonor, but her colonists brought the laws, sentiments, usages and customs, by which these things were done, with them from England, adhered to them a few years only, and then in the grandeur of the freedom of which they just began to taste, threw off the yoke of bondage and religious persecution, and established a platform of civil freedom such as the sun had never before shone upon, and such that the English government sought, for nearly one hundred years, with many inventions, to deprive them of, but failed, and that failure established the nation called the United States of America.

---

12 History of Dissenters, i. 98, and following.

14 Ibid, 100.

The Act of Toleration, under King James II. of England was established in 1687, eighteen years after the like act was made a law in Connecticut. " It suspended all penal laws against all classes of non-conformists; authorized Roman Catholics and Protestant dissenters to perform public worship; forbade the molestation of any religious assembly; abrogated all laws imposing religious test as a qualification for office; and granted entire liberty of conscience, to all the King's subjects."[14]

This act, although planned and executed by the King for another end than freedom, was, nevertheless, a law of great progress and value, compared with the terrible laws of religious persecution which had been in existence unto that day; but Connecticut had already adopted like regulations, and these from England were readily accepted by her.

One thing has been charged to the discredit of the forefathers of Connecticut with less consideration and with greater censure than all others put together; namely, the union of church and state, and thereby the levying of taxes by law to support the ministry.

To this but two things need be named in reply; one, that they knew no other way: and the other, that it seemed to them a self-evident law, that those who were benefited, should, in proportion to their ability, pay for the benefits received.

As to the first it was the law of the land whence they came, all their experiences had been under that discipline, and when they left their mother country they had made no complaint whatever at being required by law to support the preaching of the gospel.

When they had effected a settlement in the wilderness, and the question of permanency arose as to the life they were to live, and the characters they hoped and proposed to form, of right and righteousness, they judged the preaching of the gospel the most important agent to be used, and for that reason made the most equitable provision for that end, of which they had any knowledge.

They stated their own case by the action of the Commis-

---

[14] Hume.

sioners for the United Colonies, September 5, 1644, which was adopted by Connecticut, thus:

" Whereas, the most considerable persons in these colonies came into these parts of America that they might injoye Christ in his ordinances, without disturbance; And, whereas, among many other precious mercyes, the ordinances are, and have been, dispensed among us with much purity and power: The Commissioners took it into serious consideration, how some due mayntenauce according to God might be provided and settled, both for the present and future, for the encouragement of the ministers who labour therein, and concluded to propound and commend it to each General Court, that those that are taught in the word in the several plantations, be called together, that every man voluntarily set down what he is willing to allow to that end and use ; and if any man refuse to pay a meet proportion, that then he be rated by authority in some just and equal way; and if after this, any man withold or delay due payment, the civil power to be exercised in other just debts.'"[15]

This was the beginning of the law which, a few years later, required every taxpayer to pay to the support of the church or churches in his plantation or town.[16] When the law was enacted to allow freedom or choice as to church preferences, and worship in 1669, it did not release the citizen from paying tax for the support of the legally established church

---

[15] Col. Rec., i. 112.

[16] *Law of Connecticut Published in 1650.*

" It is ordered by this Court and Authority thereof, that every inhabitant shall henceforth contribute to all charges, both in Church and Commonwealth, whereof he doth or may receive benefit, and every such inhabitant who doth not voluntarily contribute proportionally to his ability with the rest of the same Towne to all common charges, both Civil and Ecclesiastical, shall be compelled thereunto by assessments and distress, to be levied by the Constable or other officer of the Towne as in other cases ; And, that the Lands and Estates of all men, wherever they dwell, shall be rated for all Towne Charges, both Civil and Ecclesiastical, as aforesaid, where the Lands and Estates shall lie, and their persons, where they shall dwell."

At this time all persons from 16 yeais old and upwards, were taxed [1st] "every person, except Magistrates and Elders of Churches. two shillings six pence per head, and [2d] all estates, bothe real and personal, at one penny for every twenty shillings." Conn. Col. Rec. i., 547.

of his community. Nor did the act of toleration in England release any one from paying to the support of the ministry in the English Church. So far had the idea of freedom in religious matters advanced in America, that, when from 1706, to 1727, the communicants of the Episcopal Church were required by law, as all others, to pay to the support of the Congregational Churches, they judged it a very grievous oppression, and some refused to do it and were imprisoned just as Congregationalists would have been if they had refused; but at the same time all denominations were taxed in England for the support of the ministers of the Episcopal Church.

There was also a great difference between the union of Church and State in England and that in Connecticut. In the former the layity had nothing to do in calling a minister or the salary paid him, while in Connecticut they controlled both, in the most democratic form then known, and the tax collected for the minister was kept separate from all others, and applied yearly, only upon the vote of the parish.

Such are some of the historical facts from which the early settlers of Connecticut had come and through which they had passed, and ·by which they were surrounded when a second denomination of Christians had become established by law in their territory.

The following extract is taken from a book called *A General History of Connecticut*, by the Rev. Samuel Peters, published first in London, England, in 1781, and at New Haven in 1829, page 166:

Mr. Peters, being a very strong loyalist in the time of the Revolution, found it to his comfort to go to England, where he published this book, in which are many things of true history and also many things without a shadow of truth, and which have the appearance of being published for the purpose of defaming the people of Connecticut.

He married in Stratford, Mary, only daughter of William Birdseye, April 20, 1773, and hence was acquainted in Stratford.

The story which he relates concerning the Indian powwow, had some foundation in tradition, and historical fact. The Indians held yearly powwows, and held ceremonies with extreme fanatical bodily exercises, but of this particular occasion we have no account only this given by Mr. Peters.

"*Stratford* lies on the west bank of Osootonoc river, having the sea or sound on the south.

There are three streets running north and south and ten east and west. The best is one mile long. On the centre square stand a meeting with a steeple and a bell, and a church with a steeple, bell, clock, and organ.

It is a beautiful place, and from the water has an appearance not inferior to that of Canterbury. Of six parishes contained in it, three are Episcopal.

The people are said to be the most polite of any in the colony, owing to the singular moderation of the town in admitting latterly, Europeans to settle among them. Many persons come also from the islands, and southern provinces, for the benefit of their health.

Here was erected the first Episcopal Church in Connecticut.

A very extraordinary story is told concerning the occasion of it, which I shall give the reader the particulars of, the people being as sanguine in their belief of it as they are of the ship's sailing over New Haven.

An ancient religious rite called the Pawwaw, was annually celebrated by the Indians; and commonly lasted several hours every night for two or three weeks. About 1690, they convented to perform it on Stratford point near the town. During the nocturnal ceremony the English saw, or imagined they saw, devils rise out of the sea, wrapped up in sheets of flame, and flying round the Indian camp, while the Indians were screaming, cutting, and prostrating themselves before their supposed fiery gods. In the midst of the tumult the devils darted in among them, seized several, and mounted with them into the air; the cries and groans issuing from whom quieted the rest. In the morning, the limbs of Indians, all shrivelled, and covered with sulphur, were found in different parts of the town. Astonished at these spectacles, the people of Stratford began to think the devils would take up their abode among them, and called together all the ministers in the neighborhood, to exorcise and lay them. The ministers began and carried on their warfare with prayer, hymns, and adjuration: but the pawwaws continued, and the devils would not obey.

The inhabitants were about to quit the town, when Mr. Nell spoke and said: "I would to God that Mr. Visey, the Episcopal minister at New York, was here; for he would expel these evil spirits." They laughed at his advice; but, on his reminding them of the little maid who directed Naaman to a cure for his leprosy, they voted him their permission to bring Mr. Visey at the next pawwaw.

Mr. Visey attended, accordingly, and as the pawwaw commenced with howlings and whoops, Mr. Visey read portions of the holy scripture, litany, etc. The sea was put into great motion; the pawwaw stopped; the Indians dispersed and never more held a pawwaw in Stratford.

The inhabitants were struck with wonder at this event, and held a conference to discover the reason why the devils and pawwawers had obeyed the prayers of one minister, and had paid no regard to those of fifty. Some thought that the reading of the holy scripture, others that the Litany and Lord's prayer; some, again, that the Episcopal power of the minister, and others, all united were the means of obtaining the heavenly blessing they had received.

Those who believed that the holy scriptures and litany were effectual against the devil and his legions, declared for the Church of England; while the majority ascribed their deliverance to a complot between the devil and the Episcopal minister, with a view to overthrow Christ's vine planted in New England. Each party acted with more zeal than prudence."

This story of expelling the devils from Stratford has about as much force against the Congregationalists as the story still told as to the cause of the mosquitoes in Stratford. That cause, it is well known, is the great salt meadow of 1,500 or 2,000 acres below Stratford on the Sound, yet a jocose story is told of another cause.

It is said, when the Rev. George Whitefield preached in Stratford, he represented all the Episcopal people as never having been converted, and they, in turn, were very severe in remarks on Mr. Whitefield; and that when he left Stratford he shook off the dust of his feet against them, saying, the curse of God would come upon them. That curse, it has been said, was the coming of the mosquitoes.

The Episcopal Burying Place. Established in 1723.

The purpose in copying these inscriptions, has been to present every one just as it is on the stone—the names, dates, verses and spelling, every word and letter on each and every stone to the date of June 10th, 1885; and much care and effort have been employed to make this record correct. There are four or five inscriptions so effaced that they could not be copied.

Inscriptions in the Episcopal Burying-place in Stratford.

Sacred to the Memory of
Clarissa, wife of the Rev. Ashbel Baldwin, & Daughter of Mr. Samuel & Mrs. Margaret Johnson of Guilford: born July 7, 1761, & departed this Life April 16, 1823, aged 62.
Blessed are the dead who die in the Lord.

Anne Barrows, of New York, died March 16, 1844, Æ. 88.

Lewis Starr, son of Samuel & Harriet Barnum, died Jan. 6, 1830, Æ. 4 yrs.
When the Arch Angel's trump shall sound
And souls to bodies join,
What crowds shall wish their lives below
Had been as short as theirs.

Ann Rebecca, daughter of Samuel & Harriet Barnum, died Aug. 29, 1837, Æ. 2 yrs.
Also
Julius Curtiss, Died Aug. 20, 1834: Æ. 7 mos. & 14 ds.
Suffer little children to come unto me & forbid them not.

Aaron Beard, Died Jan. 11, 1853, Æ. 59.

Beneath this stone repose the remains of *Francis M. Beard,* who died May 5, 1843 : Aged 19 years.

In Memory of
Mr. Abijah Beardslee, who died Sept. 3, 1839, in the 76th year of his age.

In Memory of
Mr. Abraham Beardslee, who died Feb. 13, 1815, Aged 88 Years.

In Memory of
Major B. Beardsley, who died Nov. 14, 1847, Aged 38.

In memory of
Charles Frederick Beardslee, son of Wilson & Louisa Beardslee, who died Oct. 13, 1843, in 20 year of his age.
Dearest son since thou hast left us
Here thy loss we deeply feel,
But 'tis God that hath bereft us.
He can all our sorrows heal.
Yet again we hope to meet thee
When the days of life are fled,
Then in heaven we hope to greet thee,
Where no farewell tear is shed.

In Memory of
Mrs. Bethia Beardslee, wife of Mr. Abraham Beardslee, who died Aug. 4th, 1801, In the 71st Year of her age.

In Memory of
Caroline, daughter of Ephraim & Sarah Beardsley, who died Jan. 24, 1827, Æ 3 yr. 6 mo.

In Memory of
Christana, wife of Henry Beardsley, who died Feb. 27th, 1823, aged 89 years.

In Memory of
Curtiss Beardeslee, who departed this Life Sept. 13th, 1796, in the 43d Year of his age.

In Memory of
Mary, wife of Curtiss Beardsley, who died Oct. 15, 1822, aged 62 years.

Ephriam, their son, died Jan. 10, 1793 : aged 16. Two Infant children of David & Rebecca Beardsley, one died 1817, the other June, 1822.

In memory of
Henry Beardslee, who died Aug. 13, 1806, aged 69 years.
O weeping friends your tears withold,
Nor mourn me as forever gone :
I go as God himself has told,
To wake at resurrection morn.

In Memory of
Nancy, wife of Abijah Beardsley, who died Oct. 8, 1811 : Æ. 45

Oliver Beardsley, died Dec. 30, 1793, Æ. 3.
Six children she has left
To mourn and lament her death.
The God that made her called her home
Because he thought it best.

In Memory of
Philo Beardslee, who died Feb. 20, 1846, Æ 80 years.

In Memory of
William Beardsley, who died August 21, 1841, aged 73 years.

Mr. Abel Beach, Departed this life December 16th, 1768, In the 38th year of his age.
His affectionate Sister Ann Johnson, erected this Stone to the Memory of a Brother whom she tenderly loved and lamented.

Here lies Inter'd the Body of
Mrs. Hannah Beach, Relict of
Mr. Isaac Beach, who Departed this
life Oct'r y[e] 15th, A.D. 1750, in the
79th year of her age.
[A TABLET.]
[The first or uppermost inscription on
this tablet is gone by the slate-stone
being removed. It was that of William Beach, who m. Sarah Hull, and
died in 1751.]
His worthy Relict
Mrs. Sarah Beach, was afterwards
married to the Reverend Dr. Johnson,
President of Kings College at New
York: and died of the small-pox
with much patience, Faith and Resignation, Feb[ry] 9th, 1763, Ætat. 61 : And
lies interred under the Chancel of
Trinity Church there.

Colo. Aaron Benjamin, Nov. 23,
1828, Aged 72 years.
He was an officer of the Revolution and served his country faithfully through the whole of
that struggle for freedom which resulted in the
complete establishment of our National Independence. He also had command of the important post of New London during the 2d war
with Great Britain.
He was a firm friend, a true patriot and an
honest man.

Dorothy Benjamin, wife of Col.
Aaron Benjamin, Born March 3, 1768,
Died Oct. 4, 1853.
Precious are the memories of Home
that was blessed with her love and virtue.
Sacred is the grave of our Mother.

John Benjamin, Son of the late
Col. Aaron Benjamin, died Sept. 22,
1816, aged 43.
He was a man beloved by all who knew him
for his benevolence, strict integrity and christian
character.

Olivia Eloiza Benjamin, Daughter of Col. Aaron Benjamin, Born
March 7, 1792, Died January 6, 1853.

Adele, Daughter of John & Hannah S.
Benjamin, died Oct. 22, 1871, Aged
10 years & 9.mos.
"Abide with me."

Alexr. Gillon Benjamin, son of
John & Anna Maria Benjamin, died
Dec. 6, 1840, aged 1 year, 9 mo. & 8
days.
We shall go to him but he will not come back
to us.

Capt. D. Pulaski Benjamin,
son of Col. Aaron Benjamin, died
Oct. 27, 1883, in his 88th year.

Susan Curtis, his wife, died Nov. 27,
1835, in her 38th year.

William Benjamin, Aged 79,
Born March, 1773, Died May, 1852.

In Memory of
Colo. John Benjamin, who departed this life Sept. 14, 1796, in the
66th year of his age.

In Memory of
Mrs. Lucretia Benjamin, Wife
of the late Colo. John Benjamin, who
died March 22[d], 1803, Aged 69 Years.

John Packinson, son of John &
Hannah S. Benjamin, Died Aug. 7,
1870, aged 1 year & 6 mos.

Here lies Buried the Body of
Mr. John Benjamin, who departed this Life April the 13th, 1773, in
y[e] 73 Year of His Age.

Laura Gertrude, Daughter of W.
M. & S. J. Benjamin, died Sept. 5,
1848, Æ. 4 yrs. & 4 mo.
Oh not in cruelty, not in wrath
The reaper came that day ;
'Twas an angel visited the green earth,
And bore our child away.

In Memory of
Mr. Philip Benjamin, who died
Feb. 20, A. D. 1815 : in the 86 year of
his age.

In Memory of
Mrs. Prudence Benjamin, Wife
of Mr. Philip Benjamin, who died
Febr. 19th, 1795 : in the 64th year of
her age.

In Memory of
Gideon Benjamin, who died Nov.
5, 1846, Aged 87 yrs.

In memory of
Sarah Benjamin, wife of Gideon
Benjamin, who died Jan. 16, 1841, in
the 81 year of her age.

Sarah Marie, wife of William Ben-
jamin, Aged 71, Born Oct. 1782, Died
April, 1853.
[MONUMENT.]
Sacred to the memory of
William Benjamin, Born January
1, 1800, Died March 2, 1862.
Mark the perfect man, and behold the
upright for the end of that man is peace.

In Memory of
William Benjamin, son of Capt.
D. Pulaski & Susan Benjamin, who
died Dec. 16, 1835, Aged 4 years.
God took him away from mortal sorrow
Before his little heart was ripen,
For a bright long day without a morrow,
To join his mother in the songs of heaven.

Here lies intered the Body of
Mr. Roger Bessin (?), late of Antigua, who departed this life Oct. y[e]
26th, 1743, Aetatis 47, Having given a
100 pounds to the Church of England
in this town.

Here lie yᵉ remains of
Eunice Anne Birdsey, Dauʳ of
Mr. Everett & Mrs. Phebe Birdsey,
who died Sept. 19, 1773, Aged 3 years
& 2 Months.

In Memory of
Everett Birdsey, who died Oct. 30,
1845, Æ. 68.

In Memory of
Mary, wife of Everett Birdsey, who
died Oct. 4, 1830, Aged 54 years.

In Memory of
Sarah Birdsey, Daugʳ of Mr. Everett & Mrs. Phoebe Birdsey, who departed this Life May 9ᵗʰ, 1773, Aged
9 Months.

In memory of
William Birdsey, Son of Mr. Ev-
erett & Mrs. Phebe Birdsey, who died
August the 12, A.D. 1776, in the 2ᵈ
Year of His Age.

Here lie the remains of
Mr. William Birdsey, who died
Sept. 10ᵗʰ, 1795, Aged 76 Years.
Reader, reflect when you these lines peruse
On thy own self, What thou art & When
The grim triumphant tyrant Death may come
Oh ! be then like to him, & meet it, good.

In Memory of
Mary Blakeman, Wife of Elijah
Blakeman, & Daughter of Samuel
Hubbell, who died Novr. 22ᵈ, 1809,
Aged 30 years & 8 months.

William Hubbell, Died in Wash-
ington, North Carolina, Oct. 1ˢᵗ, 1809
Æt. 32.
Behold and see as you pass by,
As you are now so once was I,
As I am now soon you will be,
Prepare for death and follow me.

Mr. Phinehas Blakeman, Died
Nov. 28, 1812 ; aged 66 yrs.

Caroline E. Bowdin, Daughter of
Rev. John Bowden, D.D., LL.D. died
Jan. 22, 1877.
Blessed are the dead who die in the Lord.

Margaret, Daughter of Rev. John
Bowden, D.D., died March 19, 1880.

Sacred to the Memory of
Mrs. Mary Bowden, Relict of the
late Rev. John Bowden, D.D., who
died Dec. 29, 1819 : aged 64 years.
The kind friend,
The affectionate Mother,
The faithful Wife,
The exemplary Christian.

Amelia J. Bowden, Died Jan. 21,
1872.

Here lyes yᵉ Body of
Mrs. Anne Brooks, Wife of Mr.
David Brooks, Who Departed this
life October yᵉ 6ᵗʰ, 1766, in yᵉ 47 year
of Her Age.

Here lyes Buried the Body of
Mr. David Brooks, Who departed
this Life June yᵉ 11ᵗʰ, 1766, in yᵉ 47ᵗʰ
year of His Age.

In Memory of
Mrs. Elizabeth Brooks, the Beloved Consort of Mr. Benjamin Brooks,
who departed this Mortal life on the
9ᵗʰ of October, 1773, in yᵉ 28 year of
Her Age.

In Memory of
Isaac Brooks, who died July 11,
1797, aged 17 years.

In memory of
Joseph Brooks, who died Oct. 22,
1787, aged 39 years.

Here lyes yᵉ Body of
Dinah Browne, Dautʳ to James &
Elizabeth Browne, Died Janʳ yᵉ 5ᵗʰ,
1739, in yᵉ 24ᵗʰ Year of Her Age.

In Memory of
Joseph Brown, who Died Octbr. yᵉ
25, A.D. 1757, Aged 70 [?] yrs. & 6
Months.

Sacred To the memory of
Ruth Brown, who was born in this
town October 10, 1779, and died in
New York, March 6ᵗʰ, 1846 : in the
67ᵗʰ year of her age.
Also of her daughter
Susan A. Chamberlin, who was
born March 3ᵈ, 1804, and died Janu-
ary 26ᵗʰ, 1826, in the 23ᵈ year of her
age.
Blessed are the dead who die in the Lord.
Rev. XIV. 13.

In Memory of
Mary, Daughter of Mr. Joseph & Mrs.
Mehetable Bryan, who died November 1, A.D. 1753, aged 3 Years & ten
days.

In Memory of
Ann, wife of Ephraim Burritt, who
died Mar. 19, 1846, Æ. 80.

This stone is erected in memory of
Mr. Ephraim Burrett, Junr.,
who departed this life Oct. 26ᵗʰ, 1802,
in the 40ᵗʰ year of his age.
And in memory of
Abel Burritt, a child 6 weeks old,
son of Ephraim Burritt, Jur. & Ann
his Wife.

In Memory of
Mr. Ephraim Burritt, who died
August 18th, 1807, in the 77th year of
his age,

Here lies Buried the body of
Mrs. Phebe Burritt, wife of Mr.
Ephraim Burritt, Who died Oct. 26th,
1708, in the 67th Year of her Age.

In Memory of
Lewis Burritt, Who died Jan. 8,
1839, in the 67 Year of his age.

In Memory of
Esther Burritt, Wife of Lewis Burritt, who died Oct. 10, 1839: in the
61 year of her age.

Here lies Buried the Body of
Mr. Charles Burroughs, Junr.,
Who Departed this Life July the 12th
A. D. 1770, in the 40th year of his age.

Here lyes ye Body of
Mrs. Elizabeth Burroughs, Wife
to Mr. Stephen Burroughs, Dautr. of
Mr. Joseph & Mrs. Parnai Brown,
Who died December 4th, 1764, in ye
36th Year of Her Age.

In Memory of
Lettice, Wife of Charles Burroughs,
who died July 16, 1802, aged 64 years.
Behold and see as you pass by,
As you are now so once was I.
As I am now so you must be,
Prepare for death and follow me.

William Butler, Died Feb. 5, 1857,
Æ 68.
"Blessed are the dead who die in the Lord."

Mary Ann, Relict of William Butler, Died July 30, 1866, Æ. 57 yrs.

In Memory of
Mr. Legrand Cannon, who departed this Life June 2d, 1789, in the
57th Year of his Age.

Here lies intered
LeGrand, son to LeGrand and Char-
ity Cannon, Who departed this Life
ye 30th of Augst, A. D. 1775, Aged 4
years.
Kind Reader,
A youthful Soul Solaced on high.
Think thou on thy Mortality.

Sacred to the Memory of
Mrs. Francis Chapman, who exchanged this Life in hope of a better
one the 30th of December, A.D. 1783,
in the 80th Year of her Age.

Sacred to the Memory of
Mr. George Chapman, who exchanged this Life in hopes of a better
on the 6th June, A. D. 1777, in the
forty eighth Year of his Age.

Bessie Coleman, Born May 30,
1875, Died April 11, 1882.

Luther Copley, Died March 28,
1846, Æ. 64.

Betsey, Wife of Luther Copley, Died
Sept. 2, 1852, Æ. 68.

Asa Curtis, died Feb. 11, 1850, Æ.
76 y'rs.

Susan, the wife of Asa Curtis, died
Feb. 2, A.D. 1859, aged 85.

Mary Eliza, daughter of Asa &
Susanna Curtis, died Oct. 28, 1722,
aged 20 years.

In Memory of
Chloe, Wife of Hannibal Curtiss, who
died April 24, 1828, Aged 72.
God has bereaved me of My wife,
His will for him I stood,
It was God and he is Kind,
He does what seemeth him good.

In Memory of
Mr. William Curtis, who died
Aug. 14th, 1803, in the 40th Year of
his Age.

Francis, Wife of William Curtis,
Died Feb. 7, 1854, Æ. 85.

Freddie, son of Claudus B. & Harriet Curtis, died Apr. 5, 1854, Æ 2
y'rs & 8 mo.

Here lyes Buried the Body of
Mrs. Hannah Curtiss, Wife to Mr.
Ephraim Curtiss, Who Departed this
life Feb. ye 2d, 1761, in ye 64th Year
of Her Age.

In Memory of
Isaac J. Curtiss, who died July 17,
1815, Æ 78 yrs. & 4 mo.

In Memory of
Charity, wife of Isaac Curtiss, who
died Dec. 16, 1846, Æ 75 Years.

Charity, Daughter of Isaac J. &
Charity Curtis, died Aug. 19, 1801.

In Memory of
Mr. Jeremiah Judson Curtiss,
who Departed this Life Sept. ye 4th,
A.D. 1782, in ye 67th year of his Age.

In memory of
Thomas Curtis, Who died May 25th
1787, Æ 47. Also of three Children
of Thomas & Anna Curtis.

Benjamin, died at Sea Sept. 1789,
Æt 19.

Catharine, Died at N. York, Jan.
17th, 1798, Æt. 21.

Reuben, Died at Sea, Feb. 8th, 1802,
Æt. 23.

[A Broken Stone.]
May 21, 1815, aged 36 years. [E. C. on the foot stone.]

Sacred to the Memory of
Elizabeth Anne Davies, Daughter of Henry Davies, Esqr., late of New York, who died on the 23d of Dec. 1799, in the 19th Year of her Age.
Rich in every Virtue & directed by a sound understanding, she was ever in pursuit of useful knowledge while the cheerfulness with which she discharged her duty endeared her to all her Relatives and Friends: having a mind stored with ever useful & ornamented acquirements, she seemed fitted for an example for the young & beautiful, & a Comfort to the Aged, When by a momentary stroke of Death she was called from health and Youth to a life of everlasting felicity. [Several lines effaced.]

Sacred to the Memory of
Henry Davies, Esqr., late of New York, and formerly of his Britanic Majesty's Navy in which he discharged many offices of trust and importance with honor to himself and integrity to his Country. After living in the constant practice of piety toward God and benevolence to MEN; after fulfilling every duty in social and domestic Life, died at this place on the 28th day of April, 1802, in the 57 year of his age in full hope of receiving that reward which a redeemer hath purchased for all who trust in him.

Charles S., son of Garry & Sally Dayton, died Aug. 8, 1825, aged 1 year and 10 months.

Betsey, daughter of Garry & Sally Dayton, died Dec. 18, 1827, aged 9 years and 9 Mo.
So fades the lovely blooming flower,
Frail smiling solace of an hour.

Sarah Dayton, Died Aug. 4, 1846, Æ 49 years.

In Memory of
Peggy, wife of Henry Dean, who died Feb. 10, 1822, in her 28 year.

Albert DeForest, died Sept. 9, 1826, aged 25 years.

Samuel E., died Sept. 11, 1810, aged 16 Mos.

Samuel 2d, died Jan. 1814, aged 2 years.
Children of Daniel & Phebe De Forest.

Ephrian DeForest, Died Oct. 27, 1848, Æ 61 yrs.

Phebe, wife of Daniel DeForest, Died March 18, 1852, Æ. 82.

Daniel DeForest, Died July 30, 1833, aged 62 years.

David, son of Mr. Samuel & Mrs. Ruth Edwards, died Oct. 6, 1815, aged 7 years.

John C. Fairchild, died Feb. 22, 1825, Aged 79.

Ruth, His Wife, Died Oct. 28, 1804, Aged 56.

Sacred to the Memory of
Sarah Avery, Daughter of John C. & Ruth Fairchild, Born in this town Feb. 28th, 1773. Died in New York, May 6th, 1837, Aged 64 years, 2 months & 6 days.
Respected and beloved by all ; a most brilliant example of virtue and loveliness she departed this life rejoicing in the hope of a glorious immortality.
Thou hast taught us to live and for death to prepare,
By example and precepts most true,
May we copy thy virtues, thy glory to share,
Adieu dearest Sister, adieu.
Thou lived'st but to merit life better than this
Where the righteous ever shall dwell ;
Thou art gone to those mansions of heavenly bliss,
Farewell dearest mother, farewell.

In Memory of
Robert Wells, son of William and Hannah Fairchild, who departed this life Sept. 18, 1805.

Lewis C., son of Benjamin & Eunice Fairchild, died April 22, 1829, aged 7 yrs. & 8 mo.
Dear little boy thy years were few,
And suffering was thy lot below.
Jesus called, thou hast obey'd
And left a world of pain and wo.

Father
Dennis Fitch, Born Nov. 19, 1798, Died Jan. 25, 1827.

Sarah Francis, Daughter of Dennis & Eunice Fitch, Born Nov. 9, 1825, Died Aug. 18, 1827.

Mother
Eunice Birdsey, Wife of Dennis Fitch, Born Aug. 25, 1799, Died Jan. 18, 1877.

Herona, Wife of Edmond Freeman, Died Aug. 4, 1855, Æ 38.

In memory of
Esther, ye Wife of Mr. Stephen Frost, who died Novemr ye 2d, 1753, in ye 30th year of Her Age.

Elizabeth Cannon, Wife of Alexander S. Gorden, Died April 7, 1876, Aged 84 yrs. 7 mo.

In Memory of
Mr. Frederick Hawley, who Departed this life March ye 16th, 1774, in ye 39th year of his age.

Charity Hubbell, Died March 21, 1866, Æ 88. Erected by the Wardens of Christ Church.

In Memory of
Elizabeth Hubbell, wife of Silas Hubbell, died Feb. 5, 1829, Æt. 74 yrs.

In Memory of
Capt. Ezra Hubbell, who was lost at sea Sept. 1801, in the 35 Year of his Age.

Mrs. Mary Alice, Wife of Capt Ezra Hubbell, Died August 11, 1811, Aged 28 Years.

In Memory of
Mr. Joseph Hubbell, who departed this life May 9th, 1804, in the 26th year of his age.
This mortal shall put on immortality.
And of
Benjamin [out—stone broken.]

Here lyes Buried the Body of
Mrs. Sarah Hubbell, Wife of Mr. Joseph Hubbell, who died March 9th, 1790, Aged 56 Years.

In Memory of
Silas Hubbell, who died Nov. 30, 1812, Aged 60 years.

William Hubbell, Died Feb. 1856, Æ 55.

In Memory of
Mrs. Elizabeth Hurd, Wife of Mr. Gilead Hurd, who departed this life Aug. 8, 1787, in the [out] year of her Age.

In Memory of
Jane, wife of Jacob Hurd, who died May 2, 1825, aged 63 Years.

In Memory of
Daniel Jackson, a Revolutionary pensioner, who died Aug. 25, 1841, aged 78 yrs.

In Memory of
Elizabeth, Wife of Daniel Jackson, who died March 17, 1839, Aged 78 yrs.

In Memory of
Daniel Jackson, who died Aug. 16, 1829, Aged 38 years.
Ah 'tis a holy rite remembrance of the dead, That will not oblivion blight around the grave be shed.

Frederick, Son of Whitney & Clemtine Jackson, who died July 5, 1836, Æ 7 years & 9 mo.

In Memory of
Charles Jarvis, late of London, who died Oct. 8, 1840, aged 76.

Here lyes ye Body of
Mrs. Sarah Jeans, Deceased October yᵉ 16, 1739, in yᵉ 72 year of her age.

Here lyes ye Body of
Mr. William Jeans, Deceased Nov'r yᵉ 17th, 1726, in yᵉ 79th Year of His Age.

Sacred to the Memory of three most affectionate Sisters, The daughters of Wᵐ. Samuel Johnson, Esqr. And Anne his Wife.

Sarah Johnson, Nata April 8th, A. D. 1754; Obiit 20th June, A. D. 1782.

Mary Johnson, Nata April 19th, A. D. 1759; Obiit. December 23d, A. D. 1783.

Gloriana Anne Alden, the affectionate Wife of Roger Alden, Esqr. Nata March 17th, A. D. 1757, Obiit. March 4th, 1785.

M. S. Samuelis Johnson, D.D., Collegii Regalis Novi Eboraci Præsidis prmi et hujus Ecclesiæ nuper Rectoris. Natus Die 14 to. Octob. 1696, Obit. 6 to. Jan. 1772.*
In decent dignity and modest mien,
The cheerful heart and countenance serene
If pure religion and unsullied truth,
His age's solace, and his search in youth,
If piety in all the paths he trod
Still rising vigorous to his Lord and God;
If Charity thro' all the race he ran,
Still willing well, and doing good to man:
If learning, free from pedantry and pride;
If Faith and Virtue, walking side by side;
If well to mark his being's aim and end,
To shine thro' life a Husband, Father, Friend,
If these ambition in thy soul can raise,
Excite thy reverence, or demand thy praise;
Reader, ere yet thou quit this earthly scene,
Revere his name, and be what he has been.
Myles Cooper.

Here lyes the body of
Mr. John Johnson, who decᵈ Feburʳ yᵉ 8th, 1725, Aged 75.

In Memory of
Mr. Archibald Jones, Who died May 24, 1800, Aged 60 years.

In Memory of
Mrs. Sarah, consort of Mr. Archibald Jones, Who died June 8th, 1792, Aged 53 years.

Hannah Jones, Died Sept. 8, 1855, Æ 81.

---

* This inscription is taken from Mr. J. W. Barber's Historical Collections, for the reason that the slate-stone inlaid on the tablet, on which the lettering was placed, is entirely gone. The same is true as to the slate-stone on several other tablets in this burying-place.

James Jones, Born March 24, 1775, Died April 6, 1853.

Esther, wife of James Jones, Born Sept. 25, 1782, Died May 5, 1854.

In Memory of
John Jones, who died Aug. 1, 1852, Aged 34 years.

Hannah Jones, wife of John Jones, Died Oct. 21, 1884, Aged 85 yrs.

Joseph Jones, Died Nov. 25, 1845, Æ. 76.

[TABLET.]
In Memory of
Mrs. Mary Jones, consort of Joel Jones and eldest daughter of Isaac J. Curtis, who departed this life Jan. 15, 1817 ; in the 25 year of her age ; leaving with her afflicted friends a tender infant which survived until April 21, 1817, when it declined the bitter cup of life and joined its departed Mother; aged 4 months & 22 days.

Also in Memory of
Julius Curtis, son of Joel & Mary Jones, who departed this life Sept. 20, 1815, aged 3 years and 5 months.
Unerring wisdom drew the awful veil
Bade the eye languish and the cheek grow pale,
From lips beloved the vital warmth retired,
And life's faint lustre silently expired ;
The immortal spirit reached its destined height,
A star forever in the realms of light.
Here also lies entombed the remains of *Dillissenea,* eldest son of Isaac J. & Charity Curtis, who after long and distressing illness which he bore with Christian fortitude, resigned his soul to God who gave it, on the 11 of June, 1817, in the 21 year of his age.
When tides of youthful blood run high,
And promised scenes of joy draw nigh,
Youth presuming, beauty blooming,
O ! how dreadful 'tis to die.

Woolsey S., son of John & Hannah Jones, Died May 16, 1849, Aged 4 years & 4 mo.

George F., Son of Samuel & Betsey Judson, died Aug. 16, 1820, aged 7 years & 4 months.

Here are Intered the Remains of *Mr. John Keyes,* who departed this Life March 29th, A. D. 1753, in his 50th year.

Here lyes y* Body of
Dr. James Laborie, Physician, Died Dec'r y* 26, 1739, in y* 48th Year of His Age.

George Lampson, Died May 22, 1870, Æ. 70 yrs.

Here lyes Buried the Body of *William Lamson,* Who Departed this Life Jany. y* 21st, A. D. 1755, Aged 60 Years, 2 Months & 27 Ds.

Charles T., Died Dec. 21, 1838, Aged 14 yrs. & 11 Mos.
Be ye also ready.

Caroline L., Died July 1, 1844, Aged 18 yrs. & 5 Mos,
In the midst of life we are in death.
Children of George & Betsey M. Lamson.

George Henry, infant son of Capt. L. H. & A. E. Layfield, died Nov. 9, 1852.

In Memory of
Capt. Agur Tomlinson Lewis, who died March 12, 1815, Aged 38 Years.
Peace to his ashes, and eternal rest to his departed spirit.

Here lyes Buried the Body of *Collo. Edmond Lewis,* Who Departed this life May 14th, 1757, in ye 78 Year of his Age.
Calm he commits his flesh to Dust,
'Till the last trumpet wakes the Just,
And he immortalized shall Rise
To mansions far beyond the skies.

Here lyes Buried y* Body of *Mrs. Hannah Lewis,* wife to Colo. Edmond Lewis, who Departed this life July y* 13th, 1756, in y* 75th Year of Her Age.

In Memory of
Daniel A. Lewis, son of Alpheus & Phebe Lewis, who died March 31, 1831, aged 11 yrs. & 1 mo.

Sacred to the Memory of
Mr. David Lewis, who departed this Life the 13th day of November, 1783, in the 74th Year of his Age.

Mr. Eli Lewis, died Dec. 24, 1818, Aged 80.

Mrs. Naomi Lewis, wife of Mr. Eli Lewis, died Feb. 3, 1814, aged 70 years.

Here lyes y* Body of
James Walker Lewis, Son of Mr. Eli Lewis, who departed this life May 11, 1772, in y* 5th Year of his Age.

In Memory of
Mrs. Hannah Lewis, Wife of Capt. James Lewis, Who died July 2d, 1756, Aged 75 Years.

Mr. Isaac Lewis, died August 31, 1804, in the 70 Year of his Age.

23

In memory of 3 Children of Mr. James & Mrs. Sarah Lewis.

James, died Sep. 12, 1777, in his 5th Year.

David Booth, died Sept. 22, 1777, in his 3d Year.

Rebecca, died Sep. 24, 1777, Aged 6 Months.

In Memory of
Capt. James Lewis, Who departed this life Janr. the 29th, 1766, Aged 89 Years.

In Memory of
Mr. James Lewis, Who departed this life August 13th, 1779, Aged 39 Years.

Just as he arrived, to those scenes
Where pleasures seemed to flow,
Just as he tasted those sweet charmes
Death struck the fatal blow.

Here Lies intered
Mr. Joseph Lewis, who died July 3d, A. D. 1756, Æt. 74.

Here lies the Body of
Mrs. Phebe Lewis, wife of Mr. Joseph Lewis, who died Septr. ye 11, 1753, Aged 62 Years.

In Memory of
Phebe Lewis, Daur. of Mr. David & Mrs. Phebe Lewis, who died October ye 2d, A. D. 1764, Aged 9 years.

Pheneas & Phebe, Son & Daughter of Mr. David & Mrs. Phebe Lewis, died Sept. ye 7, 1751. Pheneas in the 17th Year of his Age: Phebe aged 3 Years.

Col. Philo Lewis, departed this life Nov. 7, 1836, Aged 78 years & 3 Mo.

Mrs. Charity Lewis, wife of Col. Philo Lewis, died Dec. 21, 1842, aged 82 Years.

In Memory of
Capt. Nathl. Sherman Lewis, who died Feb. 14, 1812, aged 82.

Mary, Wife of Capt. N. S. Lewis, died April 10, 1819, age 83.

Francis, their daughter, died July 1, 1804, aged 37.

James, son of James & Hannah Lockwood, Died Febr. 21, 1818, Aged 10 yrs. & 9 ds.

Here lies the Body of
Mr. Nehemiah Loring, Aged 44 Years, 6 Mo. & 29 Ds. Departed this Life January the 9th, 1730-31.

Here lyes the Body of
Mrs. Elizabeth Loring, wife of Mr. Nehemiah Loring. Aged 57 Years, 1 m. & 6 days, Died July 20, 1797.

In Memory of
Capt. Phinehas Lovejoy, Junr. who departed this life Sept. 26, 1803, Æt. 41.

Death like an overflowing stream,
Sweeps us away, our life's a dream,
An empty tale: a morning flower,
Cut down and withered in and hour.

In Memory of
Anna Roberts Lynus, Daughter of Mr. Robert & Mrs. Mary Linus, who departed this Life May 5th, 1786, Aged 1 year 6 months & 18 days.

Henry Lundy, died June 14, 1879, Aged 70.

Charlotte, wife of Henry Lundy, died Nov. 17, 1857, Aged 50.

And now she lies with folded hands
In an untroubled sleep;
With tearless eyes and peaceful heart,
Where none can make her weep.

In Memory of
Elijah Marshall, who died May 3, 1839, aged 57.

In Memory of
Lucy, wife of Elijah Marshall, who died April 1, 1840, aged 56.

Here lieth the Body of
Mr. Paul Maverick, who Departed this Life Janry. the 20th, Anno Dom 1745-6 in the 52nd year of his age.

In Memory of
Ann, wife of John McEwen, who died Dec. 4, 1824, Aged 72 Years.

In Memory of
John McEwen, a Revolutionary soldier who died Sept. 29, 1842, aged 98 years.

In Memory of
Nancy McEwen, who departed this life Feb. 7, 1831, Æ 45.

William McEwen, Died Aug. 18, 1851, Æ. 40.

William McEwen, Died Nov. 10, 1871, Aged 96.

In Memory of
Mary McEwen, wife of William McEwen, who died Dec. 28, 1842, Aged 62 Yrs.

Sarah Maria, Daughter of William & Mary McEwen, died Nov. 11, 1836, Æ. 18 yrs. & 8 mo.

Two children of Mr. Aaron & Mrs. Chloe Nichols,

Proctor Thomas, died August 26, 1815, aged 2 yrs. & 8 mo.

Isabella, died August 30, 1815, aged 11 months.

[The following 23 inscriptions are found in the Nicoll's plot.]

[MONUMENT.]

Sacred to the Memory of

Francis H. Nicoll, son of the late Genl. Matthias Nicoll, who died Sept. 24, 1842, aged 57 years.

It may be truly said of him that he was a father to the fatherless, a friend to the widow, kind and benevolent to the poor.

This stone is erected by his surviving brother and sisters, who live to mourn his loss.

Our Mother's Grave.

[MONUMENT—West side.]

Genl. Matthias Nicoll, Born 11th October, 1758, Died 11th February, 1830.

At Peace with his God,
Himself and the world,
He died lamented,
By all who knew him.

[South side.]

Sarah, Relict of Genl. Matthias Nicoll, Decd. Jan. 6, 1848, Aged 90 Years.

The righteous shall be had in everlasting remembrance.

[East side.]

Died at Canton, in China, on the first day of November, 1829, where his remains are interred.

George Robert Dowdall, Son-in-law of Genl. Matthias Nicoll, in the 47th year of his age.

Commander of the ship Ajax. In his profession he was inferior to none, And in the discharge of all Social duties as Husband, Father, Friend and Citizen, few excelled him.

[North side.]

Also Died at Canton, on the 27th of October, 1829, in the 31st year of his age,

Edward Nicoll, First officer of the ship Ajax, And Son of Genl. Matthias Nicoll.

He was beloved by all who knew him.

In Memory of

Mary Magalene Nicoll Clinch, died Sept. 3, 1822, aged 9 months and 11 days.

David Poore, Died April 5, 1853, Æ. 70.

In Memory of

Louisa, the wife of David Poore and daughter of General Matthias Nicoll, who departed this life January 19th, 1832 ; Aged 34 Years.

She sleeps but to wake at the call of her God.

In Memory of

Samuel Charles Nicoll, Infant son of David & Louisa Poore, who departed this life June 5, 1833, Aged 17 Months and 11 days.

"I shall go to him, but he shall not return to me." 2 Samuel, 12 C., 25 V.

[MONUMENT.]

Francis Holland.

Fanny.

Children of J. L. & A. F. Hubbard.

Anna G. Chevallie, wife of the late Henry Chevallie, of Richmond, Va. Died June 8, 1870.

Edward H. Turk, died March 4, 1841, aged 16 yrs.

In Memory of

Catharine Jones, late wife of David Jones, of New York, Merchant, who departed this life in this town on the 21st day of April, 1798, in the 63 year of her Age.

Beloved while living by all her Relatives and acquaintance, and much lamented by them at her death.

Elizabeth H., Daughter of the late A. H. Turk, died Jan. 9, 1847, Æ 17 yrs.

In death as well as in life she was truly a lovely character, a flower unfaded yet prepared to die.

Sacred to the Memory of

David Jones, late of New York, Merchant, A Man who to the keenest Sensibility to the Distresses of others, possessed the greatest Fortitude in supporting his own.

Placed in the most trying Situations of life no murmur at the Dispensations of Providence passed his Lips, After a Life of strict Integrity, he met Death with that cheerful Resignation which true Christianity alone can inspire.

He died at this place on the 11th day of October, 1806, in the 73d Year of his Age.

Elizah, Widow of Geo. R. Dowdall, Died Sept. 7, 1851, Æ 65.

A devoted Mother, a kind friend, a sincere Christian. Her record is on high.

[MONUMENT.]

Samuel C. Nicoll, Born May 13, 1782, Died May 1, 1850.

In full communion with the Christian Church, he died lamented as he had lived beloved.

Elvira Nicoll, wife of Samuel C. Nicoll, and daughter of Col. Aaron Benjamin, Born Feb. 8, 1794, Died April 9, 1851.

As wife, daughter, sister, woman, a light and blessing in our pathway which even death cannot extinguish, She yet lives in our Memory and love.

Violetta Seabury Gore, Widow of Richard Gore, and eldest daughter of the late Genl. Matthias Nicoll, Born in Stratford, 29ᵗʰ December, 1783; Died in New York, 5ᵗʰ November, 1854.
> O may I find in death
> A hiding place with God,
> Secure from woe and sin till called
> To share his blessed abode.

Elizabeth Nicoll, Widow of John Springs, of South Carolina, and daughter of the late Genl. Matthias Nicoll, of Stratford, Born Sept. 21, 1800, Decd. in Petersburgh, Va., March 13, 1872.
> "I know that my Redeemer liveth, and that He shall Stand at the latter day upon the Earth, and though after my skin worms destroy this body, yet in my flesh shall I see God."

Sacred to the Memory of
Maria Nicoll, wife of Ahasuerus Turk, deceased: Born Mar. 30, 1791, Died April 17, 1882.

In Memory of
Isaac Nichols, who died May 22, A. D. 1776, in the 41ˢᵗ Year of his Age.

In Memory of
Mrs. Sarah Nichols, Relict of Mr. Isaac Nichols, who died Oct. 5, 1815, Aged 81 years.

Here lies Buried the Body of
Theophilus Nichols, Esqr., Who departed this Life April the 7ᵗʰ, 1774, Aged 71 Years.

Here lies Buried the Body of
Sarah Nichols, Wife to Theophilus Nichols, Esqr., Who departed this Life sept. the 26ᵗʰ, 1769, in the 68ᵗʰ Year of Her Age.

Here Lyes Buried the Body of
Mrs. Mehetable Nichols, Wife of Theophilus Nichols, Esq. Who died September ye 20ᵗʰ, 1771, Aged 52 Years.

[TABLET.]
In Memory of
Mrs. Abigail Norris, Wife of Robert Norris, who departed this life August 19ᵗʰ, 1805, aged 26 Years, 2 Months & 9 Days.
I shall be satisfied When I awake with thy likeness.

In Memory of
Betsey, wife of Capt. Samuel Peck, who died Jan. 4, 1835, Æ 54 yrs.

In Memory of
Capt. Samuel Peck, who died Aug. 11, 1837, Æ. 59 yrs.

In Memory of
Delia, dau. of Capt. Samuel Peck, who died March 21, 1835, Aged 14 Years and 5 Months.

Henry, son of Capt. Samuel & Betsey Peck, died May 7, 1826, aged 9 years.

Here lyes Buried yᵉ Body of
Mr. Jonathan Pitman, Who died December 1st, 1731, Aged 91 Years.

David, the Son of Mr. Peter & Mrs. Mary Pixlee, Died Sept. the 18, 1751, in yᵉ 9 year of his age.

Blessed are the dead who die in the Lord.
Emeline A., Daughter of Samuel & Eliza Plumb, died Jan. 8, 1851, Æ. 20 yrs.
The Choir of Christ Church erect this stone to the memory of their late associate.

Frederick F. Plumb, Son of Samuel & Eliza Plumb, died Feb. 14, 1862, Æ. 19.

In Memory of
Lucius Plumb, who died June 7, 1862, Æ. 70.
Rest in Peace.

Our Mother.
Julia, wife of Lucius Plumb, died Oct. 12, 1857, Æ. 55 yrs. & 6 Mo.
"Blessed are the dead who die in the Lord."

In Memory of
Miss Mary Porter, who died Jan. 7, 1829, Aged 28 years.

Here lies Interr'd the Body of
Mr. John Pryn, late of Antigua, who Departed this Life November the 23ʳᵈ, 1751, Aged 51 Years.

Harriet E., Relict of James E. Richardson, Died Oct. 5, 1858, In the 41ˢᵗ year of her age.

John Nisbit, son of James E. & Harriet E. Richardson, died Oct. 31, 1854, Æ. 8 yrs. & 9 mo.

James, son of Patrick & Catharine Riley, Died Oct. 25, 1845: aged 13 Months,

In Memory of
Obed Roberts, who died Dec. 1, 1824: Aged 72.

Alfred, son of John & Mary Roosevelt, Died Sept. 27, 1810, aged 71 years.

In Memory of
John Roosevelt, who died Nov. 14, 1810, aged 57 years.

In Memory of
Ann Roosevelt, wife of John Roosevelt, who died Feb. 15, 1834: Æ 78.

Here rests in Peace the body of
Elizabeth, wife of Jacob June, who
departed this life the 2ᵈ day of September, A. D. 1799, of the then prevailing Epidemic: Aged 39 years,
6 mo. and 26 days.
To her Memory this token of affectionate
esteem is dedicated by her surviving partner.

Of lovely form, kind and sincere,
Was she that now reposes here,
In her each milder virtue met,
Virtues that I can never forget,
But patiently those joys resign,
Which heaven decreed no longer mine.

Mary Wells, the wife of John Roosevelt, died March 1, 1863, Æ. 82 Years.

In Memory of
Mary E., daughter of John & Mary
Roosevelt, who died March 9, 1839,
aged 24 years.

In Memory of
Ann Satterly, who died June 2,
1828, in the 32 year of her age.

Here lies the Body of
Mr. Thomas Salmon, who was
born in Chippenham, in England,
was a worthy member of yᵉ Church
of England here, & yᵉ ingenious
Architect of the Church, & Departed
this Life Jany. 20ᵗʰ, 1749-50, in yᵉ 57ᵗʰ
year of his age.

Here lies yᵉ Body of
Mrs. Sarah Salmon, the wife of
Mr. Thos. Salmon, who departed this
life March yᵉ 15ᵗʰ, 1750, aged 55
Years.

Charles Scott, died Dec. 21, 1827,
Æ. 13.

Here lies the Body of
Mr. Ebenezer Sherman, Junr.,
who departed this life January 14ᵗʰ,
A. D. 1764, in the 44ᵗʰ Year of His
Age.

Here lyes Buried yᵉ Body of
Mrs. Mary Sherman, Wife to Mr.
Ebenezer Sherman, Who Departed
this Life March yᵉ 30ᵗʰ, A. D. 1752,
Aged 35 years & 4 mo.

In Memory of
Mrs. Elizabeth Sherman, Wife to
Mr. Timothy Sherman: who died
December 10ᵗʰ, 1766, in yᵉ 52ᵈ Year
of Her Age.

In Memory of
Mrs. Naomi Sherman, Wife to
Mr. Timothy Sherman, who departed
this life Jany. 27ᵗʰ, 1797, In the 85ᵗʰ
Year of her Age.

William E., son of John & Mariah
Sherman, Died April 7, 1833, Æ 2 yrs.
& 3 mo.

In Memory of
Capt. John Silby, who died May 1,
1825, aged 55 years.

In Memory of
Mrs. Betsey Silby, wife of Mr. John
Silbey, who died Feb. 4, 1822, aged 44
years & 9 months.

This Stone is erected by John Silby,
Jr., In Memory of his Father,
Mr. John Silby, who died Decr.
25th, 1800.

Everett Davis, Son of Isaac & Sarah
C. Sniffin, Died Jan. 14, 1843, Aged
8 mo.

John Stratton, Died Nov. 22, 1850,
Æ. 79.

Charity, Wife of John Stratton, Died
Nov. 15, 1871, Aged 89.

In Memory of
Elizabeth Thatcher, who died
April 10, 1817, Æ. 70 yrs.

In Memory of 2 Children of Mr. Joseph & Mrs. Mary Thompson, viz:
Isaac, who died Octr. 17ᵗʰ, 1776, aged
3 years, 4 months & 18 days, & also
Joel, who died October 1716, aged 1
Year.

In Memory of
Mr. Joseph Thompson, Junr.,
who departed this Life Octr. 17, A. D.
1776, Aged 29 years & 19 days.

Mrs. Temperance Thompson,
Wife of Mr. Joseph Thompson, Departed this Life Jany 8ᵗʰ, 1790, In
the 70 Year of her Age.

In Memory of
Mrs. Esther, relict of Doct. Abraham
Tomlinson, who died Dec. 28, 1831,
aged 66 yrs. & 4 mo.

John, Son of Wᵐ. & Diana Vance,
died Mar. 18, 1828, Æt. 2 yrs.

Here lies Intered the Body of
Mr. Peter Viou, who Departed this
life November the 11ᵗʰ, 1751, in the
25ᵗʰ year of his age.

Miss Frances Waldecker, died
Sept. 22, 1813, aged 67 years.

Miss Sarah Waldecker, died
April 10, 1812, aged 58 years.

In Memory of
James Walker, Esqr., Who departed this Life June 9ᵗʰ, 1796, In the
81ˢᵗ Year of his Age.

Mrs. Jerusha Walker, Relict of James Walker, Esqr. Died July 8th, 1803, in the 87th year of her age.

In Memory of
Benjamin Wells, who died June 8, 1818, age 73 years.

In Memory of
Elizabeth, wife of Benjamin Wells, who died Oct. 29, 1822, aged 71 years.

In Memory of
Curtiss J. Wells, who died June 4, 1847, Æ. 77 years.

Ruth Hawley, the wife of Curtiss J. Wells, died April 24, 1863, Æ. 86 Years.

In Memory of
Legrand Wells, who died April 15, 1848, Æ. 84.

In Memory of
Phebe, wife of Legrand Wells, who died Oct. 23, 1810, Aged 76 Years.

In Memory of Two Children of Le-Grand & Cate Wells,
Susana, died Oct. 8th, 1803, aged 9 years.
Martha Carline, died August 29th, 1803, aged 2 Years.

In Memory of
Lewis Wells, 3rd, who died April 3rd, 1841, Æ. 41.

Julia, Wife of Lewis Wells, 3rd, Died Jan. 20, 1850, Æ. 50.

Reuben Wells, died June 12, 1859, Æ. 85.

In Memory of
Samuel W. Wells, who died June 11, 1822, Aged 54.
Also
Mary E. Wells, Wife of Samuel W. Wells, died July 1, 1850, aged 81.

Charles S. Whiting, Died Nov. 7, 1845, Æ. 65.
Sally, his wife, Died Nov. 20, 1842, Æ. 62.

Curtis J. Whiting, Died June 14, 1854, Æ. 76 yrs.

Fanny Mott, Wife of Curtis J. Whiting, Died Aug. 22, 1872, Æ. 80 Yrs., 6 Mo.

Catharine A., Daughter of Curtis J. & Fannie M. Whiting, Died Aug. 12, 1874, Æ. 65 Yrs., 6 Mo.

Here lyes Buried the Body of
Mrs. Sarah Wilcox, Wife to Mr. Elisha Wilcox, who died Feb. 10th, 1788, in the 43^d Year of her Age.

Sacred to the Memory of
Mrs. Sarah Ann, the wife of Mr. Daniel Worden, of Goshen, N. Y., who died August 4, 1825, aged 32.

Here lyes Buried ye Body of
Capt. Abram Wooster, Died Sept. ye 1, 1741 (?), In ye 70 Year of his Age.

[TABLET.]
Sacred to the Memory of
Colonel Joseph Wooster, who died December 30th, 1791, Aged 89 Years.
Also of
Mrs. Lucy Wooster, Wife of Colonel Joseph Wooster, who died October 18th, 1760, Aged 32 Years.
And I heard a voice from Heaven saying unto me, Write Blessed are the dead who die in in the Lord.

CHAPTER XIV.

ECCLESIASTICAL PROGRESS.

IN the great excitement and religious controversy following Whitefield's visit to Stratford, considerable changes occurred, some in favor of, and others against, the prosperity of the place. Those things which resulted in renewed religious activity by which two new houses of worship were erected, were in favor, and those which caused the removal from the town of a number of first-class citizens were against the best interests of the place.

Whitefield's stay in Stratford extended to a few hours only. He preached in New Haven on Sunday, and on Monday morning came to Stratford, preached at the meeting-house, probably outside, in the open air; dined with the Rev. Mr. Gold, then went to Fairfield, where he preached in the afternoon of the same day.

The idea of charging Whitefield with extravagancies and turning "the world upside down," in one sermon or in a few hours, is too simple, unless there was something more than human in his preaching, in which case it would be still more dishonorable to make the charge. There had been an unusual revival of religious interest in New England for several years, and Whitefield's preaching was in accord with that revival. After Mr. Whitefield's departure, unlettered, and unlearned men, as well as some who were learned, made vastly more trouble by extravagancies and unwise proceedings than Whitefield ever countenanced, or probably ever dreamed of.

There was great excitement in Stratford, unquestionably, and the one thought or doctrine that produced it, was the question of a decided, definite, clear understanding, as to a personal experience, or " change of heart" in religious things. This was an old orthodox doctrine, then revived, especially in the Calvinistic form. In the Congregational churches some accepted this doctrine as the only assurance of heaven, while others held more to the efficiency of a careful, dutiful life of obedience to, and support of, Bible teachings, to secure the same end. Mr. Gold held to the former—which view has been termed in Congregational churches, as well as others, for over one hundred years, the evangelical—and some of Mr. Gold's leading men held to the latter; and hence, desired and finally secured Mr. Gold's dismission.

In the midst of this controversy and excitement, which lasted ten years, the Rev. Richardson Miner of Unity, an acceptable Congregational minister, and a much esteemed practising physician, resigned his pastorate and joined the Church of England, in 1744. Several families in Stratford had made a like change previous to this, and some followed. The result is seen in the officers of the Episcopal Church.

From 1725, until 1737 or 8, a few men had served in those offices, so far as the records show; namely, John Benjamin, John Kee, Nehemiah Loring and Richard Rogers. In 1739, a much longer list is recorded,[1] indicating, either the increase

---

[1] "Easter Monday, 1739. Church Wardens chosen and appointed to gather the minister's rate and to give our account of it to the Commissary for the year were:

For Stratford {	John Benjamin	
	Zachary Clarke.	
For Ripton {	Joseph Shelton	
	John Beardsley.	

Vestry {
William Smith.
Samuel French.
Samuel Blagge.
William Beach.
Joseph Brown.
Gershom Edwards.
Captain Hubbell.
Ephraim Curtiss.
Lieutenant Fairchild.
Doctor Laborie.
Millar Frost.
Thomas Lattin.
Hugh Curland.

"The same day, Voted that we pay this year towards the support of our minister 4 pence farthing upon the pound of our Ratable Estate." In 1748 the Vestry ' Voted the same Rate to Dr. Johnson that the Dissenters pay to Mr. Gold."

of numbers or a more complete organization and the keeping of a full record.

In 1741, others appear, as: " Edmund Lewis, Esq., Mr. Joseph Lewis, Mr. Jonathan Curtiss, Capt. James Lewis, Mr. Ebenezer Hurd and Dr. William Russell;" and in 1746, Capt. Theophilus Nichols; all but Dr. Russell were of the old Stratford families.

Several of these men had been members in full communion in the Congregational Church from fifteen to twenty years—Edmund Lewis, Esq., and Capt. James Lewis, from fifteen to eighteen, and Capt. Theophilus Nichols and his wife over twenty years.

Hence, it appears that a number of persons of the old way of thinking or the conservative element, who were opposed to the New Light movement, left the Congregational and joined the Episcopal Church, while Mr. Gold continued to preach, and when he was dismissed in 1752, a number of leading men in favor of his preaching, removed from the parish, to North Stratford, Ripton, New Haven; and others went further—to Waterbury, Newtown and New Milford; thus affecting, decidedly, the strength and numbers of the old church and society.

But the increased interest in religion, soon led to new efforts to promote the cause, and hence, as has been recorded, in a previous chapter, the Congregational people built them a new house of worship in 1743, raising the money by a tax on the property held by the members of the society.

The Episcopal Society built a house also in 1743; but on the principle of stock ownership, and not by a public tax; and so far as the author of this history has learned, it was the first house of worship built on this plan in this region of country.

The subscription[1] to secure the money to build this house

---

[1] " We whose names are hereunto subscribed being convinced that it is our duty to contribute what we are able towards building a Church for y* Honour and Glory of God in this town to be set apart for his worship and service according to the excellent method of the Church of England Do hereby cheerfully and seriously devote to God the following sums (in the old tenor) annexed to our several names to be employed for the promoting of that pious undertaking.

Stratford February y* 2ᵈ, 1742-3.

is dated in February, 1742-3, and gives the names, probably, of nearly all the contributors at that time.

The money to build the church being secured, the next great question was where to locate it. Two deeds for sites were recorded; one, of a lot on Watch-house hill, and the other near that of the present church, in both of which it is

Sm. Johnson, a bell, ...£300 00 00	Bemslee Peters £10 00 00
Wm. Beach..... ....250 00 00	Sam^{ll} Preston 10 00 00
Wm. Russell 5 00 00	Sam^{ll} Folsom................. 12 00 00
Abm. Savage............... 5 00 00	Eph. Osburn 10 00 00
Charles Curtiss............. 30 00 00	Edmond Lewis............... 70 00 00
Richd Salmon 3 00 00	Ephra^m Curtiss............. 50 00 00
Israel Curtiss............... 4 00 00	James Lewis 30 00 00
Joseph Lewis, Jr. 2 00 00	Abel Burdsey 60 00 00
Samuel Thompson........... 2 00 00	Daniel Hawley 40 00 00
Peter Foot 15 00 00	Joseph Lewis............... 40 00 00
Ephraim Fairchild 10 00 00	Ambrous Thompson 30 00 00
John Barly 5 00 00	Gersh^m Edwards............. 50 00 00
Jeremiah French............. 10 00 00	John Benjamin 50 00 00
George Tyley............... 10 00 00	Joseph Browne............... 30 00 00
Joseph Lamson............. 2 00 00	James Dunlop............... 40 00 00
John Brooks 5 00 00	Benjamin Peirce............. 8 00 00
Daniel Munson............. 3 00 00	Paul Maverick 10 00 00
By a person unknown........ 10 00 00	Joseph Prince............... 20 00 00
John Kiely................. 2 00 00	Ebenezer Curtiss 15 00 00
David Lewis............... 20 00 00	Eliphelet Curtiss 60 00 00
Eliezer Newhall 20 00 00	Joseph Thompson 20 00 00
Timo. Bontecou 15 00 00	James Lewis, Jun. 15 00 00
Edmond Booth............... 10 00 00	Sam^{ll} Jones 10 00 00
David Brooks 4 00 00	Tim^o Sherman................. 35 00 00
Ephraim Burrit............. 10 00 00	Hew Curland 3 00 00
Ebenezer Sherman 5 00 00	Ephraim Hawley 15 00 00
Joseph Burdsey 12 00 00	Ephraim Lewis 15 00 00
Ebenezer Hurd.............. 30 00 00	David Fansher 5 00 00
Josh. Foot 00 00 00	Abra^m Blackman 6 00 00
John Arnold 00 10 00	James Frost................. 3 00 00
James Beach 5 00 00	Thos Stratton............... 4 02 00
Wm. Lamson............... 40 00 00	Joseph Laine............... 5 00 00
Nehemiah Beardslee 7 00 00	Edmund Lewis 20 00 00
Sam^{ll} Benjamin............... 20 00 00	William Wells............ ...... 10 00 00
Wm Leese 5 05 05	Joseph Gorham............... 5 00 00
Elnathan Peet............... 60 00 00	Daniel Foot.................. 3 00 00
Nathan Peet................. 20 00 00	Natt^{ll} Lamson............ ... 2 00 00
Edward Allen 25 00 00	William Beach ....-750 00 00

A true copy.   John Benjamin, Clerk."

stated that the purpose was to erect a church upon them, and the latter one was retained and occupied, while the other was sold.

Tradition says, as well as the Rev. Samuel Peters, that there was much excitement about securing this site; that the Congregationalists opposed the proposition of locating it on the hill near the meeting-house. It is said, the site on the hill was secured first and afterwards the one on Main street, but the deeds are dated quite the reverse—the one on Main street, April 16, 1743, and the one on the hill, May 24, 1743.

The building committee were as follows:

"February y⁰ 2, 1742–3. Unanimously chosen by y⁰ members of the Church of England in Stratford Town a committee to take care for y⁰ building a new church in Stratford.

Coll. Edmond Lewis.	John Benjamin.
Capt. James Lewis.	Mr. Ambrose Thompson.
Mr. Ephraim Curtiss.	Capt. Gershom Edwards.
Mr. Daniel Hawley.	Mr. Joseph Lewis.
Mr. Joseph Brown.	Mr. Thomas Lattin.

July, 1744. Voted that Theo⁰. Nickols, Esqr., also be one of the committee, and Mr. Wm. Lamson.

"Voted the same time that whatsoever shall be done by the Church Wardens for y⁰ time being, and any five of the Comᵗ. shall be held valid by y⁰ whole community."

The seating of the church was arranged according to the following: "It was unanimously voted y⁰ 1st day of January, 1744–5, that the proprietors of y⁰ church should chuse their ground for their pews according to what they have given towards building the same."

The property was secured to the church by the following:

"January ye 14, 1744–5. It was unanimously voted by y⁰ minister and Church Wardens and committee of y⁰ new church in Stratford, called Christ'⁰ Church, that if any persons that have or ever hereafter shall have Rights in pews in sd. Church, that if they shall leave sd. Church, they and their heirs; that in that case y⁰ Rights they have in said Church shall be Resigned for the Benefit of sd. Church; to be dis-

Titherton and Wm. Smith.

Wm. Beach.

Nathaniel Lamson.

Mr. Daniel Hawley. — Wm. Willcockson.

Mr. Wm. Lamson. — Mr. Ephm. Curtiss.

Mr. Nathan Peet. Capt. Elnath'n Peet. — Coll. Joseph Wooster.

John Brooks. David Brooks. — Sam'll Jones.

Abraham Blackman. — John Barley.

Benjm. Peirce.

Thomas Selby and Mrs. Allen. — Capt. Elnan. Peet.

David Lewis. Ephm. Burrit.	Wm. Smith. Mr. French. Richd. Blackleach. Both Blaggs. Capt. Hubbil. M. Porter.
Ebenr. Hurd. Mr. Newhall.	Eliph. Curtiss.
Mr. Joseph Lewis. Benjm. Lewis.	Charles Curtiss. Jerh. French.
Abrm. Savage. Mrs. Tree.	Thomas Lattin. Mr. Prys.
Samuel Preston. Ebenr. Sherman.	Mr. Joseph Shelton. Capt. Jos. Wooster.
John Hurd. Thos. Lake. Benj. Pierce.	Thos. Stratton. Thos. Daskem. Ricd. Burton.

Minister's Pew.

| Amba. Thompson. Doct. Munson. Capt. Coldwell. |
Coll. Lewis and Capt. Lewis.	Mr. Abel and Joseph Burdsey.
Paul Maverick.	Capt. Joseph Prince. Mrs. Serles.
Rev. Dr. S. Johnson.	John Benjamin.
Capt. Gershom Edwards.	Timothy Sherman. Samll. Benjamin.
Peter Foot. Samuel Folsom.	Jos. Thompson. Neh. Beardslee. Jos. Nichols.
Thos. Salmon. Mrs. Loring and family.	C. Burroughs. Stephen Frost.
Abraham Patterson. William Watkins.	Samuel Fairchild.

Wm. Beach. Sold to Henry Davis.

Eph. Lewis. John Lewis. Rented May 10, 1797.

Capt. James Dunlop. — Edw. Allen.

Mr. John Keys. Wm. Wells. Aba. Curtiss.

James Lewis. — Joseph Browne.

Eph. Hawley. — Eph. Osburn.

Doct. Russell. George Tyley. Jeremiah Judson Curtiss.

| Timo. Bountecou. | James Frost. | Doct. Benjm. Warner. |

| Mrs. Laborie. Benjm. Arnold. Mrs. Whitnee. | Capt. Theos. Nickols. |

PEWS AND OCCUPANTS IN THE EPISCOPAL CHURCH, STRATFORD, IN 1745.

posed of as y⁰ minister, Church Wardens and vestry then in being shall think most for the advantage of the same Church."

Some of the material for this church may have been, brought from England, but it was only a small proportion if any (the pulpit, and perhaps the chancel ornaments), as the Warden's record book now shows. A credit to Colonel Edmund Lewis stands: "about 12 loads of timber got in his land, 34 trees, £03–08." Lieut. Joseph Wooster furnished in "July, 1743, 12,000 feet of pine siding at ten pounds per thousand, and 2,000 feet of sash plank at £14 per thousand; 244 feet of pine boards at 20 s. per thousand; and "iron for y⁰ spindle for y⁰ weathercock." In August, 1744, Capt. James Lewis is credited, by "John rending 3400 lath for the church, ⅞4–05 :" and soon after to 1250 more lath; which shows that the edifice was not completed until the autumn of 1744.

Several items of credit on the account book show that the workmen were engaged nine days in raising the frame of this church ; and from many items recorded it is certain that the amount of timber in it was very great.

The Rev. Samuel Peters, in connection with his account of the Indian powwow on Stratford point, makes the following record in reference to the building of this church, or the one preceding it, for it is difficult to determine which he intended :

"When the Episcopalians had collected timber for a church, they found the devils had not left the town, but only changed their habitations—had left the savages and entered into fanatics and wood. In the night before the church was to be begun, the timber set up a country dance, skipping about, and flying in the air, with as much agility and sulphurous stench as ever the devils had exhibited around the camp of the Indian pawwawers. This alarming circumstance would have ruined the credit of the church, had not the Episcopalians ventured to look into the phenomenon, and found the timber to have been bored with augurs, charged with gun powder, and fired off by matches :—a discovery, however, of bad consequence in one respect—it has prevented the annalists of New England from publishing this among the rest of their miracles.'"

---

* History of Connecticut by the Rev. Samuel Peters.

This sketch, with many others in Mr. Peters' book, might easily be taken for a moderately good burlesque but for the fact that some historians quote the book seriously as authentic history.

The following record concerning the clock is of interest, although it is unfortunate that they did not write more particulars about it:

"An agreement made this 25th day of Feb^y, 1750–51, between the Church Wardens of Christ Church in Stratford, and John Davis, clock maker, a stranger, and is as followeth:

"That the said Davis is to keep the clock of said church in good repair for two years from the date hereof and to have for his labour five pounds for each year, provided the said clock goes well the said time; if not, he is to have nothing for his labor, and the first five pounds to be paid at the end of the first year, and the other five pounds at the second year; and that the Church Wardens are not to be put to more trouble about paying the money than to pay it either in Stratford or Fairfield; and to be paid in old tenor money."

Two full years were occupied, apparently, in building and finishing this church edifice; for much, if not all the lathing and plastering were done in the summer of 1744, and the regulations for seating the church were not made until January, 1744–5. The work for obtaining lime, is indicated by charges for drawing loads of wood for burning loads of shells, and was no small item in the finishing of such an edifice.

When the church was completed and the clock placed in the tower, there was one thing lacking, the privation of which they endured until the beginning of the year 1756, when they undertook the enterprise of securing an organ for their house of worship. A subscription[4] was raised for annual payments

---

"Stratford, February 16th, 1756.

[4] "The following proposals for the purchase of an organ for the use of Christ Church in this town are offered by Mr. Gilbert Deblois of Boston, Merchant.

"That the price of the said organ is to be fixed at Sixty pounds sterling.

"That the time allowed for the payment of the said sum be six years from the time of its being delivered, and this to be made in the six equal payments of ten pounds sterling per annum, without any demand of interest. That the said organ be delivered at Stratford by the last of April next, if it can be completed by that

during six successive years, at ten pound a year, and by it the instrument was obtained, and was in its place in the "organ loft," March 27, 1758, when the officers of the church appointed Mr. John Benjamin, organist, and from that time he was yearly elected by the same authority to the same office until 1773; serving the church in that capacity sixteen years,

---

time and there should be a convenient opportunity for shipping it. That the said Mr. Gilbert Doblois do take upon himself all the risque in transporting the s⁴ organ round from Boston to Stratford.

"We the subscribers do hereby accept the above mentioned proposals, and do hereby oblige ourselves and our heirs to the just payment of the respective sums yearly which are with our names herein expressed, to continue during the term of the six next succeeding years.

"Witness our hands. The money to be collected above, we also agree to pay into the hands of Mr. John Benjamin.

	Lawful Money.
Edmund Lewis two dollars and a half	£0-15
David Lewis five dollars a year	1-10
David Brooks three dollars a year	0-18
James Willoughby one dollar a year	0- 6
Nathaniel Curtis of N. Stratford one dollar pr. year	0- 6
Charles Curtis two dollars pr. year	0-12
Jere Judson Curtiss two dollars pr. year	0-12
Wᵐ Samuel Johnson 20/ per ann.	1-00
John Benjamin twelve shillings pr. year	0-12
Gershom Edwards one dollar and half	0- 9
Madam Beach a sett of Curtains and fringes for the Organ loft	
Edward Winslow two dollars pr. annum	0-12
Joseph Lewis two dollars pr. annum	0-12
Joseph Lewis, Jr. one dollar pr. annum	0- 6
Watman Duncan one dollar pr. annum	0- 6
Timothy Sherman three dollars pr. annum	0-18
Joseph Nickols three dollars pr. annum	0-18

	Lawful Money.
Andrew Hurd one dollar pr. annum	£0- 6
Alexander Zuill	0- 8
Abijah Beach twenty shillings pr. annum	1-00
John Backus one and a half dollars pr. annum	0- 9
John Robertson three dollars pr. annum	0-18
Abraham Patterson one dollar pr. year	0- 6
Abel Beach four dollars pr. annum	1- 4
Samuel Jones two dollars pr. annum	0-12
LeGrand Cannon two dollars and half	0-12*
Edward Hawley one dollar and half pr. annum	0- 9
Theophilus Niculls three dollars pr. year	0-18
Edmund Burritt half a dollar	0-03
Ambrose Thompson two dollars pr. annum	0-12
Edward Allen two dollars pr. annum	0-12
Harpin Jr. one dollar pr. annum	0- 6
Jean Harpin two dollars	0-12

* This is so carried out on the record.

and perhaps several years longer, since the records make no mention of an organist from 1773 to 1779, when Capt. George Benjamin is appointed to that service. So far as seen, no mention is made of remuneration to the organist until 1786. In 1780 Philip Benjamin was appointed organist; and in 1783, Asa Benjamin was elected to that place. In 1786 they voted to give the organist twenty dollars per year for his services.

On the 8th of July, 1744, the new church was opened with a sermon by Dr. Johnson, although it was not then plastered, and probably the pews were not then made.

Ten years he preached in this church, seeing large and encouraging results from his own labors and those of his brethren, and then he accepted the presidency of the college at New York. He neither resigned his parish at Stratford nor removed his family. The parish continued to raise his salary and when he could not hold service with them he secured one to do it. After some years this course secured the following entry in the Warden's record book:

" Stratford April 8, 1765.

" To prevent misunderstanding what I propose with regard to the money rates is this; not to take any of it to myself but after crossing out the names of such as I think subjects of Charity, to order the Church wardens to see that it be punctually collected and let out at interest and pre-served to the sole purpose of establishing a fund towards the better support of my successor excepting only so much as from time to time shall be found needful to use in rewarding any gentleman whom I shall need to call to assist me in cases of infirmity.   Samuel Johnson."

Judging from the history of one hundred and forty years, the sudden and rapid progress of the Episcopal Church in Stratford, for about ten years, resulting in the completion of a new Church about 1750, was of very great importance to the success of that denomination in America. The accession of a few prominent citizens of Stratford to this church added greatly to the prominence of Dr. Johnson and his people in the Colonies, and the more than ordinary elegance of the new church edifice contributed also to the same result.

Dr. Johnson seems to have appreciated these facts in his letter to the Society, September 29, 1748, when he says:

" As to the Church in this town, it is in a flourishing condition, one family having been added, and more looking forward, and thirty-one have been baptized, and eight added to the communion, since my last; our new Church is almost finished, in a very neat and elegant manner, the architecture being allowed in some things to exceed anything done before in New England. We have had some valuable contributions, and my people have done as well as could be expected from their circumstances, which are generally but slender; but there is one of them who deserves to be mentioned in particular for his generosity,—Mr. Beach, brother of the Reverend Mr. Beach, who, though he has a considerable family, has contributed above three thousand pounds, our currency, to it already, and is daily doing more, and designs to leave an annuity, *in perpetuum*, toward keeping it in repair."[*]

This edifice was not only remarkable in its architecture and finish, but also returned a full compensation for all the expense put upon it, in its durability, for it continued in use until the present Church was opened on the 29th of July, 1858, having served the purpose of its construction one hundred and fourteen years.

The height of the progress of this Church, for many years, seems to have been attained about the time Dr. Johnson became president of the College at New York. Having attained a good degree of strength and numbers it did well until the opening of the Revolutionary War, when all out-

---

[*] History of the Church in Conn., i. 157.

24

ward circumstances were against its progress, yet it continued its services probably until July, 1776.

Dr. Johnson remained the Rector until his decease in 1772; but his strength failed him somewhat so that an assistant became necessary and was secured, as shown by the parish vote, January 6, 1768, when "it was unanimously voted that the Rev. Mr. Ebenezer Kneeland be an assistant to the Rev. Doct' Johnson our pastor, and also our missionary during his natural life."

Rev. Ebenezer Kneeland was a graduate of Yale College in 1761; went to England for ordination three years later, returned to this country and served for a time as chaplain in a British regiment, and settled in Stratford according to the above vote.[1]

Upon the decease of Dr. Johnson, Mr. Kneeland succeeded to the Mission in Stratford, with all the emoluments of his predecessor. The church wardens and others, in requesting his appointment, gave these reasons for claiming a continuance of the Society's bounty:

"As Stratford is situate upon the great road from Boston to New York, Mr. Kneeland must inevitably be at a greater expense than any Missionary in the interior towns; so that from the decline of trade, the death and failure of several of our principal members, from the increasing price of the necessaries of life, the scarcity of money, and the extraordinary expenses a missionary must be at here, we may truly say we have not needed the assistance of the Venerable Society more for fifteen years past than we do at present. . . . We are now endeavoring to raise money to enlarge the glebe, but, for the reasons before mentioned, fear we shall meet with little success; however, our best endeavors shall not be wanting to complete the same."[2]

Mr. Kneeland served the parish until his decease, April 17, 1777.

Rev. Samuel Johnson, D.D.,[3] was born in Guilford,

---

[1] History of the Church, i. 269.

[2] Dr. Beardsley's History of the Church, i. 297.

[3] This sketch of Dr. Johnson is taken largely from the Rev. Dr. E. E. Beardsley's "Life and Correspondence of Samuel Johnson."

Connecticut, Oct. 14, 1696, and was the son of Dea. Samuel and Mary (Sage) Johnson; the grandson of Dea. William Johnson,—and his wife Elizabeth Bushnell,—who came to America when twelve years of age, with his father, Robert Johnson, from Kingston upon Hull in Yorkshire, England, and was at New Haven in 1641.

Samuel Johnson passed his preparatory studies largely by private instruction and entered Yale College and was graduated in 1714, the college then being at Saybrook. He soon after commenced ·teaching in his native town, where he received, the next year, some of the Yale students and acted as their tutor until the college was settled at New Haven, when he was elected one of the tutors for that institution, and served until the election of the Rev. Timothy Cutler to the rectorship or presidency of that institution in 1719. March 20, 1720, he was ordained pastor of the Congregational Church at West Haven, where he continued to serve two years when he with three others—Mr. Timothy Cutler, Mr. Daniel Brown, and Mr. James Wetmore declared themselves in favor of the Episcopal Church. The same year they went to England for ordination, and Mr. Johnson, after securing it, and the honorary degree of Master of Arts bestowed by Oxford University, returned to his native land under a commission from the Society for the Propagation of the Gospel in Foreign Parts as a missionary to Stratford, where he arrived, November 4, 1723.

Here he found a few communicants of his church and a number of others in adjoining towns, looking to him for occasional services, and that therefore the work was great and laborious. This would have been true if there had been no opposition to the introduction and success of another denomination, but as it was, the difficulties and labor were great and for a time almost insurmountable and disheartening, but Mr. Johnson was just the man for the place; patient, not particularly sensitive, not enthusiastic, but enduring in hope and devoted to his work. He very soon saw evidences of success, indeed no faithful pastor could labor under like circumstances without success, and therefore as he had been sent here to establish and build a Church, and had a heart to do it, at just that time and place, he was successful in a very honorable degree. He had a decided literary and educational taste, and therefore not only found employment as a minister, but also in efforts to lift up the masses in intellectual attainments and enterprises. He continued to exert a helpful influence at Yale College, which fact gave him a much larger influence in the State than he otherwise could have had. He found not only satisfaction in high educational attainments, but a force or popular influence which always reacted for his success as a minister, even though not put·forth for that end, but in a spirit of general benevolence.

On the 26th of September, 1725, he married Charity Nicoll, widow of Benjamin Nicoll, of Islip, L. I., and daughter of Col. Richard Floyd, of Brookhaven, L. I. She had by her former husband two sons and one daughter, and he at once began to prepare the sons for Yale College, where they were both graduated in 1734, and he doubtless had other students much if not all of the time he could devote to such work. There are evidences that his higher ambition and tastes in learning won for him and his church much favor even under the adverse circumstances in which he was placed. The record given on page 322 of this book as to the liberty to erect a school-house, indicates a public sentiment to this effect.

Mr. Johnson's labors as a missionary extended to several towns in the State, whenever occasion required. He visited Ripton, Newtown, Reading, Fairfield, Stamford, and as far east as New London, and occasionally Rhode Island. Besides his labors in preaching and administering the sacraments, he had of necessity, as the first and most prominent clergyman in his church, a general oversight of the interests of that body in Connecticut; in correspondence, in commending men who went to England to receive orders, and in consulting with companies in various places who desired to organize churches and secure the services of ministers. All these he attended with great fidelity and discretion, and his labors were accompanied by a large degree of success, but nothing very especially satisfactory until about 1740, when the great religious interests and controversies of the New Light movement occurred in the Congregational churches.

At the Rev. George Whitefield's first visit in Connecticut, in 1740, there was but little opposition to him from the Congregational people. Very many went to hear him preach, and also many were very much stirred in their religious thoughts on the subject of being saved through Jesus, the only Saviour. And it is very certain there was great need of such awakening to the subject. The Rev. Mr. Gold had pursued a course of pastoral labor and preaching for eighteen years that readily accepted Mr. Whitefield's preaching, and many in his own congregation were awakened to, and greatly interested in the subject.

Some way, how is not clearly revealed, Mr. Johnson and Mr. Gold became involved in a controversial correspondence. To illustrate the character of that controversy, and the excited, deep, sincere feeling on both sides, and as revealing some history of the times, a letter from each is here produced, with the assurance that it is no fault of the historian that Mr. Johnson's letter is twice as long as Mr. Gold's.

Mr. Johnson's Letter.[10]

"July 6, 1741.

"Sir,—. . . I thought it my duty to write a few lines to you, in the spirit of Christian meekness, on this subject. And I assure you I am nothing exasperated at these hard censures, much less will I return them upon you. No, Sir! God forbid I should censure you as you censure me! I have not so learned Christ! I will rather use the words of my dear Saviour concerning those that censure so, and say, 'Father, forgive them, for they know not what they do.'

"As to my having no business here, I will only say that to me it appears most evident that I have as much business here at least as you have,—being appointed by a Society in England incorporated by Royal Charter to provide ministers for the Church people in America; nor does his Majesty allow of any establishment here, exclusive of the Church, much less of anything that should preclude the Society he has incorporated from providing and sending ministers to

---

[10] These letters are taken from the "Life and Correspondence of Samuel Johnson," by the Rev. E. E. Beardsley, D.D.

the Church people in these countries. And as to my being a robber of churches, I appeal to God and all his people, of both denominations, whether I have ever uncharitably censured you, or said or done anything to disaffect or disunite your people from you, as on many occasions I might have done; on the other hand, whether I have not on all occasions put people upon making the kindest constructions possible upon your proceedings, and whether there has ever been anything in mine or my people's conduct that could be justly interpreted to savor of spite or malice, though we have met with much of it from some of our neighbors.

"If any of your people have left you, I appeal to them whether it has been owing to any insinuations of mine, and whether it has not been many times owing to your own conducting otherwise than in prudence you might have done, that they have been led to inquire, and upon inquiring to conform to this Church. And pray why have not Dissenters here as much liberty to go to church, if they see good reason for it (as they will soon do if they seriously inquire), as Church people to go to meeting if they see fit, as some have done, without my charging you so highly? In short, all I have done which could be the occasion of any people leaving you, has been to vindicate our best of churches from injurious misrepresentations she has labored under from you and others; and this it was my bounden duty to do.

"And indeed I shall think myself obliged in conscience to take yet more pains with Dissenters as well as Church people than I have ever yet done, if I see them in danger of being misled by doctrines so contrary to the very truth and spirit of the Gospel as have lately been preached among us up and down in this country.

"And as to my Church being open to all wickedness, I appeal to God and all that know me and my proceedings whether I have not as constantly borne witness against all kinds of wickedness as you have, and been as far from patronizing it as you have been, and must think my people are generally as serious and virtuous as yours. And lastly as to your censuring me and my people as being unconverted, etc., I will only beg you to consider whether you act the truly Christian part in thus endeavoring to disaffect my people towards my ministrations, and weaken and render abortive my endeavors for the good of their souls, when I know not that I have given you any occasion to judge me unconverted,—much less to set me out in such a formidable light to them. However, I leave these things, Sir, to your serious consideration, and beg you will either take an opportunity to converse with me where and when you please, or rather return me a few lines, wherein (as you have judged me unconverted, etc.) I entreat you will plainly give me your reasons why you think me so; for as bad as I am, I hope I am open to conviction, and earnestly desirous not to be mistaken in an affair of so great importance, and the rather because I have not only my own, but many other souls to answer for, whom I shall doubtless mislead if I am misled myself. In compassion, therefore, to them and me, pray be so kind as to give us your reasons why you think us in such a deplorable condition.

"In hopes of which I remain, Sir, your real well-wisher and humble servant   S. J."

The immediate reply to the above letter is not at hand, but another in reply to others is available. It is stated that Mr. Gold denied having made the severe statements alleged in the above letter.

Mr. Gold's Letter.

"Sir,—I don't wonder that a man is not afraid of sinning that believes he has power in himself to repent whenever he pleases, nor is it strange for one who dares to utter falsehoods of others to be ready at any time to confirm them with the solemnity of an oath,—especially since he adheres to a minister whom he believes has power to wash him from all his sins by a full and final absolution upon his saying he is sorry for them, etc.; and as for the pleas which you make for Col. Lewis, and others that have broke away disorderly from our Church, I think there's neither weight nor truth in them; nor do I believe such poor shifts will stand them nor you in any stead in the awful day of account; and as for your

saying that as bad as you are yet you lie open to conviction,
—for my part I find no reason to think you do, seeing you
are so free and full in denying plain matters of fact; and as
for your notion about charity from that I Cor. xiii., my
opinion is that a man may abound with love to God and
man, and yet bear testimony against disorderly walkers,
without being in the least guilty of the want of charity
towards them. What! must a man be judged uncharitable
because he don't think well nor uphold the willful miscar-
riages and evil doings of others? This is surely a perverse
interpretation of the Apostle's meaning. I don't think it
worth my while to say anything further in the affair, and as
you began the controversy against rule or justice, so I hope
modesty will induce you to desist; and do assure you that if
you see cause to make any more replies, my purpose is,
without reading them, to put them under the pot among
my other thorns and there let one flame quench the matter.
These, sir, from your sincere friend and servant in all things
lawful and laudable.　　　　　　　　　Hez. Gold."
　　"Stratford, July 21, 1741."

　　In February, 1743, Mr. Johnson and his people began the
proceedings which secured, within two years, a new church
edifice; and shortly after commencing this work he learned
that in that same month the University of Oxford, England,
had conferred on him the degree of Doctor of Divinity.

　　The new Church was opened, though unfinished, by a
sermon from Doctor Johnson, July 8, 1744, and he enjoyed the
privilege of preaching in it regularly ten years, when in 1754
he accepted the presidency of the New York College, although he neither resigned his pastorate nor removed his
family from Stratford.

　　His wife Charity died June 1, 1758, and while in the college in 1761, he married Mrs. Sarah, widow of William Beach
of Stratford. She was the daughter of Capt. Joseph Hull, of
Derby, born in 1701, and was great aunt to Gen. William
Hull. She died of the small pox Feb. 9, 1763, in New York.
Soon after this Dr. Johnson returned to Stratford where he
had a home with his son Wm. Samuel until his decease, Jan.
6, 1772.

The interesting details of the ministerial, religious, and literary life and character of Dr. Johnson are well portrayed in his "Life and Correspondence," by the Rev. E. E. Beardsley, D.D.; of New Haven, Conn., in a volume of 380 pages, with a fine steel portrait.

In the history of the Colony and State of Connecticut, he will ever hold a prominent place, and in that of the Episcopal Church in America it would be ingratitude not to accord him the honor of being its founder, and earliest as well as most successful champion and builder.

Thomas Salmon, born in Chippenham, England, came from London to Stratford, and married Sarah, daughter of William Jeans, about 1719. He was an architect and superintended the building of the first Episcopal Church at Stratford. The tradition in the family says, he brought the ceiling, the sounding-board, the pulpit, and other ornamental work in that Church with him from England.[11] If this was so, then it seems that there must have been some movement or efforts in Stratford to build a Church in 1718 or 1719, of which there is no record so far as known, or Mr. Salmon was sent to England for them. His gravestone, which, with that of his wife, is in the Episcopal burying-place, says he was "a worthy member of the Church of England here, and the ingenius architect of the Church and departed this life January 20, 1749–50, in the 57th year of his age." From this it may be inferred that he was the architect of the second Church, built in 1743, and if so he was "an ingenius" and superior builder.

John Benjamin came to Stratford about 1726, and in Jan. 1726–7, purchased "a certain messuage tenement and shop . . . . at a place called Pond brook, and one-quarter of an acre of land whereon the house and shop stand, the land being 'bounded all round with highways and common land.'" This property he exchanged in 1736 with Richard Rogers of New London, for a dwelling house near Stratford Ferry, and this he exchanged with Josiah Curtiss for land and a dwelling house and barn, "lying near the said Stratford Old Society's

---

[11] Giddings Family, by Mr. M. S. Giddings, 49.

meeting-house," and six acres of land "lying at a place called Intact."

Mr. Benjamin at once united in the support of the Episcopal Church and his name is prominent among its officers nearly to his decease, April 13, 1773, in the 73d year of his age. His descendants are still prominent in the town. His grandson Aaron entered the Revolutionary Army when quite young, and served his country as a brave soldier and Colonel through that war, and lived over forty years to enjoy the honor and privileges of the national liberty secured by that great conflict.

Col. John Benjamin, Jr., was a prominent citizen, and served as organist in the Episcopal Church about sixteen years, most of the time, apparently, without compensation. He was prominent in sustaining the Revolutionary War, serving some of the time in the army, and in some of the most important committees and public positions at home during the contest. He was captain of the train band or militia, made Colonel of the same after the Revolution. It is said he was a goldsmith and made the weather-cock still standing on the Episcopal Church. He was town treasurer in 1777.

William Beach, son of Isaac, the son of John, the first of the name in Stratford, was born in 1694, and died July 26, 1751. He married Sarah, the daughter of Capt. Joseph Hull in 1725. Her father belonged to one of the wealthiest and most influential families in Derby. After the death of Mr. Beach she married Dr. Samuel Johnson and died in New York in 1763.

William Beach was the brother of the Rev. John Beach, a Congregational and afterwards an Episcopal clergyman of prominence, and he became a prominent citizen in this his native town. His father, Isaac Beach, was a tailor by trade and does not appear largely in the offices of the town or as a land holder. He married Hannah, daughter of John Birdsey, Jr., in 1693, and died in 1750, in his 71st year.

William Beach joined the Episcopal Church not long after his brother's ordination in that Church in 1732. In the building of the second Episcopal house of worship he was the largest contributor, and in that relation did a very important and benevolent work. Dr. Johnson said he "contributed above three thousand pounds, our currency;" and although the Connecticut currency was at that time a great way below par, yet the contribution was a very large one for those days; and represents him as the foremost person in the town at that time, in giving to such an enterprise, including the Congregationalists, who built a meeting-house the same year.

Some extracts are here introduced from the "*Historical Discourse*, delivered in Christ Church, Stratford, Conn., on the fifth Sunday in Lent, March 28th, 1855, by the Rev. John A. Paddock, M.A., Rector."

This discourse was prepared with much care, research and unbiassed fidelity to historic truth, and was a very honorable production."[19]

"There is no record of the baptismal, or other offices being performed here from the beginning of the Revolution till after the close 'of the war."[18] But there seems reason for

---

[19] Mr. Paddock's discourse furnishes the following as to the first efforts of the Episcopal people of Stratford to secure a minister.

"A petition from the parish for a clergyman, addressed to the Bishop of London on the first of April, 1707, bears the signature of the following nineteen men, acting 'in behalf of the rest:' Richard Blacklatch, Isaac Knell, Daniel Shelton, Wm. Rawlinson, Jonathan Pitman, John Peat, Samuel Gaskill, Samuel Hawley, William Smith, John Skidmore, Timothy Titharton, Archibald Dunlop, Thomas Edwards, Isaac Brint, Daniel Bennett, Richard Blacklatch, Jr., Thomas Brooks, Isaac Stiles, Samuel Henry. (Sermon, page 8).

"Letter from the Wardens and Vestry to the Venerable Society, 1712. The names of the Wardens and Vestry first appear this year. Wardens: Timothy Titharton, William Smith. Vestry: William Rawlinson, William Jeanes, John Johnson, Richard Blacklatch, Daniel Shelton, Archibald Dunlop, James Humphreys, James Clarke, Edward Borroughs." (Sermon, page 9.)

"In 1724, the wardens and vestry were chosen from Stratford, Fairfield, Newtown, and Ripton, as follows: Wardens for Stratford, Nehemiah Loring, Thomas Salmon; for Fairfield, Dougal Mackenzie; for Newtown, John Glover; for Ripton, Daniel Shelton, Charles Lane. Vestry for Stratford, Wm. Jeanes, Jonathan Pitman, John Johnson, Richard Blacklatch, William Smith, Samuel French, Samuel Watkins, Samuel Blagg, James Laborie, Jr.; for Fairfield, James Laborie, Sen., Benjamin Sturgis; for Newtown, Samuel Beers, Robert Seeley; for Ripton, James Wakelee, Richard Blacklatch, Nathaniel Cogswell."

[18] A little before the war there is this record, April 20, 1772: "Voted that the pew next to the pulpit be given to Capt. Philip Nichols, he building the Christening pew."

"The last record is the baptism of Asa, son of Thomas and Ann Curtiss on the 3d of February, 1776.

supposing that the churchmen of this town were generally patriots.

"The parish seems to have been destitute of clerical services for some time after Mr. Kneeland's death. In April, 1778, the use of the glebe was granted to his widow until the appointment of another incumbent to the parish.

"In 1783, the Independence of the United States was acknowledged by Great Britain, and with this ended the aid extended to the parish by the society in England, it being deemed incompatible with their charter to carry on missionary operations beyond the dominions of the British crown.

"The parish was now thrown entirely upon its own resources, and, notwithstanding the trials of the previous ten years, it soon gave proofs of life and vigor. On the 18th of April, 1784, the Rev. Jeremiah Leaming, D.D., was called to the Rectorship and immediately entered upon his duties, which he continued until Easter, 1790, when, suffering from the infirmities of age, he resigned his position.

"An aged communicant, Mrs. Susan Johnson, of the parish, who received the statement from members of the family of a former generation, informs me that Bishop Seabury's first confirmation, and hence the first administration of the rite in America, was in this church in which we are now worshiping.

"On the first of April, 1793, the Rev. Ashbel Baldwin, then of Litchfield, was called to the rectorship to officiate here two-thirds of the time. He accepted the call, devoting to the Church at Tashua the remaining Sundays."

Rev. Ashbel Baldwin was born in Litchfield on the 7th of March, 1757, of Congregational parents, and was graduated at Yale College in 1776. He held for some time, during the Revolutionary War, the appointment of a quartermaster in the Continental Army and received a pension from the Government, which was his principal means of support in his latter days.

He became a clergyman of the Episcopal Church and the change of denomination is accounted for as follows:

"After leaving college, he engaged himself, temporarily, as a private tutor in the family of a gentleman on Long Island.

The family belonged to the Church of England, and, at that date, where the Episcopal house of worship was, for any cause, closed on Sunday, it was customary for the stanchest churchmen to turn their parlors into chapels and have the regular morning service. Mr. Baldwin, being the educated member of the household, was required to act as the family lay reader, and, ashamed to confess his ignorance of the Prayer Book, he sought the aid and friendship of the gardener, who instructed him in the use of the 'Order for Morning Prayre;' and soon his love and admiration of the Liturgy and conversion to the Church followed."[14]

He was one of the first four candidates at the first ordination by Bishop Seabury at Middletown in 1785, and after preaching at Litchfield nearly eight years, was invited to the rectorship of the Church in Stratford, April 1, 1793, which he accepted, the parish then including the Church at Tashua. This position he held until his resignation in 1824. He served the Church in other offices most efficiently many years and departed this life February 27, 1825, and was buried in the Episcopal burying place.

The Rev. Edward Rutledge succeeded Mr. Baldwin, and served until the spring of 1829, when he accepted a situation as professor in the University of Pennsylvania at Philadelphia.

For a short time after Mr. Rutledge, the Rev. Ashbel Steele officiated in this Church, but was not rector.

The Rev. George C. Shephard followed him from Nov. 1, 1829, until Easter, 1839.

Several other clergymen followed these in succession, the Rev. Edwin W. Wiltbank, the Rev. Alfred A. Miller, the Rev. John Morgan, the Rev. James Scott, and on the 28th of October, 1849, the Rev. John A. Paddock commenced his labors here, and the next April 30th was admitted to the order of priests by Bishop Brownell.

---

[14] History of the Church in Connecticut, ii. 345 and 425.

CHAPTER XV.

THE REVOLUTIONARY WAR.

INGS and monarchs have nearly always estimated too lightly the power of the common people they pretended and sought to govern, until it was too late to govern at all. King George III. of Great Britain, and his Ministers of State, were no exceptions to this law or want of wisdom, in 1776, and hence the American Revolution and the Independence of the United States.

The loyalty of New England had been exhibited previously, by its aid in the war between England and France, by the number, energy and success of volunteers and the expenses borne. In the capture of Louisburgh the Connecticut soldiers under Capt. David Wooster bore an honorable part; there being, however, only one memorandum concerning it on the Stratford town records, so far as seen.

"Zebulon Lorin of Stratford having been a soldier in the reduction of Louisburgh and the Island of Cape Brittain, in the Col. Goreham Regiment and in Capt. Lumber's Company, sold for ten pounds current money to Capt. David Wooster of New Haven, all title to his right in 'Plunder, stock of plunder, captures, stock of captures and all my right, title, interest and claim to the soil, land and appertenances upon or in the said Island of Cape Brittain and parts adjoining.' March 27, 1746,—19th year of the Reign of Our Sovereign Lord George II. King, &c."

No account of the part Stratford had in the French war has been obtained except that which appears incidentally in the following record of the acts of the General Assembly, but a careful perusal of the colony records shows Connecticut to have done grandly in soldiers and money in that war.

The following is one item only, amounting in the aggregate to £2376–11ˢ–6ᵈ.

"October 1758. On the memorial of the inhabitants of the towns of Fairfield, Milford, Stratford, Norwalk and Stanford, praying for the reimbursement of the charge and expense for quartering Col. Frasiers Highland Battalion the last winter; Resolved by this Assembly that the treasurer of this Colony be and hereby is ordered and directed to pay out the Colony treasury to the inhabitants of the town of Fairfield the sum of £449–16ˢ–3ᵈ; Milford the sum of £429–12ˢ–4½ᵈ; Stratford £435–10ˢ–11½ᵈ; Norwalk, £349–7ˢ–2½ᵈ; Stanford, £369–13ˢ–4½ᵈ, for charges and expenses referred to."

But these appropriations did not settle the matter, for it came before the Assembly the next spring, and a committee was appointed to investigate the expenses and make report, and the next October another committee was appointed to complete the examination of the matter, but the towns preferred to bring the matter before that body at that time, and it ordered the following sums paid: Fairfield, £491–15ˢ–7ᵈ; Milford, £491–10ˢ–9ᵈ; Stratford, £472–5ˢ–11ᵈ; Norwalk, £487 –5ˢ–6ᵈ; and Stanford, £433–13ˢ–11ᵈ, in full satisfaction of their said respective accounts."

The Regiment of Col. Frasier or a part of it lay encamped in Stratford, during the winter of 1757 and 8, on the common east of the old Episcopal burying-ground. He and his commissioned officers occupied the house then recently built, but never occupied, by the Rev. Izrahiah Wetmore.[1] Col. Frasier was he who said that with one regiment he could march through North America.

The Rev. I. Wetmore recorded Jan. 29, 1758, the baptism of Bettee the daughter of Daniel Gunn, drum Major in Col. Frasier's regiment.

He also records: "On October 6, 1760, baptised Victory the son of Iz. Wetmore, born the 8th of September previous, the day Montreal was taken."

---

[1] Vol. ii. Town Records.

It is said that Col. Frasier's men amused themselves at times in shooting at the weather-cock at the top of the Episcopal Church spire, which they pierced several times, as may still be witnessed by climbing to it.[1]

The records of Stratford introduce us to the part which that town was to take in the Revolution by three votes in town meeting.

"December 19, 1774, Ichabod Lewis moderator. In the meeting were read the proceedings of the Continental Congress, and the association therein recommended, and unanimously appeared as the most peaceable and likely method to be pursued at present, and that we will firmly adhere to the measures proposed in said association until the next General Congress, unless we obtain redress of our grievances before that time. Passed without contradiction.

"Voted N. C. D.[2] that a committee be chosen in the several parts of this town to observe the conduct of all persons relative to said association and proceed thereon according to the advice therein given : and Mess. Robert Fairchild, Deacon Johnson, John Brooks, Esqr., Capt. Isaiah Brown, Capt. Samuel Whiting, Capt. Daniel Judson, Isaac Nichols, William Pixlee, Mr. Nathan Birdsey, Mr. Joseph Curtiss, Maj. Agur Judson, Ichabod Lewis, Daniel Fairchild, Esqr., Capt. Abraham Brinsmade, Capt. Nathan Booth, Capt. Samuel Blakeman, Capt. Stephen Burroughs, Elnathan Curtiss and Abijah Starling were chosen a committee for the purpose abovesaid."

The first great overt war act of the British government towards the colonies was the blockading of Boston. No act

---

[1] The officers of Col. Frasier's Highland Regiment quartered in Stratford and Milford in 1757 and 8 were :

Hon. Col. Simon Frasier,	Lieut. Alexander McLoud,
Capt. John McPherson,	Lieut. Simon Frasier,
Capt. John Campbell,	Lieut. William McDonald,
Capt. Charles Bailey,	Lieut. Hector McDonald,
Lieut. John Cuthbert,	Ensign Simon Frasier,
Lieut. Charles McDonald,	Ensign John Chisholm,
Lieut. John Frasier,	Adjutant Hugh Frasier.

In 1759, Sergt. William Young and Captain Gordon of the 48th Regiment.

[2] *Nemine contra dicente.* Without one dissenting voice.

could have been more fortunate for America and unfortunate for England, since nothing could move the sympathies of the people throughout the country as the causing of indiscriminate suffering of helpless women and children of the poorer classes. This is clearly set forth in the resolution of the town when assembled, December 19, 1774.

"The meeting then took into their serious consideration of the unhappy circumstances of the poor people of Boston, now suffering in the common cause of American liberty under the oppressive acts of the British Parliament called the Boston Post Bill; and thereupon unanimously voted, that a subscription be immediately opened, and collection be made and sent as soon as may be, for the relief of the poor sufferers in that town; and Mess⁹. Philip Nichols, Josiah Hubbell, David Hawley, Nathan Bennitt, Stephen Burroughs and Legrand Cannon, are appointed a committee to solicit and transmit to Boston such donations as they shall receive, by any safe opportunity, addressed to the committee appointed to take care of, and employ the poor of that place.

"Attest, Robert Fairchild, Town Clerk."

In this list of names may be seen Episcopalians as well as Congregationalists; and the same is true throughout the struggle to the end of the war.

The next year—Dec. 18, 1775—the town appointed as a "Committee of Observation," the following persons:

"Robert Fairchild, Daniel Fairchild, Esqr.,
John Brooks, Esq., Capt. Abram Brinsmade,
Capt. Isaiah Brown, Capt. Nathan Booth,
Col. Samuel Whiting. Capt. Lemuel Blackman,
Daniel Judson, Esq., Capt. Stephen Burroughs,
Mr. William Pixlee, Mr. Elnathan Curtiss,
Mr. Isaac Nichols, Mr. Abijah Starling,
Mr. Joseph Curtiss, David Wilcockson, Esq.,
Maj. Agur Judson, Mr. George Thompson."
Col. Ichabod Lewis,

The battle of Lexington, Mass., occurred on the 19th of April, 1775, and the above seems to be the first vote of Stratford in sustaining the war. The next year, in December,

25

1776, after the Declaration of Independence, a like committee was appointed, but it was called the "Committee of Inspection," and consisted of the following persons:

"Capt. Ebenezer Coe,
Capt. Nathaniel Wheeler,
John Benjamin,
William Thompson,
Capt. Isaiah Brown,
William Pixley,
Capt. Samuel Beers,
Abijah Sterling,

Daniel Bennitt,
Benjamin Deforest,
Maj. Agur Judson,
Edmund Leavenworth,
Capt. Abraham Brinsmade,
Stephen Middlebrook,
David Wells,
Thomas Hawley,
Nehemiah Deforest."

At the same time they passed the following:

"Voted, that watch and ward be kept in this town at the discretion of civil authority and selectmen as to the number from time to time, and to appoint a grand officer or officers to superintend said watch who shall be under the discretion of said authority and selectmen, and obey their instructions, and said grand officers shall be rewarded for their time while on duty not exceeding soldier's wages.

"January 13, 1777, Messrs. Joseph Curtiss, Capt. John Sherwood, John Hinman, William Wordin and Aaron Hawley, were added to the above committee of inspection."

A special town meeting was called, and met at Trumbull, probably, as being more central and convenient for the whole township, since no part of the original township had then been taken from it by the formation of any other town; and decided action was taken.

"At a meeting of the inhabitants of the town of Stratford, holden at North Stratford Parish at said Parish meeting house, on Monday the 7th of April, 1777, in consequence of an order or requisition made by his honor the Governor and Council of Safety holden at Lebanon on ye 18th March, ult., said meeting being duly warned, chosen Mr. Nathan Birdsey, moderator, and John Brooks, clerk. Committees chosen: for the old society, Capt. Samuel Beers, Lieut. Ephraim Willcockson and William Pixlee; for Ripton, Maj. Agur Judson and Elisha Mills; for North Stratford, Stephen Middlebrook and Eliakim Walker; for Stratfield, Nathan Nichols and Jabez Summers; for New Stratford, Capt. Nathan Booth and Dea. John Judson; for New Stratford, west part, Benjamin Beardsley.

"The meeting proceeded to vote unanimously that they will give as an additional bounty to all such as shall or have inlisted themselves into the Continental service for the time of three years or during the war, the sum of ten pounds lawful money, and that this donation shall be paid to such only as are inlisted to it and belong to the quota of men this town is to raise.

"Voted, also a tax or rate on the pound of eight pence for the purpose abovesaid, on the list for the year 1776, and that Capt. John Benjamin collect the same, and that the collector pay the same into the hands of the selectmen from time to time for the purpose above mentioned."

The following is a sample of the drafting and of paying fines at the early stage of the war, as shown by the dates. It is said that Daniel McEwen was a locksmith and his trade at this time in making and repairing guns was so profitable that he could afford to pay his fine every few months, besides remaining at home, somewhat shielded from danger.

"STRATFORD, May 14, 1777.
"To MR. DANIEL McEWEN, Sen.
 In pursuance of Regimental Orders after a fair Lot drawn ; you are to equip yourself; and you are detached to serve as a guard under the Command of Col. Samuel Whiting until January next unless sooner discharged.
JOHN BENJAMIN, *Captain.*"

"STRATFORD, May 15, 1777.
 Then Received of Mr. Daniel McEwen, five pounds lawful money in full for a fine for not serving until January next under the command of Col. Samuel Whiting, when drafted.   Recd per me
JOHN BENJAMIN, *Town Treasurer.*"

"STRATFORD, Sept. 30, 1777.
 Recd of Mr. Daniel McEwen, five pounds L. Money for a fine for neglect of duty when drafted to serve under Col. John Mead.
            Recd per me
JOHN BENJAMIN, *T. Treasurer.*"

At another special meeting held Nov. 10, 1777, they made the following record :

"The laws were read in said meeting respecting the providing of necessaries for the Continental soldiers, &c., and were of opinion it ought to be done, and thereupon appointed Messrs. Mr. Joseph Curtiss, Capt. John Benjamin, Capt. Joseph Birdsey, Mr. Zechariah Lewis, Capt. Joseph Burton, Daniel Fairchild, Esqr., Mr. David Wells, Nehemiah Deforest, Capt. Robert Hawley, and Capt. John Sherwood, a committee to provide immediately all those necessaries for said soldiers as the law directs.

"Voted in said meeting that Messrs. Ephraim Willcockson, William Pixlee, Maj. Agur Judson, Elisha Mills, Esqr., Stephen Middlebrook, Eliakim Walker, Nathan Nichols, Jabez Summers, Capt. Nathan Booth, Dea. John Judson, and Benjamin Beardslee are reappointed a committee for the purpose of supplying the families of such soldiers as are in the Continental service, as the law directs."

One month later, Dec. 22, 1777, a committee was appointed to receive all provisions the people were disposed to give for the support of the soldiers' families, and another was appointed to distribute the same; and a tax was laid of sixpence on the pound. This made two taxes voted in one year, amounting to fourteen pence per pound.

Also, a committee of inspection was appointed as usual for the year.

Capt. Ebenezer Coe, who was elected deacon in the Congregational Church in 1784, was a captain in the American army and left the following brief record of his service and misfortunes in that war.

"An account of the singular misfortune and deliverances which befel me during the contest.

"Aug. 13, 1776, marched to New York with my company as Lieutenant at the time, and on the 15th of September, providentially escaped from the enemy to Harlem hills and arrived home on the 17th, after which I was sick some months.

"On the 25th of April, 1777, twelve o'clock at night, marched to Fairfield. The next day to Danbury; 27th to Ridgefield, it being Lord's day; attacked the enemy; received a musket ball through my head, cutting off a part of my right ear and carrying away my right eye. I fell, as dead, lay a time, but recovered to my thoughts, after being inhumanly stabbed with a bayonet in my side and right hand while l lay unfeelingly as dead ; which perhaps was the means, by turning the stream of blood another way, of saving my life.

"At this time, being come to my thoughts, was abused, robbed, and repeatedly threatened with instant death. But blessed be the name of the Lord, who delivered me from death and from the hand of my enemies, who heard my cry in the night of distress, as in the 142d Psalm, and brought me to my house, the 21st day of May. ' Bless the Lord, O my soul and forget not all his benefits.' "

Tradition explains further, that while Captain Coe lay on the field wounded a British soldier was about to pierce him with a bayonet when a superior officer severely reprimanded him, took up Captain Coe, carried him to a school house near by, examined his commission which was in his pocket, expressed his sorrow at being unable to give him further aid and withdrew.

The Captain recovered and lived many years afterwards.

"Dec. 31, 1781. On motion in town meeting, it was voted that the house purchased by the selectmen from Mr. Silas Nichols for the horse-neck service, be given and granted as a free donation to Capt. Ebenezer Coe, as a compensation in part for his suffering and loss occasioned by the enemy landing on Stratford Point last summer.

"William Thompson was also present from Stratford at the fight at Danbury. At Ridgefield he was wounded, and while in that condition a British soldier stepped up and blew out his brains with his gun."

The following resolves sent to Stratford for their consideration and adoption, manifest a remarkable degree of clear perception and discriminating judgment, precisely as to what the people intended to secure by their resistance to England ; and the people of Stratford on hearing them read, quickly decided to pass them without alteration ; and here is a forcible illustration that the people understood that they were contending for great principles of government that were worthy of the efforts and sacrifices they were making to secure them.

"Stratford, Second Monday of January, 1778.

The meeting took into consideration the Articles of Confederation proposed and recommended by the Continental Congress, and being read and deliberately considered, paragraph by paragraph, and were adopted and approved by said meeting, and the Representatives be instructed to give their voice for the approbation in General Assembly.

" The meeting then proceeded to adopt several resolves of the town of Norwich which was thought of such importance to the privileges of the people, and so seasonably presented to the meeting as to need no emendation.

" First. The Representatives of the freemen of this town, use their utmost influence in the General Assembly to have the Delegates in Congress chosen by the freemen of this State in the same manner as the Assistants in this State are chosen.

" 2dly. That they use their influence to procure an alteration of the mode of taxation in such a manner that the same may be levied on the inhabitants in proportion to the worth of their whole estate, which method alone we conceive to be equitable.

" 3dly. That they endeavor to procure an act to be made and passed that all male persons in this State who are obliged by law to give in their list and able to pay taxes and are of sober life and conversation, and have taken the oath to the State (and of Freemen) may have the privilege of voting in all Freemen's Towns and Societies meetings, when they are liable to pay taxes in consequence of those votes.

" 4thly. That they also endeavor to have the debates in the Assembly be made as public as may be, and that the yeas and nays in every important question be noted in the Journal and published that the towns may have them.

" 5thly. That they use their influence that the Delegates of this State in Congress be instructed to transmit to the Assembly a list of the yeas and nays in every important question, and that the publication of the Journal of Congress may be printed with the greatest dispatch and sent to the different States.

" The foregoing several Resolves the Clerk is directed to give in writing to the Representatives of this Town.

" The several matters, causes and complaints of several persons who, deserted from the Fish Kills and Peeks Kills in the company in October last, for which desertion they have been prosecuted and fined, and said fine secured or to be secured in the town treasury : On motion, voted, that Samuel Whiting, Abraham Brinsmade, Esqr., Mr. Nathan Birdsey, and Deacon Daniel Bennitt be and are hereby appointed a committee to hear and enquire into the causes of their said desertion, and if it shall appear to the satisfaction of said committee that the aforesaid deserters have reason sufficient to excuse themselves from said fine the committee are accordingly to make their report to proper authority, and the town voted to give up their fines, yet not so as to make this a precedent or to countenance desertion in future."

" Mar. 20, 1778. The meeting proceeded, as was designed in the warning, to read, particularly and distinctly the present act of the General Assembly made at Hartford on the 12th day of February, 1778, entitled an act for the regulation of the prices of labour, produce, manufactures, and commodities within this State ; likewise the doings, requisitions and statings of civil authority and selectmen of this town, on the several articles, &c., &c., not particularly enumerated in said act, which duty as aforesaid, the said act does enjoin; at the same time also was laid and read before said meeting a Resolve of the General Assembly of this State at their session in Hartford on the 2d Tuesday of January, 1778, requiring this town to procure a quantity of clothing for the Continental troops, &c., as per sd Resolve.

" The meeting after hearing the foregoing act, Stating of the town and Resolves of the Assembly ; and approved thereof, did proceed to vote, 1st. that this meeting does recommend that a suitable number of men in each society of the Town do enter into an association and mutual engagement with each other, to assist the civil magistrate and all informing officers, to carry effectually into execution all breaches of the present regulating act of Assembly, and the doings and statings of the civil authority and selectmen of this town thereon, and this meeting by their vote also do earnestly recommend that the members of which this association may be composed, be vigilant in complaining of and prosecuting all breaches of this act, which shall be considered by this meeting as rendering (not only this town) but the public the most essential service.

" Voted secondly, that Mr. Joseph Curtiss, Mr. Nathan Birdsey and Capt. Benjamin of this Society; Capt. Joseph Burton and Mr. Daniel Hawley, of North Stratford parish, Woolcot Hawley of Stratfield parish, Zechariah Lewis and Samuel Beard of Ripton parish, Nehemiah DeForest and Lieut. David Wells of New Stratford parish, and Capt. John Sherwood of North Fairfield parish, be and they are each and every of them appointed as a committee in behalf of this town to purchase and procure clothing, &c.,' for the Continental troops agreeable to the directions of the aforesaid resolve of Assembly.

NORTH STRATFORD, March 11, 1778.

The following is an exact account of the donations of the parish of North Stratford, for the Continental soldiers in the southern army, Valley Ford, belonging to this place, sent down by Lieut. Beebe, being fifteen in number, to be divided equally between them, viz : the following persons : John Downs, Jeames Downs, Abraham Hawley, Truman French, William Dascom, Daniel Evis, Nathan Hawley, Reuben Beach, Joel Mosher, John Craford, Samuel Henman, Daniel Sherwood, Toney Turney, Cæsar Edwards, and Nero Hawley.

The following persons were the donors :

	£	s.	d.		£	s.	d.
Daniel Beers,	o	1	10	Ichabod Hawley,	o	5	o
Jonathan Beers,	o	3	oo	Eliakim Beach,	o	6	o
Nathaniel Mosour,	o	3	o	Daniel Beach,	o	2	o
David Stratton,	o	3	o	Thomas Edward's wife,	o	3	9
Hawkins Nichols,	o	3	o	Joshua Henman,	o	6	o
Daniel Turney,	o	3	o	John Beach,	o	5	o
David Turney,	o	2	o	Reuben Sherwood,	o	6	o
Elnathan Turney,	o	3	o	Enoch Henman,	o	6	o
John Turney,	o	12	o	Josiah Henman,	o	6	o
Robert Turney,	o	5	6	Samuel Turney,	o	3	o
Gideon Peet,	o	5	o	Joseph Burroughs,	o	5	o
David Edwards, Jr.,	o	2	o	Samuel Edwards,	o	3	o
John Hains,	o	3	o	Edmon Curtis,	o	3	o
David Barsley,	o	3	o	Gershom Turney,	o	3	o
Thaddeus Barsley,	o	1	9	Ephraim Sterling,	o	12	o
James Barsley,	o	3	o	Peter Beers,	o	1	o
David French,	o	4	o	Stephen Middlebrook,	o	6	o
John Burton,	o	6	o				

"On representation made to this meeting by Col. Whiting and Capt. Joseph Birdsey, that the lines at the Sawpitts were in a defenceless condition for want of men, and much exposed to the enemy and that although there had been a late draft from the militia and alarm list companies of this town, and regimental orders issued to them to march, join and take part at the said Saw-Pitts under the command of said Capt. Joseph Birdsey, notwithstanding which order many had refused to join said Captain as aforesaid, in consequence of which default orders were now issuing for a new draft to supply the deficiency aforesaid. Therefore, in order to encourage the soldiery, on motion it was voted that this town will give a bounty of five pounds to the non-commissioned officers and soldiers that have joined or shall speedily join said company at said post under the command of said Joseph

The subscribers that gave cheese.

	lbs.	oz.		lbs.	oz.
David Salmon,	5	4	Josiah Henman,	5	o
Jabez Beach,	3	12	John Edwards, 3d,	6	o
Mrs. Starling,	4	4	David Edwards, 3d,	6	o
Mrs. Beach,	4	12	John Edwards, 4th,	5	o
Joseph Burton,	7	4	Abigail Mosour,	4	2
Benjamin Burton,	6	o	Eliakim Walker,	5	4
John French,	6	8			
John Wheeler,	6	o		70	10

Subscribers for gammon.

	lbs.	oz.		lbs.	oz.
Andrew Beach,	1	8	John Hinman,	4	12
Abel Beach,	4	o	Reuben Sherwood,	5	8
William Burritt, neat tongue,			John Turney,	4	o
Mrs. Hinman,	2	8	Agur Beach,	4	4
Josiah Hinman,	4	8			

Small packs sent—

	lbs.	oz.		lbs.	oz.
By Elnathan Seeley,	15	4	By Andrew Hawley,	8	8
By Daniel Hawley,	6	o	By Peter Lewis,	4	8

NORTH STRATFORD, 12th March, 1778.

Then received of Mr. Stephen Middlebrook, the sum of seven pounds, three shillings and ten pence, lawful money, for the purpose of paying the expenses of transporting a donation in provisions, from the parish of North Stratford to the Continental soldiers of that parish, Genl. Washington's Headquarters.

pr. JAMES BEEBEE, *Captain.*" *

* Manuscript of Major L. N. Middlebrook of Bridgeport.

Birdsey; provided they thus continue on duty the term of two months, or are sooner discharged, and that the fines drawn from the delinquents or to be recovered from them be appropriated for the aforementioned purpose.

October 12, 1778. Voted that Mess' Capt. Samuel Beers and John Brooks Esqr. be and they are hereby appointed a committee to receive and take into their stores and keeping a certain quantity of salt, supposed to be about seventy-five bushels, the property of the town, and hold and dispose of same in the following way and manner (viz:) to deal and deliver out said salt to every society as nearly as may be according to their respective lists, and that a committee be appointed in each society to receive their proportion of said salt, barter and exchange the same to the inhabitants of said societies respectively for necessary provisions, &c., and no man shall be allowed to purchase by exchange more than half a bushel of said salt, and some less as their circumstances may be, at the discretion of the committee who deal out and exchange said salt; and the avails of said salt shall be appropriated to the support of the soldiers' families and poor of the town as the law requires; and said committees to render their accounts to the next town meeting of their doings thereon.

"And for the first society, John Brooks, Esqr., for the society of Ripton Mr. Ebenezer Blackman, for North Stratford Mr. Sylvanus Starling, for Stratfield Mr. Wm. Wardon, for New Stratford Capt. Samuel Blackman, and for North Fairfield, part, Capt. John Sherwood, are chosen a committee to receive the proportionable part of salt belonging to each society according to their respective list."

The year 1779 was one of great discouragement to the Colonies because many things seemed to forebode defeat to the objects for which the strife had continued for four years. In July Governor Tryon came up the Sound with several hundred soldiers to burn and destroy the villages along the shore. On the 7th of that month they plundered New Haven and on the 11th burned Fairfield.

Some of the Stratford people were greatly frightened, and engaged in an effort to secure the place against future calamity, by entreaty, by circulating a subscription paper, with the following heading:

"We, the subscribers, being exceedingly desirous, if possible, to save the town from the destruction it is now threatened with by the invasion of the British fleet and army, do hereby request and desire Doctor William Samuel Johnson, Captain Philip Nichols, Captain George Benjamin, and Mr. Ebenezer Allen to use their influence, either in person or by letter, with the British Admiral and General to save the town. And we do hereby promise and most sacredly engage to support them in the execution of their design, and to protect and defend them from any insult, injury, or abuse, either in their persons, properties, or families, on account of their making such application: as witness our hands this 12th day of July, 1779."[4]

Intelligence of these proceedings soon reached General Oliver Wolcott's headquarters at Horseneck, who sent Col. Jonathan Dimon to Stratford to make inquiry, and upon his report the General gave him the following order:

"*Sir,*—Your favour of yesterday is received. I shall make no observations upon the tendency, or rather the conclusive effect of those men's conduct who could wish to supplicate the clemency of an enemy whose unparalleled barbarity has put a dishonor on human nature. To a mind enlightened by science, and which views acts with their consequences, it is impossible that it should not comprehend that the step which was intended to be taken must, by inevitable consequences, involve in it the most abject submission to a tyranny rendered, if possible, ten times more detestable than it was before, by the very means by which it was designed to be established. These are times when the usual forms of proceeding are to give place to a regard for the public safety, and the love of country is to be preferred at all times to the friendship of youth.

"You are therefore, Sir, directed to send, under guard or otherwise, Dr. William Samuel Johnson, of Stratford, to the town of Farmington, and deliver him to the care and custody

---

4 Life and Times of Wm. Samuel Johnson, 113.

of the civil authority of that town, and request of them that they would secure or keep him under such proper restraints as to prevent his having any correspondence with the enemy."

The further record of this matter is as follows,[1] as given by the Rev. Dr. Beardsley:

"A detachment of troops was sent to carry out this order, and Johnson was made a prisoner, but conscious of his innocence, and wishing to avoid a public disturbance, he persuaded the officer to accept his word of honor that he would proceed at once to Farmington, and place himself voluntarily in the custody of the selectmen. One of that board was John Treadwell, an acquaintance of his, who declared, after consultation with his colleagues, that they had no business with him, and that if they put him under any restraint it would be a false imprisonment. Johnson said he knew this, but suggested that, for their sakes and his, it was necessary that they should do something; and proposed that they should permit him to pass to the Governor and Council of Safety, in whose hands at that time was lodged the military authority of the Colony, and whose decision alone would quiet the people."

"Having given his parole[2] and received his pass, he started on his solitary journey, and arriving at Norwich, where the Council of Safety sat, unfortunately found that body not in session. But he proceeded to Lebanon, the residence of Governor Trumbull, and stated his condition

---

[1] Life and Times of Wm. Samuel Johnson, by the Rev. E. E. Beardsley, D.D., 115.

[2] *William Samuel Johnson's Parole.*

"Farmington, July 23, A. D. 1779.

"I, the subscriber, having been sent by order from Major General Oliver Wolcott, as a prisoner to the care of the civil authority of the town of Farmington, and by them permitted to go from thence to Lebanon on business with his Excellency the Governor and Council of Safety, do pass my word that on said journey and business I will do nothing directly or indirectly against the interest and welfare of the United States; and that, on my having accomplished said business, will return and put myself under the immediate care of said authority, unless his Excellency the Governor and Council of Safety, or his Excellency the Governor only, shall direct otherwise.

"Wm. Samuel Johnson."

and the object of his appearing in his presence. As his
Excellency knew his character well, and the principles on
which he had acted from the beginning of the war, it did not
require any urgent entreaty to enlist his sympathy and gain
his favor. He informed Dr. Johnson that the Council would
meet again in two days, when he could appear, and the
matter would be laid before them, and the result communicated. The Council met, and his own statement went to
show that he had no inclination to aid the enemy; that he
had encouraged the enlistment of soldiers; contributed of
his property for that purpose, hired his man to serve for him
during the war, and was ready to take the oath of fidelity
required by law.

"After hearing the case, the Governor was advised to
permit him, until further orders, to return and remain in
Stratford, which place he speedily reached to the great joy
of his family and friends."

While Dr. Johnson was on his journey to the Governor
and returning, the town of Stratford was also in great commotion, as seen in the following records:

"At a town meeting specially warned and convened at
the town-house in Stratford July 21, 1779, for the purpose of
exculpating the town from the imputations of some scandalous reports spread abroad to the disadvantage of the town,
purporting that the people were about carrying on a traitor-
ous correspondence with the enemy, and laying down their
arms and submitting to the British Government, &c., Daniel
Fairchild Esqr. moderator of said meeting:

"Voted unanimously that an address be made to the
public for the purpose abovesaid,—and Capt. Ebenezer Coe,
Samuel Adams, Esqr. Stephen Burroughs, Esqr. Abraham
Brinsmade, Esqr. and Capt. Blakman were appointed a
committee to prepare a draft for that purpose and lay it
before the meeting in their next adjournment. The meeting
adjourned to the 29th instant one o'clock afternoon to North
Stratford meeting-house. Test Robert Fairchild, Clerk.

July 29, 1779. The meeting convened and opened at
North Stratford meeting-house. Daniel Fairchild, Esqr.
moderator. The above committee made their Report which

was read, received and approved and ordered to be published
in New Haven paper with the names of those who had subscribed a certain subscription paper as recited in said report
now on file, and on motion suggesting that Daniel Judson,
Esqr., John Brooks, Esqr. and Mr. George Lewis had so far
encouraged the signing said paper recited in said report that
their names ought to be inserted in the paper, the said
Brooks and Lewis shewed to the meeting to their satisfaction, that they were not at all concerned in procuring said
paper, nor encouraging the signing thereof, and were discharged by the meeting.

The said Judson acknowledged that he had been too
forward in encouraging people to sign, but without any
design of making a confession to the prejudice of his country,
but was innocent of any ill design, and was still a fast friend
of the cause of America; and desired the town would overlook his misconduct and receive him into friendship again.

Whereupon voted that the said Daniel Judson, Esqr.
should have liberty to insert his name in said paper, and his
reflection or leave it out at his election, and Stephen Burroughs, Esqr. was desired to fit said report and address for
the press, and procure the same to be published.'

Test, Robert Fairchild, T. Clerk.

Other Town Acts during the Revolution.

"Town meeting at the Town-house July 29, 1779. In
said meeting Elisha Mills, Esqr., Daniel Bennitt, Esqr., Stephen Burroughs, Esqr. and Capt. John Benjamin were appointed a committee to meet the county committee, at a time
and place to be agreed upon by other towns in this county to
consult and devise some proper method to prevent a further
depreciation, to retrieve and establish the credit of our
currency.

"Resolved in said meeting that Isaac Wells Shelton shall
not reside in this town, and Robert Fairchild, Esqr. is desired
to inform Hartford County Sheriff thereof.

"Resolved that no inimical person now with the enemy

' See Appendix for a copy of this address.

shall return and reside in the town, unless they have the approbation of the town in their meeting."

"Sept. 21, 1779. In said meeting the regulation of prices stated by Reading committee were read. The meeting then chose Capt. Isaiah Brown, Capt. Ebenezer Coe, William Pixlee, Capt. Nathaniel Wheeler, Sylvanus Starling, Stephen Middlebrook, Capt. Zechariah Coe, Capt. Wm. Worden, Abram Hubbell, Capt. Edmund Leavenworth, Benjamin Mallory, James Blakman, Ebenezer Blakman, Samuel Beard, Capt. Phineas Sherman, David Wells, Elijah Curtiss and Elle Curtiss a committee to assist and inform the informing officers of all breaches of laws that shall come to their knowledge, that all the wicked tribe of monopolizers, engrossers, forestallers and stock-jobbers who enhance the prices of the necessaries of life, and depreciate our currency, may be brought to condign punishment, that their pernicious practices may be prevented.

"Test, Robert Fairchild, T. Clerk."

In June, 1780, the town in a meeting offered a bounty of "ten pounds lawful silver money, or gold, or provisions equivalent, to each effective man who would enlist and serve, for the town, in the Continental army until the last day of the next December.

"Voted, that each able bodied man who shall enlist to serve in the Continental army for three years or during the war shall receive a bounty, over and above the said ten pounds, of six pounds lawful silver money annually so long as he shall continue in said service."

"On November 20, 1780, the town voted, in addition to other taxes and supplies called for, "to provid 100 shirts, 100 pair of mittens, 100 pair of stockings and 100 pair of shoes, for our soldiers belonging to this town who are now in the service in the Connecticut lines."

In June, 1781, the town authorized the Recruiting committee to fill the quota required "for six months or twelve months on the best terms they can;" and the same directions were given the next year, and at this time—1782—for the first time the town voted, to borrow money to pay the bounties.

At the same meeting a tax of four pence hard money on the pound was voted, to raise beef supplies for the army, and the town appointed William Pixlee as collector to seize the cattle and have them estimated and delivered to the receiver, and give credit for them, or pay for them from the town treasury.

"Dec. 31, 1781. On motion it was voted that the select-men be directed carefully to inspect all persons who shall come into this town, and such as do not come well recommended as being friends to this country, or do not manifest the same to their satisfaction, they do forthwith warn out, and if need be prosecute them."

"December 31, 1781. On motion it was voted that the town treasurer be directed to pay unto John Daskum as a gratuity for his former service in the Continental army from the commencement of the war to the present day, the sum of six pounds, hard money, and to be paid as soon as may be."

Capt. Joseph Hull, whose son Isaac in 1812 became Commodore in the American Navy, was a native of Derby in this state, and commanded one of the light crafts known as "Commission boats," which were employed in privateering service against the British and Tories. Upon one occasion he ran down to an inlet or arm of the sound near Throg's Neck, where the British, then occupying New York, were accustomed to send vessels for firewood. He found there, under convoy of a schooner mounting ten guns, and of ninety tons burthen, which lay at anchor in the stream, a number of these wood vessels loading, and surprised and captured one of them that night. The two sailors who composed her crew, he caused to be secured below, and with his own men numbering about fifty, carefully concealed on board, he weighed anchor with the captured craft, a little after midnight, and bore down upon the British gunboat.

When hailed his reply disarmed suspicion, although he was warned by the sentry to have a care or he would run foul of them. "No, no! room enough!" he replied, still keeping on his course till he ran under the bows of the

---

* Maj. W. B. Hink's Historical Sketches, 42.

schooner, and then with all his men leaped on board. After a short but fierce struggle, the schooner was taken; when, with the two vessels, both under British colors, and his own boat hoisted upon the deck of one of them, Captain Hull set out upon his return, passed unsuspected three armed vessels of the enemy lying at anchor off Eaton's Neck, and brought his prizes safely into Black Rock harbor.

David Blakeman, of Monroe, a descendant of the Rev. Adam Blakeman, the first minister at Stratford, was among Captain Hull's crew upon this occasion. In the act of boarding he was wounded across the abdomen by a cutlass so that his bowels protruded, but he held the wound together, laying quietly upon his back until the vessel was captured, when the British surgeon dressed his wound. He recovered and lived to be an old man. He, in consequence of a peculiarity of voice, was known as " Squeaking David."[9]

Zechariah Blakeman, of Stratford, another descendant from the same clergyman, was killed by the British on the day. when Fairfield was burned, July 11, 1779. His body was brought to Stratford and laid under the shade of an old buttonwood tree on the green, where numbers of people flocked to view it. It was afterward buried in the graveyard near the place where a stone still bears the name of his son Abijah, who was lost at sea. The story goes that when Mr. Blakeman heard that the British had landed at Fairfield, he with others hurried to the scene of action, saying as he did so that he would bring down at least one red-coat, but was shot through the body by one of the enemy's sentinels while in the act of taking aim.

Washington passing through Stratford.

There are related[10] two incidents connected with Washington's progress through this part of the country during and subsequent to the Revolution. The first was related by Mrs. Alice Thompson, daughter of George Benjamin, of Stratford,

---

[9] Manuscript of the Rev. B. L. Swan.

[10] Maj. W. B. Hink's Historical Sketches, 44.

who died in May, 1862, aged nearly ninety-eight years. She was eleven years of age in 1775, and may have been thirteen or fourteen when she saw Washington. On that occasion she with other girls were picking berries on the banks of the Housatonic near the ferry, when suddenly a cry was heard that soldiers were crossing the river, and presently an officer with a number of others landed and asked the ferryman to direct them to the tavern. He replied: "Yonder is the tavern-keeper's daughter," and calling Alice bade her show General Lafayette the way to her father's house. She walked beside his horse on their way to the village, Lafayette talking to her in his charming broken English, telling her of his children and asking if she would not like to go to France with him to see them. On reaching home she found that General Washington had arrived by the western road. Her mother thus unexpectedly called upon to provide a dinner for two such distinguished guests would have apologized for her fare, but was reassured by Washington, who told her that all he wanted was simple food, and that what was good enough for her family was good enough for him.

Mrs. Benjamin happened to have some potatoes, then a great rarity, and Alice obtained leave to place them upon the table. In doing this she stepped between Washington and Lafayette, when the former, placing his hand on her head and turning her face toward him asked her name, and after some other questions told her to be a good girl and gave her his blessing. It may easily be supposed that she never forgot the circumstances.

The late Mrs. Benjamin Fairchild, who died a few years since aged over eighty, well remembered another visit made by Washington to Stratford while on his tour through New England in October, 1789. At that time Capt. Alison Benjamin lived at Old Mill, about half-way down the western slope of the hill; the house is still standing and is owned by Mr. Judson. This Capt. Benjamin built a sloop of forty-five tons burthen called the "Hunter of Berkshire," in a field south of the road, just opposite his own door, although there was no water in sight. It was nearly completed when Washington passed, and surprised at the sight, he alighted, went over to the place and questioned the workmen as to how they expected to get the vessel to the water. In reply, he was told that strong ways were to be built beneath the craft, to serve as a sled, upon which when winter came it would glide down hill to the creek, a branch of Yellow Mill stream, fully a quarter of a mile away, and in the spring would settle through the ice into the water, and by this plan it was subsequently launched.

A Midnight Party of Regulars.

In the winter of 1777 or 1778, the house of Joseph Lewis on Old Mill Hill was visited by a party of British soldiers on one of their plundering expeditions from Long Island. The family being roused at dead of night by the crashing in of the door, were unable to offer the slightest resistance, and therefore the soldiers not only stripped the house of all supplies of food stored for the winter, but, taking the quilts and coverings from the beds, spread them on the floor and emptied into them the contents of all the drawers and chests, and even the wearing apparel in daily use, tied them and carried all away.

Mr. Lewis besought them to leave for his use the Continental bills found in the till of one of the chests, as they could be no service to the regulars, but the officer in command tauntingly answered that they "would serve for a bonfire," and carried them with the rest of the booty.

Phebe Lewis, a girl of twelve years, had that winter finished her first spinning stint. As she lay in her trundle-bed while the soldiers were collecting the goods, she saw the large roll of wool, dyed dark blue, ready for the weaving, tossed upon the heap of plunder. It rolled to the edge nearest her bed, and as the soldier on guard turned his back for an instant, she grasped it, drew it into the bed and lay upon it. Of all the family stores and supplies this was the only article saved. The occupants of the beds were left shivering under a single sheet, and in the morning were fed and clothed by the charity of their neighbors.

Jabez Huntington Tomlinson, a student of Yale, and engaged to be married to Rebecca Lewis, was spending the night at the house. The soldiers on leaving ordered him to rise, dress and accompany them. He was taken to Long Island, thence to New York, and imprisoned in the Old Sugar House. After a confinement of nearly two years, he succeeded, through the connivance of a guard, in sending a letter to Sir Henry Clinton, detailing the circumstances of his capture and imprisonment, and praying for release. Clinton, surprised to receive so scholarly an epistle from one of the despised Yankees, granted the young man an interview and subsequently allowed him to return to his friends.[11]

Gen. David Wooster, son of Abraham and grandson of Edward Wooster, one of the first settlers of Derby, was born at Oronoke, in Stratford, March 2d, 1710–11. His father, Abraham Wooster, from Derby. settled at Stratford about 1706, in the southeast corner of what is now Huntington, where he remained until about 1720, when he settled at Quaker's Farms, in Derby, where he died.

David Wooster was graduated at Yale College in 1738. Something more would probably have been known of his early life but for the burning of all his family papers by the British when they pillaged New Haven in 1779.

When the Spanish war broke out in 1739 he was employed as first lieutenant, and in 1745 as captain of a coast guard.

In 1746, he married, in New Haven, the beautiful and accomplished daughter of Thomas Clapp, president of Yale College; but neither the society of a charming companion, his love of classic lore, nor his youthful inclination for a learned profession could restrain his devotion to the interests of his country. He continued in the service and was appointed captain in Colonel Burr's regiment, which formed a part of the troops sent by Connecticut in the celebrated successful expedition against Louisburg in 1745.

For a time he was retained among the colonial troops to keep possession of the conquest he had assisted in effecting, and he was soon after elected among the American officers to take charge of a cartel ship for France and England. He was

---

[11] Manuscript of Mrs. Rufus W. Bunnell.

not permitted to land in France, but was received in England with distinguished honor.

The young American officer, as he was called, was presented to the King and became a favorite of the court and people. The King admitted him into the regular service and presented him with a captaincy in Sir William Pepperell's regiment, with half-pay for life. His likeness at full length was taken and transferred to the periodicals of that day. The peace of Aix-la-Chapelle, which took place in 1748, restored Louisburg to France, and the young American officer to his home and family.

In the French war of 1756, he was appointed colonel of a regiment raised in Connecticut, and afterwards to the command of a brigade, in which station he remained until the peace of 1763, when he returned again to his family.

Soon after this he engaged in mercantile business in New Haven, and held the office of his majesty's collector of the customs of that port.

When the Revolutionary troubles began, although an officer in the British regular army, entitled to half-pay for life, he did not hesitate to take sides with his native country, and his pen and sword were actively employed in the defense of its rights.

After the battle of Lexington, he, with a few others, while engaged in the General Assembly in May, 1775, planned the expedition from Connecticut to seize and retain the fort at Ticonderoga, and to enable them to carry their plans into execution they privately obtained a loan of eighteen hundred dollars from the treasury of the state, for which they became personally responsible ; the result being that on the 10th of May, this fort was surprised and delivered up to Allen and Arnold, and their brave followers.

Congress, when informed of this transaction, recommended that an inventory of the cannon and military stores found in the fort should be taken, " in order," as they say, " that they may be safely returned when the restoration of the former harmony between Great Britain and these colonies shall render it prudent and consistent with the overruling care of self-preservation."

The military experience, as well as the daring spirit of General Wooster, recommended him to Congress when raising an army of defence, and among the eight brigadier generals appointed by that body on the 22d of June, 1775, he was the third in rank.

During the campaign of 1776 General Wooster was employed principally along the Canada line, and at one time he had the command of the Continental troops in that quarter.

After this expedition he returned home and was appointed first major-general of the militia of his state. During the winter of 1776 and 1777 he was employed in protecting Connecticut against the enemy, and particularly the neighborhood of Danbury, where large magazines of provisions and other articles had been collected by the Americans. He had just returned to New Haven from one of his tours when he heard on Friday, the 15th of April, 1777, that a body of two thousand men, sent from New York on the preceding day, had effected a landing at Norwalk and Fairfield for the purpose of destroying the magazines at Danbury, which object they accomplished the next day.

On hearing this news Generals Wooster and Arnold set off from New Haven to join the militia hastily collected by General Silliman, who numbered about six hundred, and with this small force it was determined to attack the enemy on their retreat, and a part of the men were put under General Wooster and a part under General Arnold. General Wooster with his men pursued the enemy the next morning, but he having inexperienced militia and the enemy having several field-pieces, his men, after doing considerable execution, were broken and gave way. The General was rallying them when he received a mortal wound. A musket ball hit him obliquely, broke his backbone, lodged within him and could not be extracted. He was removed from the field, his wounds dressed and he was conveyed to Danbury where all possible care was taken of him. His wife and son were sent for and came, but skill and kindness could not save him, for he died on the second day of May, 1777, at the age of sixty-six years.

Much care has been exercised to secure lists of Revolutionary soldiers from Stratford, with very little success. If anything further shall be obtained it will be placed in the Appendix of this book. In another town of this State, some years since, an aged woman was asked who of the town went to the war as soldiers. Her answer was: "Who went? They all went." This answer, apparently, is appropriate to Stratford.

Gen. Joseph Walker. The inscription on his tombstone says: "He entered the American Army in the year 1777, served his country in the several grades of office, from a Captain to a Major General."

Capt. Ebenezer Coe, wounded at Ridgefield, April 27, 1777.

Capt. Nehemiah Gorham served through the war. He died Feb. 17, 1836, aged 83 years.

Capt. Beach Tomlinson, of Ripton, was in the army.

William Thompson was killed at Ridgefield, April 27, 1777; and on May 4, 1777, the Sunday after his death, the Rev. Izrahiah Wetmore preached his funeral sermon at Stratford. Text, Isaiah ix. 5. The manuscript sermon is still preserved by the Wetmore family.

George Thompson, son of Daniel, is recorded in Ripton, in 1776, as "died in the army."

Agur Tomlinson, of Ripton, son of Capt. Beach Tomlinson, was in the army.

Samuel DeForest, born in July, 1758,

Abel DeForest, born in April, 1761,

Mills DeForest, born in May. 1763,

Gideon DeForest, born in September, 1765; all sons of Joseph DeForest of Stratford, were in the war; all drew pensions many years, and all met in a reunion at Gideon's home at Edmeston, Otsego County, N. Y., in 1835, fifty-four years after the war closed, when the youngest was 70 years of age and the eldest 77.

Capt. Stephen Middlebrook and his company were in the war as represented by receipts.

"Received, March 15, 1779, of Silvanus Starling, one of the Selectmen of Stratford, Fifty-seven pounds, twelve shillings lawful money, which is in full for my services, and the persons under my command, in keeping guard at North Fairfield in April, 1777.

Rec⁴ per STEPHEN MIDDLEBROOK."

Nathan Gorham was born in 1751 and died May 28, 1839, aged 88 years.

Before the Revolution he and John Barlow sailed together in the West India trade, but when the war broke out, they discontinued the business through fear of the British war vessels by whom they might be captured. After a little time Barlow obtained command of an American privateer, to sail from Boston, and engaged Gorham as his mate and sail maker.

"Ride and Tie."

Their journey to Boston was accomplished in the following manner, called "Ride and Tie." They purchased an old horse for seven dollars, with which they started, one riding and going ahead a number of miles then tying the horse so it could eat grass, pursued his journey on foot. When the other came to the horse he rode him, and passing his fellow traveler continued his stipulated number of miles then tied the horse to eat and took his journey on foot as before. When they had in this manner reached near Boston they turned the horse into the highway to care for himself, and went to their boat.

They sailed with the purpose of capturing vessels from England with supplies for British troops in America. After sailing around about ten days, they sighted a ship and giving chase, she made more sail as if trying to escape being captured, and the privateer being a fast sailer soon came up, and running along side, commanded her to strike—or in other words, to surrender. Upon this she opened her ports, showing herself a man of war, and being so near, the privateer could only surrender, and the men were taken as prisoners of war. They were all sent to New York and put on board the Jersey, a prison ship lying in the East river.

Camp disorder (which was diarrhœa), soon broke out among the prisoners, carrying off from ten to fifteen a day. Mr. Gorham being a good oarsman was detailed as one of the boatmen to take the dead ashore and bury them, and thereby he escaped severe illness. This burying was performed where the Navy Yard is now in the city of Brooklyn. A large excavation was made and when a corpse was put in some earth was thrown upon it, and thus one after another, until the place was filled, and then another excavation was made. All were taken ill, but many not severely, enlisted in the British service as the only way to escape death, as they were immediately transferred to healthy quarters. As soon as Mr. Gorham was taken ill he enlisted and was put on board a war vessel, in which they sailed to the southward. One morning they fell in with a privateer and tried to decoy her alongside, but did not succeed. The privateer was armed with a long 32 pounder, while the war vessel had short guns, and the firing of the former was very dangerous to the latter, but she kept at a distance, and at evening disappeared. To repair damages the war vessel put into St. Augustine, Florida, that being then a Spanish port, and while repairing, the soldiers were at liberty in the port. Mr. Gorham and two others finding an old canoe agreed to try to make their escape, although at great hazard. They saved from their rations enough to last them two or three days. The canoe being leaky Gorham stole a calking iron to make it tight when they should reach a place out of danger of being captured. They coasted the canoe most of the way in sounds and inland waters to the north part of North Carolina, going ashore nights and begging what they needed to eat, in which effort they would have had but little difficulty had it not been for the savage dogs, which were so fierce that they several times feared being torn in pieces. When they left the canoe to come on land Mr. Gorham put the calking iron in his pocket thinking he might sell it for a few pennies or something to eat. He did not part with it, however, but brought it to Stratford and kept it. About 1830 Mr. Nathan Birdsey McEwen, grand-son of Nathan Gorham, had built a boat and desiring to calk it went to his grandfather to borrow a calking iron, upon which he gave him this iron that he stole from the British war ship and told him this history how he came by it, and Mr. McEwen named it "The Story of the Calking Iron." In the year 1884, Mr. McEwen being eighty years of age, and the iron having been in possession of himself and his grandfather over one hundred years, he gave it and its history to his nephew, Robert W. Curtis, for transmission as a relic of the hardships of the American Revolution. The iron has a stamp of the British crown upon it."

Nathan Gorham was in active service in the Revolution, at New York City, and told the following story, a part of which has already been published as Revolutionary history:

"I was in the retreat from Long Island and barely escaped with life. The Stratford Company was the last to leave, and just as the last boat was leaving the British Lighthorse were coming down upon it, and it was so loaded that three men were left—John Benjamin, myself and another. We ran up the river where the Navy Yard now is, and finding a small boat, although dried and leaky, we launched it and jumped in and with pieces of a rail rowed as well as we could for the New York shore, bailing with our hats. We drifted with the tide up to a place called Corlear's Hook and almost to where the British had commenced crossing, our boat sinking under us as we struck the shore. We started on a run fearing we would be cut off. The day being very hot we suffered dreadfully with thirst, when seeing a well the third man said he must have some water or he should die. Benjamin and myself, not daring to go, advised him not to, but he went. Benjamin, and myself narrowly escaped being cut off, but the man who went to the well was never heard of again. In Frost's History of the United States (II. 211), the three are reported as staying behind for plunder, but afterwards returning to their ranks, which is a decided error."

Nathan Gorham, although three years in the service, enlisted only three months at a time, and therefore received only a pension of thirty-six dollars per year. He died May 28, 1839, aged 88 years.

---

[12] Manuscript of Nathan B. McEwen.

"John Barlow died May 4, 1786, in the 37th year of his age. His tombstone is in the Congregational Cemetery, on which is the following inscription, which he copied from the monument of an English Admiral's tomb in the West Indies:

"Though Boreas' blasts and Neptune's waves
Have tossed me to and fro ;
In spite of death, by God's decree
I harbor here below,
Where I do now at anchor ride
With many of our fleet.
Yet once again I must set sail
Our Admiral Christ to meet."

The following is a copy of the Roll of Lieut. William Hall's Company of Guard, stationed for four years—from 1777 to 1782—in the old Borroughs store building on the wharf of Bridgeport, furnished by Wildman Hall, one of the members of the company and its last survivor, to Dea. Isaac Sherman. The said Wildman Hall died July 10, 1851.

Officers in 1781.

Lieut. William Hall, Sargt. Isaac Patchen,
Corpl. Joel Parish.

Privates.

Thomas Cooke,	Samuel French, clerk,
Ebenezer Hawley,	Lyman Hall,
Samuel Wheeler,	Ichabod Beardsley,
Zachariah Wheeler,	Salmon Patchin,
Gideon Wells,	James Gregory,
James Crawford,	Josiah Burritt,
John Porter,	Sherman Burritt,
William Hubbell,	Denton Seeley,
Lyman Knapp,	John McEnzie,
Ebenezer Gregory,	Seth Bulkley,
Wildman Hall.	Joseph Hawes.

A Substitute Paid for.

"Stratford in Connecticut, Febru^y 20th, 1778.
"This may certify that Phillip Benjamin and Stephen Beers, both of the town of Stratford in Fairfield County, have hired Joel Beers, an able bodied Man, to Inlist himself

to serve during the present war between the American States and Great Britain, in one of the sixteen Battallions raised and commanded by Samuel B. Webb, Esqr.

"per me Joseph Walker, Lieu. Sd. Reg."

Mr. Nathan B. McEwen gave the following, told to him by his father:

" In the war of the Revolution my grandfather and great uncle Daniel McEwen owned land in the Great Neck, near Stratford Point, and fearing they might be taken prisoners, when British vessels were on the Sound or by boats coming from Long Island for that purpose, they placed my father, then a small boy, on Round Hill—the highest land on the Neck—to watch for any vessel that might land, and give the alarm. Many a tedious hour, he said, he spent there for that purpose.

" At one time there came two vessels and cruised off and on most of the day. The town was alarmed and the militia were called out, and a small gun which in derision was called the Clister pipe, was taken down the neck to oppose the landing of the British.

" While there a squall came up sudden and struck the brig Kingfisher, which immediately sank. Then a great shout went up from those on shore. Her masts being out of water the crew took refuge in the riging. It was not known whether any were lost except two men they had taken prisoners at Branford, and their bodies drifted ashore near where they were taken prisoners."

A Traditionary Story well authenticated.

During the Revolution there was much contraband traffic between Connecticut and Long Island, where the British soldiers were quartered much of the time, which was very profitable if the parties were not detected, and so much so that loyal men would sometimes engage in it. Many fast rowing boats were kept for this purpose, so many that it was difficult to obtain witnesses against anyone, because nearly all boatmen were interested, and they were seldom caught except by government boats employed for that purpose.

In one case,[14] in the month of March, the weather being fine, several young men—John Thompson, William Southworth, William Beers, and others, hired a sailor by the name of Crowell, who came in with a boat of codfish from the east, and Nathan Gorham, another sailor, and started on a trip, of the kind which was called Corderoy. The name was in consequence of the kind of cloth obtained in exchange for the truck carried over.

They went over in the night and did their trading in the forenoon of the next day, and came back in the afternoon near evening. Arriving near the north shore of the Sound, they saw a government boat beating off and on at the mouth of Stratford harbor, and therefore kept off in the Sound waiting to run in under cover of darkness. But unfortunately, a snow squall came up, and they were compelled to run before it, the wind blowing very hard, the sea high and frequently breaking into the boat.

Crowell and Gorham, clothed with heavy pea jackets, sat in the stern of the boat and thereby breaking off much of the sea, each holding an oar to steer the boat, soon became coated with ice which kept them warm, while the others bailed the boat, suffering with the cold.

They thus scud the boat nearly to the east end of Long Island, where they run ashore. Some of them went for a light and on returning found Beers frozen to death. Crowell's and Gorham's pea-jackets were so frozen that it was necessary for them to get out of and leave them where they sat. The snow having become deep there were only two of them able to reach a house, where they found a gang of men on a carouse, who at once went and helped bring in the others, safely, although some had frozen hands, except Beers, who was dead.

After staying there until they were in condition to return home, and having rewarded their preservers with goods they had purchased, they returned home safely, but found their friends had given them up as lost.

William Beers was a young man, just out of his appren-

---

[14] Manuscript of the late Nathan B. McEwen.

ticeship, but twenty-one years of age, having worked in a
warm shoe shop all winter and therefore could not endure
the cold.

John Thompson, the father of Joseph Thompson, lost the
ends of his thumb and fingers.

A Great Jubilee Day in North Stratford.

"The 26th day of May, 1783, the inhabitants of North
Stratford set apart as a day of Public Rejoicing for the late
publications of peace. At one o'clock, P. M., the people being convened at the Meeting House, public worship was
opened by singing. The Rev. Mr. Beebee then made a
prayer well adapted and suitable for the occasion. They
then sung a .Psalm. Mr. Lewis Beebee, a student in Yale
College, made an oration with great propriety. The congregation then sung an anthem. The Rev. Mr. Beebee, then requested the Ladies to take their seats prepared on an eminence for their reception when they walked in procession,
and upwards of 300 being seated the committee who were
appointed to wait on them supplied their table with necessaries for refreshments. In the meantime the two companies
of malitia being drawn up performed many maneuvers, and
firing by plattoons, genl¹ volleys and street firing, and the
artillery discharging their cannon between each volley with
much regularity and accuracy. After which a stage was prepared in the center and the following toasts were given:

1st. The United States in Congress Assembled.

2d. Genˡ Washington and the brave Officers and soldiers
of his command.

3d. Our Faithful and Illustrious Allies.

4th. The Friendly Powers of Europe.

5th. The Governor and Company of the State of Connecticut.

6th. May the present peace prove a glorious one and last
forever.

7th. May tyranny and despotism sink, and rise no more.

8th. May the late war prove an admonition to Great
Britain, and the present peace teach its inhabitants their true
interests.

9th. The Navy of the United States of America.

10th. May the Union of these States be perpetual and uninterrupted.

11th. May our Trade and Navigation Extend to both Indies and the Balance be found in our favour.

12th. May the American Flag always be a scourge to tyrants.

13th. May the Virtuous Daughters of America bestow their favours only on those who have Courage to defend them.

14th. May Vermont be received into the Federal Union and the Green Mountain Boys flourish."

"At the end of each toast a cannon was discharged.

"The whole was conducted with the greatest decency and every mind seemed to show satisfaction."

CHAPTER XVI.

AFTER THE WAR.

ONG was the struggle for the Independence of the United States, and immensely great was the victory. Lord Cornwallis surrendered his army and navy on the 19th of October, 1781, which was the virtual close of the war, although peace was not lawfully proclaimed until after the treaty was signed by the King, September 3, 1783, a preliminary treaty having been signed November 30, 1782.

Naturally it might be expected that the spirit and enterprise of the people, by such a seven years' struggle, would be broken and greatly reduced, but the contrary were the precise facts, notwithstanding the fact that the waste and death resulting from the war had been very great. This statement is warranted by the doings of the inhabitants in the town meeting, and by subsequent history. Before the war closed, the increase of numbers and the prosperity of the people are manifested in the following action to divide the township:

"March 20, 1780. The meeting then took into consideration the expediency of dividing the town into two townships, and voted that on condition that they could agree on a proper line of division they would apply to the General Assembly for the privilege of being made and established into two townships, and thereupon Messrs. Mr. Nathan Birdsey, Daniel Judson, Esqr., Mr. Joseph Curtiss, Col. Samuel Whiting, Samuel Adams, Esqr., Maj. Agur Judson, Elisha Mills, Esqr., Capt. Nathan Booth, Capt. Samuel Blakeman, Capt. Benjamin Nichols, Abraham Brinsmade, Esqr., Mr. Stephen Middlebrook, Capt. John Sherwood, Capt. Zechariah Coe, Stephen Burroughs, Esqr., Daniel Bennitt, Esqr., Mr. Silas Nichols, Mr. Judson Curtiss, and Mr. Zechariah Summers were appointed a committee to view and affix a line where it shall be most convenient to divide the town into two townships and make report to this meeting at their next adjournment."

The next year another committee was appointed for the same purpose, and upon their report, which was to divide the town by a line running east and west, setting off six miles in width of the north end of the township for a new town, a protest was made, and a delegation was appointed to go to the General Assembly and oppose the petition prepared to be sent to that body, and here the matter ended.

Soon after the surrender of Cornwallis, that is, December 31, 1781, another effort was made for a new township.

"After much debate it was finally motioned and unanimously voted that the parish of New Stratford and that part of North Fairfield parish that belongs to Stratford and such part of the Northerly part of North Stratford parish as may be agreed on by and between the said parishes aforesaid, be set off for a separate distinct town."

This proposition was not granted by the Legislature, but it reveals the spirit and courage of progress.

The next year a proposition was brought before the town to allow a dam and mill to be built on the Pequonnock river, which resulted, some years later, in the establishment of the Berkshire mills.[1]

William Pixlee, the son of Peter and grandson of William, one of the early settlers on Old Mill green, was a man of good standing, owned the old Pixlee homestead, and

---

[1] Dec. 30, 1782. On motion made by William Pixlee, showing to this meeting that there was a very convenient place to erect a tide mill on Pequonnock River, joining his home lot, which would be very serviceable to the town and at Great service to the public in general ; and asked the advice and approbation of this meeting in said motion ; Voted that they have no objections against the erecting a mill at the place proposed in case no damage be done thereby to the public by obstructing the navigation in said river ; nor any private injury to the property of any private person.

27

in the proposition to build this mill was following out the enterprise of his grandfather, who was a spirited, energetic man.

Mr. Pixlee built his mill, in all probability, and a bridge across the Pequonnock river, and opened a road or highway from near his dwelling at Old Mill Green down to it, it being the street now known as the Huntington road, for, in a town vote in March, 1792, the selectmen were authorized "to employ persons to keep in good repair the bridges called Pixlee's Bridge and Benjamin's Bridge;" Pixlee's bridge being at what has been since called Berkshire Mills.

On January 9, 1786, another proposition for town improvement was accepted by the town, which was known several years as Benjamin's Bridge.

"Voted, that upon consideration that a highway is opened through the Newfield to the Old Mill Creek and a good substantial cart-bridge erected across said creek and a highway opened to New Pasture Point by John Benjamin and others by the last day of December next, then said Benjamin and others shall be entitled to receive one-half penny on the pound out of the 2½ tax laid on the list of 1785, of the town treasurer."

The bridge was built and the road opened, which is now the Stratford road, and after six years the town, in March, 1792, granted another privilege in conjunction with it.

" Upon application of Joseph Walker of Stratford, praying liberty for the exclusive privilege of the salt water River or Creek running on the east side of New Pasture Point, being the same over which Benjamin's Bridge so-called is erected, for the purpose of building a Grist Mill:

Voted, That liberty is granted the said Walker, his heirs and assigns forever, for the purpose aforesaid; provided that said mill and dam be erected within seven years from this date; and also provided the mill dam does not injure the bridge erected across said river or creek; and also provided he makes all damages good to private property."

Three years later, some of the people of Stratford instituted measures for depriving General Walker of this privilege, and he being an old Revolutionary soldier, and having a will of his own, determined not to be defeated. He had then expended much money and time, and therefore petitioned the legislature, at the October session of 1795, for action on the matter, with advantageous result:

"Upon the petition of Joseph Walker of Stratford, in the County of Fairfield, showing to this Assembly that the inhabitants of the town of Stratford at a legal town meeting held on the 5th day of March, 1792, granted to him, his heirs and assigns the exclusive privilege of a certain salt water creek or arm of the sea on the easterly side of the Newfield Harbour in said town, being known and called by the name of Old Mill Creek, for the purpose of erecting a tide mill, and that he has proceeded to improve said grant, and laid out and expended large sums of money in prosecuting said business, and that he now finds some individuals in said town object to his proceedings to improve said grant, praying relief as per petition on file:

Resolved by this Assembly, That said grant of said town of Stratford, as aforesaid, made to the petitioner be and the same is hereby ratified and confirmed; and liberty is hereby granted to the petitioner, his heirs and assigns to erect and build a dam across said creek or river, at or near Benjamin's Bridge, in such manner as to use and employ the mill or mills that may be there erected to the greatest advantage; provided, nevertheless, that nothing in said resolve shall be construed to bar said town of Stratford from compelling the petitioner, his heirs and assigns, to repair any injury he or they may do said Benjamin's Bridge by erecting said mill-dam; and also provided that nothing in this resolve contained shall be construed to bar or affect the right which any individual may have to any action against the petitioner, his heirs and assigns in case they are damnified by the overflowing of the waters occasioned by said dam."

Old Mill creek is what is now called the Yellow Mill-pond and Pembroke lake, and extended northward to Old Mill Green. The elder residents of Stratford remember when vessels of considerable size were built at the head of the creek and floated down and over the causeway, at high water, to the harbor.

The tide in this creek always set back to Old Mill until the railroad culvert was built, which stopped the water from flowing above that point.

This mill, built by Gen. Joseph Walker, had a number of owners, the last of whom was Mr. George F. Cook, and he was the unfortunate loser when it was set afire and burned down in 1884.

The mill was painted yellow, and had been known many years as the Yellow Mill.

The desire for a new township or townships continued with increased interest and effort and in 1786, in town meeting, they gave consent that Ripton, North Stratford and New Stratford might become separate towns, and in 1789, Ripton and New Stratford were made a separate township.

In August, 1787, the following action as to the ferry road was taken: " Voted, that the selectmen procure an highway at New Pasture Point to accommodate the Ferry, and if they cannot agree with the owners of the land, to apply to the County Court for the purpose aforesaid."

The road was secured, and passed around the point from where the Steel Works now stand, along the shore to Benjamin's Bridge.

The only public road or highway coming to this Point was what is now Pembroke street, which had been in use probably more than one hundred years.

The Congregational Church and Meeting-house.

The third meeting-house in Stratford village had served the congregation well about forty years, was in good repair, when, on the afternoon of June 17, 1785, it was burned to the ground, being struck by lightning. This edifice stood on Watch-house Hill, and the destruction of it, so soon after the Revolutionary War, was a great calamity to the society and people.

Some description of this unfortunate occurrence, and the building of a new house, has been preserved by the thoughtfulness of one of Stratford's own citizens, having been written in an Almanac for that same year, which is now just one hundred years ago ; and it is here produced with pleasure.

In this house Mr. Gold had preached about eight years, and Mr. lzrahiah Wetmore twenty-seven years, but had resigned his pastorate five years before, and Mr. Stephen W. Stebbins had preached in it about one year when it was burned.

The burning of the Stratford Meeting-house as recorded by John Brooks.

"On Friday, the 17th day of June, 1785, at about 6 o'clock in the afternoon, Stratford meeting-house was struck with lightning and within about one hour and a half it was totally reduced to ashes. The fire broke out from the steeple, round the plate on the south side, all in an instant. The house on that side was one continued blaze instantaneously. The quantity of fire contained in the clap or explosion, was supposed to be very great, and all efforts to save the house was in vain.

" The Society having collected timber and other materials erected another house of the same dimensions as the former and placed it on Hiell's hill, so-called. The frame of this new house they commenced raising on Friday, the 17th of May, 1786, and finished it on Saturday the 18th at about sundown.

" The society with united zeal proceeded with this building and completed, painted, glazed and plastered it on Saturday, the 11th day of November, in just 25 weeks after it was erected; and on the Sunday following, Nov. 12, 1786, the congregation met in it in the forenoon for the purpose of public worship which was conducted by the Rev. Stephen W. Sebbins, who introduced the services by singing the 102d Psalm, 2d part. Next in succession followed a very pertinent extempore prayer suitable to the occasion and dedication of said house. The 1st text was from the 107 psalm at the 7th verse. The subject matter of the sermon was upon the duty of attending the public worship and other ordinances of Christ's Church, with becoming reverance and fear; and the sacrament of the Lord's supper was administered the same forenoon.

" In the afternoon the service began at 3 o'clock, introduced in the usual manner, and a sermon delivered by the Rev. Mr. Stebbins before a very numerous audience composed of the two Societies, in this place, unitedly convened with their respective pastors—the Rev. Mr. Leaming, the Episcopal Rector—and a number of gentlemen from the other parishes of the town. The sermon was on the subject of God's recording his name in his temple; and William Brooks had a child baptized by the name of Anna,[2] the first to whom that ordinance was administered in said house.'"

This was a commodious edifice, located near the site of the present house of worship of the same society, and it continued in use until the one now standing was built in 1858. Of this building a good picture is preserved, showing it to have been an imposing structure for the times, built with much skill of architecture and workmanship. This is especially exhibited by the representation of the interior of the house. There were doors on the south side and the two ends, it being the same style of meeting-house that prevailed for a hundred years or more in this State, the first one of the kind having been built at Farmington.

When this house was to be torn down, and the carpenters had commenced their work, Mr. Rufus W. Bunnell, on the morning of November 1, 1858, stepped into the front door to take a last look at the familiar seats and walls, when the thought struck him—yes, struck him—to make a drawing as it then appeared. This he did, on an old scrap of paper, so perfectly that the wood engraver[4] has produced the accompanying finely-finished illustration of the sacred old inclosure. The paneling, table, carpet, windows, pulpit and sounding-board over it are to be seen in life-like vividness, as they were when the congregation last departed from that long familiar place. The sounding-board was finished in a more ornamental style than was usual, by the dome-like paneling

---

[2] The family record says Polly.

[3] This record was made by John Brooks in the back part of a Connecticut *Register* for 1785—Green's first Register—the calculations being made by Nathan Daboll, of the academy in Plainfield. (Manuscript of the Rev. B. L. Swan.)

[4] Mr. John E. Sweet, of Bridgeport.

INTERIOR OF THE CONGREGATIONAL CHURCH TAKEN NOVEMBER 1, 1858.

above it, forming a much more imposing appearance than was customary in the meeting-houses of that day. It was not the intention of the artist to represent the pews, but only the main aisle and the side of the house on which the pulpit stood.

It is with much satisfaction that the accompanying cut is secured for this work.

This was the fourth house of worship for this, the old society, and in 1858 they commenced the fifth, which was completed in modern style inside and out, and was dedicated on the 27th of October, 1859, an ornament to the village, and a pleasant house of worship.

The Manual of this Congregational Church of Stratford is a more than usually historical, extensive and valuable work of the kind, having been published in 1881, containing 84 pages. From it are taken the following sketches of Ministers and list of Deacons:

"*Rev. Izrahiah Wetmore,*' the third son of Rev. Izrahiah and Sarah (Booth) Wetmore, born August 30, 1729, at Stratford, was graduated at Yale College in 1748, received the degree of A.M. from the same institution in 1751; studied theology and entered the ministry; was settled pastor at Stratford from May, 1753, until 1780, at Trumbull from 1785 until 1798.

" He preached the Election Sermon before the Legislature of Connecticut in 1773; also a sermon in pamphlet form at the ordination of David Lewis Beebe to the pastorate of the first Church of Christ at Woodbridge, February 23, 1791 : and other autograph sermons still preserved.

' " He was warmly attached to the cause of Independence, and it is related of him that, ' When the news of the surrender of Lord Cornwallis to General Washington reached Stratford it was on Sunday and during worship. Word was immediately taken to the pulpit, while parson Wetmore was delivering his discourse. Straightening himself to his full height, and making known the intelligence, he said: It is no

---

⁵ This sketch is taken from the *Wetmore Genealogy.*

place for boisterous demonstrations in the house of God, but we may, in giving three cheers, only go through with the motions.' "

"*Rev. Stephen William Stebbins,* son of Stephen Stebbins, was born in East Long Meadow, Mass., June 26, 1758, graduated at Yale College in 1781, and ordained pastor of this Church, July 7, 1784. Just before his ordination, the Church made declaration of independency and reaffirmed the half-way covenant. He was dismissed in August, 1813, and afterwards settled in West Haven.

"*Rev. Matthew R. Dutton* was born in Watertown, Conn., June 3, 1783, graduated at Yale College in 1808, and was ordained in Stratford, September 20, 1814, having declined an urgent call from the Church in Portsmouth, N. H., Mr. Dutton continued pastor, universally esteemed and beloved, until the autumn of 1821, when he accepted the appointment of Professor of Mathematics and Natural Philosophy in Yale College. He died July 17, 1825.

" When Mr. Dutton was called to the Church, its spiritual condition was very low. Various causes, long operating, had greatly adulterated the doctrinal belief of many members. Some of the most prominent had become believers in Universalism. The enforcement of discipline, for errors in belief, had become wholly impracticable. Mr. Dutton, as a condition of accepting the call, stipulated for an open, thorough re-confession by the Church, of sound doctrine, and an assent to a solemn covenant to enforce discipline. The Confession of Faith and the Covenant now in use were, at that time, adopted, and only those who would assent to it were enrolled as members of the Church.

" Mr. Dutton's ministry was blessed to the spiritual life and efficiency of the Church. In 1821, on one Sunday, seventy persons were added to the Church.

"*Rev. Joshua Leavitt, D.D.,* was born in Heth, Franklin county, Mass., Sept. 8, 1794, graduated at Yale College, in September, 1814, and ordained pastor of this Church in February, 1825. He was dismissed in 1828, to become the Agent of the American Seamen's Friend Society in New

York. After that he was connected with the religious and secular press, and also with several institutions of Christian benevolence and moral reform. He died in 1873.

"*Rev. Thomas Robbins* was born in Norfolk, Conn., August 11, 1777, entered Yale College in 1792, and at the close of the Junior year he left and joined the Senior class in Williams College, where he was graduated in August, 1796. In September following he took the same degree, B.A., in his former class at Yale. In 1803 he was ordained Missionary of the Home Missionary Society, to the northern part of Ohio, where he labored until impaired health obliged him to return East. In May, 1809, he was installed pastor over the Church in East Windsor, Conn., where he continued until 1827, when he was dismissed at his own request. In February, 1830, he was installed pastor of this Church, and on September 9th, the following year, he was dismissed. He removed to Metapoisett, Mass., where for fourteen years he labored as pastor, and then resigning his charge became librarian of the Connecticut Historical Society at Hartford. He died at Colebrook, September 13, 1856, in the 80th year of his age.

"*Rev. Frederick W. Chapman* was born in Canfield, Trumbull county, Ohio, November 17, 1806; graduated at Yale College in 1828, and ordained pastor of this Church, September 5, 1832. He was dismissed April 16, 1839, and subsequently settled over the Church at Glastonbury. He died in 1876.

"*Rev. William Bouton Weed* was born in Canaan, March 22, 1811, graduated at Yale College in 1830, and for several years devoted himself to teaching. He was converted under a sermon which he heard at Chilicothe, Ohio, from the text, 'Be ye thankful.' In 1836, he began the study of the law, but abandoned it for the ministry and was ordained at Stratford pastor of this Church, December 4, 1839.

" During his ministry, which was a most successful one, Mr. Weed received many flattering calls to other pastorates. At length, thinking that a new field of labor might conduce to the invigoration of his enfeebled health, he accepted the invitation of the First Church in Norwalk, Conn., where he was installed June 27, 1855. He died December 3, 1860.

Mr. Weed was held in prominent regard by the ministers and churches of the State, as a man of eminent ability, and his teachings are gratefully remembered by those who were permitted to receive them. A book of his sermons, to which is prefixed a biographical notice, has been published.

"*Rev. Joseph R. Page* was born in New Brunswick, N. J., and was ordained pastor of the Presbyterian Church in Perry, Wyoming county, N. Y., February 6, 1839, from which place he came to Stratford, where he was installed pastor February 11, 1857. In October, 1858, he was dismissed, and soon assumed again the pastoral charge of his former Church at Perry. In June, 1868, he removed to East Avon, where, for about five years, he was acting pastor of the Presbyterian Church. In November, 1872, he removed to Rochester, where he served as missionary of the Rochester Presbytery. In February, 1875, he was installed pastor of the Presbyterian Church in Brighton, N. Y. In 1876, the degree of D.D. was conferred on him by Hamilton College.

Rev. Benjamin L. Swan was born in Medford, Mass., July 31, 1813; entered College in the Junior Class, but was providentially hindered from completing the course. He received the honorary degree of A.M. from Yale in 1844. He was ordained pastor of the Church in Fair Haven, Conn., in 1836; was installed pastor of the Church in Litchfield, Conn., in 1846. He was acting pastor at the South Church in Bridgeport, from June, 1856, to November, 1858. In September, 1858, he accepted the invitation of this Church, and was installed in October, 1858, and dismissed in 1863. In the spring of 1866, he became pastor of the Presbyterian Church in Oyster Bay, N. Y., where he labored until the Autumn of 1875, when domestic bereavement and ill health obliged him to resign his pastorate.

Rev. Lewis Charpiot was installed pastor of this Church May 25, 1864, and dismissed April 12, 1866.

Rev. William K. Hall was born in Boston, Mass., Nov. 4, 1836, was graduated at Yale College in 1859; pursued his theological studies in New Haven and Berlin, Germany, and was ordained October 17, 1862, chaplain of the Connecticut Volunteers. He was installed pastor of this Church, October 24, 1866, and the relation was dissolved at his request in May, 1872. In January, 1873, he accepted a call from the First Presbyterian Church in Newburgh, N. Y. He was chosen moderator of the New York Synod in 1878, and in the following year was appointed by the Secretary of War as one of the Board of Visitors at West Point.

Rev. Frank S. Fitch was born in Geneva, Ohio, February 24, 1846. He was graduated at Oberlin College in 1870, and at Yale Divinity School in 1873. He was ordained pastor of this Church June 17, 1873, and resigned in October, 1878, and on November 21st of the same year was installed pastor of the Seventh Street Congregational Church, Cincinnati, Ohio.

Rev. S. H. Dana was installed pastor March 12, 1879, and dismissed December 31, 1881.

Rev. Joel Stone Ives, son of the Rev. Alfred E., and Harriet P. (Stone) Ives, was born in Colebrook, Conn., Dec. 5, 1847; graduated at Amherst College, July 16, 1870, and from Yale Divinity School, May 14, 1874; licensed to preach by the New Haven Centre Association, May 4, 1873, and ordained the tenth pastor of the first church in East Hampton, September 29, 1874. From this church he was dismissed October 31, 1883; began to preach in Stratford November 1, and was installed pastor November 20, 1883.

He married, July 15, 1874, Emma S., daughter of Mr. Joel Ives Butler, of Meriden, Conn. Their children are Anne Emma, Mabel Sarah, died in 1879, and Joel Butler.

This Church has given to the Ministry the following named persons from her members :

"*Rev. Benjamin Blakeman,* son of the first pastor, was graduated at Harvard College in 1663. Closed a ministry at Malden, Mass., in 1678. He afterwards preached at Scarborough, and was subsequently in secular business.

Rev. Charles Chauncey, son of the pastor Israel, was the first pastor of the Stratfield Church and Society from 1695 to 1714, he having preached for that people considerably if not regularly two or more years before 1695. He died in 1714.

Rev. Isaac Chauncey, son of the pastor Israel Chauncey, was pastor at Hadley, Mass., from 1696 to 1745, when he died.

Rev. Nathaniel Chauncey, nephew of Israel Chauncey, the pastor, was the first recorded graduate of Yale College, and was pastor at Durham, Conn., from 1711 to 1756, when he died.

Rev. John Beach, son of Isaac Beach, of Stratford, was the pastor of the Congregational Church at Newtown from 1725 to 1732, and Rector of the Episcopal Church of the same place from 1732 to 1782, when he died.

Rev. John Goodsell, first pastor of the Church on Greenfield Hill from 1726 to 1756, when he died. He was only twenty years of age when he settled in the parish, the Church being organized at the time of his settlement, with twenty-six members, and at the close of the year 1741 the number was one hundred and sixty.

Rev. Jeremiah Curtis was the first pastor at Southington, and labored there from 1728 to 1755. He died there in 1795, aged eighty-nine years.

Rev. Jonathan Ingersoll was pastor at Ridgefield, from 1740 to 1778, when he died.

Rev. Mark Leavenworth was pastor at Waterbury from 1740 to 1797, when he died.

Rev. Nathan Birdsey was pastor at West Haven from 1742 to 1758, when from domestic considerations he retired to his homestead at Oronoke in Stratford, where he died in 1818, aged 103 years 5 months and 9 days. When one hundred years old he made the prayer at the ordination of Mr. Dutton. He had twelve children, and at his death his grandchildren had numbered seventy-six, his great grandchildren one hundred and sixty-three. The Rev. Joseph P. Thompson, D.D., was a descendant.

Rev. David Judson was pastor of the Congregational Church at Newtown from 1743 until 1776, when he died.

Rev. Hezekiah Gold, the son of the pastor, was pastor at Cornwall from 1755 until 1790, when he died.

Rev. Eden Burroughs was pastor of a Church at South Killingly, from 1760 until 1763, then pastor at Hanover, N. H., from 1772 until 1809. He preached at Hartford, Vt., from 1809 until 1813, when he died, aged seventy-five years. The Rev. E. B. Foster was a descendant.

Rev. Andrew Judson was pastor at Eastford from 1778 until 1804, when he died.

Rev. Nehemiah Beach Beardsley was ordained in 1816 and died in 1868.

Rev. Spencer F. Beard was ordained in 1829, and died at Andover, Mass. in 1876. The Rev. William H. Beard and the Rev. Edwin S. Beard are his sons.

Rev. William Russell, son of Alden and Sarah (Norton) Russell, was born in Stratford, February 15, 1815, graduated at Yale College in 1837, and Yale Divinity School in 1841. In 1842 he was settled in Wakeman, Ohio, where he remained three years. In January, 1846, he commenced preaching for the Congregational Church at Easthampton, Conn., and on October 14th was settled there as the seventh pastor of that Church, remaining until October 11, 1855, when he was dismissed. The next year he was installed pastor of the Second Congregational Church of New Ipswich, N. H., where after remaining three years he found the climate too severe for his health and was dismissed. In 1860, he became pastor of the Church in Sherman, Conn., and remained three years, at which time an asthmatic affection of long standing obliged him to relinquish the pulpit.

Since that time he has resided in Washington, D. C., in the service of the Government.

He married, May 10, 1842, Sarah Elizabeth Brown, of New Haven. Their children are Hattie Hamlin, b. Mar. 1, 1844; Sarah Norton, b. July 6, 1847, and Minnie Williams, b. Nov. 22, 1851.

Rev. Phineas Blakeman, ordained in 1843.

Rev. Charles Henry Russell, ordained in 1859.

Rev. Henry Samuel Barnum was graduated at Yale College in 1862 and became a Missionary of the A. B. C. F. M. in Persia in 1867.

Rev. Samuel F. Emerson was graduated at Yale College in 1872 and Union Theological Seminary in 1879.

Rev. Joyce Curtis, son of Solomon and Jerusha (Walker) Curtis, was born in 1787 and died in 1861.

Rev. Hezekiah Gold Ufford, son of Samuel and Abigail (Gold) Ufford, was born in 1779, graduated at Yale College in 1806, and died, January 23, 1863, aged 84 years.

George Wm. Judson, son of George T. Judson, was graduated at Yale College in 1884, and is now in Yale Divinity School.

Elder and Deacons of this Church.

" Philip Groves was the only Ruling Elder in this Church from near its organization to his death in 1676. He was Deputy to the General Court from this town as early as 1652, and in 1654 was chosen Assistant and as such was ' empowered to marry persons.'

" John Birdsey is referred to as Deacon in 1678. He died in 1690.

" Timothy Wilcockson is referred to as a Deacon in 1678. He died in 1714.

" Thomas Welles is mentioned as Deacon in 1707. He died in 1721.

" Robert Walker is named as a Deacon in 1722. He died in 1743.

" John Thompson is also mentioned as a Deacon in 1722. He died in 1765.

" Job Peck is styled Deacon on his grave stone, although no record of his appointment has been seen. He died in 1782.

Elnathan Wheeler, appointed in 1751, and died in 1761.
Isaiah Brown, appointed in 1755, and died in 1793.
Ebenezer Coe, appointed in 1784, and died in 1820.
Nathan McEwen, appointed in 1791, and died in 1810.
Samuel Ufford, appointed in 1801, and died in 1821.
Agur Curtiss, appointed in 1801, and died in 1838.
Philo Curtiss, appointed in ——, and died in 1852.
Agur Curtiss, appointed in ——, and died in 1868.
David P. Judson, appointed in 1837, and died in 1869.
Agur T. Curtiss, appointed in 1858.
Lewis Beers, appointed in 1858, and died in 1870.
Charles C. Welles, appointed in 1867.
Samuel T. Houghton, appointed in 1877.
Samuel E. Curtis, appointed in 1877.

Sketches of Prominent Men.

Hon. William Samuel Johnson, son of the Rev. Samuel Johnson, D.D., was born in Stratford, October 7, 1727, and died November 14th, 1819, aged 92 years and two months. His mother was Charity, widow of Benjamin Nicoll, of Islip, L. I., and daughter of Richard Floyd, of Brookhaven, L. I. He was fitted for college by his father and was graduated at Yale in 1744.

After this he pursued his studies in several classical lines while fitting himself for the profession of the law, upon which he soon entered, and gave, at once, much promise of a remarkably successful and honorable life work.

He married, at the age of twenty-two years, Ann, daughter of William Beach, of Stratford, in 1749, and made his residence in his native town.

In 1754, he was commissioned as lieutenant in the Stratford militia company.

In 1761, he was chosen Representative for Stratford, and again in 1765; and the next year he was elected an Assistant at the General Court.

When the first Continental Congress assembled in New York City in 1765, the representatives in that body, from Connecticut, were William Samuel Johnson, Eliphalet Dyer and David Rowland.

The next January 23, 1766, the University of Oxford, England, conferred on him the degree of Doctor of Laws.

His next service to the Colony of Connecticut was in reference to its title to land obtained of the Mohegan Indians, concerning which the Rev. E. E. Beardsley, D.D., makes the following brief statement :[6]

" In February, 1766, Connecticut was cited to appear before the King and Lords in Council, to answer in a matter which had been kept in agitation for nearly seventy years, and concerned the title to a large tract of land that Lieut. Governor Mason was appointed to obtain for the Colony, from the Mohegan Indians. He took the deed to himself, and the fact remained unnoticed until after his death, when the property was claimed by his heirs for services rendered to the Indians, as their agent. It was a part of their suit, too, to oppose the claim of Connecticut under pretense of protecting the rights of the Indians; and they appealed from the legal decisions against them in this country to the highest tribunal in England : while the title of the land was valuable, the most important question was one which affected the chartered rights of the Colony; for had they succeeded, ' the conduct of Mason would have been adjudged fraudulent, and the British Government would have made it a ground for taking away the charter.'

" Dr. Johnson was appointed by the General Assembly at its October session in 1766, to proceed to England and defend in that case. In obedience to this direction he arrived in London on the 8th of February," expecting to remain there a few months at longest; but it was nearly five years before he returned to his home.

His long stay in England, in which he was largely successful in retaining for the Colony the right of soil to the Mohegan lands, enabled him to become thoroughly acquainted with the public sentiment in that country towards the Colonies, which knowledge was of great service to this country after his return, when the Revolutionary conflict began.

---

[6] Life and Times of William Samuel Johnson, 35.

28

At the May session of the General Assembly, in 1772, Dr. Johnson was appointed one of the Judges of the Superior Court, which position allowed him favorable opportunities to continue his literary pursuits and correspondences which he had industriously improved up to this time, and which course he followed to the close of life.

In 1774, he was elected one of three to represent Connecticut in the Congress of the Colonies to meet in Philadelphia on the 5th of September, but having accepted previously an appointment as arbitrator on the estate of Van Renselaer of Albany, he was excused from serving and his place was filled by Silas Deane.

After the Declaration of Independence he remained at home most of the time except as related on page 421 of this book, maintaining, in regard to public acts, neutral ground to a considerable extent in relation to the great conflict for the liberty of the United States, until peace was declared.

In 1782, he came prominently before the public in his profession as an advocate in behalf of the State of Connecticut, in the great trial of the claims of this State to the Susquehanna lands in Pennsylvania.

From November, 1784, until May, 1787, he was a representative in Congress, from his native State.

The delegates sent by the Connecticut Legislature to form the Constitution of the United States, in 1787, consisted of William Samuel Johnson, Roger Sherman, a signer of the Declaration of Independence, and Oliver Ellsworth ; and in this great work each of these men rendered distinguished service.

While thus serving his country he was elected, on the 21st of May, 1787, president of Columbia College in New York City, which he accepted and removed his residence to that place where he remained, serving with much honor, until his resignation in the year 1800, when he retired to his old home in Stratford.

Dr. Johnson was reared in the Episcopal Church and to it he maintained his loyalty and devotion to the last, and as such exerted a large influence in behalf of that Church in the Colony and State of Connecticut and in the United States.

His literary attainments and culture were among the most complete and attractive of any among Americans, and his elegance of diction and charm of delivery were in few cases, if any, surpassed in his day.

Adopting the Constitution.

The question of adopting the Constitution of the United States excited great interest in Stratford, and at the town meeting held to elect delegates to a State convention to ratify or reject that instrument, there was much excitement, debate and anxiety, there being considerable strong opposition to it. The town meeting meet in the town house but adjourned to the meeting house, probably because of the great number present.

By the favor of Professor Charles F. Johnson, of Trinity College, Hartford, the following letter of Robert Charles Johnson, son of Dr. Wm. Samuel Johnson, to his father, is, upon solicitation, submitted to be published. This letter, although from a young man of only twenty-one years, gives some insight into the excitement and contest of that occasion, and of what a sincere, earnest young person can do if wisely trained, for it must be remembered that he had been greatly favored in his advantages of education and in public society. The letter was written to his father with no idea that it would ever be seen by any other person.

"Stratford November 1787.

Honored Sir: This afternoon I spoke in the town meeting. I observed the outlines of the declamation you read, and chained down the attention of a numerous audience for upwards of three-quarters of an hour. Silas Hubbell at the begining of the debate made a motion, that as I had been much with you, I should be requested to deliver my sentiments of the Constitution. The proposition was laughed at and rejected. I was then determined I would speak. Major [Joseph] Walker held me by the arm and said I should ruin everything. I waited till the moderator called for the votes, and then broke from him, jumped over the seats, mounted the pulpit stairs and succeeded beyond my expectations, equal to my wishes, and closed, with launching an empire on the sea of glory,' amidst a general clap of hands. Every one I met shook me by the hand and told me I was an honor to Stratford. [Indeed he was.] Then I went to hand in my vote, and the moderator—Major Judson—rose from his seat, shook me by the hand, and said, he 'publickly thanked me for the information and pleasure I had given, and that I was an honor to Stratford.' The Selectmen unitedly requested that I would preserve the train of my arguments, that they might print it, for that 'it was a pitty that they should be lost after making such an impression.' Can I not now by working the outlines of the declamation, and by close logical reasons intermingled submit it to men of sense and confirm my reputation? Sir, please write me as soon as cónvenient, as the Selectmen have already called on me for a copy of my speech. You, sir,' and Esquire Mills are chosen. I should certainly have been elected had not every one been persuaded from my information that you would attend. Esquire Bennett and myself were equally balanced, and had I had intriguing on ṁy side should have carried it against Esquire Mills. Forgive me this effusion of vanity."

In another letter to his brother who was in the Bermudas, a few days later, Dec. 3d, he further reveals the spirit of the occasion: "The new Constitution is almost the only subject of conversation. A town meeting was called at Stratford for the choice of delegates to the Constitutional Convention. All our Stratford orators spoke and were heard with impatience by a powerful opposition. Deacon Bennet was to be the man known to be a violent opposer of the Constitution.
. . . . After I sat down the temper of the house seemed to be changed, and they almost unanimously voted in my father and Esquire Mills. The Constitution, we flatter ourselves, will be adopted. The Pennsylvania convention is in favor of it. In Connecticut a decided superiority. General Parsons says he can engage to raise 15,000 volunteers who will stake their lives and fortunes on the event. Delaware, it is thought,

---

[1] Dr. Johnson was then President of Columbia College, and hence was in New York City.

will follow Pennsylvania, Massachusetts doubtful, but expected in favour. Virginia and Georgia in all probability, will adopt. New York against. Rhode Island out of the question; as much the scorn and derision of America as America is of the rest of the world.

"If not accepted, America will in all probability be a scene of anarchy and confusion. If adopted it will be some time before peace and serenity prevail. I will sacrifice my life in defence of it. I will wade up to my knees in blood that it may be established."

Such were the perils over which sailed the ship of state, and such the spirit of the young men who manned her; a spirit which has been manifested more grandly, if possible, in recent days, in preserving the Union, for which the Forefathers suffered so much.

Capt. William Birdsey, previous to 1762, owned and lived in a house that had been his father's, which stood at the foot of Main street, facing up the street. It was an old house.

In this year Mr. Birdsey then built a fine house on the northeast corner of the streets where now resides Dea. Samuel E. Curtis.

Capt. William Birdsey married in 1745, Eunice Benjamin, and was a wealthy, prosperous farmer, and not far from the time the new house was built, the Rev. Samuel Peters married his daughter.

Mr. Birdsey lived in this house until 1779 or '80, when the discouragements as to the success of the Revolution were very many and great; he, fearing if the British won the day he should lose all his property, went over and joined the British army on Long Island, where he remained until the war was over. Then he returned to Stratford to find that the government had confiscated his property, and that it was to be sold at auction.

The people of Stratford, knowing him to have been a very fine citizen, and true several years to the cause of American freedom, pitied him, and agreed among themselves not to bid on certain portions of the property, at the sale, so as to allow him to bid it in at a low price. This was done and he secured and retained the old house, and much of his land which had been in the family from the first. It is said that at the sale, one of his neighbors, Samuel Ufford, bid on one piece of land that seemed quite desirable, but this created such excitement that he came near being mobbed. Mr. Birdsey lived in the old house until his death.

In 1802, his son Everit Birdsey started to build a house on the site of the old house fronting up Main street. But as soon as he had removed the old building, the town authorities appeared and laid the highway directly over the site through the field southward, as it is at present, and in 1808, Everit Birdsey built his house on the corner directly east of the old site.

Abel Beach, in 1767, built the first house and barn on Stratford Point. It stood about twenty rods west of the lighthouse. His own residence was in the village across the street from the site of the first meeting-house at Sandy Hollow. He was a prominent man in business and enterprise.

Legrand Cannon, a merchant from New York City, bought the house and estate of Abel Beach at Stratford Point, about 1768, and Mr. Beach's homestead in the village east of Sandy Hollow opposite the site of the first meeting-house. This house was built by Nathan Beach, father of Abel, in 1722, who left it to his son Abel. Mr. Cannon bought also a brig of Abel Beach, which he run to the West Indies.

Edward DeForest married a daughter of Legrand Cannon, and to this daughter the father gave the house and land at the Point, and Mr. DeForest lived there several years until he killed his wife's slave-woman by stabbing her with a pitchfork, which created much talk, but nothing was done about it.[1]

Old Time Hospitality runs some risks not to be coveted. The late Nathan B. McEwen left the following record connected with his grandmother:

"The house known on Lindsley's Map as the Hon. Robert Fairchild's was built, in 1770, by my great-grandfather, Josiah Beers, for a good size homestead.

---

[1] Manuscript of Nathan B. McEwen.

" Tramps and travellers in those days had to find lodging and food in private families when too poor to pay for them at the Inn, which was easy to do, as it was considered an act of charity to care for such.

" A poor man called on Mr. Beers, late in the day, for food and lodging, saying he was sick and unable to go any further, and Mr. Beers took him into his home. The next morning he was much worse and could not go. He had a fever and at the end of about two weeks he died. Both Beers and his wife took the fever, and died leaving four young children, one son and three daughters.

" They had three uncles in good circumstances; each took a girl to bring up, and the boy was put out to work, being old enough to earn his living. The house and land were sold to maintain and bring up the girls.

" My grandmother was taken by Stephen Porter, who lived on the corner of Elm street and Michell's Lane in the lower part of the village. The other girls were taken by their uncles to Stepney in Monroe. Eunice married Stephen French, and the other married John Summers Hawley, and both raised a family.

" My grandmother, Sally, married Nathan Gorham. The son William Beers, married and had children, Lewis and Mary. He was a sailor and acquired some property."

Hon. Robert Walker was one of the most noted men that Stratford ever produced. He was born in 1704 and died in 1772, aged 68 years. The brief summary of his life as given on his tombstone appears to have been very true and appropriate. " He sustained many important offices in civil life, for many years before and at the time of his death. He was one of his Majesty's Council for the Colony of Connecticut, one of the Judges of the Superior Court, and a Colonel of the Militia; all which offices he discharged with fidelity and honor. He firmly believed and conscientiously practiced the Christian religion; was a kind husband, a tender parent, and faithful friend."

This inscription was doubtless written by his pastor and son-in-law, the Rev. Izrahiah Wetmore, who had known him intimately nineteen years, and it would be difficult to improve the epitaph.

Hon. Robert Walker was the son of Robert and Ruth (Wilcoxson) Walker, who was the son of Joseph and Abigail (Prudden) Walker, the son of Robert Walker, one of the founders of the Old South Church of Boston, Mass., and could therefore boast of as staunch puritan blood as any. His father was deacon in the Congregational Church, a man of influence and high standing in the town as well as in the Church, who died in 1743.

Robert, the son, after graduation at Yale College in 1730, became a lawyer, and as such was quite celebrated, having but few equals in his day, not excepting his rival the Hon. William Samuel Johnson, between whom and himself there was great friendship. He was first sent to the legislature in 1745, and served in that body fourteen sessions, and where he is styled first Mr., then Captain, and then Colonel, and in 1766, he was chosen an Assistant or member of the upper house in which position he served two years.

He was appointed Judge of the Superior Court first in 1762, and held that position five years. He was also Justice of the peace in his own township several years.

Robert Walker, Jr., son of the above, was also a prominent citizen, a lawyer, judge and influential man. He was graduated at Yale College in 1765, and was appointed by the General Court, October, 1766, " Surveyor of lands for the county of Fairfield, in the room of Mr. Judah Kellogg, resigned."[*] This was a fine beginning for a young man not twenty-one years of age. What position he took in the Revolution is not known, but soon after he became prominent as a lawyer, became Judge of Probate, serving a number of years ; Justice of the peace, and a well known and well tried public citizen. He died in 1810, and his epitaph, found on page 233 of this work, and probably written by his pastor the Rev. Timothy Cutler, gives high praise to his life and character. He was town clerk from 1789 to 1804.

Gen. Joseph Walker, brother of Robert, Jr., above, was born in 1756 ; graduated at Yale College in 1774, served

---

* Coll. Rec., xii, 502.

through the Revolution, beginning in 1777 as captain and closed a Major General. He was a number of times a representative to the legislature; was a prominent business man after the war. He built the first mill at Benjamin's Bridge, known for many years lately as the Yellow Mill at Pembroke Pond or Lake. His dwelling house, which he may have built, stands a few doors north of the railroad, on Main street in Stratford village. It is the old style of a long-roofed house with the end to the road and two immense elm trees in front of the lot in the street. There was a stone in the front, near the top of the chimney with the date, no doubt, on it, but this stone long since disappeared, very much to the regret of the historian if no one else.

Robert Fairchild, Esqr., was born in 1703 and died in 1793, "In the 90th year of his age," says his tombstone. He was one of the remarkable men of Stratford.

He probably practiced law, but held the office of Probate Judge many years. His house, which was built by Josiah Beers, in 1770, is still standing by a well of most delicious water, on Main street, first one south of the railroad, with the little office still attached where he spent much of his time for many years. He was town clerk from 1759 until 1789, and during the Revolution he was a firm patriot, and some of the resolutions recorded and printed in this book were probably the work of his pen, and if so, they show the energy, decision and earnestness with which he labored and used his pen during that great conflict. His fame as town clerk and probate judge is still spoken of as remarkable, and very honorable to the town, as well as to himself.

Rev. Nathan Birdsey died in Stratford, Jan. 28, 1818, aged 103 yrs. 5 months and 9 days. He was born Aug. 19, 1714; took his degree in Yale College in 1736, was settled as a minister in West Haven, 1742; preached there 16 years, then removed to his patrimonial estate at Oronoque in this town where he resided until his death. He married but once and lived with his wife 69 yrs. She died at the age of 88 yrs. He had 12 children, 76 grandchildren, 103 great-grand-children, and 7 of the 5th generation at his decease. Of his

12 children 6 were sons and 6 daughters, a daughter being born next after a son in every instance. His funeral was attended by a large concourse of people. among whom were about 100 of his posterity. A sermon was delivered on the occasion by the Rev. Stephen W. Stebbins from the text, "All the days of Methuselah were," etc.

Mr. Birdsey, after he left West Haven, continued to preach occasionally for many years. When he was over 100 years he officiated in the pulpit in Stratford. (See Sprague's Annals.) He retained his mental faculties in a remarkable degree until his death, although nearly blind and quite deaf at the last. (From Sprague's Annals.)

Mr. Birdsey married Dolly Hawley of Ridgefield, who was brought up by her aunt Cheney in Boston, of whom she learned to make wax figures or statuary. Some of her productions in this line are still preserved among her descendants, by the family of Aaron Benjamin.

Mr. Birdsey attended personally the ordination in Stratford of Rev. Hez. Gold in 1722 ; the Rev. Izrahiah Wetmore in 1753 ; the Rev. S. W. Stebbins in 1784 ; the Rev. Matthew R. Dutton in 1814, at the last, he being then 100 years old, offered the ordaining prayer, and afterwards dined with the council.

It is stated as tradition, that Mr. Birdsey, when a young and single man, dreamed that he should pass the night somewhere in his travels where the supper table would be set by a young lady wearing on her neck a blue bandanna handkerchief with white spots, and that he should marry her. This all came to pass at Mr. Hawley's in the person of Dorothy, whom he married.

There is preserved an account of the finding of a very good spring of water by the Rev. Nathan Birdsey in answer to prayer. While the question of his piety and true Christian life is not doubted, it is nevertheless true that if he had looked for a spring of water with the same earnestness any other time he would have found it just the same. One effect of prayer is to move persons to do their own duty and work, and then the Great Ruler of the Universe does his, or has it already done, long before the prayer is made.

The War of 1812.

No town acts are recorded in reference to this war. A few items have been gathered, while hurriedly collecting the the material for this work.

During this war against England, the United States employed vessels owned by individuals as privateers, or in other words, granted Letters of Marque to capture English vessels wherever found. Capt. Samuel C. Nicoll being a qualified person was thus engaged and some account of his services are here given. In such cases the engaging in this kind of employment is regarded the same as going to the field of battle in the army. The work of a privateer is very different from that of pirates. The following brief account of Capt. Nicoll is taken from Cogshall's History of the American Privateers, chapter vii.; published in 1856.

"The privateers Scourge and Rattlesnake appear to merit something more than a passing remark, as they were often in company in a distant sea, on the same cruising ground, and as they were very fortunate in capturing and annoying the enemy's trade and commerce, I shall devote a separate notice to them as their just due.

Though the worthy captains of both these vessels have passed away from earthly scenes, I hope their acts and deeds in their country's service will ever be appreciated, while bravery and patriotism are held in high regard by civilized nations.

"The Scourge was owned in New York, and commanded by Capt. Samuel Nicoll, a native of Stratford, Conn. He was a worthy, intelligent, enterprising man, and a good patriot.

"The Scourge was a large schooner privateer, mounting 15 guns, with musketry, etc., and suitably officered and manned for a long cruise. She sailed from New York in April, 1813, for the north coast of England and Norway.

"Captain Nicoll was a man of sound judgment, and a good financier. After he had made one or two successful cruises, he found it more to his advantage to remain on shore in the different parts of Norway, where he sent in most of his prizes, and attend to the sale of them than to go to sea, and

leave the management of his rich prizes in the hands of dis-
honest or incompetent persons.

"On the 19th of July, while Captain Nicoll was off the
North Cape in the Scourge, he fell in with and cruised for
several days in company with Commodore Rodgers, in the
United States frigate President, who was then cruising in
those high northern latitudes.

"After Commodore Rodgers left that region for a more
southerly one, the Scourge proceeded off the coast of Norway, and alternately off the North Cape, to intercept British
ships sailing to and from Archangel.

"The following list comprises a portion, but by no means
all the prizes captured by the Scourge. A great number
were sent into the different ports in the United States and
Norway, particularly into the harbor of Drontheim, and
many others were disposed of in various ways.

"Brigs Nottingham, 266 tons and 4 guns, and Britania,
4 guns, both from Onega, Russia, for Hull, cargoes lumber;
after an action of fifteen minutes, no lives lost; taken by the
Scourge.   •

"Prosperous, 260 tons and 4 guns, in ballast, from New-.
castle; given up to dispose of the prisoners by the Scourge.

"Latona, of Shields, by the Scourge.

"Experiment, of Aberdeen, by the Scourge.

"Ship Brutus, taken by the Scourge and Rattlesnake;
given up to dispose of the prisoners.

"Westmoreland, from London, partly laden with sugars;
taken by the Scourge.

"The Brothers, of 126 tons, from Lancaster; by the
Scourge.

"Brig. Burton, Ludlin, of 266 tons, and 4 guns, from
Onega for Hull; by the Scourge. •

"Brig Hope, 260 tons, 4 guns, cargo of linseed; also the
Economy, of 181 tons, and 2 guns, with tar; both from
Archangel for England; by the Scourge.   ▪

"After these captures the Scourge was refitted, at Drontheim, and rigged into a brig, for a new cruise under the
command of Capt. J. R. Perry, Captain Nicoll remained in
Drontheim to look after the prizes.

The Chandelier.

It is said that during these cruising voyages as a privateer, Captain Nicoll obtained the very elegant chandelier which he gave to the Episcopal Church of Stratford, and which was used many years for lighting the Church. It was a richly ornamented article, for which he was offered in New York eighteen hundred dollars, and if it was still preserved whole would be worth a large sum of money, but it was distributed some years since in pieces, to any who desired.

Scatter, Men, Scatter.[10]

In this conflict of 1812, with Great Britain, vessels of war frequently came up the Sound and lay off Stratford to obtain supplies from the Housatonic river; and their presence was alarming to the people of Stratford, they fearing the soldiers would land, plunder or burn the town or carry off men as prisoners of war. To prevent such calamities a guard of soldiers was stationed at the mouth of the river to keep watch and give alarm, should there be any occasion.

One afternoon such a war vessel came and lay off the harbor late in the afternoon, and just at night Sergeant James Coe, with several soldiers under his command, was sent as a guard to watch the movements of the enemy. It being near dark when they took their post of observation, and hence they thought they saw several men, in groups, slightly moving, as if in consultation, ready to move forward. Charles Burritt, who had worked about there in the day time, and had guarded there in the night, knew that what seemed to be groups of soldiers were only bunches of thistles which grew there and were moved by the wind, said softly to Sergeant Coe, "Shall I shoot? I have two in range; I can kill them both." "No, no!" said the sergeant, "don't fire, but *Scatter boys! Scatter!* or we shall all be killed." And scatter they did, in double quick, still carrying on the joke. Soon

---

[10] Manuscript of Nathan B. McEwen.

the story was taken up by the younger men, and the sergeant being a man easily teased, did not soon hear the last of " Scatter, men! scatter!" which was the proper command to be given had there been real danger.

The Old Pump of the Cedar of Lebanon would furnish quite a history if it could reveal secrets.

Capt. Samuel C. Nicoll built the dyke at the Lordship farm about 1815. In 1818, the dwelling and barns were built. That year he brought from New York a red or Spanish cedar pump, some say a cedar of Lebanon, taken from a Spanish vessel that was being repaired at that port; the pump being old and hence unfit for further service. He set it in his yard for watering his cattle at the Lordship farm.

After standing there about forty-three years, it was taken out, somewhat rotten at the lower end, but was afterwards used by the Spiritualists to pump water from the hole at the gold diggings about a mile east from the Lordship farm, near the shore.

The old pump was made of two pieces bound together with iron hoops. After a time it was brought to the village and became the property of Nathan B. McEwen for some work he did in pay.

So the old pump, after being transported in active service over the great seas, many years, did about sixty years service on land, and then, although much of the wood was filled with nails yet Mr. McEwen secured quite a number of beautiful canes, and thus, in parts, the old cedar pump travels on.

Mosquitoes sure. It is said mosketoes are not as plentiful as they were fifty years ago.

In 1822, the lighthouse keeper lost a cow by the mosquitoes. He shut the cow in the barn, but the mosquitoes attacked her so numerously that she broke out of the barn in order to get away from the torment. Then they came in clouds and stung her so that she swelled as large as a hogshead and died from the effect."

---

[11] Manuscript of Nathan B. McEwen.

John Selby lived near the lower wharf in Stratford. He was a young man who had worked his way to the command of a brig running to the West Indies. In an evil hour he was tempted to smuggle a few hogsheads of rum, the doing of which proved his ruin.

He commanded a brig built all of mahogany in the West Indies, with which he came into and went up the Housatonic river to Friar's Head, where in the night he unloaded some casks of rum and put them into a building to save the tariff or duties. A young man being near, courting late in the night, discovered the transaction and complained to the authorities that he might get the reward, which was half the vessel and half the cargo. The vessel was seized by the government, condemned and sold. Capt. Selby was fined and imprisoned. After lying in prison a long time, his wife smuggled a saw in to him with which he broke jail and went pirating, and was gone several years.

Finally, becoming tired of the business, and desiring to see his family, which consisted of a wife and three children, he, through agents, made a compromise with the government and was pardoned by paying nine thousand dollars. He came home a dissipated, wretched man."

Oysters are now a commodity of large growth and commerce.

When the white settlers first came they found piles of oyster shells in various places on Great Neck and where now the village of Stratford is located. These beds of oyster shells when now dug up as they frequently are, reveal the fact that many of the oysters that the Indians gathered were remarkably large, and probably very rich as food.

There has been found no town acts for the first one hundred years restricting the taking of oysters by the Indians or inhabitants of the town.

In December, 1764, for the first is found a vote of the town restricting the time for taking oysters, thus: "That if any parties should take oysters between April 20th and the 10th day of September they should pay a fine of ten shillings," and a committee was appointed to prosecute if necessary.

" Manuscript of Nathan B. McEwen.

From 1790, to 1810, the matter received considerable attention, restricting not only the time for taking them but also the instruments with which the work should be done.

At present the territory for oyster beds is mapped out, bought and sold, and deeded with as much precision as the cultivated land on the shore, and every year the matter assumes new interest and additional proportions.

Ferries in Stratford.

The Ferry was started by Moses Wheeler, as heretofore stated, but while the ferry property belonged to Mr. Wheeler the privilege of conducting a ferry across the river did not. This privilege was given to Mr. Wheeler for the first twenty-one years, and afterwards leased to him and other parties.

In January, 1690, a committee of the town was appointed, who leased " the Stratford Ferry to Samuel Wheeler, son of Moses Wheeler for 21 years from the 18th of November next."

To this record Moses Wheeler appended the following, he being then ninety-two years of age.

" To yᵉ Committee of yᵉ town of Stratford, Gentᵐ. These may inform you that for the natural love and affection yᵗ I have to my dearly beloved son Samuel Wheeler, I doe by these presents transmit all my right, title and interest of yᵉ ferry in the bounds aforesaid with all benefits and profitable improvements accrewing thereunto by virtue of any gift, grant or lease whatsoever in as full and ample manner as ever it was made to me or intended, as witness my hand this 6ᵗʰ day of January, 1690.

MOSES WHEELER.

Signed in presence of
  Thomas Hicks. }

Previous to 1719, Richard Blackleach had leased and conducted the ferry some years, and a town committee was appointed to lease it twenty-one years longer.

In 1727 the Assembly granted the liberty to the town of Milford to establish a ferry and keep a boat on the east side of the river. Whether the ferry on the east side was established or not, or how long it continued, if at all, is not known, but in May, 1758, the subject came up again before the Assembly and they gave notice for the towns and ferry-man—Josiah Curtiss of the Stratford side—to appear in the next October session and give their reasons, if any, why a ferry should not be established on the east side, and at that session they ordered that "there be a boat kept on the east side of Stratford Ferry River for transporting passengers, etc.;" and the privilege was granted to the town of Milford, upon the condition of their erecting a dwelling house at or near said ferry place, commodious for the reception and entertainment of travellers, and procuring and keeping a good boat, etc."

In May, 1761, Peter Hepburn, of Milford, having taken the ferry on the east side, petitioned the Assembly and received liberty "to keep a house of public entertainment at said ferry the year ensuing."

In this way the ferry was continued until a little after the year 1800.

In 1802, the Legislature, upon the petition of Jonathan Sturges and others, incorporated a company to build a bridge across the Housatonic river at or near the ferry place between Stratford and Milford, by the name of The Milford and Stratford Bridge Company, and in 1803, the same body changed the name to that of Washington Bridge.

In 1807, the company were released from building the bridge on "stone abutments and stone piers," and were allowed to build it "on piers and abutments constructed with wood and stone, in a substantial and workmanlike manner; and the privilege of a lottery was granted to raise money in aid of building the bridge, provided the bridge should be built within five years.

In 1813 the bridge was standing, and rates of toll were established.

This Washington Bridge is still a standing institution of very complete and substantial construction, but how many times it has been rebuilt is not known.

The Zoar Bridge Company was granted incorporation in May, 1807, and rates of toll established. This was

then at the northern extremity of Huntington, but before
1789 the place was at the north end of Stratford.

In 1762, the privilege was granted to Edmund Leavenworth to establish a ferry "at the narrows a little above
Derby Neck."

In May, 1716, Sergt. Joseph Hawkins was granted liberty
by the Assembly to establish a ferry across the Housatonic
river at what is now Birmingham Point, and also to run
across the mouth of the Naugatuck river a little below, whenever he had occasion.

In 1737, the Assembly granted this privilege to Moses
Hawkins, son of Sergt. Joseph, he having the exclusive right
at that place.

In 1745, Capt. Moses Hawkins being deceased, the Assembly granted this ferry privilege to Joseph Hawkins.

In 1763, John Stephens had a ferry at Derby Narrows,
across to Stratford side. When this ferry was removed from
Hawkins Point down to the Narrows, the Leavenworth ferry
was established above Derby Neck.

The ferry at Derby Narrows continued many years after
the year 1800, and was often called the Huntington ferry, as
it landed passengers on the west side of the river, in the town
of Huntington.

More about Mills.

In 1730, Robert Wheeler was granted liberty to " set up
a grist mill on the east sprain of the Farmill river below Pine
Swamp, a little below the beaver dam."

"December 31, 1739. Voted liberty to Mr. Nathan Curtiss and Judson Burton to make a dam and erect a sawmill
over Unkaway mill river, so-called, being west of Tashua on
their own land."

The Tide Mill at the Eagle's Nest was built first on the
east side of Nesumpaws creek, and was the first flouring mill
in Stratford, and was probably conducted by the Hurd family
at first; then some years by the Blakeman families, the two
sons of Rev. Adam, James and Samuel. After that it is prob-

able that this mill was left and went to decay, and no mill
was there for nearly one hundred years. To this first mill
there seems to have been a road or horse path from the
southern end of Stratford village, southwest across the
swamp, perhaps near or in the path still called Chauncey's
Lane ; the Rev. Mr. Chauncey having owned land on that
lane it was called after his name.

In 1765, a new mill was built on the old site, still on the
east side of the stream, and a house was also built the same
year on Eagles' Nest, the highest land in that vicinity, by
Samuel Judson; the cellar of which was plainly to be seen a
few years since.

Afterwards the mill was kept for a time by Nicholas
Darrow. About the year 1800 a great freshet carried away
the foundations, the mill and several rods of earth where it
stood, making the stream much wider. There was a dike
about three feet high around the mill inclosing considerable
land, to keep out the high tide, which was also destroyed, and
drowned all the miller's hogs and poultry.

After a short time a large mill was built at the same
place, on the west side of the stream, but using the same dam.
This mill was four and a half stories high, about 60 feet in
length and 40 in width. It was built of very heavy timber,
the posts being twelve inches square, for the purpose of stor-
ing corn, which was ground, kiln-dried and shipped to the
West Indies, packed in large hogsheads. Within the memory of the late Nathan B. McEwen, William S. Johnson and
William A. Tomlinson were engaged in this enterprise. The
mill was also used to grind wheat and rye, as a grist mill.

The mill was owned and kept by William Samuel Johnson and afterwards by his son Edward, as a grist mill, until
August 30, 1851, when it was consumed by fire.

The water was so deep that large sloops came to the side
of the mill and took on their loads for the West Indies.

Vessels were owned, built and sailed from Stratford.
Many have been the men who were owners and part owners,
sailors and masters of vessels which sailed from Stratford,
and the list of the sons of Stratford whose dust was buried in
the deep, deep sea is a long one. The items or particulars,

and names of these which have been gathered for record here are scarcely worth mentioning, yet by time and search much fuller record could be secured.

Among the first ship owners and ship builders at Stratford was Joseph Hawley.

" October 27, 1678. This writing witnesseth that I, John Rogers, of New London, in the Colony of Connecticut, doe acknowledge that I have received of Joseph Hawley of Stratford the full and just sum of fifty-eight pounds one shilling two pence; which said money was improved in the building of a ship, which said ship now rideth in Fairfield harbor, called the John and Esther."

In the remainder of the record, this sum is said to be one-eighth of the value of the ship.

In 1680 John Prentice bought of Joseph Hawley one-eighth part of this ship.

In 1679, Richard Blackleach bought one-eighth part of a vessel called the " Katch Tryall of Milford," for sixty pounds money.

James Bennitt, a shipwright, built a vessel at Stratford in 1696.

Stratford was among the established ports of entry in 1702, but had been the same many years before, probably from the first, since there was a collector of customs here soon after the settlement.[18]

---

[18] " May, 1702. Be it enacted by the Deputy Governor, Council, and Representatives, in General Court assembled, and by the authority of the same: That the maritime towns and places hereafter named and no others shall be held, deemed and adjudged to be Lawful Ports within this Colony, that is to say, New London, Saybrook, Gilford, Newhaven, Milford, Stratford, Fairfield and Stamford, at every of which aforesaid ports an officer shall be held and kept for the entring and clearing of all ships and other vessels trading to or from this Colony, to be called and known by the name of the Navall Office, with such fees as have been accustomed ; and at one of the ports aforesaid and not elsewhere, all ships or other vessells is trading to or from this Colony shall lade and unlade all goods, commodities, wares and merchandise whatsoever, which they shall import or export."

Col. Rec., vi. 374.

The Universalist Church of Stratford.

A church of this denomination was built in Stratford, as appears from the following extract from the paper of that day called the " Universalist Union."

"The Church recently completed at Stratford by the First Society of Universalists in that place was solemnly dedicated to the service of ' God the Saviour of all men, especially those that believe,' on the 24th of November, 1837. The day was unusually fine and the house well filled with attentive worshippers. This small, but neat and commodious edifice has been tastefully planned and finished in a style which does great credit to the architect. It is thirty by forty feet, has a gallery at one end, the pews are arranged in the modern style and it will seat comfortably from 200 to 250 persons. It does not stand on so high ground as the other churches of the place, nor reach quite so high towards heaven, but we are fully justified in the belief that its proprietors and attendants rank as high in point of moral worth, sincerity, zeal, and pious devotion as any church in Stratford.

" The order of exercises on the occasion were: Voluntary by the choir; Reading the Scriptures by Br. F. Hitchcock; Hymn; Introductory prayer by Br. F. Hitchcock; Hymn; Sermon by Br. S. J. Hillyer, text I. Chron. xvi. 29; Dedicatory prayer by Br. B. B. Hallock; Hymn; Benediction.

"The morning, afternoon and evening services were attended by large congregations." Mr. F. Hitchcock was the pastor of this Church.

In the Manual of the Congregational Church of this place it is stated that " when Mr. Dutton was called to this Church, its spiritual condition was very low. Various causes, long operating, had greatly adulterated the doctrinal belief of many members. Some of the most prominent had become believers in Universalism."

This belief resulted in a new society and a church edifice in 1837, as recorded above.

The Methodist Episcopal Church in Stratford.[14]

Tradition says that the Rev. Jesse Lee preached in Stratford on the 4th of July, 1789, it being the first sermon preached here by a Methodist minister. The first Methodist class was organized here on the 19th of May, 1790, by Mr. Lee, consisting of John Smith, John Peck, and Margaret and Amy Plumb. Bishop Asbury preached in the town house on June 7, 1791, and met the class, which, organized only a little over one year before, now numbered twenty members. From this time to about 1810, when the first house of worship was ✸ erected, the preaching services were held in private houses; much of the time in the residences of Capt. John Peck and Elnathan Wheeler. No record is known to be preserved of the precise date when the first church was built, nor of the names of the first officers and members. The Conference records show that in 1810, Nathan Emery and John Russell were preachers on the Stratford Circuit, and Joseph Crawford was the presiding elder; in 1811, Aaron Hunt, Oliver Sykes and J. Reynolds were preachers, and William Anson was presiding elder; in 1812, Seth Crowell, Gilbert Lyon and S. Beach were the preachers, and Elijah Hawley was presiding elder; in 1813, E. Washburn, James Coleman were preachers, and Nathan Bangs, presiding elder.

The preachers from 1814 to 1879 were as follows: 1814, E. Wolsey and H. Ames; in 1815, E. Hibbard and B. English; in 1816, R. Harris and —— Dickerson; in 1817, R. Harris and E. Canfield; in 1818, S. Bushnell and A. Pierce; in 1819, B. Northrop and D. Miller; in 1820, Bela Smith and D. Miller; in 1821, Bela Smith and James Coleman; in 1822, Laban Clark and Eli Bennett; in 1823, Laban Clark and John Nixon; in 1824, E. Denniston and William Pease; in 1825, E. Denniston and Julius Field; in 1826, S. D. Ferguson and V Buck; in 1827, E. Bennett and V. Buck; in 1828–9, John Lovejoy and J. H. Romer; in 1830–31, H. Bartlett and Charles Sherman; in 1832, S. Martindale and L. C. Cheney; in 1833, J. P. Youngs and J. Tackaberry; in 1834, R. Gilbert; in 1835,

---

[14] Compiled for the Fairfield County History by Mr. H. A. Sutton.

D. Miller; in 1836, D. Miller; in 1837, C. W. Turner; in 1838, Clark Fuller a part of the year, and Asahel Brons the other part; in 1839-40, Abram S. Francis, during whose pastorate the present church was built; in 1841-42, Paul R. Brown, under whose labors a number were added to the Church; in 1843-44, Daniel Smith, a successful laborer; in 1845-46, Harvey Husted; 1847, ——— Frost; in 1848-9, C. Kelsey; in 1850-51, Morris Hill; 1852-53, Jacob Shaw; in 1854, G. C. Creevy; in 1855-56, L. D. Nickerson; in 1857-58, William T. Hill; in 1859-60, S. A. Seaman; in 1861-62, J. W. Simpson; in 1863-65, Bennett T. Abbott; in 1866-67, T. D. Littlewood; in 1868-70, Joseph Smith; in 1871-73, Joseph Vinton; in 1874-76, A. V. R. Abbott; in 1877-79, Benjamin Pillsbury; in 1880, S. A. Seaman.

Summerfield M. E. Church in Stratford.[15]

About the 1st of January, 1871, the following persons met in a room on Barnum street, West Stratford, and established a mission: Rev. W. W. Bowditch, pastor of Washington Park M. E. Church, Rev. George A. Parkington, George W. Bacon, Solomon Bachelor, W. W. Stannard, and a number of others.

Rev. George A. Parkington, then a local preacher, but since a member of the New York East Conference, was selected to preach in the mission. He preached his first sermon here January 15, 1871, and on January 29, 1871, a Sunday-school was organized, with Wesley W. Botsford, Superintendent; Frank N. Cox, Secretary and Treasurer, and David Clark, Librarian. The school began with thirty members, and in due time a membership class and regular prayer meeting were established, with Solomon Batchelor as class leader.

Soon after a committee was chosen to proceed in preparing for and building a church, consisting of George W. Bacon, Solomon Batchelor, Calvin Hall, I. Hurd and L. B. Vaill; and George A. Parkington, having joined the Conference in

---

[15] Fairfield County History, 765.

April, 1872, was sent to the Summerfield Church, this being the name selected for the new enterprise.

The subscription list commenced with the name of Susan Hubbell, who gave five hundred dollars, and George W. Bacon gave the same amount, which were followed by Solomon Batchelor, Isaac Hurd, P. T. Barnum and Francis Ford, who each gave one hundred dollars. A site was selected, the building commenced, and on March 16, 1873, the edifice was dedicated by Bishop Edmund S. Janes.

The Trustees elected June 3, 1872, were Solomon Batchelor, L. B. Vaill, James Lobdell, Calvin Hall, Smith Lewis, Sylvester Bradley, Gilead L. Andrews, Emmanuel Sciviter and Frank Fairchild.

The pastors have been: 1872–73, George A. Parkington ; 1874–76, A. P. Chapman ; 1876–78, Larmon W. Abbott; 1878, Edward L. Bray.

Trinity Memorial Church in West Stratford.[18]

On the 20th of September, 1871, the first of a series of Wednesday evening services was held in West Stratford, at the house of Silas Scofield, Esq., in Rivere Place, by the Rev. Sylvester Clarke, Rector of Trinity Church, Bridgeport. On the following Sunday, September 24th, a Sunday-school was begun in the school house of the same Newfield district. The corner-stone of a chapel was laid by the Rt. Rev. Bishop Williams, of Connecticut, on Wednesday, Nov. 29, 1871. The building, after being inclosed, waited through the winter before it was plastered.

The first service in it was the celebration of the holy communion on Sunday morning, May 19, 1872.

The chapel is in memory of the Rev. Gurdon Saltonstall Coit, D.D., rector for nearly thirty years of St. John's Church, Bridgeport, who died in Southport, Conn., Nov. 10, 1869.

This parish is a mission of Trinity Church, Bridgeport.

---

[18] From Fairfield County History, page 766.

Newfield M. E. Church in West Stratford.[17]

On the second Sunday of May, 1871, D. W. Currier and Theodore Courtright called on the neighbors of Newfield School District, and gave notice that they would open a Sunday-school on the following Sunday afternoon in the barn of Nirum Hawley. At the appointed time two children met, and the next Sunday there were fifteen present. Mr. Courtright was elected superintendent. The school increased in numbers and interest until the barn became too small, when they removed to a more commodious place in a store building owned by John French.

In the mean time a society was established, and a Sunday-school organized on Sunday, September 24, 1871, called a Union Sunday-school. This school met in the district school house until the completion of a chapel, which was erected and ready for use on the 3d day of March, 1872.

These two schools united in one, August 18, 1872, and the whole was turned over to the Rev. A. C. Eggleston, pastor of the Washington Park M. E. Church.

This organization was called the Newfield Methodist Episcopal Society, which assumed all debts and purchased the property, securing the chapel and the site.

The following spring, 1873, they applied to the Conference, and the Rev. R. S. Eldridge was sent to them as their pastor, who labored successfully one year. The next year the Rev. E. A. Blake was appointed as their pastor, who served one year. Since that time the church has had no regular pastor, but has been supplied from other churches.

Schools in Stratford.

Teaching children to read and write was attended to in the families by the first settlers. Very soon the Colony made some provisions for educating children.

The town of Stratford gave early attention to providing schooling for the children in it.

---

[17] From Fairfield County History, page 766.

In October, 1678, the town voted twenty pounds of money " for maintainance of a school master, the rest of the money to be levied upon the children privileged by the school." In December of the same year they voted a school master " to teach small children to read and write."

A special provision was made by the town as follows:

" October 31, 1687. Also it was voted at the same meeting that what land the town hath at or near the ferry, upland and meadow now in the possession of Moses Wheeler, sen^r., that the produce and benefit thereof shall henceforth forever be paid and improved for and towards the maintaining of a publique school for and in the town of Stratford."

This was land the use of which was granted to Moses Wheeler twenty-one years, gratuitously in view of his maintaining a ferry across the Housatonic river, and his twenty-one years having expired they thenceforward devoted the income to the support of " a publique school." That is, it was so much towards a free school, which is the earliest provision of the kind seen on record by the author of this work.

So far as seen there was but one school in the town until December 13, 1715, when it was voted that "our neighbors north of Tanner's Brook, may set up a school house at the north end of the town, they doing it at their own expense."

The next year there were two schools in the village, and in January, 1716–17, they voted that "the farmers at Long hill, Oronock, Putnee, Mohegin hills, Trapfalls, Fairchilds, and Nichol's Lakes and Pambrook, shall have the use of their part of the 40 shillings pr. thousand allowed by law for seven years ensuing, provided they educate their children according to law," and Sergt. John Hurd and Sergt. Andrew Patterson were chosen a committee for Pembroke.

This shows that there were forty shillings drawn from the Colony upon each one thousand pounds on the town list for schools.

In 1722, Capt. Josiah Curtiss, Samuel Uffoot and Abel Birdsey were the committee for the South School, and Thomas Welles, James Judson and Ephraim Clark for the North School. Hence, Thomas Welles was living within this district, and possibly on what is now the Elias Welles place, where the great elm tree stands; and that tree was in all probability set there about twenty years later.

In 1740, the schools being under the care of the Ecclesiastical Society, were named the South School, North School, Pembrook School and Putnee School. In 1741, the names were a little changed and they were called the South End School, the North End School, Oronoke and Putnee and Pembrook School.

After this period schools increased, new districts were organized until the whole town was under a thorough system of common school education. Those young men who desired to go to college were prepared in their education by the parish ministers, until the erection of the Academy.

The Stratford Academy.

"Town Meeting December 17, 1804. Whereas, Samuel W. Johnson, Ezekiel Lovejoy and other inhabitants of this town have subscribed one thousand dollars for the building of a school house or academy for the education of youth, and have applied to this town for liberty to erect the same on the public square called the Meetinghouse Hill.

" Voted, that the applicants have liberty to erect a house for the purpose aforesaid on the Meetinghouse Hill, where the old meetinghouse formerly stood, with the privilege of enclosing the same with a fence suitable for ornament and convenience not exceeding three rods from each side of said house.

Test, AARON BENJAMIN, Town Clerk."

In May, 1806, the proprietors were made a corporate body, by the following declaration: " Resolved by this Assembly, That Samuel Wm. Johnson, Jabez H. Tomlinson, Stephen W. Stebbins, Ashbel Baldwin, Robert Fairchild, Roswell Judson and Solomon Curtis, the present trustees of said Academy, and others who now or hereafter may be proprietors of said Academy, be, and they are hereby created and made a body corporate, by the name of " The Proprietors of the Stratford Academy."

In 1836, this Academy was still standing, and the hill had become known as Academy Hill, which name is still frequently used.

Stratford Union School.

The year 1883 marks a new era in educational enterprise, spirit and accomplishments, for in that year a union of four districts was formed; and a new, two-story brick school house was built in 1884–85, at a cost of $20,000, and the school was opened in it with a full complement of teachers, September 14, 1885.

The following was the first School Committee after the consolidation; George H. Spall, Howard J. Curtis and Chas. B. Curtis; and Edwin F. Hall, Clerk, and Albert Wilcoxson, Treasurer.

The following are the names of the Building Committee: Robert H. Russell, Rufus W. Bunnell, Charles B. Curtis, Charles D. Curtiss, and David W. Judson.

The school opened with the following list of teachers: Mr. Wilfred M. Peck, Principal; Miss Addie T. Gilman, Miss Mary E. Cable, Miss H. Lina Lobdell, Miss Eleanor A. Peck, and Miss Minnie Judson.

Samuel Fulsom came from Windham, Conn., to Stratford, probably in the spring of 1743, he having then a wife Ann, and two children. His descendants have the tradition that he came specially to do the iron work on the Episcopal Church then to be built, he being a blacksmith. It is also said that he brought other blacksmiths with him to work, and who did work in his shop.

He became a communicant in the Episcopal Church here in 1743, and purchased his first land in Stratford in 1745, it being the corner where now Mrs. Hudson's dwelling stands. This lot of one acre had been owned some years by John Moss, who had died, leaving it with a house and barn on it, to his two children Joseph and Mary Moss. After Mary's part was taken off, Joseph sold his right to John Benjamin and Samuel Fulsom, who afterwards divided it, Mr. Fulsom retaining the corner. On this homestead lived the Fulsom family, the father continuing many years the work of a blacksmith.

Glorianna Fulsom, the last but one of this family of nine children, was born December 24, 1753, and grew to be a very beautiful young lady at the age of sixteen years, the charming companion of many like her in Stratford at that day, only she is said to have been more beautiful than any other. She possessed light brown hair, bright, sparkling blue eyes, a fine personal figure with a lively, entertaining manner, and all the modest culture of those frugal days.

In the autumn of the year 1770, when the beauty of the country was all aglow with preparations for the coming winter, there came into Stratford a stranger, of rather remarkable appearance, who stopped at Benjamin's tavern, then located where the dwelling of Mr. Frederick A. Benjamin now stands. He was John Sterling, from Edinburgh, Scotland, the son of a Baronet, and he had been sent out by his father on a visiting tour to America, going first to Canada and thence to New York. By what fatality he came to Stratford is not known, nor can it be guessed unless it was to find the very cradle of liberty, which it has always been understood he did find, both in politics and marriage. His manner was pleasant and entertaining, but he seemed to be a person without any object of worldly or religious business, and therefore was viewed as a suspicious character.

He saw the beautiful Glorianna in church, he saw her in singing-school; he went wherever he could see her, became acquainted with her, and sought her in marriage. This proposition all opposed except the father and "sweet sixteen." The mother imposed every opposition, so did Anna, the eldest sister, but Johnny won the race, and came out Mr. Sterling with Mrs. Glorianna Sterling as mate, March 10, 1771.

He then tarried in Stratford, and after a time wrote home for money. The father sent some, and wrote him to return home, but he wrote that he was married and could not come, so say the descendants of the Fulsom family; others say, he did not write home, which is improbable, but that his father heard of his son's marriage and the beauty of his wife, by some mariners, who were there from Stratford.

When funds ran low again, Mr. Sterling, like a true Yankee, engaged in teaching school, "in the old Pendleton house," where he continued several months, if not more than a year.

In December, 1771, the daughter Mary Glorianna was baptized, and a pupil was taken in charge, to board in the family.

In the autumn of 1772, the Baronet in Edinburgh, became impatient at the stay of his son in America and wrote a peremptory requirement for his son to come home and bring his wife with him, but this latter seemed impossible then, and he departed alone, assuring her he would send for her as soon as possible.

When he had departed, the whole town was musical with whisperings, suspicions and reports that the great Mr. Sterling had deserted his wife and that she would see and hear no more of him.

On March 14, 1773, another daughter, named Maria Jane was baptized in Stratford.

Soon a letter came from Mr. Sterling that a ship, fitted for her special comfort, would be in New York at a certain time, to convey her to Scotland in the best style possible; that he had sent her a quantity of goods, of elegant material, which she must have made in New York, and that he had sent servants to attend to the necessary work and preparations for her journey. Her relatives in Stratford have pieces of the silk for the dress which she was to wear at her reception when she should arrive at her home in Scotland, which though now changed in color was originally white embossed silk, with colored flowers in small boquets scattered sparsely over it.

After making her wardrobe as complete as possible, Mrs. Sterling sailed for Europe with her two children and two servants, a nurse and maid, who had been sent out to attend her. Mr. Sterling sent an invitation to his sister-in-law Anna Fulsom to accompany his wife, and goods for her outfit, but her mother would not give her consent, although it was much to Anna's regret, saying, it was enough to bury one, for she should never see Glorianna again, and she could not bury two. Mrs. Sterling wrote back that when she arrived in Scotland there were so many carriages on the wharf that she was at a great loss to know what it meant, but found they were all there to meet her.

After her arrival she had governesses in the house to teach her the accomplishments befitting the future Lady of Sterling Castle. She never returned to America, although she always intended to do so, but she kept up a continued correspondence with her family, often sending them valuable presents, especially to her mother and her sister Anna. Quite a number of these articles are still preserved in Stratford; also a razor case left by Mr. Sterling, and the remains of what was once a very beautiful doll, which was sent with a complete doll's outfit to her little niece, the six-year old daughter of her sister Anna, who had become the second wife of Abraham Tomlinson, the father of Mjss Huldah and Miss Polly Tomlinson. Their mother, the first wife, was a daughter of parson Gold.

During the Revolution Mrs. Sterling had very little communication with her friends in America, but as soon as peace was declared correspondence was resumed and she sent presents of various kinds. There is still preserved quite a good sized box that came from her filled with presents.

She was very anxious that members of her family should visit her, and was much delighted when her brother, Nathan Fulsom wrote that he would go and see her. She directed him where to go when he arrived in Liverpool and have an outfit made at her expense. He went, and after remaining some months he returned, bringing glowing accounts of the grandeur with which his sister was surrounded.

Her husband, upon the decease of his father, in 1791, succeeded to the office of a Baronet, which he held to his death, and the Baronness, although so widely separated from her family in America, kept up a most cordial intercourse with them as long as she lived, sending several of her children to visit them. Her youngest brother, John Fulsom, visited at her home after his brother Nathan had been there.

In Playfair's Baronetage of Scotland it is stated that Sir John and Glorianna Sterling had nineteen children in the first eighteen years of their marriage. It is said by the descendants of her relatives here that she was the mother of twenty-two children. The Baronetage of Scotland shows that one of her sons succeeded his father in that office and that her descendants held the office in 1879.

It may be seen by the above dates which are taken from Stratford town records and those of the Episcopal Church, that the story which connects Sir John Sterling with the American Revolution cannot be correct, since he was married and he and his wife Glorianna and their children were at home in Scotland before the war in America began. Then, also, the above dates correspond and confirm all the leading facts of the story as given by Misses Elizabeth and Maria Peck, still living in Stratford, whose mother was the daughter of Anna Fulsom, the eldest sister of Glorianna. These ladies well remember their grandmother, and heard her as well as their own mother narrate the story, often, in their early years, and their mother many times in later years ; and they are authority for the above plain statement of facts. It is very pleasant to the author of this work, that by the assistance of several persons of Stratford, the above true, straightforward and agreeable history has been obtained, since a variety of versions have been heretofore given to it.

St. John's Lodge, No. 8, of Free and Accepted Masons.

The following history of St. John's Lodge has been collected and arranged by Mr. Nathan B. Wells, from a historical address by the Rev. C. H. W. Stocking in 1866, and the Manuel of the lodge and other records:

"The original charter of St. John's Lodge, Stratford, was granted by the R. W. George Harrison, Provincial Grand Master of the Colony of New York, dated April 22, 1766. On the 7th of May following, a preliminary meeting to the formal opening of the lodge was held, and Monday, the 12th day of May, designated as the day for organizing.

"On the appointed evening there were present Joseph Clark, W. M.; James Dunn, S. W.; John Harpin, J. W., *pro tem.*, and ' visitant ' Brother Lemuel Brooks. The lodge having been ' opened in due form and cloathed with all their honors, after having dedicated the same to the Holy St. John, they proceeded to raise the following Brethren to the Sublime Degree of Master Mason, to wit : Brother Henry Van Dyck,

Brother Ephraim Peet, Brother Abijah Beach, Brother William McIntosh.'

"On the 15th of the same month 'the four new brethren were appointed to the subordinate offices. Henry Van Dyck, S. W.; Ephraim Peet, J. W.; Abijah Beach, Treas.; James Dunn, Sec.

"The element of discipline early entered into the workings of the lodge. Refusal to obey the Master's gavel was punished by a fine of two shillings, to be paid immediately, or suffer expulsion. Obscenity paid a fine of one shilling; talking, one shilling; profanity, two shillings. Initiation fees were £3, to the box, and three shillings to the Tyler.

"Twelve successive times Samuel Benjamin represented the lodge at the annual communication of the Grand Lodge, walking the distance with glad though weary feet, that so his candlestick should not be removed. Matthias Nicoll, Benjamin Fairchild and Rev. Ashbel Baldwin appear as frequently representing their lodge at the grand communications in honest discharge of their Masonic obligations.

"This lodge worked under its old colonial charter as St. John's, No. 1, until October 9, 1792. It then came in under another charter from the newly formed Grand Lodge of the State, as St. John's, No. 8. The Nicolls, the Benjamins, the Fairchilds, the Johnsons, and others who might be mentioned, appear among their fellows as zealous craftsmen who knew their work and wrought it well.

"The following are the names of the Past Masters of this lodge, with their terms of office: 1766–68, Joseph Clarke; 1768–69, Henry Van Dyke; 1769–70, Joseph Clarke; 1770–73, Stiles Lewis; 1773–79, Joseph Clarke; 1779–80, Stiles Lewis; 1780–84, John Thatcher; 1784–86, Peter Nicoll; 1786–88, Matthias Nicoll; 1788–90, John Thatcher; 1790–95, J. L. Wooster; 1795–96, John Thompson; 1796–97, Matthias Nicoll; 1797–98, Ashbel Baldwin; 1798–1804, Matthias Nicoll; 1804–7, John Thompson; 1807–8, Nathaniel Kennedy; 1808–11, Ashbel Baldwin; 1811–12, George Smith; 1812–15, Matthias Nicoll; 1815–21, William T. Shelton; 1821–27, Matthias Nicoll; 1827–33, Samuel Benjamin; 1833–36, Benjamin Fairchild; 1836–40, John Goulding; 1860–62, A. B. Judd; 1862–

63, Nathan B. Wells; 1863–66, George Jewell; 1867–68, Ezra Whiting; 1868–70; William A. Lewis; 1870–72, Walter J. Bristol; 1872–73, Melville J. Curtis; 1873–75, Henry G. B. Cuzner; 1875–77, Lasper K. Whitney; 1877–79, Samuel A. Patterson; 1880–81, Nathan F. Wilcoxson; 1882–3, John W. Beach; 1884, Henry F. Mechan.

The officers for the year 1885, are: Nelson E. Dorman, W. M.; George W. Cradduck, S. W.; Daniel C. Wood, J. W.; Samuel A. Patterson, Secretary; Ezra Whiting, Treasurer. John W. Beach, George H. Zink and Henry P. Stagg, Trustees; Charles F. Judson, S. D.; Frederick P. Welles, J. D.; Bernard H. Merrick, S. S.; Charles E. Lovell, J. S.; Lasper K. Whiting, Marshall; Rev. Thomas J. Watt, Chaplain; George W. Lampson and George H. Spall, Auditors; and Joseph W. Dufour, Tyler.

The number of members at present is about one hundred and thirty.

"*Oronoque Lodge, No. 90, I. O. O. F.*"

This lodge was instituted by Grand Master A. W. Phelps, in the old Masonic Hall. The first officers installed were: J. W. Dufow, N. G.; G. T. Lewis, V. G.; Charles D. Curtis, Treas.; H. A. Sutton, Sec.

"Charter members: Joseph W. Dufow, George T. Lewis, Francis S. Avery, Lucius E. Hendric, H. A. Sutton, John Cradduck, Charles D. Curtis, William Shilston, Perry Beardsley, C. Lester Young, Laspore K. Whitman, Lewis S. Hubbell, Abram T. Peck.

"The following is a list of Noble Grands from the organization to 1881: Joseph W. Dufow, George T. Lewis, John Cradduck, Francis S. Avery, Laspore K. Whitney, John Kugler, Charles E. Curtis, A. S. Allen, D. W. Judson, A. C. Ellis, William Young, Lewis S. Hubbell, A. C. Ellis, A. McEwen, George Cradduck, William Blaney."

---

18 Fairfield County History, 768.

The Borough of West Stratford.

West Stratford, as a borough was organized July 3, 1873. The officers for 1873 and 1874, were: A. W. Lewis, Warden; Alfred Beers, James Bounds, E. B. Peck, John French, William H. Bunnell, and Harvey Birdsey, Burgesses; Charles H. Hinman, Clerk; H. B. Drew, Treasurer; D. C. Wood, Collector; H. T. Quire, Bailiff; J. R. Lockwood, and Frank Bacon, Registrars of Voters.

This is a rapidly growing borough, and will without doubt, soon become a part of the city of Bridgeport.

The Bridgeport Hospital is located within its boundaries. There are two school houses; the one in the lower district has four teachers and about 290 scholars, and in the upper district 200 scholars.

The Public Greens of Stratford Village.

It has been represented that these greens were always the property of the town, but the records show quite the contrary.

In 1745, Hezekiah Gold, Joshua Judson, Joseph Booth, Ebenezer Beech, David Judson, John Wilcoxson, Abram Curtis and Daniel Curtis, gave four pieces of land to the town for public greens; three of them constituted the green at Academy Hill in the rear of the Episcopal Church, and one of them the Uptown Green. The deed is to be found in the records of the Town Acts, Book No. 5, page 153.

From the Revolution to 1850, there were in Stratford about fifty men of noted prominence, as indicated in the list of Representatives,[19] of whom it would be a satisfaction and pleasure to make biographical sketches, if time and space in this book would allow, but as the facts are, these must be left for the genealogies and a future historian.

---

[19] The list of Representatives will be found in the Appendix to this book.

Besides the following sketches of descendants of the older families, space is allowed for brief notices of two or three persons who with their families, became residents of this town more recently, and whose literary productions and beneficent public labors call for the notice and space here cordially given.

The Benjamin Family of Connecticut.

From the manuscripts of Governors Eaton and Winthrop are obtained the following account of the first settler in this country of the family of Benjamin.

"*John Benjamin, Esqr.*, Gentleman, was the first of that name who came to this country. His ancestors were Welch and were among the first of the landed Gentry of England. He came in company with Governor Winthrop to the Massachusetts colony in July, 1630, and settled in Watertown of the same colony [adjoining the present Cambridge] and died in that town, June, 1645. His house, accidentally destroyed by fire, was unsurpassed in elegance and comfort by any in the vicinity. It was the mansion of intelligence, refinement, religion and hospitality: visited by the clergy of all denominations and by the *literati* from far and near. He called his eldest son John and after the father's death the family removed to Connecticut."

Col. John Benjamin, the third in descent from John Benjamin, Gent., of Gov. Winthrop's colonists, was born in Stratford, Conn., in 1731. He was married to Lucretia Backus, of Windham, Conn., daughter of Dr. Backus, an eminent physician of that place. He is described as a man of comely person and strong mental powers, of philosophic tastes and studies, of which honorable mention was made by President Stiles of Yale College. He was an earnest and energetic patriot of '76. He took part in the battle of Ridgefield, and received a ball in the shoulder on that occasion which he carried to the end of his life. He died in Stratford, Conn., Sept. 14, 1796. He left four daughters, one of whom married Josiah Meigs and was the mother of the late Dr. Chas. Meigs, of

Philadelphia, and of Mrs. John Forsyth, wife of the Secretary of State, in the administrations of Jackson and Van Buren. He also left six sons, one of whom,

Col. Aaron Benjamin, was the hero of that generation of the family. Col. Aaron Benjamin was born in Stratford, Conn., Aug. 17, 1757. He entered the Revolutionary army in July, 1775, when not quite 18 years of age, and remained with it in active duty till the peace of 1783. He was in nearly all of the principal battles of that memorable war. Among his experiences were Montgomery's expedition to Canada, the battles of White Plains, Princeton, Monmouth, Germantown, Fort Mifflin, Stony Point, the winter at Valley Forge, innumerable encounters with the enemy, which have no record in history, hand to hand fights as perilous as " the imminent and deadly breach."

It is said that he was more than a hundred times under fire.

At Stony Point he was on the forlorn hope and he was the second man to enter the fort in that famous midnight victory. He was a Lieutenant and Adjutant during most of the Revolutionary war, and his son, Hon. Frederick A. Benjamin, has in his possession many volumes of Order Books in his father's handwriting. In these books, among many other interesting items is the complete plan of the attack on Stony Point, arranged with great precision and embraced in the Order for the preceding day.

Many were the incidents of the war related by this gallant actor on its battle fields; most of them have no place in History, but are preserved as sacred traditions among his descendants. After thirty years of peace this veteran of the War of Independence received a commission of Lieut. Col. and was again called into the service of his country in the War of 1812. During most of this conflict he commanded the military post of New London.

In person he was of medium stature, but commanding presence. He was a man of large humanity, of great purity of character, of iron energy, and equally unyielding integrity and honor.

He died in November, 1828, leaving a widow, four sons, and four daughters.

Hon. Frederick A. Benjamin, residing in Stratford, on the old place of his ancestors, is the only survivor of these eight children. He was for many years a merchant in the city of New York, and after retiring from business he returned to his native state and town, making it his home. Mr. Benjamin was a member of the State Senate in 1862, and of the Electoral College in 1864.

Among the descendants of Col. Aaron Benjamin his military mantle has fallen upon his grandson, Col. Samuel N. Benjamin, now one of the Adjutant Generals of the U. S. army, whose brilliant record in the War of the Rebellion was worthy of his grandsire.

Jesse Olney, A.M.," was born at Union, Tolland County, Oct. 12, 1798. He exhibited in childhood a remarkable fondness for geography, as well as aptness in classical studies; was for twelve years a teacher in the Hartford Grammar School, where he was the first American teacher to introduce the method, now generally adopted, of separating geography from astronomy, and beginning the former study by familiarizing the pupil with the description and surroundings of his own town, county and state, advancing thence to national and foreign geography.

His School Geography and Atlas, first issued in 1828, almost immediately became a standard throughout the country, has had a sale of several millions of copies, and has been the model of which all subsequent school geographies have more or less been imitations.

In 1831, appears the National Preceptor, a reading manual far superior to any predecessor in the United States, which was followed by a series of readers and outline maps, an Arithmetic, and a School History of the United States.

Mr. Olney was also author of a small volume of poems, anonymously published at Hartford. To perfect himself in his favorite studies he visited Europe several times, residing at Paris for considerable periods.

His residence was at Southington from 1834 to 1854, and at Stratford for the remainder of his life. He served ten

---

" Johnson's New Universal Cyclopædia, vol. iii. 949.

terms in the Connecticut legislature, where he was an active worker in behalf of educational interests, and was elected State Comptroller of public accounts in 1867. He died at Stratford, July 30, 1872.

Rev. James Harvey Linsley, son of James and Sarah (Maltby) Linsley, was born in Hartford, Conn., May 5, 1787. His ancestors came from the town of Lindley, near London, England. His was the eighth generation of his family in this country.

He graduated at Yale College in 1817. While there, a temporary illness obliged him to postpone his preparation for the ministry, that goal of his desires, and aim of his studies.

During this period of waiting he was made principal of the Academy at New Haven, and of that at New Canaan. Later he opened a private school of his own, the object of which was to prepare young men for College; although at this time he was offered the charge of five other academies, in as many different towns.

He came to Stratford in 1821 with his highly cultured and accomplished wife, Mrs. Sophia B. Linsley. This lady was the daughter of Col. William Lyon, of New Haven.

As an instructor Mr. Linsley was widely known and eminently successful. He dismissed his school in 1831, thus closing this portion of his life.

On the 9th of June, 1831, he was ordained to the ministry at the Baptist State Convention of Connecticut. He had already opened a mission at the lower wharf, in Stratford, wholly at his own expense. Here he held services and preached gratuitously for about five months. In 1832 he established a Baptist Church in Milford, and in 1835, the First Baptist Church in Bridgeport. During this period he supplied for a while the pulpit in Milford, and for a longer time, that in Stratfield. He was constantly invited to the pastorate in other places, and in this last year, 1835, he received calls from five or six different churches, most of them among the first of the denomination in the State. But he declined them all. He preached his farewell to his latest charge, his people in Stratfield, on the first Sunday in 1836.

Again the loss of health caused his physicians to forbid

him further public speaking.   Brief as this part of his life
was he had reached the position of one of the most prominent
and influential clergymen of his denomination.

Mr. Linsley was among the earliest and most fearless
pioneers in the temperance movement.   In 1830 he addressed
crowded houses on this theme, and he was one of the first
clergymen in the State who sent on his name as a subscriber
to the total abstinence pledge.   He was the leader in organizing the first temperance society in Stratford, of which he was
made president.   For his persistent and undaunted efforts in
the cause of temperance, then so unpopular everywhere, he
had the honor of being burnt in effigy.   The parties to this
transaction selected an evening when Mr. Linsley was absent
from Stratford.   The effigy was carried on a bier to Academy
Hill, where it was consumed, with expensive but appropriate
orgies.   When these ended one or two of the ringleaders had
become so helplessly intoxicated that the same bier conveyed
them to their homes.

For the twenty-five years preceding his death Mr. Linsley's contributions to the press, religious, literary and scientific, were too great in number for mention in this brief sketch.

But the achievements which crowned this successful life ;
which gave his name the widest publicity, and which will continue to illumine it in the records of history, were those won
in the difficult fields of science.   Many as were his attainments
in other sciences, in that of the Natural History of his native
State he was without a peer.   His catalogues of the Zoology
of Connecticut, including the five classes, Mammalia, Birds,
Reptiles, Fishes and Shells, were first published in the American Journal of Science for 1842, 1843 and 1844.   Of Mammalia
he discovered several more species than had been found elsewhere in New England, one new; of Birds, many more than
Wilson, the distinguished ornithologist had found in the
United States; of Amphibia and Reptiles he detected species
unseen elsewhere in New England ; and of Shells he ascertained more than double the number supposed by other nat-
uralists to be resident in the State, and of these, many were
entirely new.

The value of this great and unprecedented work on the

Zoology of Connecticut can not be estimated. It was rapidly accepted by the scientific world as acknowledged authority, and such it still remains.

During the progress of these studies, which Mr. Linsley accomplished in the brief period from 1837 to 1843, he was elected to the membership of various scientific societies of the highest importance.

Numberless publications, American and European, religious, literary and scientific, contain notices, sketches and biographies of this most useful and distinguished life. And the acts and opinions of one so upright and so learned, find constant mention in the diversified literature of the present time.

Mr. Linsley died at his residence in Stratford, Dec. 26, 1843, leaving a widow and two daughters.

Gideon Tomlinson was for four years from 1827 Governor of Connecticut, and six years from 1831 Senator of the United States. For special reasons the further record of his life is placed with the genealogy of the Tomlinson family.

David Plant was for four years from 1823 Lieutenant Governor of Connecticut and a very widely known and influential lawyer, politician and citizen. (See genealogy of his family).

Dea. David Plant Judson, son of Daniel and Sarah (Plant) Judson, was born in Stratford, April 16, 1809; graduated at Yale College in 1831, a classmate of Dr. Porter, now President of Yale College. He read law two years, but did not follow the profession.

Here in his native town the remainder of his life was passed, in the fine old house built by his father in 1803, much of it as an invalid, except a small portion passed at the South, during several successive winters, in the hope of benefiting his health and prolonging his life.

In 1853, he married Elizabeth S., daughter of Rev. Frederick Gridley, of East Lyme, who, together with their three children, a daughter and two sons survive him. He died May 24, 1869. He was a highly esteemed citizen. He gave considerable attention to his family genealogy.

Several remarkable relics of the Judson family are still preserved, especially the old court cupboard and chest brought to America by William Judson, the first of the name here. It is of English oak—both dark and light shades—six feet high, five feet wide, two feet and two inches deep, highly ornamented with engraved work. The chest is also ornamented in the same style, being four feet long, three feet four inches in height, and twenty-one inches deep, and remarkably beautiful. There is also a large chair brought to this country by the same person, which is a beautiful article.

Several articles of much interest are preserved by this family, which belonged to parson Wetmore more than one hundred years ago; his inkstand, his punch bowl and others.

Of these large court cupboards, there were three brought to Stratford by the earliest settlers: one by William Judson, one by John Welles and one by Robert Coe. The one which belonged to the Welles family has gone to ashes, but the one brought by Robert Coe is in the possession of Mrs. George A. Talbott, of Stratford, which is a particularly quaint article.

What Might have been Written.

Very much that is not recorded in this book is just as worthy to be here as anything in it, but the fact that the author could not obtain it in the time allowed for the collection of material, is the *only* excuse or reason why such matter is not here.

It is hoped that the perusal of this book will stimulate many persons to write for preservation, general public occurrences, and their family histories, so that future historians may have more ready access to them.

There will be found in the genealogical part of this book many brief sketches of persons and families.

CHAPTER XVII.

STRATFIELD SOCIETY.

BRIDGEPORT, denominated Park City, stands on the shore of Long Island Sound, fifty-five miles from New York City. The locality, when first seen by English people, was the site of an Indian village of about one hundred and fifty wigwams, occupied by five or six hundred Indians, of the Pequonnock settlement or tribe. The southern part of the territory for about a mile in width was a part of a fertile plain of a sandy, and loamy soil, extending along the shore of the Sound from the mouth of the Housatonic River to Southport, a distance of twelve miles. This plain when discovered by the English was covered with forests only in part, there being intervening fields, which in places were cultivated by the Indians in raising corn. At a distance of about a mile from the shore, the hills begin to rise, and continue gradually northward for twelve or fifteen miles, furnishing a fine farming country, and many most picturesque localities.

The City of Bridgeport being so favorably situated, it could, if it should ever see fit, extend itself to a half million of inhabitants, with perfect safety to health, ease of access, charming picturesqueness of local parts, and unsurpassed salubrity of atmosphere from the great ocean and the hills of the country.

With these advantages in its favor, Bridgeport has become a city of about forty thousand inhabitants, and the story of its growth, from the first few families which sat down among the Indians about the year 1665, until it reached its present maturity of numbers, is to be briefly told in the succeeding pages.

Two families at first located west of the Pequonnock river within the township of Stratford. These were Henry Summers, Sen., and Samuel Gregory, and their first houses

THE LOG HOUSE OF 1665.

were probably log houses,[1] located near the present junction of Park and Washington avenues.

---

[1] The accompanying cut of the log-house was drawn by Esquire Isaac Sherman, as representing the kind of house some of his ancestors at Pequonnock resided in at their first settlement here.

At that time there were no highways laid out in the vicinity. A reservation of four rods wide on the east side of the boundary line between Fairfield and Stratford, for a highway, had been made in laying out the lots of land along that line, but the highway had not been surveyed. A well-worn Indian path, which served as a cartway, passed to the northeast over Golden Hill where now Washington avenue is located; which was made a legal highway in 1686, and passed diagonally through the Indians' Reservation. The, one hundred and more wigwams were mostly located near the springs on the southern declivity of Golden Hill.

It was in 1687, when the King's highway, now North avenue, was laid out, and still later when the Toilsome Hill road, now Park avenue, was surveyed.

The one relieving social comfort to these earliest settlers, although there were a few neighbors residing at Old Mill Green, was the fact that the Fairfield men had crowded out eastward nearly to Stratford line, for Col. John Burr's home had been established some years, when the celebrated Indian council was held under the historic oak tree in May, 1681, which was about half a mile west from Samuel Gregory's house.

The Indians were so numerous that the children of these families were afraid to go out of their dwellings, and if they were out and saw an Indian coming they ran with great fright to get into their houses. Persons are now living who have seen those who heard others tell how dreadfully afraid they were of the Indians when they were children, and had many times run to enter their homes to escape the coming Indians; and the Indian children, it is said, were equally afraid of the white people.

Thus began the home of the white man, where now sits the queen of the realm—the city of Bridgeport, with her towering spires, fine public buildings, elegant residences and ·beautiful parks. Then there were only two families, now there are ten thousand, nearly. But it was so long ago! two hundred and fifteen years. The first hundred years produced only a farming community, with beautiful fields, comely residences and a numerous, toiling, happy people, with now and

then a vessel sailing out of the harbor. The next fifty-nine
years gave the embryo city, and the life of that city for sixty-
one years gives the aggregate of nearly forty thousand living

THE BURR HOUSE AND THE HISTORIC OAK TREE. (*See page 49.*)

souls. Then there were two log houses and a hundred wig-wams; now the blazing sunlight is dazzled by its own re-flected rays, from ten thousand roofs, spires, minarets, castles and domes lifted towards the king of day by skilled, artistic hands. Then the weary ox dragged slowly the jolting cart along the stumpy highway as if an age were too short for the journey of a day, now the flying monster engine drives along upon the polished steel as if a day were too long for the journey of an age, and the blazing electric fires dispel the midnight darkness that of yore was far too long for the sleep of man. The farmer in his manly frock of tow plowed the smooth fields and gathered in his abundant harvest from year to year with increasing pleasure and gain; while his womanly wife spun the tow to make the frock and provided the frugal, healthful repast, by the strength of which the harvests were gathered and the homes made comfortable, cheerful and attractive to kindred and friends far and near. But the charming old country homes have long since departed to give place to their burnished city successors.

Such was the ordinary life eighty and a hundred years ago, where now the streets are thronged with rich costumes of silks and satins, and gay, brilliantly ornamented equipages, the product of a marvelous growth of industrial and com-mercial enterprises, such as is not frequent in New England.

Here grew up on these farms a multitude of strong, enter-prising young men, who, fortunately, are not all yet departed to the land of rest, by the strength of their paternal, physical and intellectual inheritances, have made a fame of honor at home and abroad, for their native place, such as to challenge the rivalry of all neighboring regions or countries; and with these young men grew up also, beautiful, intelligent and finely cultivated young ladies, the equal in every respect to their accomplished brothers and successful men of the community.

But in order to a full understanding of the great changes which have taken place in this locality, and the success which has marked the enterprising efforts of the people, it is neces-sary to review the history of two hundred and twenty years, or from 1665 to 1885, by an abbreviated account of the various stages through which the citizens of this locality have passed.

The third and fourth settlers in this place were apparently Capt. John Beardsley, near Samuel Gregory's home, on now Park avenue, and his brother Samuel Beardsley, east of the site of the present Bridgeport jail, or as one of the deeds says, " west of Ireland's brook and north of the Fairfield road."

Not long after, Samuel Wells, son of the first John, established his home in what is now the southern part of Bridgeport, east side of Park avenue, and there dwelt until his decease and his descendants after him for about one hundred years.

Then soon came other settlers in the northern part of Bridgeport, a Hawley family, a Booth family and Sherman family, and others, pushing the settlement several miles back into the woods. There came also a number of families from Fairfield, and one, Samuel French, from Derby. Although the progress was slow they continued to grow in numbers and wealth. At the end of twenty-two years they petitioned for church privileges, but did not succeed until twenty-five years had passed.

The Stratfield Ecclesiastical Society.

The movement began by the organization of a school, which is described by Maj. Wm. B. Hincks in his " Historical Notes," as follows :[1]

" The oldest document signed by the inhabitants of the plantation as such, that I have been able to find any account of, is a petition to the General Court dated May, 1678, subscribed by Isaac Wheeler, John Odell, S[r]., and Matthew Sherwood, in behalf of the people of the place. The distance of nearly four miles that separates them from Fairfield Centre is too great, they say, to be easily traversed by the children, especially the younger ones, and therefore they had set up a school of their own, and employed an experienced teacher. Forty-seven children were already in attendance. The ex-

---

[1] Historical Notes, 32.

pense of the school they propose to bear themselves, but ask to be freed from taxation for the benefit of the one in Fairfield. Rev. Samuel Wakeman, minister at Fairfield, adds a favorable indorsement to the petition, though most of his parishioners were opposed to granting it. The General Court referred the matter to the Fairfield county Court, with power to act, and recommended that body to make an allowance to the petitioners, equal to or greater than their annual school-tax."[3]

This action of the General Assembly applied only to the inhabitants of Fairfield, residing at Pequonnock, for the inhabitants of Pequonnock, in Stratford township, had a school on the east side of the line very early, at least soon after the organization of the Fairfield Village Society; and it is probable that before that they attended school at Stratford village.

Whether the people of Pequonnock held services before the year 1690, may be a question, since Mr. Chauncey gave a receipt, as follows, except a little part of it which is torn from the page of the record book.

"—— said inhabitants to me the said —— the year sixteen hundred eyghtey and eight to the year sixteen hundred ninetey and foure exclusively, that I doe fully and freely——as above said inhabitants and their heirs forever from —— as above said from me or my heirs, &c.: I doe —— of December, seventeen hundred ——.

Subscribed, CHARLES CHAUNCEY."

This indicates that he had served the people as a minister from 1688 to 1694, but had given no receipt for the salary they were obligated to pay him, and hence the receipt was given in 1700.

The first page of the earliest Society's book contains the following record:

"The Records of the Acts of the Society of Fairfield Village, began in the year 1693.

It was then voted pr. the said Society that Mr. Charles Chauncey for his encouragement in the ministry in this place shall have sixty pounds in good provisions for the year ensu-

---

[3] Col. Rec., iii. 8.

ing to be paid him by way of Rate, each man according to the list of his estate given in.

"March 19, 1694. At a meeting of the Society of this place it was voted that Mr. Charles Chauncey should have for his encouragement in the ministry sixty pounds in good provisions pay, for the year ensuing, to be raised by way of Rate according to custom."

The proprietors of undivided lands in Stratford, having given certain lands to other societies in the town, gave to this, in 1719, several acres of land, and afterward added to the number. "Granted to our neighbors of Stratfield parish that belong to Stratford fifteen acres of pasture land . . . for and towards the support of a Presbyterian minister amongst them forever, for the only benefit of our neighbors belonging to Stratford."

"1704, Mr. Jos. Bennitt of Stratfield, having payd full satisfaction ——— majority of merchants in Stratfield for his trading in said place—Merchant: the said society do acknowledge the same and authorize it to be entered on the record of Stratfield, Joseph Bennit, Merchant. Voted as above.

SAMUEL HUBBELL, Clerk."

This shows that a merchant was established in the place by the vote of the society.

Twelve years later another petition was sent to the General Assembly, signed by forty-six tax-payers for ecclesiastical privileges, which furnishes, probably, nearly a complete list of the householders in the settlement in the year 1690.[4]

---

[4] STATE PAPERS, ECCLESIASTICAL, I, 105. COPY FURNISHED TO MAJ. WM. B. HINCKS, BY THE COURTESY OF MR. C. J. HOADLY, STATE LIBRARIAN.

Petition for Ecclesiastical Privileges.

"To the Gen[ll] Court of Connecticut (whom we honor), in their next session at Hartford.

We, the inhabitants and persons of Poquannock, do in all humility address and apply ourselves unto you in mann[r] method and form following:

Manifesting unto this hono[rd] respected representative body that this vicinity of Poquonnock afores[d] appertaineth part to the town of Fairfield, and part to the town of Stratford, unto which two townships it hath been fully responsible according to obligations, for meeting house and school dues, rates and assessments; we, the dwellers there, have to the towns we have been engaged to, ever punct-

At that time, Fairfield opposed the request of the petitioners, and it was not granted, but in May, 1694, they renewed their request, and no opposition being offered, liberty was granted to organize a society. The acquiescence of the Fairfield and Stratford churches was perhaps due to the influence of the Rev. Israel Chauncey, who had interested himself in their behalf.

Of the forty-six names attached to the petition of 1790, thirteen of them, and perhaps others, were inhabitants of Stratford, residing west of the Pequonnock river.

---

ually paid our acknowledgements, taxes and charges, as we have from time to time been laid under such bonds and indisputable engagem[ts]. But now since we are by the blessing and grace of Almighty God, risen and advanced to somewhat more maturity and ripeness, and grown more populous than before, in capacity to stand within ourselves, without running for succor six or seven miles on one hand, and at least four on the other; we doe make it our joynt ardent request and passionate petition to this honour'd esteem'd Court, that you would in the greatness of your goodness, and out of your sincere zeal to the comfort of this part every way, so order it in your new convention that wee, every one of us, that are settled inhabitants of and steady dwellers in Poquonnock, may be exempted and relaxed from any minister's rate or rates and schooll mastours salerys, either in Fairfield or Stratford afores[d], purposing (God smiling on and favouring our enterprises) to suit o'selves in time convenient wth such meet instrum[ts] for ye pulpit and scholl, as may most and best serve the interest of our God, and do our souls and children most good; such as shall bee most painfull pious and profitable for these ends to w[ch] they were ordain'd, and are improv'd. And your humb. petitioners shall ever continue to pray for your long life and prosperity, subsigning this our address, dated 2[d] May, 1690.

John Bardsle, S[r].,	Sam[ll] Hubbell,	Ephraim Wheller,
Richard Hobbell, S[r].,	Sam[ll] Bardsley, S[r].,	Daniel Bardsle,
Matthew Sherwood,	Samuel Hall, .	Samuel French,
Sam[ll] Wells,	David Sherman,	Samu[ll] Hubbell,
Isaac Wheeler,	Richard Hubell,	Timothy Wheller,
James Benitt,	Samuel Gregory,	Thomas Benit,
David Reynolds,	Sam[ll] Tredwell,	Ed. Tredwell,
Nathn[ll] Knap,	John Odell, S[r].,	Jacob Joy,
Will Barsley,	Izhak Hall,	John Odell, Junr.,
Matthew Sharwood, Jr.,	John Wheller,	John Benitt, Jnr.,
Isack Wheeler, S[r].,	Thomas Wheller,	Thos. Morhous, Jr.,
Thomas Griffin,	Joseph Seely,	John Sherwood,
Roburd Bishop,	Moses Jackson, Jr.,	Joseph Joy,
Sam[ll] Morhous,	Samu[ll] Jackson,	Sam[ll] Sumers.
Jacobe Wakelen,	Matthew Sherwood, Jr.,	
Samuel Bardsle,	Moses Jackson, S[r].,	

In May, 1691, the Court granted liberty to the inhabitants at Pequonnock " to procure and settle an orthodox minister among them if they find themselves able so to do, and provided that those of Paquonnock that do belong to Fairfield township shall pay their just proportion of rate towards the maintenance of the ministry in Fairfield till they can obtain freedom of Fairfield or from this Court."

The next October they were released from paying to the support of the ministry at Fairfield while they supported a minister among themselves.

In May, 1694, permission was given to organize a church and the name Pequonnock was changed to Fairfield Village; and this name was changed by the Court in May, 1701, to Stratfield.

The town of Stratford treated the Stratfield people with a good degree of friendship and favor.

" December 29, 1692. The neighbors at Paquonnock requested of the town liberty that in case the good people at Paquonnock should see cause to build a meeting house there at Paquonnock the liberty to set the said house part upon Stratford bounds, and said town by vote granted the same."

Therefore the probability is that the first meeting-house was located on the boundary line, half on Stratford, and half on Fairfield territory.

In 1696,' and 1697, and perhaps several years after, the town remitted to the society one-third part of their town taxes.

" In 1693, the foundation of a house of worship was laid on an eminence in the upper part of Division street [Park avenue] a few rods south of the King's highway [North avenue]. This height affords a pleasant view of the surrounding

---

ᵇ " Jan. 13, 1696. Lt. John Beardsley with ye rest of our loving neighbors at Paquonnock, inhabitants of Stratford, requesting yt. ye town would be pleased to consider them in the present town rate and make them some abatement in consideration yt they apprehend themselves not equally privileged with ye rest of ye town in some causes of expense, and the town did by vote grant the request and give order to ye town treasurer to give to them our said neighbors credit one-third of their town rate respectively."

" Jan. 19, 1697. It was voted that our loving neighbors at ye Village should be allowed one-third part of their town rate for ye year past."

country and is still called Meetinghouse Hill. The building, though small, was not completed until 1695, and in the mean time it is probable that the people gathered upon the Sabbath in a private house, having already provided themselves with a pastor.[6]

The Stratfield Ecclesiastical Society was the first one in the Colony, not being a town, fully organized as independent of all other societies, and hence it was necessary for the General Assembly to define its privileges and powers. This was done as follows :

"August 1, 1699. Liberties granted to Fairfield Village by the Assembly :

" 1 Impr. To make choice annually of two or three persons who shall have power to order meetings of the society, their ministers' rates, and what concerns may be about their meeting house.

" 2d. To choose collectors of the rates, and that they shall have power by virtue of a writ from lawful authority of non-payment to distrain.

" 3d. To choose a constable whose power shall reach from west side of Pequonnock River unto the utmost bounds of the village, westward according to the limitations granted Commission officers : the village consisting partly of Fairfield and of Stratford.

" 4th. That they shall have liberty to choose annually a society recorder to be sworn to that work."

In 1717, the privileges and powers of ecclesiastical societies were further defined ; and in 1723, still further.[7]

In the case of the second society organized by law in Stratford village, to which Mr. Zachariah Walker ministered, it was in part under the officers and control of the first society, or the town, for so far as seen it had no officers elected by the town ; but the Stratfield society was granted several offices to be filled by its own election, in 1699. Previous to this, a part of the time at least if not all, its recorder was that of the town of Fairfield ; and its own special officers, if it had any, had not civil authority.

---

[6] Historical Notes, by Major W. B. Hincks, 35.

[7] See foot note on pages 302 and 303 of this book.

The boundaries of the Fairfield Village on the western side were not particularly specified as became necessary, and on petition the General Assembly in May, 1701, established them definitely, and changed the name from Fairfield Village to that of Stratfield,[8] a name formed from the first part of the words Stratford and the last part of Fairfield.

In May, 1702, this society received its part of the State money for schools according to the following act:[9]

"Ordered by this Assembly, that the constable or constables of Fairfield and Stratford, or those to whom orders shall be sent annually for the payment of the schools there, shall pay to the schoolmaster of Stratfield, so much as ariseth upon their part of the list at forty shillings upon every thousand pounds, according to the late law for Schools."

The ecclesiastical Society being fully organized, it thereby became the territory for a military company, and hence in October, 1703, "David Sherman was appointed Ensign of the train band in Stratfield."[10]

The next spring the complement of officers was made more complete by the appointment of "Lieut. John Beardsley to be Captain of the train band of Stratfield, and Lieut. James Bennet to be their Lieutenant."[11] Capt. John Beardsley

---

[8] "May 1701. This Assembly having heard and considered the petition or request of the inhabitants of Fairfield Village presented to them by Lieut. James Bennett, desiring that the Court would state and settle for them a line for the west boundary to their plantation, &c., do order and enact: That the line to be the west boundary of the said plantation shall run so that it may take in and include within their bounds, one Moses Jackson, miller, his housing and lands, and run on the west side of old Jackson's lotts (viz): pasture, building lot, and long lot, upwards or northwards to the upward or northern end of the bounds of the town of Fairfield, and that all such person or persons as have built or shall build and inhabit on the east side of the abovesaid line, and on the west side of Poquanack River, shall pay to all public charges that shall arise in the said plantation his ratable part thereof.

"Provided always: That this act shall in no wise hinder or abridge the inhabitants of said plantation, of using and holding the priviledge of feeding sheep to the westward of the abovesaid line, as it was granted to them formerly by the inhabitants of the town of Fairfield.

"And further it is enacted by the authority aforesaid: That the said plantation (formerly called Poquannuck and Fairfield village) shall for the future be called by the name of Stratfield."—Col. Rec., iv. 356.

[9] Col. Rec., iv. 384.   [10] Col. Rec., iv. 445.   [11] Col. Rec., iv. 476.

had been lieutenant at Stratford many years, and James Bennett the same at Fairfield.

The following is a copy of the first page of the Stratfield earliest church record book.

" The Church of Christ in Stratfield (formerly called Poquannuck) was gathered, and Charles Chauncey was ordained the Pastor thereof, June 13, 1695.

" The Names of those that at that time were embodied into Church estate were as followeth :

"CHARLES CHAUNCEY, Past^r.

" Richard Hubble, sen^r,	Mathew Sherman,
Isaac Wheeler, sen^r,	Richd Hubble, jun^r,
James Bennit, sen^r,	David Sherman,
Samu^{ll} Beardsley,	Jno Odill, jun^r.
Samuel Gregory, sen^r,	

" The Names of those that were afterwards received by vertue of Letters Dissmissory or Recommendatory from other Churches were as followeth :

From Fairfield Church.
{
Mary Sherwood,
Anne Wheeler,
Mary Odill,
Rebecca Gregory,
Ruth Tredwell,
Mercy Wheeler,
Abigaill Wells,
Elizabeth Sherwood,
Sarah Odill.
Their letter was read and accepted Anno 1695.
}

From Stratford Church.
{
Abigaill Hubble,
Mary Bennit,
Abigaill Beardsley,
Abigaill Wakely,
Temperance Hubble,
Mercy Sherman,
Their letter was read and accepted, July 10, 1695.
}

" Concord. Joseph Wheeler and his wife. Their letter was read and accepted.

" From the Church of Christ, Norwalk ; Mary Jackson, her letter was read December 20, 1697, and accepted.

" Stratford. Hannah Fairchild ; her letter was read and accepted by the Church September 10, 1699.

" Thomas Hawley, his letter was read and accepted.

" Fairfield Church ; Mary Beardsley, Jno's wife ; her letter was read and accepted, July 26, 1702.

" Woodbury ; Abegaill Tredwell's letter was read and accepted, Nov. 24, 1704.

"Concord; Sarah Whitacus, her letter was read and accepted June 17, 1705.

"Charlestown; Zachariah Ferris, sen', his letter was read and accepted, Sept. 9, 1705."

Besides the above there were added to this Church by profession, in full communion, during Mr. Chauncey's labors, to the end of the year 1714, the time of his death, 64 persons, making 97 in all.

During the same time there were 133 who united under the Halfway Covenant.

As to the meaning of this latter relation, Mr. Chauncey says, in heading the list with a prefatory statement:

"The Names of those who have renewed their Covenant, and personally subjected themselves to the government of Christ in his Church, and particularly in this Church, together with the time of their doing it."

This indicates that the relationship of the Halfway Covenant church members, was not regarded as of less seriousness or solemn obligation than that of full membership. The requirements in the Covenant itself were nearly the same as those of full communion; and it was not a trifling matter as it has so often been represented. Many persons at the present day are received to full membership in evangelical Churches without placing themselves under anything like the solemn promises that the Halfway Covenant imposed," in those days of strict religious principle.

---

[19] The following is a copy of the Halfway Covenant which stands upon the records of the Church of Ripton at the date of 1773, the use of which was discontinued in 1817:

"You do now, before God and these witnesses, avouch the Lord Jehovah to be your covenant God and Father, viewing yourself under solemn bonds and obligations to be the Lord's by your baptismal vows. You do, so far as you know your own heart, make choice of Jesus Christ to be your only Saviour and Redeemer, and the Holy Ghost to be your Sanctifier, solemnly engaging to serve the Lord and him only, as he shall by his grace enable you; that you will deny all ungodliness and worldly lusts; that you will be careful to keep a conscience void of offence, so as to do honor to God and the religion you profess; that you will endeavor by strength from God to walk in all his commandments and ordinances blameless, desiring to put yourself under the watch and care of this Church, to be trained up in the school of Christ for his heavenly kingdom; promising also that you will give up your children to God, in baptism, and to bring

The part which this Church had in the establishment of the Saybrook Platform is seen in the resolution and action recorded:

"July 27, 1708. Voted on the Sabbath that Leut. Bennet or Ensigne Sherman or both, be the messengers of this Church at the meeting of the elders at Fairfield on the 28ᵗʰ of the same month by the appointment of the General Assembly at Hartford in May last, the end of which meeting of elders and messengers to Consider the matter of Church discipline."

When the result of the Saybrook convention had been confirmed by the General Assembly, Mr. Chauncey made the following entry in the Church book:

"February 16, 1708–9. I published the Confession of Faith, the Articles of union between the united Presbyterians and Congregational men in England, also read the regulations for Church discipline agreed upon by said Colony, and confirmed by authority; None among the brethren objecting."[13]

The Rev. Charles Chauncey[14] was the first pastor of the Stratfield Congregational Church. He was a son of the Rev. Israel Chauncey, of Stratford, and grandson of President Chauncey of Harvard College, and was born at Stratford, September 3, 1668. He was graduated at Harvard in 1686, and married at Pequonnock, June 29, 1692, Sarah, daughter of Major John Burr, and great-granddaughter of Mr. Jehu Burr, one of the original settlers of Fairfield.

Mr. Chauncey was made freeman in Fairfield, March 18, 16⅞⅞, which indicates his residence there either as a school

---

them up in the fear of the Lord; and to attend upon all the ordinances of Christ as administered in this place; also that it is your full purpose to obey God in the ordinance of the Holy Supper as God shall give you light, and show you his will herein. And you covenant, and you promise, relying for help, strength and ability on the blood of the everlasting covenant, to perform all and every duty to the praise and glory of God."—*See Ecclesiastical Contributions,* 411.

[13] This account of the action of this Church, as to the Saybrook platform, and the record of the meeting of the first Consociation of Fairfield County, printed on pages 310 to 313 of this book, in foot note, are taken from the Stratfield Church Record book.

[14] See sermon by the Rev. Charles Ray Palmer, pub. 1876.

teacher—which is probable—or serving as a minister under his father in lectures on week day evenings. It is evident that he served as a preacher, soon after, from the fact that in 1692, the town of Fairfield gave him land to descend to his heirs "if he shall die in the work of his ministry at Poquonnock."

The privileges of a society were granted in 1691, and the Church was organized and Mr. Chauncey ordained, as seen above, June 13, 1695.

On the corner of Major Burr's farm, in what has since been known as Cooke's Lane, a house was built, and in it, in 1693, Mr. Chauncey and his wife took up their abode, and he commenced his regular ministerial labors.

In 1697, his wife Sarah died, and he married 2d, Sarah, daughter of Henry Wolcott, of Windsor, March 16, 1698. She died Jan. 5, 1702, and he married, 3d, Elizabeth Sherwood, March 14, 1710.

Mr. Chauncey was a member of the Council at Saybrook, and one of the founders of the Fairfield Consociation. Under his ministry both the church and the settlement steadily increased in numbers. His salary was at first £60 per annum, payable in produce at market rates, but afterwards it was increased to £80. He had, independently of his support, property in Stratford and in England, and left an estate valued at £743.

Mr. Chauncey died December 31, 1714, leaving a widow and several children.

The first Deacon of Mr. Chauncey's Church was David Sherman, a large farmer, and one of the first settlers in Pequonnock. He was born in Stratford in 1665; was a man of good abilities, gifted in prayer, and much esteemed. In the absence of the minister he took the lead of religious services.

The Second Meeting-house in Stratfield.

Mr. Samuel Cooke commenced preaching for this people soon after July 11, 1715, and was ordained pastor February 14, 1715-16.

In December, 1715, the Society proceeded to the election of officers in which they called their most prominent officers " Selectmen," it being probable that they intended by that term simply the society's committee. They also voted, " that the drum shall bee beaten round the meeting house on Sabbath days;" and Richard Hubbell, Thomas Hawley, James Seeley, were chosen a committee to consult some carpenters about the enlargement of the meeting-house.

In July, 1716, further action was taken : " Voted, that they will inlarge and repair the meeting-house ;" and a large committee was appointed to have the work done as soon as convenient, at the charge of the society."

In the progress of events, the work being delayed, another plan seems to have come under discussion, and probably was brought up at the next annual meeting, which meeting was adjourned several days, and when they came together in December, 1716, they voted, " that the place for the setting of the new meeting-house, if they shall afterward agree to build one, shall be near the corner of Joseph Trowbridge's orchard, late deceased, on the norwest side of the road between that and the widow Sharman's, deceased. Also voted at the same time, that they will build a new meeting-house, of these following dimensions : twenty-four feet between joints ; forty-eight feet long : thirty-eight feet wide and a long roof. Major John Burr, Capt. David Sharman, Left. Richard Hubbell, Jr., Samuel Sherwood, Mr. Benjamin Fairwether, were chosen a committee to build the above said house, on the charge of the abovesaid inhabitants; and what the major part of the committee agree to, shall be binding, not exceeding four hundred and fifty pounds, besides the charge of raising said house."

At another meeting, on December 31, 1716, they "granted by a major vote a Rate of one hundred pounds money to be raised on them according to their lists the last year, to be laid out towards the building of the new meeting-house."

In March, 17⅟₇ the following request was received by the meeting of the society : " Your petitioner requests your favour so far as to grant me the liberty of making a pew for my wife and children at my own charge in the new meeting-

house, on the women's side up by the pulpit. Pray be so
kind as to gratify me in this instance, both with respect to
the thing itself and the situation of it. I remain your s. in
all things I may.   Sam᷊ᴸ Cooke.

 Passed in the affirmative at the abovesaid meeting."

 "May 23ᵈ, 1717, then voted and agreed that the committee shall hire men to raise the meeting-house and give
them 3ˢ per day, they finding themselves."

STRATFIELD SECOND MEETING–HOUSE ERECTED IN 1717.

 On December 30, 1717, they proceeded to make the rules
for seating the meeting-house: "Voted that the meeting-
house shall be seated by dignity, age, and estate by the present list; and also that David Sharman, Richard Hubbell, John
Odell, Samuel Sherwood and John Burr be a committee to
seat the meeting-house, and have power to seat from time to
time as they see occasion.

 "At a meeting of the society, March 7, 17¼⅛, then voted
that Major John Burr sit with his family in the pew that he

has built in the meetinghouse during the pleasure of the society."

In 1718, an appropriation of sixteen pound and six shillings was made by the society for building a gallery in the meeting-house, and Capt. David Sherman, Thomas Hawley, and Samuel Gregory, were appointed the committee to build it.

This meeting-house was considerably altered as shown by the vote, December 17, 1765 : " Liberty was granted to the following persons, each, to build a pew at the east end of the meetinghouse where the short seats are, they building at their own cost and paying the several sums affixed to each of their names, to the treasurer of this society in three months from this time ; for them and to be for their benefit during their pleasure to sit in :

Nehemiah Smith Odell,	13ˢ 2ᵈ	Seth Gregory,	13ˢ 2ᵈ
Hezekiah Hubbell,	12ˢ 1ᵈ	Benjamin Hubbell, Jr.,	12ˢ 6ᵈ
Edward Rowland,	13ˢ 3ᵈ	Jabez Hubbell,	12ˢ 2ᵈ
Wolcott Hawley,	13ˢ 0ᵈ	Gideon Hubbell,	12ˢ 1ᵈ
Aaron Hawley,	12ˢ 8ᵈ	Thomas Hawley,	12ˢ 0ᵈ
Isaac Hunt,	13ˢ 1ᵈ	Elnathan Sherman,	11ˢ 4ᵈ

" December 20, 1769. Voted that the society are willing to build a steeple at the west end of the Presbyterian meeting house."

The committee to do the work consisted of " John Burr, Esq., Lieut. Benjamin Fayerweather, Lieut. Abel Seelye, Mr. Stephen Starling, and Mr. Benjamin Wheeler," and they were to do the work by subscription.

The subscription, however, was not sufficient to complete the work, for on September 19, 1770, the society voted that they were " willing to tax themselves to finish the steeple ;" but changing their minds somewhat, they voted to make further efforts with the subscription, and it is probable that it was finished without a tax.

The steeple was not finished, when on the 28th of July, 1771, it was struck with lightning while the people were worshiping in the house, but was not greatly injured, although two men, John Burr, Esq., and Mr. David Sherman, being in the house at worship, were killed. No other persons were seriously injured by the shock.

On August 5th, 1771, they voted to repair and finish the steeple; and the next April they voted "that there may be an iron rod put up at the steple by subscription."

Another improvement was secured by the following society act: "Mar. 8, 1774. Voted that they will have a bell; also that the society will get a bell by subscription, and Joseph Strong, Gideon Hubbell, and Edward Boroughs shall be the committee to get the bell."

"September 12, 1774. Voted that yᵉ Society are willing to have the bell ringed at yᵉ usual time on Sabbath days, and other days at 12 of yᵉ clock in yᵉ day and at 9 o'clock at night, and also on lecture day; and whereas Mr. Wolcott Hawley offers to ring yᵉ Bell at yᵉ rate of £4 10ˢ by yᵉ year for yᵉ first three months, it was agreed to by yᵉ meeting."

There seems to have been some failure in the bell, for in November the society voted that they were "willing to run the bell over again and pay for it by subscription." This was probably done, since they continued afterwards to appoint a person to ring the bell from year to year.

Rev. Samuel Cooke,[18] son of Thomas Cooke, Jr., and Sarah (Mason) Cook, of Guilford, Conn.,. was born in Guilford, November 22, 1687. His father died suddenly in 1701, before the son entered college, and the General Court granted, in May, 1703, a petition from the boy and his guardian (John Parmelee) for the sale of a house and lot to gain funds to carry out "the great desire of Thomas Cooke, deceased, to bring up this his son in learning." He graduated at Yale College in 1705.

He perhaps studied divinity immediately after graduation. In January, 1707, he became the rector of the Hopkins Grammar School in New Haven, and held that position at a salary of £60 a year, also occasionally preaching, until the close of the year 1715. He was also a deputy to the General Assembly from New Haven, for the six sessions from October,

---

[18] This sketch is taken from " Biographical Sketches of the Graduates of Yale College," by F. B. Dexter, M.A.

1712, to May, 1715, serving as Clerk of the House for the last five. He married, November 30, 1708, Anne, only daughter of John Trowbridge, of New Haven, and granddaughter of Governor Leete, of Guilford.

In 1714, the Church in Stratfield lost by death its first pastor, the Rev. Charles Chauncey; and on June 16, 1715, a call was extended to Mr. Cooke to become his successor. The church in New Haven was also pastorless, owing to the death of the Rev. James Pierpont; and on July 1, 1715, this society met " to nominate a man to carry on the work of the ministry on probation." Mr. Cooke was put in nomination, and the place was probably more attractive to him than was Stratfield; but the vote stood 86 for Mr. Joseph Noyes to 45 for Mr. Cooke.

Accordingly, the call to Stratfield was accepted July 11, and Mr. Cooke appears to have begun his ministry there at once, though fulfilling his engagement with the New Haven Grammar School, until the end of the year 1715. His ordination is said to have taken place February 14, 1715–16. The salary was £100 a year, with firewood.[16]

He retained this pastorate until his death, December 2, 1747, at the age of 60. His latter years were troubled by an alleged backwardness on the part of his people to make good the salary promised him; and after his death his executors brought suit for the sum of £3000 arrears due his estate.[17]

In 1717, at the very beginning of his ministry, a new meeting-house was erected, which was used until the present century. In the events which followed the great revival of 1740, Mr. Cooke was a zealous advocate of what were known

---

[16] *Specimen of Mr. Cooke's Receipts.*

"Stratfield, July ye 14, 1716. Received of henry Wakely and Sam¹¹ Wells, Jnʳ, Collectors of the Minister's Rate or accepted as Received the sum of one hundred pounds six shillings and fore pence as money in full of the Rate that by agreement was to have been paid me on or Before the first day of March last passed and acordingly acquit the Society of Stratfield of one full years Rate and one myself endebted to the sᵈ Society ye sum of six shillings and fore pence.

Witness my hand, SAMˡˡ COOKE.

[17] A considerable part of this sum, probably, grew out of claims, in consequence of the depreciation of the currency.

32

as "New Light" measures; and particularly, in May, 1742, he took an active part in the organization of a new church in New Haven. He had been since September, 1732, one of the Trustees of Yale College, but the predominant "Old Light" convictions of the other trustees led finally to the following vote, found in the original records of the Corporation for September, 1745: "Whereas, this board have at this and former meetings signified to Mr. Cook their dissatisfaction with sundry things in his conduct, and he could not conveniently tarry to make any distinct answer thereunto at this time by reason of sickness in his family, Voted, that the President, with the rest of the standing Committee of this Board be desired to signifie to Mr. Cooke the reasons of their dissatisfaction in writing and desire his answer thereto."

It is but fair to read between the lines, and bearing in mind that this was the first meeting convened after the new charter of 1745 had passed the legislature, which gave power (not in the former charter) to six of the Trustees to remove a Trustee from his place, we may conclude that the writing sent to Mr. Cooke forced upon him the resignation of his trusteeship, which was announced to the Corporation at their next meeting, in April, 1746.

The New Haven County Association of Ministers had previously, September 25, 1744, sent a letter to Mr. Cooke signifying their uneasiness with, and offense at the proceedings of said Mr. Cooke, etc., in pretendedly gathering a Church among the Separatists at New Haven in opposition to the pastor and 1st church there. His letter in reply was voted "not satisfactory," September 24, 1745.

On the other hand the Fairfield Eastern Association of Ministers, in which Mr. Cooke was a leading member, passed, April 15, 1746, a series of resolutions, evidently bearing reference to his citation before the Trustees, and to this effect: in view of the Assembly's having granted "a new College Charter with large privileges and a new form of government, and particularly by investing the newly incorporated body with powers of taking away as well as giving College honors, as the said Corporation see just cause; Therefore,

"1. Voted and Agreed, That no person or future member of this Association shall be looked upon by us obliged to answer before sd. authority for any such fact or facts as were committed by such member before sd. Corporation's Investiture with such new authority.

"2. Voted and Agreed that no member of this Association is obliged to answer to sd. Corporation for any of their Doctrines or Conduct as ministers of the gospel. . . . ."

"He was," says his present successor, "a man whose personal dignity was long remembered in the parish, and was held in the highest respect—somewhat in fear. He was particularly careful in his personal appearance. This comprised a heavy curled wig, black coat and small clothes, shoes with silver buckles, and over all a black gown or cloak."

His first wife was born July 22, 1688, and died August 11, 1721; and he married, May 3, 1722, Esther, daughter of Nathaniel Burr, and widow of John Sloss, both of Fairfield; she died in less than a year. He married, thirdly, Elizabeth, daughter of Joseph Platt, of Norwalk, Conn., born December 2, 1701, and died May 16, 1732, "of an apoplexy;" and fourthly, Aug. 6, 1733, Abigail, daughter of the Rev. Samuel Russell, of Branford, and widow of the Rev. Joseph Moss, of Derby, Conn., who survived him. His children were, three sons and four daughters by his first wife, and three sons by his third wife. Three of his sons, Samuel, William, and Joseph Platt, graduated at Yale College in 1730, 1747, and 1750, respectively. One of his daughters married the Rev. Robert Silliman.

The inventory of his estate amounted to £2,787; it included 61 books and 173 pamphlets.

He published two sermons:

1. A sermon preached at the funeral of Rev. John Davenport, of Stamford, published in 1731.

2. A sermon preached before the Eastern Association of Fairfield County, on a publick lecture in Danbury, July 29, 1741.

This sermon was introduced into a spirited controversy between Jonathan Dickinson and Samuel Johnson. Johnson published, in 1744, "A Letter from Aristocles Authades, concerning the Sovereignty and Promises of God," and Dickin-

son, in replying, in 1746, with "A Vindication of God's Sovereign free Grace," interpreted Johnson's imagined antagonist (Authades) as Mr. Cooke, whose views (as printed in his
sermon) he certainly seemed to be controverting; Johnson,
however, in "A Letter to Mr. Jonathan Dickinson," disclaimed
the intention of a precise reference to Cooke's sermon.

Besides these sermons should be mentioned:

3. " Invitations to the Rev. Mr. Whitefield from the Eastern Consociation of the County of Fairfield. With a Letter
from the Rev. Mr. Samuel Cooke, of Stratfield, to a Minister
in Boston, Concerning the former success of Mr. Whitefield's
Ministry there."

This pamphlet contains a letter by Mr. Cooke to one of
the Boston ministers, dated May 15, 1745. This letter is an
urgent appeal that Mr. Whitefield may come and preach in
the churches of Fairfield County; and to show the spirit of
some of these churches he prefixes a vote of the Consociation
at a meeting held in Stratfield, October 7, 1740, of which he
was Moderator and Scribe, inviting Whitefield.

This publication was quite possibly an additional motive
for the action taken in September, 1745, by the College
Trustees.

History of the Porter Property.[18]

Much interesting history is connected with the premises
of No. 532 Main street and the house recently demolished to
make room for a block of stores. The territory of nearly
seven acres, on the east side of Main street from a point at or
near Golden Hill street to Congress street, bounded easterly
by the harbor, was purchased by Samuel Porter, sen.,[19] from
Zachariah Hawley, Feb. 5, 1759. A plot of the premises

---

[18] Manuscript of Dea. R. B. Lacey, written for this work.

[19] *A portion of the old Samuel Porter deed.*

To all persons . . . Greeting. Know ye that I, Zakry Hawley, of Stratford
and County of Fairfield and Colony of Connecticut in New England. For the
Consideration of One Hundred and two pounds York money by me in hand received to my full satisfaction of Samuel Porter of Stratford, and County and Colony aforesaid, do give grant bargain sell to his heirs and assigns forever my

copied from the original, made by Wolcott Hawley, surveyor, found among the Porter papers, is given with this record.

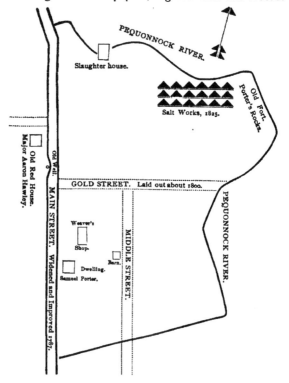

THE PORTER PROPERTY.

Dwelling house and Land whereon it stands on Golden Hill, called ye old fort, and is Bounded South on Deacon Joseph Booth's Land Easterly and Northerly on ye creek and West on highway—the sd house and Land with all the appertenances thereunto belonging for him the said Samuel Porter forever. To have and to hold . . . forever.

Witness my Hand and Seal the 5th day of Feb. in the 32d year of the Reign of our Sovereign Lord GEORGE the second of Great Britain. . . . . King, Annoque Domini, 1759.

ZACHARIAH HAWLEY."

Signed and sealed in presence of
　　Theophilus Nichols.
　　Joseph Nichols.

There was a dwelling house on the plot in 1759, but not the one which has just been taken down. The latter was probably erected by Samuel Porter, sen., soon after the close of the Revolutionary war, and, with the " Old Red House" which stood on the west side of the highway,—Main street— the site of the present wooden block of Mr. Nathaniel Wheeler, was among the very first residences of a good class erected upon the Newfield, as Bridgeport was then called. James and Zachariah Hawley were sons of Gideon, and third in descent from the original Joseph Hawley, of Stratford, through first, Ephraim and Sarah Wells, and second, Gideon and Ann Bennett. They were pioneers here. The Hawley family were large land owners. James seems to have settled on the west side of the highway. His son, Deacon Elijah, was a house carpenter, and probably built and occupied the old red house. Isaac Sherman says of him : " He removed to the West very early, and died in Ohio in 1825, aged 84 years. He had a son by the name of Jesse, who was born in the old red house. This Jesse removed to the state of New York in early life and died there in 1843, at the age of 70 years. It is said that he was the projector of the Erie canal by communicating his ideas of such an enterprise to Governor DeWitt Clinton.

Major Aaron Hawley, a brother of Deacon Elijah, appears to have been the owner of the old red house in 1787, at which period the "upright highway "—Main street—was widened and the site of the famous well in front, which stood its width in the street, was excepted and liberty was given to fence around it. The same well exists to-day covered by the sidewalk stone. Zachariah Hawley married Bethia Austin of Suffield, Ct., and probably removed to Massachusetts, for none of his descendants appear in this part of Connecticut.

Samuel Porter, sen., died September 15, 1795. The Porter purchase remained intact as field land during his life, except at the south end, where he gave a house lot as an advancement to his daughter Mary, who married Lewis Sturges. The old house, now a portion of the Elisha Hubbell property at the northeast corner of Main and Golden Hill streets, was the residence of Isaac Sturges, son of Lewis. His son Joseph

P. Sturges—commonly called Porter Sturges—had his residence a little way south. The original house is standing but it has a brick front and has been raised an additional story. The main building is occupied by Cohen (millinery) and Bain (a tea and coffee store.) It was a double house with hallway and kitchen wings both on the north and south. Porter Sturges occupied the south house, and Henry Coty and the late Thomas Hutchins successively occupied the north part for many years.

There was a vacant lot between the two Sturges houses through which Golden Hill street was extended in 1847, from Main street easterly, leaving a strip of land on the south side of the street, which was leased by the city and an engine house, for the original No. 5 hand engine, was erected thereon. The same building is now occupied as a bakery by Mr. A. Brennan.

The survey from which the accompanying diagram is taken was made by Wolcott Hawley, a brother of Major Aaron and Deacon Elijah Hawley, October 20, 1795, to aid the distribution of the estate of Samuel Porter, Sen. The original has the dotted lines showing the portions set out to the two heirs, Samuel Porter, Jr., who had a double portion and his sister, Mary Sturges.

Lewis and Isaac Sturges with their families went West about 1820, and afterwards settled in Wisconsin. Rev. Albert Sturges, the veteran missionary of the American Board in Micronesia, is of this family.

They sold their interest in the remnant of this property on the death of Samuel Porter, Jr., who died without children, September 9, 1842.

The Rev. Thomas B. Sturges, of Greenfield Hill, Conn., is the only son and heir of Joseph P. Sturges. He inherited the undivided half of the old Porter house, lot No. 532, Main street, and came into possession of it on the death of the widow of Samuel Porter, Jr., April 12, 1867.

Recently, there has been a division by which he has acquired sole ownership of the entire Main street front, and is putting it to use by erecting the one-story block of stores now being built.

This plot of land is referred to in the deed, as being located on Golden Hill, showing that the name was applied to
the land extending to the Pequonnock river. It was also
called "Y* Old Fort." Referring to the diagram on the
right hand side, bordering on the creek at the extreme point,
the position of the fort may be seen. These are the only
allusions to a fort here, now known, and its previous existence
must have been traditionary in 1795. It could hardly have
been built by the English settlers, or there would have been
some record of it, or in connection with its erection and use.
Therefore it must have been an Indian fortification.

The location was a rocky promontory jutting out into
the creek from a beautiful plateau which extended back to
the highway. Later, for three-quarters of a century it was
universally known as Porter's Rocks. It retained nearly its
pristine beauty until 1838, and was a favorite resort for sports
and bathing, by the young men and boys of the period, a few
of whom survive to this day. There was the round rock and
the flat rock; both extending out so as to afford at their base
considerable depth of water at high tide; the latter was at
the extreme point and was a favorite place for fishing, especially for frost fish in their season. A short distance from the
point on the northern bank was the round rock, from which
the bathers took their leap headforemost into the briny
waters. The bank here was skirted with cedars, which
afforded a good cover for this sport.

Just before the present century, a new spirit of enterprise
was awakened here. Previous to the Revolutionary War
the parish of Stratfield was a quiet farming community.
Nothing had been done, specially, to develope the place.
Long Island Sound had indeed become a highway of commerce. The frequent disturbances, at that period in the
political atmosphere of the Old World, were soon felt here,
and the infant settlements, unprotected as they were, and
their trading vessels especially, were a tempting and easy
prey to the privateers, which swarmed on the American
coast.

The harbors and settlements lying close upon the Sound
were most exposed. Pequonnock river, however, was excep-

tionally safe. There was fully as much depth of water above the neck, now the site of Berkshire bridge, as on the bar outside, and plenty of space also. The wooded bluffs on the shore, some of them jutting out into bold promontories, shut out this portion from the open harbor and Sound, affording a safe retreat, almost a hiding place. Under the then existing state of things it is no wonder commerce was early developed at this place. Theophilus Nichols and his son Philip had their store and wharf at the extreme head of navigation near what is now known as the Plumb place. They built and sailed vessels from there, as did also Capt. Stephen Burroughs, Sen. The shore opposite the old red brick house on North avenue was long known and designated the Shipyard. The commercial and trading interests to this period with Boston and New York were not large, yet were sufficient to foster a spirit of enterprise and educate and prepare the more ambitious young men to improve their opportunities.

The establishment of our national independence not only infused new life, but brought greater security to our coast and coasting trade. The surrounding country naturally centering here was rich in agricultural resources. Boston, New York, the Southern Atlantic States and the West Indies, were the markets. Water street had been laid out from the present Fairfield avenue, three rods wide to Welles' Tongue. Wharves and stores began to be built upon it. Men with their families, who had lived from one to two miles in the interior, settled on the shore and entered vigorously into trade and commerce. Among these may be mentioned the families of Nichols, Hawley, Hubbell, Sherman, Burroughs, Sterlings and Summers. The advantages of the location began to be appreciated and an enterprising element came into the place, from the surrounding towns and from a greater distance. Isaac Sherman mentioned by name, in 1857, not less than forty men who came from abroad and settled here between the years 1790 and 1806, who became prominent as successful business men.

The names of these persons with the date when they came, and their business occupations, are here given ; the stars indicating those whose descendants are known, still remain in the city.

1786, Daniel Young, merchant, from Norwich, Conn.

1790, Salmon Hubbell, merchant, from Wilton, Conn.

1790, Capt. Abraham Hubbell, merchant, from Wilton, Conn.

1792, John S. Cannon, merchant and banker, from Norwalk, Conn.

1792, Robert and Prosper Wetmore, merchants, from Stratford, Conn.

1792, David and John DeForest, merchants, from New Haven, Conn.

1792, Thomas Gouge, hatter, from New York State.

1793, Reuben Tweedy,* hatter, from Danbury, Conn.

1793, Nathaniel Wade,* watchmaker and merchant from Norwich, Conn.

1794, Capt. Thaddeus Hubbell, seaman, from Wilton, Conn.

1794, Isaac Hinman,* merchant, from Trumbull, Conn.

1794, Thaddeus Benedict, attorney, from Reading, Conn.

1794, Lambert Lockwood, merchant, from Wilton, Conn.

1794, Hull and Lyon, merchants, successors to David and John DeForest.

1794, Capt. Jonathan Baker,* seaman, from an eastern town.

1794, Richard Hyde,* merchant, from Norwich, Conn.

1794, Samuel Burr, merchant, from Fairfield, Conn.

1796–1803, Ezra Gregory,* inn keeper, from Wilton, Conn.

[The following came between the years 1796 and 1803.]

Ephraim Middlebrook,* joiner, from Trumbull, Conn.

Stephen Hull,* blacksmith, from Wilton, Conn.

Dea. William DeForest,* merchant, from Weston (now Easton), Conn.

Robert Linus,* packer, from Stratford, Conn.

Capt. John Brooks,* seaman, from Stratford, Conn.

Capt. Joseph Sterling Edwards, seaman, from Trumbull, Conn.

Sylvanus Sterling, merchant, from Trumbull, Conn.

Jesse Sterling,* merchant, from Trumbull, Conn.

Capt. Ezekiel Hubbell, seaman, from Greenfield Hill, Conn.

William H. Peabody, cabinet maker, from Norwich, Conn.

Ira Peck,* merchant, from Brookfield, Conn.

Lemuel Hubbell, cabinet maker, from Stratford, Conn.

Benjamin Hall, attorney, from Weston (now Easton), Conn.

Joseph Backus, attorney, from Glastonbury, Conn.

Maj. Benjamin M. Woolsey, merchant, from Long Island, N. Y.

1806, Smith Tweedy, hatter, from Danbury, Conn.

1806, Samuel Penney, merchant.

1806, Hezekiah Ripley, printer.

1806, Lazarus Beach, printer, from Redding, Conn.

1806, Stiles Nichols,* printer, from Danbury, Conn.

1806, James E. Beach,* physician, from New Haven, Conn.

1803, Thomas Woodward, merchant.

1805, Josiah Prindle, merchant, from Derby, Conn.

1805, Mordeca Prindle, merchant, from Derby, Conn.

1805, Joseph H. Prindle, merchant, from Derby, Conn.

In 1797–8, the first drawbridge across the harbor was chartered and built.

In 1800, the borough of Bridgeport—the first in the State and a pattern for others—was chartered, and as a commercial and manufacturing community, BRIDGEPORT commenced her career of enterprise and·progress.

Several new streets had been laid out, which were now recognized and named; among them Gold street from Main to the harbor, two rods wide. Mr. Nathaniel Wade, a watchmaker by trade, from Norwich, Conn., afterward a merchant, bought land of Mr. Porter, and erected his house, the same is now standing on the southeast corner of Main and Gold streets. Philo and DeLuzern DeForest secured the northeast corner and erected the house now standing there, so long owned and occupied by Isaac Sherman, Esq., and now by his descendants. Capt. Joseph Sterling Edwards, from Trumbull, bought and built on the south side of Gold street, from Middle to Water street. His widow left this with other property, to her brother, Isaac Burroughs, Esq., which has served to swell the Pettengill estate, from which such munificent public benefactions are now being realized.

Mr. Jesse Sterling, also from Trumbull, a merchant, purchased the site on the north side of Gold street at the head of Water street, and erected the house more recently owned and occupied by Mr. Abel Drew. The same was removed in 1870 for the extension of Water street. Later, on Main street, next north of Isaac Sherman, Captain Gershom E. Hubbell located. Next to him was Mr. George Smith, and last on the plot was Captain William Goodsell, who had his slaughter house on the bank of the creek in the rear of the dwellings.

Isaac Sherman sold a part of his Main street front to Capt. Joseph H. Hand from Long Island—the same property being now owned by Jacob Sutter, and occupied by Mr. C. P. Coe's wholesale and retail grocery.

A Weaver's Shop is seen on the diagram, standing northerly of the dwelling house of Samuel Porter, back from the highway. It was occupied by both Samuel Porter and his son of the same name, who were weavers by trade, and supplied the settlement with the elegant woolen bed coverlets,—specimens of which are still preserved in the old families, woolen cloth and blankets, damask and plain linen.

So far as appears, this building was the first exclusively devoted to the manufacturing of goods within the limits of Bridgeport, and is in very striking contrast with the splendid and extensive structures of the present day.

The Salt Works. For some reason, probably the scarcity of salt during and after the close of the second war with Great Britain, about the year 1818, it was deemed a wise measure to secure salt of home manufacture, and so prudent and sagacious man as the late Isaac Sherman was persuaded that it was safe to invest capital and labor in it. The beautiful plateau north of Gold street, the property of his brother-in-law, Samuel Porter, Jr., was selected as the site for the operations. The location of the evaporating vats is shown on the diagram. The salt water was pumped from the bay or creek into the vats, by means of a windmill stationed at or near the point. No statistics are extant as to the quantity or quality of the product, but merchantable salt was made.

One mistake as to location became apparent, that the water of the creek at this point was too much diluted with the fresh water of its tributaries, which with the increased facilities for procuring the West India product, conspired to render the enterprise unprofitable. The Salt Works, as they were called, were mentioned in the will of Samuel Porter, Jr., written in 1828. The unused vats were admirably adapted to, and improved by the young people, for the game of hide and seek. They disappeared soon after the year 1830, as remembered by persons still living.

The Slaughter House is also represented on the diagram. Capt. William Goodsell, who early lived in the old yellow house which was removed from Main street in 1871 in order to open Congress street, is believed to have been the first to fit up and occupy a regular slaughter house here. It was a barn-like structure standing on the edge of the bluff and extending almost its whole size over the bank—which was well washed by each flood tide—the building being supported by substantial posts. Its site was included in the purchase of the late Benjamin Ray, who had much difficulty in getting the boundary lines established satisfactorily. In his numerous and vigorous talks about the matter, well remembered by many, very frequent allusions were made to " Capt. Goodsell's slaughter house yard."

It is interesting to note how the progress of the settlement moved back the slaughter houses. The next location was that of Gideon and Eli Thompson on the westerly side of North Washington avenue, not far from the present location of Mulloy's lane, from 1833 to 1843.

From this the same parties removed to what is now the Thompson farm, a little south of the toll-gate on the Huntington turnpike, while Smith and Stratton, and their successors, and Captain Terry, located theirs on the Newtown turnpike about two miles out of town.

The heavy beef is now mostly dressed for this market in Chicago, Ill.; transported in refrigerator cars and distributed from refrigerator depots—two of them located on this same territory—to be dispensed in steaks and roasts from the refrigerators of the local markets.

Saddle Boxes were made also on this territory. The shipment to markets in the South, of large quantities of saddles and harness, manufactured here from 1815 to 1860, required many strong boxes of special form and size. Up to 1849, these were almost exclusively made without machinery, by Porter Sturges, whose shop and lumber yard were on Middle street at the present corner of Golden Hill street, occupied now by the Naugatuck Valley Ice Company. His assistant when needed, was the late David Wheeler, who lived on Arch street, and later on the Newtown turnpike near Beach street.

This work afforded reliable and steady employment for these men, and with the frugality for which they were both noted, laid the foundation of handsome estates for each one.

The increased quantity needed and the competition of machinery, diverted the source of supply to the shops of L. C. Shepard & Co., about 1850, then located at the site of the north end of the Atlantic Hotel, the Union House being a part; and later to Lyon & Curtis, on Simon's wharf.

Comb Making, as a business, was established and conducted here for a while, by Moss K. Botsford, from Newtown, who purchased of Jesse Sterling, the house on the bank on the north side of Gold street, at the head of Water street. This business was very prosperous from about 1830 to 1835. Bethel and Newtown were largely engaged in it. Some manufacturers were successful for a time, but the fashions were extremely changeable, and the business fitful, which led to many failures; and hence it continued here but a short time. Mr. Abel Drew, from Derby, was the next owner of the above-mentioned house.

Cooperage. The commerce of the place, especially the West India trade, and for a number of years the whaling business, required a great many casks, and made a lively business for the coopers. Mr. Drew's shop was on the south shore of the point, where he employed a number of men, and he, seeing, embraced his opportunity, and thus laid the foundation for his handsome estate.

The Housatonic Railroad was chartered in 1836, for a line from Bridgeport to the northern boundary of the state in the town of Canaan, Litchfield County. The company was organized, capital subscribed, and right of way secured to New Milford in 1838. Commencing at a point near the west approach to the Bridgeport bridge—Fairfield avenue—it extended northerly across the mud flats and over this Porter property, making quite a deep cut across it. The company not only purchased the usual right of way over this property for main tracks, but secured the entire point east of its main line, graded it down, using the material towards filling the roadway across the adjacent mud flats, and then located their engine house, turn-tables and car-shop thereon. A wharf was constructed at the extreme point, and the Long Island skipper connected with Mr. Roswell Lewis' coal and wood yard, landed thereon the pine wood which was then used at this end of the line for fuel for the locomotives. Thus the beautiful bluff was invaded, and its glory departed before the march of modern utility and progress. The construction and opening of the railroad developed the need of a foundry and machine shops. This need was measurably supplied by the late David Wheeler of Park avenue, who was in 1843 joined by George and J. R. Young, and had their works in a wooden building on the same site as the present Bridgeport Iron Works, which is made land on the mud flats fronting this Porter property.

The First Center Bridge. When, in 1852, Hon. P. T. Barnum joined Gen. Wm. H. Noble for the development of East Bridgeport, they at once realized that they must have more direct and easier communication with the business portion of the city on the west side of the harbor. Hence they procured a charter for a bridge; the eastern terminus about identical with the present Center bridge, while the western end, spanning the Housatonic railroad track, landed upon the high bank of this Porter property, for which they made an appropriate purchase of Mrs. Ellen Porter, the widow of Samuel Porter, Jr., November 19, 1852. This was reached by a street which had been opened as a highway by Mr. Porter, and named by him Summer street, extending northerly from Gold street a little east of the line of Middle street extended. After the location of the bridge it was called Bridge street. By the kindness of General Noble the Historical society has a picture of this bridge on its walls, painted in water colors, showing a condition of the surroundings now most thoroughly changed.

When the present Center bridge was constructed in 1869, the western terminus was changed to Congress street, crossing the railroad at grade. Middle street was soon after extended thereto in a direct line and Bridge street was discontinued. In November, 1864, the city purchased this bridge and appurtenances with the other bridges across the harbor, and in the adjustment of property interests affected by these changes, and the extension of Middle street, the city obtained the site of the present No. 5 engine house.

Previous to the extension of Congress street for the western terminus of the Center bridge, in 1869, the mud flats and low ground on the west side of the Housatonic railroad track from the Porter property to Lumber street, was flooded through a water way at the old mill located near the line of Lumber street and the face of the wharf at that point. The water was changed and purified each flood tide, but the gate in the water way retained enough to give at all times a depth of several feet in the southern portion near this property.

Previous to the introduction of the present water supply of the city, much dependence was placed upon the salt water of the harbor for extinguishing fires. This vicinity was practically shut off from the water front, especially at low tide, and to remedy this, Mrs. Ellen Porter deeded to the city an addition to the Bridge street highway, May 19, 1859, and opened a way to the water above described, where the city constructed a platform sufficient to accommodate one of the hand engines of that period and its company in actual service.

About 1846, the Housatonic Railroad Company removed their depot both for passengers and freight from near Fairfield avenue southerly, nearly to the present elevator. A few years afterwards, having filled and made solid ground of the mud flats still further south they put up there a round house, and other necessary shops and buildings. The old engine house and the long car house remained in their places on the Porter property many years; also a blacksmith business by several parties. The veteran blacksmith, Mr. Joseph C. Barum, had his shop there for many years until his decease, February 25, 1883, aged 80 years.

The Bridgeport Boiler Works commenced operations n 1869, on this (Porter's) point, utilizing some of the old buildngs, and erecting others. This company embraced the folowing names: Humphrey, Watson, Farrel, and Chatfield.

In 1870, Farrel and Chatfield retired, and the business was continued by Humphrey and Watson, until 1872, when Mr. William Lowe took the place of Mr. Humphrey. Messrs. Lowe and Watson continued the making of steam boilers successfully for ten years, until they were burned out, April 24, 1882. As they were unable to obtain a lease of the premises for a term of years, they secured a location of Mr. William H. Perry, adjoining the Housatonic railroad track, farther orth.

The late Mr. Hanford Lyon purchased the water front of a ortion of this property. and improved it, in connection with lat which he previously owned, adjoining it on the south. his has been occupied as a coal yard by C. M. Noble and ompany, and by Courtland Kelsey, and is now a part of the ttensive yards of Messrs. Miller and Strickland.

Mr. Julius Hawley purchased of the Burroughs family, e Edwards property, on the south side of Gold street, exnding to the channel of the harbor, which he has improved, d upon which is located the extensive lumber yards and am saw-mill of the Bridgeport Lumber Company.

Messrs. Henry N. and Alonzo J. Beardsley purchased the iter front of Mr. Abel Drew, which carried one-half of the dth of Gold street from the east side of the tracks of the insolidated railroads to the channel, which they are leis-, ely filling, and which will become a very valuable property.

The Housatonic Railroad Company have here a fine iperty, partly mud-flats, which they will no doubt fill to : harbor line at no distant day. This done, it will afford im for the return to this point of their engine houses, thus ieving the crowded condition in the present locality of ir buildings, and facilitating the removal of the tracks of the nsolidated road from lower Water street, an object most nestly to be desired.

33

The whole plot, much of it forty years ago so quiet a
so pleasant for family homes of the best sort, is now alm
wholly given over to business.

The following list of names of householders, found or
separate sheet, with the date partly torn off, in the handwi
ing of the Rev. Samuel Cooke, the second pastor of the Str
field Church, was preserved by the late Isaac Sherman, Esc
and pasted upon a leaf of the manuscript book of his " Re
ollections." From the names found upon it, and others w
known which are omitted, the date is known to have be
1733 or 1734. The list contains the names of heads of famil
then residing in the parish of Stratfield, and upon an estima
of five persons to each family there were about seven hundr
persons in the parish.

"A List of the Householders in Stratfield Anno Domini, 17-
Disposed Alphabetically.

James Bennitt, Sen',
Isaac Bennitt,
William Bennitt,
James Bennitt, Jun',
Stephen Bennitt,
William Beardsle, Sen',
Daniel Beardsle,
John Beardsle, Sen',
Nathan Beardsle,
William Beardsle, Jun',
Ebenezer Beardsle,
David Beardsle,
John Beardsle, Jun',
Obadiah Beardsle,
Joseph Booth,
John Burr, Sen',
John Burr, Jun',
Charles Burrett,
Stephen Burrows,
Samuel Cable,
Israel Chauncey,
Robert Chauncey,
Caleb Cole,
Daniel Comestock,
Samuel Cooke,
Elijah Crane,
Jonah Curtiss,

John Edwards, Sen',
Thomas Edwards,
John Edwards, Jun',
Sarah Fayerweather,
John Fayerweather,
Abigail Fayerweather,
Deborah Fairchild,
James Fairchild,
Samuel French's widow,
Samuel French,
Ebenezer French,
Samuel Gregory,
Benjamin Gregory,
Ebenezer Gregory,
Thaddeus Gregory,
Enock Gregory,
Francis Hall, Sen',
John Hall,
Samuel Hall,
Burgess Hall,
Francis Hall, Jun',
Richard Hall,
Elnathan Hall,
Ebenezer Hawley,
James Hawley,
William Hodgden,
Matthew Horn,

Richard Hubbell, Sen',
James Hubbell,
John Hubbell,
Daniel Hubbell,
————
Stephen Hubbell,
David Hubbell,
Joseph Hubbell,
Ebenezer Hubbell,
Zechariah Hubbell,
Richard Hubbell, Jun',
Andrew Hubbell,
Nathan Hurd,
Moses Jackson,
John Jackson's widow,
Gabriel Jackson,
John Jackson,
David Jackson, Sen',
David Jackson, Jun',
John Jones,
Edward Lacy,
John Lacy,
Ebenezer Lacy,
Zechariah Lawrence,
Matthew McHard,
John Mallet, Sen',
David Mallet, Jun',

John Man,
Samuel Martin,
Nicholas Masters,
Zechariah Mead,
John Middlebrook,
Noah Morehouse,
John Odell,
Samuel Odell's widow,
William Odell,
Hezekiah Odell,
Samuel Odell,
Samuel Patchen,
Benjamin Phippeny,
John Porter,
Valentine Rowell,
Henry Rowland,
Zechariah Sanford,
Ezekiel Sanford,
Thomas Sanford,
James Seelye's widow,
Joseph Seelye,

David Sherman, Sen,
David Sherman, Jun,
Enos Sherman,
John Sherwood,
Nathaniel Sherwood,
Matthew Sherwood,
William Smith, Sen,
William Smith, Jun,
John Smith's widow,
Jacob Starling,
Henry Stevens,
Peter Stevens,
Thomas Stoddard,
Samuel Summer's widow,
Henry Summers,
John Summers,
David Summers,
Nathan Summers,
Edward Tredwell,
Deborah Tredwell,
Benjamin Tredwell,

Zechariah Tredwell,
Hezekiah Tredwell,
Samuel Tredwell,
Jacob Tredwell,
Samuel Trowbridge, Sen,
Samuel Trowbridge, Jun,
Jonah Turny,
Robert Turny,
Jonathan Wakely, Sen,
Henry Wakely,
Joseph Wakely,
Israel Wakely,
Nathaniel Wakely,
Jonathan Wakely, Jun,
Samuel Well's widow,
Samuel Wells,
John Wheeler,
Timothy Wheeler,
Isaac Wheeler,
Ebenezer Wheeler,
Richard Whitny."

CHAPTER XVIII.

STRATFIELD'S EARLY SETTLERS.

OCATING the homes of the early settlers is a work costing much time for research and study, and but for the manuscript book of Dea. Isaac Sherman, no attempt would have been made, either to provide the accompanying map, or to prepare the following biographical sketches. But, since that book was in existence, largely by the forethought and perseverance of Dea. Rowland B. Lacey in fixing Deacon Sherman's attention to it, before he died, this list became possible, and has been completed with a considerable degree of accuracy, so far as it goes. It is not claimed that the list includes all the early settlers, nor all that could be said of them, because Deacon Sherman gave only his recollections of what he had heard and known personally, and there could not be taken time sufficient to search the records so thoroughly as to perfect the work, although much that is given by Deacon Sherman has been confirmed by the town and society books.[1]

---

[1]   *Recollections of Isaac Sherman.*

The long life of Isaac Sherman in this community and his extensive personal acquaintance, his familiarity with the church and parish records, his respect for his own ancestry and his genealogical studies, his intercourse with and fondness for elderly people, his extensive business associations, his investigations for the establishment of pension claims, his experience in connection with the settlement and distribution of estates, all contributed to furnish his observant and retentive mind with a fund of information in regard to the early settlement and history of Stratfield and Bridgeport. He could give the exact location of the old families and much about their descendants, the settlement of the Newfields—now the city of Bridgeport—the rise and progress of business, and business firms, how composed, where

No. 1. Isaac Wheeler, son of Ephraim, one of the first settlers in Fairfield, in 1644, was a farmer and a large landholder, for his mother in 1681, paid tax on 706 acres of land, Isaac having received his proportion before his father's death in 1670.

He was one of the nine male members of the first Stratfield Church at its organization under Rev. Charles Chauncey, June 13, 1695; which Church is now located in Bridgeport, called the First Congregational Church.

No. 2. Samuel Welles was a farmer with a good farm, Welles' Tongue being a small part of it. He was the son of John Welles, and grandson of Governor Thomas Welles, and. this land or farm was first laid out to John Welles and given in his will to this son Samuel. He had one son, named David Wakeman Welles.

No. 3. John Mallett was a Frenchman and a farmer. Lewis Mallett who resided on the old place was a descendant. All the Malletts at Tashua are descendants of said John Mallett.

No. 4. Benjamin Hubbell was a farmer. He married a half sister of Doct. Stephen Middlebrook, of Trumbull. They had one son, John Hubbell, who married Betty, daughter of Joseph Brothwell, and had five daughters: Betsey, who married Timothy Risley; Polly, who married Howell Hough; Anna, who married Zalmon Hawley. Zalmon Hawley had Maria, who married Capt. John Brooks, Jr.; Marietta, who married Capt. Burr Knapp; and one son John, who died young.

---

located, and whether successful or not. No one had attempted to cover the field, and no one living could do it as he could, and, unless by himself committed to paper, before his decease, it was certain that very much would be inevitably lost.

This consideration was frequently urged upon him for years without success. After his retirement from public business, his consent to enter upon the work was gained, the plan as laid out for him pursued, with success, and the result is manifest in these sketches, numbered in regular order for reference to the accompanying map.

To the labors of Esquire Sherman, Dea. Rowland B. Lacey has added about forty sketches, upon much careful enquiry and research, and the whole forms a valuable portion of the history of Bridgeport.

No. 5. Benjamin Wheeler was a farmer, and was a grandson of Isaac Wheeler.[1] Said Benjamin was the father of Timothy, and grandfather of Benjamin, Ezra and Hannah.

No. 6. Samuel Odell, a farmer, was justice of the peace, and an active member of the church and society. One of his daughters is now [1856] living, and is over 90 years of age. She is the widow of Samuel Wheeler. Her name is Julia Wheeler, and she draws a pension for the services of said Samuel in the Revolution. Samuel Odell had one son by the name of Maline Odell, who was lost at sea about the year 1800, in a clipper-built schooner, commanded by Capt. Benjamin Wheeler, a descendant of Isaac, who with all his crew was lost in said schooner, for they were never heard from after they sailed from New York. Said Capt. Benjamin Wheeler left a wife and the following children: Ira B.; Daniel Odell; Sally, who married Moses Platt; Betsey, who married David Ufford, and Marrietta, who married Gideon Thompson.

No. 7. Capt. Abel Wakelee, a sailor, was lost at sea in the brig Julius Cæsar on a voyage from the West Indies bound to Bridgeport with a load of salt. The crew and officers were all saved in the long boat when the brig sunk, except Abel and a colored man named Ned, who was a slave to Capt. Amos Hubbell, the owner of the brig.

Capt. Abel Wakelee's descendants were Charles and Walker, who have died leaving no children. His widow's name was Grace.

No. 8. William Rose, a Frenchman, was one of the little colony of Frenchmen in Nova Scotia, at the time Canada was taken from the French by the English when the colony was broken up by the order of the English Government before the Revolution, and distributed among the different thirteen states. Mr. Rose was landed in this parish and Dr. Fogg, also, was one of said neutral French who settled in Fairfield. Mr. Rose was a gardener, and he married Jennette Mann. His children were: Peter, Mabel, Charity and Polly.

---

[1] This is doubtful. See Wheeler Genealogy.

Doctor Fogg was settled in Fairfield and was an acceptable physician. He died since the Revolution.

William Rose used to fish at a fishweir in Bridgeport harbor, in a boat alone, accompanied by his faithful dog, Lyon. On one of the fishing days he had the misfortune to fall overboard and was near being drowned when the dog swam to him and he clasped the dog's tail and directed him to swim for the shore. When the dog had towed his master almost to the shore he turned about to swim off, when Mr. Rose in his broken French, called, "tudder way, Lyon," and, obeying his master, drew him to the shore. William Rose died April 21, 1812, aged 90 years.

No. 9. Hezekiah Wheeler, a tailor by trade, was employed in making buckskin breeches, which were in his day the common wear for men and boys, and were used in some families as late as the year 1800. He had one son, a sailor, named Wilson, who was lost at sea. Hezekiah Wheeler, and his son now living in New York, are descendants of said Isaac Wheeler.

No. A. Bridgeport and Stratfield Burying Ground. From the earliest settlement up to 1812, the "Old Stratfield Burial Ground" was made the resting place of the dead in Stratfield Parish. At this period, even with the addition of 1772, the old ground had become too strait, and, upon petition of James E. Beach and others, to the October session of the General Assembly of 1811, showing that they had purchased a piece of land bounded north on Silas Sherman; east on highway (Division street), south and west on Abijah Hawley's land, the said proprietors and their associates were duly incorporated to be known by the name of "The Bridgeport and Stratfield Burying Ground Association." Lambert Lockwood was named as the first clerk, and it was especially provided that "said burying ground shall forever remain and be used as and for a burying ground, and for that purpose only." Provision was made for its layout into lots and the proprietor of a lot became a legal member of the Corporation, and he, his heirs, successors, or assigns, entitled to one vote for every lot he or they possessed. A son of Mr. Ezra Wheeler was the first child and Mr. Elijah

Burr was the first adult buried in this ground in 1812. Upon petition to the General Assembly at the May session, 1835, an addition was made at the west end.

Here nearly two generations were laid from 1812 to 1850, about 4,000 interments.

For some years the immediate vicinity had become so thickly settled that it had become an unsuitable place for a cemetery, and in 1849 Mountain Grove Cemetery was inaugurated. About 1860, special efforts began to be made to get a vote in this association for removal to Mountain Grove or some other point, but met with most decided opposition, as did repeated efforts.

The agitation of the subject for a general removal made many proprietors timid in respect to the permanency of their tenure, and numerous voluntary removals were made to Mountain Grove and elsewhere. The vacated and unused lots were bought up by parties desiring removal until they held a majority, and under an Act or Resolution of the General Assembly of May, 1873, the removal was consummated during the years 1873 and 1874, under commissioners named in said Act. Hon. P. T. Barnum became the purchaser of the entire territory through David W. Sherwood, his agent, and the removals were made largely under supervision of George Poole to the westerly side of the grounds in Mountain Grove Cemetery, numbering in all over three thousand. The site on the westerly side of Park avenue is now, in 1885, mostly covered by streets and cottages, and no vestige of its former use appears.

No. 10. William Hubbell was by occupation a house painter. His children were David, and Grizell, and other daughters.

Justin Smith,[1] a native of Springfield, Mass., was a stone-cutter, specially skilled in working the brown stone of the Chatham, now Portland, quarries in Connecticut. In 1789, he embarked from that place with a vessel load of the Chatham stone, his family and household goods destined for Mill river at Fairfield, but his load was not consigned.

---

[1] This name is not located on the map.

In a stress of weather he ran his vessel into Bridgeport harbor, where, while weather bound, he made some acquaintance, through which some of the leading men learned who he was, what his cargo, and his skill as a stone-cutter, and persuaded him to unload the vessel and establish himself and business here.

The many fine brown stone tablets and head-stones in the old Stratfield burying-ground and many others that were put up in the Division Street (Stratfield and Bridgeport) cemetery, and removed thence to Mountain Grove Cemetery, attest his skill and industry. His residence was on the site now occupied by the dwelling of Mr. F. W. Marsh, No. 240 Park avenue, and he was a most excellent Christian man. He died March 17, 1835, aged 81 years. His wife was Mary Fox, of Chatham. She survived her husband fourteen years and died May 21, 1849, at the great age of 92 years.

Their children were Abner and Justin, who both died young, and Sophia, Mary and Mehitable. Sophia married Robert Treadwell, son of David, and removed to Southbury. Mary married Agur Beach, of Trumbull, and Mehitable married Eli Gilman and lived in Hartford.

Mary (Smith) Beach still survives and lacks but a few days of 93 years of age—bright and well, although a little lame,—and is anticipating great pleasure in celebrating her 93d birth-day, on the 24th of September, 1885.

Her husband, Agur, was the son of Everett Beach and his wife Rebecca, daughter of the Rev. James Beebe, of North Stratford. He died of fever in New York city, where he was in business, October 7, 1822, aged 31 years, leaving a widow and two young daughters with slender means.

On the death of her father she established herself at the parental homestead and took the entire care of her aged mother while she lived.

For many years, each season has brought out a store of her handiwork in knitted articles of personal wear and of bed quilts, nicely pieced for quilting, for the Home Missionary boxes. With the completion of the pair of hose now nearly done, she will have knitted for and donated one hundred pair of stockings to the Home of the Friendless in New York

City, besides her numerous gifts in her more immediate vicinity.

She is probably the oldest person living in the town of Bridgeport, at least the oldest native born, and seems likely to become a centenarian.

No. 11. Capt. Samuel Wakelee, a shipmaster, employed before the Revolution in transporting passengers from Europe. He was a brother of Zebulon Wakelee. On one of his voyages his provisions failed and he and the crew were reduced to a state of starvation before they obtained relief.

No. 12. Capt. William Worden was a farmer and house carpenter. He was captain of a militia company, called Householders, in the Revolution. The company was raised in the parish, and they were not liable to do ordinary military duty.

He was a tall, spare built, leading man in the town and society, and was quite aged at the time of his death. He came here from an eastern town, and was a strong Whig, as most of the inhabitants were at the time of the Revolution. He had sons Samuel and William, and grandsons Thomas Cook, William, Levi, Abijah and Daniel. Capt. William Worden married a daughter of Samuel Odell, Esqr.

No. 13. Justus Burr was a farmer, and son of Col. John Burr. His children were, John, Aaron, Comfort, and two other daughters. I'

Justus Burr was killed in his own barn, when he was drawing in a load of hay. being crushed by the oxen running through a small door.

No. 14. Ezra Kirtland was a blacksmith by trade. He came to this place before the Revolution, from Wallingford. He owned a farm on the old Golden Hill road, now called Washington avenue, which contained a part of the land on which the village of the Pequonnock Indians was located at the first settlement of the parish. The Kirtland family appear to have owned all the land south of Washington ave. as far east as the spring lot beyond Courtland street and south to the present line of Fairfield avenue. He was the ancestor of all the Kirtlands of this parish. He married a daughter of Zebulon Wakelee and had two sons—Zebulon and Ezra. Zebulon, Jr., married Betty Cook, a grand-daughter of the Rev. Samuel Cook, and Ezra married Sarah, daughter of Benjamin Wheeler.

No. 15. Capt. Joseph Knapp, Sen., was for many years master of a coasting vessel employed in carrying grain and other products for the farmers, from this place to Boston, which coasting trade was profitable from the first settlement of the parish down to about the year 1835.

Before the Revolution there were four or five vessels employed in this trade, but after the war there was an average number of about ten.

The first merchants in Bridgeport purchased their goods in Boston until about the year 1790, after which they purchased in New York.

He was a thin, spare man about five feet nine inches; was prominent in the town and society and lived to be quite aged. He had three children: Joseph, Jr., Patience and Ruth. Joseph, Jr., was recently killed by the fall of a tree when he was about 80 years of age. He was a shoemaker by trade and occupied the same house his father did.

No. 16. Thaddeus Gregory was a merchant and house joiner. On being chosen to some military office he came out in front of the company with his hat off to make his acknowledgments, but when he had proceeded so far in a speech as to say, "fellow soldiers," he gave up in despair, and putting his hand on his breast exclaimed, "it is in here but I cannot get it out." He and his wife were both members of the church in 1731. He died in 1777 aged 77 years.

No. 17. Zebulon Wakelee, a farmer, lived on the east side of Division street on old Meeting-house Hill, nearly opposite where the first meeting-house was built.

He had one daughter, named Olive, who married Ezra Kirtland, Sen. Zebulon Wakelee died in 1767, aged 55 years.

No. 18. The old first Congregational meeting-house in the wilderness on Meeting-house Hill was built about the year 1693. The church was gathered, June 13, 1695, and the Rev. Charles Chauncey, a son of the Rev. Israel Chauncey of Stratford, was ordained their pastor.

The first settlers were called together by the beat of the drum, and carried arms to defend the congregation from an attack by Indians.

This first meeting-house was probably located on the town line between Fairfield and Stratford, half in one town and half in the other, or directly in the middle of the highway, on the hill, for the town of Stratford voted the liberty to set part of it on its territory.[4] It was a small house, and was in use only twenty-four years, when the second one was built.

No. 19. Rev. Charles Chauncey was the first pastor of the "Church of Christ in Stratfield." For a sketch of him see page 479 of this book.

No. 20. Andrew Sherwood was a farmer and blacksmith. His sons were David and Zachariah Sherwood.

No. 21. The School House of the old south district was located, previous to about 1830, on the westerly side of Division street, a few rods south of the present North avenue. The traveled roadway diverged to the east at that point to avoid a ledge of rocks, under the lea of which, at the southerly side, there was a level space of sufficient size to accommodate the house.

The character of the school at that time was rather superior, since some of the older scholars at the Fresh Pond district attended here because of the advantages it afforded.

No. 22. The Second Meeting-house[a] was located on the old Fairfield and Stratford country road; was erected in 1717, and taken down about the year 1835. It was occupied by the First Congregational Society until the year 1807, when this society built by subscription a new frame meeting-house in the village of Bridgeport on land donated by Richard and Amos Hubbell, on the corner of Bank, Broad and John

---

[4] See page 474 of this book. [a] See page 482.

streets, which frame church was sold to Christ Church and removed into John street, where a few years later it was burned. The first Congregational Society erected their fourth church, built in 1850, on the same site where the third stood.

No. 23. Rev. Samuel Cooke was the second pastor of the Church of Christ at Stratfield. For a sketch of him see page 484 of this book.

No. 24. Lewis Angevine, a Frenchman, and by occupation a weaver, left no descendants, if he had any. Mrs. W. R. Bunnell owns the land on which his house stood. An anecdote has been related of him, which gives an insight into his character.

"When he was courting his wife at a place where he was not known, he represented to her that he was well off as to property, and that if she would marry him she should never wash her hands in cold water. Soon after marriage she reminded him of this promise, upon which he replied that she need not wash in cold water for she could warm it."

No. 25. Capt. Thaddeus Bennett, a shoemaker and farmer, was the captain of the trainband at the commencement of the Revolutionary War and went to New York with his company in August, 1776, to defend the city against the British troops. His company suffered considerable loss by death, and the captain died soon after returning home from the campaign in 1777. He left two sons—Joseph Wilson Bennett and Thaddeus Bennett, and two daughters, Grizell and Sarah Bennett, both of whom were pensioners for the service of their husbands in the Revolution. Grizell married Isaac Odell, who was a sergeant in the army, and Sarah married Nathan Fairchild.

No. 26. Lieut. David Sherman was a farmer, and lieutenant of the militia company of Stratfield, and a leading public man in the town and society. He was the son of Matthew Sherman, and died aged 60 years, and was buried in the old parish burying ground. He erected the old two-story, long-back-roof dwelling house in the year 1717. It was in the common style of New England farm houses, and stood near the spot where Mr. John H. Beach's house now stands. His homestead contained about one hundred acres, besides woodland at Toilsome and a large farm at Tashua. Lieut. David Sherman was nephew to Deacon David Sherman, who says in his will: "I do make and ordain my well-beloved kinsman, David Sherman, my sole executor of this my last will and testament." He had three sons—Elnathan, Jonathan and David. Jonathan never married. Elnathan married Eunice Gregory.

David married Mary Sterling and occupied his father's house and homestead. He was killed by lightning in the old Pequonnock meeting-house July 28, 1771.

The said David that was killed in the meeting-house had three children—Huldah, who married Doct. James E. Beach, David, the father of Esquire Isaac Sherman, the author of these sketches, and Isaac, who died young.

No. 27.   Doctor James Eaton Beach, was a descendant on his mother's side of Gov. Theophilus Eaton, of the New Haven Colony, and came from New Haven to Stratfield about the year 1778, where he settled as a parish physician.

He married, about 1780, Huldah, daughter of David Sherman, Jr., and Mary (Sterling) Sherman, and erected his dwelling on the Sherman property a few rods north of the homestead.

He had a wide practice, was a capable and public spirited man. He was especially helpful to young men of good character and habits in starting in business, aiding them by his name, counsel and capital.

He was the responsible member of the following firms, and perhaps others:

Beach and Sterling, in 1794 (David Sterling), who were merchants in dry goods, groceries and drugs.

Beach and Sterling, in 1804 (Jesse Sterling), merchants in dry-goods, groceries and drugs.

Beach and Sterling, in 1815 (Sylvanus Sterling), merchants in dry goods, groceries and drugs.

Beach and Sherman (Isaac Sherman and Sterling Sherman) groceries, grain business, and New York packeting.

The Juniors in each of these firms were the active partners. and conducted the business, while Doctor Beach furnished the capital and for which he received interest and a
share of the profits, which appear to have been very satisfactory.

Doctor Beach was active and influential in the Stratfield
Congregational Church, and for many years served it as
chorister. He was deacon from 1806 to 1830, and gave a silver tankard for the communion service, which is still in use,
in the First Congregational Church of Bridgeport. He died
in 1838, aged 75 years.

His children were, a son Isaac Eaton, and daughters
Polly and Laura.

Isaac Eaton Beach lived at the homestead, enlarged for
his accommodation, and his descendants occupy the ancestral
lands.

Polly Beach married Sylvanus Sterling and lived at what
is now No. 84 Golden Hill street. Mr. Sterling died in 1848,
and Mrs. Sterling in 1866, leaving no children, but a considerable estate.

By the will of Mrs. Sterling the homestead was given to
the First Congregational Society of Bridgeport for a parsonage, and after providing for friends, the residue was given to
the society known as the Bridgeport Protestant Widows'
Relief Society for the establishment of a Home and for general aid, and the society has become one of the leading charities of Bridgeport.[1]

Laura Beach married Ira Sherman, a descendant of Lieut.
David (No. 26) through Elnathan (No. 34), and always resided
at what is now No. 247 Main street, dying at an advanced
age. Their only daughter, Mary B. Sherman, married James
C. Loomis, Esq.

Both Mrs. Sterling and Mrs. Sherman were remarkable
for their large charities while living, giving liberally in the
line of the religious charities of the Congregational Church
with which they were connected; and also to numerous

---

[1] The Sterling Home was incorporated at the January session of the General
Assembly in 1885.

widows, orphans and families whose needy circumstances came to their knowledge.

No. 28. Jabez Sherman was a farmer and removed to New Haven about the time of the Revolutionary War.

No. 29. Josiah Treadwell was a weaver by trade. His house was in the common style, two stories, and lighted with diamond window glass set in lead sash. His children were: Josiah, Jr., Samuel, Elijah, and three daughters. One married Thomas Cook, one married John Wheeler, and one married Mr. Turney, of Fairfield. His house being old was taken down soon after he died in 1798.

No. 30. Samuel Treadwell was a weaver, and son of Josiah. He married first Rachel Barnum, and had sons Samuel, Jr., and Barnum. He married second, Mercy Babcock, from Rhode Island. She was high-spirited and used to say she was of high blood, and that she did not come from any mean family.

They were low in circumstances, some years, during which a friend coming to see her, she remarked: "My husband is generally a good provider, although he is a little slack just now."

No. 31. Enoch Gregory was a large farmer and slave holder. He had one slave named Neptune, born in Africa, who had a son called after the master's family, Tony Gregory, who was an honest Negro. Enoch Gregory's children, Samuel, Daniel and Plumb, and others, settled at Tashua.

No. 32. Andrew Beardsley was a weaver. John W. Beardsley, and Henry and Rufus Burr, and the wife of Mr. Joseph Mott, all residents of Bridgeport, are among his descendants.

No. 33. John Hall was a weaver. His descendants are not remembered, except a daughter Julia, who married Squire Lacey as first husband, and afterwards the Rev. Nathaniel Ruggles, who, in connection with the Rev. John N. Maffit, was the founder of the first M. E. Church in the city of Bridgeport in 1822.

No. 34. Elnathan Sherman was a son of Lieutenant David. His wife, Eunice (Gregory) Sherman, died in 1793, in a fit, while kneading bread. They had sons: Abijah and Ebenezer, and daughters, Sarah, who married Stephen Sterling, Hannah, and Mary. One of these married Thomas Edwards.

No. 35. Joseph Hall, a farmer and a buckskin leather dresser, died at Toilsome, aged 94 years. He and his children were among the first Methodists in this parish. He had one son, named Hezekiah, and three daughters: Alice, married Ebenezer Brown; Molly married Stephen Wells, and Ruth never married. The whole family lived to a good old age and never disgracêd their religious profession.

No. 36. Capt. Samuel Sherwood was a farmer and a slave owner. He married Ann, daughter of Theophilus Nichols, by whom he came into possession of a portion of New Pasture Point, which was afterwards called Sherwood's Point, from which vessels were loaded for the West Indies. His children were: Lucy, who married Capt. David Barlow; Philemon, who married Hepzibah Burr, a daughter of Justus Burr and granddaughter of Col. John Burr, and David, who never married.

No. 37. The Toilsome School-house, in Toilsome district, was occupied many years by a school-master who bore the honorable title of Master Wheeler.[1] He married Dolly, daughter of Deacon David Sherman; had a daughter named Dolly, and one named Eunice. Deacon Sherman died in 1753, after which Master Wheeler occupied his house. Also, he had another daughter, who married Abijah Beardsley. She drew a pension for her husband's service in the Revolution. She lived to a good old age at Fresh Pond, near the brick house now occupied by Joseph Seeley, Esqr.

No. 38. Samuel Brinsmade, a cabinet-maker, married Peninah Burritt, and had no children. He was the only

---

[1] His name was John Wheeler.

34

very proud man in the parish; was a fine looking man. He cultivated peaches, pears and apples for market.

No. 39. Dea. Henry Rowland, a farmer, married Dea. David Sherman's daughter Tamar in 1718. He was the grandson of Henry Rowland, who came to Fairfield from the county of Essex in England. He was chosen Deacon of the Stratfield Church in 1756 and died 1775 at the age of 84 years. Rev. David Sherman Rowland, of Windsor, Conn., was his son. Dea. Rowland B. Lacey, of Bridgeport, is also a descendant, through another son Edmund.

No. 40. Dea. David Sherman was a large farmer and one of the first generation of settlers in said parish. His house and homestead were on the top of Toilsome Hill—a large, two-story dwelling with a long back roof, built in the best style of his day, with a high porch in front and small diamond windows, set in lead sash. He was one of the first nine male members of the first Congregational Church. He was the son of Mr. Samuel Sherman, of Stratford, who came from the town of Dedham, county of Essex in England.

Old Mr. Elijah Burritt, when he was 96 years of age, told me that David Sherman was the first deacon of said Church, that he had been well acquainted with him; was at his funeral, and that he was gifted in prayer and took the lead in the meetings when the pastor was absent;[1] and was very much esteemed in the parish. His gravestone, standing in the western part of the old burying-place, bears the titled inscription, "Capt. David Sherman." He had nine daughters, all of whom were married and appear to have been well settled in life.

No. 41. Samuel Edwards was a farmer. His son, Shelton Edwards, when a lad about fifteen years of age, was clerk in the store of David and John DeForest; the store then standing on the corner of State and Water streets in Bridgeport in 1796. In the autumn of the year about ten o'clock in the evening, young Edwards was murdered in the store by his skull being broken in three places by a shoe-

---

[1] Esquire Isaac Sherman says this.

maker's hammer, and his throat cut from ear to ear. His body was then wrapped in his bed clothes and put under the counter and the store set on fire. David and John DeForest were young men unmarried, and affirmed that their store was robbed of over one thousand dollars in hard money at the time of said murder. There was no bank-note currency at that time. No clue to said murder has ever been found. The store was soon discovered to be on fire, and the fire was put out before much damage was done. A piece of broadcloth was found under a lot of boards near the store. This casualty caused the failure of the DeForest brothers. David went to the Brazils, where he made a fortune and obtained the title Don David DeForest. He married a Miss Wooster and returned to New Haven, where he built a house.

No. 42. Ebenezer Hall was a farmer, and married for his second wife the widow of Capt. Thaddeus Bennett. Seth Hall was his son, and was a poet and post-rider for many years. He and his father were both old men when they died. The Halls in this parish appear to be a long-lived race.

No. 43. Nathaniel Sherwood was an early settler and a farmer. He was the son of Samuel, the son of Matthew. He lived on Toilsome Hill, and married one of the nine daughters of Dea. David Sherman. He had one son, Samuel, and a daughter, Eunice, who married Abijah Sterling.

No. 44. Gurdon Sherwood was a farmer and married Hannah Hawley. He died young, leaving no children. He died with the small-pox taken the natural way. His widow married a Mr. Penfield of Fairfield. She gave in her will one share of Connecticut bank stock to the First Congregational Society in Bridgeport, the interest or dividend to be applied to the use of said society forever. She was a member of this Church, and died aged about 83 years.

No. 45. Capt. John Edwards was a native of Scotland, and came to this country about the year 1700. He was an officer in the army in Scotland when he was taken prisoner, and as he was a rebel against the government he was sentenced to be shot, and on the way to the place of execution, guarded by a company of light horse, he made his escape and hid himself under a bridge. They searched for him under the bridge where he was, but did not find him. From this place he made his way to a vessel, on board of which he came to this country. It is supposed that he landed at Black Rock harbor, and that he built his house on Chestnut Hill, the country being a wilderness, so that he would be concealed from any ships that might be looking after him. From his dwelling he could overlook Black Rock harbor. He was known by the title of Duke, but on his gravestone he bears the title of Captain. He died aged 88 years, about the year 1740, and is buried with his wife Mary in the old Stratfield burying-place, near the southwest corner.

He gave a silver cup to the first Congregational Church in Bridgeport that is now used in the communion service.

He is the ancestor of nearly all by the name of Edwards in this region of country. "He was," says Esquire Sherman, "grandfather to my grandmother, Betty Edwards, who married my grandfather, John French. So that I am part Scotch blood and part English."

No. 46. Dea. Abel Seeley was a farmer, but left no descendants. He left his estate to Capt. Elijah Peet, his adopted son.

No. 47. Jackson's Mill. The first settler here by the name of Jackson was Henry, who came from Watertown, Mass. The family was prominent and somewhat numerous in the early period of Fairfield and Stratfield, though now scarcely represented.

Henry Jackson, who sold his Fairfield Mill to Thomas Morehouse, probably erected a mill on this location about 1667. Mary Jackson was admitted to full fellowship in the Stratfield Church from the Church in Norwalk, Conn., Dec. 20, 1697.

In the Acts of the General Assembly, May, 1701, defining the boundary line of Stratfield Parish: It is ordered and enacted, "That the line to be the west boundary of the said plantation shall run so that it may include within their bounds one Moses Jackson, Miller, his housing and lands, and run on the west side of old Jackson's lotts, viz., pasture, building lot and long lot."

In Fairfield Town Record,[*] under date Aug. 14, 1731, Moses Jackson is said to have "had quiet possession of his mill for fifteen years last past." In the list of Householders, made by Rev. Samuel Cooke, in 1733 or 1734, the following names occur: Moses Jackson, John Jackson, widow Gabriel Jackson, John Jackson, David Jackson, Sen., David Jackson, Jr. The lands of this family seem to have been located on the westerly side of Truck street.

No. 48. Silas Hawley was a farmer and has no descendants now living in this parish. His house was owned and occupied by Amos Burr, Esqr.

No. 49. John Nichols was a farmer, blacksmith and inn-keeper. General Washington stopped at his house as he was going to meet General Lafayette at Rhode Island. Opposite to his house there is now standing one of the mile stones

BENJAMIN FRANKLIN'S MILE-STONE.

erected by Benjamin Franklin before the Revolution, when he was Colonial Postmaster General. He measured the old

---

[*] Book B., page 520.

country stage-road from Philadelphia to Boston, by an ingenious device affixed to his carriage as he passed over the road,
which marked the miles, and at the end of each mile he
caused a stone to be erected with the number of miles from
one important place to another, cut on each stone.

The Nichols house is still standing on the corner of said
road, and the public parade ground is near it and near the
old burying-place.

John Nichols owned a slave named Tom, who ran away
from his master and was never recovered.

No. 50. William Burr, Esq., was a merchant and
justice of the peace, and a descendant of Col. John Burr.
The site of his house is now occupied by the new house of
Sherwood Sterling, Esq.

No. 51. Joseph Strong, Esq., was a farmer, and justice of the peace. His children were John Strong, the only
son; and daughters Deborah, Sarah, Charity, Ann, and Comfort. Deborah married David Sterling. Charity married Ira
Jones, the first printer of a paper called the American Tele-
graph, in Bridgeport, in company with Lazarus Beach, about
the year 1796.

No. 52. Rev. Robert Ross was born in America, in
1726, of Irish parents; was graduated at Princeton College
in 1751, receiving his diploma from President Burr, and ordained pastor of the Stratfield Church, November 28, 1753,
and labored as such for more than forty-two years. He was
a strong Whig in the Revolution, and when the first military
company was raised in 1775 to go to Canada to take Fort St.
John's it was mustered in his door yard, where they all
kneeled down while he offered prayer, and I believe it to be
a fact that all of the company returned in safety, says Esquire
Sherman.

He published a sermon, from these words: " And there
were great searchings of heart for the divisions of Reuben."
He also made a grammar and spelling book for schools.

He was about six feet in height, well-proportioned, and
of rather imposing presence. He wore a wig, cocked hat,

ruffled bosomed shirt, black coat, vest and breeches, with white topped boots, cramped so as to set tight on the instep. As he was once on a journey he got them wet, and, having pulled them off to dry could not get them on again; therefore he tied them with his mail straps to his saddle, and on his way he met parson Bellamy, when they commenced the old dispute about foreordination and free will.

Parson Ross was of the Old Light party, and was considered orthodox, and parson Bellamy was of the New Light party. "Now," said parson Ross, "You think you can reconcile foreordination with free will?" "Yes." "Well, you can even tell why my boots are tied on behind me?" This he could not do, and in it parson Ross had an illustration, for he believed in election, foreordination and free will, but denied the power of man to reconcile them.

Parson Ross, on a certain occasion preached a sermon before the Association; and tradition reports that at the close of the sermon he said: "My brethren, we are charged in the text to be wise as the serpent and harmless as the dove, but I think we ought to be cunninger than the serpent, which is the Devil; we ought to outwit him."

Parson Ross was a slave-holder and owned one African slave by the name of Pedro. He held no slaves after the Revolution.

He resigned his pastorate April 30, 1796, and died August 29, 1799, of a fever, and within twenty-four hours Mrs. Ross died of the same disease, and they were both buried in the same grave. Their only son then living, Merrick Ross, died nine days after, and was buried also in the same grave. He had an elder son who was drowned in his father's well. He also had a daughter Sarah.

No. 53. Benjamin Fayerweather was a farmer, and was the owner of Fayerweather's Island, where Black Rock light house now stands. He had one son, Nathaniel, who married Charity Summers, and they had, James, Daniel, and Polly, who married William Eaton. Nathaniel Fayerweather was taken prisoner by the British on Long Island Sound and confined in prison in what was afterward Dr. Spring's old

Brick Church, which was then in possession of the enemy and was used as a prison. He died of small-pox in this prison. His widow died in this parish aged over 90 years. She was a convert of the Rev. Samuel Blatchford, and was a mother in Israel.

No. 54. First Protestant Episcopal Church in the parish. The Episcopalians in the parish of Stratfield, erected in 1748, a small frame church with a steeple surmounted with a gilt weather-cock; that device being used as emblematical of the crowing of the cock when the Apostle Peter denied his Lord.

Said Church was opened for service in 1749, and called St. John's Church. lt was built near Church lane, about a quarter of a mile west of the Pequonnock meeting-house. It was not finished until 1789, when it was consecrated by the Right Rev. Bishop Seabury.

This Church was taken down in the year 1801 and rebuilt at the city of Bridgeport on the corner of State and Broad streets, retaining the same name, and it being the same church that is now, in 1856, under the pastoral care of the Rev. Gurdon S. Coit. The Rev. Philo Shelton was its first pastor, who commenced his labors in 1779, and died in 1825, aged about 70 years.

The principal proprietors in building this Stratfield Church were Col. John Burr, John Holburton, Timothy Wheeler, Joseph Seeley, John Nichols, Richard Hall and Samuel Beardsley. The land on which the Church stood was opened to commons on the east side of Church lane, and contained about half an acre.

No. 55. John Holburton, from England, was a farmer. He had children, Thomas, William, and one daughter, who married Capt. Stephen Summers, of Cow Hill. She was the mother of one son, Stephen, who married Betsey Young, and of four daughters,—Charity, who married Capt. Wilson Hawley; Polly, who married Capt. Abijah Hawley; Grizell, who married Capt. Aaron Hawley, and Ruth, who married Mr. Nathaniel Wade.

No. 56. Samuel Cable, a cooper by trade and inn-keeper, was a large, strong man and lived to a good old age. He had sons Samuel and William, and daughters Charity and Ann. Samuel Cable, Sen., came here from a place called Compo, near Saugatuck. He married, first, Mary Porter, of Stratford.

No. 57. Sergt. Jabez Summers was a farmer. His children were: Jabez, Jr., and Mary, who married Mr. Seth Sherman; and Alice, who never married. He was a slave-holder.

No. B. The Parsonage Lot, containing three acres of land at Pequonnock, was given to the Stratfield Society by the wife of the Rev. Robert Ross, for the use and benefit of the pastor for the time being. The deeds are recorded in the Society's book, and in Fairfield and Stratford town records.

No. 58. Abel Lewis was by occupation a cabinet-maker, and was the father of Ichabod Lewis, who removed from the place since the Revolutionary War. There are none of his descendants now living in this parish.

No. 59. Jacob Sterling, an early settler, came from England, and was a ship carpenter. He came to Cape Cod, thence to Haverhill, from which place he fled at the time the Indians massacred most of the inhabitants. He went to Lyme, Conn., and came thence to this parish. My paternal grandmother was his granddaughter and the wife of David Sherman, who was killed by lightning in the old Pequonnock meeting-house in 1771.

Jacob Sterling married Mrs. Hannah (Odell) Seeley, of Fairfield. His descendants are quite numerous. He resided first at Fresh Pond.

No. 60. Abijah Sterling, Esqr., son of Stephen and grandson of Jacob Sterling, No. 59, was a farmer, a public spirited man, for many years a representative to the General Assembly, and was a fine looking man,—one of nature's noblemen. He had only a common school education; was justice of the peace, and general arbitrator and peace maker in the parish. He owned a carriage, called a chaise, in the autumn of 1776, it being without a top. He heard that my father, David Sherman and Esquire Sterling, brother of Stephen, then with the Stratfield militia company, under command of Capt. Thaddeus Bennett in the city of New York, were, with many of the company, sick and dying with dysentery, and he went after them with his carriage. He found the two sick in a barn at Harlem, Capt. Bennett having discharged them so that they might try to get home. He, like the good Samaritan, put them both into his carriage, and then led the horse until they arrived at home, where both recovered.

Lieut. Edward Burroughs of the same company and of this parish, died with the same distemper after he reached home.

No. 61. James Hawley, was a farmer, and a descendant of Joseph Hawley, one of the first settlers in the old town plot of Stratford. Stephen Hawley, now living in Bridgeport, is descended from him.

No. 62. Dea. Joseph Booth was a farmer and a leading man in the town and church. He was chosen Deacon of the Stratfield Church in 1733, and died in 1763.

No. 63. Eliphalet Jennings was a farmer at Fresh Pond, and lived on the place now occupied by James Porter. He married Sarah, the only daughter of Parson Ross. They have descendants now (1856), living, namely: Capt. Robert R. Jennings and James Jennings and others, children of said Captain Jennings. These are the only descendants of parson Ross.

No. 64. Deacon Seth Sherman was descended from Lieut. David Sherman, through Elnathan and Ebenezer Sherman, and conducted a tanning and currying business on these premises. He was Deacon of the Stratfield Congregational Church from 1799 to his death, August 7, 1807. He married Mary, daughter of Jabez Summers. His children were Anson, who married Priscilla Hoyt; Rowland, who died young, and Polly, who married ———— Southard.

The tanning and currying business was continued here a number of years by Samuel Peet and James French. The late John Plumb, E. Allen Parrott, and Thomas Ward, Jr., were among their apprentices. The fine residence now located upon the premises was built by Eli Thompson about 1857.

No. 65. Samuel French was a farmer at Fresh Pond, and lived where the house of Eben French now (1856) stands. He married a daughter of Samuel Sherman, of Old Mill, and is the ancestor of all who bear the name of French in this region of country.

No. 66. Rope Walk of A. & W. Hawley.

No. 67. Benont French, the son of Samuel French, was a farmer and lived in the house (1856) owned by Henry Olmstead. He had no sons and only one daughter, who married Freeman Lewis, the father of the late Alanson Lewis, and Mrs. Eliakim Hough.

No. 68. District School House at Fresh Pond.

No. 69. Abijah Beardsley was a farmer and black-smith. He married Drusilla, daughter of Master Wheeler, of Toilsome Hill. She was about 90′ years of age when she died. She received a pension for the services of her husband in the Revolution. They had sons Anson, Wheeler and Abijah. Abijah, Jr., when about twenty years of age went as a seaman from Bridgeport in 1805, in a brig commanded by Capt. Samuel Hawley, to Antigua, on which voyage he was taken by an English press-gang and forced on board an English man-of-war, where he was put on ship's duty for a cruise for several months, until the man-of-war returned to Antigua.

Through the aid of Sylvanus Sterling and Robert South-worth, who were then doing business there, he was liberated from the man-of-war and sent home in a brig bound for Washington, North Carolina in the month of January, 1806. I was then employed in a schooner belonging to the owner of said brig, of which schooner my brother David Sherman was master. Both vessels being at anchor at Ocracock Bar, we went on board the brig to make the captain a visit. Soon after we got on board the captain said: "I have a country-man of yours on board, I will call him and see if you know him." Soon a poor ragged sailor boy came into the cabin, and, although we were intimate with him at home, we could not recognize him because his sufferings had been so great on the brig, they having been on allowance of a potato a day for a number of days. His joy at seeing us was very great, but still greater when we told him we would furnish him suitable clothing and give him a passage to New York. We brought him home, to the great joy of his widowed mother.

Soon after he shipped on board of a schooner belonging to the Prindles of Bridgeport, and sailed for the West Indies, which schooner was lost in a hurricane in 1806, and all on board perished.

No. 70. Jacob Sterling's Shipyard.

No. 71. Charles Burritt, Jr., was a farmer.

No. 72. Joel Parish was a shoemaker. He married a sister of Maj. Aaron Hawley; had three daughters. One died with consumption, and the others removed to New Jersey.

No. 73. Stephen Burroughs, Esqr., was a farmer, ship-builder, Boston coaster, ship-master, mathematician, astronomer, and surveyor—a self-made man. He was about five feet eight inches in height, strong built, was never sick during his long life, a cold water man, and died in 1817, aged 88 years. He was an active Whig in the Revolution, when he raised a militia company called Householders, of which he was chosen captain. He was often chosen representative, and was justice of the peace for many years. He owned the parish grist mill called the Burroughs mill, that stood where the Pequonnock woolen mills now stand.

He was blind for several years before his decease. It is said he invented, about the year 1798, the system of Federal Money as now used in the United States.

His children were, Stephen, Isaac, David, and Abijah, sons, one of which, Abijah, was lost at sea, and David died of a fever caught in Boston, and was buried at Martha's Vineyard, about the year 1796; and he had three daughters— Eunice, married a Pendleton, of Stratford; Betsey, married

Capt. Joseph Sterling Edwards, and Huldah married Joseph Backus, Esqr., of Bridgeport, Conn.

No. 74. Shipyard and store of Stephen Burroughs, well known for many years.

No. 75. Elijah Burritt was a blacksmith, buckskin leather dresser, cooper and farmer, and died at the advanced age of 98 years. He was six feet in height, well made, fine presence, and was never sick until the last year of his life. He had one son, Daniel, and three daughters. His first wife was the daughter of John Hall. He died, Sept. 23, 1841.

It was from him that I derived much of the information
relative to the early settlers of this parish.

Mr. Burritt retained his faculties until the year 1840, when he failed slowly until his death. I asked him about a year before his death, if death did not appear to be very near. He replied, "Not any nearer than forty years ago;" that he had "always felt that he might die any day, but when he came to reflect that he was 97 years of age, his reason and judgment satisfied him that death must be very near.

No. 76. The Burroughs Gristmill of Revolutionary times. This was an old mill site, as seen on page 280 of this book, granted first to the Sherwood family.

No. 77. Josiah Smith was a miller at the Burroughs mill. He had one son, Josiah, and one daughter, Comfort.

No. 78. Philip Nichols, son of Theophilus, was born in January, 1726. Beginning business life for himself about 1747 he had twenty-five years cotemporary with his father, and they seem to have been well and advantageously improved, and after his father's decease he continued probably an active business life twenty-five years longer, dying in 1807, in his 82d year.

While his father thought that Newpasture Point would develope into a city and shipping place, Philip inclined to the opinion that the west side of the harbor would first become a city, and therefore made considerable purchases of land where now much of the business portion of the city of Bridgeport stands, which investments furnished his children with considerable valuable property.

His dwelling was at No. 78, on the map at the corner of the roads, and a large portion of his business life was connected with the brick store and shipyard near the house on the shore. The shipping trade of Bridgeport was first developed at that place on the Pequonnock river, and afterwards came down gradually to its present localities.

Philip Nichols was a prominent communicant of the Episcopal Church at Stratford. The parish book shows the following record:

"At a parish meeting of Christ Church, Stratford, held Easter Monday, April 20, 1772, it was voted that the pew next to the pulpit be given to Captain Philip Nichols, he building the Christening Pew."

His descendants were prominent in the community and other parts of the country, many years.

No. 79. *John Peet* appears to have owned this place in 1694, according to the land records, with perhaps a dwelling on it, but considerable portion of Mr. Peet's land at this place was purchased by Richard or Theophilus Nichols, and in the inventory of the latter's estate it is called "Captain Peat's lot;" twenty-three acres being valued at £126–10.

No. 80. *William Pixlee*, son of William of Hadley, Massachusetts; was born June 27, 1669; came to Stratford when twenty-one years of age and purchased his first land of Abraham Mitchell, three acres, at what is now the southwestern corner of Old Mill Green, on the 21st day of April, 1690. He continued to buy land in that vicinity, almost yearly, so that in twelve years he had about fifty acres, besides pieces in other parts of the town. One piece that he purchased, in 1694, adjoining his own land, was bounded "on the south with the trench that dreans the pond, and on the east with the pond." This shows that an effort had been made at that early day, to drain that pond.

William Pixlee married Grace, daughter of David Mitchell, in November, 1701, when he had a good farm and home of his own. He had two sons, Peter and David, the latter died in 1742, aged 38 years. Peter occupied the home-stead with his mother as long as she lived, probably, and he, after having been a prominent and influential citizen, died in 1788, aged 85 years.

William Pixlee, the father, died in the early part of the year 1712, the inventory of his property being taken March 17, 1712, to which his widow made oath April 2, 1712.

Peter Pixlee, the son, had a son William who lived on the old homestead, and was the first to receive liberty from the town to build a mill at what is now known as the Berkshire Mills.[9] He was a prominent business man of the town.

No. 81. Richard Nichols, son of Isaac, Jr., grandson of Isaac, Sen., and great-grandson of Francis Nichols, the first of the name at Stratford, was born at Stratford, November 26, 1678, and was twelve years of age when his father died, after which his mother and her three sons removed to, and resided at, Newtown, L. I.

Richard seems to have returned to Stratford about the year 1700, and on June 2, 1702, married Comfort, daughter of Theophilus Sherman.[10]

Richard Nichols purchased land at Old Mill Green as early as the spring of 1710, and thereafter for several years he purchased land almost yearly in the same vicinity.

A number of settlers had been living at Old Mill from thirty to forty years when Richard Nichols came there, namely: Samuel Sherman, Jr., Benjamin Sherman, John Hurd, John Peet, and Samuel Blakeman's family.

His home was established on what is now the corner of Old Mill Green and East Main street, where he resided until his death in 1756, in his 78th year. Mr. Nichols was a prominent man in the first ecclesiastical society in the town. In the building of the third meeting-house, in 1743, he was one with Captain Robert Walker and David Porter as committee, to secure a committee from the General Court to select the site for that house. He was engaged frequently in the settle-ment of the estates of deceased persons.

---

[9] See page 405 of this book.

[10] This relation is proved by a deed in which the fact is stated (see genealogy).

He was the leading man, apparently, in securing to the
public generally the wide street called Old Mill Green, called
at that day Pembroke street, and to him and those associated
with him in that public enterprise, the people, and especially
those of the City of Bridgeport, will ever be grateful."

In his will, dated September 25, 1755, and proved fourteen days after, he gave his homestead to his son Joseph, containing about thirty-five acres, " with buildings, and the remainder of my pasture lot nigh to John Hurd's homestead,
and all my lot of land at Daniel's Farm, southward of the
Park, about twenty-five acres, also the whole of my lot of
wood land at Ireland's Brook, about six acres."

He says further: " I give to my son Nathaniel Nichols,
one piece of land that I purchased of Jabez Beardslee, lying
northward of Totocock (so called) in the bounds of said Stratford.

---

[11] *Sequestered Land for Pembroke Street.*

" Know all men by these presents, that we, Richard Nichols, Nathaniel
Sherman, Samuel Judson, Peter Pixlee, Ebenezer Hurd, Theophilus Nichols,
Samuel Shearman, Timothy Shearman and Joseph Nichols, all of the town of
Stratford in the County of Fairfield, for and in consideration of the love and good
will we have for the town of Stratford and the inhabitants thereof, and in order to
preserve the common good thereof, said town being the land of our nativity and
the inhabitants the first of our acquaintance here on earth, We do give, grant,
make over and confirm unto Mr. Benjamin Sherman of the said town of Stratford
and to their successors, inhabitants of said town forever, a certain tract of land
being and lying in said Stratford township in Pembroke street so called, containing in quantity about six acres of land, little more or less, and it is butted and
bounded on all points with common land as may appear by the survey bill thereof
on Stratford records, for him the said Benjamin Shearman and the rest of the said
inhabitants of the said town of Stratford :—To have and to hold the above described tract of land to be and lye a perpetual common to and for the use of them
their successors throughout all generations to the end of time.

" Affirming at the time of this grant we are well seized of the premises and have
in ourselves full power to grant the same as in manner above expressed and that
our true intent is, the same should be for a common use of all the Inhabitants of
the town of Stratford and their successors forever, never to be severed in any
manner whatsoever. To confirm all above written promises We have hereunto
set our hands and seals this 25th day of November, A. D. 1740 :

" Richard Nichols, Nathaniel Shearman, Samuel Judson, Peter Pixlee, Ebenezer Hurd, Theoph* Nichols, Samuel Shearman, Timothy Shearman, Joseph
Nichols."

No. 82. John Judson was the owner of this place and perhaps residing on it in 1702, according to a deed received by William Pixlee and given by Nathaniel Sherman, of the land lying between it and the road on the west side of it.

No. 83. Theophilus Nichols, Esq., son of Richard Nichols, was born, March 31, 1703. He married, January 1723-4, Sarah, daughter of Lt. Ebenezer Curtiss, and settled on the north side of the street nearly opposite his father's residence, where he resided until his decease in 1774. This home was held by the Nichols family until 1807, then by the Judson family of that locality.

His father, doubtless, gave him the land for his homestead when he was married, and he became a prosperous farmer. He also engaged in ship building and mercantile business to a considerable extent, probably, before as well as after his father's decease in 1756, but in his father's will there is no mention of stores or shipyard. In that will the father gave to Theophilus, with other pieces of land, "one lot in Newpasture Field called Gaspin's Point, about twenty-four acres." In the inventory of the estate of Theophilus, dated May 23, 1774, this property is mentioned, thus: "twelve acres of land on the north end of the point lot £93-10," and "three acres of land in do. with the house, store and wharf, £190." This indicates that within eighteen years he had built the house, store and wharf, at what is now the south end of Pembroke street. In the same inventory is mentioned, "three rods of land and the brick house, and shipyard adjoining," and "one acre of land adjoining on the south side." This was previously the Sterling shipyard.

This shipyard may have been the property of Theophilus before his father's death. The inventory mentions also, "the one-eighth part of a schooner, the President, £25," and £150 worth of merchandise.

Besides his business life Theophilus Nichols was a public servant and honored citizen. He was a deputy to the General Assembly twenty-three years; was a captain of the militia a number of years and a justice of the peace a number of years near the close of his life.

35

In 1745, at the time of the Great Revival in the Congregational Churches, he united with the Episcopal Church, and thereafter rendered great service to that cause. Also, the Probate records of Fairfield show that he was often selected by private individuals and appointed by the Court to the service of executor and overseer of wills and estates.

He died in 1774, aged 71 years.

No. 84. John Fulsom, son of Samuel, of Stratford, was a blacksmith and carried on his trade a number of years at this place. He died about 1815, and the house becoming old was pulled down.

No. 85. Samuel Sherman, Jr., was the first settler at this place on Old Mill Green, as far as can be ascertained. In 1663, Samuel Sherman, Sen., purchased James Blakeman's half of the mill property at this place, which comprised twenty acres of upland and several acres of meadow, while Samuel Blakeman owned the other half, of an equal number of acres. In 1680, Samuel Sherman, Jr., received this land by gift from his father, but probably had resided on it a number of years before that date, perhaps from 1663.

The highway, now called Pembroke street, began at Mr. Sherman's house, with a gate in the common fence on the south side of the Green. This road after having been used seventy years or more, was re-surveyed in 1749, by Theophilus Nichols and others, as Proprietors' committee, down to the point, and made "full three rods wide."

Stiles Lewis and his son after him, owned this place many years. The frame of the old house still stands, but the covering has been renewed, perhaps, more than once, and the exterior much changed. The father kept a tavern here, and the north front room is said to have been occupied by Washington while on one of his trips through the country.

The son sold the place to Benjamin Stillman and removed to New York.

No. 86. Samuel Blakeman, probably resided here, he having purchased of his brother James in 1662, half of the mill property, including twenty acres of farming land besides meadow; and he died in 1668. His widow married

Jacob Walker. The other half of the mill property was purchased by Samuel Sherman, Sen., in 1663, as represented in No. 85.

No. 87. Stephen Burritt; his descendants are all gone.

No. 87.ᵃ The Hurd Place. This land, including No. 87, was originally laid out to John Hurd, Sen., and by his will bequeathed to his son Isaac, who seems to have died, leaving no children, and the property descended apparently to his brother John and his children, according to his father's will, and it was the Hurd homestead for several generations.

Ebenezer Hurd, son of John 2d, as above, resided on this farm probably nearly all his life, being born April 7, 1703. He became a widely known person according to the following : "This same year (1775), Ebenezer Hurd,[18] a regular post rider, closed a service of forty-eight years, having begun it in 1727. Once in a fortnight, during that entire period, he had made a journey from New York to Saybrook and back, 274 miles. In other words—for such is the computation— during those forty eight years he had traveled over as much space as twelve and a half times around the world, or as far as to the moon and half-way back. Meantime, what of the wife? Bringing up the children, managing the farm and during one year at least, 1767, spinning not less that five hundred yards of wool and flax, all raised on the place, making and mending, especially for that indefatigable rider, who was doubtless "hard on his clothes."

This Ebenezer Hurd married in January, 1732, Abigail Hubbell, and they had fifteen children. Their gravestone stands in Huntington burying place, both inscriptions being on one stone. They are :

"Mr. Ebenezer Hurd, died May 7, 1788, aged 87 years.
Mrs. Rebecca, His Wife, died April 16, 1783, Aged —
years."

One of the sons was Ebenezer, Jr., who was also a post rider, according to the following : "The 28th of November,

---

[18] Magazine of American History, by Mrs. Martha J. Lamb, 1885, page 118.

died at Stratford, in Connecticut, of a short illness, Mrs. Elizabeth Hurd, wife of Ebenezer Hurd, Jun., Post Rider of that Place, aged 24 Years and three Months; Her Death is greatly lamented by all her Relations. She was the daughter of the Rev. Christopher Newton, of Stratford."

Andrew Hurd, eldest son of the first Ebenezer, and born in 1731, was also a post rider, and resided on the homestead on Old Mill Green until his death, April 29, 1819, aged 89 years. He is still remembered, and tradition says he used to call out when he was to stop, " Open the gate for the King's Post."

From these last items it is probable that the sons often rode post in place of their father.

No. 88. Site of the Old Mill, built in 1652 and 3, and from which Old Mill Hill and Old Mill Green take their names.

No. 89. Sergt. Charles Burritt was a descendant of Stephen Burritt of Stratford, the celebrated Indian fighter in King Philip's War, and the ancestor of the Hon. Elihu Burritt, the Learned Blacksmith.

No. 90. Dea. Thomas Hawley was a farmer and a descendant of Joseph, the first of the name in Stratford; through Samuel the eldest son. Most of the Hawleys of this parish are his descendants. He was chosen deacon of the Stratfield church in 1712, and died in 1722, aged 44 years. His son, Captain Ezra Hawley, seems to have succeeded him on the paternal homestead, and also his grandson, Ezra Hawley, Jr. Among the sons of the last was Wilson, a well known and leading farmer and merchant of this place; and Abram, who married Alice Burton of Trumbull, settled in Waterbury, and had, among other children, George B., a distinguished physician and public spirited citizen of Hartford, Connecticut.

No. 91. Gurdon Hawley was a farmer, a descendant of Dea. Thomas Hawley, through Captain Ezra and Ezra, Jr.

---

[13] Magazine of American History, 1885, page 206; taken from Rivington's N. Y. Gazetteer, Dec. 15, 1774.

George Benjamin Hawley, M. D., the son of Abraham and Alice (Burton) Hawley, was born in Bridgeport, February 13, 1812.

While he was yet an infant his parents removed to Watertown, Conn., where he spent his boyhood on his father's farm. He fitted for college at Goshen Academy, entered Yale College in 1829, and was graduated in 1833. He also studied medicine at Yale and received his diploma as an M. D. in 1836. After some preliminary work and practice he in 1840 settled down to the regular practice of his profession in Hartford, which he continued successfully over forty years.

He was a man of prodigious nervous energy and physical endurance, which were brought into full play in the practice of his chosen profession, and in many other interests and objects of a business and philanthropic nature.

The Hartford Hospital and the more recent Old People's Home of Hartford owe their inception and success more to Dr. Hawley than to any other man. He was interested in the local corporations and enterprises of Hartford—to the success of which he contributed in large degree. The woven wire mattress he viewed in a sanitary light, and overcoming some of the earlier defects, brought it to a high state of perfection and great pecuniary success. He became interested in the mechanical setting and distributing of type, and for twenty years devoted much time and money to its development. He was President of the Farnham Type-Setting Machine Company, which finally adopted the Page machine, and which, under his fostering interest and efforts, has been brought to a surprising state of practical efficiency. He did not live (as he hoped) to see it manufactured and in use in the large printing establishments in the country. .

Dr. Hawley died April 18, 1883. He was twice married and left a widow and one son (by his first wife), Dr. George Fuller Hawley, now of Chicago.

G. B. Hawley

Gurdon married Ann, daughter of Thomas, his father's brother. They had one son, Anson, who married Fanny, daughter of Dea. David Sherwood, a daughter Eliza, who married Isaac E. Beach.

No. 92. Captain Stephen Summers was a farmer and Boston coaster. He had an only son, Stephen, and daughters, Charity, Grizzell, Polly and Ruth. Stephen, Jr., was master of the brig William, bound from Bridgeport to New Providence. She sailed in November, 1810, and was lost at sea and all on board perished.

No. 93. Daniel Summers was a farmer.

No. 94. James Gregory was a farmer; married Philena Burritt, and removed, about 1808, to Kentucky.

No. 95. Dea. Lemuel Sherwood, son of Matthew, and born about 1687, was a farmer. He was chosen deacon of the Stratfield church in 1722, and served until his death in 1732. His father, Matthew, is represented in the Communion set of the first Congregational Church by a cup, the oldest piece in the set, inscribed as given in 1713.

Dea. David Sherwood, a descendant of Matthew, through Samuel, John and Stephen, purchased this farm owned by Dea. Lemuel one hundred years before, consisting of one hundred acres, in 1830. He was chosen deacon of the First Church, in 1831, and served about twenty-five years. He died January 24, 1873, at the age of 94 years.

He cultivated and kept his farm nearly intact until his decease. The population and improvements had so surrounded him, that his land had become very valuable. He died with the impression that he was very rich. The land has been mostly sold, streets have been laid over it, and these acres are covered with manufactures, stores and fine residences; and a teeming, busy, population, with a school house and chapels.

No. 96. Colonel John Burr was a farmer, an early settler and a leading man in building the first Episcopal Church. His farm is the same that Polly Burr, a granddaughter, now owns. His ancestor, Colonel John Burr, of the same name, held a meeting with the Indians under a large oak tree near to where he built his house, which tree is now standing (1856), but has marks of old age in its branches. It was evidently a large tree when the parish was first settled. Thirty years ago (1826) it was green and flourishing.

He had sons, William, Ozias, who died at the age of 98 years, and Captain John Burr, who was killed by lightning in 1771.

No. 97. *Watrous Hubbell* was a farmer, and resided at the place now occupied by the descendants of the Rev. Philo Shelton. Some of his descendants are now living in Bridgeport. Gershom E. Hubbell is a grandson, and the children of David Hubbell, 3d, Elbert E. and George Hubbell, are great-grandchildren of the said Watrous Hubbell.

No. 98. *Captain Amos Hubbell* was a farmer, Boston coaster, a West India trader and an active Whig in the Revolution, as were also all his brothers and nephews. He was a merchant at Newfield, now Bridgeport. Soon after the Revolution he built the wharf near the foot of Bank street, and was the first Warden of the Borough of Bridgeport—a man much respected.

He had one ship and two brigs built for himself, but his commercial business was not generally successful.

About the year 1798, while France and the United States were at war, Captain Wilson Hubbell, a son of Captain Amos, while on a voyage homeward bound from the West Indies, was taken by a French privateer, who took out William Cable, his mate, and one seaman, leaving Captain Wilson Hubbell with Samuel Cable, seaman, and Josiah Burr, the cook, on board. The privateer then put on board of Captain Hubbell's sloop a prize master and two French seamen.

After the privateer had left, the weather being moderate, Samuel Cable was put at the helm and the sloop was left by the French Prize Master to the care of the two French seamen. When the Prize Master went into the cabin and lay down, having laid his sword and pistols by him, as soon as he was asleep Captain Hubbell secured his arms and locked him in the cabin. He then secured the two French sailors and confined them. He now secured his money, which was in gold, in his silk handkerchief tied around his body unknown to the Prize Master.

He then unwisely held a parley with the cunning Frenchman, who made him such fair promises of his good behavior that Captain Hubbell allowed him to come on deck and to have his liberty. The Frenchman having won his confidence, he sat down with him on the quarter-rail to smoke. When the Frenchman dropped his cigar between Captain Hubbell's feet and reached down and took it up; he continued his French palaver, but soon dropped it again, and, stooping down again to pick it up, he caught Captain Hubbell by his feet and threw him overboard head foremost. The sea was calm, and when he came up he swam after the sloop, begging for his life, but the cruel Frenchman was deaf to his cry and let him drown with his gold about him.

Captain Amos Hubbell had four sons, Captain Wilson and Amos, Jr., who both died young; Anson, and also Charles B. Hubbell, who is now President of the Pequonnock Bank. He had one daughter, Catharine, who married Captain Ezekiel Hubbell, formerly President of the Connecticut Bank.

No. 99. Richard Hubbell, Sen., an early settler at Pequonnock, was a cooper and farmer. He was supposed to have emigrated to this country from the county of Essex in England about the year 1670. He had one son, Richard, and they were two of the nine male members of the first Congregational Church at its organization.

Richard, a grandson, occupied the homestead, and died at the advanced age of 93 years. He was a deacon in this church when it was under the pastoral care of the Rev. Samuel Cooke and the Rev. Robert Ross, for thirty years. He lived with his wife, who survived him, about 63 years. He gave the church a silver tankard for communion service, which is still in use in this church. He had sons, Richard, Amos, Hezekiah, Watrous and Benjamin, and one daughter, who married Edward Burroughs. He died in 1788.

No. 100. Richard Hubbell, 3d, was a farmer and a
merchant at Newfield, and died in the city of New York
about the year 1830, aged about 94 years. He formerly resided in the parish of Stratfield, where Joseph Banks, Esq., now
resides. He married a sister of Elijah Burritt. Their children were: Richard, Philo and Eli, and Pamelia, who married Captain Whitmore; Polly, who married Asa Hurd, of
Old Mill, and Penelope, who never married, and is now living
in the city of New York at the advanced age of about 90
years.

No. 101. Captain John Burr was a farmer, and the
son of Colonel John Burr, who is described under No. 74.

Captain Burr was killed by lightning in the meeting
house in 1771, at the same time my grandfather, David Sherman was killed, as described under No. 27.

His children were: Jesse, Eunice, who married William
Holburton, and Katy, who married John Duncombe. Eunice
was a small, black-eyed woman, and died at the age of 88
years. She drew a pension for the services of her husband
in the Revolutionary war.

No. 102. Training Ground. In 1703, the Stratfield
Train-band was organized, and David Sherman appointed its
Ensign. The next year John Beardsley, of Stratford, was
confirmed its Captain, and James Bennett, of Fairfield, its
Lieutenant.

It has been current tradition that this plot at the corner
of the King's highway (North avenue) and the highway leading to Truck street, was donated for this purpose by the first
Richard Hubbell or one of his immediate descendants. It
seems to have been in use for training down to, and perhaps
after, the Revolution.

On a certain training day, among the spectators present
was a party of Indians, who had been behaving insolently,
and one of them, a burly, athletic fellow, finally challenged
the whites to choose their best man, and he would defeat him
in a wrestling match. No one appeared ready to meet the
challenge of the Indian, whose muscular frame plainly showed
him to be a formidable antagonist, although all felt it import-

ant, for the moral effect, that some one should do it. After some deliberation it was decided that Captain John Sherwood was the only man able to vanquish him, but doubts were expressed whether he would be willing to engage in a wrestling match now that he had become so active in religious matters. A deputation came to him as he was drilling his men upon the parade ground, and after hearing their story he briefly answered that his present duty was to drill his company, but that afterward he would attend to the matter.

When the parade was over and he had laid aside his regimentals, he approached the Indian champion, who was naked to his waist and shining with grease. This was decidedly to the advantage of the native, since it gave his antagonist a small chance to grasp the well oiled skin, while his opponent, dressed in ordinary clothing, presented a fair opportunity for the grasp of the savage.

Captain Sherwood advanced without any skirmishing, and laying his hand on the naked shoulder of the Indian, found himself able to get a good grip on the skin and flesh, then exerting his great strength, at once laid his antagonist flat upon his back, not caring to soften the violence of the fall, to the utter astonishment of the Indian allies. The victory was complete, confessed, and the natives withdrew quietly and never repeated the challenge.

No. 103. The Old Stratfield Burial Ground seems to have been laid out on the Black Rock road. The first burials were made upon the high ground, now the central part of the plot, which appears to have been quite fully occupied. There are numerous field stones which mark the places of interments, many of them being marked only with initial letters, date and age, and others with initials roughly cut. These dates run from 1688 to 1712.

About the oldest slate stones of the stereotyped pattern, fully inscribed, are those of Rev. Charles Chauncey, 1714, and Captain Matthew Sherwood, 1715. The ground was undoubtedly regarded as the property of the parish, for on December 29, 1772, an addition of one-half of an acre was made on the southeastern side, extending to the Training ground, securing a new entrance. This addition was purchased by the

Stratfield society, of Daniel Morris, for nine pounds ten shillings, lawful money, and the deed was recorded in the society's book and also on the land records of Fairfield. This portion is very fully occupied.

These grounds have been very little used since the year 1812, and were for many years very much neglected. For more than sixty years the society has not exercised any special supervision over it.

About 1848, a picket fence was constructed around it under the auspices of the late Isaac Sherman. A small fund remained in the hands of Mr. Wilson of Fairfield, at the time of the annexation of contiguous Fairfield territory to Bridgeport in 1871, and at a subsequent town meeting of Bridgeport, Sherwood Sterling, Joseph Banks and Albert Wilson were appointed a committee for the care of the ground. No money was appropriated and little care bestowed. Mr. Sterling and Mr. Banks died and Mr. Wilson became very infirm. The present committee having it in charge are Rowland B. Lacey, Henry R. Parrott and Daniel G. Fowler, who were appointed by the town meeting.

The present improved condition of this ground, which is very decided, is due to the persevering labors and oversight of Dea. R. B. Lacey, during a number of years past, and if his attention and efforts are aided by others, a few years more it will be a comely place for burial as well as visitation.

No. 104. James Morris was an early settler, a farmer and an innkeeper. None of his descendants are known to be living.

No. 105. Nathan Seeley, a son of Dea. Seth Seeley, a merchant and farmer removed to Bethel, where he died at a good old age. His descendants are living in Bethel and Danbury.

Nathan Seeley, when a young man, was a constable in Stratfield parish and had a writ to serve for a debt; and the law was at that time, such that the person on whom a writ was served must be touched with the paper to make the arrest legal. He rode a large, powerful horse, and found his man loading his cart with manure with a pitchfork. He told the constable to keep away and kept the fork raised for his defence. Upon this said Nathan put spurs to his horse and made him jump on the man so that he touched him with the writ. After having done that he had the power to call out the militia to make the arrest complete.

Nathan Seeley married Hannah, daughter of Major Aaron Hawley of Bridgeport.

No. 106. Dea. Seth Seeley was a farmer and for many years a deacon of the parish church. His children were: Nathan, Seth, Jr., and Samuel O. The last now occupies the homestead. Dea. Seeley married a daughter of Samuel Odell, Esq.; was an active Whig in the Revolution, and an old man at the time of his death.

No. 107. Capt. Josiah Lacey, a house joiner by trade. He was commissioned in 1777 by Governor John Hancock to raise a company for the Continental Army. This he did in the parish and was its captain for three years. The company was attached to Col. Philip Bradley's Regiment in Gen. Huntington's Brigade. His residence before the Revolution was on Truck street, whence he removed to the city of Bridgeport, where he built a house—now No. 237—on the south side of State street. He was a justice of the peace for many years, and died in the year 1812, in the 67th year of his age.

He had sons Winthrop who was lost at sea, and Josiah, who died young. His daughters were Chloe, who married Capt. Nathaniel Silliman, and Polly, who married Matthew Curtis, Esqr.

No. 108. John Lacey, son of John and grandson of Edward and Sarah Lacey, was baptized by Rev. Charles Chauncey, Oct. 22, 1710. He married Mary, daughter of Daniel Hubbell, and lived upon what is understood to have been the original homestead of the family, on the corner of Truck street and one of the cross roads leading to Toilsome Hill. The first settler is said to have come from Nottingham, England.

The family first appears upon the records of the Church of Christ in Fairfield, January 13, 1694, when Sarah, wife of Edward Lacey, was admitted as a member. June 20, 1694, their six children were baptized—viz: Edward, John, Henry, Sarah, Mary, Elizabeth.   This John of the second generation died in 1754.   His will was dated May 30, 1754, and mentions the following children: John, Edward, David, Ephraim, Eunice, Sarah.

John, of the 3d generation, whose name heads this article, appears on the Stratfield Parish records in 1759 and 1760, as one of the Society's Committee and is there called John Lacey, Jr.   He died Feb. 10, 1793, in his 84th year.   His wife Mary survived him seventeen years, and died April 1, 1810, aged 91 years.   She was an excellent woman and is spoken of as " a mother in Israel."

No. 109. Capt. Daniel Lacey, son of John, No. 108, was captain over all the companies of Guards, stationed during the Revolution, from Division street to Saugatuck river. He succeeded Capt. Nash, who first commanded the same.

His children were John, Daniel, who settled out West, Michael, Squire, and Sarah, who married Seeley Sherwood. His mother was the widow Mary Lacey, who resided in the old first homestead of the first settler in the parish by the name of Lacey.

John and Michael settled at what was known as Lacey's mill, but more recently at Plattville on the Easton Turnpike, and their remains, with those of their brother Squire Lacey, rest in the old Stratfield burial-ground.

Daniel went West.   The daughter Sarah, who married Seeley Sherwood, lived on the old road a little north of the Stratfield Baptist meeting-house.

No. 110. Joseph Brothwell was a shoemaker from Scotland.   He came to Stratfield about 1750 and had his residence at Truck street on the west side of the highway opposite No. 105 on the map, and there reared his family of four sons and three daughters.   He was a strong Presbyterian and Revolutionary Whig.   He married Hannah Fayerweather, a sister of Benjamin.   Their sons were Benjamin, Joseph Fayerweather, William and Thomas, who all lived to old age; and daughters, Betty who married John Hubbell, whose residence was on Division street, Grizel and Abigail.

Joseph F. Brothwell married a daughter of Benjamin Lacey, and removed to Woodbury, Conn., about the year 1798.

Joseph Brothwell was an active member of the parish when Mr. Ross was first settled, and to show the character o the man I will relate the following anecdote.

He was chosen Lieutenant of a company of militia called the Householders, and was a terror to the Tories. On a certain occasion when the heroes of the Revolution were gathered at Nichols' tavern, he pulled out his sword from its sheath and threw it down on the table—"There, there," said he, " I have unsheathed my sword and it shall not be sheathed again until this contest is ended."

He became blind several years before his death.

No. 111.[14] *Edward Lacey,* a farmer, son of John and grandson of Edward, the first settler of the name Lacey, in Fairfield (Stratfield), appears upon the Stratfield Parish records, Dec. 30, 1755, when Stephen Fairchild, Richard Hall, and Edward Lacey, Jr., were chosen School Committee. In 1757, he, with Dea. William Bennett and others, joined the " North Company " in the settlement of North Fairfield, now the town of Easton, which company appears to have been under the jurisdiction of the Stratfield Parish for some years. He purchased lands of —— Jackson, on the west side of the highway (now Easton turnpike) at a point about eight miles from Bridgeport, it being the same that the late Anson Bennett owned for many years. In 1761 Edward Lacey was chosen by Stratfield Parish, collector of ministerial, society and school rates within the limits of the North Company, and receipts for money paid by him to Rev. Robert Ross, and also from Rev. Joseph Lamson, of the Church of England, appears on the Parish records. It is said that the early religious meetings of the place were held at his house.

He was first married to Hannah Summers, by whom he had nine children. Eleven months after the birth of the two youngest (twins), October, 1755, she died and was buried at Stratfield. Subsequently he married Deborah Odell and had

---

[14] This may not be the exact location, but is near it.

five children. Rowland B. Lacey is a descendant through Zachariah (one of the twins above mentioned), and his wife Betty Rowland, and his son Jesse and Edna (Munson) Lacey. Edward Lacey died in North Fairfield (Easton), June 18, 1772, in his 61st year, and a fine old slate stone marks his grave in the cemetery near the Baptist Church, where also lie the remains of Zachariah and Jesse Lacey, above named.

His descendants are numerous and widely scattered through the country, but very few of the name remain in Connecticut.

No. 112. Benjamin Lacey, a tanner and currier, and shoemaker, having his shop and vats westerly from the house, convenient to the stream of water. Among his apprentices were Joseph Fayerweather Brothwell, Zachariah Lacey, and his own son David Lacey. Zachariah Lacey and J. F. Brothwell were of the same age and their terms of apprenticeship expired at the commencement of the Revolution. They together enlisted in a company commanded by Capt. Josiah Lacey and marched to New York. On the expiration of their time they re-enlisted and served nearly four years, when they united in hiring a man by the name of Jackson to serve during the war, by which they were exempted.

Benjamin Lacey married Margaret Hall. In 1767, and for many years thereafter, he was collector of ministerial rates, in Stratfield Parish, for the Church of England. He died in 1784, aged 45 years.

Joseph F. Brothwell married Molly (or Mary), daughter of Benjamin Lacey and removed to Woodbury.

David, son of Benjamin Lacey succeeded his father at the homestead and was known as David Lacey, the shoemaker. His children were David, Eleazer, Benjamin, Ruth, and Ellen. David was a large owner in, and the well known manager of the Washington bridge over the Housatonic river for many years. Eleazer Lacy was early engaged in the lumber business in Bridgeport; was next the cashier of the Middlesex County Bank, succeeding Charles Foote, who was called to the Connecticut Bank in 1834. At a later period he was the first cashier of the (Bridgeport) City Bank at its organization. Benjamin Lacey resided in Southport.

No. 113. Benjamin Brothwell, son of Joseph (No. 110), married Anna Beach, of Rock House district, in North Fairfield, now Easton. He resided first at No. 110, but after the death of his father he built a new house on this site, and reared a family of four sons and four daughters. Roswell, the third son, was the best known and most thoroughly identified with this community. He was considerable of a farmer as well as his father, much interested in agriculture, and was often engaged as manager at the county and local fairs. His residence was on the site designated as No. 115. He died in 1883, at the advanced age of 81 years. His wife was Julia Ann Hall, who survives him at the age of 83 years. Their only son, Benjamin Beach Brothwell, succeeds his father on the same premises.

No. 114. Error on the map.

No. 115. Amos Merriman was a cooper by trade. He came from Cheshire, Conn., about 1795. One of the early Baptist ministers was Elder Royce, who came here from Cheshire, and it is understood that his acquaintance with and interest in Elder Royce induced Mr. Merriman to remove to Stratfield. He built his house and cooper shop on this spot and resided here until about 1815, when he removed to Kentucky and left no representatives here.

Roswell Brothwell afterwards became the owner and made his residence here. He built the house and made the fine improvements which at present appear, some years before his death.

No. 116. Lemuel Bangs was by trade a blacksmith. His residence was in Truck street, a little way south of the first Baptist meeting-house. His children were born there.

Mr. Bangs was a poor man, but a zealous Whig in the Revolution. Two of his sons, the Rev. Nathan Bangs, D.D., of New York City, and Elder Heman Bangs, were schoolmates with Capt. Daniel Sterling, at the district school. The family left this part of the country about the year 1790. The two sons were very large men and were in the ministry of the M. E. Church many years.

Lemuel Bangs met in the time of the Revolution with other Whigs at Nichols' tavern, parson Ross, also a strong Whig, being of the number. During the discussions Lemuel Bangs said, he would be willing to die and suffer eternal punishment if he could be the means of making America free. Mr. Ross replied, " it is a good thing to be zealous but not to be too zealous. Where is my hat, I must be going."

No. 117. The Stratfield Baptist Church was first gathered in October, 1751. It was a result, in part, of the " Great Awakening," or " New Light" movement in 1740 and 41. The Rev. Samuel Cooke of the Stratfield parish was in favor of Whitefield and his preaching, but there was a considerable sentiment opposed to Mr. Cooke's views, and some of the opposition went to the Episcopal Church.

Upon the death of Mr. Cooke in 1747, a successor in the pastorate—Rev. Lyman Hall—was secured, who was opposed to New Light methods, and this increased the feeling of dissatisfaction towards the old parish and church.

The Separatist feeling, finally, took form under the leadership of Capt. John Sherwood and the preaching of the Rev. Joshua Moss (or Morse) in 1751.

Mr. Moss was a convert under the preaching of Whitefield, in Rhode Island, and had united with the Baptist Church, entertaining its sentiments in regard to baptism, close communion and preparation for the ministry, namely, that a liberal education was unnecessary ; the requisites being, the divine call, hallowed fire and spiritual enlightenment.

Mr. Moss had preached in the place repeatedly and on the second Lord's day in October, 1751, being assembled at the house of John Sherwood, he preached and after the sermon the following persons, Zechariah Mead, Nathaniel Seeley, Elihu Mash (Marsh), John Sherwood, Ebenezer Sanford and Samuel Beardsley, six men with a number of women, after the covenant services, were baptized by Elder Moss, and the Lord's Supper was administered. These services, as then judged, constituted the organization of the Church.

From this organization for six years there are found no records of this church. Some difficulty followed, between the members of this Baptist Church and the Old Stratfield Society about the collection of ministerial rates. The former thought that, under the law they should be exempt, the latter claimed of them rates the same as of others, since they were not an organized society, as the law required in order to be exempt, and tradition says that Captain Sherwood suffered his rate to be collected under distraint on his personal property, and in 1755, brought a suit in the Superior Court to recover sums which had been so collected. The result is not known, except that at the annual meeting of the Stratfield Society, December 29, 1757, shortly after the ordination of Capt. Sherwood as the first resident pastor of this Church, the ministerial rates of John Sherwood, Nathaniel Seeley, Zachariah Mead and Ebenezer Sanford were remitted for the year 1756 and 1757, and that they should be exempt from the rates of the following year.

Captain John Sherwood was ordained as an elder, in the Baptist Church, on the third Tuesday in December, 1757, by the Elders and Messengers of the Churches in New London and Groton, assembled with the Baptist Church in Stratfield, and he became the settled pastor of this church.

At the end of the first ten years, sixteen persons had been received into membership, and these had their residences in Ridgefield, Redding, Wilton and Newtown.

Elder Sherwood died in 1779, aged 75 years. He was a man of strong convictions, and was faithful to them while a member of the old Stratfield Church, as well as after he became a Baptist. He labored devotedly and with much energy, and hence successfully, not only in Stratfield but extensively in Fairfield county. He had great physical powers, as appears in his encounter with the Indian, as related in No. 102.

It is no disparagement to either to say that his grit reappeared remarkably in his well known grandson, Dea. David Sherwood, who died in 1873 at the great age of 94 years.

36

No. 118. The Parsonage of the Stratfield Baptist Society of the "olden time" was located here. It was the residence of Elder Seth Higby, Elder Royce, and others.

The house was long since taken down and the property now belongs to the estate of the late Roswell Brothwell.

The location of the present Parsonage is designated on the map as No. 116, the place formerly occupied by Lemuel Bangs. It was the toll house of the Easton turnpike for many years from about 1835.

No. 116. Capt. John Sherwood, a prominent farmer in the Stratfield Society, became a Baptist Elder, and pastor of the Stratfield Baptist Church in 1757, which he served faithfully about ten years. He died in 1779, at the age of 75 years. See No. 102 and 117.

No. 120. Patrick Keeler, from the north of Ireland, came to this parish during the period of the Revolution. He married first, Anne, daughter of Onessimus Hubbell, and 2d, Sarah Holburton. His daughter, Polly, married Nathan Seeley Meeker, son of David Meeker, who lived at the place designated on the map as No. 105. The 2d daughter, Anne, married Joseph Brothwell, son of Benjamin, and after the death of Patrick Keeler they continued to reside on the place. The children of Joseph and Anne (Keeler) Brothwell are Charles H. (of Bridgeport) and John (of Greenfield, Connecticut), and Emily, who married Charles Plumb. Charles H. is the well known agent of Hon. P. T. Barnum, and now a prominent member of the Board of Public Works of the City of Bridgeport. Patrick Keeler was strongly attached to Parson Shelton and the Protestant Episcopal Church. He was specially helpful to Mr. Shelton in many ways, but particularly enjoyed in his younger years the Christmas illumination of the old church, insisting on a candle at every pane of glass in the prominent windows.

120ᵃ.¹⁸ John Hopkins came to Stratfield from the north of Ireland in company with Patrick Keeler, who was about three years his senior.

---

¹⁸ Not located on the map.

Hopkins was a strong Presbyterian, and, though differing in religious sentiment from his neighbor Keeler, they ever remained fast friends. Hopkins located on the Valley road, so called, a few rods from where it leaves the upper cross-road leading from Truck Street to Toilsome Hill school house. He married Mehitabel Smith. Their children were James, John, Mary Ann, and Catharine. James married, first, Sarah Wilson; and second, Mary Sherwood. He lived on the old homestead, and after his second marriage built a new house. He left no children.

John was a shoemaker and dealer in Bridgeport. He married Abigail Booth, dau. of James Booth of Stratford. His children are Lewis Miles, and Alfred, both well known merchants and manufacturers of stoves, household goods and plumbing. Mary Ann married Nathaniel Thorp of Fairfield. She lived many years a widow at what is now No. 276 Lafayette street. A son Levi survives her.

No. 121. Onessimus Hubbell, son of Daniel, was baptized November 16, 1755, was a farmer, and died September 14, 1824.

No. 122. Thaddeus Hubbell, a brother of Onessimus, was a farmer. They descended from the first Richard, through Samuel; born 1657; Daniel born 1691; Daniel born 1724. Thaddeus had children Mary, who married Eli B. Nichols, Esther, who married John Parrott, Joseph and Rebecca.

No. 122ᵃ.[15] *Jedediah Wells.* His house was on the south side of the highway at Fresh Pond near the district school house—No. 68. He was son of Capt. Jedediah Wells, who was lost at sea about 1758, and grandson of Samuel Wells, located at No. 2 on the map—a large land owner in the south part of the settlement. This family are in direct line from Governor Thomas Wells. See genealogy. The only descendants of Jedediah are from his daughter Lucy, who married Abraham Parrott. Frederick Wells Parrott and Henry R. Parrott are (in 1885) owners of the ancestral property on North avenue and North Washington avenue.

---

[15] Not located on the map.

No. 123. Golden Hill Indians. The spot of ground containing eighty acres where the Golden Hill tribe of Indians lived at the time the parish began to be settled, contained at least one hundred wigwams, and was their cornfield. It was situated in the city of Bridgeport on the old Golden Hill road, now called Washington avenue. Golden Hill was so called by the English from the rocks that contained a yellow isinglass resembling gold. But it is not all gold that shines.

No. 123ª. An Indian Wigwam, occupied about 1798 by an Indian called Tom Sherman. This Indian house stood on, or near, the site of the dwelling house of the late Capt. Daniel Sterling, near a living spring called the Indian spring. It appears that there were about eight acres of land around it, which was the last of the old Indian field, on which the Golden Hill Indians inhabited.

No. 124. Capt. Daniel Sterling, a native of Stratfield, built his house on the east side of Main street, on the Indian lot, so called, in the year 1804, where he resided for many years until his death. He was for a long time a successful ship-master, from New York in the Liverpool trade.

No. 125. Ebenezer Allen, son of Nehemiah, was a shoemaker. His children were Samuel, James, Justus and Ruth, who married William Parrott, and Edri, who married Nicholas Burr.

No. 126. Dea. Elijah Hawley was a house carpenter. He was a deacon of the First Congregational Church until 1790, and died in the State of Ohio in 1825, aged 84 years. He had one son, named Jesse, who was born in the old red house, standing on Main street nearly opposite Gold street. Jesse Hawley removed to the State of New York in early life, where he died aged about 70 years. It is said that he was the projector of the Erie Canal, which project he communicated to Governor Clinton, which resulted in the building of that great work. Major Aaron Hawley, a brother of Dea. Elijah, became the owner of the place before 1787, and occupied it until his death in 1803. His son, Capt. Samuel, succeeded him. He and his descendants held and occupied it until about 1840.

No. 127. Samuel Porter was a farmer and weaver. He owned the farm called Porter's Point in the City of Bridgeport, Gold street crossing the same. He married Abiah Hubbell, who had a brother named Abel Hubbell, who lived to the extreme old age of over 103 years. I saw the old man a short time before he died. He was then in good health, but deaf and blind. He could recite hymns and portions of the Bible which he had learned in his youth. No other man in this parish has ever attained the age of 100 years. Mr. Elijah Burritt and Ozias Burr both reached 98 years; and there was a woman buried in the old parish ground by the name of Molly Jackson, who died at the age of 101 years.

Samuel Porter had a son, Samuel, Jr., who married my sister Ellen Sherman. He was a farmer and weaver; had no children. Samuel, Sen., had a daughter, named Mary, who married Lewis Sturges. They had two sons, Isaac and Joseph P. Sturges. The Rev. Thomas B. Sturges of Greenfield is an only child of Joseph P. Sturges.

This Porter property is treated at considerable length on page 489 and following, the reason being that quite a number of historical events cluster around and upon it.

No. 128. Capt. James Hayt owned this property. He came here from Norwalk. Samuel Peet purchased the property of him and erected on it a frame dwelling, which has given place to the present brick block of Mr. L. F. Curtis.

No. 129. Doct. Daniel Clifford was the first resident physician in this parish.

No. 130. Dea. Elijah Hawley erected a dwelling at this place and sold it about 1796 to Silas Sherman, who was a merchant, and married Abigail, daughter of Thomas Hawley. The late Ira Sherman was their son. His daughter, Caroline, married Nicholas Northrop.

No. 130ª. [16] *Capt. David Hawley,* son of James, owned this, the first brick house built within the present city

---

[16] Not located on the map.

limits. It was located on the corner of Water and Gilbert streets.

Capt. Hawley was with Arnold in the battle of the flotillas on Lake Champlain, in the Revolution, and he also led the expedition that captured Judge Thomas Jones, of Hempstead, L. I., who was afterwards exchanged for Gen. G. S. Silliman, an American officer. Capt. Hawley died in 1807, and his brick house was afterwards occupied as a saddle factory by Seth B. Jones, and was the arena of great theological discussions among the workmen, specially Joshua Lord, William Wright, Edwin B. Gregory and Alexander S. Gordon.

No. 131. *Timothy Shaylor* resided at this place with his brother. Isaac Sherman wrote of them, " I believe they were seafaring men."

No. 131ᵃ. *Capt. Abijah Hawley,* was the son of Thomas, No. 133. He was a prominent merchant, and in early life sailed in different vessels in the Boston coasting trade. Among his descendants in 1885 are Munson Hawley, President of the Bridgeport National Bank; Marcus C. Hawley, formerly of the hardware firm of Thomas Hawley and Company, now engaged extensively in the same business in California ; Dea. Edward Sterling, and others.

No. 132. *Nehemiah Allen* was a shoemaker and farmer. He came from Stratford before the Revolution and settled near Baker's Pond. His sons were : Nehemiah, Capt. James, who built the Stanley House, and Ebenezer. He had one daughter, Hannah, who married Capt. Charles Wing.

No. 133. *Thomas Hawley,* son of Capt. Ezra, No. 90, was a farmer. His son Zalmon is said to have transplanted the large elm tree on the premises of J. De Ver Warner, carrying it on his shoulder from the adjacent forest.

No. 134. *Mather's Point,* purchased from Mrs. Lucy Barlow, daughter of Capt. Samuel Sherwood by Capt. Titus C. Mather from Long Island, about 1829, for a shipyard. It was previously known as Sherwood's Point and earlier as New Pasture Point.

No. 135. Hon. Pierrepont Edwards, who died in Bridgeport, April 14, 1826, aged 76 years. See list of Bridgeport lawyers.

No. 136. Ephraim Wilcox was a boat builder and came from Stratford. It is said he possessed, for his day, an unsually extensive library, of which he made good use. He, Elijah Burritt, and Philip Nichols, were the literary trio of their period, or what would have been called then, "well read men." Mr. Wilcox had no children. Ira Curtis, from Stratford, was his apprentice and successor, and inherited his property and library, most of it being now in the possession of his son Lewis Curtis.

No. 137. The Old Yellow Mill, which was destroyed by fire in 1884. See page 407.

No. 138. An old dwelling, removed on the opening or extension of East Main street in 1800.

No. 139. ——— Hollins; occupation unknown.

No. 140. Capt. Nathan Sherman, a farmer, resided at this place, and died September 10, 1827. He was the ancestor of Messrs. O. W. and William Sherman, and of the Rev. H. B. Sherman of Torrington, Conn.

No. 141. James Walker was the owner of this homestead many years, from about 1739, but it is now in the possession of Mr. James W. Beardsley by inheritance through his mother, the daughter of James Walker.

The land of this homestead, most of it, was first laid out to Robert Walker, the father of James, described in part thus: "February 25, 1714–15. Then laid out one tract of land to Robert Walker on the east side of Pequonnock River, below the falls, 230 rods from north to south, 36 rods wide at the north end and 16 rods at the south end, and 66 wide in the middle, bounded west with the Pequonnock river, east with the highway, it being 61 acres, and 15 acres on the east side of the highway."

This is the territory now denominated the Beardsley Park, it having been given to the city of Bridgeport for a park by Mr. James W. Beardsley.

James Walker built the house, now standing, in 1739, and resided in it thereafter until his decease. The house is well preserved after the service of one hundred and forty-six years.

James Walker was the brother of the Hon. Robert Walker of Stratford, one of the most distinguished men that Stratford ever raised. James was Justice of the Peace in Stratford many years, and a prominent man in the society of North Stratford. Many quaint, curious and interesting papers and documents are still preserved which were collected by him in his long services as Justice of the Peace.

No. 142. Eben Booth was a farmer at this place quite a number of years since 1800. His family consisted of a wife and eight daughters. His daughter Eliza married Eli Baldwin and removed to Auburn, N. Y.; his daughter Nancy married Col. Lyman Baldwin, removed to Auburn and thence to Detroit, Michigan, where he was high sheriff, and afterwards mayor of the city; and his daughter Alice married Peter Hayden, a very wealthy hardware merchant of Cincinnati, O., and more recently a resident of New York city. The other daughters went west with their sisters.

The Stratfield (or Pequonnock) Burying Place.[17]

In memory of
Ebenezer Allen, who died May 6, 1830, in his 77 year.

Hannah Allen, wife of Ebenezer Allen, died Jan. 18, 1828, aged 68 years, 4 months.

In memory of
Ebenezer Allen, who died July 6, 1797, aged 11 years.

Also
Joseph, Edri, Joseph B., Justus, Joseph & Mary; Children of Ebenezer & Hannah Allen.

Justus Allen, Died Aug. 2, 1863, Æ. 63.

Adaline, Died July 12, 1857, Æ. 18.

Mary C., Died Aug. 4, 1863, Æ. 18. Daughters of Justus & Julia Allen.

In memory of
Mr. Nehemiah Allen, who died March 7th, 1810, in the 81st year of his age.

In memory of
Mrs. Edra Allen, wife of Mr. Nehemiah Allen, who died Feby. 20th, 1809, in the 74 year of her age.

In Memory of
Nehemiah Allen, who died Sept. 25, 1820, in his 40 year.

Here another Guest we bring,
Seraphs of celestial wing,
To our fun'ral altar come
Waft a Friend & Brother home.

In memory of
Samuel B. Allen, who died July 18, 1818, in the 36 year of his age.

In memory of
Theodore Allen, who died April 5th, 1810, aged 2 months & 15 days.

Waldomir Backus, son of Joseph Backus, Esqr. and Mrs. Huldah, his wife, born Jan. 7, 1803, died Dec. 14, 1809.

In memory of an
Infant daughter of Joseph & Huldah Backus, who died Feb. 17, 1799.

Laura, wife of Joseph Banks, & daughter of Philemon Sherwood, died Nov. 17, 1826, aged 28 years & 7 months.

In memory of
Mary Ann, daughter of Elbert & Polly Banks, who died Aug. 8, 1833, Æ. 16 yrs. & 3 mo.

In memory of
Jane, who died Jan. 26, 1816, Æ. 10 mo. & 10 d.

Also of
Stephen Henry, who died June 30, 1828, Æ. 7 mo.
Son and daughter of John & Sarah Bartlet.

Here lies the body of an
Infant son of James & Huldah Beach, who died Decr 19th, 1806, twelve hours old.

In memory of
Ensn Abijah Beardslee, who departed this Life Novr 2d, 1789, in the 40th Year of his Age.

In memory of
Drusilla, widow of Abijah Beardsley, who died April 1, 1839, in her 87 year.

In memory of
Sarah Beardsley, who died Aug. 1, 1850, in her 64 year.

Blessed are the dead
who die in the Lord.

Our Parents
Anson Beardsley, Died May 19, 1866, Æ. 83.

Nancy Treadwell, his wife, died June 12, 1866, Æ. 77.

Only resting till the morning.

Thaddeus Benedict, Esqr., departed this life Octo 6th, 1799, in the 51st year of his age.

Thaddeus Benedict, youngest son of Thaddeus & Deborah Benedict, who died 27th March, 1800, Æt. 8 years, 4 months & 4 days.

Gentle Reader what is this life?
Tis nothing. Tis everything.

Here lies the Body of
Mrs. Hannah, the wife of Mr. William Bennitt, who died Novr ye 28, 1743, in ye 31st year of her age.

In memory of
Huldah Bennett, who died Oct. 2, 1839, aged 56 yrs.

---

[17] See page 541 of this book.

Here lyes yᵉ Body of
Sarah Bennit, Wife to Mr. James Bennit, Decᵈ Novʳ yᵉ 28ᵗʰ, 1726, in yᵉ 73ᵈ year of her age.

Edwards Blackman, died Oct. 15, 1845, aged 58.

Julia, wife of Edwards Blackman, Died Aug. 5, 1839, Æ. 45.

Israel Blakeman, died June 5, 1853, Æ. 72.

In memory of
Polly, Wife of Israel Blakeman, who died Apr. 28, 1848, In her 68ᵗʰ year.

    Calm on the bosom of thy God,
      Sweet spirit rest thee now !
    E'en while with us thy foot steps trod
      His seal was on thy brow.

Here lyeth the Body of
James Blakeman, who departed this life in the 23 year of His Age, October 29, 1709.

In memory of
Susan, Daughter of Israel & Polly Blakeman, who died July 27, 1805, Æ. 2 yrs. & 9 mos.

In Memory of
Ebenezer Booth, who died Dec. 29, 1820, aged 47.

In memory of
Comphy, widow of Ebenezer Booth, who died March 11, 1843, aged 66 yrs.

In memory of
Elizabeth Booth, who died Dec. 29, 1820, aged 47.

Here lyes Buried the Body of
Deacon Joseph Booth, Who departed this Life May the 2ⁿᵈ, 1763, in the 75ᵗʰ year of his age.

Here lyes the Body of
Mrs. Sarah Booth, who died April —, AD. 1784, in the 76 Year of her age.

Anna, Daughter of Mr. Joseph & Betsey Booth, died March 26, 1793 or 5, Aged 7 days.

In memory of
Richard Walker Booth, son of Mr. Samuel & Mrs. Jerusha Booth, who died Decʳ 10ᵗʰ, 1789, Aged 3 years, 9 months & 14 Days.

Mary Ann, Daughter of Francis & Ruth Botsford, died Apl. 20ᵗʰ, 1800, aged 9 weeks.

Ann, wife of Hezekiah Bradley, died Dec. 26, 1822.

Erected to the memory of
Mr. Samuel Brinsmade, who was born March 19ᵗʰ, 1750, and died March 20ᵗʰ, 1808, aged 58 years and 1 day.
    But now is Christ risen from the dead and become the first fruits of them that slept.

In memory of
Sarah M., Daughter of Henry and Sarah Bristol, who died June 16, 1832, Æ. 1 year & 4 mo.
    Sleep, sweet babe, and take thy rest ;
    God called thee home, he thought it best.

Emery Brothwell, Died Sept. 4, 1859, aged 56 years.

Ruth Polina, wife of Emery Brothwell, Died March 14, 1848, in the 49ᵗʰ year of her age.

Sarah Ann, Daughter of Emery Brothwell, Died Mar. 22, 1867, Æ. 36 yrs.

Lucy M., Daughter of Emery & Polina Brothwell, died July 30, 1832, Æ. 4 yrs. & 4 mo.

This stone is erected in memory of
Betsey Brothwell, Daughter of Thomas & Hannah Brothwell, who died Sept. 13, 1810, in the 16ᵗʰ year of her age.

In memory of
Hannah Brothwell, who died Nov. 1, 1829, aged 63 years & 5 months.

Joseph Brothwell died Jan. 27, 1811, in the 84 year of his age.

Hannah, his Relict, died June 4, 1815, in the 85 year of her age.
    Why do we mourn departing friends
      Or shake at death's alarms !
    'Tis but the voice that Jesus sends
      To call them to his arms.

In memory of
Mary Brothwell, wife of Alden Brothwell, who died May 28, 1834, aged 27 years & 8 mo.

In Memory of
Mary Josephine, daughter of Alden & Mary Brothwell, who died Oct. 30, 1835, Æ. 1 yr. & 6 mo.

Harriet S., Daughter of Alden & Mary Brothwell, Died Dec. 7, 1853, Aged 21.

In memory of
Thomas Brothwell, who died April 14, 1842, in the 76ᵗʰ year of his age.

In memory of
William Brothwell, who died April 13, 1828, aged 72 years.

Mr. William Brothwell, son of Thomas & Hannah Brothwell, Died March 7, 1818, in the 26 year of his age.

Praise on tombs are titles vainly spent,
A man's good name is his best monument.

In memory of
Ebenezer Brown, who died June 14, 1863, Æ. 82 yrs.

In memory of
Sarah, wife of Ebenezer Brown, who died Sept. 28, 1853, Æ. 75.

In memory of
Mr. Aaron Burr, who died Aug.st 23d, 1814, in the 57th year of his age.

Here lyes yᵉ Body of
Amos Burr, son of Mr. John & Mrs. Katharine Burr, Died September 27th, 1743, in yᵉ 3d year of his age.

Here lyes the Body of
Mrs. Charity Burr, Wife to William Burr, Esqr., Who Departed this life, October yᵉ 2d, 1769, in yᵉ 48th year of Her Age.

In memory of
Mrs. Hepzibah Burr, Relict of Mr. Justus Burr, who died Octᵒ 24th, 1810, aged 78 years.

Here lyes Buried the Body of
Colo. John Burr, Who Departed this Life June 13th, *Anno Domni,* 1750, in yᵉ 79th Year of His Age.

Here lyes Buried yᵉ Body of
Mrs. Deborah Burr, Wife of Major John Burr, Who decd Decembr 4th, 1726, in yᵉ 52d year of Her Age.

Here lyes Buried yᵉ Body of
Deborah Burr, Daughter of Major John & Mrs. Deborah Burr, Who Decd November yᵉ 28th, 1726, in yᵉ 22d Year of Her Age.

Here lyes Buried the Body of
Capt. John Burr, Who Departed this Life Septr 13, O. S. A. D. 1752, in yᵉ 55th Year of His Age.

Here lyes Buried the Body of
Mrs. Catharine Burr, Widow of Capt. John Burr, Who Departed this Life Sept. yᵉ 25th, A. D. 1753, in yᵉ 53d year of Her Age.

Here lyes Buried the Body of
John Burr, Esq., Who departed this Life July 28th, 1771, in yᵉ 44th year of his Age.*

---

* He was killed by lightning, while attending worship in the meeting-house.

Here lyes Buried the Body of
Mr. Justus Burr, Who died suddenly July the 13th, 1766, in ye 32d Year of His Age.

In memory of
Ozias Burr, who died Sept. 5, 1836, in the 98 year of his age.

In memory of
Sarah, Wife of Ozias Burr, who died Sept. 2, 1820, in her 82 year.

In memory of
Charity, daur of Ozias & Sarah Burr who died Aug. 19, 1794, in her 27 year.

In memory of
Rebecca, dauir of Ozias & Sarah Burr who died Aug. 23, 1794, in her 29 year.

In memory of
Philo, Son of Ozias & Sarah Burr, who died Sept. 12, 1794, in his 13 year.

To the Memory of
Mrs. Susanna Burr, Wife of Capt. Gershom Burr, and daughter of Mr. Daniel and Mrs. Margaret Young, who departed this life Feb. 12th, 1797, in the 24th year of her age.

Also of
Susanna Burr, Junr, only Daughter of Capt. Gershom and Mrs. Susanna Burr, who died Febr 4th, 1797, aged 4 years.

They are not dead but gone before,
Why do we mourn departed friends?
Or shake at death's alarms,
'Tis but the voice that Jesus sends
To call them to his arms.

William Burr, Son of Mr. William & Mrs. Mary Burr, Died June 20th, A. D. 1739, In his 13th month.

Here lyes Buried yᵉ Body of
Mrs. Mary Burr, Wife of William Burr, M.A., Who died March 19th, *Anno Domni,* 174⅓, in yᵉ 33d year of Her Age.

Here lyes Buried the Body of
William Burr, Esq., Who departed this Life May the 5th, 1769, in yᵉ 58 year of His Age.

In memory of
Mr. Charles Burritt, Who died Novr 12th, 1801, in the 80th year of his age.

In memory of
Mrs. Lucy Burritt, Wife of Mr. Charles Burritt, who departed this life, June 26, 1789, In the 61st year of his age.

This monument is erected to perpetuate the memory of
Mrs. Sarah Burritt, Wife of Mr.
Elijah Burritt, who died Jan. 12th,
1805, in the 63d year of her age.

In memory of
Isaac Burritt, son of Mr. Elihu &
Mrs. Eunice Burritt, who died March
16, 1766, in ye 4th year of his age.

Cornelia, Daughter of Mr. Isaac and
Mrs. Rebecca Burroughs, died Oct.
8th, 1805, aged 5 years & 28 days.

In memory of
Mr. Edward Burroughs, who de-
parted this 'Life Sept. the 14th, 1776,
in the 42d year of his age.
Glory with all her lamps shall burn,
And watch the Warrior's sleeping Clay
Rest his dear sword beneath his head,
Round him his faithful Arms shall stand
The Guards and Honors of our Land.

Mrs. Grizzel Burroughs, Widow
of the late Mr. Edward Burroughs,
died Novr 19th, 1812, aged 78 years.
Rejoicing in hope, patient in tribulation, continuing instant in Prayer.

Stephen Burroughs, Esq. A man
distinguished by his industry & his
talents & acquirements, self-taught,
and original, he explored the vast
field of Mathematical & Astronomical
Science beyond all the efforts of a
Cassini or a Newton, & made discoveries of the most useful & astonishing
nature. But in consequence of blind-
ness his discoveries are lost to the
world. He died Aug. 2, 1817, aged 88.
This monument is erected by Pixley Judson.

In memory of
Mrs. Huldah Burroughs, Wife
of Stephen Burroughs, Esqr., and
Daughter of Mr. Peter and Mrs. Mary
Pixlee, who departed this life July 9th,
1803, in the 66th year of her age.

Here lies Interred the Body of
Mrs. Ruth Burton, ye wife of Mr.
Solomon Burton, who Decd Nov. ye
9, 1748, in ye 30th year of her age.

Abby Jane, Daughter of George &
Sarah Butler, Died Nov. 1st, 1873, Æ.
21.

Sarah, Daughter of George & Sarah
Butler, Died May 1st, 1882, Æ. 21.

Wm. H. Butler, Died Dec. 29, 1879,
aged 36 years.
Dear father we miss you,
Gone but not forgotten.

In Memory of
Daniel Porter Cable, Son of Mr.
Samuel & Mrs. Mary Cable, Who
died April 20, 1765, in ye 4th year of
his Age.

In memory of
Mrs. Mary, Wife of Mr. Samuel
Cable, who departed this life Decr 7th,
1793, Aged 54 years.

In Memory of
Mrs. Rebekah Cable, Relict of Mr.
Andrew Cable, who died Feby 23d,
1799, aged 80 years & 9 days.

In Memory of
Mr. Wheeler Cable, who departed
this life June 3d, 1782, in the 24th year
of his age.
I pass the gloomy vale of death,
From all danger free,
And trust to live with Christ
To all eternity.

*Ye Reverend Mr. Charles
Chauncey,* Minister of ye Gospel
at Stratfield, aged 48 years. Died
December — 1714.

Here lies the Body of
Abiah Chauncey, Daughtr to Mr.
Robert & Mrs. Hannah Chauncey,
who decd Novr ye 10, 1748, in ye 19th
year of her age.

To the Memory of
Frances Maria Clarke, daughter
of Mr. Ransom Clark and Mrs. Mary
Anna Clark, his wife, deceased August 2d, 1792, aged 2 years & 67 days.

In Memory of an
Infant son of Mr. Ransom Clark &
Mrs. Mary Anna, his Wife, departed
this life, 16th Febr 1792, aged 3 days.

Eusebia Clark, Daughter of Mr.
Daniel & Mrs. Caty Clark, died Sept.
14th, 1812, aged 1 year & 9 months.

Patience Maria, Daughter of Eleazer & Patience Edgerton, Feby 15th,
1811, Aged 13 days.

Mary Elizabeth, Daughter of Eleazer & Patience Edgerton, died Decr
30th, 1821, Aged 7 months & 6 days.
Sleep on sweet babe and take thy rest,
God called thee home, he see 'twas best.

Here lyes Interr'd ye Body of ye
Revd. Mr. Samuel Cooke, Late
Faithfull minister of Stratfield, Who
died Decr 2d, 1747, Aged 63 Years.

Here lyes Buried ye Body of
Mrs. Anne Cooke, Wife to ye Revd
Mr. Samuel Cooke, Who Died Aug-
ust 11th, 1721, in ye 34th Year of Her
Age.

Here
Lyes Interr'd
ye Body of ye Rev.D
MR SAMUEL COOKE
Late Faithfull
Minifter of Stratfield
who died Dec.r 2.d
1747 Aged 63
Years.

In memory of
Mary Dewhirst, who died June, 5, 1843, aged 47 Years.

John Edwards—See next page.

Here lyes Buried the Body of
Mrs. Mary Edwards, Relict of Mr. John Edwards, who Died March 6, 1749, in ye 82nd year of her age.

Eunice, Daughter of Joseph and Prudence (Wakelee) Edwards, died 1731, aged 1 month.

Within the Compass of this narrow grave lies the remains of
Mercy, Daughter of Nathaniel & Hannah Ells, who died Nov. 6th, 1798. Aged 4 months.
Peace to thy ashes thou lovely babe.

In memory of
Lt. Benjamin Fayerweather, who departed this Life, June 20th, 1791, In the 74th year of his age.

Joseph, Son of Mr. James & Mrs. Marcy Fayerweather, was born Jan'y 13th and died Augst 13th, 1798.

Maria, Daughter of Mr. James & Mrs. Marcy Fayerweather, died Septr 7th, 1805, Aged 16 months.

B. F. [In line with the Burrs.]

Here lyes the Body of
Mr. Benjamin Fayreweather, Decd —— 6th, 1725, —— Year of Age.

Here lyes Buried the Body of
Mrs. Sarah Noquier, Widow of
Mr. Benjamin Fayreweather & Mr.
Antony Noquier, who departed this
life May the 25th, A. D. 1743, in y⁰ 67
year of Her Age.

In Memory of
Ann, Wife of John Fayerweather, who
was Born April 27, 1712, at 5 in the
morning & Died Sept. 24, 1773.

Walter Fayreweather, Aged 6
Years, Died Dec. 26, 1717.

S. W., Decemb' 18, 1707. [In the
Fayerweather line.]

D.D., 1688. [In the Fayerweather line.]

In memory of
Gilbert Fowler, who died Mar. 5,
1848, aged 52 years, 6 ms. & 10 ds.

In Memory of
Anna, wife of Gilbert Fowler, who
died April 12, 1844, aged 44 years, 2
ms. & 10 ds.

In memory of
Benoni French, who died Dec. 20,
1823, aged 85 years.

In memory of
Mihitable, wife of Benoni French,
who died August 12, 1814, Æ. 71.

In memory of
Drucilla, wife of Capt. Joseph B.
French, who died June 25, 1830, in
her 42 year.

Drusilla Wheeler French, daughter of Mr. Joseph B. & Mrs. Drusilla
French, died Aug' 29th, 1810, aged 10
months.

In Memory of
Gamaliel French, Jun., who died
June 28, 1828, aged 72 Years.

In Memory of
Susannah, wife of Gamaliel French,
who died March 18, 1835, aged 74
years.

Here lyes Buried y⁰ Body of
Mrs. Hannah French, Wife to
Gamaliel French, Who Departed this
life October the 10th, 1745, Aged 33
years.

Here lyes Buried y⁰ Body of
Mrs. Sarah French, Wife to Mr.
Gamaliel French, Who Departed this
life May y⁰ 27th, 1758, in y⁰ 32ᵈ year
of Her Age.

In Memory of
James R. French, who died Jan.
14, 1835, in the 83 year of his age.

In Memory of

Anna, wife of James R. French, Died March 18, 1841, Æ. 70 years.

Julia Ann, daughter of James R. & Ann French, died April 20th, 1825, in her 17 year.

In bloom of life death laid me down
Till the last joyful trump shall sound,
Then burst the chains with sweet surprise
And in my Saviour's image rise.

In Memory of

Mrs. Mary French, Wife of Mr. James French, who died Febr 10th, 1803, aged 45 years & 10 months.

Here lyes ye Body of

Sergt. Samuel French, aged 65 years. Decesd Decr ye 20, 1732.

In memory of

Mabe, Relict of Samuel French, who died May 2, 1837, Aged 76 years.

Salmon Patchen, hur first husband, died April 19, 1807, aged 40 yrs.

In memory of

Daniel Glover, who died Nov. 8, 1830, Aged 87 yrs. 8 mo. & 6 days.

In memory of

Sally Glover, who departed this life Oct. 8, A. D. 1804, aged 57 years & 6 months.

George Boughton Gouge, Son of Mr. Thomas & Mrs. Ruth Gouge, decd Febry 21st, 1801, aged 5 years & 11 months.

In memory of

Esther Gregory, Wife of Mr. Enoch Gregory, Who departed this life July 16th, 1790, in the 83d year of her age.

Lilly Maria, Daughter of Mr. James & Mrs. Philena Gregory, died Jany 30th, 1792, aged 1 year & 14 days.

Here lveth ye Body of

Mary Gregory, an infant whose birth enriched her parents on March ye 8th, 1725, & she died in ye 14th month of her age April ye 17, 1726.

In memory of

Ruth Gregory, late amiable Consort of Ens. Seth Gregory, who died Octr 11, A.D. 1772, aged 36 years & 6 months wanting 1 D.

How loved, how valued once
avails thee not,
To whom related
or by whom forgot
A heap of dust alone
remains of thee.

In memory of

Samuel Gregory, son of Mr. Seth & Mrs. Ruth Gregory, who died Decembr 1st, 1766, in ye 6th year of his age.

Here lyes Buried ye Body of

Ensign Samuel Gregory, Who Departed this Life Decemb. ye 11th, *Anno Domini* 1743, in ye 66th Year of His Age.

In memory of

Mr. Thaddeus Gregory, who died Dec. 30th, 1777, in the 77th year of His Age.

Here lyes ye Body of

Mr. Selah Gregory, son of Mr. Thaddeus & Mrs. Rebeckah Gregory, who Departed this life Sept. ye 15th, 1758, in ye 26th Year of His Age.

In memory of

Miss Huldah Gregory, Daughter of Mr. Thaddeus Gregory Junr and Mrs. Huldah his Wife, Who was born 4 months after the Death of her Father, and died July 24th, 1798, in the 21st year of her age.

Here lyes ye Body of

Benjamin Hall, son of Mr. Francis & Mrs. Margaret Hall, who Died Aug. 25th, 1738, in ye 21st year of his age.

Here lyes the Body of

David Hall, aged 10 years & 7 mo. Decd February ye 15th, 1725/6.

Ephraim Hall, son of Mr. Elnathan & Mrs. Hannah Hall, Died April 22d, 1739, aged 1 year & 3 Days.

I. H., 1719.

Ephraim Hall, son of Mr. Elnathan & Mrs. Hannah Hall, Died July 2d, 1740, Aged 14 Days.

Here lyes Buried ye Body of

Mr. Francis Hall, Junr., Who Died February 26th, *Anno Domni* 1734/5, in ye 30th year of his age.

Here lyes Buried ye Body of

Mrs. Hannah Hall, Wife to Mr. Elnathan Hall, who Departed this life April 9th, *Anno Domni* 1741, in ye 26th year of her age.

In memory of

Mrs. Huldah Hall, Dau. of Mr. Richard & Mrs. Hannah Hall, who Departed this life Aug. 17th, 1773, in the 20th year of her age.

In memory of

James Seley Hall, son of Mr. James & Mrs. Abigail Hall, Who died April ye 29th, 1770, in ye 2d year of His Age.

Here lies Interrd the Body of

Mr. John Hall, who decd April ye 17, 1749, in the 71st year of his Age.

Here lyes y⁰ Body of
Garsham, son of John & Abigail
Hall, Dec⁴ Nov' y⁰ 16ᵗʰ, 1746, in y⁰
26 year of his Age.

Here lyes y⁰ Body of
Mrs. Sarah Hall, Wife to Mr. John
Hall, who died April 6, *Anno Dom⁻¹*
1739, Aged 26 years.

Here lyes the Body of
Martha Hall, Dec⁴ Nov' y⁰ 13ᵗʰ,
1747, in y⁰ 31ˢᵗ year of her Age.

In memory of
Richard Hall, who died Sept. 23,
1826, aged 47 years.

In memory of
Sally, wife of Richard Hall, who died
March 12, 1840, aged 61 years.

Orrin M., son of Richard & Sally
Hall, died Jan. 4, 1820, aged 4 years
& 10 months.

Delia F. Hall, daughter of Richard
& Sally Hall, died Aug. 16, 1826,
aged 18 years.

This lovely youth so young & fair,
Called hence by early doom,
Just come to show how bright a flower
In paradise could bloom.

Here lyes y⁰ Body of
Daniel Harmon, son of Deacon
John & Mrs. Mary Harmon of Suffield, who died at Stratford, June y⁰
22ⁿᵈ, 1763, in y⁰ 21ˢᵗ year of his age.

Major Aaron Hawley in his turn
received the Shaft of Death, July 21ˢᵗ,
1803, in 63ᵈ year of his age, and was
here deposited in hopes of a glorious
Resurrection.

Man needs but little, nor that little long,
How soon must he resign his very dust
Which frugal nature lent him for an hour.

Here lies the body of
Elizabeth Hawley, wife of Mr.
Aaron Hawley, Daughter of Capt.
Ezra Hawley & Mrs. Abigail Hawley, who departed this Life July the
8ᵗʰ, 1776, aged 35 years, 4 months &
6 days.

In memory of
Mrs. Sarah Hawley, wife of Mr.
Aaron Hawley and Daughter of Mr.
John Comstock, who departed this
life May 3ᵈ, A. D. 1786, aged 39
years, 6 months.

In memory of
William Hawley, Son of Mr. Aaron
& Mrs. Sarah Hawley, who dec⁴ Jan.
8, A. D. 1787, Aged 1 year, 9 Months
& 10 Days.

Here lyes Buried the Body of
Capt. Ezra Hawley, who departed
this life April the 27ᵗʰ, 1773, in y⁰ 62ᵈ
Year of His Age.

In memory of
Mrs. Abigail Hawley, Wife of
Capt. Ezra Hawley, who Departed
this Life April 18ᵗʰ, 1786, in the 71ˢᵗ
year of her Age.

Thrice happy she who walked the Christian road
And now enjoys her Saviour and her God.

Thomas Hawley, son of Mr. Ezra
& Mrs. Abigail Hawley, died Nov.'
28ᵗʰ, 1736, aged 10 months.

In memory of
Mr. Ezra Hawley, who departed
May 9ᵗʰ, 1796, in the 50ᵗʰ year of his
Age.

Here lyes y⁰ Body of
Mrs. Abigail Hawley, wife of Mr.
Ezra Hawley, who departed this life
Sept. y⁰ 2ⁿᵈ, 1772, in y⁰ 24ᵗʰ year of
her age.

Ruth Hawley, Wife of Ezra Hawley,
died Jan. 4, 1829, aged 75 years.

Eliza Hawley, Daughter of Mr.
Abijah & Mrs. Polly Hawley, died
March 28ᵗʰ, 1802, aged 14 months.

In Memory of
Ephraim Hawley, Junr., Son of
Mr. Ephraim & Mrs. Sarah Hawley,
who died April 11, 1777, aged 30
years; Also

William Hawley. This son Died
Janr'— 1783, aged 47 years.

Here lyes Buried
Mrs. Annah Halley, Wife to Mr.
Gideon Halley, Dec⁴ Nov' y⁰ 14ᵗʰ,
1727, in y⁰ 36ᵗʰ Year of her age.

Here lyes y⁰ Body of
Mr. Gideon Halley, Dec⁴ Feb'y y⁰
16ᵗʰ, 17⅒ in y⁰ 43ᵈ year of His Age.

Here lyes y⁰ Body of
Mrs. Annah Hawley, wife to Mr.
Gideon Hawley, Dec⁴ Nov. y⁰ 14,
1727, in y⁰ 36ᵗʰ year of her age.

Isaac Ebenezer, Son of Mr. Zalmon
& Mrs. Anna Hawley, died May 26ᵗʰ,
1811, aged 2 years & 5 months.

Here lyes Buried the Body of
Sergt. James Hawley, Who Departed this Life Oct'ᵇʳ 7ᵗʰ, A. D., 1746,
in y⁰ 34ᵗʰ year of his age.

Mrs. Eunice Bennitt, First Widow
of James Hawley & after, of Isaac
Bennitt, departed Sept. 6ᵗʰ, 1796, in
the 82ᵈ year of her age.

Eunice Hawley Chapman, Born in Bridgeport, Died in Brooklyn, N. Y., May 12, 1863, aged 85 yrs.
She was a light in the age in which she lived.

After three years incessant labour she obtained from the Legislature of New York, in the year 1818, the first law ever enacted in any country which gives to married women rights over their children and property. This has since been amended and adopted by most of the States of the Union.
Woman Call her Blessed.

Anna Hawley, Dau^tr of Mr. James & Mrs. Eunice Hawley, Died Sept. 26, 1736, Aged 10 months & 10 Days.

Lucy, daughter of Mr. Samuel & Mrs. Lucy Hawley, died June 7, 1797, Aged 3 months.

Elizabeth, daughter of Mr. Samuel & Mrs. Lucy Hawley, Dece^d June 7th, 1792, Aged 7 months.

In Memory of
Mrs. Molly Hawley, Dau^tr of Mr. Samuel & Mrs. Sarah Hawley, who departed this life April 4th, 1765, Aged 17 years.

In memory of
Mrs. Sarah Hawley, Wife of Capt. David Hawley, who departed this life Feb^ry the 8th, 1781, Aged 36 Years wanting 11 Days.

Here lyes Buried the Body of
Mr. Samuel Hawley, Who Departed this Life September 11th *Anno Dom.* 1749, Aged 31 years.

Here lyes ye Body of
Deacon Thomas Hawley, Aged 44 years, Who dec^d May ye 6th, 1722.

Here lyes ye Body of
Mrs. Joanna Hawley, widow of Deacon Thomas Hawley, Who departed this life Jan. ye 28, 1761, in ye 84th year of her age.

In memory of
Mr. Thomas Hawley, who departed this Life Novr 19th, 1797, In the 59th year of his age.

In memory of
Mrs. Anna Hawley, Relict of Mr. Thomas Hawley, who died Dec. 24th, 1810, aged 67 years.

In memory of
Mr. Wolcott Hawley, who departed this Life Jany 9th, 1799, In the 62^d Year of His Age.

In memory of
Mrs. Ellen Hawley, Relict of Mr. Wolcott Hawley, who died Feby 9th, 1823, aged 81 years.

Interred is the remains of
Capt. James Hayt, who died Novr 7th, 1787, aged 54 years.
He was a Seaman in every sense of the word, and as such will be remembered.

Interred is the remains of
Mrs. Sarah Hayt, Relict of Capt. James Hayt, who died May 19th, 1807, aged 73 years.
As her death is regretted may her conduct in life be remembered.

In Memory of
Jenny, the faithful servant of Capt. James and Mrs. Sarah Hayt. She died in June, 1807, a few weeks after her old mistress, regretting she could not go with her.
Born in Africa and supposed to be near 60 years old.
Worth does not depend on color.

This stone is erected in memory of
Mr. James Hayt, who departed this life May 5, 1804, aged 48 years.

Mercy Nichols Hayt, Born Jan. 23^d, 1759. Died Sept. 8, 1839.

Mary Elizabeth Hayt, Born Aug. 11, 1781.

James Nichols Hayt, Born Mar. 16, 1784. Died at sea.

Munson Hayt, Born Aug. 12, 1786.

Philip Hayt, Born Sept. 3, 1789, Died Sept. 25, 1840.

James Hayt, Born Sept. 3, 1789, Died Oct. 6, 1789.

Frances Augusta Hayt, Born Aug. 19, 1800, Died Oct. 24, 1819.

Interred are the remains of
Josiah Sturgis Hayt, son of George & Deborah Hayt, Born 4th of April, 1800, Died 4th Jan. 1802.

In Memory of
George Holberton, son of Mr. Thomas & Mrs. Ruth Holberton, who died Oct. ye 5th, 1777, aged 20 months.

Eunice Holberton, Died Sept. 20, 1848, Æ. 66 [or 68] years.

John Hopkins, Died June 28, 1808, Aged 51.

Mehetable, wife of John Hopkins, Died Sept. 16, 1824, In her 51 year.

In memory of
Susan, wife of James Hopkins, who died Jan. 6, 1837, Æ. 36 yrs.
Modesty and meekness adorned her life, Faith and hope supported her in death.

In memory of
Catharine Hopkins, who died Sept. 20, 1825, in her 22 year.
The last enemy that shall be destroyed is death.

In memory of
Aaron Hubbell, who died Oct. 13, 1848, Æ. 87 years.

In memory of
Sarah, Wife of Aaron Hubbell, died March 15, 1851, Æ. 84 years.

In memory of
Abel Hubbell, who died Jan. 6, 1832, aged 103 yrs. 6 mo. & 26 ds.

Abell Hubbell, died May 28, 1852, aged 62 years.

Ruth, wife of Abel Hubbell, died Feb. 10, 1864, Æ. 69 yrs. 10 mo. & 4 ds.

This Stone is erected in memory of
Capt. Amos Hubbell, who died July 2d, 1801, aged 55 years. Which also records the death of his two sons,

Amos and **Wilson ;** The former of whom died at the Havannah on the 15th day of October, 1798, by a malignant fever, aged 18 years. And the latter was deprived of life whilst in the proper discharge of the duties of his profession by an unprincipled officer of a French Privateer, who deaf to the claims of justice and the cries of humanity, plunged the sufferer into the ocean and left him to perish in the waves, on the 5th day of April, 1799, aged 26 years.

When sweet content serenely smiles around,
Like a fair summer evening, Ah ! how soon
The charming scene is lost, the deepening shades
Prevail and night approaches, dark and sad,
Till the last beams, faint glimering die away.

In memory of
Mrs. Catharine Hubbell, Wife of Mr. Amos Hubbell, who departed this life January 4th, 1776, eight days after the birth of her third child, in the 23d year of her age.
In youthful bloom death laid me down
Here to await the Trumpet's sound.
When God commands then Will I rise
And meet my Saviour in the skies.

In memory of
Amos Hubbell, son of Mr. Amos & Mrs. Catharine Hubbell, Who died Sept. 10th, 1777, in ye 7th year of his Age.

In memory of
Eleanor Hubbell, Daughter of Mr. Amos & Mrs. Eleanor Hubbell, who departed this life March 22d, 1786, Aged 1 year 9 months and 10 days.

In Memory of
Mr. Benjamin Hubbell, who departed this life Febry 24th, 1793, in the 76th year of his age.

In memory of
Mrs. Mary Hubbell, Relict of Mr. Benjamin Hubbell, who died Augst 29th, 1813, aged 92 years & 1 month.

In Memory of
Mr. John Hubbell, Son of Mr. Benjamin and Mrs. Mary Hubbell, who died Febry 7th, 1806, aged 63 years, 3 months & 7 days.

In memory of
Elizabeth, wife of Mr. John Hubbell, Died March 13, 1840, In the 90th year of her age.

Here lyes the Body of
Mrs. Anne Hubbell, only daughter of Mr. Benjamin & Mrs. Mary Hubbell, who departed this life May ye 9th, 1770, in ye 23d year of her age.

Catharine Maria, Daughter of Capt. Ezra & Mrs. Mary Alice Hubbell, died Augt 8th, 1801, aged 2 years wanting 8 days.

Here lyes ye Body of
Capt. Daniel Hubbell, Died December ye 11th, 1735, in ye 45th year of his Age.

In memory of
Eunice Hubbell, relict of Mr. Abraham Hubbell, who departed this life Sept. 4, 1794, in the 38th year of her age.

In memory of
Mr. Daniel Hubbell, who died March 4th, 1801, in the 77th year of his age.

In memory of
Mrs. Sarah Hubbell, Relict of Mr. Daniel Hubbell, who died April 11, 1801, in the 73d year of her age.

In memory of
Miss Esther Hubbell, daughter of Mr. Daniel & Mrs. Sarah Hubbell, who died Novr 7th, 1802, in the 36th year of her age.

In memory of
Miss Rebeckah Hubbell, Daughter of Mr. Daniel & Mrs. Sarah Hubbell, who died May 8, 1796, in the 39th year of her age.

In memory of
Daniel Hubbell, Junr., son of Mr. Daniel & Mrs. Sarah Hubbell, who departed this life Jan. 12th, 1778, In the 28th Year of his age.

You mourners all that see me die
Must quickly follow me.
Come and see me where I lie
A mouldering in the earth.

In memory of
Sarah Hubbell, who died Oct. 9, 1842, aged 81 yrs.

In memory of
Hezekiah Hubbell, Esqr., Son of Richard & Penelope Hubbell, Who Dep.^{td} this life July 19th, 1784, Aged 56 years 4 months & 12 days.

Here lies interred the remains of
Capt. Isaac Hubbell, who departed this life May the 22^d, 1787, in the 40 year of His Age.

Here lies interred the remains of
Mrs. Francis Hubbell, wife of Capt. Isaac Hubbell, Who departed this Life May the 21st, 1786, in the 34th year of her Age.

In memory of
James Hubbell, who died Sept. 15, 1827, aged 70 years.

In memory of
Mr. John Hubbell, who departed this life April 8th, 1774, In the 85th Year of his Age.

In memory of
Josiah Hubbull, son of Mr. Walter & Mrs. Ruth Hubbell, Who died Octr 14, 1765, Aged 15 months.

In memory of
David Hubbell, son of Mr. Walter & Mrs. Ruth Hubbell, who died Octr ye 1st, 1777, Aged 16 months and 17 Days.

In memory of
Onessimus Hubbell, who died Sept. 14th, 1824, in the 69th year of his age.

Here lyes Buried the Body of
Onesimus Hubbell, son of Mr. Joseph & Mrs. Keziah Hubbell, who departed this life Dec.^{br} 3^d, 1754, in ye 23^d year of his age.

In memory of
Deac.ⁿ Richard Hubbell, who departed this Life June 27th, 1787, In the 93^d Year of his Age.
Blessed are the dead which die in the Lord.

In memory of
Mrs. Penelope Hubbell, Relict to Deac.ⁿ Richard Hubbell, who departed this Life Aug.st 29th, 1791, In the 87th year of her Age.
For they rest from their labors and their works do follow them.

In memory of
Mr. Benjamin Hubbell, Eldest Son of Deac.ⁿ Richard Hubbell, who departed this Life Septr 17th, AD 1788, in the 62^d Year of his age.
Blessed are the dead who die in the Lord.

In memory of
Richard Hubbell, who died at the city of N. Y., July 16, 1829, in his 87 year.

In memory of
Roxana, wife of Richard Hubbell, who died Dec. 28, 1805, in her 60 year.

In memory of
Charles Hubbell, son of Mr. Richard & Mrs. Roxana Hubbell, who departed this Life June 15th, 1786, Aged 1 Year & 7 Days.

In memory of
Penelope, Daughter of Richard & Roxana Hubbell, who died Feb. 21, 1864, Æ. 92 years.

Here lies ye Body of
Phylo Hubbill, Son of Mr. Richard Hubbill, Jun. & Mrs. Roxane his wife who departed this Life Feb.^r the 13, 1774, Aged 4 years.
Happy the child who privileged by Fate
to Shorten labour & Lighter wait,
Received but yesterday the gift of breath
ordered to morrow to return to death.

In memory of
Sarah, Wife of Jabez Hubbell, died Jany ye 12th, 1754, in ye 22 year of her age.

In memory of
Mr. Stephen Hubbell, who departed this life April 29th, 1792, In the 98th year of his age.

In memory of
Mrs. Abigail, Wife of Mr. Stephen Hubbell, Who died Aug.st 1st, 1777, In the 84 year of her age.

Here lyes Buried ye Body of
Rebeckah Hubbell, Daughter of Mr. Stephen & Mrs. Rebeckah Hubbell, Who departed this life, Novr ye 9, 1754, ye 19th year of her age.

In memory of
Thaddeus Hubbell, who died Nov. 30, 1849, Æ. 85 yrs.

In memory of
Eunice Hubbell, wife of Thaddeus Hubbell, who died May 1, 1838, aged 68 yrs.

Bille Jackson, Son of Mr. Isaac & Mrs. Rachel Jackson, Died Aug.st 2^d, 1739, Aged 5 days.

Henry Jackson, who died September 15, 1717, aged 38 years.

James, Son of Mr. Samuel & Mrs. Peninah Jackson, Departed this life March y.^e 19th, 1757, In y.^e 6th Year of his Age.

Here lies the Body of
Joseph Jackson, Died the 29 of
Septemb[r], 1714.

M. J., Nov. 13, 1712. [Probably a
Jackson.]

R. J. M[y] 14, 1712. [Probably a
Jackson.]

R. J. D. S.

E. P. 1731.

In memory of
Eliphalet Jennings, who died
Aug. 22, 1839, aged 85 yrs.

In memory of
Sarah Ross, wife of Eliphalet Jennings, who died June 6, 1839, aged 83
years.

James Jennings, Died Feb. 4,
1869, Aged 76.

Mary E., daughter of Thomas &
Mary E. Jenkins, died Oct. 19, 1842,
Æ. 4 ys.

Ira Jones, died May 25th, 1836, Aged
65 years.

Charity, Wife of Ira Jones, died May
14, 1845, Aged 73 years.

Mary B., Daughter of Christopher
& Margaret Keiser, died Mar. 6, 1862,
Æ. 3 yrs. 10 mos. & 10 ds.

In memory of
Mr. Patrick Keeler, who died Oct[o]
15th, 1829, in the 76th year of his age.

In memory of
Mrs. Anna Keeler, Wife of Mr.
Patrick Keeler, who died Dec[r] 21st,
1815, in the 63[d] year of her age.

Sarah, Wife of Patrick Keeler, Died
Aug. 20, 1851, Æ. 80.

J. & W. K.

In memory of
Mr. Ezra Kirtland, who died Aug.
22[d], 1800, in the 70 year of his age.

In Memory of
Mrs. Olive Kirtland, Relict of Mr.
Ezra Kirtland, who died Sept. 23[d],
1803, in the 69th year of her age.

In Memory of
Olive Kirtland, Daughter of Ezra
Kirtland, Jun., who died July 15,
1775, in the 3[d] year of her Age.

In memory of
Mr. Ezra Kirtland, Jr., who died
Dec. 27th, 1799, in the 47th year of his
age.

In memory of
Olive Kirtland, Daughter of Mr.
Ezra & Mrs. Sarah Kirtland, who
died Aug. 14th, 1790, Aged 14 years
& 2 months.

In memory of
Mr. Zebulon Kirtland, who died
Jan[y] 2[d], 1803, in the 48th year of his
age.

In memory of
Elizabeth, widow of Zebulon Kirtland, who died Jan. 5, 1842, aged 90
years.

In memory of
Mrs. Freelove Knapp, Wife of
Mr. Joseph Knapp & Dau[tr] of Mr.
Ebenezer & Mrs. Patience Plumb,
who died Nov[r] 24th, 1771, in y[e] 31st
year of her age.

In memory of
Joseph Knapp, Jun., Son of Mr.
Joseph & Mrs. Freelove Knapp, died
Augst the 20th, 1767, Aged 2 years.

In memory of
Mr. John Knapp, who died August 3d, 1795, in the 82 year of his age.

In memory of
Mrs. Hannah Knapp, Wife of
Mr. John Knapp, who died Jany. 28th,
1796, in the 76th year of her age.

In memory of
Robert Knapp, who died April 11,
1834, aged 52 years & 10 months.

Mother
Sally, wife of Robert Knapp, Died
Aug. 15, 1861, Aged 76 yrs. 1 mo. &
8 Ds.

To the memory of
Mahala Willson Knapp, Daughter of Mr. Robert & Mrs. Sally Knapp
(a very promising child) born July
10th, 1804, and died July 18th, 1807,
aged 3 years & 8 days.

In memory of
Mrs. Anna Knowles, first the wife
of Mr. Joseph Sturges, late of Stamford, decd. and last the wife of Mr.
William Knowles, late of New Milford, decd. She died July 26th, 1801,
in the 80th year of Her Age.

Mrs. Abigail Lacey.

Hannah Summers, Wife of Edward Lacey, died Oct. 14, 1755, aged
about 43 years.

In memory of
Mr. Benjamin Lacey, who departed this life Sept. 13th, AD 1784,
aged 45 years on the same day.

In memory of
Mrs. Margaret Lacy, Wife of ye
late Mr. Benjamin Lacey, who departed this life, Sept. 1. A. D., 1792,
in the 52d year of her age.

Daniel Lacey, died Dec. 17, 1828,
in his 86 year.

Tabitha Lacey, wife of Daniel Lacey, died Aug. 9, 1814, in the 64 year
of her age.

John Lacey, died June 25, 1856, Æ.
79 yrs. & 9 mo.

In memory of
Eunice, wife of John Lacey, who died
Feb. 17, 1840, aged 56 years.

In memory of
Mr. John Lacey, who departed
this Life Feby 10th, 1793, In the 84th
year of his age.

In memory of
Mrs. Mary Lacey, Relict of Mr.
John Lacey, who died April 1, 1810,
in the 91st year of her age.

Josiah Lacey, Esq., departed this
life Oct. 28th, 1812, in the 67th Year
of his age.
He was a Captain in the Revolutionary
Army and a leading citizen.

In memory of
Mrs. Judith Lacey, Wife of Capt.
Josiah Lacey, who departed this life
June ye 3d, 1780, aged 31 years & 5
months wanting 3 days.

In memory of
Mrs. Ruth Lacey, Wife to Capt.
Josiah Lacey, who departed this life
April 18th, 1788, aged 27 years & 8
months wanting 1 Day.

In memory of
Mrs. Molly Lacey, Wife of Capt.
Josiah Lacey, who departed this Life
Jany 30th, 1793, aged 32 years 8
months & 12 days.

In memory of
Mrs. Anna Lacey, Wife of Josiah
Lacey, Esqr., Who departed this life
April 7, A. D. 1812, aged 46 years 3
months and 2 days.

Nathaniel Hazard, son to Capt.
Josiah & Mrs. Molly Lacey, Departed this life May 9, 1792, aged 14
months, wanting 5 Days.

Levi L. Lacey, Died April 1, 1845,
Aged 33 yrs.

In memory of
Michael Lacey, who died Nov. 12,
1835, Æ. 51 yrs.

In memory of
Betsey, wife of Michael Lacey, who
died Dec. 14, 1823, aged 38 years.

Robert Lacey, died Nov. 23, 1832,
aged 22 years.

In memory of
Sarah Lacey, who died May 3, 1838,
aged 65 years.

In memory of
Squire Lacey, who died Dec. 27,
1819, in his 31st year.

Urban Lacey, died March 20, 1877,
Aged 72 yrs.

In memory of her that was once
Miss Ruth Winton, Born Dec. 2d,
1731; married to Mr. Joseph Brinsmaid Octr, 1748; and secondly to Dr.
Wm Little, Novr 2d, 1762. She departed this Life for Immortality Decr
2d, 1784, aged 53 Years.
Her remains are buried beneath this Stone.

In memory of
Elenor, wife of Eaden Leavens, who died June 30, 1835, Æ. 55 years.

In memory of
Mrs. Eunice, Relict of Mr. George Lyman, who died Oct. 10, 1819, aged 67 years.

Here lves Buried yᵉ Body of
Mr. Mathew Mackhard, Who Died Febʳ yᵉ 9ᵗʰ, Anno Domni 1736/7, in yᵉ 28ᵗʰ Year of His Age.

Here lyes Buried yᵉ Body of
Mr. Mathew Mackhard, son of Mr. Mathew & Mrs. Sarah Mackhard, Who was drowned July yᵉ 22ᵈ, 1757, in yᵉ 21ˢᵗ Year of His Age.

Mary Mackhard, Dauᵗʳ of Mr. Mathew & Mrs. Sarah Mackhard, Died Janʸ 30ᵗʰ, 1737, Aged 2 years & 6 months.

Here lyes Buried yᵉ Body of
Mr. John Mallet, who Departed this life September 28ᵗʰ, *Anno Domⁿⁱ* 1745, in yᵉ 72ᵈ year of his age.

Here lyes the body of
Sarah Mallit, Wife of John Mallit, Died Decʳ yᵉ 5ᵗʰ, 1742, in yᵉ 26 year of her age.

Here lyes yᵉ Bodv of
Mrs. Joanna Mallit, widow to Mr. John Mallit, who departed this life Sept yᵉ 16, 1764, in yᵉ 101ˢᵗ year of her age.

Here lyes yᵉ Body of
Huldah Mallett, Dauᵗʳ of Mr. John Mallett, Junr., who died Oct. yᵉ 29, 1758, in yᵉ 2ᵈ year of her age.

Laura, Daughter of Mr. Lewis & Mrs. Anna Mallet, died April 3ᵈ, 1795, Aged 2 years 1 month & 8 days.

Henry Manning, Died Jan. 5, 1852, Æ. 48 years.

In memory of
Mr. David Meaker, who died Nov. 24ᵗʰ, 1828, in the 73ᵈ year of his age.

In memory of
Esther Meaker, Wife of Mr. David Meaker, who died May 26ᵗʰ, 1812, in the 48ᵗʰ year of her age.

Mrs. Polly Meeker, Died Aug. 29, 1817, Æ. 26 yrs.

Nathan S. Meeker, Died of Yellow Fever at Staten Island, N. Y., Sept. 27, 1821, Æ. 31 yrs.

Ann R. Middlebrook, Died Dec. 1, 1850, Æ. 24 yrs.

In memory of
Anne, wife of Anson Morehouse, who died May 11, 1823, aged 37 years.

In memory of
Lorintha, dauᵗʳ of Anson & Anne Morehouse, who died Sept. 10, 1841, Aged 30 years.

In memory of
Mrs. Eunice Morehouse, Wife of Mr. Lyman Morehouse, Who died March 14ᵗʰ, 1800, In the 27ᵗʰ year of her age.

In memory of
Sarah Morehouse, wife of Isaac Morehouse, who died Aug. 22, 1837, aged 86.

In memory of
Abigail, wife of Samuel Morehouse, who died Aug. 29, 1826, aged 44 years.

Here lyes Buried the Body of
Mrs. Sarah Morris, wife to Mr. Daniel Morris, who departed this life April the 16, 1761, in yᵉ 48ᵗʰ year of her age.

Here lyes the Body of
Huldah Nicholls, wife to Mr. John Nicholls, who died April 16, 1759, in yᵉ 49ᵗʰ year of her age.

In memorv of
Charles S., who died March 23, 1835, aged 3 yrs. & 6 mo.

Also of
John A., who died Nov. 15, 1836, aged 14 mo.
Sons of John W. & Susan Nichols.

In memory of
Mr. John Nichols, who died Nov. 21ˢᵗ, 1801, in the 57ᵗʰ year of his age.

In memory of
Phebe, relict of Mr. John Nichols, who died March 3, 1835, Æ. 82 years.

In Memory of
Mrs. Mehetable Nichols, Wife of Mr. John Nichols, who departed this life, April 9ᵗʰ, 1785, in yᵉ 32ᵈ year of her age.

[A TABLET.]
Sacred to the Memory of
Philip Nichols, Esq., who departed this Life May 13ᵗʰ, 1807, in the 82ᵈ year of his age.

Tears in regret in sympathy we give,
That such superior excellence should die;
But dear to memory wilt thou ever live,
Blest shade whose meed is immortality.

Sacred to the memory of
PHILIP NICHOLS Esq.
who departed this Life
May 13th. 1807.
in the 82d year of his age.

Tears of regret in sympathy we give,
That such superior excellence should die,
But dear to memory will thou ever live,
Blest shade whose meed is immortality.

Sacred to the memory of
Mrs MARY NICHOLS late Consort
of PHILIP NICHOLS Esq.
who departed this life
May 13th 1811.
In the 78th year of her age.

The soul of origin divine
God's glorious image free'd from day
In heaven's eternal sphere shall shine
A star of day.

Sacred to the memory of
Mrs. Mary Nichols, late Consort
of Philip Nichols, Esq., who departed
this life, May 13th, 1811, in the 78th
year of her age.
  The soul of origin divine,
  God's glorious image freed from clay,
  In Heaven's eternal sphere shall shine,
        A star of day.

Here lyes Buried y[e] Body of
Mrs. Rebeckah Nickols, wife to
Mr. John Nickols, who departed this
life, Sept. 12th, 1749, in y[e] 36th year of
her age.

Here lyes y[e] Body of
Huldah Nichols, Dau[tr] of Mr. John
& Mrs. Rebeckah Nichols, who died
Sept. 4th, 1753, in y[e] 13th year of her
age.

Here lyes ye Body of
Sarah Nichols, Dau[tr] of Elijah &
Mrs. Huldah Nichols, who departed
this life June ye 4th, 1753, in ye 19th
year of her Age.

William Nichols, Died July 21,
1837, Aged 82 yrs.

Philip E., his son, Died Sept. 26,
1855, Aged 48 years.

Hannah Nichols, Died Oct. 14,
1855, Æ. 69.

Here lyes the Body of
Mrs. Abigail Odell, Wife to William Odell, who died Jan.——— 40th
year of her age.*

Here lyes y[e] Body of
Mrs. Deborah Odell, wife of Lieut.
Hezekiah Odell, who departed this
life June 27, 1756, in y[e] 55th year of
her age.

Here lyes y[e] Body of
Bulah Odell, Dau[tr] of Lieut. Hezekiah & Mrs. Deborah Odell, who died
June 22[d], 1756, in y[e] 27th year of her
age.

Here lyes buried y[e] Body of
Mr. John Odell, Who Departed
this life June 1st, *Anno Dom.* 1743,
Aged 77 Years.

Here lyes Buried y[e] Body of
Mrs. Sarah Odell, wife to Serg.
John Odell, who died Octob[r] 25th,
A. D. 1743, in y[e] 79th year of her age.

In memory of
Samuel Odell, Esqr., who Departed this Life June the 7th, A. D. 1775,
in the 69th year of his Age.

---

* The dates are entirely gone by the falling
off of a part of the slate stone.

In memory of
Mrs. Johannah Odell, Wife of
Mr. Samuel Odell, who departed this
Life June 11th, 1776, in the 37th year
of her age.

Justis Odell, died January y[e] 29th,
1767, Aged 3 Days & 4 hours.

Squire Odell, died January y[e] 29,
1767, Aged 3 Days & 4 months.
  The Twins of Mr. Nehemiah
Smith Odell & Mrs. Eunice his Wife.

In memory of
Miss Temperance Odell, who de-
parted this life Octob[r] 17, 1794, Aged
27 years 8 months & 3 days.
  Too early lost, just in the bloom of youth,
  Go noblest patern of exalted truth,
  Absolved from earth that peaceful shore ascend
  Where love inhabits, love that knows no end.

Here lyes y[e] Body of
Nehemiah, son of Will[m] Odell, Dec[d]
March y[e] 26, 1727, in y[e] 8th year of
his age.

Here lyes y[e] Body of
Nathaniel Odell, Son of Mr. William & Mrs. Sarah Odell, Who Died
July 15th, 1746, in y[e] 3[d] year of his
age.

Here lyes y[e] Body of
Ebenezr Odell, Son of Mr. William
Odell, Who died Octo[r] 7th, 1743, in y[e]
19th Year of his age.

In memory of
Mrs. Abigail, Wife of Joel Parish,
who died June 1st, 1777, in her 37th
year.

Abraham Parrott, died Nov. 16,
1825, Æ. 48.
  Lord we commit our souls to thee,
  Accept the sacred trust.

Lucy Wells, Wife of Abraham Parrott, Died Sept. 8, 1856, Æ. 80.
    Revive this nobler part of ours
    And watch our sleeping dust.

In memory of
Henry O. Parrott, Son of Abraham
& Lucy Parrott, who died July 8, 1826,
aged 13 yrs. 11 mos. & 16 days.

In memory of
Mary E. Parrott, daughter of
Abraham & Lucy Parrott, who died
Sept. 23, 1826, aged 15 yrs. & 11 mo.

Thomas Parrott, died Dec. 8, 1851,
Æ. 58.

Sally, Wife of Thomas Parrott, died
Aug. 17, 1839, Æ. 49.

In memory of
Isaac Patchin, who died Feb. 11,
1832, aged 85 yrs.

In memory of
Elijah Peet, who died Nov. 26, 1841, aged 81 years.

In memory of
Anna Peet, wife of Elijah Peet, who died June 1, 1843, aged 76 years.

This monument is sacred to the memory of
Mrs. Anne Pixley, Relict of Mr. William Pixley, who died Sept. 20th, 1800, in the 69th year of her age.

Here lyes Buried ye Body of
Mrs. Hannah Porter, Wife to Ensign John Porter, Who departed this life Octobr ye 28th, 1763, in ye 61st year of her age.

Nathaniel Porter, son of John & Lucy Porter, died June 21st, 1800, in the 14th year of his age.

In memory of
Mr. Samuel Porter, who departed this life Septr 13th, 1795, In the 78th year of his Age.

In memory of
Mrs. Abiah Porter, Relict of Mr. Samuel Porter, who died July 9th, 1801, In the 76th year of her age.

In memory of
Mrs. Sarah Porter, Wife of Mr. Samuel Porter, Junr, who died April 3d, 1805, In the 25th year of her age.

Depository of
Miss Betsey Raymond, who, in the bloom of life was snatched from her friends, and ye companions of her youth, Jany 14th, A. D. 1792, In the 17th year of her age.

Mrs. Ruth Risley, Relict of Mr. Timothy Risley, of Egg Harbour, decd, and Daughter of Mr. David Wells of this Town, Decd, died Janr 2d, 1794, aged 36 years.

Here lies entombed the Remains of
The Reverend Robert Ross, Sarah Ross, his Wife, and James Merrick Ross, their Son.

The Reverend Robert Ross, A.M., a native of Ireland; in his infancy brought into this Country. Was sometime a Tutor at the College of New Jersey, where he also received his education; Afterwards Pastor of the Presbyterian Church in this Society, over which he was ordained November 28th, 1753, and in which he labored in word and doctrine, 43 years.

A person who long sustained a high character for Christian Literature and general knowledge. In his principles, orthodox; In his preaching practical and judicious. He advocated the truths of the Gospel by doctrine and example, and was, therefore, a pious guide & Instructor.

He died Augst. 29, 1799, aged 73 years.

Mrs. Sarah Ross, died the same day with her husband, aged 52. And *James Merrick Ross,* 13 days after his parents, aged 10 years.

O thou gloomy monarch!
Are these the trophies of thy conquering arms?
Nor reverend hoary age, nor blooming youth,
Nor boasted strength escape thy fatal dart!
These seem to speak
With silent horror to my shivering heart;
Bid me survey my swift approaching doom,
And view the dark retreat which waits my coming.

This monument is erected by Eliphalet Jennings, to the memory of his Father-in-law and family, —— 1801.

Here lyes Buried
James Ross, son of Rev. Robert & Mrs. Sarah Ross, Born Sept. 12, 1758, Drowned Sept. 10, 1760.

Sacred to the memory of
Revd Stephen Royce, who departed this life Augst 3d, 1802, in the 47th year of his age.

Here in death's cold embrace this body lies,
The soul is gone to mansions in the skies;
His dust must sleep, his voice be heard no more,
Till the last trump shall sound from shore to shore,
Then burst the bands of death with sweet surprise,
And in his Saviour's glorious form arise.

Here lyes Buried the Body of
Mr. Edmund Rowland, who departed this life April the 13th, 1769, in the 41st year of his age.

In memory of
Henry Rowland, who died June 19th, 1775, aged about 84 years. Erected by Rowland B. Lacey in 1879.

Here lyes Buried ye Body of
Mrs. Tamar Rowland, wife to Mr. Henry Rowland, who died April ye 21st, A. D. 1737, in ye 42d year of her age.

Here lyes Buried the Body of
Mr. Thomas Sanford, who departed this life May ye 20, 1757, in ye 83d year of his age.

Here lyes ye Body of
Mrs. Hannah Sanford, wife to Mr. Thomas Sanford, who Departed this life May 18th, 1755, in ye 75 year of her age.

In memory of
Deacon Abel Seelye, who died May 9th, 1810, in the 85th year of his age.

Marcy, wife of Dea. Abel Seeley, died March 5, 1819, aged 98.

Hannah, Daughter of Mr. Abel & Mrs. Marcy Seely, died Novr ye 19, 1746, aged 1 year & 11 months.

This Stone was erected by Seth Seelye, Jun. in commemoration of his late wife,
Abigail Seelye, who died July 8th, 1800, in the 31st year of her age.

In memory of
Ezra Seeley, died Aug. 14, 1827, aged 61 years.

Mary, wife of Ezra Seeley, died Aug. 7, 1822, Æ. 81.

Here lyes Buried yᵉ Body of
Ensign Nathan Seelye, who departed this life April 30, 1766, in yᵉ 52ᵈ year of his age.

Here lyeth yᵉ Body of
Eunice, yᵉ wife of Nathan Seelye, who died June 6th, 1745, in yᵉ 28th year of her Age.

Jennett E., wife of George B. Seeley, died Jan. 7, 1850, Æ. 35.

Mary E., their daughter, died Dec. 22, 1847, Æ. 6 yrs. & 2 months.

In Memory of
Nathaniel Seelye, who departed this life March 27, 1786, in yᵉ 85 year of His Age.

In memory of
Mrs. Elizabeth Seelye, wife of Mr. Nathaniel Seelye, who departed this life December 9th, 1781, in yᵉ 79th year of Her Age.

In memory of
Lieut. Nathan Seelye, who departed this Life June 24th, 1787, Aged 44 Years wanting 21 days.

In memory of
Mrs. Deborah Seelye, Relict of Lieut. Nathan Seelye, who died Sept. 22ᵈ, 1811, in the 69th year of her age.

In memory of
Polly, wife of Roswell Seeley, who died Sept. 9, 1838, aged 46 years.

James H., son of Roswell & Polly Seeley, Died Nov. 23, 1848, Æ. 19.

In memory of
Ruth Seeley, wife of Joseph Seeley, who died Oct. 8, 1815, aged 29 years.

In memory of
Mrs. Betsey Seeley, wife of Mr. Joseph Seeley, who died Dec. 24, 1824, aged 40 years.

In memory of
Mary E., daughter of Joseph & Ruth Seeley, who died May 11, 1835, aged 24 years.

Here lyes the Body of
Seth Seelye, Decᵈ July yᵉ 29th, 1727, in yᵉ 18th year of His Age.

In Memory of
Deacᵒⁿ Seth Seelye, who died May 23ᵈ, 1817, in the 79 yr of his age.
Blessed are the dead who die in the Lord.

In Memory of
Mrs. Joanna Seelye, Wife of Deacᵃ Seth Seelye, Who departed this life Febʳʸ 25th, 1797, In the 62ᵈ year of her age.

In Memory of
Miss Anne Seelye, Daughter of Deacᵃ Seth & Mrs. Joanna Seelye, who died June 25th, 1815, in the 53ᵈ year of her age.

In memory of
Seth Seeley, who died Nov. 2, 1844, aged 28 yrs.
Don't mourn my wife and children so dear,
  I am not dead but sleeping here ;
My peace is made, my grave you see,
Prepare for death and follow me.
  We know that our redeemer lives,
  We trust the promises he gives.
  And part in hope to meet above
  Where all is joy and all is love.

Seth Seeley, son of Mr. Samuel O. & Mrs. Sally Seelye, died March 30th, 1814, aged 16 months & 16 days.

Abiah Sherman, Died May 28, 1717, aged 19 years.

Elnathan Sherman, aged about 8 years old, Who died April 15, 1717.

Here lyes Buried yᵉ Body of
Mr. Amos Sherman, Who Departed this life, Decemʳ 11th, 1760, in yᵉ 36th year of his age.

Sacred to the memory of
Anson Sherman, who died at Orange Springs, New Jersey, July 19, 1835, Æ. 44 yrs.

Here lyes Buried the Body of
Capt. David Sherman, who departed this life Janʳ yᵉ 1 *Anno Domni,* 1753, in yᵉ 88th year of his age.

[See opposite.]

Here lyes Buried the Body of
Mrs. Marcy Sherman, Wife to Capt. David Sherman Who Departed this life Aug. 19 A. D. 1745, in yᵉ 75th year of her age.

Here lyes Buried the Body of
Lieut. David Sherman, Who Departed this life July yᵉ 8th *Anno Domni,* 1752, in yᵉ 60 year of His Age.

Here lyes the Body of
Mrs. Dinah Sherman, Wife to Mr. David Sherman, Decᵈ April yᵉ 13th, 1732, in ye 37th Year of Her Age.

Sarah Thompson, 2ᵈ Wife of Lieut. David Sherman, ———.

Here lyes Buried the Body of **Mr. David Sherman,** Who was killed by lightning in the House of God at public worship on the 28ᵗʰ of July. 1771, in yᵉ 35ᵗʰ Year of His Age.

Here lyes yᵉ Body of **Mrs. Mary Sherman,** Wife to Mr. David Sherman and Dauᵗʳ of Mr. Stephen & Mrs. Eunice Starling, Who departed this Life May yᵉ 28ᵗʰ, 1765, in yᵉ 25ᵗʰ Year of Her Age.

This Stone is erected to the memory of **Capt. David Sherman,** who died August 22ᵈ, 1810, in the 54ᵗʰ year of his age.

Also of his son,

David Sherman, who was supposed to be lost on his passage from Washington in North Carolina to New York with his whole crew in the schooner Recovery about the 20ᵗʰ of Decemᵇʳ, 1800, in the 25ᵗʰ year of his age.

In Memory of **Mrs. Rebecca,** Wife of Capt. David Sherman, who died Mar. 4, 1825, aged 70 years.

In Memory of **Isaac Sherman,** son of Mr. David & Mrs. Rebecca Sherman, died March yᵉ 19ᵗʰ, A. D. 1784, Aged 14 months & 5 days.

In memory of **Mr. Ebenezer Sherman,** who died Sept. 28ᵗʰ, 1819, aged 66 years.

Hervey Sherman, son of Mr. Sterling & Mrs. Anna Sherman, died July 1ˢᵗ, 1805, aged 2 months & 15 days.

In memory of **Mrs. Jemima Sherman,** Relict of Mr. Nathaniel Sherman, who died Febʸ 10ᵗʰ, 1806, in the 77ᵗʰ year of her age.

Matthew Sherman, born Oct. 21, A. D., 1645, died ——— A.D., 1698.

And

Hannah Bulkley, his wife, died about 1712.

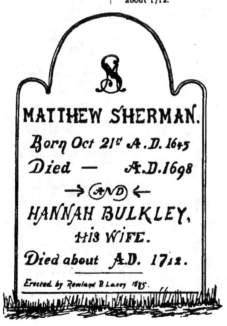

MATTHEW SHERMAN.

Born Oct 21ˢᵗ A.D. 1645

Died —   A.D. 1698

→ (AND) ←

HANNAH BULKLEY,

HIS WIFE.

Died about A.D. 1712.

Erected by Rowland B Lacey 1815.

Here lies the body of
Deac *Seth Sherman,* Who de-
parted this life, August 7th, 1807, in
the 53 year of his age.
Pause and consider where the good man lies,
Mark well his path and follow to the skies.

Here lyes Buried the Body of
Mr. Andrew Sherwood, Who departed this Life, Nov' 23d, 1767, in
the 47th Year of His Age.

In Memory of
Anna W., daughter of Charles &
Miranda B. Sherwood, who died July
19, 1837, Æ. 3 mos. & 22 ds.

David Sherwood, 1763.
This monument is erected to the
memory of
Capt. David Sherwood, who de-
parted this life, July 17th, 1811, in the
49th year of his age.
Time was, like me, he life possessest,
And time shall be when I shall rest.

Ephraim S. Sherwood, died Nov.
3, 1867, Æ. 89 yrs. & 9 mo.

In memory of
Sally, wife of Ephraim Sherwood, who
died Oct. 25, 1826, aged 44 years.

Sarah, wife of Ephraim S. Sherwood,
died April 4, 1857, Æ. 76 ys. & 10 mo.

Here lyes Buried the Body of
Mr. Gurdon Sherwood, who departed this life August y' 22nd, 1772,
in y' 32nd year of his age.

Here lyes Buried the Body of
Capt. John Sherwood, who departed this Life Sept. the 17th, 1779,
in y' 74th year of His Age.

Here lyes y' Body of
Mrs. Mary Sherwood, Wife to
Capt. John Sherwood, Who departed
this Life June y' 12th, 1767, in y' 58th
year of Her Age.

Lucy, Daughter of Mr. Philemon and
Mrs. Hepzibah Sherwood, was born
June 10, 1795, & died March 27, 1799.

Here lyes the Body of
Capt. Matthew Sherwood, departed this life y' 26th of October,
1715, in y' 72 Year of his age.

Here lyes the Body of
Mrs. Mary Sherwood, wife to
Capt. Matthew Sherwood, aged about
87 years. Dec'd December 25, 1730.

Here lyes the Body of
Matthew Sherwood, that deces'd
22 year, 1700 [or 1709.]

Here lies the Body of
Nathaniel Sherwood, who died
Octob' 2d, 1784, in the 78th year of his
age.

In memory of
Mrs. Mercy Sherwood, Wife of
Mr. Nathaniel Sherwood, who died
July 26, 1779, in the 76th year of her
age.

Philemon Sherwood, died April
19, 1838, aged 76 years.

Hepsibah, wife of the late Philemon
Sherwood, died Sept. 9, 1848, Æ. 82
yrs.

In memory of
Nathaniel Sherwood, son of Mr.
Philemon and Mrs. Hepzibah Sherwood, who was drowned May 11,
1807, in the 20th year of his age.

Dear lovely Son and Brother
Vain is the wish that calls thee back again,
Vain is the wish, heaven is thy natal shore;
There free from sorrow, free from every pain
To thee the ills of life are known no more.

Rebecca J., daughter of Mr. Charles
& Mrs. Lois Sherwood, died Dec. 30,
1818, aged 7 months & 23 days.

Here lyes Buried the Body of
Capt. Samuel Sherwood, Decd
Novr yo 10, *Anno Domini* 1732, in the
52 year of His Age.

Here lyes the Body of
Rebekah Sharwood, Wife to Capt.
Samuel Sharwood, Aged 40 Years.
Decd May 16th, 1721-2.

Here lyes yo Body of
Mrs. Mary Sherwood, Widow of
Capt. Samuel Sherwood, Who died
Sept. 18th, 1743, in yo 61st year of her
age.

In memory of
Capt. Samuel Sherwood, who
died Sept. 10th, 1802, in the 71st year
of his age.

In memory of
Ann, relict of Hezekiah Bradley, formerly the wife of Capt. Samuel Sherwood, who died Dec. 26, 1822, aged
84.

In memory of
Stephen Sherwood, who died July
12, 1837, aged 89 years.

Here lyes the Body of
Doctr. Thomas Sherwood, who
Decd May yo 7th, 1727, in yo 41st year
of his age.

Amanda Louisa, only child of Stephen & Harriet Silliman, who died
Feb. 8, 1838, Æ. 17 mo. 8 ds.

In memory of
Daniel Silliman, Esqr., who departed this Life Febr 25th, A. D. 1773,
in the 52 Year of his age.

In memory of
Mrs. Sarah Silliman, Wife of Mr.
Daniel Silliman, that departed this
life February yo 22d, A. D. 1773, aged
48 years.

Hannah Silliman, Daugr of Nathaniel & Hannah Silliman, Decd
Febry yo 18, 1826, Aged 2 years & 10
mo.

Sacred to the memory of
Loretta, Daughter of Capt. Nathaniel
& Mrs. Chloe Silliman, who was born
Sept. 23, 1791, & died Augst 24, 1794,
aged 2 years 11 months 1 day.

Here lyes Buried yo Body of
Mrs. Ruth Silliman, Wife to Mr.
Robert Silliman, Who Departed this
life March yo 15th, 1756, Aged 58 years
1 month & 15 Das.

Rhoda Silliman, Daugr of Mr.
Robert & Mrs. Ruth Silliman, Died
April 22d, A. D. 1739, aged 3 years,
9 months & 16 Days.

Here lyes yo Body of
Ruth Silliman, yo Daur of Robert
& Ruth Silliman, aged 6 years 1 mo.
& 2 days; who Died Sept. 23, 1727.

In memory of
Capt. Seth Silliman, who died
March 31st, 1808, in the 67th year of
his age.

In memory of
Mrs. Lois Silliman, wife to Capt.
Seth Silliman, who Died July 13, 1807,
in the 63d year of her age.

In memory of
Mr. Seth Silliman, son of Capt.
Seth & Mrs. Lois Silliman, who died
Decr 1st, 1794, aged 21 years, 1 month
& 7 days.

In memory of
Elizabeth, wife of Seth Silliman, who
died Oct. 10, 1826, aged 54 years.

In memory of
Mr. Josiah Smith, who departed
this Life August 26th, 1794, Aged 37
years.

In memory of
Lewis, son of Tertullus Stephenson &
Sarah his Wife, who died Sept. 11,
1805, Æ. 9 years.

In memory of
Abijah Sterling, Esqr., who died
March 17th, 1802, in the 57th year of
his age.

In memory of
Mrs. Eunice Sterling, relict of
Abijah Sterling, Esq., who died Feb.
15, 1816, in the 73 year of her age.

George, Son of Mr. David & Mrs.
Deborah Sterling, died March 5th,
1802, aged 1 year & 2 days.

Here lyes yo Body of
Mrs. Hannah Starling, wife to
Mr. Jacob Starling, who departed
this life June yo 14th, 1756, in yo 77th
year of her age.

Here lyes Buried the Body of Mr JACOB STARLING Who departed this life Janu^ry ŷ 9 1765 in ŷ 88th Year of His Age

Here lyes the Body of
Mary Sterling, Daugh^tr of Mr.
Jacob & Mrs. Hannah Sterling, who
died March 2nd, *Anno Dom.* 1737, in
ye 23^d year of her age.

In memory of
Mr. Sherwood Sterling, who died
Sept. 22^d, 1802, in the 29th year of his
age.

In memory of
Mr. Stephen Sterling, who departed this life Oct^o 23^d, 1797, in the 43
year of his age.

In Memory of
Mr. Stephen Sterling, who departed this life March 19th, 1793, in the
81st year of his age.

To the memory of
Eunice Sterling, wife of Stephen
Sterling, who died October 8, 1808,
aged 88 years.

Sacred to the memory of
Nehemiah Strong, Esq., Formerly
Professor of Mathematiks and Nat-
ural Philosophy in Yale College,
He died August 13, 1807, in the 80th
year of his Age.

Sacred the memory of
Mrs. Mary Strong, late Consort of
Nehemiah Strong, Esqr., formerly
Professor of Mathematics and natural
Philosophy in Yale College. She
died January 23^d, A. D. 1807, Anno
Ætat sue 76.
Death like an overflowing stream
Sweeps us away, our life's a dream.

Joseph Strong, died March 23, 1816,
in the 75 year of his age.

In memory of
Mrs. Comfort Strong, Wife of
Joseph Strong, Esqr., who died Feb.
14th, 1804, in the 65th year of her age.

In memory of
Comfort, Wife of Joseph Strong, who
died Sept. 13, 1841, Aged 77 years.

In memory of
Charity Strong, Dau^tr of Mr. Joseph & Mrs. Comfort Strong, Who
departed this life August ye 5th, 1776,
in the 19th month of her age.

Miss Anna, Daughter of Joseph
Strong, Esqr., and Mrs. Comfort his
Wife, departed this life July 2^d, 1798,
In the 19th Year of her Age.
Rest in sweet slumbers, lovely Sister, rest,
Thy life be copied and thy memory blest.

In memory of
Miss Comfort Strong, Daughter of Joseph Strong, Esqr., and Mrs. Comfort his wife, who departed this life March 7th, 1801, in the 20th year of her age.

Stop friend and drop the pittying tear
O'er these lov'd remains beneath this sod,
Yet think their spirits rest not here
But in the bosom of their God.

In memory of
Miss Sarah Strong, Daughter of Joseph Strong. Esqr. & Mrs. Comfort Strong, who died Octo 18th, 1804, in the 33d year of her age.

In memory of
Tryphena, wife of John Strong, of Fairfield, who died Sept. 10, 1829, aged 56 years & 6 months.

In memory of
Aaron Summers, who died Feb. 24, 1826, aged 81 years.

In memory of
Huldah Summers, wife of Aaron Summers, who died April 22, 1837, aged 83 years.

In Memory of
Alice Summers, who died March 26, 1823, aged 62 years.

In memory of
Elnathan Summers, who died Dec. 9, 1831, aged 85 years.

Urania, daughter of Elnathan Summers, died Dec. 7, 1849, Aged 68 years.

Here lyes ye body of
Enoch Summers, son of Mr. Daniel and Mrs. Eunice Summers, who departed this life March ye 12th, 1759, in ye 15th year of his age.

In memory of
Mr. Jabez Summers, who died Augst 21st, 1801, aged 80 years & 27 days.

In Memory of
Mrs. Abiah Summers, who died Septr 8th, 1807, in the 84th year of her age.

In memory of
Mary Summers, who died Jan. 12, 1824, aged 80 years.

Precious in the sight of the Lord is the death of his saints.

In memory of
Mrs. Mary Summers, who died April 19th, 1806, in the 25th year of her age.

In memory of
Mary Summers, wife of Samuel Summers. who died Feb. 2d, 1811, in the 66th year of her age.

In memory of
Miss Rhoda Summers, who died Aug. 12, 1823, in her 37 year.

Here lyes Buried the Body of
Mr. Nathan Summers, Who Departed this Life Decemr ye 13, 1772, in ye 70th year of His Age.

Here lyes the Body of
Mrs. Comfort Summers, Wife of Mr. Nathan Summers, Who departed this life Octobr ye 4th, 1763, in ye 63d Year of Her Age.

Here lies the body of
Mrs. Martha Summers, Wife of Nathan Summers, who died Oct. 26th, 1751, in ye 50th year of her Age.

In memory of
Samuel Summers, who died June 16th, 1810, in the 74th year of his age.

Here lyes ye Body of
Mrs. Eunice Summers, Wife of Mr. Samuel Summers, Who departed this Life Febry 8th, 1766, in ye 25th Year of Her Age.

In memory of
Capt. Stephen Summers, who died July 16th, 1811, in the 68th year of his age.

Also of his son,
Stephen Summers, Junr., Master of the Brig William, who with his crew were lost Novr 1810, aged 34 years.

Nathaniel Thorp, died Jan. 9, 1836, Æ. 38.

Died Jan. 26, 1826, an
Infant, daughter of Nathaniel and Mary Ann Thorp, aged 4 mo. & 18 days.

Died Jan. 7, 1828,
Emily, daughter of Nathaniel & Mary Ann Thorp, aged 11 mo. & 17 days.

Grandison B. Treadwell, died Sept. 24, 1865, Æ. 61 years, 4 Mo.

Ruth Ann, his wife, died April 22, 1869, Æ. 55 yrs. 2 Mo.

Naomy, daughter to Lieut. Hezekiah & Mrs. Mehitable Tredwell, who died A. D., August the 12th, 1744, in the 12th year of her age.

Elizabeth Treadwell, Deceased May 10, 1709, In Her 4th year.

Here lyes the Body of
H. Treadwell, Dessed Apl. ——
In Her 23 —.

Here lyes the Body of
Samuel Treadwell, Died Febray
the 28, 1717.

Here lyes Buried yᵉ Body of
Mr. Stephen Treadwell, Who Departed this Life Novʳ 23ᵈ, Anno Domini, 1753, in yᵉ 44ᵗʰ year of His Age.

Here lyes yᵉ Body of
Timothy Tredwell, of this place,
Who decd Septʳ about yᵉ 20ᵗʰ, aged
about 37 years, 1720.

S. T. [Probably a Treadwell.]

Sarah Treadwell, Died Dec. 24ᵗʰ,
1709.

R. T., 1699. [In the Treadwell row
of stones.]

D. T., 1696. [In Treadwell row.]

E. T. [and] *E.* [and] *M.—B.* [In
Treadwell row.]

E. T., 1708. [In the Treadwell row.]

Clark M. Tuttle, died December 8,
1867. aged 59 yrs. 3 mos. & 21 days.

Lorintha, wife of Clark M. Tuttle
& daughter of Abel & Ruth Hubbell,
died May 19, 1852, Æ. 38.

Here lyes yᵉ Body of yᵉ
Rev. Mr. Nathaniel Tucker,
Who died December 20ᵗʰ, 1747, in yᵉ
23ᵈ Year of His Age ; Who was Rector of the Church of Christ in Connecticut Farms in Elizabeth Town in
New Jersey.

Here lyes Buried the Body of
Mr. Henry Wakeling, who Died
Januʳʸ 9ᵗʰ *Anno Domⁿⁱ*, 1743, in yᵉ
60ᵗʰ year of his age.

Here lyeth the Body of
Rachel Waklin, Who Departed this
life in the —— year of Her Age,
March 10, 1708.

Here lyes Buried the Body of
Mr. Zebulon Wakelee, who departed this life, July 1ˢᵗ, 1767, in yᵉ
55ᵗʰ year of his age.

Sarah B., Daughter of Rufus and
Mary Way, died July 30, 1859, aged
3 mo. and 9 ds.
Sleep on dear Babe and take thy rest,
We mourn thy absence now but
Soon the trump of God shall sound
And we again Behold thy lovely face.

In memory of
Capt. William Worden, who died
Octᵒ 27ᵗʰ, 1808, in the 75ᵗʰ year of his
age.

In memory of
Anna Wordin, Wife of Capt. William Wordin, who died Augˢᵗ 27ᵗʰ,
1805, in the 68ᵗʰ year of his age.

Here lyes the Body of
Elizabeth Wel—, [probably Wells]
that deceased in the year 1706.

In memory of
Jedediah Wells, who died March 9,
1827, aged 75.

In memory of
Hannah, Wife of Jedediah Wells,
who died June 5, 1838, aged 84 years.

In memory of
Charity Wells, who died Oct. 2,
1841, Æ. 61 yrs.

Ellen Wells, Wife of Henry Manning, Died Sept. 20, 1867 ; Æ. 83
years 6 mos.

Here lyes Buried yᵉ Body of
Mrs. Lucy Wells, Wife to Mr.
Jedediah Wells, who departed this
life Octʳ yᵉ 28, A. D. 1751, in yᵉ 23ᵈ
year of her age.

Behold as you pass by
As you are now so once was I,
As I am now so you must be,
Prepare for death and follow me.

Here lyes yᵉ Body of
Mrs. Ruth Wells, wife to Mr. David
Wells, who departed this life July yᵉ
3ᵈ, 1766, in ye 35ᵗʰ year of her age.

In Memory of
Mr. Stephen Wells, who died Sept.
11, 1825, aged 70 years.

In memory of
Mrs. Mary, relict of Mr. Stephen
Wells, who died Sept. 11, 1827, aged
69 years.

Frances Caroline, Daughter of
Robert W. & Amelia Wetmore, died
April 1ˢᵗ, 1797, Aged 14 days.

In memory of
Mr. Benjamin Wheeler, who departed this Life Decʳ 26ᵗʰ, 1798, In
the 74ᵗʰ Year of his Age.

In memory of
Mrs. Mary Wheeler, Wife of Mr.
Benjamin Wheeler, who departed this
life Augˢᵗ 13ᵗʰ, 1798, In the 71ˢᵗ year
of her Age.

Chauncey Wheeler, died April —,
1803, Æ. 52.

38

Caroline M., his wife, died May 13, 1853, Æ. 92.

Here lyes the Body of
Isaac Wheeler, that Deceased Apr. 1, 1712, Age 70 yrs.

Here lyes Buried y⁰ Body of
Doctr. John Wheeler, Who Departed this life Sept⁰ 12ᵗʰ, 1747, in y⁰ 64ᵗʰ year of his Age.

In Memory of
Mr. John Wheeler, Who died Sept. 12ᵗʰ, 1790, aged 80 years 10 months & 3 days.

In memory of
Mrs. Dorothy Wheeler, Relict of Mr. John Wheeler, who died Oct. 9ᵗʰ, 1800, in the 87ᵗʰ year of her age.

Here lyes y⁰ Body of
Lucy Wheeler, Daughter of Mr. Hezekiah & Mrs. Abigail Wheeler, Who departed this Life Nov. y⁰ 26ᵗʰ, 1768, in y⁰ 14ᵗʰ Year of Her Age.

Here lyes Buried y⁰ Body of
Nehemiah Wheeler, son of Doct. John & Mrs. Hannah Wheeler, Who Decᵈ Novembʳ ye 28ᵗʰ, Anno 1726, in y⁰ 7ᵗʰ year of His Age.

Nichols C. Wheeler, died Feb. 6, 1859, Æ. 65.

Polly, wife of Nicholas C. Wheeler, died Aug. 29, 1853, Æ. 61.

In memory of
Miss Sarah Wheeler, Dauʳ of Amos Wheeler, Esqr., of Brookfield, who died Aug. 13, 1805, in the 14ᵗʰ year of her age.

Stay passenger, this stone demands thy tears,
Here lies a parent's hope of tender years,
Our sorrows now, but late our joy and praise,
Lost in the mild aurora of her days,
What virtue might have graced her fuller day!
But ah! the charm just shown, and snatched away,
Friendship, love, nature; all reclaim in vain,
Heaven when it will refuses its gifts again.

Here lyes Buried the Body of
Mr. Timothy Wheeler, who died March 5ᵗʰ, 1752, in y⁰ 62ᵈ year of his his age.

Here lyes y⁰ Body of
Mrs. Ann Wheeler, widow of Mr. Timothy Wheeler, who departed this life July the 18ᵗʰ, 1764, in y⁰ 72ᵈ year of her age.

Timothy Wheeler, son of Mr. Timothy & Mrs. Grissel Wheeler, was born Sept. 3ᵈ & died Septʳ 28ᵗʰ, 1790.

In Memory of
Wm. B. Wheeler, who decd July 20, 1842, aged 33 yrs.
Don't mourn my friends and parents dear,
I am not dead, but sleeping here;
My peace is made, my grave you see,
Prepare for death and follow me.

In memory of
Elizabeth, daughtʳ of Bennet & Susan C. Whitney, Died Dec. 29, 1839, Æ. 11 weeks.

In memory of
Aaron W. Whiting, who died Nov. 3ᵈ, 1833, Æ. 52 yrs.

Sally, Relict of Aaron W. Whiting, Died Mar. 2, 1866, Æ. 85 years, 9 mos.

In memory of
Polly, daughter of Capt. Daniel Wildman, formerly of Danbury, who died June 29, 1814, Æ. 17.

The grave of
Abraham Wilson, who died Sept. 27, 1839, aged 62 years.

Eunice, Wife of Abraham Wilson, died Feb. 28, 1854, Æ. 71.

In memory of
Mrs. Eleanor Wilson, Wife of Mr. Amos Wilson & Daughter to Mr. Benjamin & Mrs. Margaret Lacey, who departed this life June 23, 1795, aged 27 years 2 months & 17 days.

In memory of
Ann Wilson, who died Dec. 10, 1856, Aged 60 years.
I am the resurrection and the life; he that believeth in me though he were dead yet shall he live.

In memory of
Mrs. Anna Wilson, who departed this life Oct. 29, 1844, aged 73 years & 3 months.
Blessed are the dead who die in the Lord.

The Grave of
Burr Wilson, who died April 12, 1850, Æ. 76 years.

Ruth, Wife of Burr Wilson, decd June 29, 1858, Aged 84 years.

In Memory of
Isaac Wilson, son of Burr & Ruth Wilson, who died June 28, 1826, aged 29 years.

In memory of
Capt. Daniel Wilson, who died May 14, 1822, aged 52 years.

Maria, daughter of Daniel & Anne Wilson, died May 8, 1850, aged 52 years.
Them also that sleep in Jesus will God bring with him.

The Grave of
Oliver Gould, son of Alfred &
Louisa Wilson, who died Feb. 15,
1837, aged 5 mo & 10 days.
Death came like a winter's day
And snatched our lovely babe away.

Eusebia Gould, Daughter of Alfred
& Louisa Wilson, dec⁴ Apr. 6, 1852,
Æ. 5 years & 25 ds.

The grave of
Fairchild Wilson, who died May
28, 1848, Æ. 35 yrs. 5 mos. & 9 ds.
Triumphant in the closing eye
The hope of glory shone ;
Joy breathed in the expiring eye,
To think the race was run.
Thy passing spirit gently fled,
Sustained by grace divine.
O may such grace on us be shed
And make our end like thine.

James Wilson, Died Nov. 24, 1852,
Æ. 82 yrs. & 8 Mo.

Sarah, wife of James Wilson, Died
April 12, 1870, Æ. 93 yrs. 8 mos.

In memory of
Mr. James Wilson, son of Mr. Rob-
ert & Mrs. Catharine Wilson, who was
seized, Sept. 4th. at Trinity, in New-
foundland, of the illness of which he
died Oct. 12, 1773, in yᵉ 32ᵈ year of
his age.
Swift as the sun revolves the day
We hasten to the dead,
Slaves to the mind we puff away,
And to the ground we tread,
We steer our course up thro' the skies,
Farewell this barren land.
There, there the Dear wealth of spirits lies
And beckoning Angels stand.

In memory of
Mrs. Sarah Wilson, wife to Mr.
James Wilson, Dauᵗʳ of Mr. Daniel
& Mrs. Sarah Morris, who departed
this life March the 29, 1771, in ye 26th
year of her age.
Come courteous friend, come drop a tear
Over these dry bones & say :
These once were strong as mine appear
And mine must be as they.
Thus should these mouldering members teach
What now our senses learn,
For dust & ashes loudest preach
Man's infinite concern.

In memory of
Mr. John Wilson, Junr., Son of
Mr. Robert & Mrs. Catharine Wilson,
who died Octʳ 20th, A. D. 1776, in yᵉ
29th year of his age.
You sacred mourners of a nobler mould
Born for a friend whose dear embraces hold
Beyond all nature's ties you that have known,
Two happy souls made intimately one,
And felt a parting stroke, 'tis you must tell,
The smart twinges & the racks I feel borne.
This soul of mine that dreadful wound has
Off from its side its dearest half is torn,
The rest lies bleeding & but lives to mourn.

In memory of
Justus Wilson, who died Dec. 14,
1839, aged 73.

In memory of
Charity, wife of Justus Wilson, who
died April 23, 1850, in the 77 year of
. her age.

Paulina Wilson, born Agst. 16,
1798, died April 28, 1879.
Her soul Rests in peace.

Robert Wilson, died May 24, 1861,
in his 74th year.

Sarah, daughter of Robert & Sarah
Wilson, died May 3, 1859, in her 24th
year.

In memory of
Mr. Robert Wilson, who died May
11th, 1813, in the 58th year of his age.
Happy the man who consecrates his hours
By vig'rous effort, and an honest aim,
At once he draws the sting of life and death ;
He walks with wisdom and her paths are peace.

In memory of
Eunice, wife of Robert Wilson, who
died Dec. 1, 1823, in her 68 year.

The grave of
Pamelia, the wife of Wyllys Lyon
and daughter of Robert & Eunice
Wilson. She died Sept. 1ˢᵗ, 1837,
Aged 39 yrs. 2 mo. 12 ds.

In memory of
Miss Eleanor Wilson, who died
Oct. 8, 1824, aged 29 years.

The Grave of
Sarah, daughter of Robert & Sarah
Wilson. She died Nov. 16, 1835, in
her 7 year.
Thou art gone, bright flower,
Deep was our grief to part
With one so lovely, innocent and fair.
Remembrance long will wring the wounded
heart
And hold thy beauteous image ever there.

In memory of
Sarah Wilson, who died Sept. 30,
1868, Æ. 68 yrs.
Asleep in Jesus.

In memory of
Silliman Wilson, who died July 8,
1833, aged 68 yrs. 5 mo. & 15 ds.

In memory of
Rhoda, wife of Silliman Wilson, who
died April 6, 1825, aged 57 years, 8
months & 2 days.

In memory of
Summers Wilson, son of Abraham
& Eunice Wilson, who died Sept. 21,
1826, aged 22 years.

In memory of
Winthrop Wilson, who died Feb.
3, 1826, aged 33 years.

Mary, Daughter of Thomas & Elizabeth Woodward, died 18th Sept. 1802.

E. H. 1694. A. 8.
J. P. 88.
E. 1689.
R. G. 1703.
R. J. D. S. F. 12, 1731.
R. J. My 14, 1712.
E. J. June 11, 1716.
M. J. Nov. 13, 1712.
D. D. 1688.
Mrs. P. C. 1706.
B. B. 1712.
S. J. 1689.
A. B. 1688.
M. B.
O. C. 1689.
——, 1690.

Here lies
M. J. 1733, D. Jan. 3.
C. J. D. M. J. 1693.
E. J. J. E. 17, 1695.
J. O. 1691, S. 12.
O. J. M. 20, 170—.

M. S. Aged 6 ys Who died June 17,
1717.

S. H. 1718.
R. H. 1696.
E. O. Aged 17, Who died Oc. 16,
1721.
J. H. 1690. D. M.
M. S. 1711.
R. T. 1707, Apl. 9, D.
S. C. 1698.
C. B. 1700.
A. B. 1688.
—— 1699.
S. B. 1690.
E. B. 1699.
M. S. 98.
A. C. 1698.
D. C. 1699.
M. B. Ds. 7, 1715.
N. T. N.,1691.
A. S. 91.
—— 1696.
I. H. 1689.
E. H. 1688.
R. H.
S. H.

Here lies the Body of
Matthew Sherwood.

CHAPTER XIX.

THE BOROUGH OF BRIDGEPORT.

ANY plans are devised at the present day to build cities as a matter of enterprise and money-making, but Bridgeport grew up without a plan or in spite of one. Before the Revolution it was supposed that New Pasture Point would develop into a city, but so far as has been ascertained, during that war a point of trade was established on the west side of the harbor, and then or soon after, was called Newfield. In 1777 the name is first found recorded, but in an accidental way, as though familiarly used.

In January, 1787, Josiah Lacey, of Stratfield, Nathan Seeley, of Danbury, and David Burr, of Fairfield, were appointed a committee by the Fairfield County Court to lay out and widen the highways now known as Main street and State street. The former is designated in the committee's report, dated April 13, 1787, as "the road at the foot of Golden Hill," and the latter as "the road from the dwelling-house of the widow Eunice Hubbell, near the stores at Newfield, to the town line between Stratford and Fairfield." State street, as a highway, was laid out soon after November 9, 1691.[1]

In May, 1787, the following resolution was passed by the Connecticut Legislature:

---

[1] *State Street laid out.*

"Nov. 9, 1691. Samuel Sherman and Robert Cune was chosen and appointed by the town to view where it is most convenient for a highway to pass in y* Fairfield to Paquonnock Harbor and to treat with y* persons through whose land said highway should pass.

"Upon report of a committee appointed in May last, which is now accepted and approved, resolved by this Assembly that the town of Stratford be and they are hereby empowered and allowed to keep and maintain a public Ferry in said town, across the creek or harbour called New Field Harbour, from the point of land called New Pasture Point, below Toby's wharf, to the opposite shore of said harbour or creek, to and on to land of Aaron Hawley, about ten rods south of said Hawley's dwelling house, and that two sufficient boats shall be constantly kept, one on each side of said creek, plying from shore to shore as occasion may require, at the places aforesaid, during the pleasure of this Assembly, all subject to the same relations that other Ferries in this State are by Law subject to."

The western terminus was near the foot of the present Union street, but the facilities afforded by it were not sufficient to accommodate the public, and in May, 1791, the town meeting of Stratford voted its consent to "build a bridge across the Pequonnock river nearly opposite Cannon and Lockwood's wharf," and in the same month the Legislature gave authority to Robert Walker, of Stratford, and others to establish a lottery to raise the funds necessary to build a bridge across Newfield harbor, and appointed a committee to view the circumstances as to what kind of a bridge would be needed, and what the expense, and report to the next session.

The next autumn the town voted to request the General Assembly that if a bridge was built by lottery the expense of maintaining it should not fall upon the town.

Upon the building of this bridge it became necessary to change the road which passed around the point along the shore, and a committee of the Legislature made the following as a part of their report concerning it:

"The alterations between Newfield Bridge and Benjamin's Bridge are grounded on the necessity of avoiding or shunning the road now traveled, under the bank where the tide flows, which renders it at times impassable, to the detriment of travellers; being likewise very crooked, which is now remedied by a straight line on good ground through Asa Benjamin's rope walk. Twenty rods of the south part thereof must be taken up and shifted to the north end, together with his wheel house, which is thirty feet in length, and subject him to the necessity of purchasing a lot of land of about seven acres at an extravagant price, beside the expense of taking up the rope walk."

The committee recommended that three hundred and thirty dollars damages should be paid to Asa Benjamin by the town of Stratford. The road was made, and liberty given to Stratford to set up a toll-gate at Lottery Bridge in Newfield, for the support of that and Benjamin's bridge, which was done in 1799. In 1797 Benjamin's bridge was voted, by the town, to be "rebuilt and made eighteen feet wide."

In March, 1800, the town voted to lay out a "new road from New Pasture Point to Old Mill road." This was what is now East Main street.

In the report of the committee fixing the place from which the ferry should start on the east side of the harbor, they say, "from a point of land called New Pasture Point below Toby's wharf." This wharf seems to have been the same as mentioned in a deed many years before, namely, March 17, 1745-6, Ephraim Watkins, of Ulster county, N. Y., sold to Peter Veiw, of Stratford, "a certain wharf in Pequonnock River, it being the lowermost wharf in said river."

A part of the township of Stratford was incorporated, by special act of the Legislature, in October, 1800, being "constituted and declared to be, from time to time, forever hereafter, one body corporate and politic, in fact and in name, by the name of '*The Warden, Burgesses and Freemen of the Borough of Bridgeport*,' and by that name they and their successors forever shall and may have perpetual succession."[1]

The origin of the idea of such an organization is made known in the following extract from a letter written by Joseph Backus, one of the earliest lawyers in Bridgeport, to Robert Walker, Esqr., dated September 20, 1822: "I say that I did of my own mere motion project the Borough incorporation (the first project of the kind in the state), and drew the

---

[1] Statute Laws of Conn., I. 106.

charter and then submitted it to the citizens to obtain its
enactment."[1]

Hence Bridgeport was the first Borough in the State of
Connecticut, and as a forerunner, in its success and prosperity, has proved itself worthy of the position thus taken.

Before the charter was granted considerable money had
been raised and expended in improvements in the village,
and it is probable that the fact of improvement suggested
the need of further organization, and hence the proposition
for a borough.

Highways, or streets, additional to those already men-
tioned, were laid out under the direction of the Warden and
Burgesses of Bridgeport, November 16, 1805, Joseph Backus,
Justice of the Peace for Fairfield county, having appointed
Samuel Gregory, Jr., Isaac Booth and Philip Sterling "to
appraise and assess the damages."

1st. The extension of Water street from Wall to a point
about one hundred and fifty feet north of Fairfield avenue.

2d. Fairfield avenue, from Main to Water street.

3d. Wall street, from Main eastwardly to the "Lottery
Bridge," which then stood at the foot of Wall street.

4th. Middle street, from Fairfield avenue to Wall street.

5th. Broad street, from State to John street.

6th. John street, from Broad to Main street.

7th. Bank street, from Main to Broad street. That portion of Bank street, from Main eastward, had been previously
deeded to the borough by Stephen Burroughs, in 1802, and
was known as Morris street.

8th. Court street, from State, southward ninety-nine feet.

At that time there were several other streets or highways in the heart of the borough; Water street, from Wall
to Baker's pond; Bank street, from Water to Main street,
and Broad street, south of State to the outer harbor, and
Gold street and Union street.

Baker's Pond was a creek extending westward across
Main street, about where South avenue is now located, but
that portion of Water street below Gilbert was simply the
shore beach by the side of the harbor.

---

[1] Esquire Isaac Sherman's Manuscript book.

The Borough at this time owned three slips, one at the foot of State street, one at the foot of Bank street and one at about the foot of Wall street.

At a borough meeting held May 3, 1808, the street names as above noted were established.

In 1801 St. John's Church edifice was erected on the corner of State and Broad streets, and that of the First Congregational Church was erected in 1803, on the corner of Broad and Bank streets.

Business Firms of the Borough.

The following is a list of the firms, with the names of the individuals who composed them, given by Esquire Isaac Sherman, from the first settlement of Bridgeport to the first day of January, 1815, being those of merchants, manufacturers, Boston and New York coasters, and West India traders, with the names of vessels employed as well as the names of the owners. The stores and places for doing business were mostly confined to Water and State streets.

The territory on which the city of Bridgeport now stands was much of it an open field of good farming land, and at the close of the Revolution Main and State streets were laid out so that access was had to the landing place on Pequonnock river or Newfield harbor; Water street and the old Golden Hill road having been opened before the Revolution. The name of the landing was called Newfield until about the year 1800, when it was changed to Bridgeport.

The first store opened for trade to the inhabitants of Stratfield, supposed to have been opened by Philip Nichols, was situated at the head of tide water, near where Noah Plumb now resides. This store may have been first started by Richard, the father of Philip Nichols, at about the year 1730. There were no bridges across the Pequonnock river until after the Revolution, except that which now crosses near the said Plumb's house There was the same depth of water at the mouth of Bridgeport harbor as there was all the way up the channel to the wharf belonging to this store, and therefore all the vessels came up and did their loading and unloading at this wharf until near the time of the Revolutionary War.

The next store, and the first that was opened within the limits of the city, was near the foot of State street, built on a wharf, by Stephen Burroughs, before the Revolution, and occupied by himself in the grain trade to Boston until about the year 1800, He also conducted a West India trade, from this store, before and after the Revolution. He built and owned several vessels during his active, business life. This store was occupied during the Revolution by Lieut. William Hall's guard, consisting of about twenty-four men. This company of guard commenced service January 1, 1777, and continued until January 1, 1782, by authority of the Council of Safety of the State of Connecticut.

The next store was built by Major Aaron Hawley soon after the Revolution, which he sold to Daniel Young, who came from Norwich, and this was the principal store for groceries and dry goods until the year 1800. It was located on Water street nearly opposite the foot of Union street, where Mr. Young was quite successful in business.

Some little time after the Revolution, but before 1815, the firm of Abijah Hawley and Company—which consisted of Abijah, Aaron and Wilson Hawley—carried on the Boston and West India coasting trade. Their Boston coaster was called the Three Sisters, and their New York packet was a sloop called Caroline. They were successful in business for many years.

Capt. Abraham Hubbell came from Wilton and built a store and wharf a little north of the foot of State street, about the year 1790, and carried on the Boston coasting business. He died in Boston, of the small pox. Richard and Amos Hubbell, of Stratfield, succeeded him in the Boston and West India trade, under the firm name of Richard and Amos Hubbell, and conducted their trade with a brig called Julius Cæsar, and had success in their business.

Afterwards, David Minot and Company carried on the Boston coasting trade from the same store, until about the year 1810, and were successful. This firm consisted of David Minot, Stephen Summers and William DeForest. Their Boston coaster was a standing topsail sloop called Hope.

The next store and wharf north of the foregoing was

built by Stephen Burroughs, Jr., about the year 1798 and owned by him until his death. It was burned at the time of the great fire in 1845. It was occupied first by the firm of Burroughs and DeForest, consisting of Stephen Burroughs, Jr., and William DeForest, engaged in the Boston coasting and West India trade, which partnership continued about ten years, and was very successful. They owned the standing topsail sloop Volusia, sailed by Capt. Harry Lewis.

After this firm the same business was continued by said Burroughs until the year 1815, when it was assumed by Stephen Burroughs and Isaac Sherman, and thus continued to 1831, with success. The names of their Boston coasters were Volusia, sloop Peacock, schooner Hero and the schooner Nassau, built by this last firm for a Boston coaster, and after one year it was sent to Mobile under a charter to some merchants from New York to St. Stevens, on the Tombigbee river, Capt. Lent M. Hitchcock, master. She entered the port in June, 1817, and was the first American vessel that entered the port of Mobile after it came into the possession of the United States. Capt. Hitchcock succeeded in getting the Nassau up the river within about thirty miles of St. Stevens, where his cargo, consisting of goods for merchants at that place, was put into lighters and carried to that place. The schooner was then loaded with red cedar logs and ash-wood for firewood. She lost two sailors by the yellow fever on the voyage. This vessel was continued under the command of Capt. Hitchcock with good success about four years, as a packet between New York and Mobile, when the trade became so much increased as to require larger vessels.

The store and wharf next north of Bank and east of Water street, was built by Amos Hubbell, and was called the Yellow store. It was occupied by him after he dissolved partnership with his brother Richard. Capt. Hubbell built a ship and a brig near his store and conducted the West India trade until his death, in 1801.

This store and wharf has been occupied since Capt. Hubbell's decease by the firm of DeForest and Hinman, consisting of William DeForest and Isaac Hinman, who conducted

the Boston grain business; their coaster being a fore topsail
schooner called the Live Oak, of one hundred tons, built by
this firm in 1804. It was next occupied by the firm of Hubbell
and Sherwood—C. B. Hubbell and Capt. Sherwood—engaged
in the West India trade. These were followed by the firm of
C. B. Hubbell and Daniel Fayreweather, in the dry goods and
. the New York and Boston coasting trade. They owned a
New York packet called the Lapwing, and a Boston coaster
called Spartan. Later, C. B. Hubbell and his brother-in-law,
John M. Thompson, from Stratford, conducted an exclusive
dry goods business in the "old yellow store" on the east side
of Water street, up to the year 1842.

The next store and wharf north was owned and occupied
by David Sterling as an iron and grocery store. In 1807 this
property was occupied by the firm of Beach and Sherman—
Doct. James E. Beach and Isaac Sherman—until 1809, when
Capt. Sterling Sherman was added to the firm. They carried
on the grocery and grain business and New York packeting
for several years; the name of their packet being The Bridgeport.

The store and wharf next north was owned by John S.
Cannon, occupied by Esquire Isaac Sherman and Capt. John
Brooks, Jr. They ran a packet from the store about four
years—from 1818 to 1822—called the Mary Ann.

The store and wharf north of this was built by the firm of
Lambert Lockwood and John S. Cannon, and occupied by
them during several years in dry goods and grocery trade,
and running a packet sloop, called the Juba, to New York,
sailed by Capt. John Brooks, Sen.

Another store and wharf north was built by Philip
Nichols, at the foot of Wall street and adjoining the first
bridge across the harbor, called Lottery Bridge, because it
was built by a lottery authorized by the General Assembly in
1791. This bridge was rebuilt further up the harbor, where
it now stands, in 1807. This store was first occupied by
Charles T. Nichols for the sale of dry goods, and for a printing office by Hezekiah Ripley.

The store north of this was built by the firm of Prosper
Whitmore and his brothers Robert and ——— Whitmore,

about the year 1792. They conducted the West India trade, carrying provisions, cattle and horses to the different islands, and bringing back rum, sugar and molasses. They had a number of vessels employed, but they failed in business in 1797.

In the year 1805, Josiah, Mordecai and Joseph H. Prindle, brothers, came from Derby and established in this store the West India business. They had three vessels employed in carrying out corn meal, horses and cattle, and bringing back rum, sugar and molasses. They lost two schooners in the fall of 1808, in a hurricane, with full cargoes of stock and corn meal, and all persons on board perished. As the result of these losses they failed, and gave up the business.‘

Very little business was done in this store after the Whitmores failed until about the year 1816, when the firm of Sheldon Smith and William Wright occupied it for conducting the saddle and harness business, which firm was the continuation of the same business carried on previously in State street in connection with William Peet, who had retired from the business.

There were but four firms on the west side of Water street previous to the year 1815.

‘ GENERAL PROSPER MONTGOMERY WETMORE, son of Robert William and grandson of Rev. Izrahiah Wetmore, was born in that part of Stratford which is now the city of Bridgeport, Feb. 14, 1798. He married Lucy Ann, daughter of Francis Ogsby, of New York City, and had twelve children, three sons and nine daughters. He resided in New York, and in 1834 and 5 represented the city in the Legislature. In 1819 he was commissioned in the State artillery service, and in 1825 he organized the Seventh Regiment of National Guards and became its first colonel. This was and is the most famous military regiment in that State. After some years he was appointed paymaster general of the State militia, which office he held until 1841. In 1834 he was elected one of the Regents of the University of the State, which office he held until after 1861. For many years he was vice-president and secretary of the Chamber of Commerce of New York City.

Mr. Wetmore was one of the founders of the American Art Union, and conducted it as its president for three years with great success. For fifteen years he devoted his best energies to the management of the New York Institute for the Deaf and Dumb, of which he was for many years the senior vice-president. He wrote much for the public papers, and in 1830 he published, in an elegant octavo volume, "Lexington, with other Fugitive Poems," which is the only collection of his writings. He did considerable other literary work. He was, however, generally known as a man of literary influence in society rather than as an author.

About the year 1794 a firm consisting of Doct. James E. Beach and David Sterling, built a story and a half wooden building for a store on the southwest corner of Water and Bank streets, where they sold dry goods, groceries and medicines until the year 1804. The same business was continued by successive firms until 1815, as described on page 514 of this work.

Another store, south of the above, fronting on Water street, was built about the year 1798, by Elijah Burritt and Ephraim W. Sherman, and occupied by them as a dry goods and grocery store until about 1817. Oliver and William Sherman, sons of Ephraim W., succeeded Burritt and Sherman and continued in the same store a retail grocery business for many years.

The next was a small wooden store on the northwest corner of Water and State streets, built by Elijah Hawley about the year 1790. It was occupied as a dry goods and grocery store until 1815, by Salmon Hubbell.

About the year 1790 a store was built on the corner of Water and the south side of State street, by Ezra Kirtland (at that time pronounced Catlin), which was occupied in 1794 by the brothers David and John DeForest as a dry goods and grocery store, which was robbed and fired, but not burned. Their clerk, a lad about fourteen years of age, by the name of Shelton Edwards, was murdered, his skull being broken by a shoe hammer in three places and his throat cut; but the perpetrators were never discovered. Owing to this catastrophe the DeForest brothers failed in business. Hull and Lyon succeeded them in this store building, in general trade to the West Indies. They built a ship in 1795, but failed in 1799.

A small store was built about the year 1791, adjoining Salmon Hubbell's on the west, fronting south on State street, which was occupied with dry goods and groceries by Seth and Silas Sherman until about the year 1800, and after that continued as a dry goods store by Silas Sherman and his son, Ira Sherman. Their store was robbed, about the year 1811, of one thousand dollars worth of dry goods, and no knowledge of the robbers was ever obtained.

Isaac Sherman

Another store was built next above the last named, fronting on State street, by David Sherman about the year 1794,
and occupied with dry goods and groceries by David Sherman and Nathan Seeley until about 1797. They carried on,
in connection with their store, the West India trade in a
large standing topsail sloop, called Minerva, commanded by
Capt. Samuel Squires, who on his last voyage for them gam-
bled away the avails of his outward bound cargo at St. Croix
and came home with ballast only, which catastrophe broke
up said firm, and Nathan Seeley removed to Bethel, where
he died an old man about 1850, while David Sherman went
back to his farm at Pequonnock, where he died August 22,
1810.

In the year 1806 Samuel Penney built a store on the
north corner of Water and Bank streets, on land leased from
Mrs. Eleanor Hubbell, which was occupied by Charles Bostwick and Samuel C. Kirtland to 1815 as a dry goods store.

Isaac Sherman, Esq., son of David and Rebecca
(French) Sherman, was born in Stratfield, Sept. 25, 1788.
Very early in life Mr. Sherman compiled and executed quite
artistically a genealogical chart, showing at a glance his
descent on his father's side from Matthew Sherman—son of
Mr. Samuel, the first in Stratford—and Jacob Sterling,
and on his mother's side from Samuel French and John
Edwards, heads of four families of first settlers in Stratfield,
with collateral branches in each generation. When sixteen
years of age he went to sea and followed it with varying successes upwards of four years, having been shipwrecked twice
on the New Jersey coast. At this time he had ninety-five
dollars, to which his mother added five, making one hundred
dollars with which to start business. To this his uncle, Dr.
James E. Beach, added nine hundred dollars as a loan, and
with this he started the firm of Beach and Sherman, located
on Water street, in the grocery business, conducted solely
by himself. In this he was so successful that his capital was
doubled by his profits at the end of the first year. Shortly
after, his brother, Capt. Sterling Sherman, was admitted a
partner, with additional capital, and in this form the business

was continued six years. In December, 1810, he married Maria, daughter of Stephen Burroughs, Jr., and purchased the house, then recently built, on the northeast corner of Main and Gold streets, which was his only home of married life for fifty-three years.

In 1815 he joined his father-in-law in the grocery, grain, Boston and New York coasting business, which was successfully continued to 1831, with the exception of an interval of four years in partnership with Capt. John Brooks, Jr., in the same line of business. The firm of Burroughs and Sherman owned a number of vessels and built the schooner Nassau for a Boston coaster, which was used four years on mercantile trips to Mobile and back, under the command of Capt. Lent M. Hitchcock.

In 1832 Mr. Sherman retired from commercial life but not from active usefulness. As early as 1819 he was appointed justice of the peace and this office he retained after his retirement from business, until 1851. He was town clerk for sixteen years from 1831, and he was town treasurer twenty-two years, and afterwards for a time he was judge of Probate and recorder of the city. He served the city in two or three offices for a short time, but declined further responsibility in its government.

That he was a most industrious man is amply attested by voluminous records, original deeds and other conveyances, wills and documents which are preserved in the archives of the town and probate, and in the private box of nearly every property holder of his time in this vicinity.

He made a specialty in procuring the pensions of Revolutionary soldiers for them and their families, being faithful both to the government and the soldiers, and his list of pensioned soldiers is probably the most complete of any in the county.

At nearly the close of his life he was induced to write his remembrances and the traditionary history of Stratfield and Bridgeport, and, although he entered upon the undertaking reluctantly, he produced a valuable manuscript book, with a map which has been used as the foundation for the map of Stratfield and the biographical sketches in connection with

BUILDING OF THE BRIDGEPORT BANK, ERECTED IN 1806.

it, and the record of the mercantile firms in the borough of Bridgeport from 1790 to 1815. This work, styled "Esquire Sherman's Recollections," is a valuable contribution to the history of the locality now comprised in the city of Bridgeport.

Mr. Sherman from early life gave attention to religious interests and in 1812 he and his wife united with the First Congregational church, the church of his fathers. In 1830 he was elected to the office of deacon, in which he continued in active service until 1858, and for a long period was the most active member of the society's committee, being also treasurer and clerk of the church. In his own estimation he had not much religion to speak of, but his life told a truthful story of "faith and works." So lived and labored Isaac Sherman, and rested November 23, 1863.

The Bridgeport Bank[5] was incorporated, by act of the General Assembly in October, 1806; which limited the capital stock to two hundred thousand dollars, and that amount having been subscribed,[6] a meeting of the stockholders was

---

[5] This sketch of this bank is taken from a pamphlet of the same published by R. B. Lacey, Esqr., in 1885.

[6] *The Bridgeport Bank.*

The subscription list was completed by the following names and shares:

Shares.		Shares.
Elijah Ufford, Stratford,	2	Eunice Hall, New Haven,	1
Henry Nevins, Norwich,	1	William Elliott, North Guilford,	1
Asa Spaulding, Norwich,	4	Samuel W. Johnson, Stratford,	5
Jonathan Sturges, Fairfield,	1	Buckley, DeForest and Co., New
George Hoyt, Bridgeport,	2	Haven,	3
James Grayham, Sandisfield,	1	Buckley and Austin, New Haven,	1
Ezekiel Curtis, Huntington,	2	Robert Fairchild, for Stratford,	6
Jeremiah Day, New Haven,	1	James Lewis, New London,	1
James E. Beach, Stratfield,	4	Samuel Kirtland and Co., Bridgeport,	2
Samuel Watkinson, Middletown,	5	Isaac Thompson, New London,	1
Elijah Hubbard, Middletown,	3	Abel Gregory, New Fairfield,	2
Levi Curtis, Stratford,	1	Foot and Nichols, Bridgeport,	1
Nathan Wheeler, Huntington,	2	Elijah Boardman, New Milford,	4
William Haywood, Stamford,	1	Elijah Waterman, Bridgeport,	1
Asahel Tuttle, New Haven,	1	Thomas Wells, New Milford,	1
Townsend & Thompson, New Haven,	1	Lambert Lockwood, Bridgeport,	3

39

held Feb. 3, 1807, at which Joseph Goodwin was chosen chairman, and the following persons were elected directors: Isaac Bronson, Birdsey Norton, Samuel W. Johnson, John S. Cannon, Salmon Hubbell, Lambert Lockwood, David Minot, Jessup Wakeman, and Ebenezer Jessup.

At a meeting of the directors of the Bridgeport Bank convened at the dwelling house of Ezra Gregory, inn-keeper in said Bridgeport, on the 3d of February, 1807, Isaac Bronson was, upon ballot, unanimously elected president of the bank; and in the same month a committee was appointed to purchase a lot and contract for a building; and the banking house was erected in 1808.

George Hoyt was elected cashier in March, 1807, with a salary of seven hundred dollars per annum, with the privilege of the banking-house to live in, which was soon after made one thousand, he paying for a clerk's assistance.

In 1810, in order to "prevent any collision of interest between the Derby and Bridgeport banks," Isaac Bronson was appointed a committee to make arrangements to that effect with the former bank.

	Shares.
John S. Cannon, Bridgeport,	11
William Peet, Bridgeport,	9
Isaac Hinman, Bridgeport,	22
Salmon Hubbell, Bridgeport,	8
John and Chauncey Deming, Farmington,	7
Hezekiah Belding, New Haven,	1
William Brintnall, New Haven,	2
Seth P. Staples, New Haven,	1
Abijah Hawley, Bridgeport,	1
Daniel Nash, Norwalk,	1
Stephen Boroughs, Bridgeport,	1
Ashbel Baldwin, Stratford,	1
Solomon Cowles, Farmington,	1
Zenas Cowles, Farmington,	4
Elijah Cowles and Co., Farmington,	9
David Judson, Fairfield,	1
Caleb Atwater, Wallingford,	3
Reuben S. Norton, Farmington,	1
Humphrey and Whitney, New York,	5

	Shares.
Henry Ward, New Haven,	4
Matthew Marvin, Wilton,	3
David Brooks, Stratford,	1
Ezra Gregory, Bridgeport,	1
William Battell, Torrington,	1
Gershom Fenn, New Haven,	1
—— Perry, Mill River,	13
Robert Fairchild, Stratford,	1
Dyer White, New Haven,	3
Ephraim J. Wilcoxson, Stratford,	1
Samuel Smedley, Fairfield,	12
Samuel Ward, Jr., New York,	2
Joseph Goodwin, Lenox,	61
Isaac Hinman and Co., Bridgeport,	16
Shipman, Dennison and Co., New Haven,	11
Birdsey Norton and Co., Goshen,	37
Nathaniel Prime, New York,	22
Isaac Bronson and Co., Greenfield,	656
Total,	1,000

BUILDING OF THE BRIDGEPORT BANK, REMODELLED IN 1857.

On January 24, 1811, in view of an apprehension of war, the bank passed the following vote: "That in the present critical situation of affairs it becomes absolutely necessary that security more than profit should be considered, and feeling that our funds in New York should be placed in the best possible situation of security, we therefore do authorize I. Bronson, Esq., to secure what sums may be due and owing to the bank in the city of New York, in any way he may judge proper for the benefit of this institution, and use his best discretion in all other matters concerning the interest of the bank to effect the purposes aforesaid."

Mr. Bronson continued in the direction of the bank for twenty-five years. He was president for the whole period, except an interval of four years, from 1823 to 1827, when he gave place to John S. Cannon, returning to the position on Mr. Cannon's death in 1827. Capt. George Hoyt continued cashier for eighteen years, until his death in 1825, when he was succeeded by his son, Josiah S. Hoyt, for seven years. During this period the bank prospered, outrode the storms of war and financial crises without the suspension of specie payments, and paid regular, and some large, extra dividends. To do this it went outside of Bridgeport and its vicinity to make loans. In 1832 Mr. Bronson sold his stock and retired from all connection with the bank.

On November 7, 1832, Ebenezer Jessup, of Saugatuck, was elected president, and a month later, the health of Josiah S. Hoyt having become impaired, Charles Hill, of Catskill, N. Y., was elected cashier. Mr. Jessup remained president until 1838, when Sylvanus Sterling, of Bridgeport, was elected president and George Burroughs cashier. Several changes were made in the amount of capital, reducing it to $110,000, but in 1838 it was again increased and made $210,000.

Sherman Hartwell was elected president July 4, 1849, and continued in the office until July 6, 1869, when he positively declined a reëlection. During this period, in 1854-5, the banking house was repaired, another story added, and the exterior improved, at a total cost of $6,000. At his retirement from the presidency of the bank, Mr. Hartwell had served it thirty-six years as a director, and twenty years as president;

and the directors passed the following: "*Resolved*, That the thanks of this board are due, and are hereby tendered to Sherman Hartwell for efficient and valuable services as president of this bank for the last twenty years, and as evidence of the prosperity of the bank it may be stated that it has during the said twenty years paid its stockholders in dividends the sum of $430,700, on a capital of $212,000, and increased its surplus $40,000." Mr. Hartwell survived in quiet retirement until January 16, 1876, when he passed away in the fulness of years, esteemed and honored.

Mr. Munson Hawley was elected president July 6, 1869, to fill the place made vacant by the retirement of Mr. Hartwell, and proved a worthy successor. His administration for more than sixteen years has been economical, efficient and successful, for there has been paid during this period the sum of $399,320 in dividends, and the surplus increased about $40,000.

George Burroughs, the veteran cashier, continued his faithful service nearly four years longer, when his labor closed suddenly as he entered the banking house on the morning of March 12, 1872, having served as cashier nearly twenty-five years and as director ten years. The following was passed by the board of directors: "Whereas, by the death of our highly esteemed friend and associate, Mr. George Burroughs, who for nearly thirty-five years faithfully performed his duties as cashier of this bank, we feel that this institution has suffered an almost irreparable loss. Always at his post of duty, kind-hearted and obliging in his business transactions, honest and true in all his dealings, we most sincerely regret his loss, not only to this institution, but to the community, and we extend our united sympathy to his afflicted family in their sad bereavement which a wise Providence has called them to sustain. *Resolved*, That as a token of our regard for our late esteemed friend, the Board of Directors of this bank will attend his funeral in a body."

At the death of Mr. Burroughs Mr. Frank N. Benham was appointed cashier and has served faithfully and acceptably for twelve years, and for the last three years as a director.

The list of directors during the existence of the bank, numbers eighty-five names.

Of the present board of directors, only one, Mr. R. B. Lacey, served under the old system, he having first entered the board in 1857, and none of the rest earlier than 1869. The names of the present board are: Munson Hawley, Thomas B. Bartram, Plumb N. Fairchild, Carlos Curtis, Thomas B. DeForest, Rowland B. Lacey, David M. Read, John M. Wheeler, Frank N. Bartram.

The bank has had seven presidents: Isaac Bronson, who served twenty-one years; John S. Cannon, four years; Ebenezer Jessup, five years; Sylvanus Sterling, eleven years; Hanford Lyon, one year; Sherman Hartwell, twenty years; Munson Hawley, sixteen years; and it has had five cashiers; George Hoyt, eighteen years; Josiah S. Hoyt, seven years; Charles Hill, five years; George Burroughs, thirty-five years; Frank N. Benham, twelve years.

Doct. Isaac Bronson, son of Isaac and Mary (Brockett) Bronson, was born in Middlebury, Conn., March 10, 1760. After improving the privileges of the common schools ahd studying medicine with Doct. Lemuel Hopkins, of Hartford, he entered the Revolutionary army as a junior surgeon, Nov. 14, 1779, in the Connecticut line under the immediate command of General Washington, and served efficiently through the war. He then made a voyage to India, traveled in Europe, returned to the United States about 1789, and soon after married Anna, daughter of Thomas Olcott, of Waterbury, but previously of Stratford. About the year 1692 he settled in Philadelphia, where he remained two years, during which that city was visited with a severe yellow fever epidemic, in which the doctor served very successfully as a physician, and it has been currently reported that he there accumulated property which was the foundation of his subsequent financial success.

After this, for a time, he pursued the business of a banker in New York City. In 1796 he purchased the property of Timothy Dwight, D.D., on Greenfield Hill, Conn., intending it for a summer residence, but it became his settled habitation, and while residing there in 1807 he became the presi-

dent of the Bridgeport bank. In this office he continued—
with an interval of four years—a faithful and honored officer
until 1832, when he retired. He died at his home on Greenfield Hill May 19, 1839, in his 80th year.

Doctor Bronson's banking career, extending, as it did,
through two great financial crises—that of 1812 and 1836 and
7—was one of extensive influence as well as financial success.
The papers of Hon. Roger Minot Sherman show that there
was much conference between himself and Doctor Bronson
in regard to financial questions, and there is good reason to
believe that the independent treasury-system of the United
States, which succeeded the breakdown of the United States
Bank under the administration of General Jackson, was formulated after and mainly in accordance with the suggestions
of these masterly minds.

Doctor Bronson gave much attention to his farm at
Greenfield Hill, supervising personally the smallest matters,
as well as the greatest, of improvement about his home, which
still exhibits his genius, skill and labor.

John S. Cannon came to Bridgeport from Norwalk
about 1790, a merchant of some wealth. His residence was
on the site of the Waller Building, corner of Water street
and Fairfield avenue, and was associated in business with
Lambert Lockwood. They built their store and wharf on
the present site of Baruch Ellis's stone yard about 1792, and
conducted a general trade in dry goods and groceries, and
run a regular packet to New York, the vessel being the sloop
Juba, sailed by Capt. John Brooks, Sen. Mr. Cannon owned
the next store south of the above, which he rented to Isaac
Sherman and John Brooks, Jr., and others.

Lambert Lockwood came to Bridgeport from Wilton,
Conn., about 1790, and had his residence on the north side of
State street, on the site of the brick block between the houses
of the late Doct. David H. Nash and Doct. Robert Hubbard.
In personal appearance he was possessed of a full stature,
fine presence and affable manner.

He was a public spirited man, connected with the Congregational church. His house, more than any other, was a

home for visiting clergymen in his time.
Lockwood, was a well known bookseller o
Another of his sons, the Rev. Peter Lockwood
Presbyterian minister. In later life he was c
books and stationery and printing, having t
Sterling, Jr., as an assistant or partner. He
the peace and grand juryman and sometimes w
to quell disturbances.

On one occasion Mr. Lockwood made a
call upon John S. Cannon, wearing a new bro
When about to leave for home it was found
severely. Mr. Lockwood remarked that he (
wet his new coat and inquired of Mr. Cannon if
coat he could wear instead of his own. Mr. C
had, and soon brought it forth. This Mr. Locl
and departed for home, leaving his new coa
reaching home he heard a rap at his door, a
Cannon appeared wearing Mr. Lockwood's coa
another shower that had overtaken him on the
the exchange before he should sleep.

Salmon Hubbell came to Bridgeport, als
about 1790, and had his residence on the bluff,
street, south of and adjoining Mr. Cannon; th
been taken down about 1873. He was a cap
master in the Continental army, and partic
taking of Stony Point fort under General Way
a peculiarly elegant hand, which may be seer
borough and town records. He conducted a
grocery store on the northwest corner of W
streets more than twenty years, to 1815. H
town clerk of Bridgeport, to which office I
several years from 1820. He was brother of (
Hubbell.

Isaac Hinman came from Trumbull. 1
on the corner of Main and Bank streets and aft
corner of Wall and Water streets, which lat
Washington Hotel and was kept for many y
the well known Capt. Munson Hinman. He

the south side of State street, but on the erection of the new block—now old—on the north side of State street, between the post office and Main street, he removed to it and opened a distinctively dry goods store. Richard Hyde married one of his daughters, and was associated with and succeeded him in the business. Mr. Hinman died in middle life. Mr. Hyde was prominently identified with the dry goods trade many years.

William Peet was a successful business man of the old school. His residence was a large old fashioned house with two front rooms with a wide hall extending from the front to the rear, standing on the site of the present post office building, fronting on State street. Though in later years it was skirted with stores on each side, yet with its liberal piazza and front yard filled with shrubbery, it was very noticeable and attractive. He was a tanner and currier, and his yard was located on Broad street between Cannon and John streets. The remains of the old vats were but recently taken from the site of Messrs. Hincks and Johnson's new factory. In connection with Sheldon Smith, as Peet and Smith, he conducted the manufacture and sale of saddlery in and over the store next east of and adjoining his residence on State street. This business was enlarged by adding to the firm William Wright, who opened a store in Charleston, S. C., soon after the close of the war of 1812, under the name of Peet, Smith and Company. The business was successful and although he retired from it early, it added much to Mr. Peet's wealth.

He reared an excellent family; among them was an Episcopal clergyman and two successful business men in New York City, while another followed the business of his father in this city. One daughter married William Wright, above mentioned, who, after a successful business career, became governor of New Jersey and United States senator from that state; and another married the late Hon. Henry K. Harral, who also followed the saddlery business in Charleston, S. C., New York city, and Bridgeport, with great success. Mr. Peet survived most of his associates and came to his death full of years.

Capt. David Minot was a man of wealth
His business firm consisted of David Minot, Step
and William DeForest. They carried on the B
trade successfully for a number of years previc
the store located a little north of the foot of
which had been previously occupied by Richa
Hubbell. He was quite a conspicuous person
munity, ranking, probably, next to John S. C
were leaders in public matters, and each retaine
tion with the bank until his death. Mr. Min
was on State street identical with the green on
of the present court-house. He died in 1830.

Samuel William Johnson, of Stratford
of Judge Wm. Samuel Johnson and grandson c
Johnson, and was a prominent citizen of the
·State. He served the bank eight years, freque
dent *pro tem.* of the meetings of the board of
relation ceasing in 1814.

Ezra Gregory, Sen., came to Bridgeport
in 1796. His house, situated on the west side o
at the head of Wall, was occupied by him for
as a public house or tavern. He was one of
stockholders of the bank and all the early me
stockholders and board of directors were held
until the bank building was completed. He w
of the bank from 1817 to 1821. His house was
many others in the great fire in 1845. He was
and a prominent citizen, as was also his son, Ezr
and many years after. His daughter married J
from Trumbull, a successful dry goods merchant
and in the later years of his life, treasurer of th
Railroad Company.

Hon. Elijah Boardman was a prominer
merchant of New Milford. He was a grandson
Daniel and Jerusha (Sherman) Boardman and th
great grandson of Dea. David Sherman, of St
business career extended from 1782 to 1819, a
successful. In 1795 he became leading membe

necticut Land Company, and therefore one of the purchasers of the Western Reserve, now comprising a considerable portion of the northern part of the State of Ohio. He attended in person to the survey and sale of a large proportion of the section divided to his company, and derived considerable income from the sale. He was a representative in his own State and in the upper house or senate from 1818 to 1821, and was a representative in the 17th congress, and having been elected to the United States senate for six years, was a member of that body at his decease, which occurred in Ohio during one of his visits there in 1823. He was a director of this bank from 1808 to 1817-18. His personal appearance was unusually elegant, affable and refined. His business talents were uncommonly good and his constancy in their use was rarely surpassed. The late Hon. William W. Boardman, of New Haven, was his son.

Capt. George Hoyt was a native of Bridgeport. He owned and resided in a house built by his father before the Revolution on the high bluff on the west side of Water street, about two hundred feet south of State street. In his earlier days he was a seaman in the employ of John S. Cannon or his firm. His fine business qualities were well known and at the organization of the Bridgeport bank he was elected the first cashier, which position he filled with great acceptance eighteen years, until his death in July, 1825.

Abijah Hawley was a representative of one of the oldest, most numerous and prominent families in the early settlement of Stratford and Stratfield. The Hawley family was among the most wealthy at the start, and as they branched out from the old homestead they were everywhere thrifty, acquiring large tracts of land, and in Bridgeport they were among the first for adventure and successful trade. "As rich as the Hawley's," was a familiar phrase among the people seventy years ago. The rule had its exceptions, but was so applicable as to become a common saying. Isaac Sherman, Esq., speaks as follows of the firm of Abijah Hawley and Company: "It was composed of Abijah, Aaron and Wilson Hawley. They carried on the Boston coasting grain business

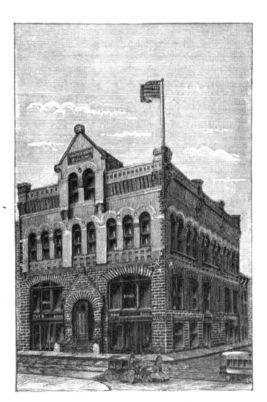

UNITED BANK BUILDING, ERECTED IN 1884 AND 85.

and West India trade. Their coaster was called the Three Sisters, probably from the wives of the partners, who were all daughters of Capt. Stephen Summers; and their New York packet was the sloop Caroline, and they were very successful for many years. Their store and wharf were on Water street a little south of State street, the grain elevator of Mr. John Hurd occupying about the same site. Abijah Hawley was the sixth generation from Joseph Hawley, the first settler of the name in Stratford, through Samuel, of Stratford; Dea. Thomas, Capt. Ezra and Thomas, of Stratfield. The last was the father of Abijah, whose residence was on the west side of Water street corner of Thomas. The following were children of Abijah and Polly (Summers) Hawley: George, Abijah, Thomas, Emeline and Munson. The first two followed the water for many years. Thomas was a merchant, the founder of the well known hardware house of T. Hawley and Company. Emeline married Dea. George Sterling, and Munson, who has been a successful merchant, and who in later years has given his attention to banking, has been for the last sixteen and a half years the efficient president of this bank, and now at the age of more than four score years it may be said of him, that his eye (to business) has not become dimmed, nor his natural force abated.

The United Bank Building, erected in 1885, by the Bridgeport National Bank and the City Savings Bank, situated on the northeast corner of Main and Bank streets, is constructed with granite copings and steps, with rock-faced Springfield brown stone extending to the height of the second story on the front and one story on the side. Above, the materials are Trenton pressed brick with brown stone trimmings. The main entrance is situated in the center of the building, on Main street, and the banking room floor is reached through a commodious vestibule by a broad flight of slate steps. The side walls of vestibule and main halls are composed of enamelled brick laid in neat geometrical patterns. The floor of the hall on the first floor and of the business portion of both banking rooms is of white marble tiles. There is a commodious staircase leading to the second floor, composed entirely of iron and slate.

The building contains three stores, accommodations for two banks, and thirteen offices; it has also ample storage room on the third floor, which is reached by a circular iron staircase. The structure is heated throughout by steam and the best of plumbing appliances have been introduced. The store and office floors are finished in pine; the banking room floors and halls in cherry in the natural wood. The vaults in the banking rooms are among the best ever built in this country and are furnished with the latest improvements of all kinds; their exterior surfaces are built of enamelled brick in the same manner as the main halls.

The building was designed for strength, convenience and utility; no effort was made for elaborate or ornate architectural display, but a general appearance of solidity and strength was aimed at: it was the aim of the designer to indicate exteriorly the purpose for which the interior was to be used. The style of architecture adopted was a modified Gothic in combination with heavy Romanesque arches; the architect relied more upon the contrasting colors of the materials used and the grouping of the entrances and windows for his effects than upon elaborate detail. He aimed not only to obtain pleasant and commodious quarters for the banks, at an easily accessible height above the sidewalk level, but at the same time to utilize the space underneath the banks for business purposes. The problem thus presented was solved by the introduction of stores with areas in front. This led to much adverse criticism while the building was being constructed, but the ready rental of the stores and their popularity is the best and most conclusive argument that the bank officials acted wisely in adopting this mode of construction.

Shipping and Shipmasters.

As early as 1760 the mouth of the Pequonnock river was called the harbor, but previously it had been called the Pequonnock river, showing that not very remote from that date vessels began to come up the river to load and unload. Previous to the death of Richard Nichols in 1756, the shipping business—whatever it was—was done at what is called the Berkshire Pond. Not long after this a store and wharf were built by Philip Nichols at the south end of Pembroke street, or the Point, and about the same time or soon after—a little before the Revolution—loading and unloading vessels began on the west side of the harbor, and this locality as early as 1777, was called Newfield, and the mouth of the river Newfield Harbor.[6]

The beginning of shipyards in the Pequonnock river must date about 1720 and continued to enlarge in proportions until after 1800; and the result was that many of the farmers held property in vessels and their sons learned to be sailors and commanders of these and other vessels. Before the Revolution, but especially after it, trade with the West Indies was of commanding proportions, and when Bridgeport began to spread out as a seaport town just after the year 1800, the coast trade to Boston, New York and Baltimore and the West Indies was largely the cause of the rapid growth of the borough. " The West India trade was a very considerable interest quite early and continued to be prosecuted as late as 1840. The parish mill site was on Pequonnock river at what is known as Pequonnock Mills. The West India trade made brisk times for the coopers and millers, and led to the construction of the Yellow Mill and Berkshire dams and mills, using tide water as a power."

" The success of the whaling business in eastern ports led to investments in that business here."[7]

The Bridgeport Whaling Company was incorporated in May, 1833, with a capital stock of one hundred thousand dollars; the following persons being named as corporators: Eben Fairchild, Daniel Tomlinson, David P. Minot, Samuel F. Hurd and David Perry.[8] This company owned and fitted the following ships—the Harvest, Hamilton, Atlantic and Steiglitz.

A company was also formed for fishing on the banks of

---

[6] Historical Notes of Major Wm. B. Hincks.

[7] Report of Bridgeport Board of Trade for 1878, p. 32.

[8] Conn. Private Acts, First Series, i. 590.

New Foundland, in charge of Captain E. Doane, but the company was not particularly successful.[*]

The Bridgeport Steamboat Company was incorporated in May, 1824; the persons named being: Daniel Sterling, Enoch Foote, Ransom C. Canfield, Isaac Sherman, Thomas C. Wordin and Wilson Hawley, with a capital stock not to exceed thirty thousand dollars. Wilson Hawley, Daniel Sterling, Thomas C. Wordin, Reuben Tweedy and Isaac Sherman were the first directors of this company.[10]

Only two companies had been previously incorporated in this State for the purpose of navigation by steam; the first was secured in October, 1818, and named "The Connecticut Steamboat Company;" the second, The Connecticut River Steamboat Company, in May, 1823.

---

[*] *Log-Book of Ship Atlantic*

On her third voyage to the south Atlantic and Indian Oceans, whaling, during the years 1837-8 and 9; having departed from Bridgeport, Conn., on July 22d, 1837, returning on April 12th, 1839.

Master, WM. POST.

1st Mate, JOB BABCOCK.

2d " JOHN LEWIS.

3d " EDWARD HOWEL.

Recapitulation.

The voyage has occupied 629 days. The ship has been at sea 567 days. According to calculations made at the end of each day the whole distance sailed is 46,640 miles. The whole number of whales seen, making no allowance for the same ones seen at different times, is 901, of which 165 are sperm. The total number struck is 75. The number of whales taken, including one found dead, is 34, of which ten were females. The whole number of pleasant days (tolerable whaling weather), is 462, as may be seen by the following table, where the pleasant or whaling days, whales seen, whales struck, and whales obtained, are arranged against the several days of the week.

Pleasant.	Whales seen.	Whales struck.	Whales obtained.
Sundays, ... 70	170	15	9
Mondays, ... 64	181	6	4
Tuesdays, ... 66	114	13	6
Wednesdays, ... 69	127	18	5
Thursdays, ... 65	123	10	4
Fridays, ... 65	86	8	5
Saturdays, ... 63	106	5	1
462	907	75	34

[10] Conn. Private Acts, First Series, ii. 1106.

The following charters were granted by the Connecticut General Assembly with and following that of Bridgeport:

The Bridgeport Steamboat Company, May, 1824.

The Hartford Steamboat Company, May, 1824.

The New Haven Steamboat Company, May, 1824.

The Norwalk and New York Steamboat Association, May, 1824.

The Ousatonic Steamboat Company, May, 1825. This company was to run steamboats between Derby and New York, and their boat "Ousatonic" was running on that line the next year.

The Stamford Steamboat Company, May, 1825.

The Steam Navigation Company, May, 1825.

By a letter to Roger M. Sherman dated January 8, 1838, it is seen that the boat named Fairfield was running on the Bridgeport line, but had then discontinued her trips for the winter. The steamboat Nimrod, Captain John Brooks, was on this line quite a number of years, and is still remembered by many individuals.

The number of men who "followed the sea" from Bridgeport as well as Stratford, would make a long list, and comprise many who were in their day well known to the merchants of New York. A few illustrations are here given at length as affording more interest than the list, if that could be obtained.

The grave-stone inscriptions of this region reveal the sad fate of many who sailed from these ports never to return. The probate records show that fathers and brothers, remembering the perils of the great deep, recorded their wills as a settlement of all earthly estates, before passing out of these harbors on their long journeys.

In addition to the illustrations here following, a list of sea captains, from fifty to one hundred, who were raised in the territory of old Stratford, might be obtained, who sailed, not as far away, but by many perils, successes and disasters, like those whose records are given.

Capt. Ezekiel Hubbell,[11] of Bridgeport, son of John
and Eleanor (Burr) Hubbell, was born in Fairfield, Conn.,
April 5, 1768. After enjoying all the advantages of an early
education, at the age of fourteen he was employed as clerk
on board of vessels belonging to Richard and Amos Hubbell,
well-known merchants trading between Newfield (Bridgeport)
and the West Indies. Soon manifesting great confidence in
himself, he not only took charge of the cargo and business of
the concern, but also the command of the vessel as a merchant
navigator, called in those days captain and supercargo, both
positions being filled by the same person. In 1797, owing to
his industry and perseverance, he became managing owner of
two fine vessels, the brig Caroline and the ship Sally and·
Betsey, and became also interested in other vessels of smaller
capacity. Next he took command of the armed ship Citizen,
of New York city, which carried sixteen guns and was
manned with a crew of fifty men, and in her he made several
voyages to Havana. The New York "Commercial Adver-
tiser" of July 15, 1798, says: "Ship Citizen, Hubbell, master,
off Newfield, Thursday last, via·Halafax, where she had been
taken by an English cruiser, and after a close examination of
the crew and papers, was released." The same paper of
December 6, 1798, says: "This day came up the armed ship
Citizen, Capt. E. Hubbell, sixteen guns, nineteen days from
Havana. Came out with eighteen vessels under convoy, and
parted with them on the coast. Left a French privateer
lying off Havana, but she did not seem inclined to come
out. Flour, $6½; sugars, 6ᵃ to 7ᵃ cwt. Cotton goods pro-
hibeted."

Early in 1799 he ventured in the same ship (Citizen) to
Vera Cruz, in the Gulf of Mexico, and endeavored to open a
trade and dispose of the investment he had on board, adapted
to the wants of the inhabitants of the city of Mexico. Disappointed in gaining permission to land his goods, he proceeded
to Honduras, thence to Havana and New York.

The information Captain Hubbell obtained at Vera Cruz
of the vast wealth of the Spaniards in their South American

---

[11] History of the Burr Family, 96.

States on the Pacific coast, and the fabulous reports of the demand for certain descriptions of goods, enabled him, on returning home, to plan an important and enterprising venture to those countries. Being a man of great prudence yet indomitable energy, he at once enlisted the confidence of his friends, purchased the ship Enterprise, of 250 tons, and joined capital with Isaac Moses and Son, and Hoyt and Tom, each owning one-third of the ship and cargo. After taking on board an invoice of costly goods, of little bulk, adapted to the wants of the Spaniards in Chili and Peru, and in addition, to guard against possible failure and disappointment, as at Vera Cruz, shipping a quantity of goods suited for traffic with the Indians on the northwest coast of America, he sailed from New York in October, 1799, with intelligent officers and a reliable crew, numbering thirty men and boys. Making slow progress in crossing the equator and coming into the high southern latitudes with lengthening days, they decided to seek a harbor on the east coast of Patagonia, which they effected in the latitude of about 45° south, where they cleaned the ship of barnacles and sea grass, for further and swifter progress. Passing Cape Horn early in February, after a stormy and tempestuous time, they were favored in the Pacific Ocean with fine southerly breezes, which carried them along the coast of Patagonia and southern Chili, and about the first of March, 1800, anchored in the harbor of Valparaiso.

As many of the crew were suffering with scurvy for the want of vegetables, of which they had been without for many months, the governor granted permission for the ship to remain in port for a reasonable time, but as no vessels except those bearing the Spanish flag were allowed to enter the port for purposes of trade, the Enterprise was closely watched and guarded by revenue officers. During this stay Captain Hubbell obtained a passport to visit the capital, Santiago de Chili, ninety miles in the interior, and was the first citizen of the United States allowed to visit that city. He was especially noticed by the Viceroy, General O'Higgins, upon whom he called, and requested to land and sell his cargo under any restrictions His Excellency might see fit to enjoin.

40

While permission was refused, yet the beautiful city was shown to him and he returned to his vessel. Lingering at Valparaiso for ten days he succeeded in making a conditional sale for the greater portion of his cargo to the governor, deliverable at Conception, a bay about three hundred miles south of Valparaiso. After arranging the terms an agent was placed on board the vessel, who, after it had sailed, examined the cargo, and following instructions, they approached Conception Bay, where a payment of 150,000 Spanish dollars was to be made on board, in advance of the delivery of the goods. The morning was fair, the scenery magnificent, a beautiful bay and harbor could be seen, overtopped by the snow-capped Cordilleras in the distance, as the ship glided to her haven. The agent landed and proceeded towards a thicket at a short distance, but instead of finding friends to answer his countersign, he was surprised by a squad of cavalry in ambush. Seeing at once the treachery of the officers and his own defeat, he sprang for his life towards the boat, into which the crew took refuge also, he barely escaping the coils of a lasso as they pushed off for the ship, which was reached in safety except a wound received by one of the officers from the ambush. Some years afterwards it was learned that the governor's friends betrayed him and the silver coin sent to Conception Bay was seized by the viceroy and confiscated.

Captain Hubbell then sailed toward the northwest coast of America, and approaching the coast of New Spain he stood into the harbor of San Blas, with the hope of landing the Spanish agent, but being fired upon from the forts he continued his course northerly to Nootka Sound. At this place and the adjacent coasts he traded such suitable goods as he had with the Indians for their valuable furs, and proceeded to China, calling at the Sandwich Islands and the Russian settlements near Kamtschatka, where he sold them at a great price, with which he purchased a large portion of a cargo of cheap Bohea tea and other goods. Sailing in January he arrived off Bridgeport, in Long Island Sound, June 27, 1802, one hundred and forty days from Canton on his way to New York City. Being the first navigator of the globe from New York, his arrival caused much excitement. Many of his friends had mourned for him as lost for he had not been heard from during his absence of nearly three years."

In the spring of 1803 Captain Hubbell purchased an interest in the Catharine Ray, a fine vessel of about 200 tons, and took command of her as captain and supercargo, on a voyage to China, with a view to an important investment in silks, which voyage was performed in regular course, returning to New York in the spring of 1804. Under a similar arrangement with the same owners he made a second voyage to China, returning home in the spring of 1805, when the vessel was sold.

In May, 1805, he resumed the command of his old ship, Citizen, under the auspices of the firm of Hoyt and Tom, and fitted her for a voyage to China, which was performed by investing $150,000 in Spanish coin in the purchase of silks, he receiving only his commission, and returned to New York in May, 1806. In October, 1807, he sailed on another voyage to China, in the ship Augustus, owned by Isaac Moses and Son, Hoyt and Tom, and himself, stopping on his way at the Isle of France, where he purchased a cargo of cotton. Disposing of his cotton at Canton he, after some unexpected delays and difficulties, shipped a cargo of tea, upon the recommendation of Houqua, the senior Hong merchant, to whom, in want of sufficient funds, he gave the following note :

CANTON, CHINA, January 15, 1808.

"$103,000. Twelve months after date, for value received, I promise to pay to the order of Houqua, Hong merchant, one hundred and three thousand dollars for cargo of tea per ship Augustus, with interest at 12 per cent. per anum.

EZEKIEL HUBBELL."

Leaving Canton he sailed for Amsterdam, Holland, for the sale of his tea, but on arriving at Plymouth, in the English Channel, found that in consequence of war between England and Holland the port of Amsterdam was blockaded. After consulting London merchants he proceeded on his

---

" It is stated that another vessel from New York had been around the globe, completing the voyage in 1799.

voyage through the North Sea, where, after some delay, lying in sight of the blockading squadron, he ran the blockade in the night. The sun rose brightly the next morning and found the good ship Augustus embeded in the sandy beach, near the main channel to Amsterdam, fully protected by the fortifications, while in the distant offing the British fleet was seen powerless to reach her. Permission being obtained from Louis Bonaparte, then King of Holland, the cargo was soon landed in the king's warehouses at Amsterdam, from which it was afterwards disposed of through the aid of London merchants, and Captain Hubbell returned to New York, arriving in December, 1808. After enormous expenses the result, still, was a large profit, leaving Captain Hubbell, for those days, not only independent, but rich. He paid his note, which was receipted as follows: " Received pay in full, with interest, as adjusted, $119,000. HOUQUA."

Under this Captain Hubbell wrote: " Paid, thank God ! E. H."

From 1809 until 1812 Captain Hubbell resided at his country home in Bridgeport, where he occupied his time in gratifying his tastes and assisting his friends in their various pursuits in life. In 1813 he entered into an extensive speculation by purchasing large tracts of woodlands near West Point, on the Hudson river, with the object of furnishing ship timber, but the enterprise proved a losing investment. This, with other losses in consequence of the war, led him again to project foreign adventure.

In 1817, after nine years spent mostly in retirement, he planned a voyage to the eastern world, and in combination with his friends Hoyt and Tom and others, sailed in his old ship, Citizen, as captain and supercargo, with ample means in Spanish dollars, for Manila. There he loaded with sugars and indigo, and returned to New York, realizing but moderate returns on the expenditures and risks. Retaining his interest in the Citizen, she was despatched again to Manila in the spring of 1819, under the command of Captain Loring, with Captain Hubbell's son George William, then twenty-three years of age, on board as supercargo in charge of the business of the ship. She loaded at Manila for Hamburg, where she arrived in May, 1820. His son, after dispatching the ship from Hamburg back to Manila, in charge of Captain Loring as master and supercargo, returned to New York, where he arrived in February, 1821.

Captain Hubbell continued to reside at his home in Bridgeport from the spring of 1818 until 1821, when he embarked in the ship Ajax, a new vessel in which he was interested, and the building of which he superintended. His two sons, George William and Henry Wilson, the former twenty-five and the latter sixteen years of age, were passengers on this voyage, and had in view the establishing of a mercantile house in Manila. The Ajax sailed from New York April 21, 1821, and arrived at Manila the following August, after 120 days passage. She loaded and returned to New York, arriving in May, 1822, leaving his sons at Manila, who during the year prepared a cargo for the Ajax on her return as a regular trader in the monsoon season. Captain Hubbell made four voyages in the Ajax, taking out valuable investments of English and French manufactures adapted to the wants of that people. The Ajax was finally sold, and within four months afterwards, in August, 1825, foundered in crossing the Atlantic on a voyage to England.

In June, 1825, he took command of the ship Sabina, and proceeded to Manila, where he loaded and arrived home April 22, 1826, bringing with him his younger son.

On December 26, 1826, he sailed on a voyage in the ship Sabina to Rio Janeiro and Valparaiso (where he landed under very different circumstances from those encountered on his former visit to Chili in 1801), thence to Lima and Pata in Peru, Guayaquil, in Ecuador, thence to the Sandwich Islands, and thence to Manila. At the latter place he loaded his ship from proceeds of treasure which was taken over in the ship from Lima, together with returns from cocoa shipped from Guayaquil, and sandal wood from the Sandwich Islands. After an absence of fifteen months and eighteen days he arrived at New York April 14, 1828, in a passage of one hundred and eighteen days from Manila. His son, Henry Wilson, in the capacity of supercargo, was with him throughout the voyage. This was Captain Hubbell's last voyage.

The following extract is from a letter written by Capt. Hubbell under date Dec. 7, 1833:

" I have retired from going to sea, some five or six years, but to give you some idea of my travels, I have traveled 245,000 geographical miles since I passed my fourteenth year, which distance was made up in eight voyages to the Indies, which average over 30,000 miles each voyage. I am 65 years of age—now set myself down in this village enjoying the fruits of my travels and for passtime accepted the Presidency of the Connecticut Bank, which has been in operation two years very successfully thus far."

Capt. Hubbell was a member of the First Congregational Church in Bridgeport, to which he was strongly attached. He died from the effects of an influenza April 1, 1834.

George William Hubbell and Henry Wilson Hubbell, sons of Capt. Ezekiel Hubbell, were captains, supercargos and merchantmen, and followed the sea most of their lives. George William, after traveling round the globe many times, performing efficient and successful service as a merchant, died at Manila, Philippine Islands, May 3, 1831, aged 35 years. Henry Wilson continued to follow the sea as a merchant more than twenty years after the decease of his brother, and his voyages in distance sailed sums up to over 370,000 miles."

Two other illustrations of Bridgeport sea captains are given in "A Centennial History" of 1876, by Major W. B. Hincks, in some sketches of men of the Revolution.

" Early in the war Capt. David Hawley, of Stratfield, sailed to the West Indies for a cargo of gunpowder, which, upon his return, was divided between the towns of Stratford and Fairfield, a part of it being stored for a time in Nichols' tavern on the old county road. In March, 1776, he sailed again from Stratford in command of a privateer sloop, but was captured, when four days out, by a British man of war, Bellona. Large inducements were offered him by his captors to change his allegiance and act as a pilot to the British fleet, but these were firmly declined. He was taken to Halifax, but after a captivity of only two weeks made his escape with eight companions in a small boat, and at length found his way back home. In August, 1776, he was commissioned by

---

[13] See History of the Hubbell Family, 144.

the legislature to raise a naval detachment for service upon Lake Champlain, and a few months later he took part in the disastrous action fought upon this lake between the British and American flotillas. After this, Long Island Sound was his cruising ground, and besides capturing Judge Jònes we find him in May, 1777, and again in August of the same year, bringing a number of prizes into Black Rock harbor. After the war he resided in Bridgeport until his decease in 1807. He built on the corner of Water and Gilbert streets the first brick house erected within the city limits."

"Capt. Samuel Smedley sailed upon the Atlantic as commander of the brig Defense, perhaps the most successful vessel in the Colonial Navy. He captured many prizes, among them the British ship Cyrus, mounting eighteen guns and laden with a cargo that sold for about £20,000, one of the most valuable captures made during the revolution. After the war Capt. Smedley was for many years collector of Customs for this district, residing and having his office at Fairfield."

Capt. Isaac Burroughs, son of Stephen Burroughs, born in Bridgeport or Newfield, Conn., in 1778, and died at his residence in Bridgeport, Conn., January 8, 1861, was also a sea captain. Like his father before him, he was extensively engaged in navigation and owned a large number of vessels, which plied between Boston, New York and nearly all the southern ports, besides visiting many of the islands of the sea. He was a large owner of real estate in this city, and a director in the old Bridgeport bank. He was a life-long Whig and Republican, and as such represented his town in the State Legislature. He was a warden for several years of St. John's Episcopal Church, and one of its most liberal supporters. He married Rebecca, daughter of Andrew Hurd, of Old Mill, Conn. Their children were six in number, all of whom are deceased. Catharine A. married A. A. Pettingill, an accomplished gentleman and scholar, of Bridgeport. She gave in her will the elegant building known as the Burroughs Block, to the Bridgeport Public Library for a perpetual library building.[14]

---

[14] See Bridgeport Public Library and Reading Room.

CHAPTER XX.

ECCLESIASTICAL HISTORY.

EWFIELD village people, both Congregational and Episcopal, went to Stratfield, a distance of one mile or more, about twenty-five years, to church, but as soon as the borough was organized in 1800 movements began to bring these churches into the borough, where then were located the post office and stores.

The Episcopal people were the first to build a church edifice here.

St. John's Church, Bridgeport.

The first edifice built as a house of worship for this church in Stratfield was erected in the summer of 1748, as indicated by the following record :[1]

"I have formerly mentioned a Church built at Stratfield, in which they are very urgent to have me officiate every third Sunday, because we have large congregations when I preach there. The people living in the town and westward are very much against it, because Mr. Caner used to keep steadily to the Church in town, but then there was neither Church nor Congregation at Stratfield."

Mr. Caner resigned his pastorate in Fairfield and removed to Boston in the year 1747, and Mr. Lamson was his successor as missionary pastor at Fairfield, and he says there was "neither Church nor congregation at Stratfield," under

---

[1] Church Documents of Connecticut, vol. i, page 246, letter of Joseph Lamson, dated Fairfield, Nov. 10, 1748.

Mr. Caner, and hence the interest in establishing a church in this locality must have taken form and the church been built after Mr. Lamson came and in the year 1748, and Mr. Lamson held services in it that year. It was called St. John's Church and was a frame building with a steeple, and stood on the corner of Church Lane (now Wood avenue, of Bridgeport). Among the contributors for its erection were Col. John Burr, John Holburton, Timothy Wheeler, Joseph Seeley, John Nichols, Richard Hall and Samuel Beardslee. For some years the Rev. Joseph Lamson officiated, dividing his labors so as to minister here and in other localities, and was succeeded by the Rev. John Sayre.

Tradition says Mr. Lamson was engaged to marry Abigail Rumsey, of Fairfield, that she went to Stratford to visit friends, was taken very ill, and being attended by her parents and Mr. Lamson in her illness, she directed just before her decease, that a string of gold beads which she wore should be taken from her neck and placed on his, which was done and he wore them as long as he lived. The following is the tombstone inscription memorial of the young lady: "Abigail Rumsey, Daughter of Mr. Benj^{mn} & Mrs. Rebecka Rumsey of Fairfield, Who Died Octb^r 14, 1743, Aged 16 years & 7 months."[1]

Although there was neither church nor congregation at Stratfield, there were communicants of the Episcopal Church residing here while Mr. Caner preached at Fairfield, for the following vote is recorded in the Stratfield society's book: "December 24, 1746. Voted a tax or rate on all the polls and ratable estate of the Society, of nine pence on the pound to defray the ministerial charges in the society, Professed Churchmen exempted." This vote, however, to exempt the churchmen was rescinded at a society meeting the next February.

It is certain that some of these men who contributed to build this Episcopal Church were prominent persons in the Congregational society until the great stir made soon after Whitefield's visit to Stratford and Fairfield in October, 1740.

---

[1] See page 227 of this book.

The following record is conclusive: "At a lawful meeting of
the Society of Stratfield held on 22 day of December, 1743,
it was voted that Capt. John Burr, David Sherman, Jr., and
Timothy Wheeler be a committee to order the prudentials
of the society for the year ensuing." Col. John Burr was
moderator of this same meeting, so that his position as a
prominent man of the Congregational society at that date is
also decided. It is indicated that Col. Burr and Timothy
Wheeler united with the Episcopal Church in the year 1744,
since in the annual meeting of the Stratfield society, December, 1744, neither of their names occurs.

John Beardslee, who has been supposed to have been a
member of the Episcopal Church some years earlier, was
moderator of the Stratfield society's meeting in October,
1743. Samuel Beardslee was not prominent in the Stratfield
society; he conformed to the Episcopal Church, probably,
with others in 1744, and after several years joined the Baptist
Church.

It is therefore quite certain that in 1740 there were very
few if any communicants of the Episcopal Church residing
within the boundaries of the Stratfield society.

The records of this St. John's Church now in existence,
begin with a copy of the summons of "those persons profess-
ors of the Episcopal Church, inhabitants of Stratfield Society,
to appear at the Church in said Society, Thursday the ninth
day of instant December, at two of the clock in the afternoon,
for the purpose of forming themselves into one body Corporate, or Society, for to chuse Society officers for the well-
ordering and governing the prudential affairs of said Episcopal Church as they in their wisdom shall judge meet and
fitting." This document bears the date December 1, 1784.
The first meeting was held on the day designated and after
choosing the parish officers it was "voted to settle Mr. Philo
Shelton in this Society." Mr. Shelton at that time was a
candidate for orders, and continued to officiate as lay reader
until the arrival of Bishop Seabury, who admitted him to the
order of Deacons of Christ Church, Middletown, and to the
order of Priesthood in Trinity Church, New Haven, in 1785.
Aside from the fact that his rectorship was the first after the

organization, and the longest that the parish has known, he is also to be remembered as the first individual who received Episcopal ordination in this country, as appears from the inscription placed over his remains, which were interred in the Episcopal Church which was at Mill Plain, Fairfield, also under his charge. The increase of business and the population in the borough of Bridgeport, necessitated a change in the locality of the church, and accordingly in 1801 the second edifice was erected at the southeast corner of State and Broad streets in Bridgeport. Mr. Shelton's rectorship continued until Easter in 1824.

The following sketch of his life and labors is taken largely from the "Seabury Centenary of Connecticut," published in 1885.

Rev. Philo Shelton, son of Samuel and grandson of Daniel Shelton, was born in Ripton—now Huntington—May 7, 1754. He was graduated at Yale College in 1775, and officiated as lay reader in several places, principally at Fairfield, Stratfield and Weston, after 1779. While waiting for ordination he married, April 20, 1781, Lucy, daughter of Philip Nichols, Esq., of Stratford—now Bridgeport. In February, 1785, a formal arrangement was made that his services in each of the three places should be proportioned to the number of churchmen residing in them respectively, and until he should be in orders it was stipulated to pay him twenty shillings lawful money for each day that he officiated. Rev. Ashbel Baldwin, his nearest neighbor in parochial work, and most intimate friend and associate in efforts to build up the church in Connecticut, used to say that the hands of Bishop Seabury were first laid upon the head of Mr. Shelton on the 3d of August, 1785, so that his name really begins the long list of clergy who have received ordination in this country by Bishops of the Protestant Episcopal Church. In the Diocesan Convention, under an established rule of that body, he invariably outranked Mr. Baldwin, and so was frequently the presiding officer in the absence of the Bishop, which is another proof that he was his senior by ordination as well as in years.

After his admission to Holy Orders, according to his own statement, Mr. Shelton took full "pastoral charge of the cure of Fairfield, including Stratfield and Weston, dividing his time equally between the three churches, with a salary of óne hundred pounds per annum from the congregations, and the use of what lands belonged to the cure." Five years passed away before the enterprise of building a new church in Fairfield was really begun, and then it was erected about a mile west of the site where the old one stood, and was only inclosed and made fit for occupancy at the time and not finished and consecrated until 1798.

Then the population was drifting from Stratfield toward the borough of Bridgeport, and in 1801 it was deemed advisable to demolish the old church and build a new one in a more central locality; and Mr. Shelton, seeing the wisdom and advantage of this movement, encouraged it.

This new church in the borough was so far completed that it was used in the beginning of Advent, 1801, and two years later "the ground floor was sold at public vendue for the purpose of building the pews and seats thereon, and finishing the church, and the money raised in the sale amounted to between six and seven hundred dollars." The building cost about thirty-five hundred dollars above this, and was met by voluntary contributions of the people. Mr. Shelton, in speaking of the whole work, said: "It has been conducted in harmony, with good prudence, strict economy, and a degree of elegance and taste which does honor to the committee and adds respectability to the place."

For nearly forty years the scene of his ministerial labors was undisturbed, and he dwelt among his people in quietness and confidence and had the satisfaction of seeing them attain to a high degree of worldly prosperity. The silent influence of a good life carried him along smoothly and left its gentle impress wherever he was known. "A faithful pastor, a guileless and godly man," is a part of the inscription upon the marble monument erected over his ashes in the Mountain Grove Cemetery at Bridgeport, a few years since, by his son William, and these words sum up very appropriately his ministerial and Christian character. While he confined himself closely to the duties of his cure, he shrank not from work put upon him by the diocese and was for twenty-four years a member of the standing committee and a firm supporter of ecclesiastical authority in seasons of trial and trouble. He was also several times chosen a deputy to the General Convention, and never failed to attend its sessions.

Mr. Shelton continued to serve in this parish until his resignation of the pastorate of St. John's Church, which took effect at Easter in 1824. After this he confined his labors regularly to the church in Fairfield, but did not long survive the change, for he died February 27, 1825, and was buried under the chancel of the old church in Mill Plain, Fairfield, where he had ministered so many years, and a marble tablet was provided by the congregation to mark his resting place, on which, among other things, were inscribed the date of his birth, graduation, admission to Holy Orders, and the words: " being the first clergyman Episcopally ordained in the United States."

The remains of Mr. Shelton now have a final resting-place with those of his wife and two of his daughters in Mountain Grove Cemetery. A monumental tablet in the wall of St. John's Church, Bridgeport, "bears an affectionate testimony to his Christian worth and ministerial fidelity." Bishop Brownell said of him: "For simplicity of character, amiable manners, unaffected piety, and a faithful devotion to the duties of the ministerial office, he has left an example by which all his surviving brethren may profit, and which few of them may hope to surpass."

His widow survived him thirteen years, being an intelligent and devout churchwoman, who, as it has been said, "left a name only to be loved and honored by her friends." Two of his sons entered the ministry. George Augustus Shelton, the younger, was a graduate of Yale College, and died rector of St. James's Church, Newtown, L. I., in 1863. The other son, William Shelton, D.D., succeeded his father for a time in Fairfield, and then went to Buffalo, where for more than half a century he was the distinguished rector of St. Paul's Church, the oldest parish in that city. Both died childless.

Rev. Henry R. Judah in 1824 succeeded the Rev. Philo Shelton in the pastorate of St. John's Church, and continued therein until the year 1833, when he was followed by the Rev. Dr. Gurdon S. Coit. In 1836 the third church edifice was built, located at the southeast corner of Broad and Cannon streets, and Dr. Coit served the parish until 1861, when he resigned.

Gurdon Saltonstall Coit, D.D., was born in New London, Conn., October 28, 1808, and was graduated at Yale College in 1828, and became rector of St. John's Church, Bridgeport, in October, 1833. In 1836, during his labors here, the third edifice of worship for this church was built on the corner of Broad and Cannon streets, a stone structure of dignified proportions and commodious capacity. It is still standing but occupied for other purposes, the congregation having removed to their new edifice on the corner of Park and Fairfield avenue.

Dr. Coit continued rector of this parish with much success until he accepted the chaplaincy of Colonel Berdan's regiment of sharp-shooters, September 26, 1861. After the war he became rector at Naugatuck and subsequently at West Haven. He died in Southport, Conn., Nov. 10, 1869.

In 1861 Dr. Coit was succeeded by the Rev. Junius M. Willey, whose brief rectorship was terminated by his untimely death on April 7, 1866. This is the only instance in the long history of the parish in which its members have been called to follow the remains of one who while yet their official head had been summoned from the labor of earth to the rest of the blessed.

Rev. Eaton W. Maxcy, D.D., became the pastor of St. John's Church at Whit Sunday, 1867, and continued in its service until his resignation took effect on Easter, 1885. During his labors here the fourth edifice of worship for this parish was erected, being located at the corner of Park and Fairfield avenues, which was occupied by the congregation the first time at Easter in 1875. It is one of the finest edifices in the city and has one of the most favorable locations. Dr. Maxcy resigned this parish after eighteen years of successful and most constant labors, at Easter, 1885, and has since become the rector of a pleasant and prosperous church in the city of Troy, N. Y.

First Congregational Church of Bridgeport.

This was originally the Stratfield Church, the history of which until 1745 has been given in a previous part of this book. The Rev. Samuel Cooke, the pastor, died December 2, 1747, and his successor was Lyman Hall.

Mr. Lyman Hall was born in Wallingford, April 12, 1724, and graduated at Yale College in 1747. He studied theology with an uncle in Cheshire, and was ordained in Stratfield, September 20, 1749, but his pastorate was short, closing June 18, 1751. He then taught school in Fairfield, studied medicine and became a physician. He married, May 20, 1752, Abigail, the accomplished daughter of Thaddeus Barr. She died July 8, 1753, as seen by the inscription on her grave-stone.[3]

Mr. Hall was in Fairfield as late as 1757, but afterwards removed to the State of Georgia, and early in 1775 took a seat in the Continental Congress as a representative of that patriotic people. He was a signer of the Declaration of Independence, and in 1783 was the first Governor of that State. He died October 19, 1790, leaving a widow but no children.[4]

---

[3] " Here lies buried the Body of Mrs. Abigail Hall, wife of Lyman Hall M.A., Daughter of Thaddeus Burr, Esqr., died July 8th, 1753, Aged 24 Years.

> Modest, yet free, with innocence adorned ;
> To please and win, by Art and Nature formed ;
> Benevolent and wise, in virtue firm ;
> Constant in Friendship, in Religion warm ;
> A partner tender, unaffected, kind ;
> A lovely Form, with a more lovely mind,—
> The scene of Life tho' short sh' improved so well,
> No charms in human forms could more excel ;
> Christ's Life her copy ; His pure law her Guide ;
> Each part She acted, perfected, and dy'd."

[4] Sermon by the Rev. Charles Ray Palmer, of Bridgeport, 1876.

Rev. Robert Ross,[1] after an interval of two years and more, succeeded Mr. Hall in the pastorate of the Stratfield Congregational Church. He was the son of Irish parents. but a native of this country. He was born in 1726, graduated at Princeton in 1751, and ordained pastor here November 28, 1753, which position he filled with much efficiency and success more than forty-two years. He lived on the old stage road, a little west of Church Lane, in a house recently taken down. He was beyond doubt a remarkable man. He was six feet in height and well proportioned. His presence was imposing, and his ruffled shirt, wig, and cocked hat seemed peculiarly in keeping with it. His usual dress was a black suit with knee breeches, and white topped boots. He was distinguished for his classical attainments and was esteemed as a sound theologian ; but he most strongly impressed himself upon the community through the warmth of his patriotism and the decisiveness of his political convictions. He became a man of influence on the patriotic side and proportionally obnoxious to the royalists. At the outbreak of the Revolutionary War he preached on the text, " For the divisions of Reuben there were great searchings of heart," in a way long to be remembered. A company of soldiers, raised to join the invasion of Canada, in the fall of 1775, mustered in his door yard and was commended to God in a fervent prayer by him, before starting on their expedition. He was a steadfast promoter of education and published some school books. He married, first, Mrs. Sarah, widow of Samuel Hawley, December 18, 1753. She was Sarah Edwards before marriage to Mr. Hawley. She died October 10, 1772. Mr. Ross married, second, Eulilia, daughter of Ebenezer and Elizabeth (Williams) Bartram, of Fairfield. She died December 9, 1785, in her 49th year, being much esteemed by the people. Mr. Ross married in 1786, Sarah, daughter of Rev. Jonathan Merrick, of North Branford. She died August 29, 1799, leaving a son, Merrick, who died September 11, 1799. By his first wife he had a son and daughter. The son, while a lad, was drowned in his father's well, but the daughter, Sarah, married Eliphalet Jennings, and her descendants are

---

[1] Sermon by the Rev. Charles Ray Palmer, of Bridgeport, 1876.

still living. Another son, of the third marriage, survived his father only a few days.

Mr. Ross resigned his charge April 30, 1796, and died August 29, 1799, of a fever, and within twenty-four hours Mrs. Ross died of the same disease. They were buried in the same grave.

The long period covered by the pastorates of Cook, Hall, and Ross—over eighty years—saw many changes in the community at Stratfield. The inhabitants were no longer solely farmers and stock growers, but had developed, before the middle of the century, in spite of all discouragements, a coasting trade of quite honorable proportions, and a race of mariners had been bred to the ocean. Mechanics and tradesmen, in a new form, had found means for living in Stratfield, and thus the simple uniformity of the earlier period passed away. Political events, too, brought about changes. The French and Indian wars introduced no foeman within the borders of Connecticut, but her sons did yeoman service in the struggles of sister colonies. The Revolution, as is well known, laid heavy burdens upon the Connecticut coast, and the long train of evils which accompanied and followed it went far toward ruining every interest of society. The last ten or twenty years of Mr. Ross's ministry were, for many reasons, times of trial. The diseases, vices, sufferings, losses, universal insolvency, which came with or were entailed by the war, made darker days than had ever been seen before. Good morals were forsaken and godliness decayed to a disastrous extent. The difficulties, depressions and straits of the church during this time must have tasked even so ardent and zealous a man as Mr. Ross. As the process of recuperation slowly went on, another change in the community worked important results. The little cluster of houses and stores which acquired the name of Newfield, on the shore of the harbor and in the vicinity of the present intersection of State and Main streets, began to increase in importance, and this was the nucleus of the future town and city of Bridgeport, in which the individuality of Stratfield was eventually to be lost.

41

Rev. Samuel Blatchford was the successor of Mr.
Ross in the pastorate of the Stratfield Church. He was the
son of Henry and Mary Blatchford, and born in Devonport,
Devonshire, England, in the year 1767. His father's family
sympathised with the American cause during the Revolution,
and he was often employed to convey means of relief to
American prisoners of war in the Mill prison. His interest
in these objects of his friends' bounty led him to an early
purpose to visit this country. He was placed at a boarding
school at Willington, in Somersetshire, and afterwards at
Homerton College, near London. After completing his studies he was employed as assistant minister, and in November,
1789, he was ordained pastor at Kingsbridge, near Dartmouth.
He married, in March, 1788, Alicia, daughter of Thomas
Windeatt, Esq., of Bridgetown, Totwas, a lady admirably
fitted for her station, and spared to him to the end of his life.
In 1791 Mr. Blatchford removed to Topsham, near Exeter,
and thence, in 1795, he emigrated to America, according to
his long cherished purpose, and arrived in New York August
1st of that year. He preached first in Bedford, N. Y.; then
for a year at Greenfield Hill, succeeding there President
Dwight.

In February, 1797, he was invited to preach in the Stratfield church for six months, with the view of a settlement,
which he afterwards accepted, and he was installed November 22 of the same year. His salary being inadequate, he
added to it by teaching an academy for boys. He lived in a
house now numbered 644 Main street, and his academy was
just below, on land now owned by Thomas Calef. He labored here until March 20, 1804, when he resigned to accept a
call to Lansingburgh, N. Y., where he continued until his
death, March 17, 1828. He was honored with the degree of
D.D. by Williams College in 1808. He had seventeen children, of whom ten survived him. While here he had not
developed his best powers, for, being unfamiliar with American life, scantily supported, burdened with work and care in
his double duties, he could not do justice to himself. But he
became an able, prominent man. As a preacher he was
instructive in matter, unaffected and impressive in manner,

He was well read in theology, and decided in his convictions. He possessed generous sympathies and was interested in all enterprises of beneficence, especially in the education of young men. His labors here were of great service to the church, and only too soon terminated. The church at his coming was low as to prosperity, but he gave it a rising impulse. A revival in 1800 added a number of persons to the membership, and in 1803 a movement to build a new house of worship was successfully inaugurated. He died December 2, 1846.

A story is told of Mr. Blatchford's ready and appropriate use of language in rendering thanks at the table of William Worden. Mr. Worden had been to short beach and just, returned with some fine clams, which Mrs. Worden had hastily cooked, as Mr. Blatchford happened to call. A very plain table was set with bread, butter, milk, tea and the clams, and Mr. Blatchford was invited to share the meal and ask a blessing, which proposition he accepted, and in giving thanks said: "O Lord, thou hast cast our lines in pleasant places and given us a goodly heritage. Thou feedest us with the finest of the wheat and givest us the milk of kine. Thou causest us to suck the abundance of the sea and treasures hid in the sand."

The removal of the Congregational place of worship was more difficult than that of the Episcopal. The movement originated in the borough and was wholly voluntary, and therefore the records of the inception do not appear on the books of the society.

The building shown in the accompanying cut as the First Congregational Church was erected and inclosed during the year 1803. On June 11, 1804, the society voted to agree to hold the meetings for public worship half the time in Bridgeport, when a house suitable for that purpose shall, without expense to the society, be so far completed as to accommodate such meetings. Ayes, 32; nays, 19.

A meeting of the society was warned and held June 20, 1808, in the new meeting house, and it was voted to hold public worship there two-thirds of the time, and during this year the change was made entire.

METHODIST.   St. John's   Second
    First Congregational.   Episcopal.   Congregational.

A View of the Churches of Bridgeport in 1835, looking from the South.

A list of pew holders in the old church at this time, not including pew owners, is recorded, namely: Josiah Lacey, Dea. John P. Austin, William DeForest, Lambert Lockwood, Lewis Sturges, Silas Sherman, Ezra Gregory, Thomas Woodward, Simon Backus, Benjamin Wheeler, Stephen Burroughs, Jr., Wilson Hawley, Samuel Hawley, Jr., Elijah Burr, Stephen Hull, Abijah Morehouse, William Benedict, Wid. Mary Sherman, Salmon Hubbell, Robert Southward, David Sterling, Thomas Gouge, Jesse Seeley, Henry May, Abijah Sherman, Samuel Wordin, Levi Silliman, Barzillai Benjamin, Anson Beardsley, Samuel Burr.

In 1830 a division occurred in this church and thirty-nine men and seventy-eight women were dismissed at their own request, to form a second Congregational church, the old church giving them one-half of the church property and funds, and also contributing two thousand dollars toward the erection of a church edifice. This new edifice, when built, being so much of an improvement in such structures, seems to have stimulated enterprise, for the Episcopal Church was enlarged and improved, and the First Congregational people also rebuilt their steeple in an improved form, and reconstructed the pulpit and galleries.[*]

This building was occupied until 1850, when it gave place to the present edifice. The former was purchased for the use of Christ Church and removed upon John street, at the site of the present works of Nichols, Peck and Co., where it was accidentally destroyed by fire in 1851.

Rev. Elijah Waterman was the successor of Mr. Blatchford. He was the son of Nehemiah and Susannah (Isham) Waterman, and born in Bozra, Conn., November 28, 1769; was graduated at Yale College in 1791, and engaged in teaching, intending to study law, but changed his purpose, and in 1792 became a student under Dr. Dwight at Green-

---

[*] A nearly complete list of pew holders in the First Congregational Church in 1835.

Officers of the Church: Rev. John Blatchford, pastor; Isaac Sherman, David Sherwood, and Sylvanus Sterling, deacons; Isaac Sherman, Hanford Lyon, and Joseph Mott, society's committee; Daniel Sterling, treasurer; N. S. Wordin, clerk; Nathaniel Wade, collector; Sylvanus Sterling, salesman.

Pew holders.

Daniel Thatcher,	Alanson Caswell,	Nichols Beardsley,
Alanson Hamlin.	Coley E. Betts,	Lemuel Coleman,
Alexander Hubbell,	James Betts,	William R. Bunnell,
Daniel Sterling,	Daniel Curtis,	Thomas Bartram,
Hanford Lyon,	Henry N. French,	Ira Peck,
Thomas C. Wordin,	Gurdon Hawley,	Joseph C. Lewis,
Samuel Niles,	Abijah Beardsley,	David Hubbell, 3d,
Charles B. Hubbell.	Wyllys Stillman,	Anson Hawley,
Doct. James E. Beach,	Alexander Black,	David Sherwood,
Sylvanus Sterling,	Nathaniel Humiston,	Robert Milne.
David Sterling,	Cyrus Botsford,	Wheeler French, Jr.,
Joel Thorp,	Titus C. Mather,	Judson Bray,
Philo C. Wheeler,	Joseph Mott,	Sturges and Smith,
John M. Thompson,	Isaac M. Conklin,	Isaac E. Beach,
Daniel Fayerweather,	Capt. E. Wicks,	Stephen Nichols,
Charles Hawley,	David Wheeler,	George Kippen,
Gideon Thompson,	David Victory Seeley,	Samuel Porter,
Benjamin Wheeler,	Joseph Knapp,	Elijah C. Spinning,
Isaac Sherman,	George Wade,	Samuel Wordin,
Nathaniel Wade,	Ezra Gregory,	Louisa Bartlett,
Legrand Sterling,	Joseph P. Sturges,	Eleazer Edgerton.
Levi Wordin,		

field Hill, and afterwards with Dr. Jonathan Edwards at New Haven. In April, 1794, he went to Windham to preach as a candidate, and the next October was ordained pastor there and served that church ten years. He married, November 18, 1795, Lucy, daughter of Shubael Abbe, of Windham. She was born May 21, 1778, and died at Bridgeport, Sunday morning, March 17, 1822. He married, second, Lucy Talcott, of Springfield, Mass., in October, 1823, who survived him.

Mr. Waterman's ministry was terminated at Windham in 1804, and on the first day of January, 1806, he was installed pastor of the church in Stratfield, where he continued until his death. He built and resided in the house on Golden Hill street now owned by the heirs of Hanford Lyon. In person he was of medium height, well built, and had the appearance of great physical strength, and possessed a fine presence. He was active in his habits, possessed a high spirit and a keen sense of favors and injuries, and was liable to sudden outbreaks of temper, yet placable. He was a vigorous thinker and his manner of delivery was animated and effective. He was a moderate Calvinist, leaning strongly to the New School side of theology in his day, but being a man of strong common sense and good will he kept his hold on men of both sides, and averted any divisions in his congregation. In 1807 his new church edifice was completed, built by subscription on the site at present occupied by the same society. At first it was occupied two Sundays out of three, but after a short time every Sunday. The borough of Bridgeport was incorporated in 1800, with two hundred and fifty inhabitants, and by a rapid growth it gradually absorbed the dwellers of the more ancient settlement. In 1821 the town of Bridgeport was erected and the parish of Stratfield, practically, ceased to exist. The church soon felt the effects of Mr. Waterman's invigorating administration. August 6, 1806, a confession of faith, a covenant, and standing rules were adopted, and from that time the half-way covenant was discontinued. In 1814 a Sunday-school was organized by Platt Benedict, which was the first in the town, and was ultimately taken under the care of the church.

In April, 1821, the church purchased the land where the chapel stands for a "conference room and academy," and a building was erected to answer both purposes. Mr. Waterman instructed a number of students in theology and proposed to establish a theological school, but did not succeed in this purpose.

When Mr. Waterman was installed the church consisted of forty-seven members. To these there was a steady growth, until in 1815, over one hundred had been added, mostly on profession of faith. Then came a powerful revival which resulted in eighty-four additions. Four more years of quiet growth followed, and then another revival season came, and seventy-seven more were added to the membership. The whole number added during his ministry was about three hundred and sixty.

In 1825, while Mr. Waterman was on a visit to Springfield, Mass., he was taken ill of typhus fever and died there October 11th of that year. The church sent a committee to bring hither his remains for interment, and thus ended a useful life and a most successful ministry.[7]

In the settlement of a successor a difference of views arose which ripened a few years later. The candidates were a son of the former pastor, the Rev. Thomas T. Waterman, and the Rev. Franklin Vail. Mr. Vail was finally chosen, but he had a short pastorate.

Thomas Tileston Waterman,[8] son of the Rev. Elijah Waterman was born in Windham, Conn., September 24, 1801, and four years after removed with his parents to Stratfield, and was prepared for college by his father and at Hartford, and was graduated at Yale in the class of 1822. He studied theology with his father, and was ordained pastor of the Richmond street Congregational Church, of Providence, R. I., December 13, 1826. In 1837 he became pastor of the Fifth Presbyterian Church, of Philadelphia, where he continued until 1843, when he returned to Providence, and was installed pastor of the Fourth Congregational Church, which

---

[7] Sermon of the Rev. C. Ray Palmer.

[8] Fairfield County History, 166.

soon after became known as the Free Evangelical Church. After leaving this church he held pastorates in the Second Presbyterian Church at Galena, Ill., and in the Congregational Churches at Winona, Minn., D'anielsonville, Conn., Spencer, Mass., and Monroe, Conn.

On December 11, 1827, Mr. Waterman married Delia, daughter of Dann Storrs, a native of Mansfield, Conn., and they had children: Thomas S., Alfred T., George I., Lucy M., and Edwin S. Waterman. The Rev. Thomas T. Waterman died in Stratford, Conn., August 7, 1873, aged 71 years.

Rev. Franklin Y. Vail was born at East Hampton, L. I., in 1797, entered Yale College, but did not graduate, studied theology in New York, and was ordained here October 4, 1826. Neither his health nor his tastes fitted him for a pastorate as well as for what became his life-work afterwards —the raising of funds for beneficent enterprises. He was for many years the general agent of the American Tract Society, and was greatly valued by that institution. He afterwards was the principal agent in founding and endowing Lane Theological Seminary at Cincinnati, Ohio, and an institution for female education in that vicinity. He died in that city June 23, 1868, aged seventy-one years. His ministry at Bridgeport ended July 8, 1828, and was notable for a revival season in the winter of 1827 and 8, after which thirty were added to the church.

In the settlement of a successor to Mr. Vail a decided difference of theological sentiment became quite prominent. Mr. John Blatchford, as a candidate in 1828, was understood to be decidedly a new school man, and the more conservative section of the church were opposed to calling him. In January, 1829, the church proved to be nearly equally divided, and the call, issued by a majority of only four, Mr. Blatchford declined. It proved impossible to harmonize the conflicting elements, and, at length, December 28, 1829, a division of the church was resolved upon. On January 24, 1830, three deacons, thirty-six other men, and seventy-eight women were dismissed from the church, at their own request, to form a second church, the old church giving them one-half of the church property and funds, and also contributed two thousand dollars toward the erection of a church edifice. One week later, January 31, 1830, those abiding in the old church, being one hundred and seventy in number, renewed the call to Mr. Blatchford. which he promptly accepted, and served them until July 26, 1836, when he was dismissed.

Rev. John Blatchford, son of the Rev. Samuel Blatchford, D.D., a former pastor of this church, was born May 24, 1799, in Stratfield, graduated at Union College in 1820, studied theology in Princeton Theological Seminary, and was ordained pastor of the Presbyterian Church at Pittstown, N. Y., in August, 1823. He was installed pastor of the Presbyterian Church in Stillwater, in April, 1825, and on February 10, 1830, he was installed here. After being dismissed as above, he removed to the West, resided successively at Jacksonville and Chicago, Ill., and at Wheeling, Va. From 1841 to 1844 he was connected with Marion College, the latter part of the period as president. He removed thence to West Ely, Mo., and thence to Quincy Ill., where he died in April, 1855. He received the degree of D.D. from Marion College in 1841. He possessed a bright, ready mind, a genial spirit and pleasing manners. His general appearance was attractive and he was almost any where an acceptable minister. A very interesting revival occurred under his labors here in Bridgeport in 1831, which added eighty-six to the church membership, and the church parted with him reluctantly.

Rev. John Woodbridge followed Mr. Blatchford, being installed here June 14, 1837, and continued about seventeen months and was in 1839 installed over the North Church in New Hartford, Conn.

Rev. John H. Hunter succeeded Dr. Woodbridge, being installed here February 27, 1839, and continued until November 13, 1845. He soon after went west to look after lands left him by his father and was not again settled in the ministry. This church grew under his ministry, especially in 1844, when twenty-five members were added at one time.

Rev. Benjamin St. John Page was installed pastor here February 10, 1847, and continued until August 30, 1853. During his pastorate here the present house of worship was erected. The old house was removed northward a short distance and occupied while building the new one, and was used by this society for public worship the last time, April 7, 1850. It was purchased for the use of Christ Church, removed to a new site on John street west of Broad, and in 1851 was accidentally destroyed by fire.[*]

The new house was built and fitted up at a cost of about $25,000—raised by subscription—the first paper bearing the date June 1, 1848. About two-thirds of the amount was in stock, bearing interest at the rate of six per cent. per annum. Most of this—both principal and interest—was subsequently given to the society. Thomas Dixon, of Stamford, Conn., was the architect. The builders were, William A. Dowd, mason, and Beardsley and Daskam, carpenters and joiners. The building committee consisted of Freeman C. Bassett, Ira Sherman, Hanford Lyon and Sherman Hartwell. The two first named were the active members of the committee.

This edifice was dedicated on Thursday, April 11, 1850, and on the Sunday following was opened for public worship, and is well represented by the accompanying engraving—in which the steeple of the former house, on its temporary site, also appears. Beyond that is faintly seen the steeple of the former St. John's Church.

In 1882 a thorough renovation and some improvement in the interior of this edifice was deemed necessary for the comfort and prosperity of the church and society. Accordingly the side galleries were removed, the walls, ceiling and ornamental plastering repaired, and all suitably decorated. Elegant stained-glass, memorial windows were furnished, also two new furnaces, new carpets and cushions, at a total cost of six thousand dollars.

---

[*] The history of the First Congregational Church and its ministers thus far given has been taken largely from the manuscript of the Rev. C. R. Palmer, cheerfully granted for this purpose, it having been obtained by him during several years' research and inquiry.

THE FIRST CONGREGATIONAL CHURCH, ERECTED IN 1848.

The following is a list of the memorial windows:

Rev. Charles Chauncey, pastor, 1695–1714.
Rev. Elijah Waterman, pastor, 1806–1825.
Rev. Samuel Blatchford, D.D., pastor, 1797–1804. }
Rev. John Blatchford, D.D., pastor, 1830–1836. }

Hanford Lyon.	Rev. Henry Jones.
Ira Sherman. }	Sherman Hartwell. }
James C. Loomis. }	Sophia Todd Hartwell. }
Dea. Sylvanus Sterling. }	Frederick W. Parrott. }
Thomas C. Wordin. }	Henry R. Parrott. }
Dea. Isaac Sherman. }	Vestibule with historical dates.
Dea. Rowland B. Lacey. }	

A List of the Deacons of the old Stratfield Church of Christ, which is now the First Congregational Church, of Bridgeport:

David Sherman, chosen in 1695, and died in 1753, aged 88 years.

Thomas Hawley, chosen in 1712, and died in 1722, aged 44 years.

Lemuel Sherwood, chosen in 1722, and died in 1732.

Joseph Booth, chosen in 1733, and died in 1763, aged 74 years.

Richard Hubbell, son of one of the first members of this church, was chosen in 1738, and died in 1788, aged 92 years. He gave to the church in 1738 the silver tankard now in use in the communion service, on which his name is engraved.

William Bennett, chosen in 1754, removed to North Fairfield —now Easton—in 1756, and died in 1788, aged 79 years.

Henry Rowland, chosen in 1756, and died in 1775.

Abel Seeley, chosen in 1775, served until 1779, and died in 1810, aged 84 years.

Elijah Hawley, chosen in 1776, removed from the town in 1790, and died in Ohio in 1825, aged 81 years.

Seth Seeley, chosen in 1779, served until 1806, when, at his own request, he was excused from further service, and died in 1817, aged 79 years.

Seth Sherman, chosen in 1806, died in 1807.

Doct. James E. Beach, chosen October 10, 1806, and died in 1838, aged 76 years. He gave to the church the silver flagon now in use in the communion service.

John P. Austin, chosen October 21, 1807, served until 1813, when he removed from the place.

William DeForest, chosen in 1813, was dismissed at his own request with others to form the Second Congregational Church.

Stephen Hawley, chosen August 31, 1821, and dismissed at his own request for the same purpose as Dea. DeForest.

Josiah B. Baldwin, chosen in 1821, dismissed the same, and for the same purpose as Dea. DeForest.

Isaac Sherman, chosen in 1830, and died November 23, 1863, aged 75 years.

Sylvanus Sterling, chosen November 4, 1831, and died in 1848, aged 61 years.

David Sherwood, chosen November 4, 1831, and died in 1873, aged 94 years.

Samuel Beach, M.D., chosen May 4, 1849, and died May 6, 1853, a victim of the railroad accident at Norwalk bridge.

Rowland B. Lacey, chosen August 30, 1850, and is still serving.

John W. Hincks, chosen Sept. 1, 1854, died Feb. 6, 1875.

Rev. Henry Jones, chosen Feb. 15, 1858, died Nov. 9, 1878.

Elbert E. Hubbell, chosen February 25, 1858.

Rev. Guy B. Day, chosen April 1, 1874, and is still serving.

Samuel R. Wilmot, chosen March, 1875, and is still serving.

William B. Hincks, chosen March, 1875, and is still serving.

The communion service of the First Congregational Church is of solid silver, and is an aggregation of gifts dating from an early period in the history of the church, consisting of various antique patterns with inscriptions, highly valued as memorials of those who have passed on to the communion of a higher sphere. The list contains the following:

One silver tankard, the gift of Lieut. Richard Hubbell to the Church of Christ in Stratfield, A. D. 1738.

One silver flagon, presented to the First Congregational Church in Bridgeport by Doct. James E. Beach, in 1830.

One silver cup, a gift to the Church of Christ in Stratfield by Matthew Sherwood, January, 1713.

One silver cup, presented by Mr. John Edwards in 1746.

One silver cup, presented to the First Congregational Church of Bridgeport, by Salmon Hubbell, in 1829.

One silver cup, presented by Isaac Sherman in 1836.
One silver cup, presented by Isaac E. Beach in 1839.
One silver cup, presented by Mrs. Sylvanus Sterling in 1839.
One silver cup, presented by Ira Sherman in 1839.
One silver cup, presented by Mrs. Ellen Porter in 1843.
Two silver cups, not inscribed.
Three silver goblets, presented by Mrs. Ira Sherman in 1868.
One silver plate, presented by the Rev. Henry Jones in 1867.
One silver plate, presented by Hanford Lyon in 1867.
One silver plate, presented by Dea. John W. Hincks in 1867.
One silver plate, presented by Dea. Rowland B. Lacey in 1867.

Rev. Joseph H. Towne became pastor of this, the First Congregational Church of Bridgeport, June 13, 1854, and continued here until June 29, 1858. He was pastor in Salem Street Church in Boston about 1838, when he was joined by a portion of his church in founding the Leyden Chapel, located in the same vicinity. This enterprise embraced some excellent men, but was not successful. They inaugurated a new departure in the order of worship, which was much commented upon at the time. It consisted in the introduction of responsive reading and chants, an order adopted since that day by many Congregational churches in New England. Mr. Towne was an able and very interesting preacher. During his pastorate the congregations were large, and in 1857 and 8 there occurred one of the most extensive revivals this church has ever known.

Rev. Matson Mier Smith, successor to Mr. Towne, was born in Harlem—now New York—April 4, 1826, was graduated at Columbia College, N. Y., in 1843, and at the Union Theological Seminary, N. Y., in 1847. He was ordained by the Presbytery of Geneva, October 23, 1849, as pastor of the church in Ovid, N. Y., and in the same year, November 14, he married Mary Stuart, daughter of Norman White, Esq., of New York City, where she was born. He resigned his charge in Ovid March 21, 1851, to accept a call to the Harvard Church, Brookline, Mass., where he was installed June 5, 1851. There he labored until he was dismissed November 23, 1858, to accept a call to this church, where he was installed January 5, 1859, and dismissed June 6, 1865. On March 6, 1866, he was ordained deacon in the Protestant Episcopal Church by Bishop Eastburn, at Boston, Mass.

Rev. George Richards, a native of New London, was graduated at Yale College in 1840, associate pastor for a time in Summer street in Boston, after that was pastor in Litchfield, Conn., from which place he came to this church and was installed January 3, 1866. He was dismissed August 24, 1870, and died October 20, 1870.

Rev. Charles Ray Palmer was born in New Haven, May 2, 1834, and was the son of the Rev. Ray Palmer, D.D., and Ann Maria, the daughter of Marmaduke Waud, Esq., of New York City. His father with his family at the time occupied the school building on the lower green as a Young Ladies' Institute. In the autumn of that year he removed eastward, and in May, 1835, to Bath, Maine, where he became pastor and continued fifteen and a half years. Charles R. Palmer's education commenced in the academy at Bath, and in September, 1849, he entered Billings Academy at Andover, Mass., in the middle class, where he was graduated in 1851, and entered Yale College. He was graduated at Yale in 1855, and went to Mississippi as a private tutor for a year in the family of John Murdock, Esq., a planter. In the autumn of 1856 he entered the Andover Theological Seminary, where he graduated in 1859. On August 29, 1860, he was ordained pastor of the Tabernacle Church of Salem, Mass., where he labored nearly twelve years. In 1865 he spent seven months in Europe. On February 10, 1869, he married Mary Chapin, eldest daughter of A. S. Barnes, Esq., of Brooklyn, N. Y. She was born in Philadelphia, Pa., but in her infancy her parents removed to Brooklyn, where she was educated.

On August 15, 1872, Mr. Palmer commenced his pastoral labors here, and on the 11th of the next September was installed pastor of this church and society. In 1875 his health failed to such a degree that he signified his willingness to resign his pastorate, but from which he was dissuaded. He went to Europe, spent five months there, returned and the next March resumed his labors.

In 1880 he again went to Europe for rest and the benefit of his health, which has become fully established, and his labors as preacher and pastor of the First Congregational Church at the present time are highly appreciated and cordially accepted.

The Second Congregational Church of Bridgeport has been earnestly pursuing the object for which it was organized, fifty-six years; has had good success and attained a strong position in the community.

On the 18th of March, 1880, it held its semi-centennial anniversary, at which time a paper, prepared by the standing committee, was read, in connection with other public addresses, from which the following history of the church is taken, mostly in the words of the committee, since better could not easily be produced :[10]

. "This church was organized January 28, 1830, by one hundred and seventeen persons"—thirty-nine men and seventy-eight women—who had been dismissed for the purpose

---

[10] This sketch of the Second Congregational Church was prepared by Edmund S. Hawley, upon the request of the committee.

[11] The following is a list of pew holders in the Second Congregational Church in 1835:

Seth B. Jones,	Sherwood Sterling,	John Brooks, Jr.,
William B. Dyer,	George Sterling,	James Jennings,
Burr Knapp,	Wilson Hawley,	Nathan Baldwin,
Josiah Hubbell,	William DeForest,	Samuel Peet,
Victory Curtis,	Lockwood DeForest,	Josiah S. Fayerweather,
Joseph Wood,	Bronson Hawley,	Josiah B. Hall,
Fitch Wheeler,	Charles B. Middlebrook,	William B. Nash,
Jesse Sterling,	Edward Burroughs,	Charles Sherman,
Charles DeForest,	Harry Judson,	George Wheeler,
Munson Hawley,	Josiah B. Baldwin,	Daniel B. Oviatt,
Abijah Hawley,	Nichols Northrop,	D. Mallory,
David Perry,	Ransom C. Canfield,	Zenas R. Moody,
Stephen Hawley,	Benjamin DeForest,	Benjamin Pilgrim,
Edwin B. Gregory,	Mrs. Talman Perry,	Nathan Shepard,
R. Thorborne,	Edwin Porter,	Capt. E. Doane,
Rowell Lewis,	James Robinson,	E. D. Bull,
Mrs. Wm. Burr,	E. C. Warren,	John Cogswell,
David Hubbell,	Bradley Gould,	William Allis.
Elliot Morris,	Samuel Morse,	

from the Stratfield—now First Congregational—Church of this city; they being recognized as such the same day by a council of ministers convened to assist in its organization; and after entering into church covenant, William DeForest, Stephen Hawley and Josiah B. Baldwin were chosen deacons. Religious services were temporarily held in the high school house on State street, while measures were at once taken for the erection of a house of worship. A lot on the corner of Broad and Gilbert streets, where the church now stands, was purchased, and its first edifice, built of wood, was erected that year. It cost about $5,000, besides the foundation and the finishing of the basement, which was done mainly by the members of the church, some furnishing materials, many working with their hands, and all doing something to forward the work; the ladies, as well, taking an active interest in everything connected with the prosperity of the church. The house was soon completed, and on November 30, 1830, it was dedicated to the worship of God, at which time the church numbered one hundred and twenty-eight members. At a meeting of the church held August 28, 1830, the Rev. Nathaniel Hewit, D.D., was unanimously invited to become its pastor, which call was accepted and he was installed December 1, 1830, Dr. Woods, of Andover, preaching the sermon.

"During Dr. Hewit's ministry of nearly twenty-three years, he had the confidence and respect of his church and the whole community. It was his custom to preach three times on the Sabbath, and lecture every Thursday evening. He was a power in the church and in the world, and it is our pleasure to bear testimony to his rare endowments and many virtues, and to render our humble tribute to his memory.

"In the summer of 1831 a friend of the cause of temperance offered to pay Dr. Hewit's expenses if he would go to England and present the cause of temperance in that country. To this the church assented, and he sailed at the short notice of four days. During his absence of nearly six months the Rev. Mr. Hermance supplied the pulpit. Protracted meetings were held, and for a considerable time prayer meetings were held in the basement of the old church in the morning

SECOND CONGREGATIONAL CHURCH, ERECTED IN 1860 AND 61.

at sunrise. In these much interest was taken and as a result forty-seven were added to this church, and a large number to the First Church.

"Dr. Hewit was an eloquent man, mighty in the Scriptures, and his warnings and denunciations against intemperance and moderate drinking, his bold and heroic rebuke of fashionable vice and immorality, at home and abroad, made a deep impression on the public mind. During the latter part of his ministry the old church edifice was altered, enlarged and repaired, at considerable expense. He continued pastor until September 21, 1853, when he was dismissed, and on October 9, seventy-eight members were, at their own request, dismissed to organize a Presbyterian church, of which Dr. Hewit became pastor. The results of Dr. Hewit's ministry are here presented as written by himself on the records of the church. 'At my installation, December 1, 1830, there were 128 members in the church. Of these 52 remain. There have been added by profession, 153; by letter, 220. Total, 373. Of these there remain 238. There are on record 131 infant baptisms. One hundred church members have departed this life. One hundred and thirty marriages have been solemnized by me. The amount taken up for charitable objects, also by legacies, subscriptions, etc., is at least $24,000, five thousand of which is a legacy of the late Alfred Bishop to the American Bible Society, and one thousand a recent donation by his widow to found a permanent scholarship in the Literary and Theological Institute at East Windsor.'

"The second pastor, the Rev. Asahel L. Brooks, was installed January 25, 1854, and continued thus a little over two years, he being dismissed March 11, 1856, during which time there was a gain of 37 members. His removal to another field of labor was much regretted by the church and society. He died recently at the residence of his son in New Jersey.

"The Rev. Benjamin L. Swan succeeded Mr. Brooks as acting pastor, and his ministry of two and a half years was very acceptable to the church and congregation. He left the church with twenty-nine members more than when he began his labors with it.

42

"The fourth pastor, the Rev. Alexander R. Thompson, entered upon his labors March 1, 1859, and continued here for three years. In the summer of 1860 two mission Sunday schools were established, through the instrumentality of Mr. Thompson, one in East Bridgeport in the old carriage factory on William street, which proved very successful and which, it is believed, resulted finally in the present large Congregational Church of East Bridgeport. The other school was among the colored children in the lower part of the city, formerly called "Liberia." This was successfully sustained some time.

"In the autumn of 1860 the old church was removed to a vacant lot on the opposite side of the street and the foundation for the present edifice was laid. Notwithstanding the calamities of the civil war, which soon began, this work went forward and the new church was dedicated January 20, 1862, the sermon being preached by the Rev. R. S. Storrs, D.D., of Brooklyn. Mr. Thompson's able and earnest preaching filled the old and the new house with attentive listeners, and his many labors of love in the church and in the whole community are still fresh in the recollections of the people."

"Mr. Thompson was succeeded by the Rev. Francis Lobdell, who was installed in April, 1863, and dismissed February, 1865. During his labors, in February, 1864, the Rev. E. P. Hammond held services with this church and fifty-three members were added. The same year a heavy debt on the church and society was removed by the generous subscriptions received.

"In the spring the Rev. Daniel Lord was invited to become, and in May, 1865, was installed pastor of this church and society. He resigned in April, 1869, to accept the pastorate of a church in Chicago. He left the church in a prosperous condition.

"The next pastor, the Rev. Edwin Johnson, was installed in November, 1870. His labors were blessed of God, and many were added to the church. He resigned his charge in

---

[11] Some special account of a number of men who went from this church in the civil war will be found in the war record of Bridgeport.

November, 1876, after a faithful and successful ministry of six years.

"The present pastor, the Rev. R. G. S. McNeille, was installed December 4, 1877, the Rev. Dr. Noble, of New Haven, preaching the sermon. The following summer our pastor was absent about four months on a tour in Europe, and on his return gave two courses of very interesting lectures on Northern Italy, the proceeds being for the ladies' sewing society."

In the summer of 1879 this church edifice was repaired, with considerable alterations and adornments, at a cost of over seven thousand dollars. Alterations and improvements, also, in the chapel were made at the expense and under the direction of the ladies of the church, at a cost of over three thousand dollars.

The present pastor of the church is the Rev. R. G. S. McNeille, and the following have been or are deacons: William DeForest, chosen in 1830, died in 1853; Stephen Hawley, chosen in 1830, resigned in 1842; Josiah B. Baldwin, chosen in 1830, resigned in 1841; Sherwood Sterling, chosen in 1833, died in 1869; Harvey Higby, chosen in 1841, died May 29, 1875; George Sterling, chosen in 1847, died September 8, 1871; Thomas Lord, chosen in 1867, resigned November 4, 1870; Edward Sterling, chosen in 1867; Edward W. Marsh, chosen in 1867; William E. Brown, chosen in 1867, died November 15, 1873; Joel Blakeslee, chosen ——; Thomas Calef, chosen November 5, 1875; Leonard Wood, chosen February 28, 1883, died February 6, 1886. Superintendent of the Sunday school, Edward W. Marsh; assistant superintendents, A. H. Warner, Miss Sarah L. Baldwin.

The First Presbyterian Church of Bridgeport was constituted October 16, 1853, at which time eighty-two persons, who had previously obtained letters of dismissal from the Second Congregational Church, entered into covenant and resolved to connect themselves with the Presbytery of New York. Dr. Hewit, who had received, at his request, letters of dismissal from the consociation, was admitted to the Presbytery of New York, October 19, 1853, and the Presbytery met at Bridgeport the same month—October 31—and took the church under its care, and installed Dr. Hewit its pastor. In 1860 this church was transferred to the Presbytery of Connecticut, and in 1870 to the Presbytery of Westchester, to which it still belongs. The services of installation were held in the Second Congregational Church edifice. At the installation of the pastor the following persons were ordained and installed ruling elders: Stephen Hawley, Thomas Hawley, John Brooks, Henry M. Hine and Stiles M. Middlebrook.

On February 1 the chapel on Myrtle avenue was dedicated, having cost about three thousand dollars. The church adjoining, on the corner of Myrtle avenue and West Liberty street, was dedicated August 8, 1855, and cost $28,000. The lot on which the church and chapel stood was the gift of Capt. John Brooks and Capt. Burr Knapp.

From this time Dr. Hewit labored, as usual, with much success until failing strength made it necessary that he should have a colleague, and hence the Rev. H. G. Hinsdale, from Germantown, Pa., and formerly of New York City, was installed pastor October 28, 1862. Upon this, or soon after, Dr. Hewit insisted on being relieved from any responsibility in the pulpit except by invitation.

Nathaniel Hewit, D.D., was born in New London, Ct., August 28, 1788, and graduated at Yale College in 1808, licensed to preach September 24, 1811, and afterwards studied theology at Andover. He was installed, in his first charge, pastor of the Presbyterian Church at Plattsburgh, N. Y., July 5, 1815. The severity of the climate necessitated his resignation, and he was dismissed October 2, 1817, and on the 14th of the next January was installed pastor of the Congregational Church at Fairfield, Conn., where he labored ten years with much success. He was a strong advocate of temperance, and in 1827 was engaged in the service of the American Temperance Society, and lectured in the principal cities of Connecticut, Rhode Island, New York and Pennsylvania, and organized many temperance societies. After great success as a temperance lecturer and organizer three years, he was installed on December 1, 1830, pastor of the Second Congregational

Church of Bridgeport. He sailed for London, where he arrived June 28, 1831, and delivered an address in Exeter Hall the next evening, and on the 19th of July assisted in the formation of the British and Foreign Temperance Society. He visited Paris and afterwards delivered addresses in London, Birmingham and Liverpool. In the autumn of the same year he returned to Bridgeport and assumed his pastoral duties and continued for more than twenty years to serve successfully this church, his fame and influence as a theologian augmenting with every year's labor.

In 1853 a division arose in his congregation in regard to procuring him an associate. A large number withdrew and formed the First Presbyterian Church, to which they called their "old, revered, and beloved pastor, whose ministrations they could not consent to forego." He was dismissed from his former charge September 21, and October 31 was installed over the latter, where "he continued to preach the Word and feed the flock of God" till nearly fourscore years of age.

Dr. Hewit was twice married. His first wife, Miss Rebecca Hillhouse, of New Haven, died January 4, 1831. His second wife, Miss Susan Eliot, of Fairfield, died May 1, 1857.

In the fall of 1858, having arrived at the age of seventy years, he tendered his resignation, which his people refused to accept. Four years later, April 1, 1862, he released his salary to the congregation, and in August of the same year Rev. Horace G. Hinsdale was called as associate pastor. To this colleague and successor he cordially handed over his charge, preaching occasionally, until on Sabbath morning, February 3, 1867, he "fell asleep."

Of the three children who survived him, one, Henry S. Hewit, M.D., late surgeon of the Army of the Cumberland, has since died; another son, Rev. Augustus F. Hewit, is one of the Paulist Fathers of New York; the other, Sarah, the widow of the late William S. Bowen, M.D., surgeon U. S. N., resides in New Haven.

A marble tablet to his memory, which was destroyed when the church edifice was burned in 1874, has been replaced in the new sanctuary by a handsome memorial baptismal font of carved stone, the gift of the children of the Sunday school. To a memorial discourse delivered on the occasion of his funeral, February 6, 1867, by Rev. Lyman H. Atwater, D.D., of Princeton, N. J., we are indebted for much of the foregoing sketch. Of him it may be well said,—

" He being dead yet speaketh."[12]

In the autumn of 1872 an organ was placed in the church at an expense of nearly $5,000.

In 1873 the chapel was taken down and a new one, costing $11,000, was erected, and the work of enlarging the church organ, already one of the finest in New England, and putting a new roof on the church, amounting to about $6,000, was also accomplished.

These and other improvements were not quite completed when, on Wednesday evening, December 9, 1874, both church and chapel, with all their contents, were destroyed by fire, probably occasioned by the careless use of candles by a workman. The burning steeple, 227 feet in height, was a brilliant spectacle. The loss upon the buildings and their contents amounted to $70,000, the insurance being $35,000. Resolutions of condolence and tenders of the use of their several edifices were made by most of the other churches in Bridgeport, but the church preferred to occupy the opera house, corner of State and Main streets, for a season. Owing to the liberality of Capt. Brooks and other members of the society, rebuilding was promptly commenced. The old site was sold and the present one on the corner of State street and Myrtle avenue was purchased, and the work commenced April 28, 1875, and on the 12th of October, 1876, the new church was dedicated, it having cost, including chapel, organ and furniture, about $94,000. With the new and advantageous facilities the people were encouraged and the work of the church prospered.

In October, 1877, Mr. Hinsdale was dismissed by the Presbytery to accept a call to the pastorate of the Presbyterian Church at Princeton, N. J. He was succeeded February 14, 1878, by the Rev. H. A. Davenport, who is at present a

---

[12] From a historical sermon by the Rev. Horace G. Hinsdale.

John Brooks

Capt. John Brooks, son of John Brooks, Senior, died at his residence 263 Main Street in Bridgeport, at eight o'clock A. M., December 7, 1881, at the advanced age of eighty-six years, having been a prominent figure in the community over seventy years. His father, also a prominent man of his time, died January 17, 1862, at the great age of ninety-seven years, so that the son was known as John Brooks, Jr., until he himself was a veteran in years as well as experience. He was born in East Bridgeport, the son of Capt. John and Mary Coe Brooks, September 18, 1795, at which time there were but ten houses on the east side of the harbor. For his education he received the advantages of the district school and of the Stratford Academy, of which the distinguished David Plant, afterward Lieutenant-Governor, was preceptor. At the age of fifteen years he went to New York to live with John Vanderbilt, and the next year, 1811, entered the store of Gershom Smith, grocer, in Peck Slip, as clerk, but soon found he had mistaken his calling, and on the breaking out of the war of 1812, came home. His father being a seafaring man, he early imbibed a fondness for the water and acquired skill as a boatman. That he was a born leader is evident from the fact· that at the early age of eighteen years he was given charge of a vessel, as well as from his subsequent history, which was that of a popular and successful steamboat commander. His life career is outlined as follows : He first sailed the sloop "Arab" in 1813, from Bridgeport to New York, the sloop "Intrepid" in 1814, the sloop "Patriot" in 1815, the sloop "Mary Ann" in 1816. On October 14, 1817, he married Mary, daughter of Zalmon Hawley, who survived him, and in the same year entered into a co-partnership with Isaac Sherman, Esq., occupying a store on Water Street, Mr. Sherman attending the store and Capt. Brooks sailing the sloop "Mary Ann" as a regular packet to and from New York until 1822. Esquire Sherman, in his reminiscences, speaks in warm terms of his agreeable relations with Capt. Brooks, and of his many acts of kindness to himself and family.

In 1824, he took charge of the steamboat "John Marshall," plying between New York and Norwalk, Bridgeport passengers being taken to Norwalk by stage. The next year he was transfered to the steamer "United States," running between New Haven and New York, and soon after to the "S. B. Hudson," a fine boat built by Montgomery Livingston, and run on the same route.

In 1826 and 1827 he commanded the steamer "Franklin" and the "Governor Wolcott," on the Hudson river. At this period he made the acquaintance of Capt. Cornelius Vanderbilt, which ripened into a warm and life-long friendship, and contributed largely to his prosperity. An incident connected with their business relations is worthy of special notice. While Capt. Brooks was running one of Cornelius Vanderbilt's boats, Mr. Vanderbilt made arrangements for and insisted on Sunday trips. Capt. Brooks at once resigned his position. This occurred when he was a young man, dependent entirely upon his own labor for livelihood. From his knowledge of Mr. Vanderbilt's character, he had no doubt that all business relations between them were at an end, but he was true to his religious principles and convictions of duty at whatever cost, and certainly the cost did seem great. After a short interval, however, Mr. Vanderbilt invited him to return to his service, with total exemption from Sunday duty, with advanced position and better pay than before, which is an instance where sturdy adherence to the right was openly rewarded ; and that too by a man who then made no pretentions to a religious character.

Subsequently, Capt. Brooks commanded the "Emerald," running between New York and Norwalk, the "Bellona" and "Thistle," to New Brunswick, N. J.

and the "Ansonia" and "Nimrod," to Norwalk, Bridgeport and Birmingham. The "Nimrod" was sold in 1864, during the war, for transportation purposes, and this closed his long career upon the water.

Capt. Brooks was appreciated by his fellow citizens in civil life, as is evident from the offices to which he was elected by their suffrages. The first office held by him under the city government was membership on the Board of Relief, to which he was successively elected in 1851, '52 and '53. On October 20, 1857, he was elected Mayor of the City, to fill a vacancy. On the 7th of October, 1864, he was again elected Mayor. He was elected Alderman April 2, 1866, and appointed by the Common Council Superintendent of Docks and Wharves, May 7, 1866. Politically, he was a decided republican from the organization of that party. Previous to that he acted with the Whig party. He naturally took great interest in Bridgeport harbor, watched its currents and the changes they wrought. In 1830–33 there was but five feet of water at low tide on the outer bar, and the larger vessels had to be lighted to get in and out. The steamers were compelled often to wait for the rising tide. He petitioned Congress, which resulted in an appropriation, and the channel was deepened, but the "ditch" was narrow and needed a light. Another successful petition was promoted by him, and a temporary light was provided, and afterwards the present substantial light-house was built. His observations suggested the breakwater and that was constructed, and he was also largely influential in the location and construction of the lighthouse on Penfield Reef, all most necessary and useful improvements.

Capt. Brooks and his wife, Maria Brooks, united with the First Congregational Church, October 7, 1821. At the division of the church in 1830, they were of the number who were dismissed to form the Second or South Church. Here he was the faithful ally and helper of that great and good man, Nathaniel Hewit, D.D. At that period Dr. Hewit was opposed to the employment of the organ in church music, but did not object to Capt. Brooks' violin nor even a second one. The South Church choir was famous for number, volume and drill. For quite a period Capt. Brooks brought up from New York the celebrated professor, Thomas Hastings, to instruct this choir. At the organization of the First Presbyterian Church, October 31, 1853, under the leadership of Dr. Hewit, he was ordained a ruling elder and was active in all church work, living the life of a faithful Christian man. The growth and prosperity of this church have been largely due to his large financial contributions. He, with the late Capt. Burr Knapp, gave the land on the corner of Myrtle Avenue and West Liberty Street, on which the first house of worship was erected, and when that building was destroyed by fire, December 9, 1874, he, although sick at the time, said the same evening: "We shall begin to rebuild before the bricks are cold." The present beautiful edifice was largely due to his efforts. He headed the subscription with a handsome sum, and when a few years later an effort was made to pay a debt of about $30,000, he subscribed more than one-third of the whole sum, and the entire amount was secured in less than a week. His characteristic Christian benevolence was wont to find an outlet through the church, but many citizens, not church members, in the humbler walks of life, can testify to his large-hearted, open-handed assistance in times of need.

He had no children, and after providing in his will for sundry bequests and legacies to relatives and friends, he left the balance of his estate to be forever appropriated to Christian and benevolent uses. His aged widow survived him about four years and was then gently called to join him in the spirit world. She also left all her estate for religious and benevolent uses.

successful pastor of the church. The late Mrs. Mary Bishop was one of the most liberal benefactors of this church, having subscribed largely to build it and also to cancel the debt incurred in its erection.

Ruling Elders in the First Presbyterian Church:

Stephen Hawley, ordained October 31, 1853, died November 4, 1861.

Thomas Hawley, ordained October 31, 1853, dismissed October 26, 1861.

John Brooks, ordained October 31, 1853, died December 7, 1881.

Stiles M. Middlebrook, ordained October 31, 1853, dismissed February 10, 1878.

Henry M. Hine, ordained October 31, 1853, dismissed in June, 1879.

Egbert Marsh, elected in April, 1860, dismissed February 10, 1878.

David F. Hollister, elected in April, 1860.

Alexander Wheeler, elected December, 1878.

Alexander Lane, elected December, 1878.

Richard H. Townsend, elected December, 1878.

Rev. Henry Adolphus Davenport is a native of Stamford, Conn., and descended in a direct line from the first minister at New Haven. He was educated at Williston Seminary, Amherst College, Mass., and the Union Theological Seminary of New York City, a part of which time he was engaged in teaching. He was ordained in June, 1873, and preached four and a half years in a chapel of the Fifth Avenue Reformed Church of New York City. He was installed pastor of the Presbyterian Church of Bridgeport February 14, 1878, and is serving this parish at present, as also heretofore, with much credit and faithfulness. The membership of this church numbers 300, and the Sunday school 350.

The German Reformed Church was organized October 1, 1860, the Rev. Andrew Schroeder being pastor from 1860 to 1864. In 1868 the church was reorganized, having for their pastor the Rev. Caspar Brunner, who still continues in that office with good success. In the same year the society purchased the Polanna Chapel, standing on State street, nearly opposite Myrtle avenue, which they occupied until the beginning of the year 1883, when they sold this property, purchased another site on Congress street near Main, running through to Chapel street, and built upon it a church edifice and parsonage, both of brick, at an expense of about $20,000. The membership numbers about 150, having made good progress during the short time since their organization.

Christ Church (Episcopal).—The call for the first meeting of "persons interested in the formation of a new parish in this city," was read by the rector of St. John's Church August 3, 1850, and a meeting of such persons was appointed for Tuesday evening, August 6, at the vestry room of St. John's Church. A meeting was holden at that time and place, at which Charles Bostwick presided and John S. Smith was secretary. At a meeting holden August 13, 1850, a resolution was passed "that a Parish of the Protestant Episcopal Church be formed," and the name "Parish of Christ Church" was formally adopted. On August 16, 1850, the parish organized by the election of the following officers: Senior Warden, Charles Bostwick; Junior Warden, Russell Tomlinson; Vestry, Charles B. Ferguson, Chauncey M. Hatch, Charles M. Booth, Samuel Stratton, Aaron T. Beardsley, Philip B. Segee; Treasurer, Henry Shelton; Clerk, John S. Smith.

The first rector was the Rev. J. Howard Smith, who was called November 7, 1850, and who was rector till April, 1854. During this time the land was bought for the present church on Courtland street, the corner stone of which was laid on Good Friday, April 9, 1852. The building committee were Stephen Tomlinson, S. B. Fergurson, and Aaron T. Beardsley. The church edifice was completed in 1853, and was consecrated by Bishop Thomas Church Brownell, on the 21st day of April of that year. It is built of brown stone, and cost about $32,000.

The rectors succeeding Mr. Smith have been as follows:

the Rev. William Preston, 1854–1856; Rev. George E. Thrall, 1856–1859; Rev. L. W. Bancroft, 1860–1861; Rev. Henry M. Stewart, 1861–1863; Rev. John Falkner Blake—subsequently John Blake Falkner, 1863–1870; Rev. John J. Harrison, April 12, 1870–November 28, 1870; Rev. N. L. Briggs, 1871–1875; Rev. Dr. H. N. Powers, 1875–1885; Rev. Beverly E. Warner, 1885, present incumbent. During its existence the following have at different times been Wardens of the church: Charles Bostwick,* S. B. Fergurson,* Russell Tomlinson,* P. H. Skidmore, S. S. Clapp,* Clapp Spooner, L. W. Clark, Daniel Hatch,* George C. Waldo, William H. Noble, George Munger. Those marked with an asterisk· are deceased. The Parish Clerks have been: John S. Smith, R. T. Clark, Robert C. Booth, John S. Beers (eight years), J. B. Hay, M. H. Tomlinson, Edwin Hurd, D. W. Kissam, L. M. Segee (five years), S. R. Tomlinson, Charles W. McCord. The church chapel, in the rear of the church, was erected in 1867 at a cost of about nine thousand dollars. During the rectorship of the Rev. M. Briggs the brick block on Courtland street opposite the church, and in which was the residence of the rector, was burned, and many of the parish records and papers were lost. Among these was the roll of the parish, containing upwards of three hundred families. At the parish meeting for 1885–6, held on April 9, the following officers were elected: Senior Warden, John McCord (Mr. McCord subsequently declined and William H. Noble was chosen in his place); Junior Warden, George Munger; Vestry, L. W. Clark, George C. Waldo, S. F. Raymond, H. H. Pyle, Clapp Spooner, F. M. Wilson, C. B. Hotchkiss, L. N. Van Keuren, A. B. Beers, John McCord, C. F. Wood, S. B. Beardsley, George Richardson, P. B. Segee, S. W. Ely, R. T. Whiting, S. S. Jarvis, A. J. Cable, John North, C. W. McCord, Blaise Soules, C. S. Lupton, C. R. Brothwell, A. H. Doolittle, John M. Wheeler, H. C. Fairchild; Treasurer, L. N. Van Keuren; Clerk, Charles W. McCord.

It will be seen that but one of these gentlemen, P. B. Segee, was a member of the original vestry at the founding of the parish. The church, in point of ecclesiastical polity, might be called a low, broad church, and its membership has been largely drawn from the liberal portion of the community. It has a large and flourishing Sunday school, which has always been an important adjunct to its work and a source of strength. It has also a very active Ladies' Aid Society, which is constant in work of a charitable and helpful character. Since the loss of the parish records no census has been taken of the membership, but the present rector, Mr. Warner, is engaged in compiling one. The church is the most centrally located Episcopal church in Bridgeport and the parish is a large and able one.

The church has suffered severely by death in the last fifteen years. Beside those marked above among its wardens as deceased, there have died of its prominent members, I. H. Whiting, Frederick Wood, Benjamin Ray, George Keeler, and Samuel Titus.

Horatio Nelson Powers, D.D., was born in Amenia, Duchess Co., N. Y., prepared for college at the Amenia Seminary, graduated at Union College, Schenectady, studied theology in the General Theological Seminary, New York, and was ordained in Trinity Church, New York, July 1, 1855. He served as assistant to the Rev. Dr. Samuel Bowman, St. James's, Lancaster, Pa., till the spring of 1857, when he married Clemence Emma, only daughter of Prof. Francis Fauvel Gouraud, of the University of France, and removed to Davenport, Iowa. He resided there as rector of St. Luke's Church, and afterwards as President of Griswold College, till the fall of 1868, when he accepted a call to St. John's Church, Chicago, where, in addition to his ministerial relations, he was a Regent of the Chicago University, President of the Foundling's Home, Corresponding Secretary of the Chicago Literary Club, of which he was one of the founders, and a lecturer before the Athenæum. In November, 1875, he took charge of Christ Church, Bridgeport. His connection with this parish terminated October, 1885. In Bridgeport he was president and one of the founders of the Scientific Society. He is an honorary member of several learned bodies, and a Fellow of the Clarendon Historical Society, of Edinburgh, Scotland. Dr. Powers received the degree of

D.D. from his Alma Mater in 1867. He has contributed, either in prose or verse, to most of the prominent periodicals in the country, such as the "Century," "Harper's Magazine," "Lippincott's," "International Review," "Literary World," New York "Evening Post," "The Independent," "Round Table," "The Critic," "The Chicago Dial." He has also been the American contributor to "*L'Art*," the great art journal of France. His books are "Through the Year," published by Roberts Brothers; poems "Early and Late," Jansen, McClurg & Co.; and "A Brief Biography of William Cullen Bryant," Appleton & Co. He has been fortunate in his friendships; Philip Gilbert Hamerton dedicated to him his beautiful work, "The Unknown River," and presented him with two of his admirable oil paintings—the only ones by this artist and critic in America. He was on intimate terms with Bryant and Bayard Taylor. Specimens of Dr. Powers' poetry are found in nearly all the important collections of the American poets—Bryant's, Longfellow's, Epes Sargent's, Stoddard's, Piatt's, F. F. Brown's, etc.

C. W. deL. Nichols, candidate for Holy Orders from Christ Church parish, is connected, through his father's family, with some of the most distinguished Episcopal clergymen of the diocese, including the last one who went to Scotland for Orders and the first one who was ordained in the United States. Mr. Nichols has had an unusually advantageous preparation for the study of divinity. He graduated from the classical department of Williston Seminary, Easthampton, Mass., in 1874, with high honors. Mr. Nichols was afterwards bred at the Johns Hopkins University, besides having spent many years elsewhere in general culture. For two years he was instructor in metaphysics and English literature in the preparatory department of Seabury Divinity School, under Bishop Whipple, at Faribault, Minnesota, until in the year 1884 he entered the General Theological Seminary at New York, where he is at present studying. Mr. Nichols is also familiar with philosophical circles in various parts of the country, and has written articles on philosophic, historic and literary themes.

Trinity Church, Bridgeport.—This parish was organized June 1, 1863, and was admitted into union with the Convention of the Diocese of Connecticut, June 10, 1863. A hall on the second floor of the New York and New Haven Railroad depot was quickly and tastefully prepared for temporary occupancy by the parish, and in it the first service was held on Sunday, June 14, 1863. The corner-stone of the church, on the corner of Fairfield avenue and Broad street, was laid on the 2d of November in the same year. The edifice was finished in the following spring and early summer, services began to be held in it Sunday, July 3, 1864, and it was consecrated by the Right Reverend John Williams, D.D., Assistant Bishop of Connecticut, on Wednesday, November 2, 1864. It is a substantial building of brown stone from the Portland quarries, Gothic—of the early English period—in its style of architecture, and has a seating capacity of six hundred.

The parish was formed by members from St. John's Church, Bridgeport. Sixty families took part in its organization. Its motive was this, viz: a desire to work for the Saviour's glory and to advance His Kingdom—a Kingdom of righteousness, mercy, truth, honor and charity. It has enjoyed nearly a quarter of a century of unbroken harmony and of quiet and steady growth, and is now one of the first parishes in the Diocese. It has had thus far but one rector, the Rev. Sylvester Clarke, who was born at Newtown, in this county, was ordained to the ministry in 1858, and became rector of the church in Oxford, Conn., coming from that parish to Bridgeport in March, 1861. Hon. Jarratt Morford has been the Senior Warden of this parish since its organization. Its Junior Wardens have been as follows: Ira Gregory, Esq.,* 1863–1883, Hon. E. B. Goodsell,* 1883–1884, Hon. D. N. Morgan, 1885, now serving.

Trinity Memorial Church, West Stratford, is a mission of Trinity Church, Bridgeport. On the 20th of September, 1871, the first of a series of Wednesday evening services was held at the residence of Silas Scofield, Esq., Newfield district. On the following Sunday, September 24, in the common school house of the same district, a Sunday school was begun. The corner-stone of a chapel was laid by Bishop Williams, November 29, 1871. This building was finished in the May succeeding. It is of wood, cost about $6,000, and will seat nearly 300 persons. The first service in it was that of the holy communion on Sunday morning (Whit Sunday), May 19, 1872. It is a memorial of the Rev. Gurdon Saltonstall Coit, D.D., twenty-eight years rector of St. John's Church, Bridgeport. At the present time about 40 families are connected with this mission, and it has an interesting Sunday school of 85 members.

The Church of the Nativity (Episcopal), a very picturesque stone building located on Sylvan avenue and Carson street, was erected mainly at the expense of the Rev. E. F. Bishop, of Bridgeport, with some assistance from Joseph Richardson, of North Bridgeport. Previous to this a mission school had been maintained by members of St. John's Church, Bridgeport, in a small building belonging to the woolen mills, then under the proprietorship of Nathaniel Green. E. F. Bishop officiated as lay reader, under the direction of the rector of St. John's Church, the Rev. Gurdon S. Coit, from the time he was licensed to that office by the Rt. Rev. Thomas C. Brownell, Bishop of Connecticut, November 21, 1856.

This church was organized June 4, 1856, the persons present being Mr. Bishop, Joseph Richardson, Eli Thompson, Ira Gregory, John Hurd, William M. Hubbell, and Henry M. Sherman, all laymen of St. John's Church. The sittings have always been free, and the service choral. The services have been conducted much of the time by Mr. Bishop himself. Rev. Gurdon S. Coit, D.D., held the rectorship until 1863 or 4. Mr. Bishop, having been ordained deacon May 21, 1860, and priest September 22, 1863, by the Rt. Rev. John Williams, assistant bishop of the diocese, was elected to the rectorship, being assisted at various times by the Rev. H. C. Stowell, the Rev. Charles H. W. Stocking, D.D., the Rev. O. L. Prescott, the Rev. Joseph W. Hill, until 1872, when the Rev. Henry Darby was elected rector and held it, nominally, until 1884, though much of the time he was absent from the charge. The services were carried on during this time partly by the priests of St. John the Evangelist, with which society he was at first connected; then by the Rev. D. Lounsbury, and Lewis W. Wells, D.D. Mr. Bishop frequently officiated here until near the time of his decease, December 7, 1883.

A choral service in this part of the country, at the time it was started in this place, was a new thing and called forth much comment.

On the day of the consecration of this church the bishop and clergy having returned to dine with Mr. Bishop at his home, were listening to the amusing incident which was being related by some one at the table, that an owl had obtained an entrance into the church in some way and lodged itself among the beams so securely that it required much trouble to eject it before the service began. Much merriment was excited by Mr. Bishop's mother (who was a Presbyterian) pithily remarking that " Perhaps it came in to make the responses."

The First Methodist Episcopal Church of Bridgeport.—In 1784 William Black, a preacher of the Methodist church in Nova Scotia, visited the United States for the purpose of consulting Dr. Coke and procuring assistance. He traveled by way of Boston, Mass., where he preached twice. He met Dr. Coke in Maryland and, either on his way thither or when returning, he preached several times in the Congregational Church in Stratfield, then standing at what is the corner of North and Park avenues. The impression made by his preaching was at first favorable, but upon a discovery of his Arminian theology he was pronounced a wolf in sheep's clothing. In one sermon, while preaching, he was interrupted by the pastor of the church, who stamped upon the floor and declared his doctrine to be damnable." He was the first Methodist preacher known to have visited the State of Connecticut or New England. There is evidence that his preaching had good results, for, according to Rev. Jesse Lee (memoirs, page 110), a desire was thereby awakened for the ministrations of Methodism. About the same time, or soon after a number of persons began to assemble for the purpose

[13] Rev. Robert Ross.

of social religious exercises. Among those who thus assembled were a Mrs. Wells and a Mrs. Wheeler, both living at the south end of Park avenue,[14] then called Mutton Lane.

In May, 1789, a Methodist conference was held in the city of New York, where Jesse Lee, the pioneer of New England Methodism, was appointed to the Stamford circuit, which appears to have included the greater part of the State lying west of the Connecticut river. On the 17th of June, 1789, he preached his first sermon in the State under a tree at Norwalk.[15] June 18th he rode to Fairfield and preached in the Court House at 6 o'clock in the evening to about forty persons. He stopped over night at a public house kept by a Mr. Penfield. The next morning Mrs. Penfield, who heard him preach, gave him a note of introduction to her sister, Mrs. Wheeler of Park avenue, representing her as interested in the subject of religion, and desiring him to call on her.

While Mr. Lee was approaching the place Mrs. Wells was at the house of Mrs. Wheeler on a visit, and the two were in conversation upon the religious interests of the neighborhood. Just at the moment of his arrival that conversation became a point of extraordinary interest. Mrs. Wells told Mrs. Wheeler that on the preceding night she had dreamed that a man rode up to a house where she was, got off his horse, took his saddle-bags on his arm, and, walking directly into the house, said: "I am a minister of the Gospel of Jesus Christ, and am come to preach to the people of this place. If you will call your neighbors together I will preach to them to-night." Then Mrs. Wells said she retained so perfect a recollection of the man's face and general appearance that she would certainly know him if she should ever see him. While she was yet speaking she looked out the window and exclaimed, "Why, there is the man now!" Mr. Lee rode up, dismounted, took his saddle-bags on his arm, entered the house, and addressing the women, said: "I am a minister of

---

[14] No. 3, on page 505.

[15] "The Rev. Cornelius Cook preached the first Methodist sermon in Norwalk, near the New Canaan parish line, in 1787 ; the Rev. Jesse Lee preached the next sermon on the 17th of June, 1789, in the highway, near the centre of the town."— *Hall's History of Norwalk, 170.*

the Gospel of Jesus Christ, and have come to preach to the people of this place. If you will call your neighbors together I will preach to them to-night." Mrs. Wells was so deeply affected as to be scarcely able to stand. Mr. Lee was welcomed, the neighbors were called together, Mr. Lee preached to them, and tradition says three conversions was the result, and that two of them were Mrs. Wells and Mrs. Wheeler. This service was held in the old yellow house on the south end and east side of Park avenue, on the 19th of June, 1789.

After visiting other places in the State Mr. Lee preached on the 3d of July at the house of Deacon Elijah Hawley, at Stratfield, and on the 5th of August preached again at the same house, though in the latter entry in his journal it is said to have been at Newfield. The house is still standing on the northwest corner of Thomas and Water streets. On the 14th of August Mr. Lee was again in this vicinity and preached at the house of Mr. Wells. The nucleus of the first Methodist society in this neighborhood, and, it is believed, the first in New England, consisted of a class organized by Mr. Lee September 26, 1789, in a house which stood on Toilsome Hill, on the west side of the highway, and hence in Fairfield. The three persons composing the class were Mrs. Wells, Miss Ruth Hall her sister, and a Mrs. Risley. These all died in great peace, within the memory of persons now connected with this church.

In 1790 Mr. Lee was made Presiding Elder of the New England work, but at that time the districts had no name, and scarcely any limits. The name of the circuit including this region of country was called Fairfield, and it extended to several townships, Redding being one of them. In this neighborhood preaching was held on week-day evenings, somewhat regularly, at the four following places: at Stephen Wells', on Division street, at widow Nichols', on Pequonnock Green, Ebenezer Brown's, on Toilsome Hill, at Father Penfield's, on Holland Hill, the house being occupied now, or recently, by Lewis Penfield. In 1797 a Methodist Church was built on Division street road north of Toilsome Hill at the corners of the roads about three miles north of the present North avenue. The late Dea. David Sherwood, who died January 24, 1873, aged 94 years, was at the raising of this

church, being then eighteen years of age. This statement was made by Dea. Sherwood to Dea. R. B. Lacey and others, and written down at the time for permanent record. After 1797 preaching was held, probably, most regularly at the new meeting house on Toilsome Hill, until 1815. During this early stage of this church the Conference, Circuit, Presiding Elders, and Preachers were:

1790. Jesse Lee, Presiding Elder, Fairfield circuit; John Bloodgood, preacher.

1791. Nathaniel B. Mills and Aaron Hunt, preachers.

1792. Jacob Brush, P. E.; Joshua Taylor and Smith Weeks, preachers.

1793. Thomas Ware, P. E.; Aaron Hunt and James Coleman, preachers.

1794. George Roberts, P. E.; Zebulon Kankey and Nicholas Sneathan, preachers.

1795. The name of the circuit was changed to Redding; George Roberts was P. E., and Daniel Dennison and Timothy Dewey, preachers.

1796. There were two P. E's, Freeborn Garretson and Sylvester Hutchinson, dividing all New England between them. The preachers for Redding circuit were Elijah Woblsey and Robert Leeds.

1797 to 1800. S. Hutchinson, P. E.; preachers: 1797, David Buck, Augustus Jocelyn; 1798, William Thatcher; 1799, David Brown.

1800. F. Garretson, P. E.; Augustus Jocelyn, preacher.

1801. The ministers began to give names to the districts; this circuit was in the New York district; F. Garretson, P. E.; S. Marvin, Isaac Candee, preachers.

1802. The same P. E.; J. Coleman and I. Candee, preachers.

1803. The same P. E.; James Campbell and N. W. Tompkins, preachers.

1804 to 1807. Wm. Thatcher, P. E.; preachers: 1804, P. Moriarty and Sylvester Foster; 1805, P. Moriarty and S. Merwin; 1806, Nathan Felch and Oliver Sykes.

1807 to 1810. Joseph Crawford, P. E.; preachers: 1807, J. M. Smith and Zalmon Lyon; 1808, Noble W. Thomas, J.

43

Lyon; 1809, Billy Hibbard and l. Candee; 1810, Nathan Emory and John Russell.

1811. Redding circuit was included in the Rhinebeck district. Wm. Anson, P. E., two years; preachers: A. Hunt, O. Sykes, J. Reynolds; 1812, S. Rowell, G. Lyon, S. Beach.

1813 to 1817. Nathan Bangs, P. E.; preachers: A. Hunt and Henry Eames; 1814, E. Washburn and Reuben Harris; 1815, E. Woolsey and R. Harris; 1816, S. Bushnell and John Boyd.

During this year the old Congregational meeting house at Pequonnock was purchased for use by the Methodists, and for about six years this was their gathering place for public worship, the services by the conference ministers being held on week-day evenings, unless some services were held on Sundays at the old meeting house at the corner of the roads on Toilsome Hill. During the year 1816 Benoni English and Elisha P. Jacobs, who were not members of the conference, preached on Sundays at the Pequonnock house.

1817. For the first time Bridgeport appears in the conference minutes, meaning the old Pequonnock church.

1817 to 1821. Ebenezer Washburn, P. E.; preacher, Aaron Hunt, who being ill, Cyrus Silliman, a local preacher, supplied; 1818, Bridgeport disappears from the minutes, being connected with Stratford circuit, Samuel Bushnell, preacher; 1819, S. Merwin, P. E.; preachers: Bela Smith and J. Coleman.

1822. The same P. E.; the preachers being Laban Clark and Eli Barnett. The Rev. John N. Maffit, the revivalist, spent a portion of this year in this place, and from this time preaching was discontinued in the old meeting house.

1823. Bridgeport again appears on the minutes with Wm. l. Pease as preacher. His pastoral care did not extend beyond the township, and under his labors the first Methodist church within the city limits was erected. .

1824. Samuel Luckey, P. E. for three years; the preacher being Humphrey Humphreys.

1825 and 6. Bridgeport was again connected with the Redding circuit, the preachers being Marvin Richardson, H. Humphreys and F. W. Sizer.

1827. Samuel Ostrander, P. E.; preachers, Henry Stead and John Lovejoy.

1828. Bridgeport was again connected with the Stratford circuit.

1829. Laban Clark, P. E.; the preachers were J. Lovejoy and James H. Romer.

1830 and 31. The preachers were H. Bartlett and Charles Sherman.

1832. Heman Bangs, P. E.; preachers: S. Martindale and Laban C. Cheney.

1833. Preachers: James Youngs and J. Tackerberry.

1834. Bridgeport becomes a permanent station on the minutes of the conference; S. Martindale, P. E., and Davis Stocking the preacher.

1835 and 6. Wm. Jewett, P. E., and Charles F. Pelton was the preacher.

1837. Harmon D. Goslin was the preacher, but becoming ill, J. W. Lefevre supplied the remaining part of the year.

1838. Daniel Smith, pastor, and Mr. Goslin died and was buried here.

1839. Nicholas White, P. E.; pastor, Daniel Smith.

1840 to 1844. Charles W. Carpenter, P. E.; the pastor in 1840 was John M. Pease; in 1841 and 2, Salmon C. Perry, and in 1843 and 4, John L. Gilder.

1844 to 1848. Laban Clark, P. E.; pastors: 1845 and 6, James H. Perry; 1847, H. Bangs.

1848 to 1852. Heman Bangs, P. E.; pastor in 1848 and 9, George Brown. At the session of the general conference held in 1848 the New York conference was divided, and Bridgeport lay within the bounds of the New York East conference, and during the second year of Mr. Brown's pastorate the present church was erected. It is a very commodious and appropriate edifice. In 1850 John B. Stratton was pastor, and in 1851 and 2, Edwin L. Janes.

1852 and 3. William H. Norris, P. E.; pastor in 1853 and 4, Thomas G. Osborn.

1853 and 4. E. L. Janes, P. E.; pastor in 1855 and 6, Charles Fletcher. In 1856 Bridgeport gives name to a district in the New York east conference.

1856 to 1860. E. E. Griswold, P. E.; pastor in 1857, John M. Reid, and in 1859, William F. Collins.

1860 to 1863. William C. Hoyt, P. E.; pastor in 1860 and 61, Albert Nash. During the pastorate of Mr. Nash there was a reunion of the church, at which time the debt, amounting to $8,000, was paid.

The following items of history are compiled from a sketch prepared, and read on that occasion, by Mr. Nash:

"After the organization of the first class in 1789, I am unable to give any satisfactory account of the members of the society for thirty-four years. It is probable that there was no register kept for a number of years, and that for several years succeeding, it was found in connection with Redding circuit. Under the labors of Mr. Maffit, in 1822, a class was formed in the city proper. In 1823, about the time the first church was erected here, we have a register of the persons then connected with the society."

---

[14] " Nathaniel Ruggles, local preacher,
Burr Penfield,
Stephen Wells,
Mary Wells,
Mary Edwards,
Julia Ruggles,
Silas Turney,
Polly Turney,
John P. McEwen,
Harriet McEwen,
James Penfield,
Mary Penfield,
Anna Turney,
Anna Wheeler,
Phoebe Nichols,
Catharine Nichols,
Hannah Penfield,
John W. Beardsley,
Betsey Porter,
Sarah Burritt,
Sophia Plumb,
Eliza Cable,
Harriet Gould,
Fanny Middlebrook,

Griswold Odell,
Elias A. Hall,
Chauncy Ward,
William Bardsley,
Ezra Morris,
Stephen Durand,
Esther Durand,
Phoebe Hawkins,
Mary Hildroup,
Betsey Downs,
Catharine Ufford,
Mary Ann Hopkins,
Samantha Mosure,
Sally S. Curtis,
Charles G. Brisco,
Charles H. Wakelee,
Susan Wakelee,
Stiles Nichols,
Ebenezer Brown,
Sally Green,
Harpin Blake,
Harriet Hubbell,
Hannah Morris,
Mary Baldwin,
Eliza Evitts,

Ann Cables,
Mary Ann Patchin,
William Daggett,
Ruth Edwards,
John Beardsley,
Marietta Wells,
Hannah Blackman,
Catharine Witherill,
Ruth Hall,
Alice Hall,
Sylvina Booth,
Sally Brown,
Patience Mitchell,
Ruth Turney,
Susannah Tupler,
William L. Peet,
Seth Turney,
Maria Nichols,
Sally Hubbell,
John Feeley,
Zilpha Feeley,
Tracy Freeman,
Diana Lewis,
Effa Freeman."

" The following is a review of church enterprises :

" Before the church at Pequonnock was abandoned in 1821, a room was procured for holding Methodist meetings in the borough in what was then called the New Block, at the corner of Main and State streets, over the drug store. This place appears to have been procured mainly by the efforts of Nathaniel Ruggles, who had been converted a few years previous under the labors of the Rev. Benoni English, at the Pequonnock Church. From my best information I conclude this hall was first occupied by our people in the winter of 1821 and 2, and that John N. Maffit then held a series of meetings in it.

" In the year 1822 measures were taken for the erection of our first house of worship in this city. The members of the society were first organized into an ecclesiastical body according to law, June 30, 1821, and the principal members are stated in the warrant to have been Nathaniel Ruggles, Burr Penfield, Agur Bassett, Richard Fuller and Stephen Durand.

"At the first meeting, held for the purpose of organization, Stiles Nichols, long and favorably known as the editor of the Republican Farmer, acted as chairman ; N. Ruggles was chosen clerk; and A. Bassett, John P. McEwen, and R. Fuller were chosen the trustees.

"On the 11th of February, 1822, the meeting voted to proceed in the erection of a house of worship, and N. Ruggles was entrusted with all the business necessary to be done in the matter. The site of the church was located at a meeting held May 13, 1823, and the house, though for some years remaining unfinished, was occupied for worship the latter part of that year, Mr. Maffit preaching the first sermon in it. The trustees at the time of its erection were Charles H. Wakeley, J. P. McEwen, B. Penfield, Abram S. Smith, and Elias A. Hall. That church stood on the site of the present one. It was forty by sixty feet, and its cost, with the lot, was about three thousand dollars. That house stood about twenty-six years, and in 1849 it was burned. Measures were immediately taken to erect the present church edifice, and while it was being built the society worshiped in Wordin's Hall, at the corner of State and Water streets. On the 14th of February, 1850, this house was dedicated—the Rev. Dr. Durbin and the Rev. Allen Steele preaching on the occasion. At its completion a debt of about nine thousand dollars remained, which was paid in 1860, Mr. Eben Fairchild generously giving half the sum upon the rest being raised by others.

"The first Sunday school in connection with this society was organized during the conference year commenceing in 1828. The records of this school were burned with the church in 1849."

The pastors in this church since 1862 have been : 1862 and 3, John Miley ; 1864 and 5, Ichabod Simmons ; 1866 and 7, Frank Bottome ; 1867, 8 and 9, James M. Carroll ; 1870, John Dickenson ; 1871, 2 and 3, S. H. Platt ; 1874, 5 and 6, Daniel O. Ferris ; 1877, 8 and 9, George A. Hubbell ; 1879, 80 and 81, Charles E. Harris ; 1881 and 82, H. Q. Judd ; 1883, 4, 5, W. W. Clark."

The Washington Park Methodist Episcopal Church was organized September 12, 1853. The first church edifice was erected on the corner of Barnum and Noble streets, and was completed and occupied in the same year. Its original cost was four thousand dollars, but in 1867 it was enlarged and improved at an expense of eleven thousand dollars. This structure was removed in 1883, and a commodious brick edifice erected on the old site, with a chapel and parlor rooms adjoining, for Sunday school and social meetings. The corner-stone of this edifice was laid May 23, 1883, and the dedication services were held March 30, 1884. Their present pastor is the Rev. Edwin G. Blake."

The Tabernacle Methodist Episcopal Church was founded in July, 1873. In March, 1874, the house of worship, which stands on North Main street, at the foot of Frank street, was completed, and in the following month the Rev. A. B. Sanford was appointed its pastor. His successors have been the Rev. S. H. Smith, the Rev. David Osborn, the Rev.

---

[17] This historical sketch is taken from a record made in the church book by the Rev. D. O. Ferris, the pastor, at the time, 1878 or 9.

[18] After the type were set for this history a pamphlet was obtained containing a full account of the church.

Joseph R. Dumble, who commenced his labors here in March, 1880. The cost of the church edifice, including the lot, was about $4,500. Their present pastor is the Rev. O. F. Tree.

The African Methodist Episcopal Chapels are two, located on Broad, near Whiting street. The older, or Bethel Church, was built in 1835; the younger and larger, known as Zion Church, was completed, as a tablet over the door informs the passer by, in June, 1843. These churches hold regular church and Sunday school services.

The German Methodist Episcopal Church is located on East Main street, and the Rev. Gustave Bobolin is pastor.

A Stillwellite Methodist Church had an existence several years in Bridgeport. The Stillwell itinerant ministers commenced preaching here, at Zoar Bridge, and in Derby in 1821 or 2. Their services here were held in the old Congregational meeting house, at the corner of North and Park avenues, which had been several years occupied by the Methodist Episcopal Church of Bridgeport. Their ministers' names were David P. Candill, Lounsbury, and Brewer. The Rev. Mr. Tuckerman came in 1824 and remained about five years, when the society was merged into the Methodist Episcopal Church. There was a class formed of the Stillwellites and a leader appointed. The following were some of the members: Anson Bradley, of Toilsome Hill, Samuel Hodges, of Bridgeport, Joel Mitchell and wife, Mills Middlebrook and wife, Benjamin Bennett, Mrs. Isaac Odell, Capt. Thomas Brothwell and wife.

The meetings were attended by the community, and Mr. Tuckerman was much esteemed, and was supported by members of various churches living in that neighborhood. He afterwards joined the Congregational church, and preached a time in Poughkeepsie, N. Y., where he died in the pulpit.

After Mr. Tuckerman left, a Protestant Methodist came and preached a short time. Lorenzo Dow preached in this old church to crowded congregations, the capacity of the house being such as to seat about four hundred.[19]

---

[19] For all the particulars of this Stillwell Church, see manuscript of Mr. S. M. Main, deposited with the Fairfield County Historical Society.

The Hebrew congregation *(Benai Israel),* in Bridge-port, was organized September 19, 1859, the first minister being the Rev. A. Jacobs, and the place of worship No. 35 Wall street. The ministers have changed frequently. For a time the congregation met at Freedman's Building, on State street opposite the court house, but it now meets every Friday evening at seven o'clock and every Saturday morning at eight o'clock, in the Curtis Building, 483 Main street. The Rev. Gustav Gumpel is the pastor.

The Advent Christian Church of Bridgeport was organized in November, 1849, with fourteen members, and has maintained regular services ever since, on Sunday and week-day evenings, although most of the time without a pastor. About eighty members have been added since the church was formed. The place of meeting is Temperance Hall, on Beach street.

The Church of Christ in Bridgeport have held meetings since the year 1871, but were not formally organized as a church until August 23, 1874, under the leadership of Dr. W. A. Belding, of Troy, N. Y. The meetings were at first held in a private house, but for several years past they have been conducted in the hall at No. 356 Main street, on Sunday and two week-day evenings. The church has had no regularly installed or employed pastor, but has had the service of revivalists, especially that of Charles Abercrombie, in May, 1880.

St. Augustine's Church—Catholic.—The Rev. Father McDermott was the first Catholic priest who celebrated mass in Bridgeport. This was in the house of Mr. Farrell, on Middle street, in the year 1834, there being then about eighteen Catholic families residing in this city. Soon afterwards, by order of Bishop Fenwick, the Rev. James Smith visited Bridgeport once a month for the purpose of holding services. He built the brick church which stood on the corner of Arch street and Washington avenue, and the church was called St. James's Church. The Rev. Michael Lynch was the first settled pastor of this church and of the Catholic people in Bridgeport, and received his appointment here in December, 1842.

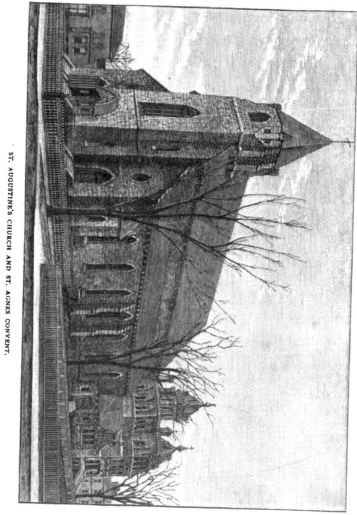

ST. AUGUSTINE'S CHURCH AND ST. AGNES CONVENT.

On September 2, 1852, the Rev. Thomas J. Synnot was appointed by Bishop O'Reilly pastor of this church. Soon after his arrival he commenced building the church of St. Mary, on Crescent avenue, in East Bridgeport, and finished it in the following year. In this same year he began St. Thomas' Church, at Fairfield, and finished it in 1854. In 1864, the brick church on Washington avenue having become too small, the foundation of the present edifice was laid on the corner of Washington avenue and Pequonnock street. This church, which is the largest in Bridgeport, was named St. Augustine Church and dedicated March 17, 1867, and cost about one hundred thousand dollars. It is built of gray granite from the quarries of North Bridgeport. It is intended to carry the spire about ninety feet higher than its present termination, making it far the highest object in the city, and the more so because of its location on Golden Hill. The whole number of Catholics embraced in the St. Augustine parish is about four thousand souls, and the average attendance at mass is estimated to be three thousand. The Sunday school contains about six hundred and fifty members. The amount raised for church purposes, parish expenses, and buildings, during the pastorate of twenty-eight years of the Rev. Father Synnot, cannot be far from a quarter of a million dollars.

Adjoining this church on the west is a large, imposing structure, built of granite from Plymouth, Conn., which is the home of the Sisters of Mercy and an academy for young ladies. It was completed in 1881 and cost about the same as the church.

Church of Sacred Heart of Jesus was erected in the year 1884, on Myrtle avenue near Prospect street. It is built of brick with granite trimmings, in the equilateral Gothic style, large and commodious, the ceiling being vaulted and groined. Rev. Dennis J. Cremin is the pastor.

St. Mary's Church—Catholic—of Bridgeport, is located on the corner of Pembroke and Steuben streets, and is a fine brick edifice with stone basement. This church was commenced as an out mission of St. James's, now St. Augustiné's, and was a frame building located on the corner of Crescent avenue and Church street, erected in 1854. The first missionaries to this church were the Reverends M. O'Neil, P. Lamb and Dr. Wallace. The first pastor was the Rev. Peter A. Smith, installed in April, 1857, who built the parsonage house and continued pastor until February 10, 1862. He afterwards died while pastor at Norwalk, Conn. He was succeeded by the Rev. Francis J. Lenihan, who continued pastor until November 1, 1866, when he was transferred to Woonsocket, R. I., where he died. He was followed by the Rev. Richard O. Gorman, who served until October 6, 1867, and was succeeded by the Rev. Thomas Dea, who continued to his death, July 23, 1873. These all ministered in the old church. The Rev. John F. Rogers was transferred from Newtown, Conn,, where he was pastor five years, to this parish the Sunday following the decease of Father Dea. He · was graduated at Mount St. Mary's College, at Emmetsburgh, Md. He commenced the new church edifice in June, 1874, located on the corner of Pembroke and Steuben streets, the corner-stone was laid May 16, 1875, and the house was dedicated October 14, 1877, by the late Bishop Galbury. The edifice is built in the Romanesque style, the basement of stone and the superstructure of brick, 74 feet front on Pembroke street and 154 feet in length, with a spire 187 feet in height. Its principal ornament inside is a Roman altar 35 feet in height. The basement is 14 feet in height, completed and occupied as a Sunday school room and for the meeting of various societies connected with ·the church. The parsonage was built in 1881, adjoining the church on the south, the lot extending to Sherman street.

The old church edifice has been remodeled into a parochial school building, the school being taught by the Sisters of Mercy, residing in the old parsonage adjoining. Mr. Rogers was the first to introduce the Sisters into Bridgeport. This parish, including West Stratford, now contains about three thousand souls.

The assistant pastor is the Rev. J. C. O'Connell, and the trustees are Patrick Cullen, John Flood; the committee, Martin Lee, John B. Sullivan, Martin Quinlan, Patrick Gil-

martin, Thomas McGovern; organist, Sister Mary Burk-
mans; the superintendents of the Sunday school are the
Sisters of Mercy.

The German Catholic Church was organized in December, 1874, and for a time held religious services in a hall
in Wheeler's Building, on Main street. From this they removed to the building No. 449 Main street. The present
house of worship, on Madison avenue near Washington, was
commenced in October, 1878, and completed in April of the
following year, at a cost, including the lot, of eight thousand
dollars. The Rev. Joseph A. Schaele, of New Haven, has
been the pastor from the organization of the church to the
present time. There were at first twenty-five families in the
congregation, which now numbers seventy-five families, or
about three hundred persons. The Sunday school has one
hundred members. Mass is celebrated and a sermon preached
every Sunday morning, the pastor returning to New Haven
at the conclusion of the services.

The Park Street Congregational Church is located
on the corner of Park and Barnum streets, fronting Washington Park. A movement toward the organization of a Congregational church in that part of the city of Bridgeport lying
east of the Pequonnock river, was made in November, 1867.
The first meeting to consider the subject was held on the 22d
of that month at the house of Mr. W. E. Smith, corner of
Barnum and William streets. The Rev. B. B. Beardsley, of
the First Congregational Church, and Mr. Thomas Lord, of
the Second, were present and offered to hire the Bethesda
Mission Chapel—now the East Washington avenue Baptist
Church—for at least one year, for the use of a Congregational
church, should one be formed, and in view of this proposition
it was thought advisable to occupy the chapel, and the Rev.
Joel H. Linsley, D.D., of Greenwich, was engaged to preach
on four Sundays.

The first public services were held November 24, 1867,
and on the 16th of December following a meeting was held in
the basement of the Bethesda Chapel, at which it was " Resolved, as the sense of this meeting, that it is expedient to

take measures for organizing a Congregational church in East Bridgeport." A council was accordingly called on the 15th of January, 1868, to devise respecting the matter, and if deemed expedient, to assist in the organization of a church. The council when convened voted that it was desirable to form a church, and proceeded in the formal services to that end. The church thus constituted, consisted of thirty-nine members, of whom twenty-three had been dismissed from the First Church, five from the Second Church, five from the church in Newington, three from the church in Westport, two from the church in Monroe, and one from the Chapel street church of New Haven.

On the 19th of March, 1868, Andrew L. Winton and James P. Bishop were elected deacons of the new church, and on the first day of July Mr. John G. Davenport, of Wilton, having supplied the pulpit for three months, and received a unanimous call to its pastorate, was ordained and installed pastor of the church and society.

A site for a house of worship having been purchased on the corner of Park and Barnum streets, the corner-stone of a church edifice was laid November 1, 1870. Services were held in the Bethesda Chapel until the 1st of July, 1871, when the basement of the new edifice was occupied, and on the 17th of October the church, having cost about $25,000, was dedicated to the worship of Almighty God.

Until the close of the year 1871 the church was under the fostering care of the Connecticut Home Missionary Society, when it became self-supporting.[10]

The following have served as deacons, each retiring at the end of four, five or six years, the present rule being that each term expires at the end of four years, any one being eligible to reëlection after an interval of one year: Andrew L. Winton, James P. Bishop, Charles M. Minor, David Wooster, Harmon Lane, James P. Bishop, Charles M. Minor, Frederick W. Storrs, David Wooster, James P. Bishop, Charles M. Minor.

The success of this church has been very marked and

---

[10] Historical sketch in the Church Manual, printed in 1881.

continuous to the present time. Mr. John G. Davenport was ordained its pastor July 1, 1868, and labored with much success until the summer of 1881, when he was dismissed to accept a call to the Second Congregational Church of Waterbury, where he was installed November 9, 1881. His successor was the Rev. George S. Thrall, who was installed in October, 1881, and after nearly three years of very acceptable service was dismissed, at his own request, on account of ill health.

The Rev. Frederick E. Hopkins, the present pastor, was installed March 26, 1884, and the prosperity of the church is continued. During the summer of 1885 an addition was made to the church edifice and considerable changes in the audience room, at a cost of about $2,500.

Olivet Church (Congregational).—About the year 1866 a mission Sunday school was commenced by members of the First Congregational Church and others in the northern part of the city. The school met at first in the upper story of No. 114 North Washington avenue, afterwards at Olivet Hall, upon the corner of Grand street. After some time the school developed into the church now known as Olivet Congregational Church, which was formally organized by a council convened for the purpose, November 16, 1870, and on December 14, 1870, the Rev. DeForest B. Dodge was ordained pastor, and he resigned October 11, 1871, and letters of dismission were granted to forty-nine members of this church to join him in forming a new ecclesiastical body. His successors as the pastors of Olivet Church have been: the Rev. S. Hopkins Emory, April, 1872; the Rev. Allen Clark, September, 1874; the Rev. John S. Wilson, August, 1879. The building now used by the society, on the corner of Main street and North avenue, was completed and occupied for worship December 24, 1876. It cost, including the site, about $3,500. The Rev. S. D. Gaylord became pastor of this church November 8, 1882, and died in office December 31, 1884. Mr. Edwin R. Holden, of Yale Divinity School, commenced the supply of the pulpit in March, 1885, and was ordained pastor June 9, 1885. This church has received assistance largely from the First Congregational Church and to some extent from other churches, for many years. It is under the care and aid of the Connecticut Home Missionary Society.

The Colorado Street Chapel is located in the western part of the city. About the end of February, 1884, a mission Sunday school was commenced under the auspices of the First Presbyterian Church, which at the end of the year they relinquished, and in May, 1885, it became a branch of the Sunday school of the First Congregational Church, under the charge of an assistant superintendent. The school met at first in an unoccupied store on State street, then in a cottage on Howard street, but the Congregational church decided at once to build a chapel, and land on Colorado street was purchased on the 11th of May, and a building erected. This was done by the Rev. C. R. Palmer and Col. Charles H. Russell, acting for the standing committee of the church. This chapel was completed September 8th and dedicated September 13th, with appropriate services. It was occupied by the Sabbath school from that date. As soon as a gas pipe had been laid through the street, so that the building could be lighted, services were held on Sabbath evenings, and these have continued until the present time. Until January 1, 1886, the pulpit was supplied by various gentlemen, under the direction of Mr. Palmer. From that date Mr. Robert W. Sharp became the stated supply. He is a member of the senior class in Yale Divinity School, to graduate in May next. The chapel has been conveyed by the builders to the First Congregational Church (an incorporated body), in the expectation that it will be conveyed ultimately to a religious society at the west end. It is valued at $4,200, with its contents.

Mr. James L. Harlem was the original superintendent of the school, when it was in Presbyterian hands, and has been continued in office by the Congregationalists. The success of it is largely due to the energy and enthusiasm which he has displayed from the beginning.

The First Baptist Church in Bridgeport was constituted September 20, 1837, with thirty-nine members. At that time the population of the city was about three thousand, and

the only Baptist church then within ten miles was at Stratfield, three miles distant, which was under the pastoral care
of the Rev. James H. Linsley, who resided in Stratford.
There were but three or four Baptists residing in the city,
one of whom, Miss Hannah Nichols, a devoted and active
member of the Stratfield church, about the year 1835 proposed the purchase of land upon which to erect a church in
the future. There were three brothers, named Whitney, also
members of the Stratfield church, residing about a mile from
the city, who had frequently consulted together, and with
Miss Nichols, the Rev. Mr. Linsley, and others, upon the
practicability of establishing a Baptist church in Bridgeport.
They were all waiting for a providential opening to enable
them to accomplish that object, when the way was opened,
sooner than they expected, by the offer of the Episcopal
society to sell their church edifice, on the corner of State and
Broad streets, for $3,650. Mr. Linsley circulated the subscrip-
tion paper until he secured $3,000, and paid it to the Episco-
pal society, and a deed was received August 8, 1835. During
this time a meeting was called and on July 24, 1835, a Baptist
society was organized, composed of six members, namely:
Benjamin Wakeman, Raymond, Roswell, Bennett Whitney,
and two other persons whose names are not known.

It was expected that the Rev. Mr. Linsley would accept
the pastorate, but failing health compelled him to relinquish
preaching, and the services of the Rev. Wm. W. Evarts, then
a student in Madison University, were temporarily secured.
Public worship commenced in the church April 23, 1837, but
five weeks afterwards Mr. Evarts returned to his studies, and
the church being unable to procure a permanent pastor,
public worship was discontinued until the latter part of 1838,
when the Rev. James W. Eaton, of Boston, became the first
settled minister of the church, and thus continued for two and
a half years, laboring faithfully and zealously until March 26,
1840, when he removed to Springfield, Mass. During his
ministry the church prospered and increased its membership
from 39 to 106. On the 18th of September, 1840, a unanimous
call was extended to the Rev. Daniel Harwington, of Fort
Ann, N. Y., and he became pastor of the church on the 3d of

the following month. He resigned October 16, 1842, the church having then 123 members. The next pastor was the Rev. William Smith, of Camden, N. J., who was settled here Nov. 21, 1842, and remained until July 8, 1845, during which time the church suffered severely by many of its members embracing the teachings of Millerism; but toward the close of his ministry many new converts were added to the church, through the labors of the Rev. Jacob Knapp.

The church was without a pastor from that time until January 3, 1846, when the Rev. William Reid was settled, after having previously occupied the pulpit for two or three months, and he continued in the pastorate for more than eight years, closing his labors May 28, 1854. At this time the number of members was reported to be 225. During this ministry the house of worship was repaired and the church debt liquidated, but towards the close of his service a division arose among its members which resulted, afterwards, in the formation of the second Baptist church of Bridgeport. After the resignation of Mr. Reid, June 1, 1854, the church extended a call to the Rev. J. R. Storrs, of New York, who accepted it, but after supplying the pulpit a few Sundays, resigned. A call was then extended to the Rev. W. C. Richards, who accepted, but resigned without entering upon his pastoral duties. The Rev. A. G. Palmer, D.D., then became the pastor of the church, and the formation of the second Baptist church, which now took place, greatly enfeebled the church and discouraged the new pastor. He commenced his pastorate October, 1855, and resigned September 27, 1857. The Rev. J. L. Hodge, D.D., succeeded him and labored for the church three years, commencing in November, 1857. During his ministry a new house of worship, commodious and substantial, was erected, and the church was placed in a better position for prosperity. Dr. Hodge labored earnestly, not only in his regular ministrations, but to bring about a union of the two churches, and to complete the new edifice. After the removal of the Rev. Dr. Hodge the church extended a call to the Rev. A. McGregor Hopper, D.D., who had just closed his labors with the Baptist church at Auburn, N. Y. He accepted the call and commenced his pastorate in March,

1861. Soon after the settlement of Dr. Hopper the second church disbanded and most of its members returned to the first church. Through the efforts of Dr. Hopper the debt remaining on the new edifice was paid, and he found much success in his work. The membership was increased to 331. Dr. Hopper resigned September 1, 1877, the Rev. M. H. Pogson became the settled pastor January 30, 1878, and labored with much success until January 2, 1884, when he resigned to accept a pastorate in New York City. The Rev. Wm. V. Garner was settled as pastor in this church June 4, 1884, being the present minister. The deacons of this church are: W. E. Payson, M. E. Morris, Albert Wisner and Louis Skinner. The present membership is 364.

The Washington Avenue Baptist Church was organized January 30, 1874, with forty-seven members, the Rev. C. W. Ray being the first pastor. The price paid for the church edifice and lot, which fronts on Washington Park, and originally belonged to the Bethesda Mission Sunday school, was $10,000, and about $3,500 additional, were expended in repairs and improvements. The Rev. Charles Coleman was pastor some years, but resigned in 1885. The Rev. W. M. Ingersoll is the present pastor, and the deacons are: P. J. Black, C. W. Scarrit, J. H. Gunn, and C. W. Beers.

St. Paul's Church (Episcopal), was organized June 4, 1858, at the house of William H. Noble, on Stratford avenue, and the Rev. G. S. Coit, D.D., of St. John's Church, was chosen rector. The Sunday school met, at first, in the coal office of D. W. Thompson, near the east end of the Centre Bridge, afterwards in rooms over a store upon the corner of Crescent avenue and East Main street. The Rev. N. S. Richardson, D.D., was the first settled pastor of this parish, his ministry beginning in January, 1868. The corner-stone of St. Paul's Church, a handsome stone building upon Kossuth street, fronting Washington Park, was laid by Bishop Williams, October 6, 1868; the edifice was dedicated and occupied for worship July 29, 1869, but not consecrated until May 18, 1880. It cost about thirty thousand dollars. Dr. Richardson, in addition to parochial duties, was editor of the

44

"Church Guardian," a newspaper published in New York City, the Rev. George S. Pine assisting him in the care of the parish. The other pastors have been Rev. M. Clark, Rev. James O. Drum, and the incumbent, Rev. Mildridge Walker.

The Church of the Redeemer (Universalist), was organized in 1850, and the brown stone edifice on Fairfield avenue, near Broad street, originally known as the Church of our Saviour, but now called the Church of the Redeemer, was dedicated near the close of the following year. The Rev. Olympia Brown—afterwards Mrs. Olympia Brown Willis— was pastor of this church from 1869 to 1875. The Rev. John Lyon,[11] the present pastor, was settled here December 3, 1876. The cost of the house of worship, including the site, was $34,000. The trustees of this church are: P. T. Barnum, James Staples, Jerome Orcutt, G. W. Longstaff, Benjamin Fletcher, Albert R. Lacey.

Public Schools.

The inhabitants in that part of Fairfield which afterwards became Pequonnock had established a school as early as 1678, and petitioned the court to release them from paying school rates at Fairfield village. At that time the inhabitants in the Stratford part of Pequonnock sent their children to the Pembroke school at Old Mill, and thus the schools continued until the Stratfield society was established in 1691, when it took charge of all school interests within its boundaries.[12] A school house, probably the second, was built in 1703, near the junction of the present Park avenue and Pequonnock street. Among the first teachers of those times was William Rogers, whose agreement with the committee, Samuel Hubbell and Benjamin Fayerweather, made in 1710, is still extant. A noted master after this, for many years, was John Wheeler, whose salary in 1736 for teaching a summer school was £63. The second school was formed in 1738, and the house built near the present Toilsome Hill school house in Fairfield. In 1766 the Stratfield society was divided into three districts, called the North, Middle and South.

---

[11] See biographical sketch of Mr. Lyon.
[12] See pages 472–4 of this book.

The schools continued to be managed by the committees chosen annually by the parish until 1796, when a school society was formed in accordance with a law enacted the previous year, which provided that the interest on moneys received from the sale of the lands of the "Western Reserve should be paid school societies respectively." These lands were sold for $1,200,000, which formed the foundation of the present State school fund. This society continued until 1856, when, with the other school societies in the State, it was abolished and its property and obligations transferred to the town. In 1801 there were five districts, called Bridgeport, Old South, Island Brook, Toilsome and North.

In 1841 authority was given by the State to the Stratfield society to maintain a school exclusively for colored children. Such a school was organized by the Bridgeport district, which occupied a building on Gregory street until 1871, when the school was transferred to a room in a wing of the Prospect street school house, which had recently been built. This was continued as a separate ungraded school until the fall of 1876, when the pupils were placed in their proper grades in the different rooms of the same building.

In 1858 the Bridgeport district, after an exciting discussion, voted to abolish the bills for tuition, or "rate bills," as they were called. This was ten years before the law was enacted by the State making it compulsory upon all the towns to support free schools.

When Bridgeport was incorporated as a town in 1821 there were two school districts in the territory east of the Pequonnock river. The northern one, called Pembroke, was established in 1717,[2] the house being erected some years later on Old Mill Green, where one still stands, and is in use. The other district was called New Pasture Point, and built its school house in 1796. In 1859 it erected the brick building on Nichols street, which is still in use.

In 1870 the Black Rock district was transferred from Fairfield to Bridgeport.

Some of the above districts were divided and new ones

---

[2] See page 280 of this book.

formed at different times, so that in 1876 there were eleven school districts in the town of Bridgeport.

During the year 1875 Mr. Henry T. Shelton published several articles in the "Standard" in favor of consolidating the public schools. These articles awakened a general interest in the subject, which was discussed and so agitated that, although there was great opposition to the measure, yet the town of Bridgeport, at its annual meeting April 3, 1876, voted to consolidate its eleven district schools under one government, by a majority of 172 votes in a total of 3,998 cast; and on Tuesday, April 11, 1876, the following named persons were elected a school committee: Andrew Burke, James Staples, Frederick W. Zingsen, Henry T. Shelton, James C. Loomis, Daniel H. Sterling, Augustus H. Abernethy, Edward Sterling, George W. Bacon, Joseph D. Alvord, David Ginand, Julius S. Hanover. These persons met and organized under the name and title of the "Board of Education." They divided themselves into three classes, the terms of office of the first four to expire in one year, the next four in two years, and the next four in four years. They elected James C. Loomis, president; Daniel H. Sterling, vice-president; Henry T. Shelton, secretary, and subsequently, Henry M. Harrington, superintendent. In the practical working of the new system it was found at the end of the first year that the money expended was more than $10,000 less per year than under the old system.

On the first day of March, 1877, the first death of a member of the board occurred, as seen by the following record:

"As co-laborer with the late Hon. Daniel H. Sterling, vice-president and chairman of the finance committee of the Board of Education, we desire to testify to his earnest and thorough work with us in the advancement of public schools, and herewith express our high appreciation of his valuable counsel and advice from our organization until the present time." It is also recorded that on the 11th day of July, 1877, the resignation of Joseph D. Alvord, on account of ill health, was accepted with sincere regrets.

During the first year of consolidation the establishment of the public high school was another of the important ad-

vances made. The adjustment of the financ
tween the districts and the town was the mc
of the work. This was done by placing all
the hands of a committee consisting of R.
Beardsley, and James King, as auditors, w
report became the basis of a full and satisfac

On March 5, 1877, Edward W. Marsh was
of Daniel H. Sterling, deceased, and on Sep
another memorial entry was made on the r
has again visited our board during the year a
first president, the Hon. James C. Loomis, o
est friends of education in the State, and men
Board of Education at the time of his deat
we will ever cherish, remembering his worth
dering our warmest sympathy to the widow,
any other, is bereaved."

On August 13, 1877, Daniel N. Morgan
Alvord, resigned, and on October 8th of the
M. Read succeeded J. C. Loomis, deceased, f
portion of the year. At the annual electio
the Rev. Thomas J. Synnott was elected for
Hon. Nathaniel Wheeler for one year, to fill

On June 21, 1877, Island Brook school h
and the present brick structure was immed
the old site. On November 12, 1877, Julius
elected president, and F. W. Zingsen, vice
ward Sterling resigned March 12, 1879, on ac
engagements, and the board made the followi
ily! in him we have lost a co-laborer—a men
since its organization—whom at all times we
to the great and important duty of educating
native city." George C. Waldo was electec
Sterling for the balance of the year; and du
of that year the new heating apparatus v
Prospect school building, and a training scl
was established. On October 27, 1879, Ec
was elected secretary of the board. At the s
1880, Peter W. Wren and George C. Waldo
three years, and following them the follow

BRIDGEPORT HIGH SCHOOL. ERECTED IN 1882.

been elected, most of them to serve three years: Rev. Caspar Brunner, Frederick Hurd, Henry Cowd, Warren W. Porter, Marshall E. Morris, Emory F. Strong, Morris B. Beardsley, Thomas F. Martin, John H. Colgan.

The completion of the high school building, on Congress street, in October, 1882, and its opening for school purposes, was the marked educational event of the year. Its novel plan for heating and ventilating was a departure from the commonly accepted theories, and its practical utility has been demonstrated during the four years since, as the best in the State, if not in the nation. The building has been visited by experts from all parts of the country, and the plan of heating and ventilation has been adopted by school boards, not only in this State, but in Vermont, Massachusetts, and New York. It was built under the supervision of a committee chosen on the part of the town and one from the Board of Education. These committees were identical and consisted of the following persons: Julius S. Hanover, Nathaniel Wheeler, Edward W. Marsh, and George C. Waldo. At the expiration of E. W. Marsh's term in 1884, he declined a reëlection.

The decease of the Rev. Thomas J. Synnot, pastor of the St. Augustine Catholic Church, April 30, 1884, was noticed by the following: " The Board of Education recognize in the death of the Rev. Thomas J. Synnot a severe loss to the cause of education and one which it will be difficult to repair,—a man of education, tact and ability, and although a clergyman, still a man without prejudice or bigotry, his was a happy and tolerant disposition. Being pastor of one church in this city for more than thirty years, he has so borne himself through this long period as to endear himself to the entire community. As a mark of respect and esteem the members of the board will attend his funeral."

During the summer of 1883 the Washington school house, on Pembroke street, was repaired, new heating apparatus placed in it, and in the autumn the new school building on the Newtown turnpike was first occupied for school purposes.

Another memorandum is made of the departed: " When this Board of Education was organized in April, 1876, Augustus H. Abernethy, M.D., was elected a member, and con-

PERSPECTIVE VIEW OF PUBLIC SCHOOLS, NOS. 2 AND 9. ERECTED IN 1884.

tinued such until his decease on the evening of November 9, 1884. We make this tribute to his memory on our records: Resolved, That in obedience to the will of him who doeth all things for the best, we bow in humble submission, with the feeling that this community, and especially the cause of education in our city, has sustained a great loss; that as an honorable, upright and highly esteemed citizen and member of this board, we will ever cherish his memory."

Two new school buildings were occupied at the commencement of the fall term of 1884, one on Myrtle avenue—school No. 2—the other on North avenue—school No. 9—corner of Oak street, which have commended themselves as models of convenience and adaptation to school purposes. They are warmed and ventilated by the same plan as the high school building, except that the air is warmed by furnaces instead of steam coils. The internal arrangement of these buildings is regarded as very advantageous and commendable. See cuts on the two following pages.

In January, 1885, the Hon. P. T. Barnum donated $1,000, the income to be expended in the purchase of two gold medals, to be presented each year to the two students in the high school who shall write and publicly pronounce the two best English orations.[14]

---

[14] Sometimes it is said that the higher grades of schools are maintained for the benefit of the wealthy classes rather than for the common people. In order to ascertain how far this view is correct, as applied to this high school, a careful examination has been made, which shows the following occupations represented among the parents of the pupils:

Mechanics	44	Farmers	2
Merchants	19	Policemen	1
Manufacturers	13	Government officer	1
Clerks and salesmen	11	Town officer	1
Laborers	9	City officer	1
Supts. or foremen of factory	7	Bank officer	1
Contractors	4	Doctor	1
Retired from business	4	Keeper of boarding house	1
Clergymen	4	Photographer	1
Builders	3	Undertaker	1
Teachers	3	Coachman	1
Laborers	3	Truckman	1
Printers	2		

In addition to the above there were the children of twenty-seven widows in attendance, making in all one hundred and sixty-seven families represented in the school. In other words, this high school fairly represents all classes in the city.

BASEMENT PLAN OF NOS. 2 AND 9.

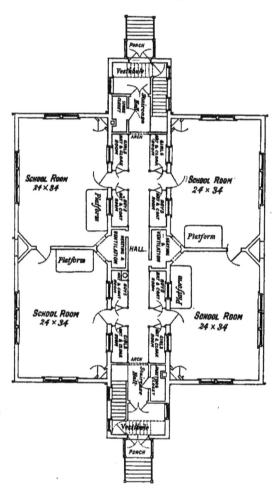

PLAN OF FIRST AND SECOND STORIES OF NOS. 2 AND 9.

The rooms for the accommodation of the Board of Education are now in the United Bank Building, corner of Main and Bank streets, they being very pleasant and commodious.

The population of the town of Bridgeport—including the city—as estimated by school enumeration, was in 1876-7, 24,745, and in January, 1886, 39,006. In 1876 there were 78 teachers, and in 1886, 120.

The cost per scholar of maintaining the Bridgeport schools, compared with others in the State as reported by the State Board of Education for the year 1884, is as follows: Hartford, $34.19; Norwich, $23.45; New Britain, $23.35; New Haven, $22.81; Stamford, $21.41; Norwalk, $20.05; Meriden, $19.65; Waterbury, $19.52; New London, $19.33; Danbury, $19.17; Middletown, $19.03; Bridgeport, $15.43.

The officers of the Board of Education for 1885-6 are: Julius S. Hanover, President; Nathaniel Wheeler, Vice-President; Morris B. Beardsley, Secretary. The members of the board are: Peter W. Wren, Henry Cowd, Frederick Hurd, Marshall E. Morris, Morris B. Beardsley, Emory F. Strong, William B. Hincks, Thomas F. Martin, Julius S. Hanover, Nathaniel Wheeler, David Ginand, John H. Colgan. H. M. Harrington, Superintendent of Schools.

The Bridgeport Public Library and Reading Room has acquired a high position in the estimation and care of the citizens of Bridgeport, as the beginning of what they hope to make a large and influential institution of culture in the city. About sixty years ago a boy wrote some brief articles which were printed in a newspaper of Bridgeport, and in them called for a public meeting of citizens for the purpose of establishing a public library. The meeting was held by a few persons, the boy being among them, but he did not at that time let it be known that he wrote the articles and called the meeting. The result of the meeting was that a library was established about, perhaps, a year or two before 1830. This library was continued until about 1855, when it purchased the library of the Calliopean Literary Society of Yale College, which had disbanded, numbering about 1,000 volumes, and the Bridgeport Library Association was established December 7, 1857. For many years it was supported as a subscription library, charging a fee for membership and its privileges.

BURROUGHS PUBLIC LIBRARY BUILDING.

In 1881 Mr. Clarence Sterling, calling upon Mr. John D. Candee, then editor of the Bridgeport "Standard," requested that the "Standard" would favor the establishing of a free public library, in accordance with a recent law of the State, granting such libraries to towns and cities, to be supported by a tax on the grand list."[15] Mr. Candee cheerfully took up the matter and Mr. Sterling started a petition to the Common Council of the city. Then upon consultation with Hon. D. B. Lockwood, president of the old library association, and others interested in it, that library was offered to the new project upon condition that the debts of the old society, amounting to about $800, should be assumed by the new society, which was accepted. Upon the matter coming before the Common Council the motion which gave to Bridgeport a free public library was carried with but one dissenting vote, and the Mayor, Hon. John L. Wessels, appointed the following board of officers: W. D. Bishop, President; John D. Candee, Vice-President; Charles Sherwood, Secretary; William B. Hincks, Treasurer; and Frederick Hurd, W. J. Hills, S. S. Blake, and Bernard Winghofer, who held their first meeting July 2, 1881.

By the lamented death of Mr. Winghofer, the removal from the city of Mr. Blake, and the resignation of the Hon. W. D. Bishop, three changes have since taken place in the . board. The successors of these gentlemen are A. B. Beers, Patrick Coughlin, and W. D. Bishop, Jr.

The rooms of the old library association, at 440 Main street, were altered and enlarged, and on the 10th of January, 1882, the Bridgeport Public Library and Reading Room opened its doors. The first ticket of membership was issued to P. T. Barnum—occupation, showman—guarantor, James Staples. By the first of June the new library had 3,193 members, and had circulated 36,547 volumes. The difficulties arising from the small number of books were tided over by the gift of a hundred dollars from Mrs. James C. Loomis, and the purchase by the Hon. P. T. Barnum of a thousand dollars worth of the best recent works in science and general literature. The original library hours were from 2 to 10 P. M. daily; but it soon became necessary to open the institution from 9 A. M. to 10 P. M. In November, 1882, at the request of

---

15 Manuscript of J. D. Candee.

many intelligent workingmen, the directors resolved to try the experiment of Sunday opening, hitherto only attempted in the New England States by the public libraries of Boston and Worcester. The change was so greatly appreciated that in 1884 they determined to conduct the library on the " never-closing" system, and the reading room is now open every day in the year.

In January, 1883, Mrs. Catharine A. Pettengill bequeathed to the public library the valuable property known as the Burroughs Building, in order that it might be converted into a permanent home for the institution. The money accruing from the rental of the building has been left to accumulate towards paying for its alteration, and it is hoped that the library will occupy its new quarters by the winter of 1887.

In 1884 the Hon. W. D. Bishop resigned the office of president, and was succeeded by John D. Candee, Esq., who had rendered the library much valuable service as vice-president and member of the book committee. The career of the library has been one of unbroken success. During the year ending July 1, 1885, 91,030 books were circulated for home use, and 15,160 were consulted in the reading room. The present membership is above 7,000. The number of volumes contained in the library is 16,400.[98]

Officers of the public library for the year 1885: President, John D. Candee; Vice-President, Frederick Hurd; Secretary, Charles Sherwood; Treasurer, William D. Bishop, Jr. The present members of the board of directors are: William D. Bishop, Jr., Frederick Hurd, William J. Hills, William B. Hincks, Charles Sherwood, Alfred B. Beers, David B. Lockwood, John D. Candee, Patrick Caughlin. Librarian, Mrs. Agnes Hills; Assistant Librarian, William J. Hills; Attendants, Theodore F. Crane, Jr., Robert Bruce Nelson.

Rev. Henry Jones, son of Daniel and Rhoda (Mather) Jones, was born in Hartford, Conn., October 15, 1801, graduated at Yale College in the class of 1820, and graduated at Andover Theological Seminary in 1824. He married Eliza

---

[98] Manuscript of William J. Hill.

S. Webster, daughter of Noah Webster, LL.D., September 5, 1825, and was ordained pastor of the second society in Berlin —now the first Congregational society of New Britain— October 12, 1825. He was dismissed at his own request December 19, 1827, and in the following year opened a select school for young ladies at Greenfield, Mass., which he conducted with success nearly ten years.

In 1838 he removed to Bridgeport and erected a cottage he ever afterward occupied on the western slope of Golden Hill. Here he opened a classical school for young men and boys, and continued it with much success as to reputation and income, over thirty years, when he gradually closed his school and ceased active labor.

When he came to Bridgeport he connected himself with the First Congregational Church, of which he remained a valued and useful member until his decease, November 9, 1878. The golden wedding of himself and wife was observed in September, 1875, and was a memorable occasion. His children were: Frances Julia, who married Rev. Thomas H. Beecher; Emily Ellsworth, married Daniel J. Day, died July 23, 1869, leaving one son, Robert Webster Day, the only grandchild; Eliza Webster, died in infancy; Henry Webster, M.D., of Chicago.

Golden Hill·Seminary for young ladies and children is located on Golden Hill street, an elevated locality, in the city of Bridgeport; Miss Emily Nelson being the proprietor and principal. Miss Nelson came from New York City, purchased the old homestead of Alfred Bishop, and established her school here in 1880. The school has a first class standing and reputation in every respect, and the principal is highly esteemed by the citizens of Bridgeport.